Toward the Twenty-First Century

A Reader in World Politics

Edited by

Glenn Hastedt
Kay Knickrehm
James Madison University

Prentice Hall, Englewood Cliffs, New Jersey 07632

Library of Congress Cataloging-in-Publication Data

Toward the twenty-first century : a reader in world politics / edited
  by Glenn Hastedt, Kay Knickrehm.
      p. cm.
      1. International relations. 2. International economic relations.
  3. Security, International. 4. Military policy. 5. World politics.
  I. Hastedt, Glenn P. II. Knickrehm, Kay M.
  JX1391.T685 1994
  327—dc20   93–23913
  ISBN 0–13–953050–9   CIP

Acquisitions editor: Julie Berrisford
Editorial/production supervision and
   interior design: Barbara Reilly
Cover design: Wendy Alling Judy
Prepress buyer: Kelly Behr
Manufacturing buyer: Mary Ann Gloriande
Copy editor: Barbara Conner
Editorial assistant: Nicole Signoretti

© 1994 by Prentice-Hall, Inc.
A Simon & Schuster Company
Englewood Cliffs, New Jersey 07632

Printed in the United States of America
10 9 8 7 6 5 4 3 2 1

ISBN   0-13-953050-9

Prentice-Hall International (UK) Limited, *London*
Prentice-Hall of Australia Pty. Limited, *Sydney*
Prentice-Hall Canada Inc., *Toronto*
Prentice-Hall Hispanoamericana, S.A., *Mexico*
Prentice-Hall of India Private Limited, *New Delhi*
Prentice-Hall of Japan, Inc., *Tokyo*
Simon & Schuster Asia Pte. Ltd., *Singapore*
Editora Prentice-Hall do Brasil, Ltda., *Rio de Janeiro*

Contents

The Global 2000 Report to the President
The Council on Environmental Quality and the Department of State

U.S. Security in a Separatist Season
Stephen P. Cohen

Preface

Academic disciplines tend to be characterized by cyclical periods of great energy followed by periods of consolidation and calm. For quite some time now the study of world politics has existed in one of those periods of calm. The debate within it has moved along well-defined paths. To be sure, methodological, conceptual, and policy disagreements have arisen, but they have been accommodated rather easily within the existing parameters of the field or have required very little stretching. All of this appears to be changing. The end of the cold war, the demise of the Soviet Union and its alliance bloc in Eastern Europe, references to a "new world order," and the approaching end of the twentieth century have combined to inject new life into the study of world politics and its teaching. Topics that once received lengthy treatment are no longer universally held to merit such attention, and others have moved from the fringes of the discipline (or the end of the semester's syllabus) to places of greater prominence. Likewise, conceptual frameworks and methodological approaches that have been hovering outside the mainstream of the field are now receiving closer attention by many practitioners and teachers.

Although invigorating, these changes also present a challenge to instructors who wish to inform students of the debate as it unfolds. Textbooks tend to pass along the accepted wisdom of a field. They are far better at recording changes that have been made than at pushing the frontiers of debate. Moreover, the current debate over the future of world politics has only recently begun. It is far too early to decipher its end point: whether the field will coalesce around existing ideas and practices, move to a new starting point, or split along several paths. As such, yet another dilemma arises: How much attention should be paid to the existing wisdom in the field compared to the more recent writings that seek to expand its boundaries?

Toward the Twenty-First Century is designed to provide instructors with a means for addressing these concerns in a systematic and coherent fashion over the course of a semester. Our goal in selecting essays for inclusion in this volume is to blend writings that present the predominant ways of thinking about a problem or issue with essays that take a fresh look. We have also included pieces on thinking about the future and commentaries on the recent past to sensitize students to the problems of predicting the course of future events. We feel that in doing so we have steered a middle ground between readers that pay primary attention to the classics in the field and those whose focus is exclusively on recent events.

A few words about the introductory essays are in order. Each set of readings is preceded by an essay that sets out some of the main issues under debate in that area. They are intended to introduce students to the subject and not to serve as a substitute for reading the essays themselves. They do not speak at any length about the essays that follow. Moreover, each of the introductory essays can stand alone; no references are made to discussions in previous chapters. Our goal in constructing them in this fashion was twofold. First, instructors who wish to give added attention to a topic might assign the introductory essay along with a textbook chapter as the required reading for that unit. Second, instructors who wish to devote less time to a topic could substitute the introductory essay for a textbook chapter with the confidence that a coherent overview of the topic will still be presented.

We should emphasize that we see *Toward the Twenty-First Century* as a volume designed for students to read. To that end we have chosen to limit the number of footnotes in the selected readings. Any article referred to in the introductory essays is cited in the reading list at its conclusion.

We owe thanks to many individuals. We are particularly grateful to Karen Horton for supporting the project and to Julie Berrisford for seeing it through to its conclusion. Thanks are also owed to the production staff at Prentice Hall for the excellent work they did in turning the manuscript into a completed book. Walter Bacon (University of Nebraska, Omaha), Howard Lehman (University of Utah), Joseph Lepgold (Georgetown University), Robert McCalla (University of Wisconsin, Madison), and Henry Shockley (Boston University) are thanked for the many comments they made in reading the manuscript at various points in its evolution. Although we were not always able to follow their counsel, it was greatly appreciated.

We dedicate this book to our families.

Chapter *1*

Studying World Politics

Making Choices

Interest in world politics proceeds at several levels. Academic writings often focus on questions of basic forces, normative standards, and methodology: Why do states go to war? What are international human rights? Should case studies or quantitative data be relied on more heavily in carrying out research? Policymakers are much more interested in problem-oriented inquiries that produce answers to the questions before them: When will economic sanctions work? When will deterrence fail? What type of international organization is best suited to deal with ocean pollution? The public at large has long been attracted to world politics by the drama of such events as large-scale movements of refugees and international crises. More recently the public has become interested in the more mundane and routine aspects of world politics for their ability to shape people's daily lives by affecting interest rates, unemployment levels, and the environmental order.

Two observations need to be made regarding these interest groupings. First, they are not self-contained. Not only do individuals such as Henry Kissinger, Jeane Kirkpatrick, and Zbigniew Brzezinski cross from one group to another, but also a full appreciation of the dynamics of world politics requires an element of all three perspectives to be present. Consider policymakers who must make a decision regarding a request for foreign aid. As noted, their primary concern is with identifying and weighing policy options: What do we want to achieve? What, if anything, will work and how much will it cost? Yet without an appreciation or interest in world politics, policymakers are not likely to pay sufficient attention to the problem even to be aware of its existence or to recognize the need to act. One of the most consistent findings by those who study world politics is that the reason policymakers are caught off guard is not because they failed to receive warnings but because they failed to listen to them. Often a type of tunnel vision sets in, and policymakers become so caught up with short-term problem-solving efforts that they fail to comprehend the severity of the problems looming on the horizon or the consequences their actions hold for other problems. At the same time, a failure to understand the structure and operation of the international economic system; the nature of the development process; and the social, political, and environmental consequences of economic growth would almost certainly doom a foreign aid initiative to failure.

Second, these three groupings are not internally consistent in their view of world politics. Terms such as *realist, liberal, Marxist, behavioralist,* and *traditionalist* are commonly used to distinguish among academics who write on world politics. Distinctions among policymakers are often made in terms of both their outlooks—hawk versus dove—and their institutional affiliations. It is not uncommon, for example, to see someone referred to as representing the State Department perspective or the congressional viewpoint. Differences in public perceptions of world politics have been organized in a number of ways. Some distinguish between those holding isolationist views and those holding internationalist views. Others make distinctions between individuals who are well informed and attentive and those who are only occasionally drawn to world politics. Finally, distinctions have been made on the basis of such characteristics as race, gender, economic class, age, and religion.

Although disagreements have always existed among those interested in world politics, the scope of the debate has not been uniform across groupings. Most notably, disagreements among academics have encompassed a larger set of issues than have disagreements among policymakers, who deal with problems on a day-to-day basis. The more limited scope of debate among the latter is understandable for several reasons. First, as policymakers are quick to point out, they must operate under time-sensitive deadlines. Whereas academics have the luxury of reformulating their ideas or gathering more data, policymakers must act even if all of the data are not there or their understanding of the problem is incomplete.

Second, domestic politics and the bureaucratic nature of government also act as constraints. Both promote incrementalism in problem solving. The tendency is to think in terms of what the government can do and what the public will accept rather than to develop and tailor programs to the problem at hand. Returning to our example of foreign aid, we see that governments and international organizations had to make decisions about giving aid to what was once the Soviet Union without really knowing the extent of the problem or who was in charge, and in formulating their plans they tended to rely on existing foreign aid programs and strategies rather than devising a new one designed to meet the specific needs of these newly independent states.

Third, and probably most important, policymakers tend to take the world as a given. For well over a quarter of a century the dominant and unchanging reality that policymakers saw when they looked at world politics was the superpower competition between the United States and the Soviet Union. This competition, although most pronounced in the military area, reached into all aspects of world politics. Succinctly summarized in the notion of a cold war, it colored virtually all thinking about what was possible in world politics and why events unfolded as they did. That perceptual anchor is now gone. In quick order the East European states began to assert their independence from Moscow with an unprecedented and unexpected degree of success, the Berlin Wall fell, the Communist party and communism lost their grip on power in the Soviet Union, and then the Soviet Union self-destructed.

Cut loose from the familiar politics of the cold war international system, policymakers now find themselves with a far wider array of policy options than most ever imagined possible. The rationale for institutions and policies that long served as the starting point for foreign-policy decision making have now been called into question, and U.S. policymakers have had to address such questions as these: What is the role of NATO (North Atlantic Treaty Organization)? What do we do with nuclear weapons? What should the relationship be between Japan and the United States? Although the questions may differ, the situation is repeated in Germany, Brazil, North Korea, Nigeria, and elsewhere around the world. At the same time that old ways of thinking and acting have been called into question a series of new foreign-policy issues (or ones previously downplayed) now also compete for positions of prominence on the foreign-policy agenda. Among these are questions regarding human rights, the promotion of democracy, environmental protection, water rights, and international health policy. No longer can they be easily dismissed as of secondary importance to a country's national interest.

Neither the enhanced freedom to choose among policy options nor the need to address new issues is necessarily welcomed by policymakers. At least in the short run, change is destabilizing, and there is also uncertainty over the end point. The inhibiting influences of domestic politics, government bureaucracy, and limited personal interest are also still present and have caused some to shy away from examining new options or tackling new problems. The point remains, however, that the range of choices in world politics open to policymakers as they face the twenty-first century is far larger than anyone would have imagined just a few short years ago.

One consequence of this expanded range of choice is that it focuses new attention on the types of "big-picture" issues and questions that academic writings on world politics have traditionally pursued. At a minimum, the changed and uncertain nature of the international system means that one can no longer expect policies to work in the future simply because they worked in the past. Some other basis for judging the merits of competing policies is needed. A theory provides one such benchmark for making judgments by supplying an organizing framework within which to fit the unfolding events of world politics. Theories accomplish this task by simplifying reality. Rather than trying to incorporate all possible explanatory factors, or variables, into the framework, theories emphasize certain points and push others to the fringes. Those factors selected for emphasis are the ones believed to be most important for explaining either the pattern of behavior or the nature of the event under study.

Choices Matter

A theory simplifies reality, but not all theories simplify reality in the same way. Depending on the theoretical perspective one starts with, one is likely to get different answers to the questions of why something happened or whether this strategy will work. Moreover, not every theoretical perspective is equally suited for all types of questions. Some theoretical perspectives are far better equipped to deal with questions relating to international conflict than to international cooperation. Others deal almost exclusively with a specific problem, such as international crises or human rights, and would be of little use in the study of other issues.

The importance of selecting a starting point can be illustrated by looking at international economic relations. Like virtually all topics in the field of world politics, international economic relations is interdisciplinary in nature. No one questions the need to bring insights from both economics and politics to bear on its study. The question is where to begin. There must be a first step, and this first step will lead down different paths. If the first step is taken from the perspective of international economics, the key organizing principles will be drawn from such concepts as the relative efficiency of foreign exchange markets, the costs and benefits of protectionism, the theory of comparative advantage, and the theory of optimum currency areas.

Susan Strange argues, however, that the proper starting point for the study of international economic relations is political science because to government officials who shape foreign-policy decisions, defense is more important than economic growth. Strange continues with a second point: Properly understood, international economic relations are a form of diplomacy and must be studied as such. Finally, she notes that starting from the vantage point of international politics casts one's study of international economic relations in terms of power, authority, and the role of the state. Strange holds that an intellectual appreciation of these terms is crucial if the study of international economic relations is to be free of "unrealistic assumptions, wild generalizations, or wishful thinking."

Joan Spero also makes a case against starting one's study solely from an economic perspective. Spero maintains that there are three ways in which political factors affect international economic outcomes. First, the structure and operation of the international economic system is shaped by the international political system. A free-trade economic order does not just happen but is brought into existence and maintained by states. Second, political concerns shape economic policy. An examination of the Bush administration's decision-making process in sending foreign aid to the former Soviet Union, placing an embargo on Haiti, or granting China most-favored-nations status would reveal the importance, if not the primacy, of political considerations. Third, international economic relations are political relations. They lend themselves quite naturally to analysis in terms of such standard concepts as conflict, cooperation, power, and influence.

Choices in the World Politics of the Twenty-first Century

Although the range of problems addressed by academics and the scope of the answers put forward have consistently outpaced those addressed by policymakers, academic writing on world politics has not been immune to the tunnel vision effect of the cold war. By far, one perspective—realism—has infused the largest amount of thinking about world politics. Realism defines the dynamics of world politics in terms of three fundamental assumptions: (1) Nation-states and their decision makers are the most important actors, (2) a clear distinction can be made between domestic and international politics, and (3) world politics is a struggle for power that pervades all foreign-policy issues. Realism emerged as a response to the values and assumptions about world politics that guided the thinking of Woodrow Wilson and other policymakers who looked at the destruction of World War I and sought to build a safer, more peaceful world. Central to their thinking was the belief that just as it was natural for a harmony of interests to exist among members of a society, it was also natural for there to exist a harmony of interests among states. They looked to public opinion, the human intellect, and international law and organization—not to the struggle for power—to provide the foundation for world politics.

Realism has never been without its critics. Just as advocates of realism criticized Woodrow Wilson and his followers for being "idealists" who were wedded to concepts that did not make sense given the realities of world politics after World War I, so too has realist thinking been criticized for not being attuned to the realities of world politics in the late twentieth century. Such criticisms come from many quarters. Students of world politics who emphasize the importance of the nonmilitary aspects of international relations as well as those who study patterns of international cooperation assert that the assumptions of realism make it ill suited for studying these topics. The same holds true for those who feel that the proper normative and empirical focus of world politics should be on individuals or groups and not on the state. Still others reject realism because of its intellectual roots, which, depending on the critic, are seen as either European in nature or gender-based. Finally, there are those critics who take exception to the claim long made by many realist scholars that realism provides the basis for an objective and all-encompassing theory of world politics. In this critical view the subjective nature of how reality is perceived and the value implications and assumptions that are often hidden in the concepts that researchers use to guide their analyses make the notion of a scientific study of world politics a dangerous illusion.

Although these challenges to realism are formidable, it is too early to consign realism to a place of secondary importance in the study of world politics. Realism has proved to be a resilient body of ideas in the face of challenges, and further adaptations are not impossible. It is also possible that a return to a more threatening international system might lend renewed credence to realist thought and discredit its challengers—such as occurred when President Reagan assumed office. The concepts of interdependence and international cooperation that guided many of the policy initiatives of the Carter administration were replaced by ones more firmly rooted in the realist view of world politics as a struggle for survival and concern for maintaining a balance of power with the Soviet Union. In fact, even as nothing more than a point of attack for other approaches, its influence would still be considerable because of its ability to influence the choice of concepts and frame debates.

It is no accident that challenges to realism have increased both in number and in intensity over the past several years. Ideas about world politics—its underlying dynamics, what the major problems are, and how they should be solved—are not formulated in a vacuum. They are very much part of the social and political atmosphere in which their proponents live. Because all theorizing is rooted in time and space, when circumstances change so, too, will thinking about world politics. What was once a high-priority policy concern may be treated as a nonproblem. A theoretical perspective once seen as holding great insight may come to be regarded as fatally flawed.

It is in this sense of ushering in an unexpected period of transition to an uncertain future that the end of the cold war has had a liberating effect on thinking about world politics. It has provided scholars, policymakers, and citizens with a sense of expanded choice and the prospect of realizing goals (and avoiding evils) that once seemed beyond reach. What the ending of the cold war has not done is identify which values are worthy of pursuit or the best method of attaining them.

The Readings

We have sought to select essays that will both help clarify our thinking about the basic nature of world politics as we enter the twenty-first century and provide at least a partial basis for judging the merits of competing policy proposals. The essays do not tell us the "right" answer. That is not their purpose. Their purpose is to provide a point of departure for our own thinking.

The first reading in this section is from Hans Morgenthau's *Politics Among Nations*, which was first published in 1948. Morgenthau was one of the founding theorists of the realist approach. He argues that like all forms of political activity, world politics is a struggle for power. Regardless of the nature of the aim being pursued (freedom, security, prosperity, etc.) the immediate aim is always power. In the selection presented here Morgenthau lays out what he perceives to be the six fundamental principles of realism.

The second reading is from Robert Keohane and Joseph Nye's *Power and Interdependence*. The first edition of this work appeared in 1978, when largely because of the oil price hikes by OPEC (Organization of Petroleum Exporting Countries) there was a growing awareness of the importance of international economic issues in world politics. Although neither its definition of realism nor its proposed alternative framework of complex interdependence were accepted by all who wrote in the field, this work quickly became influential and the basis for much subsequent theorizing about world politics. The selection presented here presents both aspects of the argument in capsule form.

In the final reading, J. Ann Tickner presents a feminist reinterpretation of Morgenthau's six principles of realism. Hers is only one example of the most recent wave of challengers to realism. Feminist theories of world politics are critical of existing theories because they neither focus on the role of women in world politics nor incorporate feminist perspectives into their analysis. For this reason, unlike many theorists, feminists see little that distinguishes realism from interdependence, world systems, globalism, or dependency-based theorizing.

Bibliography

Cox, Robert. "Social Forces, States, and World Order: Beyond International Relations Theory." *Millenium* 2 (1981), 128–37.

Dougherty, James, and Robert Pfaltzgraff, Jr. *Contending Theories of International Relations: A Comprehensive Survey*, 3rd ed. New York: Harper & Row, 1990.

Ferguson, Yale, and Richard Mansbach. "Between Celebration and Despair: Constructive Suggestions for Future International Relations Theory." *International Studies Quarterly* 35 (1991), 363–86.

Kober, Stanley. "Idealpolitik." *Foreign Policy* 79 (1990), 3–24.

Magrhroori, Ray, and Bennett Ramberg (eds.). *Globalism Versus Realism: International Relations' Third Debate*. Boulder, CO: Westview, 1982.

Spero, Joan. *The Politics of International Economic Relations*, 4th ed. New York: St. Martins Press, 1990.

Strange, Susan (ed.). *Paths to International Political Economy*. London: Unwin Hyman, 1984.

Sylvester, Christine. "The Emperor's Theories and Transformations: Looking at the Field Through Feminist Lenses." In Dennis Pirages and Christine Sylvester (eds.), *Transformations in the Global Political Economy*. London: Macmillan, 1990, pp. 230–53.

Vasquez, John. "Coloring It Morgenthau: New Evidence for an Old Thesis on Quantitative International Politics." *British Journal of International Studies* 5 (1979), 210–28.

Viotti, Paul, and Mark Kauppi. *International Relations Theory: Realism, Pluralism, Globalism*. New York: Macmillan, 1987.

A Realist Theory
of International Politics

Hans Morgenthau

. . . The history of modern political thought is the story of a contest between two schools that differ fundamentally in their conceptions of the nature of man, society, and politics. One believes that a rational and moral political order, derived from universally valid abstract principles, can be achieved here and now. It assumes the essential goodness and infinite malleability of human nature, and blames the failure of the social order to measure up to the rational standards on lack of knowledge and understanding, obsolescent social institutions, or the depravity of certain isolated individuals or groups. It trusts in education, reform, and the sporadic use of force to remedy these defects.

The other school believes that the world, imperfect as it is from the rational point of view, is the result of forces inherent in human nature. To improve the world one must work with those forces, not against them. This being inherently a world of opposing interests and of conflict among them, moral principles can never be fully realized, but must at best be approximated through the ever temporary balancing of interests and the ever precarious settlement of conflicts. This school, then, sees in a system of checks and balances a universal principle for all pluralist societies. It appeals to historic precedent rather than to abstract principles, and aims at the realization of the lesser evil rather than of the absolute good.

This theoretical concern with human nature as it actually is, and with the historic processes as they actually take place, has earned for the theory presented here the name of realism. What are the tenets of political realism? No systematic exposition of the philosophy of political realism can be attempted here; it will suffice to single out six fundamental principles, which have frequently been misunderstood.

Six Principles of Political Realism

1. Political realism believes that politics, like society in general, is governed by objective laws that have their roots in human nature. In order to improve society it is first necessary to understand the laws by which society lives. The operation of these laws being impervious to our preferences, men will challenge them only at the risk of failure.

Realism, believing as it does in the objectivity of the laws of politics, must also believe in the possibility of developing a rational theory that reflects, however imperfectly and one-sidedly, these objective laws. It believes also, then, in the possibility of distinguishing in politics between truth and opinion—between what is true objectively and rationally, supported by evidence and illuminated by reason, and what is only a subjective judgment, divorced from the facts as they are and informed by prejudice and wishful thinking.

. . . For realism, theory consists in ascertaining facts and giving them meaning through reason. It assumes that the character of a foreign policy can be ascertained only through the examination of the political acts performed and of the foreseeable consequences of these acts. Thus, we can find out what statesmen have actually done, and from the foreseeable consequences of their acts we can surmise what their objectives might have been.

Yet examination of the facts is not enough. To give meaning to the factual raw material of foreign policy, we must approach political reality with a kind of rational outline, a map that suggests to us the possible meanings of foreign policy. In other words, we put ourselves in the position of a statesman who must meet a certain problem of foreign policy under certain circumstances, and we ask ourselves what the rational alternatives are from which a statesman may choose who must meet this problem under these circumstances (presuming always that he acts in a rational manner), and which of these rational alternatives this particular statesman, acting under these circumstances, is likely to choose. It is the testing of this rational hypothesis against the actual facts and their consequences that gives meaning to the facts of international politics and makes a theory of politics possible.

2. The main signpost that helps political realism to find its way through the landscape of international politics is the concept of interest defined in terms of power. This concept provides the link between reason trying to understand international politics and the facts to be understood. It sets politics as an autonomous sphere of action and understanding apart from other spheres, such as economics (understood in terms of interest defined as wealth), ethics, aesthetics, or religion. Without such a concept a

theory of politics, international or domestic, would be altogether impossible, for without it we could not distinguish between political and nonpolitical facts, nor could we bring at least a measure of systematic order to the political sphere. . . .

The concept of interest defined as power imposes intellectual discipline upon the observer, infuses rational order into the subject matter of politics, and thus makes the theoretical understanding of politics possible. On the side of the actor, it provides for rational discipline in action and creates that astounding continuity in foreign policy which makes American, British, or Russian foreign policy appear as an intelligible, rational continuum, by and large consistent within itself, regardless of the different motives, preferences, and intellectual and moral qualities of successive statesmen. A realist theory of international politics, then, will guard against two popular fallacies: the concern with motives and the concern with ideological preferences. . . .

Good motives give assurance against deliberately bad policies; they do not guarantee the moral goodness and political success of the policies they inspire. What it is important to know, if one wants to understand foreign policy, is not primarily the motives of a statesman, but his intellectual ability to comprehend the essentials of foreign policy, as well as his political ability to translate what he has comprehended into successful political action. It follows that while ethics in the abstract judges the moral qualities of motives, political theory must judge the political qualities of intellect, will, and action.

A realist theory of international politics will also avoid the other popular fallacy of equating the foreign policies of a statesman with his philosophic or political sympathies, and of deducing the former from the latter. Statesmen, especially under contemporary conditions, may well make a habit of presenting their foreign policies in terms of their philosophic and political sympathies in order to gain popular support for them. Yet they will distinguish with Lincoln between their *"official* duty," which is to think and act in terms of the national interest, and their *personal* wish," which is to see their own moral values and political principles realized throughout the world. Political realism does not require, nor does it condone, indifference to political ideals and moral principles, but it requires indeed a sharp distinction between the desirable and the possible—between what is desirable everywhere and at all times and what is possible under the concrete circumstances of time and place.

It stands to reason that not all foreign policies have always followed so rational, objective, and unemotional a course. The contingent elements of personality, prejudice, and subjective preference, and of all the weaknesses of intellect and will which flesh is heir to, are bound to deflect foreign policies from their rational course. Especially where foreign policy is conducted under the conditions of democratic control, the need to marshal popular emotions to the support of foreign policy cannot fail to impair the rationality of foreign policy itself. Yet a theory of foreign policy which aims at rationality must for the time being, as it were, abstract from these irrational elements and seek to paint a picture of foreign policy which presents the rational essence to be found in experience, without the contingent deviations from rationality which are also found in experience.

The difference between international politics as it actually is and a rational theory derived from it is like the difference between a photograph and a painted portrait. The photograph shows everything that can be seen by the naked eye, the painted portrait does not show everything that can be seen by the naked eye, but it shows, or at least seeks to show, one thing that the naked eye cannot see: the human essence of the person portrayed.

Political realism contains not only a theoretical but also a normative element. It knows that political reality is replete with contingencies and points to the typical influences they exert upon foreign policy. Yet it shares with all social theory the need, for the sake of theoretical understanding, to stress the rational elements of political reality; for it is these rational elements that make reality intelligible for theory. Political realism presents the theoretical construct of a rational foreign policy which experience can never completely achieve.

3. Realism does not endow its key concept of interest defined as power with a meaning that is fixed once and for all. The idea of interest is indeed of the essence of politics and is unaffected by the circumstances of time and place. Thucydides' statement, born of the experiences of ancient Greece, that "identity of interest is the surest of bonds whether between states or individuals" was taken up in the nineteenth century by Lord Salisbury's remark that "the only bond of union that endures among nations is "the absence of all clashing interests." . . . It was echoed and enlarged upon in our century by Max Weber's observation:

> Interests (material and ideal), not ideas, dominate directly the actions of men. Yet the "images of the world" created by these ideas have very often served as switches determining the tracks on which the dynamism of interests kept actions moving.[1]

Yet the kind of interest determining political action in a particular period of history depends upon the political and cultural context within which foreign policy is formulated. The goals that might be pursued by nations in their foreign policy can run the whole gamut of objectives any nation has ever pursued or might possibly pursue.

The same observations apply to the concept of power. Its content and the manner of its use are determined by the political and cultural environment. Power may comprise anything that establishes and maintains the control of man over man. Thus power covers all social relationships which serve that end, from physical violence to the most subtle psychological ties by which one mind controls another. Power covers the domination of man by man, both when it is disciplined by moral ends and controlled by constitutional

[1]Marianne Weber, *Max Weber* (Tuebingen: J. C. B. Mohr, 1926), pp. 347–348.

safeguards, as in Western democracies, and when it is that untamed and barbaric force which finds its laws in nothing but its own strength and its sole justification in its aggrandizement.

Political realism does not assume that the contemporary conditions under which foreign policy operates, with their extreme instability and the ever present threat of large violence, cannot be changed. The balance of power, for instance, is indeed a perennial element of all pluralistic societies, as the authors of *The Federalist* papers well knew; yet it is capable of operating, as it does in the United States, under the conditions of relative stability and peaceful conflict. If the factors that have given rise to these conditions can be duplicated on the international scene, similar conditions of stability and peace will then prevail there, as they have over long stretches of history among certain nations.

What is true of the general character of international relations is also true of the nation state as the ultimate point of reference of contemporary foreign policy. While the realist indeed believes that interest is the perennial standard by which political action must be judged and directed, the contemporary connection between interest and the national state is a product of history, and is therefore bound to disappear in the course of history. Nothing in the realist position militates against the assumption that the present division of the political world into nation states will be replaced by larger units of a quite different character, more in keeping with the technical potentialities and the moral requirements of the contemporary world.

The realist parts company with other schools of thought before the all-important question of how the contemporary world is to be transformed. The realist is persuaded that this transformation can be achieved only through the workmanlike manipulation of the perennial forces that have shaped the past as they will the future. The realist cannot be persuaded that we can bring about that transformation by confronting a political reality that has its own laws with an abstract ideal that refuses to take those laws into account.

4. Political realism is aware of the moral significance of political action. It is also aware of the ineluctable tension between the moral command and the requirements of successful political action. And it is unwilling to gloss over and obliterate that tension and thus to obfuscate both the moral and the political issue by making it appear as though the stark facts of politics were morally more satisfying than they actually are, and the moral law less exacting than it actually is.

Realism maintains that universal moral principles cannot be applied to the actions of states in their abstract universal formulation, but that they must be filtered through the concrete circumstances of time and place. The individual may say for himself: "*Fiat jusitia, pereat mundus* (Let justice be done, even if the world perish)," but the state has no right to say so in the name of those who are in its care. Both individual and state must judge political action by universal moral principles, such as that of liberty. Yet while the individual has a moral right to sacrifice himself in defense of such a moral principle, the state has no right to let its moral disapprobation of the infringement of liberty get in the way of successful political action, itself inspired by the moral principle of national survival. There can be no political morality without prudence; that is, without consideration of the political consequences of seemingly moral action. Realism, then, considers prudence—the weighing of the consequences of alternative political actions—to be the supreme virtue in politics. Ethics in the abstract judges action by its conformity with the moral law; political ethics judges action by its political consequences. . . .

5. Political realism refuses to identify the moral aspirations of a particular nation with the moral laws that govern the universe. As it distinguishes between truth and opinion, so it distinguishes between truth and idolatry. All nations are tempted—and few have been able to resist the temptation for long—to clothe their own particular aspirations and actions in the moral purposes of the universe. To know that nations are subject to the moral law is one thing, while to pretend to know with certainty what is good and evil in the relations among nations is quite another. There is a world of difference between the belief that all nations stand under the judgment of God, inscrutable to the human mind, and the blasphemous conviction that God is always on one's side and that what one wills oneself cannot fail to be willed by God also.

The lighthearted equation between a particular nationalism and the counsels of Providence is morally indefensible, for it is that very sin of pride against which the Greek tragedians and the Biblical prophets have warned rulers and ruled. That equation is also politically pernicious, for it is liable to engender the distortion in judgment which, in the blindness of crusading frenzy, destroys nations and civilizations—in the name of moral principle, ideal, or God himself.

On the other hand, it is exactly the concept of interest defined in terms of power that saves us from both that moral excess and that political folly. For if we look at all nations, our own included, as political entities pursuing their respective interests defined in terms of power, we are able to do justice to all of them. And we are able to do justice to all of them in a dual sense: We are able to judge other nations as we judge our own and, having judged them in this fashion, we are then capable of pursuing policies that respect the interests of other nations, while protecting and promoting those of our own. Moderation in policy cannot fail to reflect the moderation of moral judgment.

6. The difference, then, between political realism and other schools of thought is real and it is profound. However much the theory of political realism may have been misunderstood and misinterpreted, there is no gainsaying its distinctive intellectual and moral attitude to matters political.

Intellectually, the political realist maintains the autonomy of the political sphere, as the economist, the lawyer, the moralist maintain theirs. He thinks in terms of interest defined as power, as the economist thinks in terms of interest defined as wealth; the lawyer, of the conformity of action with legal rules; the moralist, of the conformity of action with moral principles. The economist asks; "How does this policy affect the wealth of society, or a segment of it?" The lawyer asks: "Is this policy in accord with the rules of law?" The moralist asks: "Is this policy in accord with moral principles?" And the political realist asks: "How does this policy affect the power of the nation?" (Or of the federal government, of Congress, of the party, of agriculture, as the case may be.)

The political realist is not unaware of the existence and relevance of standards of thought other than political ones. As political realist, he cannot but subordinate these other standards to those of politics. And he parts company with other schools when they impose standards of thought appropriate to other spheres upon the political sphere. It is here that political realism takes issue with the "legalistic-moralistic approach" to international politics. . . .

This realist defense of the autonomy of the political sphere against its subversion by other modes of thought does not imply disregard for the existence and importance of these other modes of thought. It rather implies that each should be assigned its proper sphere and function. Political realism is based upon a pluralistic conception of human nature. Real man is a composite of "economic man," "political man," "moral man," "religious man," etc. A man who was nothing but "political man" would be a beast, for he would be completely lacking in moral restraints. A man who was nothing but "moral man" would be a fool, for he would be completely lacking in prudence. A man who was nothing but "religious man" would be a saint, for he would be completely lacking in worldly desires.

Recognizing that these different facets of human nature exist, political realism also recognizes that in order to understand one of them one has to deal with it on its own terms. That is to say, if I want to understand "religious man," I must for the time being abstract from the other aspects of human nature and deal with its religious aspect as if it were the only one. Furthermore, I must apply to the religious sphere the standards of thought appropriate to it, always remaining aware of the existence of other standards and their actual influence upon the religious qualities of man. What is true of this facet of human nature is true of all the others. No modern economist, for instance, would conceive of his science and its relations to other sciences of man in any other way. It is exactly through such a process of emancipation from other standards of thought, and the development of one appropriate to its subject matter, that economics has developed as an autonomous theory of the economic activities of man. To contribute to a similar development in the field of politics is indeed the purpose of political realism.

It is in the nature of things that a theory of politics which is based upon such principles will not meet with unanimous approval—nor does, for that matter, such a foreign policy. For theory and policy alike run counter to two trends in our culture which are not able to reconcile themselves to the assumptions and results of a rational, objective theory of politics. One of these trends disparages the role of power in society on grounds that stem from the experience and philosophy of the nineteenth century. . . . The other trend, opposed to the realist theory and practice of politics, stems from the very relationship that exists, and must exist, between the human mind and the political sphere. . . . The human mind in its day-by-day operations cannot bear to look the truth of politics straight in the face. It must disguise, distort, belittle, and embellish the truth—the more so, the more the individual is involved actively in the processes of politics, and particularly in those of international politics. For only by deceiving himself about the nature of politics and the role he plays on the political scene is man able to live contentedly as a political animal with himself and his fellow men.

Thus it is inevitable that a theory which tries to understand international politics as it actually is and as it ought to be in view of its intrinsic nature, rather than as people would like to see it, must overcome a psychological resistance that most other branches of learning need not face. A book devoted to the theoretical understanding of international politics therefore requires a special explanation and justification.

Realism and Complex Interdependence

Robert Keohane
Joseph Nye

One's assumptions about world politics profoundly affect what one sees and how one constructs theories to explain events. We believe that the assumptions of political realists, whose theories dominated the postwar period, are often an inadequate basis for analyzing the politics of interdependence. The realist assumptions about world politics can be seen as defining an extreme set of conditions or *ideal type*. One could also imagine very different conditions. In this chapter, we shall construct another ideal type, the opposite of realism. We call it *complex interdependence*. After establishing the differences between realism and complex interdependence, we shall argue that complex interdependence sometimes comes closer to reality than does realism. When it does, traditional explanations of change in international regimes become questionable and the search for new explanatory models becomes more urgent.

For political realists, international politics, like all other politics, is a struggle for power but, unlike domestic politics, a struggle dominated by organized violence. In the words of the most influential postwar textbook, "All history shows that nations active in international politics are continuously preparing for, actively involved in, or recovering from organized violence in the form of war."[1] Three assumptions are integral to the realist vision. First, states as coherent units are the dominant actors in world politics. This is a double assumption: states are predominant; and they act as coherent units. Second, realists assume that force is a usable and effective instrument of policy. Other instruments may also be employed, but using or threatening force is the most effective means of wielding power. Third, partly because of their second assumption, realists assume a hierarchy of issues in world politics, headed by questions of military security: the "high politics" of military security dominates the "low politics" of economic and social affairs. . . .

The Characteristics of Complex Interdependence

Complex interdependence has three main characteristics:

1. *Multiple channels* connect societies, including: informal ties between governmental elites as well as formal foreign office arrangements; informal ties among nongovernmental elites (face-to-face and through telecommunications); and transnational organizations (such as multinational banks or corporations). These channels can be summarized as interstate, transgovernmental, and transnational relations. *Interstate* relations are the normal channels assumed by realists. *Transgovernmental* applies when we relax the realist assumption that states act coherently as units; *transnational* applies when we relax the assumption that states are the only units.

2. The agenda of interstate relationships consists of multiple issues that are not arranged in a clear or consistent hierarchy. This *absence of hierarchy among issues* means, among other things, that military security does not consistently dominate the agenda. Many issues arise from what used to be considered domestic policy, and the distinction between domestic and foreign issues becomes blurred. These issues are considered in several government departments (not just foreign offices), and at several levels. Inadequate policy coordination on these issues involves significant costs. Different issues generate different coalitions, both within governments and across them, and involve different degrees of conflict. Politics does not stop at the waters' edge.

3. Military force is not used by governments toward other governments within the region, or on the issues, when complex interdependence prevails. It may, however, be important in these governments' relations with governments outside that region, or on other issues. Military force could, for instance, be irrelevant to resolving disagreements on economic issues among members of an alliance, yet at the same time be very important for that alliance's political and military relations with a rival bloc. For the former relationships this condition of complex interdependence would be met; for the latter, it would not.

Traditional theories of international politics implicitly or explicitly deny the accuracy of these three assumptions. Traditionalists are therefore tempted also to deny the relevance of criticisms based on the complex interdependence ideal type. We believe, however, that our three conditions are fairly well approximated on some global issues of economic and ecological interdependence and that they come close to characterizing the entire relationship between some countries. . . .

The Political Processes of Complex Interdependence

The three main characteristics of complex interdependence give rise to distinctive political processes, which translate power resources into power as control of outcomes. As we argued earlier, something is usually lost or added in the translation. Under conditions of complex interdependence the translation will be different than under realist conditions, and our predictions about outcomes will need to be adjusted accordingly.

In the realist world, military security will be the dominant goal of states. It will even affect issues that are not directly involved with military power or territorial defense. Nonmilitary problems will not only be subordinated to military ones; they will be studied for their politico-military implications. Balance of payments issues, for instance, will be considered at least as much in the light of their implications for world power generally as for their purely financial ramifications. McGeorge Bundy conformed to realist expectations when he argued in 1964 that devaluation of the dollar should be seriously considered if necessary to fight the war in Vietnam.[2] To some extent, so did former Treasury Secretary Henry Fowler when he contended in 1971 that the United States needed a trade surplus of $4 billion to $6 billion in order to lead in Western defense.

In a world of complex interdependence, however, one expects some officials, particularly at lower levels, to emphasize the *variety* of state goals that must be pursued. In the absence of a clear hierarchy of issues, goals will vary by issue, and may not be closely related. Each bureaucracy will pursue its own concerns; and although several agencies may reach compromises on issues that affect them all, they will find that a consistent pattern of policy is difficult to maintain. Moreover, transnational actors will introduce different goals into various groups of issues.

Linkage Strategies

Goals will therefore vary by issue area under complex interdependence, but so will the distribution of power and the typical political processes. Traditional analysis focuses on *the* international system, and leads us to anticipate similar political processes on a variety of issues. Militarily and economically strong states will dominate a variety of organizations and a variety of issues, by linking their own policies on some issues to other states' policies on other issues. By using their overall dominance to prevail on their weak issues, the strongest states will, in the traditional model, ensure a congruence between the overall structure of military and economic power and the pattern of outcomes on any one issue area. Thus world politics can be treated as a seamless web.

Under complex interdependence, such congruence is less likely to occur. As military force is devalued, militarily strong states will find it more difficult to use their overall dominance to control outcomes on issues in which they are weak. And since the distribution of power resources in trade, shipping, or oil, for example, may be quite different, patterns of outcomes and distinctive political processes are likely to vary from one set of issues to another. If force were readily applicable, and military security were the highest foreign policy goal, these variations in the issue structures of power would not matter very much. The linkages drawn from them to military issues would ensure consistent dominance by the overall strongest states. But when military force is largely immobilized, strong states will find that linkage is less effective. They may still attempt such links, but in the absence of a hierarchy of issues, their success will be problematic. . . .

The differentiation among issue areas in complex interdependence means that linkages among issues will become more problematic and will tend to reduce rather than reinforce international hierarchy. Linkage strategies, and defense against them, will pose critical strategic choices for states. Should issues be considered separately or as a package? If linkages are to be drawn, which issues should be linked, and on which of the linked issues should concessions be made? How far can one push a linkage before it becomes counterproductive? For instance, should one seek formal agreements or informal, but less politically sensitive, understandings? The fact that world politics under complex interdependence is not a seamless web leads us to expect that efforts to stitch seams together advantageously, as reflected in linkage strategies, will, very often, determine the shape of the fabric. . . .

Agenda Setting

Our second assumption of complex interdependence, the lack of clear hierarchy among multiple issues, leads us to expect that the politics of agenda formation and control will become more important. Traditional analyses lead statesmen to focus on politico-military issues and to pay little attention to the broader politics of agenda formation. Statesmen assume that the agenda will be set by shifts in the balance of power, actual or anticipated, and by perceived threats to the security of states. Other issues will only be very important when they seem to affect security and military power. In these cases, agendas will be influenced strongly by considerations of the overall balance of power.

Yet, today, some nonmilitary issues are emphasized in interstate relations at one time, whereas others of seemingly equal importance are neglected or quietly handled at a technical level. International monetary politics, problems of commodity terms of trade, oil, food, and multinational corporations have all been important during the last decade; but not all have been high on interstate agendas throughout that period.

Traditional analysts of international politics have paid little attention to agenda formation: to how issues come to receive sustained attention by high officials. . . .

Under complex interdependence we can expect the agenda to be affected by the international and domestic problems created by economic growth and increasing sensitivity interdependence that we described in the last chapter. Discontented domestic groups will politicize issues and force more issues once considered domestic onto the interstate agenda. Shifts in the distribution of power resources within sets of issues will also affect agendas. During the early 1970s the increased power of oil-producing governments over the transnational corporations and the consumer countries dramatically altered the policy agenda. Moreover, agendas for one group of issues may change as a result of linkages from other groups in which power resources are changing; for example, the broader agenda of North-South trade issues changed after the OPEC price rises and the oil embargo of 1973–74. Even if capabilities among states do not change, agendas may be affected by shifts in the importance of transnational actors. The publicity surrounding multinational corporations in the early 1970s, coupled with their rapid growth over the past twenty years, put the regulation of such corporations higher on both the United Nations agenda and national agendas. . . .

The technical characteristics and institutional setting in which issues are raised will strongly affect politicization patterns. In the United States, congressional attention is an effective instrument of politicization. Generally, we expect transnational economic organizations and transgovernmental networks of bureaucrats to seek to avoid politicization. Domestically based groups (such as trade unions) and domestically oriented bureaucracies will tend to use politicization (particularly congressional attention) against their transnationally mobile competitors. At the international level, we expect states and actors to "shop among forums" and struggle to get issues raised in international organizations that will maximize their advantage by broadening or narrowing the agenda.

Transnational and Transgovernmental Relations

Our third condition of complex interdependence, multiple channels of contact among societies, further blurs the distinction between domestic and international politics. The availability of partners in political coalitions is not necessarily limited by national boundaries as traditional analysis assumes. The nearer a situation is to complex interdependence, the more we expect the outcomes of political bargaining to be affected by transnational relations. Multinational corporations may be significant both as independent actors and as instruments manipulated by governments. The attitudes and policy stands of domestic groups are likely to be affected by communications, organized or not, between them and their counterparts abroad. . . .

The multiple channels of contact found in complex interdependence are not limited to nongovernmental actors. Contacts between governmental bureaucracies charged with similar tasks may not only alter their perspectives but lead to transgovernmental coalitions on particular policy questions. To improve their chances of success, government agencies attempt to bring actors from other governments into their own decision-making processes as allies. Agencies of powerful states such as the United States have used such coalitions to penetrate weaker governments in such countries as Turkey and Chile. They have also been used to help agencies of other governments penetrate the United States bureaucracy.[3] . . .

The existence of transgovernmental policy networks leads to a different interpretation of one of the standard propositions about international policies—that states act in their own interest. Under complex interdependence, this conventional wisdom begs two important questions: which self and which interest? A government agency may pursue its own interests under the guise of the national interest; and recurrent interactions can change official perceptions of their interests. . . .

Role of International Organizations

Finally, the existence of multiple channels leads one to predict a different and significant role for international organizations in world politics. Realists in the tradition of Hans J. Morgenthau have portrayed a world in which states, acting from self-interest, struggle for "power and peace." Security issues are dominant; war threatens. In such a world, one may assume that international institutions will have a minor role, limited by the rare congruence of such interests. International organizations are then clearly peripheral to world politics. But in a world of multiple issues imperfectly linked, in which coalitions are formed transnationally and transgovernmentally, the potential role of international institutions in political bargaining is greatly increased. In particular, they help set the international agenda, and act as catalysts for coalition-formation and as arenas for political initiatives and linkage by weak states.

Governments must organize themselves to cope with the flow of business generated by international organizations. By defining the salient issues, and deciding which issues can be grouped together, organizations may help to determine governmental priorities and the nature of interdepartmental committees and other arrangements within governments. . . .

By bringing officials together, organizations help to activate potential coalitions in world politics. It is quite obvious that international organizations have been very important in bringing together representatives of less developed countries, most of which do not maintain embassies in one another's capitals. Third World strategies of solidarity among poor countries have been developed in and for a series of international conferences, mostly under the auspices of the United Nations.[4] International organizations also allow agencies of governments, which might not otherwise come into contact, to turn potential or tacit coalitions into explicit transgovernmental coalitions characterized by direct communications. In some cases, international secretariats deliberately promote this process by forming coalitions with groups of governments, or with units of governments, as well as with nongovernmental organizations having similar interests.[5] . . .

Complex interdependence therefore yields different political patterns than does the realist conception of the world. . . . Thus, one would expect traditional theories to fail to explain international regime change in situations of complex interdependence. But, for a situation that approximates realist conditions, traditional theories should be appropriate. . . .

NOTES

1. Hans J. Morgenthau, *Politics Among Nations: The Struggle for Power and Peace*, 4th ed. (New York: Knopf, 1967), p. 36.
2. Henry Brandon, *The Retreat of American Power* (New York: Doubleday, 1974), p. 218.
3. For a more detailed discussion, see Robert O. Keohane and Joseph S. Nye, Jr., "Transgovernmental Relations and International Organizations," *World Politics* 27, no. 1 (October 1974): 39–62.
4. Branislav Gosovic and John Gerard Ruggie, "On the Creation of a New International Economic Order: Issue Linkage and the Seventh Special Session of the UN General Assembly," *International Organization* 30, no. 2 (Spring 1976): 309–346.
5. Robert W. Cox, "The Executive Head," *International Organization* 23, no. 2 (Spring 1969): 205–230.

Hans Morgenthau's Principles of Political Realism

A Feminist Reformulation

J. Ann Tickner

In order to investigate the claim that the discipline of international relations, as it has traditionally been defined by realism, is based on a masculine world view, I propose to examine the six principles of political realism formulated by Hans Morgenthau in his classic work *Politics Among Nations*. I shall use some ideas from feminist theory to show that the way in which Morgenthau describes and explains international politics, and the prescriptions that ensue, are embedded in a masculine perspective. Then I shall suggest some ways in which feminist theory might help us begin to conceptualize a world view from a feminine perspective and to formulate a feminist epistemology of international relations. Drawing on these observations I shall conclude with a reformulation of Morgenthau's six principles. Male critics of contemporary realism have already raised many of the same questions about realism that I shall address. However, in undertaking this exercise, I hope to make a link between a growing critical perspective on international relations theory and feminist writers interested in global issues. Adding a feminist perspective to its discourse could also help to make the field of international relations more accessible to women scholars and practitioners.

From Rebecca Grant and Kathleen Newland (eds.), *Gender and International Relations* (England: Open University Press, 1991).

Hans Morgenthau's Principles of Political Realism: A Masculine Perspective?

I am not going to argue that Morgenthau is incorrect in his portrayal of the international system. I do believe, however, that it is a partial description of international politics because it is based on assumptions about human nature that are partial and that privilege masculinity. First, it is necessary to define masculinity and femininity. According to almost all feminist theorists, masculinity and femininity refer to a set of socially constructed categories, which vary in time and place, rather than to biological determinants. In the West, conceptual dichotomies such as objectivity vs subjectivity, reason vs emotion, mind vs body, culture vs nature, self vs other or autonomy vs relatedness, knowing vs being and public vs private have typically been used to describe male/female differences by feminists and non-feminists alike. In the United States, psychological tests conducted across different socioeconomic groups confirm that individuals perceive these dichotomies as masculine and feminine and also that the characteristics associated with masculinity are more highly valued by men and women alike.[1] It is important to stress, however, that these characteristics are stereotypical; they do not necessarily describe individual men or women, who can exhibit characteristics and modes of thought associated with the opposite sex.

Using a vocabulary that contains many of the words associated with masculinity as I have identified it, Morgenthau asserts that it is possible to develop a rational (and unemotional) theory of international politics based on objective laws that have their roots in human nature. Since Morgenthau wrote the first edition of *Politics Among Nations* in 1948, this search for an objective science of international politics based on the model of the natural sciences has been an important part of the realist and neorealist agenda. In her feminist critique of the natural sciences, Evelyn Fox Keller points out that most scientific communities share the 'assumption that the universe they study is directly accessible, represented by concepts and shaped not by language but only by the demands of logic and experiment'.[2] The laws of nature, according to this view of science, are 'beyond the relativity of language'. Like most feminists, Keller rejects this view of science which, she asserts, imposes a coercive, hierarchical and conformist pattern on scientific inquiry. Feminists in general are sceptical about the possibility of finding a universal and objective foundation for knowledge, which Morgenthau claims is possible. Most share the belief that knowledge is socially constructed: since it is language that transmits knowledge, the use of language and its claims to objectivity must continually be questioned.

Keller argues that objectivity, as it is usually defined in our culture, is associated with masculinity. She identifies it as 'a network of interactions between gender development, a belief system that equates objectivity with masculinity, and a set of cultural values that simultaneously (and cojointly) elevates what is defined as scientific and what is defined as masculine'.[3]

Keller links the separation of self from other, an important stage of masculine gender development, with this notion of objectivity. Translated into scientific inquiry this becomes the striving for the separation of subject and object, an important goal of modern science and one which, Keller asserts, is based on the need for control; hence objectivity becomes associated with power and domination.

The need for control has been an important motivating force for modern realism. To begin his search for an objective, rational theory of international politics, which could impose order on a chaotic and conflictual world, Morgenthau constructs an abstraction which he calls political man, a beast completely lacking in moral restraints. Morgenthau is deeply aware that real men, like real states, are both moral and bestial but, because states do not live up to the universal moral laws that govern the universe, those who behave morally in international politics are doomed to failure because of the immoral actions of others. To solve this tension Morgenthau postulates a realm of international politics in which the amoral behaviour of political man is not only permissible but prudent. It is a Hobbesian world, separate and distinct from the world of domestic order. In it, states may act like beasts, for survival depends on a maximization of power and a willingness to fight.

Having long argued that the personal is political, most feminist theory would reject the validity of constructing an autonomous political sphere around which boundaries of permissible modes of conduct have been drawn. As Keller maintains, 'the demarcation between public and private not only defines and defends the boundaries of the political but also helps form its content and style'.[4] Morgenthau's political man is a social construct based on a partial representation of human nature. One might well ask where the women were in Hobbes's state of nature; presumably they must have been involved in reproduction and childrearing, rather than warfare, if life was to go on for more than one generation.[5] Morgenthau's emphasis on the conflictual aspects of the international system contributes to a tendency, shared by other realists, to de-emphasize elements of cooperation and regeneration which are also aspects of international relations.

Morgenthau's construction of an amoral realm of international power politics is an attempt to resolve what he sees as a fundamental tension between the moral laws that govern the universe and the requirements of successful political action in a world where states use morality as a cloak to justify the pursuit of their own national interests. Morgenthau's universalistic morality postulates the highest form of morality as an abstract ideal, similar to the Golden Rule, to which states seldom adhere: the morality of states, by contrast, is an instrumental morality guided by self-interest.

. . . Using examples from feminist literature I have suggested that Morgenthau's attempt to construct an objective universal theory of international politics is rooted in assumptions about human nature and morality that, in modern Western culture, are associated with masculinity. Further evidence that Morgenthau's principles are not the basis for a universalistic and objective theory is contained in his frequent references to the failure of what he calls the 'legalistic–moralistic' or idealist approach to world politics which he claims was largely responsible for both the world wars. Having laid the blame for the Second World War on the misguided morality of appeasement, Morgenthau's *realpolitik* prescriptions for successful political action appear as prescriptions for avoiding the mistakes of the 1930s rather than as prescriptions with timeless applicability.

If Morgenthau's world view is embedded in the traumas of the Second World War, are his prescriptions still valid as we move further away from this event? I share with other critics of realism the view that, in a rapidly changing world, we must begin to search for modes of behaviour different from those prescribed by Morgenthau. Given that any war between the major powers is likely to be nuclear, increasing security by increasing power could be suicidal. Moreover, the nation state, the primary constitutive element of the international system for Morgenthau and other realists, is no longer able to deal with an increasingly pluralistic array of problems ranging from economic interdependence to environmental degradation. Could feminist theory make a contribution to international relations theory by constructing an alternative, feminist perspective on international politics that might help us to search for more appropriate solutions?

A Feminist Perspective on International Relations?

Morgenthau's definition of power, the control of man over man, is typical of the way power is usually defined in international relations. Nancy Hartsock argues that this type of power-as-domination has always been associated with masculinity, since the exercise of power has generally been a masculine activity: rarely have women exercised legitimized power in the public domain. When women write about power they stress energy, capacity and potential, says Hartsock. She notes that women theorists, even when they have little else in common, offer similar definitions of power which differ substantially from the understanding of power as domination.[6]

Hannah Arendt, frequently cited by feminists writing about power, defines power as the human ability to act in concert, or to take action in connection with others who share similar concerns.[7] This definition of power is similar to that of psychologist David McClelland's portrayal of female power, which he describes as shared rather than assertive.[8] Jane Jaquette argues that, since women have had less access to the instruments of coercion, they have been more apt to rely on power as persuasion; she compares women's domestic activities to coalition building.[9]

All of these writers are portraying power as a relationship of mutual enablement. Tying her definition of female power to international relations, Jaquette sees similarities between female strategies of persuasion and strategies of small states operating from a position of weakness in the international system. There are also examples of states' behaviour that contain elements of the female strategy of coalition building. One such example is the Southern African Development Coordination Conference (SADCC), which is designed to build regional infrastructure based on mutual cooperation and collective self-reliance in order to decrease dependence on the South African economy. Another is the European Community, which has had considerable success in building mutual cooperation in an area of the world whose history would not predict such a course of events. It is rare, however, that cooperative outcomes in international relations are described in these terms, although Karl Deutsch's notion of pluralistic security communities might be one such example where power is associated with building community. I am not denying that power as domination is a pervasive reality in international relations. However, there are also instances of cooperation in inter-state relations, which tend to be obscured when power is seen solely as domination. Thinking about power in this multidimensional sense may help us to think constructively about the potential for cooperation as well as conflict, an aspect of international relations generally played down by realism.

Redefining national security is another way in which feminist theory could contribute to new thinking about international relations. Traditionally in the West, the concept of national security has been tied to military strength and its role in the physical protection of the nation state from external threats. Morgenthau's notion of defending the national interest in terms of power is consistent with this definition. But this traditional definition of national security is partial at best in today's world.[10] The technologically advanced states are highly interdependent, and rely on weapons whose effects would be equally devastating to winners and losers alike. For them to defend national security by relying on war as the last resort no longer appears very useful. Moreover, if one thinks of security in North–South rather than East–West terms, for a large portion of the world's population security has as much to do with the satisfaction of basic material needs as with military threats. According to Johan Galtung's notion of structural violence, to suffer a lower life expectancy by virtue of one's place of birth is a form of violence whose effects can be as devastating as war.[11]

Basic needs satisfaction has a great deal to do with women, but only recently have women's roles as providers of basic needs, and in development more generally, become visible as important components in development strategies.[12] Traditionally the development literature has focused on aspects of the development process that are in the public sphere, are technologically complex and are usually undertaken by men. Thinking about the role of women in development and the way in which we can define development and basic needs satisfaction to be inclusive of women's roles and needs are topics that deserve higher priority on the international agenda. Typically, however, this is an area about which traditional international relations theory, with the priority it gives to order over justice, has had very little to say.

A further threat to national security, more broadly defined, which has also been missing from the agenda of traditional international relations, concerns the environment. Carolyn Merchant argues that a mechanistic view of nature, contained in modern science, has helped to guide an industrial and technological development which has resulted in environmental damage that has now become a matter of global concern. In the introduction to her book *The Death of Nature,* Merchant suggests that, 'Women and nature have an age-old association—an affiliation that has persisted throughout culture, language, and history.'[13] Hence she maintains that the ecology movement, which is growing up in response to environmental threats, and the women's movement are deeply interconnected. Both stress living in equilibrium with nature rather than dominating it, both see nature as a living non-hierarchical entity in which each part is mutually dependent on the whole. Ecologists, as well as many feminists, are now suggesting that only such a fundamental change of world view will allow the human species to survive the damage it is inflicting on the environment.

Thinking about military, economic and environmental security in interdependent terms suggests the need for new methods of conflict resolution that seek to achieve mutually beneficial, rather than zero sum, outcomes. One such method comes from Sara Ruddick's work on 'maternal thinking'.[14] Ruddick describes maternal thinking as focused on the preservation of life and the growth of children. To foster a domestic environment conducive to these goals, tranquillity must be preserved by avoiding conflict where possible, engaging in it non-violently and restoring community when it is over. In such an environment the ends for which disputes are fought are subordinate to the means by which they are resolved. This method of conflict resolution involves making contextual judgements rather than appealing to absolute standards and thus has much in common with Gilligan's definition of female morality.

While non-violent resolution of conflict in the domestic sphere is a widely accepted norm, passive resistance in the public realm is regarded as deviant. But, as Ruddick argues, the peaceful resolution of conflict by mothers does not usually extend to the children of one's enemies, an important reason why women have been ready to support men's wars. The question for Ruddick then becomes how to get maternal thinking, a mode of thinking which she believes can be found in men as well as women, out into the public realm. Ruddick believes that finding a common humanity among one's opponents has become a condition of survival in the nuclear age when the notion of winners and losers has become questionable. Portraying the adversary as less than human has all too often been a technique of the nation state to command loyalty and to increase its legitimacy in the eyes of its citizens. Such behaviour in an age of weapons of mass destruction may be self-defeating.

We might also look to Gilligan's work for a feminist perspective on conflict resolution. Reporting on a study of playground behaviour of American boys and girls, Gilligan argues that girls are less able to tolerate high levels of conflict, and more likely than boys to play games that involve taking turns and in which the success of one does not depend on the failure of another.[15] While Gilligan's study does not take into account attitudes toward other groups (racial, ethnic, economic or national), it does suggest the validity of investigating whether girls are socialized to use different modes of problem solving when dealing with conflict, and whether such behaviour might be useful in thinking about international conflict resolution.

Toward a Feminist Epistemology of International Relations

I am deeply aware that there is no *one* feminist approach but many, which come out of various disciplines and intellectual traditions. Yet there are common themes in the different feminist literatures that I have reviewed which could help us to begin to formulate a feminist epistemology of international relations. Morgenthau encourages us to try to stand back from the world and to think about theory building in terms of constructing a rational outline or map that has universal applications. In contrast, the feminist literature reviewed here emphasizes connection and contingency. Keller argues for a form of knowledge, which she calls 'dynamic objectivity', 'that grants to the world around us its independent integrity, but does so in a way that remains cognizant of, indeed relies on, our connectivity with that world'. Keller illustrates this mode of thinking in her study of Barbara McClintock, whose work on genetic transposition won her a Nobel prize after many years of marginalization by the scientific community. McClintock, Keller argues, was a scientist with a respect for complexity, diversity and individual difference whose methodology allowed her data to speak rather than imposing explanations on it.

Keller's portrayal of McClintock's science contains parallels with what Sandra Harding calls an African world view. Harding tells us that the Western liberal notion of rational economic man, an individualist and a welfare maximizer, similar to the image of rational political man on which realism has based its theoretical investigations, does not make any sense in the African world view where the individual is seen as part of the social order acting within that order rather than upon it. Harding believes that this view of human behaviour has much in common with a feminist perspective. If we combine this view of human behaviour with Merchant's holistic perspective which stresses the interconnectedness of all things, including nature, it may help us to begin to think from a more global perspective. Such a perspective appreciates cultural diversity but at the same time recognizes a growing interdependence, which makes anachronistic the exclusionary thinking fostered by the nation state system.

Keller's dynamic objectivity, Harding's African world view and Merchant's ecological thinking all point us in the direction of an appreciation of the 'other' as a subject whose views are as legitimate as our own, a way of thinking that has been sadly lacking in the history of international relations.

Just as Keller cautions us against the construction of a feminist science which could perpetuate similar exclusionary attitudes, Harding warns us against schema that contrast people by race, gender or class and that originate within projects of social domination. Feminist thinkers generally dislike dichotomization and the distancing of subject from object that goes with abstract thinking, both of which, they believe, encourage a we/they attitude characteristic of international relations. Instead, feminist literature urges us to construct epistemologies that value ambiguity and difference. These qualities could stand us in good stead as we begin to build a human or ungendered theory of international relations which contains elements of both masculine and feminine modes of thought.

Morgenthau's Principles of Political Realism: A Feminist Reformulation

. . . This conclusion will present a feminist reformulation of Morgenthau's six principles of political realism, outlined earlier in this paper, which might help us to begin to think differently about international relations. I shall not use the term realism since feminists believe that there are multiple realities: a truly realistic picture of international politics must recognize elements of cooperation as well as conflict, morality as well as *realpolitik*, and the strivings for justice as well as order. This reformulation may help us to think in these multidimensional terms.

1. A feminist perspective believes that objectivity, as it is culturally defined, is associated with masculinity. Therefore, supposedly 'objective' laws of human nature are based on a partial, masculine view of human nature. Human nature is both masculine and feminine; it contains elements of social reproduction and development as well as political domination. Dynamic objectivity offers us a more connected view of objectivity with less potential for domination.

2. A feminist perspective believes that the national interest is multidimensional and contextually contingent. Therefore, it cannot be defined solely in terms of power. In the contemporary world the national interest demands cooperative rather than zero sum solutions to a set of interdependent global problems which include nuclear war, economic well-being and environmental degradation.

3. Power cannot be infused with meaning that is universally valid. Power as domination and control privileges masculinity and ignores the possibility of collective empowerment, another aspect of power often associated with femininity.

4. A feminist perspective rejects the possibility of separating moral command from political action. All political action has moral significance. The realist agenda for maximizing order through power and control gives priority to the moral command of order over those of justice and the satisfaction of basic needs necessary to ensure social reproduction.

5. While recognizing that the moral aspirations of particular nations cannot be equated with universal moral principles, a feminist perspective seeks to find

common moral elements in human aspirations which could become the basis for de-escalating international conflict and building international community.

6. A feminist perspective denies the autonomy of the political. Since autonomy is associated with masculinity in Western culture, disciplinary efforts to construct a world view which does not rest on a pluralistic conception of human nature are partial and masculine. Building boundaries around a narrowly defined political realm defines political in a way that excludes the concerns and contributions of women.

To construct this feminist alternative is not to deny the validity of Morgenthau's work. But adding a feminist perspective to the epistemology of international relations is a stage through which we must pass if we are to think about constructing an ungendered or human science of international politics which is sensitive to, but goes beyond, both masculine and feminine perspectives. Such inclusionary thinking, as Simone de Beauvoir tells us, values the bringing forth of life as much as the risking of life; it is becoming imperative in a world in which the technology of war and a fragile natural environment threaten human existence. An ungendered, or human, discourse becomes possible only when women are adequately represented in the discipline and when there is equal respect for the contributions of women and men alike.

NOTES

1. Inge K. Broverman, Susan R. Vogel, Donald M. Broverman, Frank E. Clarkson, and Paul S. Rosenkranz, "Sex-role Stereotypes: A Current Appraisal," *Journal of Social Issues* 28, no. 2 (1972); 59–78. Replication of this research in the 1980s confirms that these perceptions still hold.
2. Evelyn Fox Keller, *Reflections on Gender and Science* (New Haven, CT: Yale University Press, 1985), p. 130.
3. Ibid., p. 89.
4. Ibid., p. 9.
5. Sara Ann Ketchum, "Female Culture, Woman Culture and Conceptual Change: Toward a Philosophy of Women's Studies," *Social Theory and Practice* 6, no. 2 (Summer 1980).
6. Nancy C. M. Hartsock, *Money, Sex and Power: Toward a Feminist Historical Materialism* (Boston: Northeastern University Press, 1983), p. 210.
7. Hannah Arendt, *On Violence* (New York: Harcourt, Brace and World, 1969), p. 44.
8. David McClelland, "Power and the Feminine Role," in David McClelland, *Power, The Inner Experience* (New York: Wiley, 1975).
9. Jane S. Jaquette, "Power as Ideology: A Feminist Analysis," in *Women's Views of the Political World of Men*, ed. Judith H. Stiehm (Dobbs Ferry, NY: Transnational Publishers, 1984).
10. This is the argument made by Edward Azar and Chung-in Moon, "Third World National Security: Toward a New Conceptual Framework," *International Interactions* 11, no. 2 (1984): 103–135.
11. Johan Galtung, "Violence, Peace, and Peace Research," in *Essays in Peace Research*, vol. I, ed. Johan Galtung (Copenhagen: Christian Ejlers, 1975).
12. See, for example, Gita Sen and Caren Grown, *Development, Crises and Alternative Visions: Third World Women's Perspectives* (New York: Monthly Review Press, 1987).
13. Carolyn Merchant, *The Death of Nature: Women, Ecology and the Scientific Revolution* (New York: Harper & Row, 1982), p. xv.
14. Sara Ruddick, "Maternal Thinking" and "Preservative Love and Military Destruction: Some Reflections on Mothering and Peace," in *Mothering: Essays in Feminist Theory*, ed. Joyce Treblicot (Totowa, NJ: Rowman and Allenhead, 1984).
15. Carol Gilligan, *In a Different Voice* (Cambridge, MA: Harvard University Press, 1982), pp. 9–10.

Chapter 2

The Passing
of the Cold War

An Overview of the Cold War

War is by far the most studied phenomenon in world politics. It should be of little surprise, then, that our thinking about the nature of world politics in the twentieth century tends to be organized around the outbreak and conclusion of wars. We speak of the period leading up to World War I, the interwar period, and the period after World War II. This last period also came to be known as the cold war. Its defining characteristics were found in the nature of the competition between the United States and the Soviet Union, a competition that shaped all aspects of world politics. It was a period of political maneuvering, diplomatic wrangling, psychological warfare, ideological hostility, economic coercion, arms races, and proxy wars.

There is disagreement about when the cold war began, although most commentators date its start to the concluding months of World War II and the years immediately following. In 1945 wartime conferences were convened at Yalta and Potsdam to lay the groundwork for a stable postwar international system. Topics on the agenda included the establishment of the United Nations, claims for war damages, Soviet participation in the war against Japan, and the shape of postwar boundaries in Eastern Europe as well as the political makeup of their governments. The results of these meetings proved disappointing. Instead of solving problems, incomplete and unsure agreements were reached as a growing sense of distrust came to divide the Allied powers. A first test of Allied unity came in Iran. American, British, and Soviet forces had all entered Iran during the war. By agreement all foreign forces were to leave within six months after its conclusion. Although British and American forces did so, Soviet forces remained and the Soviet Union announced its intention of creating an "autonomous republic" of Azerbaijan in northern Iran. It was only under the cloud of a U.S. ultimatum that Stalin withdrew his army.

An early turning point in the evolution of the cold war came in 1947. In February, Great Britain informed the United States that because of financial problems it would no longer be able to honor its long standing defense commitments to Greece and Turkey. Both of these states had been under growing Soviet pressure. The American response came to be known as the Truman Doctrine, which pledged the United States to "support free peoples who are resisting attempted subjugation by armed minorities or outside pressure." Later in 1947 the Truman administration signaled its willingness to help underwrite European economic recovery by establishing the Marshall Plan, under which the recovery plans were drawn up by the European states themselves. Although a formal invitation to participate in the Marshall Plan was extended to the Soviet Union, it decided not to do so and pressured the East European states to decline as well. In 1949 the emerging economic division of Europe into East and West was reinforced by a military division. In that year the North Atlantic Treaty Organization (NATO) was founded. As a countermove the Soviet Union organized its East European allies into the Warsaw Pact Treaty organization.

Over the next decade a series of East-West crises erupted in Europe. Rioting in East Germany, Poland, and Hungary had its roots in Stalin's death and the resulting political turmoil. Berlin was the most frequent trouble spot. The former capital of Germany had been divided into four occupation zones and was located entirely within the Soviet zone of what became East Germany. In 1948 the Soviet Union imposed a land blockade around the city. The West responded with a massive air-supply operation, and after 348 days the blockade was lifted. In 1958, following closely on the heels of the Soviet Union's successful testing of a satellite (Sputnik) and an intercontinental missile, Khrushchev placed a six-month deadline on "solving" the Berlin problem. The deadline passed without incident, but in 1961 the Berlin Wall was erected.

The cold war was not confined to Europe. It spread to Asia in the late 1940s. American policymakers virtually took it for granted that China would emerge as a postwar ally. It therefore came as a shock when Mao Zedong defeated Chiang Kai-shek in that country's civil war, forcing the pro–U.S. forces to flee to Taiwan. Mao's 1949 victory and his alignment with the Soviet Union provided the backdrop from which the United States viewed North Korea's 1950 surprise attack on South Korea. Before the attack American policymakers had not regarded South Korea as vital to U.S. security interests, but once the attack took place they reversed course and sent forces to fight under the flag of the United Nations.

Since the early 1960s the primary cold war battlegrounds have been in the Third World. For very different reasons the two most visible points of conflict were Cuba and Vietnam. It is generally conceded that the 1962 Cuban missile crisis is the point at which the cold war came the closest to becoming World

War III. Cuba had become an obsession with U.S. policymakers ever since Fidel Castro assumed power in 1959. In 1960 the United States tried and failed to remove him from power by organizing an invasion force made up of Cuban exiles that landed at the Bay of Pigs. Cuba was important to the Soviet Union both for symbolic purposes and because of its geographic location. Rumors that Soviet offensive missiles might be in Cuba had begun to build during the summer of 1962, but it was not until October that the evidence became conclusive enough to act on. The American response was to place a naval blockade around Cuba. This response had the virtue of giving an appearance of toughness without at the same time provoking an immediate nuclear confrontation. Its primary weakness was that although it stopped more missiles from reaching Cuba, it did nothing about the missiles already there. The crisis ended on October 28 when Khrushchev publicly agreed to remove the missiles from Cuba in return for a public American pledge not to intervene in Cuba and a secret promise to remove missiles from Turkey that were pointed at the Soviet Union.

The American involvement in Vietnam spanned the terms of six presidents. President Truman ended his terms in office by providing France with $30 million in aid to defeat Ho Chi Minh. This sum proved insufficient, and in the Eisenhower administration it rose to $500 million, or approximately one-half of the cost of the French war effort. Although Eisenhower was willing to pay more, he balked at the French request for direct military help, and as a result the French were forced to leave Vietnam. Under Kennedy military advisors were sent to Vietnam to help the new South Vietnamese government in its fight with the Communist Vietcong guerrillas. This effort also proved to be insufficient, and President Johnson authorized U.S. bombing of North Vietnam and sent in U.S. ground forces. President Nixon began a program of Vietnamization, which was designed to allow the United States to disengage itself from the fighting. As part of this policy there was renewed and intensified bombing of North Vietnam and the ground war expanded into Cambodia. It was under President Ford that the U.S. involvement in Vietnam finally came to an end.

Vietnam was a pivotal event in the cold war because by the time the American involvement ended the post–World War II consensus that had been built up around the doctrine of containment and the need for a globally activist and militarily involved America was shattered. In its place there existed a "three-headed eagle." Along with this perspective there were now two other schools of thought: One favored as much of a return as possible to the pre–World War II policy of isolationism, and a second favored continued American involvement in the world but involvement geared to economic and humanitarian goals and lacking any significant military dimension.

When the U.S. involvement in Vietnam ended in 1975, there followed a period of relaxed tensions between the United States and Soviet Union. President Nixon and his national security advisor Henry Kissinger had worked to bring about this state of affairs by setting in place a series of rewards and punishments that would contain the Soviet Union without requiring the use of American military power. Détente was the name given to this policy, which was most successful in the area of arms control. Détente's major failing was an inability to curb Soviet support for anti-Western forces in the Third World in such places as

Afghanistan, Angola, the Horn of Africa, and Central America. Collectively these actions created an image of Soviet adventurism and produced a twofold American counterresponse. First, the United States undertook a large-scale expansion and modernization of U.S. military capabilities in an effort to catch up with the Soviet Union and close what the Reagan administration argued was an American "window of vulnerability." Second, the Reagan administration undertook a series of military actions designed to reestablish American military credibility. Included were low-risk but high-profile military actions such as the invasion of Grenada and attacks on Libya and a heightened level of open support of anti-Communist forces in Afghanistan, Nicaragua, and Angola.

Understanding Where We Have Been: The Cold War as History

Perhaps just as important to our understanding of the cold war as its defining characteristics was the expectation that it would continue largely unchanged into the foreseeable future. Although many held out the hope for a more relaxed or restrained pattern of competition between the two superpowers, few expected the cold war's underlying dynamic to be supplanted by fully cooperative relations. Hardly anyone expected it to come to an abrupt end. But so it did as the 1980s drew to a close and the 1990s began. First came the political revolutions in Eastern Europe. They were soon followed by independence movements in the Baltic states. As these events unfolded Gorbachev's domestic power base continued to erode. His reform program of *peristroika* (restructuring) and *glasnost* (openness) did not produce nearly enough accomplishments to offset the mounting challenges to his right to rule. For its part the West applauded Gorbachev's bold arms-control initiatives but responded hesitantly to his calls for economic help. By the end of 1991 the Soviet Union no longer existed and was replaced by a vaguely defined Commonwealth of Independent States.

One of the most startling revelations that has come from writing about the cold war in the past tense is the extent to which we do not fully understand it. Our understanding is most complete at the level of tactics and strategy, and it becomes progressively weaker and more open to challenge as we move to questions of underlying dynamics. We can even expect our sense of confidence in our understanding of tactical and strategic issues to be shaken as the Soviet side of the cold war begins to emerge with greater clarity. This effect has already occurred in our reading of the Cuban missile crisis; as a result of meetings between U.S. and Soviet scholars and the participants themselves, we have begun to change our explanation for why the crisis unfolded as it did.

The central organizing concept that guided the selection of American tactics and strategy for much of the cold war was containment. As originally put forward by George Kennan, containment was a strategy designed to enhance American national security by modifying the behavior of the one state (the Soviet Union) that possessed both the hostility and military capacity to threaten key areas of interest to the United States. At the heart of the proposed policy was the injunction that the United States must counter Soviet challenges by applying counterpressure at carefully selected points. Continually frustrated in their efforts to expand, Soviet leaders would eventually be faced with the choice of losing power or curbing their expansionist tendencies. Kennan had no doubt they would choose the latter. Containment as put into practice was often at odds with this vision. American interests, rather than being limited in nature, often became global in scope; the Soviet threat often came to be defined solely in terms of ideology; and the problem of limited resources, which the original containment doctrine took as a given, was often replaced by an almost blank check to stop communism by military means.

In looking back to how the United States implemented its containment policy, John Gaddis, in "The Long Peace," finds a pattern: a shifting back and forth between a policy of symmetrical containment, in which the Soviet challenge was to be met at the place it occurred with an equal amount of force, and one of asymmetrical containment, in which the United States felt free to respond at places of its own choosing and with whatever amount of force it felt was appropriate. The rearmament plan and its rationale contained in NSC-68, Kennedy's policy of flexible response, and Reagan's policy are examples of symmetrical containment. Kennan's original statement of containment, Eisenhower's massive retaliation policy, and détente are examples of asymmetrical containment. Gaddis looks to American politics (the need for administrations to appear to be doing something different than their predecessors and the lack of any type of institutional memory within the government) and American economics (a healthy or weak economy) to account for the alteration between asymmetrical and symmetrical containment. Finally, he finds Soviet behavior to be largely unchanged through the cold war and certainly incapable of providing a stimulus for the frequent changes in U.S. policy.

Gaddis's analysis of U.S. strategy and tactics is important because it raises a series of troubling questions about the nature of U.S. foreign policy in the post–cold war world, the most important of which is this: Will the United States change its foreign policy as conditions abroad change or will the turbulence of domestic politics dictate what foreign-policy positions are adopted? If Gaddis is correct, U.S. foreign policy in the post–cold war world will quickly become trapped in the same type of cycle that gripped its cold war policies. Instead of being an era of hope, the post–cold war period may take on the same limiting characteristics as those of the cold war.

At least two possible lines of rebuttal are open to those who disagree with Gaddis's argument or would prefer to escape its logical implications. First, it is possible that Gaddis has misread either the pattern of tactics and strategic choices made by the United States or the forces that produced them. For example, writing in 1972, Zbigniew Brzezinski constructed a very different picture of American cold war foreign-policy selection. Examining both U.S. and Soviet policy, he found that the cold war had a cyclical quality in which each side alternated between offensive and defensive phases. Brzezinski sought to explain this pattern by examining the international standing of the two superpowers, their military and economic power, and their domestic policy base. Only when most of these factors were in its favor did American policymakers become assertive.

Second, it is possible to argue that the choices made by U.S. policymakers were not really that important for what occurred (or for what did not occur, namely, war between the United States and Soviet Union). Looked at from this perspective, the cold war was not the fault of either U.S. or Soviet officials but was the product of much more fundamental forces that shaped U.S. and Soviet policy. Thus, not only did they have little freedom of choice in selecting a policy option but also the consequences of that choice were largely predetermined. A recent study of U.S. arms-control policy points to just such a conclusion. It argues that the successful conclusion of the Intermediate Nuclear Forces Treaty (INF) was not due to the U.S. strategy of bargaining from strength but rather to domestic political conditions in the Soviet Union. Thomas Risse-Kappen concludes that although Western behavior was not irrelevant to ending the cold war, the crucial factor was the state of Soviet domestic politics.

The Cold War as the Long Peace

Risse-Kappen's argument about why the cold war ended as it did shifts our attention away from strategies and tactics to underlying forces. It is at this level that our understanding of the cold war is least clear. At the center of the controversy is the question of why the cold war remained just that—a cold war. Why did it never escalate into open warfare between the United States and the Soviet Union? Commentators have noted that the period from 1945 to the end of the cold war, around 1989–1990, marks the longest single period of peace between great powers in the history of the modern state system. The only two periods that approach it are those following the Congress of Vienna (1815–1848) and the Franco-Prussian War (1871–1914). As a result many have begun referring to the cold war as "the long peace."

Numerous explanations have been put forward to explain this absence of war. Four different explanations will be presented here, although they do not exhaust the possibilities. Moreover, although each does point to a different aspect of world politics as being of primary importance, they are not necessarily mutually exclusive. One line of thought emphasizes the conflict-inhibiting influence of nuclear weapons. Their destructive power is acknowledged by all to be so great that not only is their use unthinkable but also policies that might trigger their use are rejected.

A second view holds that it is too narrow to focus exclusively on nuclear weapons. Instead the spotlight must be placed on the broader bipolar structure of the international system that characterized the cold war era. Nuclear weapons were an important contributing force to bipolarity but not its sole ingredient. Also important were the conventional forces possessed by each side, the competing alliance systems, and the presence of ideological conflict. Bipolarity is seen as contributing to peace by directing the attention of policymakers toward a single enemy, thereby reducing the likelihood of either surprise or misperception. Both of these conditions are felt to become more pronounced as the number of threatening power centers increases, thereby requiring policymakers to pay attention to more and more enemies.

A third position holds that the most important factor at work in the history of the cold war was the emergence of a U.S.-Soviet security regime. Regimes are informal rules that evolve over time and give policymakers guidance about how to act in certain situations and about what type of behavior to expect from others. Although regime rules may have their origins in power politics, over time they come to have a life of their own and will continue to shape behavior even when the distribution of power in world politics changes. What is especially important about regime rules is that they bring an element of predictability to world politics that would otherwise not be present. For some analysts such was the case with the cold war. They would argue that after a series of initial crises in the 1950s and early 1960s, the cold war competition between the two superpowers settled down into a fairly predictable and restrained test of wills. In fact, the early cold war crises in places such as Berlin, Korea, and Cuba occurred (and were so dangerous) primarily because the United States and Soviet Union were new adversaries and did not know how the other would behave.

A fourth explanation sees the absence of war between the superpowers as primarily the result of timing. Many analysts view world politics as operating through a series of long waves or cycles of war and peace. In this view the presence or absence of war is largely a product of what point in the cycle the period in question is positioned. War is most likely when the dominant state in the system is in decline and a new challenger has emerged, producing a struggle for global leadership—the case in World War II. There is no agreement on how to date the beginning and end points for these long cycles, but two of the leading studies in this area place the most likely dates for the onset of the next global war at 2025 and 2030.

Each of these four explanations suggests that there may be good reason to worry about how peaceful the post–cold war era will be. Two-power nuclear parity has been replaced by one-power nuclear supremacy, bipolarity has been replaced by a more multipolar system, with the demise of the Soviet Union a U.S.-Soviet security regime can barely be said to exist, and the current long cycle is moving toward its conclusion. One need not accept the inevitability of such pessimistic scenarios, however. As was the case with cold war strategy and tactics, their accuracy depends on the soundness of their assumptions. For example, a very different set of assumptions supports the argument put forward by Francis Fukuyama, who argues that the end of the cold war represents the demise of communism as a viable alternative to Western liberalism. Thus, in his words, we have reached the "end of history." Western liberal democracy is now firmly established as the final form of government. International conflicts will continue, but robbed of their ideological element large-scale conflicts between major (democratic) powers will disappear.

It is also possible to argue that those who lament the passing of the cold war because it may signal the end of the long peace are fundamentally mistaken in making this equation. True, the superpower war that many feared never did occur, but when viewed in a broader perspective the cold war international system was anything but peaceful. The absence of war between the United States and the Soviet Union coexisted with (some might argue required) a great deal of violence elsewhere in the world. One study identified 251 international crises between June 1945 and the end of 1985, among them conflicts between India and Pakistan (1947–1948), Afghanistan and Pakistan (1955, 1961–1962), Egypt and the Sudan (1958), Ghana and Togo (1960), China and India (1960–1962), Guyana and Venezuela (1968, 1981–1983), Zambia and South

Africa (1971, 1973), Greece and Turkey (1974, 1976), Argentina and Great Britain (1982), Botswana and South Africa (1985), and Burkina Faso and Mali (1985–1986).

Thus, although the factual support for defining the cold war as a period of peace is open to challenge, viewing the cold war in this manner does raise interesting questions about how best to think about the future. As indicated earlier, war is the most studied phenomenon in world politics. But can one study peace in the same way? For example, it is common to speak of underlying forces and triggering events when studying war. Does the same hold true for studying peace? Are the same factors that produce war the relevant factors in studying peace? Do the same factors (or their opposites) that trigger war also trigger peace? Can we speak of triggering peace, or is peace simply a condition in which no war-triggering event is present? On this last point, many scholars distinguish between negative peace (the absence of war) and positive peace (a situation in which exploitation is minimized or eliminated).

Uncovering what the cold war can tell us about creating and maintaining peace as well as avoiding war may therefore require a new set of questions and a reexamination of stock answers. One important but seldom asked question is this: If the United States won the cold war, who did it defeat? The obvious temptation is to say the Soviet Union and/or communism. According to Gaddis, however, in "Coping with Victory," this may not be the correct answer. The United States needs the Soviet Union to survive as a great power and therefore will need to help resurrect it, just as America did with Japan and Germany after World War II. The answer is not communism because it had long since lost its coherence and vigor as an ideology. The United States also did not defeat the Russian people because they were never the enemy. It should not have wanted to defeat Gorbachev, who was attempting to engineer a major transformation in Soviet foreign and domestic policy that would move it in directions favored by the United States. Gaddis argues that it was authoritarianism that was defeated in the cold war. However, unlike Fukuyama, Gaddis is not optimistic about the future. He sees the victory of liberalism as being short-lived, with new challenges sure to surface.

The Readings

Four essays make up the readings in this section. The first two attempt to decipher what shape the post–cold war world will take. John Gaddis, in "Toward the Post–Cold War World," presents an analysis of what the future "geopolitical cartography" may look like in terms of a contest between the forces of integration and fragmentation. The second essay, "The Making of NATO's New Strategy," by Michael Legge, examines the efforts of one of the major cold war alliance systems to adjust to the new political realities of Europe. In the third essay, "The Essential Irrelevance of Nuclear Weapons," John Mueller takes exception to the conventional wisdom that nuclear weapons were vital in maintaining the peace—even in their absence, he argues, other factors promoting peace were at work. In the fourth reading, "The Springtime of Nations," Michael Howard compares the evolving post–cold war world in Europe with earlier periods of European history.

Bibliography

BARASH, DAVID. *Introduction to Peace Studies.* Belmont CA: Wadsworth, 1991.

BRZEZINSKI ZBIGNIEW. "How the Cold War Was Played," *Foreign Affairs* 61 (1972), 180–209.

DIEBEL, TERRY, and JOHN GADDIS (eds.). *Containing the Soviet Union.* New York: Pergamon-Brassey's, 1987.

FUKUYAMA, FRANCIS. "The End of History." *The National Interest* 16 (1989), 3–16.

GADDIS, JOHN. "Coping with Victory." *The Atlantic Monthly* 264 (October 1989), 49–60.

GADDIS, JOHN. "The Long Peace: Elements of Stability in the Postwar International System." *International Security* 10 (1986), 99–142.

KEGLEY, CHARLES, JR. (ed.). *The Long Postwar Peace: Contending Explanations and Projections.* New York: HarperCollins, 1991.

LYNN-JONES, SEAN (ed.). *The Cold War and After: Prospects for Peace.* Cambridge, MA: MIT Press, 1991.

NOGEE, JOSEPH, and JOHN SPANIER. *Peace Impossible—War Unlikely: The Cold War Between the United States and the Soviet Union.* Glenview, IL: Scott, Foresman, 1988.

RISSE-KAPPEN, THOMAS. "Did 'Peace Through Strength' End the Cold War?" *International Security* 16 (1991), 162–88.

YERGIN, DANIEL. *Shattered Peace: The Origins of the Cold War and the National Security State.* Boston: Houghton Mifflin, 1978.

Toward the Post–Cold War World

John Lewis Gaddis

For the first time in over half a century, no single great power, or coalition of powers, poses a "clear and present danger" to the national security of the United States. The end of the Cold War has left Americans in the fortunate position of being without an obvious major adversary. Given the costs of confronting adversaries who have been all too obvious since the beginning of World War II, that is a condition worthy of greater appreciation than it has so far received.

It would be foolish to claim, though, that the United States after 1991 can return to the role it played in world affairs before 1941. For as the history of the 1930s suggests, the absence of imminent threat is no guarantee that threats do not exist. Nor will the isolationism of that era be possible in the 1990s. Advances in military technology and the progress of economic integration have long since removed the insulation from the rest of the world that geographical distance used to provide. The passing of the Cold War world by no means implies an end to American involvement in whatever world is to follow; it only means that the nature and the extent of that involvement are not yet clear.

Finding one's way through unfamiliar terrain generally requires a map of some sort. Cartography, like cognition itself, is a necessary simplification that allows us to see where we are, and where we may be going. The assertion that the world was divided between the forces of democracy and

From *Foreign Affairs* 70 (Spring 1991). Reprinted by permission of *Foreign Affairs*.

those of totalitarianism—to use the precise distinction made in president Harry S Truman's announcement of the Truman Doctrine—was of course a vast simplification of what was actually happening in 1947. But it was probably a necessary one: it was an exercise in geopolitical cartography that depicted the international landscape in terms everyone could understand, and so doing prepared the way for the more sophisticated strategy of containment that was soon to follow.

The end of the Cold War was too sweeping a defeat for totalitarianism—and too sweeping a victory for democracy—for this old geopolitical map to be of use any longer. But another form of competition has been emerging that could be just as stark and just as pervasive as was the rivalry between democracy and totalitarianism at the height of the Cold War: it is the contest between forces of integration and fragmentation in the contemporary international environment. The search for a new geopolitical cartography might well begin here.

II

I use the term "integration" in its most general sense, which is the act of bringing things together to constitute something that is whole. It involves breaking down barriers that have historically separated nations and peoples in such diverse areas as politics, economics, religion, technology and culture. It means, quite literally, the approach to what we might call—echoing some of the most visionary language of World War II—one world.

Integration is happening in a variety of ways. Consider, first, the communications revolution, which has made it impossible for any nation to deny its citizens knowledge of what is going on elsewhere. This is a new condition in international politics, the importance of which became clear as revolution swept through eastern Europe in the fall of 1989. A new kind of domino theory has emerged, in which the achievement of liberty in one country causes repressive regimes to topple, or at least to wobble, in others. Integration through communications has largely brought this about.

Consider, next, economics. These days, no nation—not even the Soviet Union, or China, or South Africa or Iraq—can maintain itself apart from the rest of the world for very long. That is because individual nations depend, for their own prosperity, upon the prosperity of others to a far greater extent than in the past. Integration also means that transnational actors like multinational corporations and economic cartels can have a powerful influence on what happens to national states. And in Europe, integration has led to the creation of a potential new superpower in the form of the European Community (EC). Europe as a whole, not just Britain, France or Germany, is already a major player in the world economy, and it may soon become one in world politics as well.

Consider, as a third manifestation of integration, security. It used to be the case that nations relied exclusively upon their own strength to ensure their safety, and that is still primarily the case. But Woodrow Wilson began the movement toward collective security after World War I with his proposal for a League of Nations, and although that organization proved ineffective, it did give rise to a United Nations that in recent years has become a major force in international diplomacy. It is significant that the United States waited to gain U.N. approval before using force in the Persian Gulf. Washington has not always been so solicitous in the past, and the fact that the Bush administration proceeded in this way suggests that it has come to see important advantages in the collective approach, which is to say the integrative approach, to security.

Then consider the integration of ideas. The combination of easy communications, unprecedented prosperity and freedom from war—which is, after all, the combination the Cold War gave us—made possible yet another integrationist phenomenon: ideas now flow more freely throughout the world than ever before. This trend has had a revolutionary effect in certain authoritarian countries, where governments found they had to educate their populations in order to continue to compete in a global economy, only to discover that the act of educating them exposed their minds to the realm of ideas and ultimately worked to undermine the legitimacy of authoritarianism itself.[1] The consequences can be seen in Chinese students who prefer statues of liberty to statues of Mao, in Soviet parliamentarians who routinely harangue their own leaders on national television and in the remarkable sight of the current president of Czechoslovakia—himself a living symbol of the power of ideas—lecturing the Congress of the United States on the virtues of Jeffersonian democracy.

Finally, consider peace. It has long been a central assumption of liberal political philosophers that if only one could maximize the flow of ideas, commodities, capital and people across international boundaries, then the causes of war would drop away. It was for a long time an idea based more on faith than on reality. But there is some reason to think that a by-product of integration since 1945 has indeed been peace, at least among the great powers. The prosperity associated with market economics tends to encourage the growth of liberal democracies; and one of the few patterns that holds up throughout modern history is that liberal democracies do not go to war with one another.[2] From this perspective, then, the old nineteenth-century liberal vision of a peaceful, integrated, interdependent and capitalist world may at last be coming true.

III

Would that it were so. Unfortunately, the forces of integration are not the only ones active in the world today. There are also forces of fragmentation at work that are resurrecting old barriers between nations and peoples—and creating new ones—even as others are tumbling. Some of these forces have begun to manifest themselves with unexpected strength, just when it looked as though integration was about to prevail. The most important of them is nationalism.

There is, to be sure, nothing new about nationalism. Given that the past half century has seen the number of sovereign states more than triple, it can hardly be said that nationalism was in a state of suspended animation during the Cold War. Still, many observers did have the sense that, among the great powers at least, nationalism after World War II had been on the wane.

The very existence of two rival superpowers, which is really to say, two supranational powers, created this impression. We rarely thought of the Cold War as a conflict between competing Soviet and American nationalism: we saw it, rather, as a contest between two great international ideologies, or between two antagonistic military blocs, or between two geographical regions we imprecisely labeled "East" and "West." One could even argue that the Cold War discouraged nationalism, particularly in western Europe and the Mediterranean, where the mutual need to contain the Soviet Union moderated old animosities like those between the French and the Germans, or the Greeks and the Turks, or the British and everybody else. Much the same thing happened, although by different and more brutal means, in eastern Europe, where Moscow used the Warsaw Pact to suppress long-simmering feuds between the Hungarians and the Romanians, or the Czechs and the Poles, or the (East) Germans and everybody else. Nationalism might still exist in other parts of the world, we used to tell each other, but it had become a historical curiosity in Europe. There were even those who argued, until quite recently, that the Germans had become such good Europeans that they were now virtually immune to nationalist appeals and so had lost whatever interest they might once have had in reunification.

Today the situation looks very different. Germany has reunified, and no one—particularly no one living alongside that new state—is quite sure of the consequences. Romanians and Hungarians threaten each other regularly now that the Warsaw Pact is defunct, and nationalist sentiments are manifesting themselves elsewhere in eastern and southeastern Europe, particularly in Yugoslavia, which appears to be on the verge of breaking up.

The same thing could even happen to the Soviet Union itself: nationalist pressures the regime thought it had smothered as far back as seven decades ago are coming to the forefront once again, to such an extent that we can no longer take for granted the continued existence of that country in the form that we have known it.

Nor should we assume that the West is immune from the fragmenting effects of nationalism. The Irish question ought to be a perpetual reminder of their durability; there is also the Basque problem in Spain, and the rivalry between the Flemings and the Walloons in Belgium. The American presence in the Philippines is becoming increasingly tenuous in the face of growing nationalism, and similar pressures are building in South Korea. Nationalism is even becoming an issue in Japan, what with recent controversies over the treatment of World War II in Japanese history textbooks and the

Shinto ceremonies that officially began the reign of the Emperor Akihito. It is worth recalling as well how close the Canadian confederation came in 1990 to breaking up—as it yet may—over the separatist aspirations of Quebec. There was even a point last year when the Mohawk Indians were demanding, from Quebec no less, recognition of their own rights as a sovereign state.

But the forces of fragmentation do not just take the form of pressures for self-determination, formidable though those may be. They also show up in the field of economics, where they manifest themselves as protectionism: the effort, by various means, to insulate individual economies from the workings of world market forces. They show up in the racial tension that can develop, both among states and within them: the recent killings of blacks by blacks in South Africa, after the release of Nelson Mandela, illustrates the problem clearly.

They certainly show up in the area of religion. The resurgence of Islam might be seen by some as an integrationist force in the Middle East. But it is surely fragmentationist to the extent that it seeks to set that particular region off from the rest of the world by reviving ancient and not-so-ancient grievances against the West, both real and imagined. Forces of fragmentation can even show up as a simple drive for power, which is the only way I can make sense out of the fiendishly complex events that have torn Lebanon apart since the civil war began there in 1975. One can look at Beirut as it has been for the past decade and a half and get a good sense of what the world would look like if the forces of fragmentation should ultimately have their way.

Fragmenting tendencies are also on the rise—they have never been wholly absent—within American society itself. It would be difficult to underestimate the disintegrative effects of the drug crisis in this country, or of the breakdown of our system for elementary and secondary education, or of the emergence of what appears to be a permanent social and economic "underclass." Well-intentioned efforts to decrease racial and sexual discrimination have increased racial and sexual—as well as constitutional—tensions. Linguistic anxieties lurk just beneath the surface, as the movement to make English the official language of the United States suggests. Immigration may well be increasing at a faster rate than cultural assimilation, which in itself has been a less than perfect process. Regional rivalries are developing over such issues as energy costs, pollution control and the bailout of the savings and loan industry. And the rise of special interest groups, together with their ability to apply instant pressure through instant communications, has thrown American politics into such disarray that elections are reduced to the unleashing of attack videos, and the preparation of the budget has come to resemble the endless haggling of rug merchants in some Oriental bazaar. When the leading light of American conservatism has to call for a return to a sense of *collective* interest, then the forces of fragmentation have proceeded very far indeed.[3]

All of this suggests that the problems we will confront in the post–Cold War world are more likely to arise from competing processes—integration versus fragmentation—than from the kinds of competing ideological visions that dominated the Cold War. Unlike the old rivalry between democracy and totalitarianism, though, the new geopolitical cartography provides no immediately obvious answer to the question of which of these processes might most threaten the future security interests of the United States.

IV

It would appear, at first glance, that the forces of integration ought to be the more benign. Those forces brought the Cold War to an end. They provided the basis for the relative prosperity that most of the developed world enjoyed during that conflict, and they offer the most plausible method of extending that prosperity into the post–Cold War era. They combine materialism and idealism in a way that seems natural to Americans, who tend to combine these traits in their own national character. And they hold out the promise of an international order in which collective, not unilateral, security becomes the norm.

But is the trend toward integration consistent with the traditional American interest, dating back to the Founding Fathers, in the balancing of power? Has that interest become obsolete in the new world that we now confront? The longstanding American commitment to the balance of power was based on the assumption that the nation would survive most comfortably in a world of diversity, not uniformity: in a homogeneous world, presumably, one would not need to balance power at all. No one would claim that the progress of integration has brought us anywhere close to such a world. Still, the contradiction that exists between the acts of balancing and integrating power ought to make us look carefully at the post–Cold War geopolitical map. Jumping to conclusions—in favor of either integrationist or fragmentationist alternatives—could be a mistake.

Consider the long-term ecological problems we are likely to face. The prospect of global warming looms as a constraint upon future economic development conducted in traditional—which is to say, polluting—ways. Integration here, in the form of expanding industrialization and enhanced agricultural productivity, has created a new kind of danger. The worldwide AIDS epidemic illustrates how one integrative force, the increasing flow of people across international boundaries, can undermine the effects of another, which is the progress made toward the conquest of disease. Population pressure, itself the result of progress in agricultural productivity and in conquering disease, is in turn magnifying disparities in living standards that already exist in certain parts of the world, with potentially disintegrative results. The forces of integration, therefore, provide no automatic protection against ecological threats: indeed, they are part of the problem. Despite classical liberal assumptions, we would be unwise in assuming that an ever-increasing flow of people, commodities and technology across international borders will necessarily, at least from the ecological standpoint, make the world a safer place.

Consider, next, the future of Europe. The reunification of Germany, together with the enfeeblement and possible breakup of the Soviet Union, is one of the most abrupt realignments of political, military and economic power in modern history. It has come about largely as a result of those integrative forces that ended the Cold War: the much-celebrated triumph of democratic politics and market economics. And yet, this victory for liberalism in Europe is producing both integrative and disintegrative consequences. In Germany, demands for self-determination have brought political integration, to be sure, but the economic effects could be disintegrative. There are concerns now over whether the progress the EC has made toward removing trade and immigration barriers will be sufficient to tie the newly unified Germany firmly to the West; or whether the new Germany will build its own center of power further to the east, with the risk that this might undo the anticipated benefits of 1992. . . .

Finally, consider one other form of regional conflict that is likely to affect the post–Cold War era: it is what we might call the "post–Marxist revolution" crisis. The most potent revolutionary force in the Third World these days may well be democracy. But it is no clearer there than it is in Europe that this supposedly integrative "triumph of liberalism" will necessarily promote peace. For just as the United States used to justify its intervention in Third World countries as a means of "inoculating" them against the "bacillus" of communism, so the post–Cold War era could see military interventions by the old democracies for the purpose of confirming in power—or restoring to power—new democracies. The violent, but overwhelmingly popular, American military operation to apprehend General Manuel Antonio Noriega in Panama could well portend things to come.

Threats can arise, though, not only from external sources; for the way in which a nation chooses to respond to threats can, under certain circumstances, pose as much of a danger to its long-term interests as do developments beyond its borders. The United States did not *have* to involve itself, to the extent that it did, in the Vietnam War. It did not *have* to become as dependent as it has on foreign oil. It did not *have* to accumulate such massive budget deficits that the government will have no choice but to allocate a significant percentage of its revenues, well into the 21st century, to paying off the accumulated debt. All of these were decisions Americans made, not their adversaries; yet their consequences have constrained, and in the case of energy dependency and the national debt, will continue to constrain, American freedom of action in the world for years to come. . . .

Which is going to win—integration or fragmentation? At first glance, it would seem that the forces of integration will almost certainly prevail. One cannot run a modern postindustrial economy without such forces, and that, many people would say, is the most important thing in the world. But that is also a parochial view. Running a postindustrial economy may not be the most important thing to the peasant in the Sudan, or to the young urban black in the United States or to the Palestinian who has spent his entire life in a refugee camp. For those people, forces that might appear to us to be fragmentationist can be profoundly integrationist, in that they give meaning to otherwise meaningless lives.

We should also recognize that the forces of integration may not be as deeply rooted as we like to think. It comes as something of a shock when one realizes that the most important of them—the global market, collective security, the "long peace" itself—were products of the Cold War. Their survival is by no means guaranteed into the post–Cold War era. Fragmentationist forces have been around much longer than integrationist forces, and now that the Cold War is over, they may grow stronger than at any point in the last half century.

We should not necessarily conclude from this, though, that it will always be in our interest to try to ensure that the forces of integration come out on top. Surely, in light of the Persian Gulf War, the international community will want to restrict future sales of arms across boundaries, and it would not be a bad idea to develop alternatives to dependency on Middle East oil as well. The increasing permeability of borders—the very thing most of the world welcomes when it comes to the free flow of ideas—will by no means be as welcome when commodities, capital and labor begin flowing with equal freedom. And Americans are already beginning to move away from the view that they can leave everything—international trade, energy resources and especially the regulation of the savings and loan industry—to the "invisible hand" of market forces that the integrationist model in principle recommends.

But swinging toward autarchy, nationalism or isolationism will not do either. The forces of fragmentation lurk just beneath the surface, and it would take little encouragement for them to reassert themselves, with all the dangers historical experience suggests would accompany such a development. We need to maintain a healthy skepticism about integration: there is no reason to turn it into some kind of sacred cow. But we also need to balance that skepticism with a keen sense of how unhealthy fragmentationist forces can be if allowed free rein.

So we are left, as usual, groping for the middle ground, for that rejection of extremes, that judicious balancing of pluses and minuses, that is typical of how articles like this are supposed to end. This one will be no exception to that rule. I would point out, though, that practical statecraft boils down, most of the time, to just this task of attempting to navigate the middle course, while avoiding the rocks and shoals that lie on either side. Certainly Americans, of all peoples, should find this a familiar procedure, for what is our own Constitution if not the most elegant political text ever composed on how to balance the forces of integration against those of fragmentation? It had been necessary, Madison wrote in *The Federalist*, no. 51, so to contrive "the interior structure of the government as that its several constituent parts may, by their mutual relations, be the means of keeping each other in their proper places." That would not be a bad design to follow with regard

to the external world as all of us think about how we might come to grips—
as the Founding Fathers had to—with the centripetal and centrifugal forces
that are already shaping our lives.

NOTES

1. See Theodore S. Hamerow, *From the Finland Station: The Graying of Revolution in the Twentieth Century* (New York: Basic Books, 1990), pp. 210–225, 300–309.
2. Michael Doyle, "Kant, Liberal Legacies, and Foreign Affairs," *Philosophy and Public Affairs*, Summer/Fall 1983, pp. 205–235, 323–335; also Doyle, "Liberalism and World Politics," *American Political Science Review*, December 1986, pp. 1151–1169.
3. William F. Buckley, Jr., *Gratitude: Reflections on What We Owe to Our Country* (New York: Random House, 1990).

The Making of NATO's New Strategy

Michael Legge

When NATO's Heads of State and Government met in London in July 1990, they agreed that the Alliance would have to adapt to reflect the revolutionary changes that had taken place in Europe.[1] As a result, over the last year, many aspects of Alliance policy have been the subject of a radical transformation, one of the most important elements of which has been a fundamental review of Alliance strategy, both political and military. The results of this review were set out in the Alliance's new Strategic Concept which was agreed and published—the first time a NATO strategy document has ever been made public—at the Rome Summit.

The new strategy marks an important development in NATO's history. It provides the conceptual foundation for the Alliance's pursuit of its security objectives, encompassing a broad approach to security which includes both an enhanced political approach and a substantial reduction and restructuring of the military forces of the Allies. While reaffirming many of the fundamental principles of Alliance security policy, the Strategic Concept contains a number of innovatory features which mark a radical departure from the past. This account of the making of the new strategy is intended to help explain how the underlying ideas were developed and to underline the important differences between this and previous approaches.

From *NATO Review* 39 (December 1991).

Evolution of NATO Strategy

The function and importance of the new NATO Strategic Concept can more easily be understood from a quick review of previous ones. The Washington Treaty of 1949, which established the Alliance, was signed with one general and one particular aim in mind. In the words of its preamble, the signatories sought generally "to promote stability and well-being in the North Atlantic area," and, more particularly, "to unite their efforts for collective self defence." In the circumstances of the time, the Alliance's wider objective of achieving peaceful and friendly relations could only be pursued once confidence had been established in a collective defence capability. Hence, the Treaty itself gave some urgency to this question. Article 9 established the North Atlantic Council and gave it as its immediate task the establishment of a Defence Committee, which in turn was to recommend measures for the implementation of Articles 3 and 5 (collective defence and resistance to aimed attack). This Committee was composed of Alliance Defence Ministers, who worked on a document originally prepared by the newly established Military Committee. The result, in December 1949, was the Alliance's first strategy, DC 6, entitled *The Strategic Concept for the Defence of the North Atlantic Treaty Area.*

The function of DC 6 was entirely practical: to encourage the greatest possible cooperation and coordination between the military forces of NATO's member nations, building on the work that had already been done under the Brussels Treaty of 1948 which had set up Western Union (later the Western European Union). Its purpose, as its title implies, was specific: to establish an effective defence posture for NATO in the face of a clearly perceived threat from the Soviet Union. It is worth noting that a number of fundamental principles that have endured throughout the evolution of NATO's strategy made their appearance in this first concept: the purely defensive nature of the Alliance, the emphasis on war prevention, the importance of collectivity, the role of nuclear weapons, and strategic unity within geographical diversity.

The strategy, as initially set out in 1949, was modified and replaced several times during the 1950s, in response to political developments in the Soviet Union and changes in the military balance. In 1950, the Military Committee approved a document, MC 14, intended as a supplement to the Strategic Concept, which provided guidance for a medium term plan to develop certain military capabilities in support of the strategy. In December 1952, the Council approved MC 14/1, which outlined the strategic basis for planning and coordination, superseding but not substantially changing DC 6. However, a fundamental change came in 1957 with the adoption of MC 14/2 (based on a Political Directive to the NATO Military Authorities issued by the Council a year earlier) which envisaged the immediate use of the Alliance's nuclear weapons in response to a major attack—the so-called strategy of massive retaliation. But the increasing Soviet nuclear capability very quickly put the credibility of this strategy in doubt and led to a debate on future Alliance strategy that was to last almost a decade. Finally, in 1967, following the departure of France from the integrated military structure, the most well-known concept of all was agreed. MC 14/3, or flexible response as it came to be known (although, as with massive retaliation, the words do not actually appear in the document), with its fully developed concepts of deterrence and defence, proved to be the most enduring of all the strategies—so much so that to some it came to be regarded as one of the Alliance's defining characteristics.

Like its predecessors, flexible response was primarily concerned about the specific requirements of credible defence. It assumed a threat in which the military capabilities of the Warsaw Pact constituted "a formidable element." It therefore concentrated, as before, on the question of countering military capabilities, setting out in full the concept of deterrence which had been a feature of Alliance strategy from the very beginning, but also considering in detail the nature of the Alliance's response to an armed attack. However, the wider political objectives of the Alliance had not been set aside. The Harmel Report on the Future Tasks of the Alliance, adopted by the Council only two days after Defence Ministers agreed to MC 14/3, underlined the Alliance's commitment to achieving progress in resolving underlying political issues, such as the division of Germany. Nevertheless, the Harmel Report acknowledged the Alliance's first function as the maintenance of adequate military strength in order to deter and, if necessary, defend. It was envisaged that the establishment of a balance of forces was a prerequisite for the creation of the climate of stability, security and confidence needed for the Alliance to carry out its second function of pursuing a more stable relationship in which the underlying political problems could be tackled. This dual approach of maintaining credible collective defence, based on the principles of MC 14/3, while at the same time pursuing a policy of seeking détente through dialogue with the Soviet Union and the countries of the Warsaw Pact, was to provide the foundation for Alliance policy for over 20 years, until the dramatic events of the Autumn of 1989 began irreversibly to transform the European strategic environment.

Development of the New Strategic Concept

It was already clear at the London Summit that, in the new circumstances, a radically different approach to strategy would be needed. The London Declaration announced the intention to enhance the political component of the Alliance. It also set out the broad outline of a new military posture for NATO's integrated military structure, reflecting some radical changes from the past. The Declaration took one step further the decision of Defence Ministers at their Defence Planning Committee meeting earlier in the year, to review NATO's military strategy and to adjust the operational concepts and doctrines which underpinned it. What was not so clear at London was how the longstanding, and to some degree separate, political and military components of Alliance policy were to be developed and modified simultaneously in a way that was harmonious and consistent.

The task of preparing the new military strategy was given by the Council to an *Ad Hoc Group on the Review of NATO's Military Strategy*—which soon became known as the Strategy Review Group. The Group was established in July 1990, less than a month after the London Summit, a first outline of a draft new Strategic Concept prepared in August and, following an initial SRG discussion in September, the first full draft was circulated in October 1990.

A consensus developed at a very early stage in the Group's discussion that the new military strategy would not only have to reflect the present security environment, but also the Alliance's political response to the changed circumstances. A complicating factor, however, was the absence of France from the work of the SRG. The strategy review had been established in London by the 15 members of the Alliance involved in collective defence planning; this reflected the status of MC 14/3 which was not agreed by France. However, as the work progressed and it became clear that it would inevitably involve a substantial political element, France decided in February 1991 to join the Group and participate fully in the preparation of a new Concept. This development was widely welcomed, and made it possible for the Concept fully to adopt a broad approach to security, integrating both the political and military elements. In the end, it was possible to reach agreement at 16 on the vast majority of the text: France reserved its position on only a few paragraphs which deal with collective defence planning and where France has traditionally maintained a separate approach.

Alliance Objectives

The work in the SRG proceeded in a fairly logical way. An early task was to redefine the objectives of the Alliance in the new security environment. It was quickly agreed that many of the the Alliance's aims were of enduring validity—the purely defensive purpose of the Alliance; the indivisibility of Alliance security; the collective nature of Allied defence; and the crucial importance of the transatlantic link. However, these had to be set into a new political framework to reflect not only the changed military environment but also developments, for example, in arms control, the CSCE and the emerging European security and defence identity. Ultimately, this task was made much easier by the development in the Council of the so-called core security functions, which were eventually published in a statement approved at the Foreign Ministers' meeting in Copenhagen in June 1991.[2] The text of this statement was subsequently incorporated verbatim in the new Strategic Concept. Given their central importance, it is worth repeating the four security functions in full:

1. To provide one of the indispensable foundations for a stable security environment in Europe, based on the growth of democratic institutions and commitment to the peaceful resolution of disputes, in which no country would be able to intimidate or coerce any European nation or to impose hegemony through the threat or use of force.
2. To serve, as provided for in Article 4 of the North Atlantic Treaty, as a transatlantic forum for Allied consultations on any issues that affect their vital interests, including possible developments posing risks for members' security, and for appropriate coordination of their efforts in fields of common concern.
3. To deter and defend against any threat of aggression against the territory of any NATO member state.
4. To preserve the strategic balance within Europe.

Risks and Challenges

Together with the redefined objectives, the other key starting point was to analyse the possible future risks to Allied security. The old massive, monolithic and immediate threat to NATO from the Soviet Union and the Warsaw Pact had clearly disappeared. But what now existed was a situation in which many of the countries on the periphery of the Alliance were faced with economic, social and political difficulties which might result in crises and in turn could lead to a range of unpredictable, multi-faceted and multi-directional risks to Allied security. Defining these risks against a constantly changing political background—the 16 months during which the SRG was working saw the unification of Germany, the disintegration of the Warsaw Pact, the Gulf War, the failure of the coup in the Soviet Union and civil war in Yugoslavia—was one of the most difficult tasks facing the SRG. The eventual outcome was a carefully balanced assessment of the risks which might arise as a result of instabilities in Central and Eastern Europe —with particular reference to the special case of the Soviet Union—and on the Southern periphery of the Alliance.

Key Features of the New Strategy

Against this background of Alliance objectives and potential risks and challenges, the heart of the new Strategic Concept lies in two sections, one on the "broad approach to security," and the second on "guidelines for defence." Two key features of the broad approach to security are worth highlighting. The first is the expansion of the former Harmel dual approach of dialogue and defence to a triad of cooperation, dialogue and defence. This commitment to cooperation with the countries of Central and Eastern Europe was first signalled in the London Declaration pledge to extend the hand of friendship to NATO's former adversaries, and reaffirmed in the Rome Declaration on Peace and Cooperation. Secondly, the new Concept places much greater stress on the importance of crisis management and conflict prevention, given the increased opportunities that exist for the successful resolution of crises at an early stage by careful selection of a range of appropriate political and military measures.

The guidelines for defence, although lying at the heart of the military strategy, proved one of the least difficult sections to draft. Most of the principles underlying an effective defence posture are unchanged; the major changes are to the way in which the Alliance's forces are organized to meet the challenges of the new environment. Many of the key features had already been identified in the London Declaration: smaller forces, many at lower levels of readiness: enhanced flexibility and mobility to replace the old static linear defence (the so-called layer cake defence concept); increased reliance on multinational forces; greater ability to build-up forces through reinforcement, mobilization and reconstitution; scaling down of training and exercises: reduced reliance on nuclear weapons and a very substantial reduction in NATO's sub-strategic nuclear stockpile in Europe. Indeed, the work on this part of the new strategy was already sufficiently under way by May 1991 to allow Defence Ministers to take important decisions on the restructuring of conventional forces in advance of approval of the Concept as a whole. These were followed by the announcement in October 1991 of 80 per cent cuts in the substrategic nuclear stockpile in Europe. Much of the debate on this section of the Concept concerned not so much the need to resolve disagreements on issues of principle, but more with deciding the amount of detail that should be included, bearing in mind that the NATO Military Authorities had been tasked with preparing a separate classified document on the implementation of the new strategy.

The Final Result

It took the SRG some 16 months to develop the new Strategic Concept. The main outlines were clear after the first few months' work, but the final version was preceded by 12 drafts, each of which was the subject of detailed scrutiny and debate. Nevertheless, the time taken to produce the new document—which, reflecting its approval by the North Atlantic Council, carries the reference number C-M(91)88—compares very favourably with the decade of debate which preceded MC 14/3. In retrospect, despite a long list of major issues, the SRG's most difficult task was not to resolve fundamental differences of view between the Allies. The broad features of the new strategy, both political and military, had been set out in London; the details had to be filled in and the ideas ordered logically in relation to each other. The major intervening events served to confirm how prescient the London Declaration had been in signalling such a major shift in approach before the characteristics of the new security environment had become clear.

The main challenge faced by the Group was to achieve a balanced, coherent and unified approach within what in practice had become an extremely wide-ranging review of the Alliance's strategy at all levels. This task was made the more difficult by the fact that the new strategy had to fulfill two quite different functions. Internally, it was urgently needed by the Alliance's military authorities and defence planners to allow them to develop a new force posture. However, the SRG had agreed at an early stage that it would be very desirable to publish the final document in order to make the Alliance's security policy clear to the widest possible audience. Harmonizing the sometimes conflicting requirements of internal defence planning and public presentation was not always easy. The final result reflects a careful balance between the political and military elements of the new strategy.

The new Strategic Concept looks forward to a security environment in which the positive developments of the last two years have come fully to fruition. The necessary changes within the Alliance have already begun. NATO's military authorities, using the guidance which the Concept contains, have much detailed work yet to do to complete the transformation of a force posture which was developed over 40 years and designed to withstand a threat which has now disappeared. While reaffirming the resolve of its members to safeguard their security, sovereignty and territorial integrity, the new Concept is designed to enable the Alliance to meet the very different challenges of the 1990s and beyond with a much broader approach to security than was possible in the past. It does this by establishing the closest possible unity of purpose and harmonization of means among the Allies in the pursuit of common security objectives. In this respect, the strategy follows from, and builds on, the successes of the past, and looks to a future where we can secure the establishment of a just and lasting peaceful order in Europe.

NOTES

1. Text of London Declaration in *NATO Review*, No.4, August 1990, pp. 32 and 33.
2. Statements and Communiqué published in *NATO Review*, No.3, June 1991, pp. 28–33.

The Essential Irrelevance of Nuclear Weapons
Stability in the Postwar World

John Mueller

It is widely assumed that, for better or worse, the existence of nuclear weapons has profoundly shaped our lives and destinies. Some find the weapons supremely beneficial. Defense analyst Edward Luttwak says, "we have lived since 1945 without another world war precisely because rational minds . . . extracted a durable peace from the very terror of nuclear weapons."[1] And Robert Art and Kenneth Waltz conclude, "the probability of war between America and Russia or between NATO and the Warsaw Pact is practically nil precisely because the military planning and deployments of each, together with the fear of escalation to general nuclear war, keep it that way."[2] Others argue that, while we may have been lucky so far, the continued existence of the weapons promises eventual calamity: The doomsday clock on the cover of the *Bulletin of the Atomic Scientists* has been pointedly hovering near midnight for over 40 years now, and in his influential bestseller, *The Fate of the Earth*, Jonathan Schell dramatically concludes that if we do not "rise up and cleanse the earth of nuclear weapons," we will "sink into the final coma and end it all."[3]

This article takes issue with both of these points of view and concludes that nuclear weapons neither crucially define a fundamental stability nor threaten severely to disturb it. . . .

Reprinted from *International Security* 13:2 (1988) John Mueller, "The Essential Irrelevance of Nuclear Weapons," by permission of MIT Press, Cambridge, MA.

The Impact of Nuclear Weapons

The postwar world might well have turned out much the same even in the absence of nuclear weapons. Without them, world war would have been discouraged by the memory of World War II, by superpower contentment with the postwar status quo, by the nature of Soviet ideology, and by the fear of escalation. Nor do the weapons seem to have been the crucial determinants of Cold War developments, of alliance patterns, or of the way the major powers have behaved in crises.

Deterrence of World War

It is true that there has been no world war since 1945 and it is also true that nuclear weapons have been developed and deployed in part to deter such a conflict. It does not follow, however, that it is the weapons that have prevented the war—that peace has been, in Winston Churchill's memorable construction, "the sturdy child of [nuclear] terror." To assert that the ominous presence of nuclear weapons has prevented a war between the two power blocs, one must assume that there would have been a war had these weapons not existed. This assumption ignores several other important war-discouraging factors in the postwar world.

The memory of World War II. A nuclear war would certainly be vastly destructive, but for the most part nuclear weapons simply compound and dramatize a military reality that by 1945 had already become appalling. Few with the experience of World War II behind them would contemplate its repetition with anything other than horror. Even before the bomb had been perfected, world war had become spectacularly costly and destructive, killing some 50 million worldwide. As former Secretary of State Alexander Haig put it in 1982: "The catastrophic consequences of another world war—with or without nuclear weapons—make deterrence our highest objective and our only rational military strategy."[4]

Postwar contentment. For many of the combatants, World War I was as destructive as World War II, but its memory did not prevent another world war. Of course . . . most nations *did* conclude from the horrors of World War I that such an event must never be repeated. If the only nations capable of starting World War II had been Britain, France, the Soviet Union, and the United States, the war would probably never have occurred. Unfortunately other major nations sought direct territorial expansion, and conflicts over these desires finally led to war.

Unlike the situation after World War I, however, the only powers capable of creating another world war since 1945 have been the big victors, the United States and the Soviet Union, each of which has emerged comfortably dominant in its respective sphere. As Waltz has observed, "the United

States, and the Soviet Union as well, have more reason to be satisfied with the status quo than most earlier great powers had."[5] (Indeed, except for the dismemberment of Germany, even Hitler might have been content with the empire his arch-enemy Stalin controlled at the end of the war.) While there have been many disputes since the war, neither power has had a grievance so essential as to make a world war—whether nuclear or not—an attractive means for removing the grievance.

Soviet ideology. Although the Soviet Union and international communism have visions of changing the world in a direction they prefer, their ideology stresses revolutionary procedures over major war. The Soviet Union may have hegemonic desires as many have argued but, with a few exceptions (especially the Korean War) to be discussed below, its tactics, inspired by the cautiously pragmatic Lenin, have stressed subversion, revolution, diplomatic and economic pressure, seduction, guerrilla warfare, local uprising, and civil war—levels at which nuclear weapons have little relevance. The communist powers have never—before or after the invention of nuclear weapons—subscribed to a Hitler-style theory of direct, Armageddon-risking conquest, and they have been extremely wary of provoking Western powers into large-scale war. Moreover, if the memory of World War II deters anyone, it probably does so to an extreme degree for the Soviets. Officially and unofficially they seem obsessed by the memory of the destruction they suffered. In 1953 Ambassador Averell Harriman, certainly no admirer of Stalin, observed that the Soviet dictator "was determined, if he could avoid it, never again to go through the horrors of another protracted world war."

The belief in escalation. Those who started World Wars I and II did so not because they felt that costly wars of attrition were desirable, but because they felt that escalation to wars of attrition could be avoided. In World War I the offensive was believed to be dominant, and it was widely assumed that conflict would be short and decisive.[6] In World War II, both Germany and Japan experienced repeated success with bluster, short wars in peripheral areas, and blitzkrieg, aided by the counterproductive effects of their opponents' appeasement and inaction.

World war in the post-1945 era has been prevented not so much by visions of nuclear horror as by the generally-accepted belief that conflict can easily escalate to a level, nuclear or not, that the essentially satisfied major powers would find intolerably costly.

To deal with the crucial issue of escalation, it is useful to assess two important phenomena of the early postwar years: the Soviet preponderance in conventional arms and the Korean War.

First, it has been argued that the Soviets would have been tempted to take advantage of their conventional strength after World War II to snap up a prize like Western Europe if its chief defender, the United States, had not possessed nuclear weapons. As Winston Churchill put it in 1950, "nothing preserves Europe from an overwhelming military attack except the devastating resources of the United States in this awful weapon."[7]

This argument requires at least three questionable assumptions: (1) that the Soviets really think of Western Europe as a prize worth taking risks for; (2) that, even without the atomic bomb to rely on, the United States would have disarmed after 1945 as substantially as it did; and (3) that the Soviets have actually ever had the strength to be quickly and overwhelmingly successful in a conventional attack in Western Europe.

However, even if one accepts these assumptions, the Soviet Union would in all probability still have been deterred from attacking Western Europe by the enormous potential of the American war machine. Even if the USSR had the ability to blitz Western Europe, it could not have stopped the United States from repeating what it did after 1941: mobilizing with deliberate speed, putting its economy onto a wartime footing, and wearing the enemy down in a protracted conventional major war of attrition massively supplied from its unapproachable rear base. . . .

After a successful attack on Western Europe the Soviets would have been in a position similar to that of Japan after Pearl Harbor: they might have gains aplenty, but they would have no way to stop the United States (and its major unapproachable allies, Canada and Japan) from eventually gearing up for, and then launching, a war of attrition. All they could hope for, like the Japanese in 1941, would be that their victories would cause the Americans to lose their fighting spirit. But if Japan's Asian and Pacific gains in 1941 propelled the United States into war, it is to be expected that the United States would find a Soviet military takeover of an area of far greater importance to it—Western Europe—to be alarming in the extreme. Not only would the U.S. be outraged at the American casualties in such an attack and at the loss of an important geographic area, but it would very likely conclude (as many Americans did conclude in the late 1940s even without a Soviet attack) that an eventual attack on the United States itself was inevitable. Any Hitler-style protests by the Soviets that they had no desire for further territorial gains would not be very credible. Thus, even assuming that the Soviets had the conventional capability easily to take over Western Europe, the credible American threat of a huge, continent-hopping war of attrition from south, west, and east could be a highly effective deterrent—all this even in the absence of nuclear weapons.

Second, there is the important issue of the Korean War. Despite the vast American superiority in atomic weapons in 1950, Stalin was willing to order, approve, or at least acquiesce in an outright attack by a communist state on a non-communist one, and it must be assumed that he would have done so at least as readily had nuclear weapons not existed. The American response was essentially the result of the lessons learned from the experiences of the 1930s: comparing this to similar incursions in Manchuria, Ethiopia, and Czechoslovakia (and partly also to previous Soviet incursions into neighboring states in East Europe and the Baltic area), Western leaders resolved that such provocations must be nipped in the bud. If they were allowed to succeed, they would only encourage more aggression in more important locales later. Consequently it seems likely that the Korean War would have occurred in much the same way had nuclear weapons not existed.

For the Soviets the lessons of the Korean War must have enhanced those of World War II: once again the United States was caught surprised and under-armed, once again it rushed hastily into action, once again it soon applied itself in a forceful way to combat—in this case for an area that it had previously declared to be of only peripheral concern. If the Korean War was a limited probe of Western resolve, it seems the Soviets drew the lessons the Truman administration intended. Unlike Germany, Japan, and Italy in the 1930s, they were tempted to try no more such probes: there have been no Koreas since Korea. It seems likely that this valuable result would have come about regardless of the existence of nuclear weapons, and it suggests that the Korean War helped to delimit vividly the methods the Soviet Union would be allowed to use to pursue its policy.

It is conceivable that the USSR, in carrying out its ideological commitment to revolution, might have been tempted to try step-by-step, Hitler-style military probes if it felt these would be reasonably cheap and free of risk. The policy of containment, of course, carrying with it the threat of escalation, was designed precisely to counter such probes. If the USSR ever had any thoughts about launching such military probes, the credible Western threat that these probes could escalate (demonstrated most clearly in Korea, but also during such episodes as the Berlin crisis of 1948–49) would be significantly deterring—whether or not nuclear weapons waited at the end of the escalator ride.

The Korean experience may have posed a somewhat similar lesson for the United States. In 1950, amid talk of "rolling back" Communism and sometimes even of liberating China, American-led forces invaded North Korea. This venture led to a costly and demoralizing, if limited, war with China, and resulted in a considerable reduction in American enthusiasm for such maneuvers. Had the United States been successful in taking over North Korea, there might well have been noisy calls for similar ventures elsewhere —though, of course, these calls might well have gone unheeded by the leadership.

It is not at all clear that the United States and the Soviet Union needed the Korean War to become viscerally convinced that escalation was dangerously easy. But the war probably reinforced that belief for both of them and, to the degree that it did, Korea was an important stabilizing event.

Cold War and Crisis

If nuclear weapons have been unnecessary to prevent world war, they also do not seem to have crucially affected other important developments, including development of the Cold War and patterns of alliance, as well as behavior of the superpowers in crisis.

The Cold War and alliance patterns. The Cold War was an outgrowth of various disagreements between the U.S. and the USSR over ideology and over the destinies of Eastern, Central and Southern Europe. The American reaction to the perceived Soviet threat in this period mainly reflects pre-nuclear thinking, especially the lessons of Munich.

For example, the formation of the North Atlantic Treaty Organization and the division of the world into alliances centered on Washington and Moscow suggests that the participants were chiefly influenced by the experience of World War II. If the major determinant of these alliance patterns had been nuclear strategy, one might expect the United States and, to a lesser extent, the Soviet Union, to be only lukewarm members, for in general the alliances include nations that contribute little to nuclear defense but possess the capability unilaterally of getting the core powers into trouble.[8] And one would expect the small countries in each alliance to tie themselves as tightly as possible to the core nuclear power in order to have maximum protection from its nuclear weapons. However, the weakening of the alliances which has taken place over the last three decades has not come from the major partners.

The structure of the alliances therefore better reflects political and ideological bipolarity than sound nuclear strategy. As military economist (and later Defense Secretary) James Schlesinger has noted, the Western alliance "was based on some rather obsolescent notions regarding the strength and importance of the European nations and the direct contribution that they could make to the security of the United States. There was a striking failure to recognize the revolutionary impact that nuclear forces would make with respect to the earlier beliefs regarding European defense."[9] Or, as Warner Schilling has observed, American policies in Europe were "essentially pre-nuclear in their rationale. The advent of nuclear weapons had not influenced the American determination to restore the European balance of power. It was, in fact, an objective which the United States would have had an even greater incentive to undertake if the fission bomb had not been developed."[10]

Crisis behavior. Because of the harrowing image of nuclear war, it is sometimes argued, the United States and the Soviet Union have been notably more restrained than they might otherwise have been, and thus crises that might have escalated to dangerous levels have been resolved safely at low levels.[11]

There is, of course, no definitive way to refute this notion since we are unable to run the events of the last forty years over, this time without nuclear weapons. And it is certainly the case that decision-makers are well aware of the horrors of nuclear war and cannot be expected to ignore the possibility that a crisis could lead to such devastation.

However, this idea—that it is the fear of nuclear war that has kept behavior restrained—looks far less convincing when its underlying assumption is directly confronted: that the major powers would have allowed their various crises to escalate if all they had to fear at the end of the escalatory ladder was something like a repetition of World War II. Whatever the rhetoric in these crises, it is difficult to see why the unaugmented horror of repeating World War II, combined with considerable comfort with the status quo, wouldn't have been enough to inspire restraint.

Once again, escalation is the key: what deters is the belief that escalation to something intolerable will occur, not so much what the details of the ultimate unbearable punishment are believed to be. Where the belief that the conflict will escalate is absent, nuclear countries *have* been militarily challenged with war—as in Korea, Vietnam, Afghanistan, Algeria, and the Falklands.

To be clear: None of this is meant to deny that the sheer horror of nuclear war is impressive and mind-concentratingly dramatic, particularly in the speed with which it could bring about massive destruction. Nor is it meant to deny that decision-makers, both in times of crisis and otherwise, are fully conscious of how horribly destructive a nuclear war could be. It is simply to stress that the sheer horror of repeating World War II is not all that much *less* impressive or dramatic, and that powers essentially satisfied with the status quo will strive to avoid anything that they feel could lead to *either* calamity. World War II did not cause total destruction in the world, but it did utterly annihilate the three national regimes that brought it about. It is probably quite a bit more terrifying to think about a jump from the 50th floor than about a jump from the 5th floor, but anyone who finds life even minimally satisfying is extremely unlikely to do either.

Did the existence of nuclear weapons keep the Korean conflict restrained? As noted, the communist venture there seems to have been a limited probe—though somewhat more adventurous than usual and one that got out of hand with the massive American and Chinese involvement. As such, there was no particular reason—or meaningful military opportunity—for the Soviets to escalate the war further. In justifying *their* restraint, the Americans continually stressed the danger of escalating to a war with the Soviet Union—something of major concern whether or not the Soviets possessed nuclear weapons.

Nor is it clear that the existence of nuclear weapons has vitally influenced other events. For example, President Harry Truman was of the opinion that his nuclear threat drove the Soviets out of Iran in 1946, and President Dwight Eisenhower, that his nuclear threat drove the Chinese into productive discussions at the end of the Korean War in 1953. McGeorge Bundy's reassessment of these events suggests that neither threat was very well communicated and that, in any event, other occurrences—the maneuverings of the Iranian government in the one case and the death of Stalin in the other—were more important in determining the outcome.[12] But even if we assume the threats *were* important, it is not clear why the threat had to be peculiarly *nuclear*—a threat to commit destruction on the order of World War II would also have been notably unpleasant and dramatic.

Much the same could be said about other instances in which there was a real or implied threat that nuclear weapons might be brought into play: the Taiwan Straits crises of 1954–55 and 1958, the Berlin blockade of 1948–49, the Soviet-Chinese confrontation of 1969, the Six-day War in 1967, the Yom Kippur War of 1973, Cold War disagreements over Lebanon in 1958, Berlin in 1958 and 1961, offensive weapons in Cuba in 1962. All were resolved, or allowed to dissipate, at rather low rungs on the escalatory ladder. While the horror of a possible nuclear war was doubtless clear to the participants, it is certainly not apparent that they would have been much more casual about escalation if the worst they had to visualize was a repetition of World War II.

Of course nuclear weapons add new elements to international politics: new pieces for the players to move around the board (missiles in and out of Cuba, for example), new terrors to contemplate. But in counter to the remark attributed to Albert Einstein that nuclear weapons have changed everything except our way of thinking, it might be suggested that nuclear weapons have changed little except our way of talking, gesturing, and spending money.

NOTES

1. Edward N. Luttwak, "Of Bombs and Men," *Commentary*, August 1983, p. 82.
2. Robert J. Art and Kenneth N. Waltz, "Technology, Strategy, and the Uses of Force," in *The Use of Force* ed. Robert J. Art and Kenneth N. Waltz (Lanham, MD: University Press of America, 1983), p. 28. See also Klaus Knorr, "Controlling Nuclear War," *International Security* 9, no. 4 (Spring 1985): 79; John J. Mearsheimer, "Nuclear Weapons and Deterrence in Europe," *International Security* 9, no. 3 (Winter 1984/85): 25–26; Robert Gilpin, *War and Change in World Politics* (Cambridge: Cambridge University Press, 1981), pp. 213–219.
3. Jonathan Schell, *The Fate of the Earth* (New York: Knopf, 1982), p. 231.
4. *New York Times*, April 7, 1982. See also Michael Mandelbaum's comment in a book which in this respect has a curious title, *The Nuclear Revolution* (Cambridge: Cambridge University Press, 1981), p. 21: "The tanks and artillery of the Second World War, and especially the aircraft that reduced Dresden and Tokyo to rubble might have been terrifying enough by themselves to keep the peace between the United States and the Soviet Union." Also see Bruce Russett, "Away from Nuclear Mythology," in *Strategies for Managing Nuclear Proliferation*, ed. Dagobert L. Brito, Michael D. Intriligator, and Adele E. Wick (Lexington, MA: Lexington, 1983), pp. 148–150. And of course, given weapons advances, a full-scale *conventional* World War III could be expected to be even more destructive than World War II.
5. Kenneth N. Waltz, *Theory of International Politics* (Reading, MA: Addison-Wesley, 1979), p. 190. See also Joseph S. Nye, Jr., "Nuclear Learning and U.S.-Soviet Security Security Regimes," *International Organization* 41, no. 3 (Summer 1987): 377.
6. Jack Snyder, *The Ideology of the Offensive* (Ithaca, NY: Cornell University Press, 1984); Stephen Van Evera, "Why Cooperation Failed in 1914," *World Politics* 38, no. 1 (October 1985): 80–117. See also the essays on "The Great War and the Nuclear Age" in *International Security* 9, no. 1 (Summer 1984): 7–186.
7. Matthew A. Evangelista, "Stalin's Postwar Army Reappraised," *International Security* 7, no. 3 (Winter 1982/83): 110.
8. As Michael May observes, "the existence of nuclear weapons, especially of nuclear weapons that can survive attack, help[s] make empires and client states questionable sources of security." "The U.S.-Soviet Approach to Nuclear Weapons," *International Security* 9, no. 4 (Spring 1985): 150.

9. James Schlesinger, *On Relating Non-technical Elements to Systems Studies*, P-3545 (Santa Monica, CA: RAND, February 1967), p. 6.

10. Warner R. Schilling, "The H-Bomb Decision," *Political Science Quarterly* 76, no. 1 (March 1961): 26. See also Waltz: "Nuclear weapons did not cause the condition of bipolarity. . . . Had the atom never been split, [the U.S. and the USSR] would far surpass others in military strength, and each would remain the greatest threat and source of potential damage to the other." Waltz, *Theory of International Politics*, pp. 180–181.

11. John Lewis Gaddis, *The Long Peace* (New York: Oxford University Press, 1987), pp. 229–232; Gilpin, *War and Change in World Politics*, p. 218; Coit D. Blacker, *Reluctant Warriors* (New York: Freeman, 1987), p. 46.

12. McGeorge Bundy, "The Unimpressive Record of Atomic Diplomacy," in *The Nuclear Crisis Reader*, ed. Gwyn Prins (New York: Vintage, 1984), pp. 44–47. For the argument that Truman never made a threat, see James A. Thorpe, "Truman's Ultimatum to Stalin in the Azerbaijan Crisis: The Making of a Myth," *Journal of Politics* 40, no. 1 (February 1978): 188–195. See also Gaddis, *Long Peace*, pp. 124–129; and Richard K. Betts, *Nuclear Blackmail and Nuclear Balance* (Washington, DC: Brookings Institution, 1987), pp. 42–47.

The Springtime of Nations

Michael Howard

In 1989, while the nations of Western Europe celebrated the bicentenary of the French Revolution, the nations of Eastern Europe reenacted it.

The similarities were striking. In every major country east of the Iron Curtain, *anciens régimes* that had lost all ideological credibility had been brought by corrupt and incompetent leadership to the point of economic collapse. As in eighteenth-century France, economic crisis precipitated mass popular discontent, led by intellectuals who had long been harassed by a censorship severe enough to infuriate but not sufficiently brutal to crush them. In some cases—the Soviet Union and Poland—the governments themselves took the initiative (as had the ministers of Louis XVI of France in summoning the Estates General) by opening consultations with opposition elements they had long tried to ignore or destroy. In others—East Germany, Czechoslovakia, Bulgaria and Romania—the regimes simply crumbled (like the French monarchy between 1789 and 1791) before repeated and implacable mass demonstrations.

The process reached a climax on the afternoon of November 9, 1989, when the Berlin Wall, a symbol of oppression at least as gruesome as the Bastille, was pierced by crowds who poured into West Berlin, dancing, singing and weeping for joy. Unlike the events of 1789 all this happened, Romania alone excepted, without the loss of a single life.

We can well understand the feelings of William Wordsworth when he wrote:

From *Foreign Affairs* 69 (1990). Reprinted by permission of *Foreign Affairs*.

Bliss was it in that dawn to be alive
But to be young was very Heaven!

The parallel is not altogether a comfortable one. Wordsworth lived to regret his youthful enthusiasm. The fall of the Bastille in 1789 was followed by events so terrible that many Frenchmen still wonder whether the revolution deserves to be celebrated at all.

II

There are other analogies yet more disquieting. The French Revolution did not set off an immediate chain reaction throughout Europe, unlike the revolutions of 1848 when, fired by the example of Paris, crowds in Brussels, Vienna, Budapest, Milan and Warsaw poured onto the streets. Barricades were erected, governments collapsed like ninepins, leaving a power vacuum into which moved eloquent but inexperienced leaders, faced with the task of translating into reality the ideals they had been preaching in opposition. They fumbled and fought among themselves. Liberals and radicals found they had as little in common as either had with the old order. The forces of reaction, scotched but not killed, bided their time and struck back. By the end of 1849 order had been restored, the revolutionary leaders were in exile, and tougher if more pragmatic gendarmes had taken charge of the European continent. That Springtime of Nations was over almost before it had begun.

Argument by analogy is an activity that professional historians properly mistrust. For one thing, the events we recall occurred in a context so richly different from our own that we are liable to misunderstand their significance. For another, the memory of those past events is itself a historical determinant. The men and women of 1848 would not have acted as they did had they not remembered the course taken by events in Paris after 1789. Lenin might not have acted as he did in 1917 had he not drawn from the events of both 1789 and 1848 the idea of establishing a "dictatorship of the proletariat" before free elections could bring moderates to power. President Mikhail Gorbachev does not need the expertise of the West to remind him of the fate of the tsar liberator, Alexander II of Russia.

The lesson of 1789 and 1848 is not that events repeat themselves in some Thucydidean fashion. It is that during long periods of peace such as those which Europe enjoyed from 1763 to 1789, 1815 to 1848 and 1945 to 1989, economic and social development engenders a political dynamic of its own. If governments are not responsive to that force they will sooner or later be swept away. Paradoxically the man who discerned and explained this process most clearly was Karl Marx himself—a great European philosopher whose works appear to have been as little studied in the Soviet Union as they are in the United States. . . .

1989 was indeed "the Year of Europe," in a far more profound sense than that announced with such Olympian condescension by Henry Kissinger

16 years ago. Events on so seismic a scale have occurred nowhere else in the world. But disturbing long-term processes have continued that may force their way to the front of tomorrow's agenda. Conflicts in the Middle East and Central America remain unresolved and apparently unresolvable. Racial confrontation continues in Southern Africa together with starvation and civil war elsewhere on the continent. Sophisticated weapons still proliferate to unstable Third World countries; and among Islamic fundamentalists there remains a sullen and inextinguishable hatred of the West and all its values.

More disquieting has been the continuing inability of Third World countries to absorb their rapidly multiplying populations, and the magnetic attraction of those wealthy Western societies that cannot prevent their poorer neighbors from crossing their borders and eking out a living; thereby creating internal social and political tensions of a deeply alarming kind. For the nations of southern Europe, Spain, Italy and France, the Mediterranean rather than the Elbe has for long been emerging as the real front line, as has the Rio Grande for the United States and perhaps the interface between European and Asiatic Russia in the Soviet Union. One can become too apocalyptic about the future. The world is not about to become engulfed in a global race war. But the end of the ideological cold war will only reveal the vast dimensions of the problems still confronting us. History will go on and it will be far from boring.

The end of ideological confrontation, however, should have one far-reaching consequence for the affairs of the world. The Soviet Union (barring its total disintegration) will remain a great power and will continue to pursue its interests throughout the world; but those interests will be as likely to lie in cooperating with the West as in opposing it. The Soviets may no longer see it to be in their national interest to support every revolutionary movement in the Third World that, professing Marxism-Leninism, turns to Moscow for help.

Conversely Washington may no longer feel it necessary to support any regime, however brutal, corrupt and arbitrary, that opposes communism. The emergence of an agreed settlement over Namibia is almost as hopeful a portent of such cooperation as events in Eastern Europe. The Soviet Union may find it as hard to control the policies of Cuba as does the United States those of Israel, but Moscow is bound to realize the profound unwisdom of even appearing to countenance revolutionary regimes in Central America. Then the United States may abandon its neurotic obsession with that unhappy region and cease picking at it like a scab, by its constant interventions creating the very wounds it is trying to heal. The United States might also come to appreciate that an Afghanistan stabilized under Soviet influence might suit U.S. interests better than one controlled by Muslim fundamentalists. Ideologues nourish one another, and the eclipse of those in Moscow should at least erode the passions of their *doppelgänger* in Washington.

What, finally, of our disquieting historical analogies? Will liberation inevitably be followed by anarchy, reaction and renewed repression as in the earlier Springtime of Nations? The exact pattern of events is unlikely to repeat itself for the reasons already given, but no one can be under the illusion that the next ten years in either the Soviet Union or in Eastern Europe will be happy or easy ones. To free oneself, as André Gide once remarked, is only the beginning. The real problem is to live in freedom.

But there is another analogy perhaps even more pertinent than those of 1789 and 1848. In 1919 President Woodrow Wilson visited Europe and was hailed by ecstatic crowds in London, Rome and Paris as a peacemaker, a statesman whose vision and wisdom had ended a terrible war and now promised perpetual peace. No less well-deserved enthusiasm has greeted Mikhail Gorbachev on his visits to the West; but as with Wilson, support for him at home is muted and his domestic problems accumulate. The question insistently presents itself: Whatever his own transcendent abilities and undeniable goodwill, can Gorbachev bring his own country with him? Or will the new European order he is trying to build collapse as did Woodrow Wilson's, for lack of the essential support that his own country alone can provide?

. . . A post-Gorbachev Soviet Union, like the post-Wilsonian United States, might relapse for a time into self-absorbed isolation within its own borders. The West could live with that outcome. Our relations with the Soviet Union would be no worse (if no better) than those with the People's Republic of China. But that is the worst outcome that can plausibly be visualized: not agreeable, certainly, but considerably more tolerable than anything that has gone on before.

Whatever happens, the structure of world politics has been changed, and changed irrevocably. The problems that those changes present to our statesmen are urgent and complex, but never has there been a better opportunity—not in 1945, not even in 1918—to construct a new order that will finally defuse Europe as a focus of world conflict and allow it to re-emerge, after nearly a century of pain and horror, as a dynamic and stable center of prosperity and peace. However inadequately those opportunities are grasped, 1989 is likely to be seen as a historic turning point, one ending the catastrophic era that began in 1914. . . .

Chapter 3

The Rise and Fall of Free Trade

Historical Overview

From the fifteenth to eighteenth centuries, international trade was characterized by mercantilism; that is, nationalism and economic interests were linked. Economic activity was regulated for the purpose of enhancing a state's power. Colonial acquisitions were pursued to provide resources and markets, and colonies were governed and their economies regulated for the good of the mother country. Economic policy was geared toward the protection of domestic industries through tariffs, import restrictions, and subsidies. During this period, there were several nation-states that were largely equal in power, and each one's perceived national interest shaped international economic policy.

In the nineteenth century, the international political system changed with the emergence of Great Britain as the most powerful state. Britain's naval superiority resulted in British control of extensive territory, particularly in Africa and Asia. By 1900, 50 percent of all colonial land area was under British control. Britain dominated overseas trade and was able to impose an international economic system thought to be in its own interests, a system of free trade. This liberal system ended, however, with the rise of Germany and the United States, both of whom challenged British dominance.

During the latter part of the nineteenth and the early twentieth centuries, the international system was characterized by imperialism and conflict, including the first and second world wars, as well as regional conflicts in areas of colonial dominance. States pursued policies designed to enrich themselves at the expense of others. After World War II, many policymakers blamed the nationalistic pursuit of economic power for both world wars, and the great powers, particularly the United States and Britain, sought to devise a system that would prove less conflictual. In 1944, representatives of the Allies met in Bretton Woods, New Hampshire to plan a system that would restore order to the international economy at the close of the war. This plan involved a return to free trade.

Bretton Woods and Economic Liberalism

The theory supporting economic liberalism, or free trade, argues that when there are no barriers to the movement of goods, services, or resources across state boundaries, everyone benefits from international trade because of the principle of comparative advantage. That is, in making decisions about what to trade, a state should concentrate its resources on producing those goods or resources that it produces most efficiently and import products that other states produce most efficiently. A state has a comparative advantage over another state if in producing some commodity it can do so at a relatively lower opportunity cost compared to alternative commodities. Under a system of free trade based on comparative advantage, each economy is operating efficiently; thus the world's resources are being used in an efficient manner, which is seen as a benefit to all humanity. Total world income and human welfare are maximized under these conditions.

The Bretton Woods conference established three institutions: the International Monetary Fund (IMF), the World Bank, and the General Agreement on Tariffs and Trade (GATT). These institutions were designed to promote a liberal economic order.

Because international trade involves the buying and selling of goods valued in different currencies, some mechanism has to exist for converting one state's currency into another's. The rate of exchange for each country consists of the rate at which the state's central bank will exchange local currency for foreign currency. A state's balance of payments includes all currency exchanged with other states, including trade and such other areas as tourism and foreign aid. Under the Articles of Agreement of the IMF, exchange rates were to be fixed without being rigid: Each country would declare a value for its currency, and an exchange rate would be maintained within 1 percent of this amount. When there was a serious imbalance, a state could alter this par value. Since states lost the ability to devalue their currency at will under this system, the IMF was established to provide reserves that each state could draw on when it reached an unfavorable balance of trade. Member nations were assigned quotas and were to pay a specified amount into the fund for later withdrawals.

The prices of goods and services flowing across international borders are affected by the current exchange rate. When one state's currency is valued highly vis-à-vis another's, the former's purchasing power expands. Imports rise, but since one state's own products are more expensive to purchasers in the other state, exports fall. In theory when exchange rates are allowed to fluctuate freely, a self-correcting mechanism is built into the system. As the value of a state's currency goes down relative to that of a trading partner, its goods become cheaper and exports increase, thus restoring a balance to trade. Because states were given a means of weathering short-term imbalances by the Bretton Woods agreement, there is less need to restrain trade.

The World Bank was established to aid in the recovery of economies after the war. It was to make loans from its own funds and to underwrite loans from private sources. Additionally, it could raise new funds by issuing securities.

Created in 1947 as a mechanism to organize and encourage world trade, GATT is a set of continuously negotiated rules governing trade as well as a set of procedures for arbitration. It has a small permanent staff based in Geneva, Switzerland, and regularly schedules conferences to negotiate tariff reductions. The rules agreed on by members of GATT are designed to promote free trade and are legally binding for member states, although there is no enforcement mechanism. Originally plans called for an institution, the International Trade Organization (ITO), to oversee trade in the way that the IMF oversees exchange. The United States failed to approve the establishment of the ITO and it was omitted from the final agreements. Members of GATT agree to abide by three principles (as well as a number of other conditions). The first principle, nondiscrimination, provides that all trading partners of a given country are treated equally. This is often referred to as the most-favored-nation principle. The second principle, transparency, requires that if there are barriers to trade, they should be primarily tariffs rather than nontariff barriers. Finally, the principle of reciprocity provides that when one country lowers its tariffs on another country's products, the latter should reciprocate.

There were six trade negotiations between 1947 and 1967. During this time the system worked well and world trade grew rapidly, although success was due largely to the efforts of the United States. It was apparent almost immediately following World War II that the World Bank and the IMF would not be able to deal with the economic damage in Europe. The United States stepped in to preserve the system. Believing that the economic recovery of Europe and Japan was vital to its own economic and security interests, the United States was willing to provide massive amounts of aid. Since it was running a large trade surplus, it also allowed Europe and Japan to pursue protectionist policies that were actually at odds with the liberal system it sought to protect. By 1971, however, the United States was no longer willing to support an open economic system at the expense of its own interests. The Nixon administration developed a New Economic Policy, which among other features imposed a 10 percent surcharge on all imports that were eligible for duties. In 1973 the Tokyo Round of GATT reduced tariffs in a number of areas and declared a continued commitment to the rules of a liberal order; however, trade has become less rather than more open in the decades following Nixon's new policy initiatives.

Decline of Free Trade

The Bretton Woods system was designed to depoliticize trade and economic relations in the belief that world peace as well as economic well-being would result. Even during the years in which the international economic system was most open, there were exceptions to free-trade rules. Under GATT, agricultural products remained protected. Also, GATT contains an escape clause that allows a country temporarily to protect other products endangered by competition and difficulties in the balance of payments. In theory each member adheres to the most-favored-nation principle (nondiscrimination), but exceptions are granted for customs unions, free-trade associations, and developing nations. There is no authority to apply sanctions or force against members who fail to comply with GATT's policies. Moreover, GATT does not establish rules governing competition and thus cannot address such issues as whether the *keiretsu* (industrial groups) in Japan constitute an unfair trade advantage.

The Bretton Woods system worked reasonably well as long as the United States was able to manage it. The abandonment of its rules on monetary policy in 1971 led to concern that protectionism or regional trading blocs would develop in the future. Analysts have argued that the existence of a dominant power (hegemon) committed to maintaining the system is essential to the survival of liberalism. In the absence of enforcement mechanisms, the hegemon is needed to ensure cooperation. That state with the most at stake in the system takes responsibility for regime management and must be willing to pay the costs of providing for stability.

The fall of the system that many predicted in the early 1970s did not occur. Its continuance is attributed in part to the internationalization of firms whose interests offset domestic demands for protection. However, many observers see a growth of nationalist sentiments, which they have labeled neomercantilism. Problems with instituting a single currency for the European Community (EC), the way in which government and business have worked together for Japanese interests, and U.S. campaigns to "buy American" all indicate that nationalism is not dead. Additionally the demise of the cold war, which united Europe, the United States, and Japan, has raised questions of how much influence the United States can continue to have. Without the threats to their national security that existed during the cold war, the Japanese and the Europeans have less incentive to bow to U.S. pressure. Within the United States, the government can no longer appeal to security issues to counter domestic interests asking for protection from imports and isolationist sentiments advocating a less active role in world affairs. Domestic concerns in the United States are prevalent in other countries as well. In times of recession, it becomes difficult to replace jobs lost to foreign competition, and demands for protection of domestic industries increase.

There are many signs that U.S. support at any cost for the liberal system is a thing of the past. One area that has evoked a lot of criticism involves voluntary restraint agreements and voluntary import agreements. Technically, because they are voluntary, these are not violations of GATT rules. Forty-seven bilateral agreements between the United States and other countries have been identified by GATT. Another set of actions that is thought to violate the spirit of liberalism (but not GATT rules) involves duties imposed to counter "dumping" (selling goods at less than they cost to make or at lower prices abroad than at home). Accusations against Japan for dumping have led to the imposition of duties. The Trade Act of 1988 contains a provision, Section 301, that allows the government to retaliate against countries thought to be using unfair trade practices, and it has been applied against Japan, Brazil, and India. Moreover, the

United States has refused requests to exhaust GATT procedures before imposing Section 301 remedies.

Without U.S. dominance it is difficult to predict what lies in store for the system of rules agreed on in past GATT negotiations. Europe and Japan may not see the liberal system as in their best interests. There is no agreement among the experts on this point.

Some argue that there was nothing inevitable about the system of rules and procedures that developed from Bretton Woods. They point out that international trade was not apolitical even when the Bretton Woods system was fully operational. During the cold war era, security concerns contributed heavily to maintenance of the system. The United States followed a policy of building up Europe and Japan as a line of defense against communism. Other examples include the use of development aid for political purposes and the Arab oil embargo. Marxists go further and see free trade as a form of imperialism. Equal competition among unequal partners is, they argue, inherently unequal.

Although most American economists agree with liberalism in principle, there are dissenters. The theory of comparative advantage rests on a number of assumptions, including perfect competition and full employment. In recognition that these assumptions do not always hold in reality, GATT allows for the protection of infant industries until they can become competitive and for remedies for dislocations in employment caused by free trade. Strategic trade theory argues that some important industries do not operate under the assumption of perfect competition. A nation's economy may be hurt if key industries are not protected through government support. Government and industry partnerships would be initiated to alter comparative advantage.

One possibility for the future is the substitution of regional trading blocs for a worldwide open system. If the rules (multilateralism) are abandoned, three major regional trading blocs are foreseen—a European, East Asian, and American bloc. Those predicting the growth of these blocs argue that there is little incentive for the EC to support liberal trade laws when it can sustain growth by turning to the former Soviet Union and Eastern Europe for raw materials and new markets. Presently the United States is working to establish the North American Free Trade Area, to include Canada and Mexico. The ultimate goal is a free trade area in the entire Western hemisphere. If regionalism does replace the GATT regime, the American bloc would be the weakest. Presently the market in the Americas is not large enough to allow for growth in the U.S. economy. Additionally, there is no indication that Latin American countries are anxious to submit to U.S. dominance in a free-trade area.

Whereas multilateralism emphasizes nondiscrimination, transparency, openness to all potential members, and trade organized on the basis of rules rather than results, regionalism features discrimination toward nonmembers, various forms of protection other than tariffs, exclusion of some nations desiring membership, and agreements that may focus on results and strategic trading rather than rules. Although many observers predict an increase in regionalism, this growth may occur within the GATT system. Presently half of the world's trade is conducted on some legal basis other than nondiscrimination, but typically nations join more than one trading group at a time. An increase in the number of trading blocs does not necessarily mean the end of multilateralism.

As long as nations continue to see the liberal order as being in their best interests, they will act together to ensure that the rules are maintained. Privileged groups of states instead of one actor may cooperate for the continuation of the rules. Many analysts argue that since international trade is mutually beneficial, we may expect to see new nonprotectionist trade agreements, although these may be negotiated among groups of countries and will not apply multilaterally.

Recent GATT Negotiations

Although there has been a rise in protectionism, particularly through the imposition of nontariff barriers (NTBs), at this point GATT members continue to express support for free trade in principle. Because GATT rules apply to those manufactured products that have been specifically covered in past negotiations, recently negotiators for 108 countries have sought to extend the rules to new areas: trade in services and trade in most agricultural products. These items were the focus of the negotiations begun in 1986 and known as the Uruguay Round.

Services are estimated to make up 20 percent or more of world trade and are increasing in importance. They include such items as banking, telecommunications, tourism, management consulting, insurance, construction, and so on. Services, particularly telecommunications and finance, are heavily regulated by states, involving standards for licensing professionals, such as lawyers or architects; price controls; requirements for safety or ethical conduct; and so on. Many of these services are products as well as inputs into other processes, and those firms involved in providing services would prefer to have them subject to GATT-type open-trade rules rather than state regulations.

Trade in services was brought before GATT in 1982 and was included on the agenda for the Uruguay Round. This trade is particularly important to the industrialized countries, where services account for as much as 70 percent of the gross domestic product (GDP). The less developed countries have been less supportive of liberalizing the rules and have requested special protection for their own service industries. At the Uruguay Round, negotiations have involved what services will be covered, what safeguards will be included, and whether exceptions should be allowed. Services covered under GATT would be subject to nondiscrimination (the most-favored-nation principle) and transparency (openness about the regulations and procedures affecting trade). Additionally states would be expected to afford equal treatment to foreign and domestic companies and would agree to the progressive lowering of barriers to trade.

One problem with liberalizing trade in services involves removing regulations that in many instances are designed to protect the consumer. The EC has dealt with this question by establishing universal standards to take the place of domestic regulations. This type of agreement is easier to achieve, however, among relatively homogeneous states. One area almost certain to be excluded from any GATT agreement is aircraft landing rights. Presently these rights are bilaterally negotiated, and there is general agreement that the most-favored-nation principle cannot be applied in this area.

Under the services plan being negotiated, a parallel organization to GATT, the General Agreement on Trade in Services (GATS), will require countries to identify any regulations that run counter to the agreement. Countries with practices in conflict will be able to ask for temporary exemptions.

A central issue in the negotiations for agricultural products has been the EC's common agricultural policy (CAP), which contains a number of costly subsidies that make it possible for European farmers to sell their crops at lower prices. Agriculture is much less efficient in Europe than elsewhere, particularly in the United States and Canada, and without subsidies European farmers would not be able to compete effectively in world markets. Conversely, these subsidies, which keep the prices of European goods artificially low, put farmers elsewhere at a disadvantage and distort trade. Many European states, in particular France, have up to 30 percent of the work force employed in agriculture (compared to about 10 percent for the United States). They consider agricultural supports to be essential for economic, political, and social reasons.

Supporting the United States in calling for a 70 percent reduction worldwide in agricultural subsidies were many less developed countries that desire a better market for their agricultural products in exchange for agreements on trade in services. Negotiations were complicated by disagreement within the EC over how much subsidies should be reduced as well as the volatility of this issue in each state. Farmers command a disproportionate amount of political power in several European countries and can be expected to continue to exert pressure.

In the spring of 1992, negotiators rushed to reach an agreement that could be passed by individual countries' legislatures in time to become effective as originally scheduled, in January 1993. A compromise on agricultural products called for a 20 percent cut in trade-distorting subsidies before 1999 and a conversion of other forms of protectionism (such as the Japanese refusal to import rice) into tariffs, which would then be reduced by 36 percent by 1999. The EC rejected this plan, but in May it proposed an alternative reform policy that would cut trade-distorting subsidies while retaining some form of support for farmers who agree to take land out of production.

The Uruguay Round has missed several deadlines for closure because an agreement had not been reached. Agreements on textiles and trade in services were held up by the agricultural issues. No one believes that the talks will collapse, but it is apparent that any agreement reached will fall far short of the liberal ideal.

The Readings

The readings in this section provide an overview of thinking on international trade. They approach the issue from three perspectives. Stephen Krasner, in "State Power and the Structure of International Trade," adopts a macro-, big-picture perspective and argues that it is the power and policies of states that bring order to international trade relations. His essay is important because it directs our thinking about the future shapes that the international trading system might take. "Competing Economies," a study by the Office of Technology Assessment, adopts a comparative perspective. It examines U.S. trade policy since World War II and compares it with that of Europe, Japan, Taiwan, and South Korea. Finally, Robin Gaster, in "Protectionism with Purpose," adopts a policy-making perspective. The author criticizes the absence of an activist U.S. policy on foreign investment, arguing that the United States ought to look to Europe for guidance on how to construct such a policy.

Bibliography

BROAD, ROBIN, and JOHN CAVANAGH. "No More NICs." *Foreign Policy* 72 (Fall 1988).

CONYBEARE, JOHN. *Trade Wars: The Theory and Practice of International Commercial Rivalry.* New York: Columbia University Press, 1987.

DRAKE, WILLIAM, and KALYPSO NICOLAIDIS. "Ideas, Interests and Institutionalization: 'Trade in Services' and the Uruquay Round." *International Organization* 46, 1 (Winter 1992).

GILPIN, ROBERT. *The Rise of the Trading State: Commerce and Conquest in the Modern World.* New York: Basic Books, 1986.

MCKEOWN, TIMOTHY. "A Liberal Trade Order? The Long-run Pattern of Imports to the Advanced Capitalist States." *International Studies Quarterly* 35 (1991), 151–72.

MILNER, HELEN. *Resisting Protectionism: Global Industries and the Politics of International Trade.* Princeton, NJ: Princeton University Press, 1988.

SPERO, JOAN. *The Politics of International Economic Relations.* New York: St. Martin's Press, 1991.

YARBROUGH, BETH, and ROBERT YARBROUGH. "Cooperation in the Liberalization of International Trade: After Hegemony, What?" *International Organization* 41, 1 (Winter 1987).

State Power
and the Structure
of International Trade

Stephen D. Krasner

Introduction

In recent years, students of international relations have multinationalized, transnationalized, bureaucratized, and transgovernmentalized the state until it has virtually ceased to exist as an analytic construct. Nowhere is that trend more apparent than in the study of the politics of international economic relations. The basic conventional assumptions have been undermined by assertions that the state is trapped by a transnational society created not by sovereigns, but by nonstate actors. Interdependence is not seen as a reflection of state policies and state choices (the perspective of balance-of-power theory), but as the result of elements beyond the control of any state or a system created by states.

This perspective is at best profoundly misleading. It may explain developments within a particular international economic structure, but it cannot explain the structure itself. That structure has many institutional and behavioral manifestations. The central continuum along which it can be described is openness. International economic structures may range from complete autarky (if all states prevent movements across their borders), to complete openness (if no restrictions exist). In this paper I will present an analysis of one aspect of the international economy—the structure of interna-

Reprinted by permission of Princeton University Press from *World Politics*, Vol. 28, 1976.

tional trade; that is, the degree of openness for the movement of goods as opposed to capital, labor, technology, or other factors of production. Since the beginning of the nineteenth century, this structure has gone through several changes. These can be explained, albeit imperfectly, by a state-power theory: an approach that begins with the assumption that the structure of international trade is determined by the interests and power of states acting to maximize national goals. The first step in this argument is to relate four basic state interests—aggregate national income, social stability, political power, and economic growth—to the degree of openness for the movement of goods. The relationship between these interests and openness depends upon the potential economic power of any given state. Potential economic power is operationalized in terms of the relative size and level of economic development of the state. The second step in the argument is to relate different distributions of potential power, such as multipolar and hegemonic, to different international trading structures. The most important conclusion of this theoretical analysis is that a hegemonic distribution of potential economic power is likely to result in an open trading structure. That argument is largely, although not completely, substantiated by empirical data. For a fully adequate analysis it is necessary to amend a state-power argument to take account of the impact of past state decisions on domestic social structures as well as on international economic ones. The two major organizers of the structure of trade since the beginning of the nineteenth century, Great Britain and the United States, have both been prevented from making policy amendments in line with state interests by particular societal groups whose power had been enhanced by earlier state policies.

The Causal Argument: State Interests, State Power, and International Trading Structures

Neoclassical trade theory is based upon the assumption that states act to maximize their aggregate economic utility. This leads to the conclusion that maximum global welfare and Pareto optimality are achieved under free trade. While particular countries might better their situations through protectionism, economic theory has generally looked askance at such policies. . . . Neoclassical theory recognizes that trade regulations can. . . be used to correct domestic distortions and to promote infant industries, but these are exceptions or temporary departures from policy conclusions that lead logically to the support of free trade.

State Preferences

Historical experience suggests that policy makers are dense, or that the assumptions of the conventional argument are wrong. Free trade has hardly been the norm. Stupidity is not a very interesting analytic category. An alternative approach to explaining international trading structures is to assume that states seek a broad range of goals. At least four major state interests affected by the structure of international trade can be identified. They are: political power, aggregate national income, economic growth, and social stability. The way in which each of these goals is affected by the degree of openness depends upon the potential economic power of the state as defined by its relative size and level of development.

Let us begin with aggregate national income because it is most straightforward. Given the exceptions noted above, conventional neo-classical theory demonstrates that the greater the degree of openness in the international trading system, the greater the level of aggregate economic income. This conclusion applies to all states regardless of their size or relative level of development. The static economic benefits of openness are, however, generally inversely related to size. Trade gives small states relatively more welfare benefits than it gives large ones. Empirically, small states have higher ratios of trade to national product. They do not have the generous factor endowments or potential for national economies of scale that are enjoyed by larger—particularly continental—states.

The impact of openness on social stability runs in the opposite direction. Greater openness exposes the domestic economy to the exigencies of the world market. That implies a higher level of factor movements than in a closed economy, because domestic production patterns must adjust to changes in international prices. Social instability is thereby increased, since there is friction in moving factors, particularly labor, from one sector to another. The impact will be stronger in small states than in large, and in relatively less developed than in more developed ones. Large states are less involved in the international economy: a smaller percentage of their total factor endowment is affected by the international market at any given level of openness. More developed states are better able to adjust factors: skilled workers can more easily be moved from one kind of production to another than can unskilled laborers or peasants. Hence social stability is, *ceteris paribus*, inversely related to openness, but the deleterious consequences of exposure to the international trading system are mitigated by larger size and greater economic development.

The relationship between political power and the international trading structure can be analyzed in terms of the relative opportunity costs of closure for trading partners. The higher the relative cost of closure, the weaker the political position of the state. Hirschman has argued that this cost can be measured in terms of direct income losses and the adjustment costs of reallocating factors. These will be smaller for large states and for relatively more developed states. Other things being equal, utility costs will be less for large states because they generally have a smaller proportion of their economy engaged in the international economic system. Real-location costs will be less for more advanced states because their factors are more mobile. Hence a state that is relatively large and more developed will find its political power enhanced by an open system because its opportunity costs of closure are less. The large state can use the threat to alter the system to secure economic or noneconomic objectives. Historically, there is one important exception to this generalization—the oil-exporting states. The level of reserves for some of the states, particularly Saudi Arabia, has reduced the economic opportunity costs of closure to a very low level despite their lack of development.

The relationship between international economic structure and economic growth is elusive. For small states, economic growth has generally been empirically associated with openness. Exposure to the international system makes possible a much more efficient allocation of resources. Openness also probably furthers the rate of growth of large countries with relatively advanced technologies because they do not need to protect infant industries and can take advantage of expanded world markets. In the long term, however, openness for capital and technology, as well as goods, may hamper the growth of large, developed countries by diverting resources from the domestic economy, and by providing potential competitors with the knowledge needed to develop their own industries. Only by maintaining its technological lead and continually developing new industries can even a very large state escape the undesired consequences of an entirely open economic system. For medium-size states, the relationship between international trading structure and growth is impossible to specify definitively, either theoretically or empirically. On the one hand, writers from the mercantilists through the American protectionists and the German historical school, and more recently analysts of *dependencia*, have argued that an entirely open system can undermine a state's effort to develop, and even lead to underdevelopment. On the other hand, adherents of more conventional neoclassical positions have maintained that exposure to international competition spurs economic transformation. The evidence is not yet in. All that can confidently be said is that openness furthers the economic growth of small states and of large ones so long as they maintain their technological edge.

From State Preferences to International Trading Structures

The next step in this argument is to relate particular distributions of potential economic power, defined by the size and level of development of individual states, to the structure of the international trading system, defined in terms of openness.

Let us consider a system composed of a large number of small, highly developed states. Such a system is likely to lead to an open international trading structure. The aggregate income and economic growth of each state are increased by an open system. The social instability produced by exposure to international competition is mitigated by the factor mobility made possible by higher levels of development. There is no loss of political power from openness because the costs of closure are symmetrical for all members of the system.

Now let us consider a system composed of a few very large, but unequally developed states. Such a distribution of potential economic power is likely to lead to a closed structure. Each state could increase its income through a more open system, but the gains would be modest. Openness would create more social instability in the less developed countries. The rate of growth for more backward areas might be frustrated, while that of the more advanced ones would be enhanced. A more open structure would leave the less developed states in a politically more vulnerable position, because their greater factor rigidity would mean a higher relative cost of closure. Because of these disadvantages, large but relatively less developed states are unlikely to accept an open trading structure. More advanced states cannot, unless they are militarily more powerful, force large backward countries to accept openness.

Finally, let us consider a hegemonic system—one in which there is a single state that is much larger and relatively more advanced than its trading partners. The costs and benefits of openness are not symmetrical for all members of the system. The hegemonic state will have a preference for an open structure. Such a structure increases its aggregate national income. It also increases its rate of growth during its ascendancy—that is, when its relative size and technological lead are increasing. Further, an open structure increases its political power, since the opportunity costs of closure are least for a large and developed state. The social instability resulting from exposure to the international system is mitigated by the hegemonic power's relatively low level of involvement in the international economy, and the mobility of its factors.

What of the other members of a hegemonic system? Small states are likely to opt for openness because the advantages in terms of aggregate income and growth are so great, and their political power is bound to be restricted regardless of what they do. The reaction of medium-size states is hard to predict; it depends at least in part on the way in which the hegemonic power utilizes its resources. The potentially dominant state has symbolic, economic, and military capabilities that can be used to entice or compel others to accept an open trading structure.

At the symbolic level, the hegemonic state stands as an example of how economic development can be achieved. Its policies may be emulated, even if they are inappropriate for other states. Where there are very dramatic asymmetries, military power can be used to coerce weaker states into an open structure. Force is not, however, a very efficient means for changing economic policies and it is unlikely to be employed against medium-size states.

Most importantly, the hegemonic state can use its economic resources to create an open structure. In terms of positive incentives, it can offer access to its large domestic market and to its relatively cheap exports. In terms of negative ones, it can withhold foreign grants and engage in competition, potentially ruinous for the weaker state, in third-country markets. The size and economic robustness of the hegemonic state also enable it to provide the confidence necessary for a stable international monetary system, and its currency can offer the liquidity needed for an increasingly open system.

In sum, openness is most likely to occur during periods when a hegemonic state is in its ascendancy. Such a state has the interest and the resources to create a structure characterized by lower tariffs, rising trade proportions, and less regionalism. There are other distributions of potential power where openness is likely, such as a system composed of many small, highly developed states. But even here, that potential might not be realized because of the problems of creating confidence in a monetary system where adequate liquidity would have to be provided by a negotiated international reserve asset or a group of national currencies. Finally, it is unlikely that very large states, particularly at unequal levels of development, would accept open trading relations.

These arguments, and the implications of other ideal typical configurations of potential economic power for the openness of trading structures, are summarized in Chart 1.

The Dependent Variable: Describing the Structure of the International Trading System

The structure of international trade has both behavioral and institutional attributes. The degree of openness can be described both by the flow of goods and by the *policies* that are followed by states with respect to trade barriers and international payments. The two are not unrelated, but they do not coincide perfectly.

In common usage, the focus of attention has been upon institutions. Openness is associated with those historical periods in which tariffs were substantially lowered: the third quarter of the nineteenth century and the period since the Second World War.

Tariffs alone, however, are not an adequate indicator of structure. They are hard to operationalize quantitatively. Tariffs do not have to be high to be effective. If cost functions are nearly identical, even low tariffs can prevent trade. Effective tariff rates may be much higher than nominal ones.

Chart 1. Probability of an Open Trading Structure with Different Distributions of Potential Economic Power

	SIZE OF STATES		
	Relatively Equal		Very Unequal
LEVEL OF DEVELOPMENT OF STATES	Small	Large	
Equal	Moderate-High	Low-Moderate	High
Unequal	Moderate	Low	Moderate-High

Non-tariff barriers to trade, which are not easily compared across states, can substitute for duties. An undervalued exchange rate can protect domestic markets from foreign competition. Tariff levels alone cannot describe the structure of international trade.

A second indicator, and one which is behavioral rather than institutional, is trade proportions—the ratios of trade to national income for different states. Like tariff levels, these involve describing the system in terms of an agglomeration of national tendencies. A period in which these ratios are increasing across time for most states can be described as one of increasing openness.

A third indicator is the concentration of trade within regions composed of states at different levels of development. The degree of such regional encapsulation is determined not so much by comparative advantage (because relative factor endowments would allow almost any backward area to trade with almost any developed one), but by political choices or dictates. Large states, attempting to protect themselves from the vagaries of a global system, seek to maximize their interests by creating regional blocs. Openness in the global economic system has in effect meant greater trade among the leading industrial states. Periods of closure are associated with the encapsulation of certain advanced states within regional systems shared with certain less developed areas.

A description of the international trading system involves, then, an exercise that is comparative rather than absolute. A period when tariffs are falling, trade proportions are rising, and regional trading patterns are becoming less extreme will be defined as one in which the structure is becoming more open. . . .

The Independent Variable: Describing the Distribution of Potential Economic Power Among States

Analysts of international relations have an almost pro forma set of variables designed to show the distribution of potential power in the international *political* system. It includes such factors as gross national product, per capita income, geographical position, and size of armed forces. A similar set of indicators can be presented for the international economic system.

Statistics are available over a long time period for per capita income, aggregate size, share of world trade, and share of world investment. They demonstrate that, since the beginning of the nineteenth century, there have been two first-rank economic powers in the world economy—Britain and the United States. The United States passed Britain in aggregate size sometime in the middle of the nineteenth century and, in the 1880's, became the largest producer of manufactures. America's lead was particularly marked in technologically advanced industries turning out sewing machines, harvesters, cash registers, locomotives, steam pumps, telephones, and petroleum. Until the

First World War, however, Great Britain had a higher per capita income, a greater share of world trade, and a greater share of world investment than any other state. The peak of British ascendance occurred around 1880, when Britain's relative per capita income, share of world trade, and share of investment flows reached their highest levels. Britain's potential dominance in 1880 and 1900 was particularly striking in the international economic system, where her share of trade and foreign investment was about twice as large as that of any other state.

It was only after the First World War that the United States became relatively larger and more developed in terms of all four indicators. This potential dominance reached new and dramatic heights between 1945 and 1960. Since then, the relative position of the United States has declined, bringing it quite close to West Germany, its nearest rival, in terms of per capita income and share of world trade. The devaluations of the dollar that have taken place since 1972 are reflected in a continuation of this downward trend for income and aggregate size. . . .

In sum, Britain was the world's most important trading state from the period after the Napoleonic Wars until 1913. Her relative position rose until about 1880 and fell thereafter. The United States became the largest and most advanced state in economic terms after the First World War, but did not equal the relative share of world trade and investment achieved by Britain in the 1880's until after the Second World War.

Testing the Argument

The contention that hegemony leads to a more open trading structure is fairly well, but not perfectly, confirmed by the empirical evidence presented in the preceding sections. The argument explains the periods 1820 to 1879, 1880 to 1900, and 1945 to 1960. It does not fully explain those from 1900 to 1913, 1919 to 1939, or 1960 to the present.

1820–1879. The period from 1820 to 1879 was one of increasing openness in the structure of international trade. It was also one of the rising hegemony. Great Britain was the instigator and supporter of the new structure. She began lowering her trade barriers in the 1820's, before any other state. The signing of the Cobden-Chevalier Tariff Treaty with France in 1860 initiated a series of bilateral tariff reductions. It is, however, important to note that the United States was hardly involved in these developments, and that America's ratio of trade to aggregate economic activity did not increase during the nineteenth century.

Britain put to use her internal flexibility and external power in securing a more open structure. At the domestic level, openness was favored by the rising industrialists. The opposition of the agrarian sector was mitigated by its capacity for adjustment: the rate of capital investment and technological innovation was high enough to prevent British agricultural incomes from falling until some thirty years after the abolition of the Corn Laws. Symbolically, the Manchester School led by Cobden and Bright provided the ideological justification for free trade. Its influence was felt throughout Europe where Britain stood as an example to at least some members of the elite.

Britain used her military strength to open many backward areas: British interventions were frequent in Latin America during the nineteenth century, and formal and informal colonial expansion opened the interior of Africa. Most importantly, Britain forced India into the international economic system. British military power was also a factor in concluding the Cobden-Chevalier Treaty, for Louis Napoleon was more concerned with cementing his relations with Britain than he was in the economic consequences of greater openness. Once this pact was signed, however, it became a catalyst for the many other treaties that followed.

Britain also put economic instruments to good use in creating an open system. The abolition of the Corn Laws offered continental grain producers the incentive of continued access to the growing British market. Britain was at the heart of the nineteenth-century international monetary system which functioned exceptionally well, at least for the core of the more developed states and the areas closely associated with them. Exchange rates were stable, and countries did not have to impose trade barriers to rectify cyclical payments difficulties. Both confidence and liquidity were, to a critical degree, provided by Britain. The use of sterling balances as opposed to specie became increasingly widespread, alleviating the liquidity problems presented by the erratic production of gold and silver. Foreign private and central banks increasingly placed their cash reserves in London, and accounts were cleared through changing bank balances rather than gold flows. Great Britain's extremely sophisticated financial institutions, centered in the City of London, was restored in the mid-twenties at values incompatible with long-term equilibrium. The British pound was overvalued, and the French franc undervalued. Britain was forced off the gold standard in September 1931, accelerating a trend that had begun with Uruguay in April 1929. The United States went off gold in 1933. France's decision to end convertibility in 1936 completed the pattern. During the 1930's the monetary system collapsed.

Constructing a stable monetary order would have been no easy task in the political environment of the 1920's and 1930's. The United States made no effort. It refused to recognize a connection between war debts and reparations, although much of the postwar flow of funds took the form of American loans to Germany, German reparations payments to France and Britain, and French and British war-debt payments to the United States. The great depression was in no small measure touched off by the contraction of American credit in the late 1920's. In the deflationary collapse that followed, the British were too weak to act as a lender of last resort, and the Americans actually undercut efforts to reconstruct the Western economy when, before the London Monetary Conference of 1933, President Roosevelt changed the basic assumptions of the meeting by taking the United States off gold. American concern was wholly with restoring the domestic economy.

That is not to say that American behavior was entirely obstreperous; but cooperation was erratic and often private. The Federal Reserve Bank of New York did try, during the late 1920's, to maintain New York interest rates below those in London to protect the value of the pound. Two Americans, Dawes and Young, lent their names to the renegotiations of German reparations payments, but most of the actual work was carried out by British experts. At the official level, the first manifestation of American leadership was President Hoover's call for a moratorium on war debts and reparations in June 1931; but in 1932 the United States refused to participate in the Lausanne Conference that in effect ended reparations.

It was not until the mid-thirties that the United States asserted any real leadership. The Reciprocal Trade Agreements Act of 1934 led to bilateral treaties with twenty-seven countries before 1945. American concessions covered 64 per cent of dutiable items, and reduced rates by an average of 44 per cent. However, tariffs were so high to begin with that the actual impact of these agreements was limited. There were also some modest steps toward tariff liberalization in Britain and France. In the monetary field, the United States, Britain, and France pledged to maintain exchange-rate stability in the Tripartite Declaration of September 1936. These actions were not adequate to create an open international economic structure. American policy during the interwar period, and particularly before the mid-thirties, fails to accord with the predictions made by a state-power explanation of the behavior of a rising hegemonic power.

1960–present. The final period not adequately dealt with by a state-power explanation is the last decade or so. In recent years, the relative size and level of development of the U.S. economy has fallen. This decline has not, however, been accompanied by a clear turn toward protectionism. The Trade Expansion Act of 1962 was extremely liberal and led to the very successful Kennedy Round of multilateral tariff cuts during the mid-sixties. The protectionist Burke-Hartke Bill did not pass. The 1974 Trade Act does include new protectionist aspects, particularly in its requirements for review of the removal of nontariff barriers by Congress and for stiffer requirements for the imposition of countervailing duties, but it still maintains the mechanism of presidential discretion on tariff cuts that has been the keystone of postwar reductions. While the Voluntary Steel Agreement, the August 1971 economic policy, and restrictions on agricultural exports all show a tendency toward protectionism, there is as yet no evidence of a basic turn away from a commitment to openness.

In terms of behavior in the international trading system, the decade of the 1960's was clearly one of greater openness. Trade proportions increased, and traditional regional trade patterns became weaker. A state-power argument would predict a downturn or at least a faltering in these indicators as American power declined.

In sum, although the general pattern of the structure of international trade conforms with the predictions of a state-power argument—two periods of openness separated by one of closure—corresponding to periods of rising British and American hegemony and an interregnum, the whole pattern is out of phase. British commitment to openness continued long after Britain's position had declined. American commitment to openness did not begin until well after the United States had become the world's leading economic power and has continued during a period of relative American decline. The state-power argument needs to be amended to take these delayed reactions into account.

Amending the Argument

The structure of the international trading system does not move in lockstep with changes in the distribution of potential power among states. Systems are initiated and ended, not as a state-power theory would predict, by close assessments of the interests of the state at every given moment, but by external events—usually cataclysmic ones. The closure that began in 1879 coincided with the Great Depression of the last part of the nineteenth century. The final dismantling of the nineteenth-century international economic system was not precipitated by a change in British trade or monetary policy, but by the First World War and the Depression. The potato famine of the 1840's prompted abolition of the Corn Laws; and the United States did not assume the mantle of world leadership until the world had been laid bare by six years of total war. Some catalytic external event seems necessary to move states to dramatic policy initiatives in line with state interests.

Once policies have been adopted, they are pursued until a new crisis demonstrates that they are no longer feasible. States become locked in by the impact of prior choices on their domestic political structures. The British decision to opt for openness in 1846 corresponded with state interests. It also strengthened the position of industrial and financial groups over time, because they had the opportunity to operate in an international system that furthered their objectives. That system eventually undermined the position of British farmers, a group that would have supported protectionism if it had survived. Once entrenched, Britain's export industries, and more importantly the City of London, resisted policies of closure. In the interwar years, the British rentier class insisted on restoring the prewar parity of the pound—a decision that placed enormous deflationary pressures on the domestic economy—because they wanted to protect the value of their investments.

Institutions created during periods of rising ascendancy remained in operation when they were no longer appropriate. For instance, the organization of British banking in the nineteenth century separated domestic and foreign operations. The Court of Directors of the Bank of England was dominated by international banking houses. Their decisions about British monetary policy were geared toward the international economy. Under a different institutional arrangement more attention might have been given after 1900 to the need to revitalize the domestic economy. The British state was unable to free itself from the domestic structures that its earlier policy decisions had created, and continued to follow policies appropriate for a rising hegemony long after Britain's star had begun to fall.

Similarly, earlier policies in the United States begat social structures and institutional arrangements that trammeled state policy. After protecting import-competing industries for a century, the United States was unable in the 1920's to opt for more open policies, even though state interests would have been furthered thereby. Institutionally, decisions about tariff reductions were taken primarily in congressional committees, giving virtually any group seeking protection easy access to the decision-making process. When there were conflicts among groups, they were resolved by raising the levels of protection for everyone. It was only after the cataclysm of the depression that the decision-making processes for trade policy were changed. The Presidency, far more insulated from the entreaties of particular societal groups than congressional committees, was then given more power. Furthermore, the American commercial banking system was unable to assume the burden of regulating the international economy during the 1920's. American institutions were geared toward the domestic economy. Only after the Second World War, and in fact not until the late 1950's, did American banks fully develop the complex institutional structures commensurate with the dollar's role in the international monetary system.

Having taken the critical decisions that created an open system after 1945, the American Government is unlikely to change its policy until it confronts some external event that it cannot control, such as a worldwide deflation, drought in the great plains, or the malicious use of petrodollars. In America perhaps more than in any other country "new policies," as E. E. Schattschneider wrote in his brilliant study of the Smoot-Hawley Tariff in 1935, "create new politics,"[1] for in America the state is weak and the society strong. State decisions taken because of state interests reinforce private societal groups that the state is unable to resist in later periods. Multinational corporations have grown and prospered since 1950. International economic policy making has passed from the Congress to the Executive. Groups favoring closure, such as organized labor, are unlikely to carry the day until some external event demonstrates that existing policies can no longer be implemented.

The structure of international trade changes in fits and starts; it does not flow smoothly with the redistribution of potential state power. Nevertheless, it is the power and the policies of states that create order where there would otherwise be chaos or at best a Lockian state of nature. The existence of various transnational, multinational, transgovernmental, and other non-state actors that have riveted scholarly attention in recent years can only be understood within the context of a broader structure that ultimately rests upon the power and interests of states, shackled though they may be by the societal consequences of their own past decisions.

NOTE

1. E. E. Schattschneider, *Politics, Pressures and the Tariff: A Study of Free Enterprise in Pressure Politics as Shown in the 1929–1930 Revision of the Tariff* (Englewood Cliffs, NJ: Prentice Hall, 1935), p. 288.

Competing Economies

America, Europe, and the Pacific Rim

Congress of the United States
Office of Technology Assessment

U.S. Trade Policy

Since World War II, the United States' overriding objective in trade policy has been to promote free trade throughout the world, using the GATT system and, to a lesser extent, bilateral negotiations. The GATT system has reduced quantitative barriers to trade (quotas and tariffs), and as a result is often given credit for the increase in world trade.

For most of the postwar period, U.S. firms prospered under this regime. To be sure, some industries had problems, even in the 1960s when most U.S. industry was at the technological forefront of global competition. The textile and apparel industries, for instance, relied heavily on unskilled and semiskilled labor, and as a result faced competitive pressure from low-wage countries quite early; treaties limiting textile imports were signed in the 1950s. Television manufacturers came under pressure from imports in the 1960s, as a result of both high production costs and, toward the end of the decade, superior technologies (solid state circuitry) in Japanese products. Until the early 1980s, the industries that had competitive trouble were regarded as outliers, which the United States could probably afford to lose as it shifted into high-technology sectors. But in the 1980s these trade troubles spread. The indisputable fact emerged that American technology development and diffusion was deficient in even the most high-technology industries.

From *Competing Economies: America, Europe, and the Pacific Rim Summary* (Washington, DC: Office of Technology Assessment, 1991).

Now, it is difficult to find an American industry that is in no competitive trouble at all, and there are a few where only fast and drastic action can preserve domestic manufacturing. Moreover, American firms are significantly behind in an increasing number of emerging technologies and industries. Trade increasingly exposes U.S. companies to competition from foreigners with superior technologies, deeper pockets, better trained workers, and governments determined to provide their indigenous firms with advantages.

Some of these advantages are nationwide—e.g., first-rate education, encouragement of household savings, and tax breaks for R&D and capital investment. Some governments, notably in Japan, Korea, and Taiwan, have also targeted for support specific industries, such as semiconductors and computers, that seem to contribute disproportionately to a nation's wealth and economic development. Developing such industries is often a race in which the firms or nations that get ahead will likely stay ahead for some time. A company with technical advantages or greater market share can reap economies of scale or learning, which will let it capture additional market share or finance more R&D than its competitors, enabling it to pull still further ahead.

Governments have targeted critical industries with both domestic policies and home market protection. Domestic policies include R&D support, special tax breaks, preferential financing, and tolerance or encouragement of cartel pricing in specific industries. R&D programs can give firms a technical advantage over competitors abroad or at home. Special tax breaks or other financial support can help domestic companies pay for their investments or charge lower prices.

Trade protection has rarely if ever been successful when used alone, but in combination with domestic policies it can be a powerful tool. A protected home market can enable domestic firms to catch up with more advanced foreign companies without having to compete with them for domestic customers. Profits in a protected home market can bankroll forays into export markets at low prices, R&D, and investment in worker training and equipment. In the short term, foreign producers could probably meet these low prices; but in the long term, foreign firms not similarly supported can lose market share and the revenues to fund new investments. Of course, protection can easily go astray, leading to an industry ill-suited to international competition, but when managed properly it can aid a nation's economic development.

Other countries' domestic programs and market protection have often delivered a one-two punch to U.S. industries. For the most part, the U.S. Government does not have comparable proactive programs to promote its own industries. U.S. trade policy plays out by noticing some of the advantages foreign firms enjoy, and then trying after-the-fact to eliminate or offset them, usually after substantial delay and often incompletely. Important foreign market barriers often persist for years, despite U.S. attempts to eliminate them. While some advantages enjoyed by foreign firms are recognized by U.S. dumping and subsidies law, various problems prevent or limit redress even in deserving cases. These problems include the expense required to prepare a petition and fight a legal case, the time it takes to conduct investigations, ways by which foreign firms circumvent duty orders, the interpretation of the injury requirement so as to inhibit timely relief, and the law's failure to recognize the impact of many subsidies.

U.S. policy thus puts important industries at risk. No matter how hard U.S. firms work, under current conditions they might not be able to compete with foreign industries backed by their governments.

Other aspects of U.S. policy are also ineffective in promoting the competitiveness of U.S. industry. While many foreign governments' procurement policies are attuned to fostering national industries, U.S. procurement policy is not. The Commerce Department's export promotion programs, while useful, are small and ineffective compared with programs in other countries. Export financing by the Export-Import Bank of the United States is sometimes less attractive than that offered by other countries' export financing agencies. Finally, U.S. national security export controls unduly hinder high-technology exports; while many controls truly are necessary for national security, some are not.

Europe and the Single Market

The United States is not alone in facing questions of what to do about lagging industries and technologies. The nations of the European Community, individually and together, have a long record of attempts to use industrial policy, and with few real successes in past attempts, are launching a new initiative. Known as the Single Market, or, after the proposed date of its inception, Europe 1992, the initiative is really a wide variety of new policies and agreements broadly aimed at increasing European unity, improving technology, and increasing competitiveness. . . .

Nearly everyone expects that removing sources of commercial friction among the 12 EC nations—impediments to movement of goods, people, services, and capital—will mean faster growth in the GNP of the European Community. The range of estimates of the increase in growth is wide. The closest thing to an official estimate of the EC is a report done in 1988 (known as the Cecchini report), which estimated gains at 4.3 to 6.4 percent of GDP accruing over a 6-year period, or up to 1 percent additional growth in GDP each year. Another 2.5 percent (over the 6 years) is possible if appropriate accompanying macroeconomic policies are added, according to this estimate. The Cecchini report has been hailed as an impressive technical work, but its growth estimates are also regarded as optimistic.[1] In contrast, the gains in GDP from the elimination of tariffs on industrial products among Common Market countries in 1968 were on the order of 1 percent, total.

What this means for the United States, in the short or long run, is murky. Additional growth, even if it were substantially below the levels estimated by the Cecchini report, would ordinarily mean increased opportunities for U.S. firms to sell goods to and produce goods in Europe. The former (increased exports) would further the national interests of the United States directly; the latter only indirectly, to the extent of contributing a bit to the prosperity of firms headquartered here. But the Cecchini report also makes it clear that some of the added growth in Europe is expected to come at the *expense* of imports from outside the EC; the Cecchini growth forecasts assume a reduction of imports from outside the EC by 7.9 to 10.2 percent. Whether there will be growth in Europe due to factors not anticipated by the Cecchini team, and whether these increase the possibilities for U.S. exports, is simply not clear. Most of the fears that EC 1992 would be a "Fortress Europe" have been put to rest, but there are a few signs of increasing protectionism in Europe. . . .

Japan

Japan is the economic phoenix of the postwar period. Throughout the nearly five decades following the war, its growth of GNP and productivity have consistently been higher than in the rest of the developed world. That it should be so was by no means obvious in the first decade after the end of the war. Japan was desperately poor, short of most raw materials, and faced labor strife. Now, one of the biggest problems Japanese bureaucrats face is how to contain the robust productive power of its premier corporations enough to avoid exacerbating trade disputes.

The Japanese Government has long used industrial policy to push its economy toward more high-value-added, knowledge-intensive industries that use more highly skilled labor and fewer natural resources. The primary tools are financial aid, government sponsorship of price, investment, and R&D cartels, and protection of the domestic market. These policies were instrumental in improving competitiveness in industries like steel, motor vehicles, semiconductors, and computers.

A few caveats are in order. The impression is often given that Japanese policies alone are responsible for Japan's economic success, and that the record of success is unblemished. In fact, Japan's policies were creative and innovative but they would have been much less effective in a society with less well educated people that placed lower value on hard work and ceaseless pursuit of improvement. Japan's culture, with its emphasis on achieving consensus, and on the performance and interests of groups rather than individuals, played a role, although the prominence given to cultural explanations of Japan's success in the popular literature is often overdone. There are also several examples of failure in Japanese industrial policies. For instance, the long-term goal of promoting an indigenous large civilian air transport industry has remained elusive, and MITI's expectations have been scaled back considerably.

There is widespread disagreement, at least among American analysts, about the overall effect of Japanese industrial policy on Japan's national income and standards of living. Japanese consumers have long been able to live less well than American consumers on an equivalent amount of income, in part because of policies that sheltered many industries from foreign competition. Some of those policies, in turn, were made to foster industrial development; the inference that Japanese consumers pay for Japan's industrial policies is quite correct. But the tradeoff is not just between Japanese industry and consumers; it is also a sacrifice of short-run gratification in favor of enhanced prospects for long-run growth. Even as Japanese standards of living and wages approach those of the richest nations, there are few signs of impending stagnation, and it is likely that faster growth of Japanese living standards will continue, surpassing ours.

That does not mean that Japanese policy remains the same as always. The hand of the government in directing industrial development is considerably less heavy than it was during the high-growth period (which ended in 1974, with the first oil shock). Japan's government has liberalized financial markets and consumer credit, reduced formal, quantitative import barriers, liberalized foreign investment, and reduced the number of cartels. Some have interpreted this as proof that Japan's economy is a modern, capitalist, free-market one along the lines of America, Canada, Germany, or Great Britain. Yet Japan's trade patterns remain peculiar by the standards of other developed countries; manufactured imports are quite low, and a strong preference remains for adding as much value as possible in Japan. Japanese direct investment abroad is more oriented to exports than the direct investment of other developed nations, and it is an outlier among developed nations in that foreign direct investment plays a much smaller role in its own economy. Many in America and Japan argue that all this is simply because foreign exporters or investors are not diligent enough; their products are inferior or their knowledge of Japanese business practice is weak. Some of that is true, but it is not the whole story.

Japan's Government is still actively involved in creating an advantageous environment for Japanese business. The computer industry was targeted for development nearly three decades ago, and within the past 5 years has come of age; many Japanese computers from mainframes to laptops are now as good as or better than American models. That payoff is the result of three decades of company diligence and experimentation, combined with tax incentives (general and specific), R&D funding in strategic areas, subsidized leasing, and market protection. Policies changed over time, in response to different industry needs, and even now, with competitive and technological advantage increasingly weighted on the side of the Japanese computer makers, policies to support specific segments continue. One such area is supercomputers, where Japanese Government support has continued through the 1980s and into the 1990s. Some support comes in the form of funding for research consortia. From 1981 to 1989, the Japanese Government spent

18.2 billion yen (about $121 million) on the High Speed Computing System for Scientific and Technological Uses Project, aimed at producing a machine with a speed of 10 Gigaflops. NTT, the Japanese telephone company, also supports supercomputer technology development in its own supercomputer project, and several public and private projects are exploring parallel and massively parallel processing.

Another important element of the strategy is procurement. Until very recently, American supercomputers were superior to Japanese supercomputers, yet while U.S. machines only were bought and installed in America and Europe, they were a small share of Japanese purchases. In 1987, for example, Cray and Control Data, American supercomputer makers, accounted for 73 percent of installed supercomputers in the world; Japanese companies for 27 percent, which consisted entirely of sales within Japan. Moreover, the Japanese companies Fujitsu, NEC, and Hitachi accounted for 87 percent of all Japanese installations, and Cray for only 13 percent. In part, that could be attributed to the Japanese preference for buying goods from and doing business with other members of *keiretsu,* but American supercomputers had a far more difficult time in the Japanese public sector than in the private sector. A few Japanese private companies bought Cray machines because they were better and faster, and buying an inferior Japanese machine would have been a real handicap; in the public sector, however, procurement was almost exclusively of Japanese machines. The Japanese Government apparently was determined to provide Japanese companies with a secure market while they worked hard to catch up to or surpass Cray's technology.

There are many who regard such practices as unfair or underhanded. In fact, they are logical, reasonable things for governments to do; Japan is hardly alone among industrialized countries in using the power of public procurement to foster domestic business and competitiveness. The story is not told for the purpose of castigating Japanese policy, but to illustrate that policies designed to create competitive advantages for Japanese firms (and compensate for the advantages of foreign firms) are not relegated to Japanese history. MITI, and other Japanese Government agencies that are *genkyoku* (sections of the bureaucracy with primary responsibility for developing and supervising policies for an industry), may have less ability to manipulate industries and the economy than they once had, but they still wield considerable power.

Is Japan at a crossroads? Legions of writers have said so; one of the most popular themes of current writing on competitiveness is how much and how fast Japan is changing. In a sense, Japan has never stopped changing; policies that supported a particular industry or activity were shifting in the 1950s and 1960s as well as the 1980s. But the implicit corollary to the "Japan is changing" genre is also that it is becoming more like us in ways that will make its industrial performance more like ours. At best, this is unproven; more likely it is a delusion. Japan's government and private sector are still working, independently and together, to improve the competitive performance and market share of Japanese companies in a wide range of industries. They will probably succeed.

Industrial Policies in Taiwan and Korea

Like Japan, Korea and Taiwan have used industrial policies to encourage the development of high-technology, high-wage industries. They, too, have been successful. Their successes indicate that industrial policies can contribute to industrial competitiveness under differing circumstances—in other words, that Japan's industrial policies were not mere adjuncts to a culture that provides hothouse conditions for business. . . .

Korean and Taiwanese industrial policies share many similarities, but there are important differences as well. They are similar in that they rely on long-term planning—overall visions of the directions of economic growth and development—and use industrial targeting in addition to broader measures to encourage industrial activity generally. They educate their people superbly and share a cultural commitment to hard work. Finally, they both forced their companies to compete with the most proficient of world competitors, using competition abroad to provide the impetus for cost reduction and productivity improvement, while shielding them from competition at home. In Korea in particular, the protected home market was also used to make firms compete more effectively; the ability of firms to import needed inputs and machinery depended on their export performance.

The differences are also interesting. The Taiwanese market has long been more open than Korea's and the industrial structure much less concentrated. Taiwanese firms have performed well across a broader range of industries than Korean firms, reflecting the choice of market niches that rely on standardized technologies that can be purchased and used effectively by small firms. Korea has organized production into large, conglomerate firms that have very few competitors at home and have performed well in many sectors where the economies of scale that large firms can gain are advantages, such as motor vehicles, consumer electronics, semiconductors.

Both countries have had setbacks. Some attempts to develop industries or rationalize production failed, as was the case in Japan. But Japan's success has also made the world a more difficult place for Taiwan and Korea; developed countries, afraid of what could happen to their own industries if "another Japan" appeared, have been much less tolerant of Korean and Taiwanese policies like controlling currency values, protecting their own markets, and loose protection of intellectual property than was true for Japan. Both countries have, in response to increasing pressure from the United States and other trading partners, liberalized controls over their markets and currencies, and permitted more imports. Their own success has made it more difficult for them to pursue the policies responsible for success. Whether they can continue to develop, and raise their living standards above levels that are still only at the high end of poverty by the standards of developed nations, will probably depend as much on the performance of American and European economies as on their own. If America and the EC are successful in getting their own manufacturing back on track, by whatever standards they adopt, the world will be a more amenable place for developing countries, including Korea and Taiwan. If, on the other hand, American and European manufacturing continue to lose competitiveness, and only Japan gains, things could be different. Japan's role in promoting world development is now larger than America's, but would Japan be able to compensate for the retaliatory and self-protective policies likely to grow if American and European industries continue to lose competitiveness? It is possible, but perhaps unlikely; Japan, too, is concerned about the economic success of her neighbors, and continues to pursue industrial policies of her own in response to the challenge of these newly industrializing countries.

NOTE

1. See, for example, Merton J. Peck, "Industrial Organization and the Gains from Europe 1992," Vittorio Grilli, "Financial Markets and 1992," Richard N. Cooper, "Europe Without Borders," and Rudiger Dornbusch, "Europe 1992: Macroeconomic Implications," all in William C. Brainard and George L. Perry, eds., *Brookings Papers on Economic Activity* 2 (Washington, DC: Brookings Institution, 1989), pp. 277–381 passim. Peck, for example, says, "It is important to emphasize this overoptimism, given the significance of the report both as a work of economic advocacy and as an impressive scientific study" (p. 278).

Protectionism with Purpose

Guiding Foreign Investment

Robin Gaster

Almost five hundred years after Columbus arrived in the New World, foreigners are again seeking fortunes in North America. This time, though, the invasion is one of capital, not of people.

During the 1980s, foreign direct investment (FDI) in the United States—defined as the acquisition of at least 10 percent ownership in a U.S. firm, enough to exert influence over its management—soared. From a total market value of $83 billion in 1980, it reached more than $407 billion in 1991. Those investments have been heavily concentrated in a few key industries (notably automobiles, chemicals, electronics, food processing, and financial services), and, in many instances, FDI helped to further erode the market shares of American-owned firms. Between 1984 and 1991, for instance, the Big Three automakers together lost more than 13 percentage points of their share of the U.S. automobile market—while the share produced by Japanese transplants climbed 12 percentage points.

As FDI in America continues to expand, the United States must decide whether to welcome it with open arms and beckoning realtors, or whether to consider it a long-run threat to American economic and military security. Even if FDI is accepted in principle as beneficial to America, new public policies may still be needed to ensure that the United States extracts the maximum possible benefit from its new guests.

Reprinted with permission from *Foreign Policy* 88 (Fall 1992). Copyright 1992 by the Carnegie Endowment for International Peace.

Those are important questions, and until now they have dominated political discussions about FDI. However, they are not in the end the most important reason to reevaluate the potential impact of FDI. Instead, FDI can be the basis for an altogether new set of economic strategies that could break the catastrophic logjam in Washington over economic policy.

The political gridlock is the result of continuing conflict between two camps: those who believe that government intervention is generally useless or counterproductive, and those who believe that leaving the U.S. economy to the mercy of market forces will bring continued economic decline. Both camps can muster substantial empirical evidence to support their positions, and both hold their beliefs in an ideological death grip. It is as though both sides see themselves as standing at the top of a glass pyramid, with slippery slopes on all sides, fearful that the slightest movement will send them sliding down to defeat or (it sometimes appears) damnation. As a consequence, U.S. economic policy largely reflects the relative political influence of the two positions, rather than the pragmatic adoption of measures appropriate to a given situation.

That is certainly true of U.S. policies on FDI. To the conservative, free-market economists who dominate the thinking of the Bush administration, free flows of capital will, by definition, benefit the economy. They argue that foreign capital brings growth and increased competition, and that any limits or constraints on FDI will reduce growth and lead to market inefficiencies. They advocate, in short, unrestrained foreign access to the U.S. economy.

In contrast, American nationalists of both the left and the right have formed something of an alliance with some big businesses and organized labor. They see FDI as a major threat to existing patterns of ownership and participation in the economy—patterns in which both management and labor have a direct stake. In addition, they claim that some FDI threatens national security, which they say depends on American ownership and control of key firms in military-related and high-technology industries. They argue for tighter controls on FDI.

Both sides suffer from the rigidity of their positions; the archaic economic policies that result from their ideological inflexibility will be no match for the increasingly competitive Europeans and Japanese. To break the logjam, the United States should instead adopt an activist national FDI strategy that has two fundamental aims. First a sound FDI strategy should seek to attract foreign investment, thus adding to the flow of capital into the United States. Second, it must guide those investment flows for the maximum long-term benefit of the U.S. economy. . . .

A European Model

In sharp contrast to the United States, governments in Europe and Japan either already have strong FDI policies or are developing them rapidly. Those governments encourage foreign firms to produce on their territory instead of importing goods. As a result, U.S. firms relocate their production abroad in response to government pressure as well as market forces. The United States thus experiences a loss of crucial production—as in the well-known case of semiconductors.

Largely ad hoc and poorly coordinated, the FDI policies being developed in Europe still constitute an important model, for three reasons. First, the Europeans have economic and political structures that are relatively similar to those of the United States. Second, they face a similar economic problem: Their policymakers are struggling to create efficient markets and reduce the tremendous pain caused by the rapid restructuring of uncompetitive industries—all in an environment of slow growth and relatively high unemployment. Finally, their policies are in most cases adaptable to American economic and political structures.

For decades, the large European markets—with the exception of Great Britain's—have been hard to invest in. Governments and tight business networks obstructed FDI, reasoning that domestic firms needed security in their home markets in order to face foreign competition.

The shift to a single market from 1985 on undermined that approach. The Treaty of Rome explicitly guarantees equal treatment to all firms, foreign or European, established within the European Community (EC). That guarantee offers an extended cloak of equal treatment to all foreign investments in the Community. On the other hand, the new strategy had no direct impact on EC trade policy, and the EC retained significant barriers to goods from abroad.

That distinction became even more important as the Europeans discovered that their policies to enhance the competitiveness of domestic firms were failing. Traditional national champion strategies were explicitly undermined by the single market itself, because a single market by definition cannot be broken up by governments trying to favor their own firms at the expense of those based in other EC countries. To their growing dismay, the governments of the EC countries found that a whole range of industrial policies, including subsidies, technology policy, and lucrative public contracts for domestic producers, was no longer practicable.

As a result, major European firms found themselves in serious trouble. The savage downsizing at Philips, the sale of part of the French computer champion Groupe Bull, the collapse of the British-owned auto industry, and the huge losses at Italy's steel mills all pointed to the uncomfortable fact that much of European industry was not competitive. It needed protection, at least during a "transition period."

The Commission of the European Communities tried to help by restricting the flow of foreign goods into the EC. Beyond tariffs and quotas, which are being shifted from the national to the EC level, the EC has instituted anti-dumping policies since the early 1980s to prevent foreign manufacturers from putting European firms out of business by flooding the market with goods at below-cost prices. During the late 1980s, the policies were largely aimed at Asian electronics producers. Along with the anti-dumping policies, the EC has set anti-circumvention standards to prevent firms from escaping trade barriers or dumping duties by exporting nearly finished products into European "screwdriver" factories for final assembly. Although a General Agreement on Tariffs and Trade (GATT) panel has found the anti-circumvention measures to be illegal, foreign firms in Europe have been forced to raise the local content of their finished products. Tighter rules of origin have also had powerful protectionist effects, especially on semiconductors. Finally, public procurement practices also function as a barrier to trade. European authorities can still reject any bid if at least half of its value would be created outside of the EC, and they must impose a mandatory 3 percent price penalty on all foreign bids.

Importers got the protectionist message. Many built up production bases within the EC, replacing imports. During the late 1980s, Europe was flooded with foreign investment drawn by the huge new single market. Japanese investment flows grew from $549 million in 1980 to $8.9 billion by 1988. Thus, the net effect of the EC's protectionist policies has been to encourage inward investment.

As foreign investment skyrocketed, the EC's FDI policy evolved. To begin, the EC tackled the difficult problem of subsidies by limiting them in size and insisting that, generally speaking, they apply only to designated depressed areas. That has helped the Commission prevent a bidding war for FDI among the EC countries. Thus, the huge subsidies Nissan was paid to set up a plant in the North of England six years ago are no longer available. Honda's new plant in Swindon is not in a depressed area and is therefore ineligible for subsidies. The EC has even forced Toyota to return some subsidies for its new Derbyshire plant.

Equally, European politicians have pressured foreign firms to bring the most lucrative phases of the assembly process to their European factories. Producing sophisticated goods forces foreign companies to train local workers and introduce advanced management practices. The Europeans have also explicitly called on foreign firms to conduct more R&D in Europe and encouraged them to set up design facilities and use local suppliers, training the suppliers to meet international standards. All those steps are crucial if FDI is to replace failing domestic firms.

The messages from Europe have been received very clearly in Japan. Key Japanese circles have recognized that they have to adapt to the new requirements of doing business in Europe. The influential Industrial Bank of Japan acknowledged that point by noting on the cover of its *Review* that Japanese investors in Europe would have to increase the levels of local content, shift design and R&D to Europe, and use local suppliers and local managers where possible. The Japanese Ministry of International Trade and Industry (MITI) understands the game too, as its own publications indicate. The private sector is also listening: Surveys by the Japan External Trade Organization indicate that about 65 percent of Japanese manufacturing establishments investing in Europe have been asked for some specific performance guarantees by the host government.

The impact of European policies is already pretty clear. Even though there are no definitive statistical measurements, the anecdotal evidence is highly suggestive. Toyota and Honda recently announced firm commitments in Europe. Toyota has formally agreed to reach 60 percent local content at its British plant by August 1993 and 90 percent two years later. Honda has also announced sourcing plans for its new British plant, now under construction. United Kingdom suppliers alone are expected to provide 50 percent of its components. In both cases, the commitments mean the transfer of all major systems to Europe.

The contrast with the United States is stark. Honda is regarded as the most American of Japanese car manufacturers. Although Honda claims to have reached 75 percent local content, it still imports high-value-added components from Japan. In 1989, at its Marysville, Ohio, plant, it imported by value 58 percent of engines, 62 percent of transmissions, and 60 percent of suspension and steering components. Domestic sources supplied predominantly lower-value components like windshields and seats. . . .

An Activist FDI Policy

It is crucial to clearly distinguish between managed protectionism aimed at encouraging FDI and random protectionism aimed at shielding uncompetitive U.S. producers. The protectionist component of a new U.S. FDI policy should have at least three parts.

First, protection should be strongly tariff-based and hence highly transparent. Nontariff barriers are bad because their real impact is obscure (no one knows the real impact of "Buy American" legislation, for example), because they can distort markets much more severely than tariffs do, and because the benefits often flow to the importers in the form of higher prices, rather than to the U.S. government. Not only do tariffs make better economic sense, but a shift back to tariffs could encourage similar changes in the policies of U.S. trading partners, encouraging them to move away from the secretive and frustrating tools, such as informal quotas and anti-dumping policies, they currently use to shelter their markets.

Second, protection should be limited. A study by the Institute for International Economics in the mid-1980s showed that if U.S. trade barriers on selected manufactures were quantified solely as tariffs, they would have ranged between 11 and 40 percent. So a tariff on the order of 25 percent could be a good starting point for discussion. Crucially, though, in exchange for higher tariffs, nontariff barriers should be removed or phased out.

Third, protection should cover the entire manufacturing sector, in order to avoid the treacherous quicksands of selecting appropriate industries and sectors for protection. Such an approach would seriously diminish the influence of trade lobbies and special interests.

In sum, the goal is to institute protection sufficient to encourage inward investment, especially in knowledge-intensive industries, without prohibiting the import of goods produced in locations that do have genuine and compelling competitive advantages. In those cases, effective protection would cost the consumer too much, and the industry should be located abroad in low-wage economies or near sources of the raw materials of production. Finally, a 25 percent tariff on manufactured goods could generate on the order of $50 billion annually—not an insignificant sum.

Yet protectionism alone is not enough. An activist policy must also attract foreign investment and at the same time manage it for the overall benefit of the U.S. economy. That means considering some or all of the following options:

Investment incentives. The federal government must end the disastrous competition between the states for capital investment. It is simply not in the interests of Americans to pay large subsidies to attract—or even retain—jobs. Should the state of Kentucky really pay Toyota $373 million to locate there? Should Illinois have paid Sears $110 million to move from downtown Chicago to the suburbs? True, discouraging state subsidies would limit states' prerogatives within the federal system—just as the single market took prerogatives away from European governments—but there are precedents for federal fiscal incentives to constrain states, such as the link between federal highway funds and states' acceptance of federal speed guidelines.

Local content. While protection helped to encourage inward investment, the Europeans used both carrots in the form of a huge, rich, single market, and sticks in the form of rules-of-origin and public procurement regulations. Together, those efforts made it very clear that the Europeans do not welcome mere "screwdriver" plants. U.S. policy should at a minimum offer preferential treatment to more complete forms of investment—perhaps in the tax code. To begin with, the government needs to define and clarify what types of investments are desired. In addition, tighter audits are needed on local content, along with the reversal of auditing rules that allow "roll-up," the practice whereby a component that is 51 percent American made is counted as 100 percent American when considering the local content of the overall product.

Technology. Much U.S. technology policy has hitherto focused on keeping American technology in American hands, but foreign firms are increasingly important sources of technical knowledge. Accepting that reality, the EC encourages foreign firms to transfer technology to Europe by opening technology programs to foreign-owned subsidiaries established in Europe. IBM, for example, is a major participant in many of the EC's ESPRIT information technology projects. As the United States develops its technology policy, it should place those considerations at the forefront.

Management. To a significant degree, the success of foreign firms has been attributed to their use of "lean production" systems, flat hierarchies, and distributed design systems that "bind in" suppliers and clients. Foreign companies should be encouraged to transfer those management techniques to the United States. More local content means more local components—and thus the inclusion of local suppliers in the production system.

Taxes. The United States will have to address the issue of transfer pricing by multinational corporations. It is more profitable for multinational corporations to fix the prices of internal transfers in order to show profits in the lowest-tax country. As recent research shows, U.S. corporate income tax rates are higher than those in most other countries, tempting corporations to show their profits—and pay their taxes—in other countries.

Profits. An important objection to a pro-FDI policy is that foreign investment siphons off profits from the United States in the form of dividends on the investment. While that may be a necessary short-term price for using foreigners' capital, it does pose a potential long-run problem. One possible solution might be for the United States to use targeted corporate tax incentives to encourage foreign firms to list their North American operations on a U.S. stock exchange, allowing U.S. savers an opportunity to buy part of the profit stream.

***Antitrust and* keiretsu.** Japanese-style *keiretsu* are historically alien to the United States, and some Americans fear them. Yet, like other foreign management practices, they probably have something to offer American managers. In particular, *keiretsu* offer long-term ties to component suppliers and clients, giving suppliers access to important corporate secrets, which in turn allows products to be tailored to the needs of the buyer. At the same time, *keiretsu* largely avoid the classic problems of complacency and inefficiency frequently encountered in long-term contracts. Those factors are at the core of *keiretsu*'s success in world markets.

Still, the United States will have to make sure that *keiretsu* do not act like classic trusts, completely shutting out outside firms. However, it seems obvious that policies designed to break such trusts are more likely to be successful once foreign corporations become financially committed to American production facilities. Tokyo's own antitrust policies seem less than adequate for the job, and need to be supplemented by the rigorous application of U.S. laws to the U.S. operations of Japanese *keiretsu*.

The proposed policies do offer a radical change of direction, and critics will no doubt focus on the likely foreign reactions, raising the specter of another Smoot-Hawley tariff and a downward spiral into worldwide protection. However, times have changed since the Great Depression, in several respects. First, the United States runs the largest trade deficit in the world, so other countries are unlikely to start a trade war with the United States that they would inevitably lose. Second, the global economy is much more integrated than it was during the inter-war years, and major corporations are far less dependent on single national markets. Thus, the major players prefer open markets over protectionism. Third, and most important, a shift from furtive protectionism to open and limited tariff-based protection would allow the United States and its trading partners to negotiate differences more openly and honestly. After all, each of the major trading partners has a strong interest in accepting a policy that recognizes that each needs a fair share of the high-value industries of the future. . . .

Chapter 4

Power

A quick sampling of newspaper and television commentaries would reveal an almost universal tendency to equate world politics with power politics. A closer look at these editorials would also reveal two important differences. More clearly visible is the fact that they differ on how this equivalence should be viewed. Some simply treat this condition as a fact of life brought on by the anarchic nature of the international system, one not to be condemned or lamented. Other commentators acknowledge that historically this has been the case but reject the notion that the two are synonymous by definition. Instead, they see it as a product of choice—a choice that has now become counterproductive to the conduct of foreign policy. If cooperation is to replace competition and conflict, power politics must be rejected. In between these two positions are those who are resigned to thinking about world politics in terms of power politics but whose interests lie in understanding and furthering international cooperation. They argue that it is only by understanding power politics and not by rejecting it that lasting international cooperation can occur.

A second difference is less noticeable but no less important. No single definition of power is used. Analysts either employ an "atmospheric" definition in which the term is never defined but used as if everyone knows what it means, or they present a very explicit definition that may or may not conform to others' use of the term. This situation reflects the larger disagreement among students of world politics over how to define power. However, there is a general consensus that power needs to be looked at in three different ways if its importance to the study of world politics is to be fully appreciated. As defined by Jeffrey Hart, these views are power as control over resources, power as control over the actions of another, and power as control over events and outcomes.

Power as Control over Resources

Traditionally the most common way to think about power is as a resource that states control or that policymakers can draw on in conducting foreign policy. The underlying logic to this approach is that the more power resources policymakers have at their disposal, the greater the range of policy options they can select from and the more likely they are to realize their objectives. Power is viewed as a type of international currency which can be spent as needed in furthering state objectives. Thinking about power in this way leads to the construction of power profiles in which the various ingredients of state power are cataloged and recorded.

An example of an attempt to construct a power profile can be found in *The World Factbook*, produced yearly by the Central Intelligence Agency (CIA). Under each country can be found information about its geography (total area, borders, maritime claims, climate, terrain, land use, and environment), people (population, birth and death rates, migration rate, ethnic divisions, literacy, and structure of the labor force), government (its structure, the names of its leaders, and membership in the international organizations), economy (gross national product, exports and imports, debt, industrial production, economic aid, and nature of industrial and agricultural production), communications (highways, ports, and telecommunications), and defense forces (manpower available and defense expenditures).

Because such a cataloging of factors often tends to overwhelm rather then enlighten, some have turned to the construction of power equations in which the various elements in a state's power profile are related to one another in a systematic manner. Although these equations can often become quite complex, Ray Cline suggests that this construction can be done in a rather straightforward fashion by using this formula: $Pp = C + E + M \times (S + W)$. In this equation C defines a country's critical mass of population and territory, E refers to its economic power, and M refers to its military power. The values of each are added together and multiplied by the sum of a country's strategy and national will. According to Cline the total value represents a state's power potential (Pp).

Several types of problems confront anyone wishing to construct a power profile or put together a power equation. The first concerns what to include in the calculations. Do we focus only on the tangible, concrete aspects of power or do we include the types of intangibles that Cline feels are important? How much control over a resource must a policymaker have before it can be included in a state's power profile? Should a power profile reflect the maximum amount of mobilized resources that are at a policymaker's disposal or the actual amount available at any given time? Put concretely, should the size of an army be measured in terms of (1) active duty personnel, (2) active duty personnel plus the reserves, or (3) active duty personnel plus the reserves plus all draft-age men and women. Finally, should one make allowances for the power resources of allies in constructing a state's power profile?

A second set of problems deals with questions of measurement. Clearly, these problems are most pronounced when dealing with such intangibles as national will and quality of leadership, but they are also present when dealing with tangible resources. First, there is the basic question of how to measure any aspect of power. Consider the problem of measuring economic wealth. The most recognizable measure is gross national product (GNP), a measure of the total amount of goods and services produced by an economy. In 1991 the Commerce Department announced that it was no longer going to use GNP because it gave a misleading picture of the health of the U.S. economy by including the value of the goods and services earned by the foreign operations of American corporations. In its place it was going to use gross domestic product (GDP), which measures only the value of the goods and services produced in the United States. The two measures give very different pictures of the state of the U.S. economy. For example, according to calculations based on GNP, the U.S. economy grew by 1.4 percent in the third quarter of 1990, whereas according to calculations based on GDP, it fell by 0.7 percent.

Another measurement problem arises from the fact that virtually every power resource holds the potential for both contributing to a state's power base and detracting from it. One example is population. Large populations are thought to add to a state's power. They permit policymakers to have large work forces and large military establishments at the same time. However, large populations have to be fed, housed, and educated, and an aged population must be cared for. Consideration must also be given to the ethnic mix of a population in judging its contribution to a state's power potential. Populations marked by centuries of hatred and bitterness are far less desirable than ones that are largely homogeneous.

Power as Control over the Actions of Others

Power viewed as control over the actions of others becomes a relational concept rather than an absolute quantity. It is a means to an end rather then an end itself. What is of concern in this approach is the ability of power resources to produce a certain result. Unlike the previous approach, this one does not take for granted the ability of power resources to produce desirable results. Instead the ability to do so is seen as highly contingent on a number of factors. From this perspective, it is the absence of these conditions that goes a long way toward explaining why small or weak states are often able to defy the wishes of more powerful states.

First, there is the engineering problem of mobilizing power resources in the appropriate fashion. For every policy option it is possible to identify a set of objective factors that are crucial for success. States may find themselves rich in power resources but poor in policy instruments. American economic power is overwhelming compared to that of Haiti, yet rather then bring about the rapid capitulation of that country's government following the ouster of President Aristide in 1992, U.S. economic sanctions only made a bad situation worse. Similarly, U.S. and EC economic power combined is overwhelming compared to that of Serbia, yet it proved to be woefully inadequate in bringing about a quick resolution of the Yugoslavian civil war. The exercise of military power faces the same paradox. As the United States discovered in Vietnam and the Soviet Union learned in Afghanistan, a state with the ability to fight a major conventional war may find itself unable to defeat an enemy conducting a guerrilla war against it.

A second factor concerns the nature of the behavior at issue. Is one trying to get another state to do something new or merely to hold to the status quo? Does the behavior in question involve a tactical adjustment on the part of the other state or a fundamental realignment in the conduct of foreign or domestic policy? Barry Blechman and Stephen Kaplan examined 275 peaceful uses of military force by the United States between 1948 and 1975. They found that success was more likely when the behavior in question had to do with domestic politics rather than international politics. It was also found that favorable outcomes were most often realized when the purpose was to reinforce the authority of a specific regime, particularly when viewed from a long-term perspective (two and one-half years). A success rate of 50 percent was achieved only when the goal was to reinforce regime behavior.

A third factor is the reciprocal influence that the target state holds over the state that is attempting to control its behavior. Even when the power relationship between two states is overwhelmingly one-sided, the weaker state may be able to exercise power over the stronger state. Several forces come together to produce this situation: the speed and character of international communications technologies, the role that domestic politics plays in foreign policymaking, and the ability of small states to bring international organizations and other states into the struggle on their side. This situation holds true both when the small state is an enemy, such as North Vietnam against the United States, and when it is an ally. During the cold war the United States and Soviet Union repeatedly found themselves either drawn into conflict or forced to take action because of the behavior of such weaker allies as South Vietnam, Taiwan, East Germany, Afghanistan, and Cuba. The question of who controls whom has also been a constant point of contention in American-Israeli relations. Viewed strictly in terms of power resources, the United States ought to be able to dictate terms to Israel, yet this has rarely been the case. Instead, critics argue that it is Israel that has set the U.S. agenda in the Middle East and alienated it from much of the Arab world.

For the United States, the inherent difficulties involved in translating power as control over resources into power as control over the actions of others have long been obscured by the abundance of power resources at its disposal. This is no longer the case. Military frustrations abroad and economic crises at home have highlighted the need to make a choice that has long confronted most states: Should it emphasize the economic or military dimensions of power?

In Richard Rosecrance's terms, the choice is between a military state or a trading state. The goal of a military state is to create an autonomous and self-contained state, which is best realized through the control of territory and resources that free it from dependence on others. Because territory and resources are limited, states find themselves in a competitive struggle to acquire and hold on to them, making military power the essential ingredient in a state's power profile. For the trading state, wealth and not security is the primary foreign-policy goal. Moreover, wealth is not measured in terms of control over land and people but in terms of control over market shares. Control here is realized not by trying to duplicate or outdo the efforts of others, as it is in the pursuit of military power; it is realized through specialization and product innovation.

The choice is not one of absolutes: military power or economic power. It is a matter of how economic and military power should be related to each other and how much of each to "purchase." For the military state, economic factors are important only to the extent that they contribute to military power. This is an updating of classical mercantalist thought, which viewed the purpose of international trade as creating wealth. In turn, wealth was one of the building blocks of state power—namely, large armies and navies. For the trading state, military power serves as an insurance policy against those challenges to its national interest for which economic power is ineffective. The problem facing the trading state is deciding how much insurance to take. Not having enough military power leaves it vulnerable to blackmail or hostile military action, whereas purchasing too much means that it has failed to invest resources in the more valued economic components of power and risks falling behind those states that have managed their power resources more astutely.

Achieving the proper mix between economic and military power is no easy task. Three sets of issues show just how tightly interwoven economic and military power considerations have become in the selection of policy instruments. The first involves the impact of national defense spending on economic performance. Is there a limit on how much a state can spend on war or the preparation for war without at the same time hurting its international economic growth? Is there such a thing as a peace dividend? Will reduced military spending lead to greater economic growth? Alternatively, can military spending be used to stimulate economic growth?

The second set of issues revolves around the impact of economic change on national security. Will the increased economic prominence of Japan and Germany necessarily translate into an expanded definition of national security and large military establishments? What are the national security implications of the increased globalization of the production process, particularly among defense industries? According to a recent Defense Department report, American firms trail behind non-American firms in one-quarter of the technologies considered to be most essential to American industry. At what point do foreign purchases of key American defense-related industries and coproduction agreements and the reliance on foreign-made technologies move from being economically justifiable to becoming possible points of leverage that could be used against the United States in times of crisis?

The third set of issues focuses on the problem of restoring American international competitiveness. An unsound economy, a troubled educational system, and an overburdened social service sector are not a foundation on which to build either a military state or a trading state. Neither are they typically thought of as foreign-policy problems. For generations they have been the heart and soul of domestic politics. The need to frame solutions to these problems that are sensitive to both their foreign and their domestic dimensions is a major challenge to the political process.

Power as Control Over Events or Outcomes

A third way to conceptualize power is in terms of the ability to control events or outcomes. The guiding assumption behind this approach is that what is really important in world politics is the bottom-line question, "What happened?" Controlling the actions of others does not guarantee that a specific outcome or event will take place. Policy implementation is never perfect. Accidents do happen, and an element of chance is always present. More significantly, today there is a range of desired outcomes in world politics that no state controls, in the sense that its actions alone can bring them about: a clean environment, the preservation of endangered species, respect for human rights, an end to poverty, and nuclear disarmament. The key to achieving these events or outcomes lies in joint, cooperative action.

But how does one go about encouraging international cooperation? The historical record is not very encouraging. Viewed from a power perspective, several factors appear to contribute to this condition. First, not all states involved in the cooperative effort will have an equal stake in bringing about the desired outcome or event. This factor may produce a situation in which the power of the states most interested in the cooperative effort will be significantly weakened and added power will be given to those whose cooperation is essential but who are either largely indifferent to the project or opposed to it. The reluctant state will find its bargaining leverage greatly enhanced as the terms for cooperation are set. The United States was all but able to dictate the terms of the agreements reached at the 1992 Environmental Summit Conference for this reason. Before the meeting, President Bush indicated his opposition to many elements in the proposed treaties. Only the acceptance of the U.S. positions ensured that he would attend and make the conference truly global in scope. The indifferent state, especially if it is small, may also be able to catch a free ride on the back of the more powerful states who want to reach an agreement. Such was the U.S. experience in NATO. The smaller West European states had little to fear from not paying their fair share of the defense burden because of the intense American interest in making NATO work.

Second, not all states will be equally able to contribute to the cooperative effort. The reasons lie as much with the nature of domestic politics as they do with international politics. At the international level, states are constrained in their ability to cooperate by such factors as the structure of the system, their overall lack of power, or their vulnerability to retaliation. At the domestic level, cooperation may be thwarted or limited by an upcoming election, reluctant bureaucracies, a divided public, incompatible elite values, or deadlocked government.

Finally, there is still a great deal of disagreement on what types of power arrangements and what types of power are most conducive to international cooperation. Some argue that there must be a single dominant state in the international system—a hegemonic state—that can either force others to change their position or bear the costs of the cooperative effort. Others believe that international cooperation can occur among relative equals. Cooperation without a hegemonic state is possible because over time a set of informal rules, norms, and policy assumptions develop that guide states' behavior as they collectively try to solve problems. Although in theory there is no international enforcement mechanism to punish those who break these rules and norms, in practice they are obeyed out of self-interest. Only by obeying them can a state expect others to reciprocate. Thus, states come to depend on these rules to protect their rights and regulate the behavior of other states. Under these conditions, coercive power will be of little use. States will have to rely more on the power of leading by example and the force of moral persuasion to get other states to cooperate.

The Readings

As our discussion shows, power is an elusive concept. It means different things to different people. One of the major issues facing analysts and policymakers in the twenty-first century will be developing a finer appreciation of what is meant by the term and a greater understanding of the proper role it plays in world politics. The first two readings take a more detailed look at economic and military power. The first, "Holding the Edge: Maintaining the Defense Technology Base," is a study done by the U.S. Congress, Office of Technology Assessment. It examines the critical issues involved in reestablishing the United States as the undisputed technological leader in the world. The second reading, "To What Ends Military Power?," is by Robert Art, who examines the future role of military power. He concludes that although it has its limitations, especially in the pursuit of economic goals, it will remain central to the conduct of foreign policy. The last two readings take a more general look at power. Paul Kennedy, in "On the 'Natural Size' of Great Powers," addresses the question of America's decline as a world power. His argument that the United States is in decline became a major focal point of debate within the academic community. Here, he introduces the idea of "natural size" to further the ongoing debate over America's future. The last reading is by Joseph Nye, Jr., who rejects the idea that America is a great power in decline. In "Soft Power," he examines the types of power resources that states will need to play a leadership role in world politics in the twenty-first century.

Bibliography

BECKMAN, PETER. *World Politics in the Twentieth Century.* Englewood Cliffs, NJ: Prentice Hall, 1984.

BLECHMAN, BARRY, and STEPHEN KAPLAN. *Force Without War: U.S. Armed forces as a Political Instrument.* Washington, DC: Brookings Institution, 1978.

CLINE, RAY. *World Power Assessment.* Washington, DC: Georgetown University Center for Strategic and International Studies, 1975.

HART, JEFFREY. "Three Approaches to the Measurement of Power," *International Organization* 30 (1976), 289–308.

HUNTINGTON, SAMUEL. "The U.S.—Decline or Renewal?" *Foreign Affairs* 67 (1988/89), 76–96.

KAPSTEIN, ETHAN. *The Political Economy of National Security: A Global Perspective.* New York: McGraw-Hill, 1992.

KEOHANE, ROBERT, and JOSEPH NYE. *Power and Interdependence,* 2nd ed. Glenview, IL: Scott, Foresman, 1989.

KNORR, KLAUS. *Power and Wealth: The Political Economy of International Power.* New York: Basic Books, 1973.

MILNER, HELEN. "International Theories of Cooperation Among Nations: Strengths and Weaknesses." *World Politics* 44 (1992), 466–96.

MORAN, THEODORE. "The Globalization of America's Defense Industries." *International Security* 15 (1990), 57–99.

NAU, HENRY. *The Myth of America's Decline.* New York: Oxford University Press, 1990.

ROSECRANCE, RICHARD. *The Rise of the Trading State.* New York: Basic Books, 1986.

Holding the Edge
Maintaining the Defense Technology Base

Congress of the United States
Office of Technology Assessment

Not long ago, the United States was the undisputed technological leader of the world. U.S. military equipment was meaningfully and undeniably more sophisticated than that of the Soviet Union, and our allies sought American technology for their own defense efforts. American companies developed and sold high-technology products to a world that could not produce them competitively. Defense-related developments led American technology and often "spun-off" into the civilian sector, creating products and whole industries. This reinforced a U.S. defense posture based on using technological superiority to offset whatever advantages the Soviet Union and other potential adversaries might have.

As we approach the 21st century, much has changed. The model of U.S. technology leading the world, with defense technology leading the United States, still retains some validity. But it is a diminishingly accurate image of reality. Soviet defense technology increasingly approaches our own, and sophisticated weapons appear in the hands of third world nations not long after their introduction into Western and Soviet arsenals. At the same time, the U.S. military has been plagued with complex systems that do not work as expected, work only after expensive fixes, or simply do not work. Most are high-priced and take a long time to develop. Increasingly, leading edge technology comes from an internationalized, civilian-oriented economy, which puts a premium on exploiting technology as well as developing it. . . .

Reprinted from "Holding the Edge: Maintaining the Defense Technology Base" (Washington, DC: Office of Technology Assessment, 1989).

Dual-Use Industries

Most of the technology that is engineered into defense systems is still developed in the "defense world" of DoD's laboratories and contractors. This is particularly true of the exotic technologies that are the centerpieces of advanced designs. But increasingly, building those systems depends on developments that take place in the civilian sector, a civilian sector that is driven by the international marketplace. This was dramatically illustrated by events during the first week of November 1988. A company called Avtex, which manufactured rayon fibers for the apparel industry, announced that it was shutting its doors in response to foreign competition in the clothing business. This sent shock-waves through DoD and NASA when it was discovered that Avtex was the only producer of fibers that were critical to the production of missiles and rockets. While other sources could be qualified, and other fibers might be found to substitute for the rayon that Avtex made, that process would take longer than the period of time the available supply of rayon would support production. Negotiations were soon completed to keep Avtex open.

High-technology industries are becoming increasingly internationalized: foreign companies and multinationals are technology drivers. Large international markets generate huge amounts of capital that fuel research and development into new products and underlying technologies. The defense components of these markets are often small, giving DoD little or no leverage over the directions developments will take. DoD has to choose between playing a follower role, or spending large amounts of money to keep a competitive leading edge capability in defense laboratories and industries. But because of the cost of developing modern technology, it seems unlikely that DoD can afford to develop all the technology it needs in parallel with the civilian sector. Dependence on the private sector is not all bad: commercial development of technology is a basic strength of the industrialized, non-Communist world. Failure to exploit developments in the civilian sector would be throwing away a major advantage over the Soviets. But relying on the private sector means that defense development and production will depend increasingly on the health of the civilian sector and on the ability of DoD and its contractors to gain access to the products of the civilian sector. Thus DoD faces two challenges: maintaining access to the technology developed in the commercial sector, and coping with the international nature of that sector.

DoD and Congress face three generic problems. The first is keeping dual-use companies interested in doing defense work. Some are leaving the defense business. Others have technology that DoD could use, but are reluctant to get into the defense business. These attitudes are based primarily on perceptions of the difficulties of doing business with the government, and the problems of doing business in both sectors simultaneously. Second, high-technology industries are moving offshore due to foreign competition. Some have almost vanished, others are on the way. Furthermore, it seems likely that in the future some new technology-based industries will develop in other nations and never take root here. Careful balance will be necessary to nurture U.S. industries while maintaining access to foreign technology. Congress will have to consider U.S. trade and industry policy carefully. Third, entire industries, individual companies, and the many-stepped trails that lead from raw materials to finished components cross many national borders. In many cases, it is nearly impossible to determine what a U.S. company is, while in others it is difficult to separate U.S. companies from their foreign partners. Congress will have to come to grips with the meaning of foreign ownership and foreign siting for the availability of technology, as well as with how dependent the United States can afford to be on foreign sources. These international relationships will complicate attempts to protect U.S. supply sources.

Barriers between Civilian and Military Industry

Since World War II, the U.S. economy has evolved relatively separate military and commercial sectors. They have different business practices, one dictated by government regulations and procurement practices and the other flowing from the marketplace. In recent years the *international* market has had a considerable effect on shaping the latter.

Government practices have made it increasingly difficult for DoD to obtain state-of-the-art technology in areas where civilian industries are leading, making defense business unattractive to innovative companies and contributing to traditional suppliers leaving the defense business. Many firms that are not heavily involved in defense business are reluctant to deal with the government because they consider it to be a bad customer. Moreover, many do not need DoD's business and can simply opt out. The barriers are not technological, but legal, institutional, and administrative. Some are the direct result of legislation, others flow from DoD regulations, including overly cautious interpretations of laws. Some commercial firms cite excessive regulation, burdensome auditing and reporting requirements, compromise of trade secrets, and loss of data rights. Large defense companies have similar complaints, but have adjusted to working under these conditions. But for smaller companies, getting into the defense business means heavy investment and reorientation of business practices.

A company can organize to do business in either sector, but can rarely do both under one administrative roof. Companies that do business in both sectors typically have separate divisions that are organized differently and almost never share staff, production and research facilities, data, and accounting procedures. These differences are profound. In large aerospace companies the commercial side responds to market conditions, whereas the military side responds to Service programs, government regulations, and the Federal budget. Their planning is "slaved" to the Federal planning and budgeting cycle. Corporate structures and rules tend to mirror those of DoD and tend to pass government encumbrances down to lower-level suppliers. Companies doing government contract work have to keep their books in formats that are compatible with government auditing rules and procedures.

Following these and other government rules adds to the costs of doing business, costs that can legitimately be passed on to the government customer. Tighter control of the defense business ultimately translates into higher costs to DoD. The United States is apparently willing to bear this increased cost as the price of other benefits—for example, knowledge that the government is trying to keep the process honest. However, imposing the same rules on dual-use industries has other, farther-reaching effects. It makes them reluctant to do business with DoD and encumbers their products with additional costs that may adversely affect their international competitive positions. When dealing in both sectors, companies can accept either the higher cost of following government business procedures, or the higher costs of maintaining two separate business practices—one for government business and one for other business. With some exceptions, DoD product specifications are also seen as encumbrances; characteristics that are of no value in the commercial marketplace are engineered into the products for sale to DoD.

Government contracts regulate profits, creating a business environment very different from that in which most high-technology companies deal. These companies are used to investing heavily in R&D, recovering their investments through large profits, and then reinvesting in the next generation of product. Moreover, their customers see only the product, whereas DoD insists on knowing how the product was made. Defense contractors get by on small profits, in part because much of their R&D costs are covered either by contract or IR&D recovery. But dual-use companies qualify for little if any IR&D recovery and are reluctant to do contract R&D. The government owns the rights to data generated by contract R&D so that it can keep the subsequent phases of a project competitive by making a data package available to all bidders. But companies that live by their innovation in the commercial market see this process as offering their trade secrets to the competition. DoD procedures provide the winner of a development contract poor profit margins, no guarantee of a continuing relationship with DoD, and little incentive to innovate and provide a superior product.

Some industries, like advanced composites, are currently so closely tied to the defense business that they are apparently willing to live with these problems. But they worry that their competitive position may be damaged as the commercial market develops. At the other extreme, the companies that produce fiber optics are reluctant to get involved in a defense market they see as always being a small part of their business: they do not necessarily see the potential payoff as worth the aggravation.

While the small amount of military fiber optics business might be seen as evidence that the industry is not really important to defense, some within the DoD see it as a critical new technology for future systems, one in which defense could gain tremendously just by exploiting what has been and is being developed in the commercial sector. But DoD has been generally slow in adopting fiber optic technology. Program managers have much to lose by inserting risky new technologies that may delay schedules and increase costs, but little to gain because the advantages of the substitution will usually become apparent only on someone else's watch.

In the software industry, the divergence between government and commercial practices has been enough to produce separate defense and commercial businesses that often do not share technology. The procedures, policies, and management of large-scale systems in the military and civilian sectors diverge starting with requirements definition, continuing in the development or acquisition of software, and throughout the entire life cycle of the software. This restricts the flow of leading-edge technology from defense into the commercial sector and reduces DoD access to readily available commercial products. Most of the differences can be attributed to the policies, regulations, standards, and directives mandated by DoD. DoD software requirements are more rigid than their commercial counterparts. Defense systems tend to be overwhelmingly custom built, while commercial systems will use as much off-the-shelf technology as possible. Software companies are particularly concerned about data rights, which they see as critical to competitiveness. Companies are reluctant to deal under DoD restrictions; in their eyes the government would be taking and possibly giving to their competitors the very basis of their business.

International Competitiveness and the Health of U.S. Industries

The Department of Defense has been concerned for some time about the implications for defense of deteriorating competitive positions of U.S. manufacturing companies in the international market.[1] The government is also concerned from a wider perspective that this trend is weakening and undermining the U.S. economy. DoD shares the concern that a weakening economy and a drain of resources into purchases of foreign goods will reduce money available to produce defense equipment, but its primary concern is the continuing availability of necessary items and technology.

The government does not as yet have a policy regarding dependence on foreign sources for defense material and technology, let alone a game plan for implementing such a policy. The Undersecretary of Defense for Acquisition has recommended a plan to bolster defense-related manufacturing in the United States.[2] The report detailing that plan does not make a statement on how much foreign dependence is tolerable, although it does imply that some is unavoidable.

The complexity of the problem is illustrated by the issue of cooperative development and production of defense equipment with the European NATO Allies. It has been long-standing U.S. policy to encourage multinational procurement of similar defense equipment to foster commonality, to get the best equipment into the forces of all the Allies, to save money, and recently, to exploit a broad multinational technology base. In recent years the Defense Department has made great progress in generating international memoranda of understanding for joint development, with the help of initiatives like the Nunn Amendment. But as the Europeans have become more interested in cooperative developments, they have also sought a greater share in generating the technology and a larger market share for their defense industries. Interest by U.S. companies in joint ventures with Europeans has been spurred, in part, by fears that several trends in European thinking could sharply curtail their sales in Europe. Thus, the cooperative programs are a two-edged sword helping U.S. sales in Europe while stimulating European sales to the United States; and helping U.S. defense policy in general, while both helping and hindering the maintenance of the U.S. defense industrial technology base. Crafting a workable policy will be a tricky job.

There are three basic policy choices:

■ demand that anything that goes into defense equipment be built in the U.S. from U.S.-sourced components, taking whatever measures are necessary to ensure that all the necessary industries are alive and well in the United States;

■ let the market dictate which industries will be healthy in the United States and look only for the best deals wherever they can be found worldwide; or

■ choose some industries that have to be located in the United States, take appropriate measures to ensure that, and let the rest go with the market.

The first and third require some sort of intervention in the international economy, either supporting the international competitiveness of U.S. companies or protecting, supporting, and subsidizing U.S. companies that cannot otherwise survive. Another approach is to design nothing into U.S. defense systems that cannot be domestically sourced. But this cuts off a great deal of modern technology, a Western strength. In making these choices, the United States will have to decide how dependent we can afford to be, and how much independence we are willing to pay for. If the United States demands self-sufficiency without taking measures to keep U.S. companies alive and competitive, the list of technologies available for defense systems is likely to decrease as time goes on.

It will be necessary to decide how to treat dependence on various nations. There are significant differences in being dependent on Canada (already defined as part of the North American industrial base), Britain, our other NATO allies, Mexico, Japan, Korea, etc. U.S. and Canadian companies are closely intertwined. Despite the recent controversy over the trade agreement and other arguments, we are each other's largest trading partners. Canada is also a NATO ally with a common security interest. The chances of being cut off from Canadian sources either by policy or by hostile act are minimal. We are also close to our European Allies; much of our defense equipment is bought to defend them. But we are separated from Europe by an ocean, and they have not always supported U.S. military actions. Other nations are much less tightly tied to the United States.

The high-technology economy is an international one and responds to international market forces. These forces are likely to continue to move industries offshore despite U.S. efforts to will (or legislate) them to stay. In the vast majority of cases, defense business is far too small to provide the necessary clout, particularly when faced with other nations that manipulate their civilian markets to keep their companies healthy. Competition comes from Japan, the smaller Asian nations—Korea, Taiwan, Singapore, etc—and Western Europe. The Europeans are taking dramatic steps to improve their international competitive position, particularly in high technology industries. These include the economic integration of the EC in 1992, and the funding and encouragement of large cooperative R&D projects.

Although all industries are different, the plight of the fiber optics industry is illustrative. While healthy in the United States, it faces increasingly stiff competition at home and continuing difficulties abroad stemming from limited access to foreign markets. Both the Europeans and the Japanese are making major pushes in fiber optics and photonics in general. U.S. technology and production costs are at least competitive. But while U.S. producers have been largely excluded from some important foreign markets, the U.S. market remains open to foreign vendors. Japanese companies can sell in foreign markets at low prices because their government has discouraged foreign competition in Japan where prices are kept artificially high. The closed domestic market supports overseas competitiveness.

The U.S. software industry faces a different sort of challenge. It is currently strong and competitive, but the rapid growth in worldwide demand for software threatens to outstrip the capacity of U.S. firms to meet it, leaving a large opening for foreign firms to penetrate the market. Japan, France, the United Kingdom, Korea, Singapore, Taiwan, and India have the capacity to penetrate the global market. And many of these nations have trade policies that either discourage sales by U.S. companies or fail to protect the intellectual property rights of those companies: "pirated" software is becoming a major problem. Moreover, the Japanese are making rapid strides in turning software design from art to manufacture, building software factories to increase productivity dramatically.

Internationalization of Industries

Efforts to protect and nurture U.S. companies will be complicated by trends toward internationalization in high-technology industries. Examples are found in the advanced composites industry in which many of the firms that appear to be American—because they have American names or U.S. facilities—are actually owned by foreign companies and in the fiber optics business where international joint ventures are used to get into otherwise closed markets. International ownership, vertical and horizontal integration, and international siting make it difficult to define in any convincing way what an American company is. Moreover, the sequence of steps that leads to a final product often crosses international boundaries many times and shifts as prices and availability of components shifts. Is a Pontiac built in Korea any more or less an American product than a Honda made in the United States or a Chevrolet/Toyota assembled in California from U.S. and Japanese parts?

Difficulties in identifying U.S. companies will produce difficulties in writing legislation to protect them or establishing DoD policy to encourage the growth of important domestic industries. Foreign plants owned by U.S. companies, U.S. plants owned by foreign companies, joint ownership, and joint ventures all offer different sets of problems.

Formulating Policy

These trends toward internationalization will complicate difficult issues that Congress and the Administration are already facing. Paramount among these is to decide whether the U.S. Government will play a major role in encouraging and supporting U.S. commercial business and industry, or whether—almost unique among the governments of major nations—it will continue to remain more or less aloof, confining its activities to a few international trade negotiations. Other governments encourage the development of commercial technology and associated industry, help to foster a domestic situation conducive to growth, and support aggressive overseas marketing.

Having decided government's role, the next issue would be to define goals. These might include:

- keeping key nondefense manufacture and development in the United States,
- keeping manufacture and development in the hands of U.S.-based (or U.S.-owned) companies;
- preserving some portion of the U.S. market for U.S.-based (or U.S.-owned) companies; and
- gaining access to foreign markets for U.S. firms.

Defining such goals will entail arriving at a working definition of a U.S. company, or at least of how location and ownership affect U.S. national security interests.

NOTES

1. For examples, see Defense Science Board, "Report of the Defense Science Board Task Force on Defense Semiconductor Dependency," prepared for the Office of the Under Secretary of Defense for Acquisition, February 1987; Report to the Secretary of Defense by the Under Secretary for Acquisition, "Bolstering Defense Industrial Competitiveness: Preserving Our Heritage, the Industrial Base, Securing Our Future" (Washington, DC: Department of Defense, 1988); and Martin Libicki, *Industrial Strength Defense: A Disquisition on Manufacturing, Surge, and War* (Washington, DC: National Defense University, 1986). See also, U.S. Congress, Office of Technology Assessment, *Paying the Bill: Manufacturing and America's Trade Deficit*, OTA-ITE-390 (Springfield, VA: National Technical Information Service, June 1988).
2. See "Bolstering Defense Industrial Competitiveness," op. cit., footnote 12.

To What Ends Military Power?

Robert J. Art

What Has Been the Impact of Nuclear Weapons?

Have nuclear weapons affected either the need that states have for force or the uses to which military power can be put? Stated succinctly, the answer is "no" and "partially."

Nuclear weapons have not obviated the need of states for military power. . . . The need for military power derives from the self-help nature of international relations, itself a consequence of anarchy. Nuclear weapons have enabled some states to help themselves better than other states heretofore could, but they have not produced an effective world government and thereby eradicated the necessity for self-help. Because nuclear weapons have left anarchy untouched, military power remains integral to every nation's foreign policy.

Rather, what nuclear weapons have done is to alter the ways in which states that possess such weapons use their military power. For those states, nuclear weapons have downgraded the function of defense, ruled out physical nuclear compellence, enhanced deterrence and nuclear swaggering, and left unclear the utility of peaceful nuclear compellence. To this statement, however, three caveats must be immediately made. First, it would be a mistake to ascribe all the changes in the ways nuclear states have used their military power simply to nuclear weapons. The changes wrought have been due as

Reprinted from *International Security* 4:4 (1980), Robert Art, "To What Ends Military Power?" by permission of MIT Press, Cambridge, MA.

much to *whom* has had them as it has been to *what* the weapons are physically capable of doing. Second, the changes have manifested themselves primarily in two sets of relations, those between the two superpowers and those between NATO and the Warsaw pact. Nuclear weapons have not left untouched the relations between each superpower and the nations of Africa, Latin America, the Middle East, and Asia; but the effects on these relations are not readily evident, uniform, nor necessarily far-reaching. Third, nuclear weapons have not eliminated the need for nuclear states to deploy non-nuclear forces, nor have they diminished for most non-nuclear states the utility that conventional forces have for attaining their foreign policy goals vis-à-vis one another. In short, nuclear weapons have profoundly affected how some states have used force; but not all states have experienced a radical transformation in the ways that they have employed their military power. One can be impressed equally by the enduring realities of international politics and by the changes nuclear weapons have wrought. . . .

What Is the Future of Force?

If the past be any guide to the future, then military power will remain central to the course of international relations. Those states that do not have the wherewithall to field large forces (for example, Denmark) or those that choose to field forces far smaller than their economies can bear (for example, Japan) will pay the price. Both will find themselves with less control over their own fate than would otherwise be the case. Those states that field powerful military forces will find themselves in greater control, but also that their great military power can produce unintended effects and that such power is not a solution to all their problems. For both the strong and the weak, however, as long as anarchy obtains, force will remain the final arbiter to resolve the disputes that arise among them. As has always been the case, most disputes will be settled short of the physical use of force. But as long as the physical use of force remains a viable option, military power will vitally affect the manner in which all states in peacetime deal with one another.

This is a conclusion not universally nor even widely held today. Three schools of thought challenge it. First are those who argue that nuclear weapons make war, nuclear or conventional, between America and Russia or between the NATO Alliance and the Warsaw pact unthinkable. Hopefully that is the case. But, as we have argued, one does not measure the utility of force simply by the frequency with which it is used physically. To argue that force is on the wane because war in Europe has not occurred is to confuse effect with cause. The probability of war between America and Russia or between NATO and the Warsaw pact is practically nil precisely because the military planning and deployments of each, together with the fears of escalation to general nuclear war, keep it that way. The absence of war in the European theater does not thereby signify the irrelevance of military power to East-West relations but rather the opposite. The estimates of relative strength between these two sets of forces, moreover, intimately affect the political and economic relations between Eastern and Western Europe. A stable balance of forces creates a political climate conducive to trade. An unstable balance of forces heightens political tensions that are disruptive to trade. The chances for general war are quite small, but the fact that it nevertheless remains possible vitally shapes the peacetime relations of the European powers to one another and to their superpower protectors.

Second are those who argue that the common problems of mankind, such as pollution, energy and other raw material scarcities, have made war and military power passé. In fact, their argument is stronger: the common problems that all nations now confront make it *imperative* that they cooperate in order to solve them. This argument, however, is less a statement of fact about the present than a fervent hope for the future. Unfortunately, proof of how the future will look is not available in the present. Cooperation among nations today, such as it is, should not make us sanguine about their ability to surmount their conflicts for the good of all. It takes a strong imagination, moreover, to assume that what some nations term common problems are viewed as such by all. One man's overpopulation, for example, is another man's source of strength. China and India are rightly concerned about the deleterious effects of their population growth on their standard of living. But Nigeria, whose source of power and influence within Africa rests partly on a population that is huge by African standards, is not. The elemental rule of international relations is that the circumstances of states differ. Hence so too do their interests and perspectives. Not only do they have different solutions to the same problem, they do not always or often agree on what are the problems. As long as anarchy obtains, therefore, there will be no agency above states powerful enough to create and enforce a consensus. As long as anarchy obtains, therefore, military power deployed by individual states will play a vital role both in defining what are the problems and in hastening or delaying their solutions. Only when world government arrives will the ability of every nation to resort to force cease to be an option. But even then the importance of force will endure. For every government has need of an army.

Finally, there are those who proclaim that the nations of the world have become so economically intertwined that military power is no longer of use because its use is no longer credible. A nation whose economic interests are deeply entangled with another's cannot use force against it because to do so would be to harm itself in the process. Interests intertwined render force unusable—so believe the "interdependencia theorists." Two of the leading proponents of this view have forcefully argued that when "military force is not used by governments toward other governments within the region," even "complex interdependence" prevails. Under such a condition:

> As military force is devalued, strong states will find it more difficult to use their overall dominance to control outcomes on issues in which they are weak. . . .
> The negligible role of force leads us to expect states to rely more on other instruments in order to wield power. . . .

Intense relationships of mutual influence exist among these countries, but on most of them force is irrelevant or unimportant as an instrument of policy.[1]

This condition of complex interdependence now obtains for the United States in its relations with its key allies—Western Europe, Canada, and Japan. And it can be expected to hold for America's relations with other nations where military power is not usable.

This view of the world is odd. How can American military power, which is the cement binding the great powers of the free world together, be "irrelevant or unimportant as a tool of policy"? American military power has created and sustained the political preconditions necessary for the evolutionary intertwining of the American, Canadian, Japanese, and Western European economies. That which the commitment of American power has created and sustained could easily unravel should the commitment be withdrawn. It is therefore strange to argue that force has no utility among states that are closely united when force has been responsible for uniting them. The Japanese, Canadians, and Western Europeans know that they remain dependent for their security on American military power, especially the American nuclear umbrella. It would be odd indeed if this dependence were not exploited by the United States on political and economic matters of interest to it. Military preeminence has never ensured political and economic preeminence. But it does put one nation in a stronger bargaining position that, if skillfully exploited, can be fashioned for non-military goals. Force cannot be irrelevant as a tool of policy for America's economic relations with her great power allies: America's military preeminence politically pervades these relations. It is the cement of economic interdependence.

A simple example will clarify the point. In 1945, convinced that competitive devaluations of currencies made the depression of the 1930s deeper and longer than need be, America pushed for fixed exchange rates. Her view prevailed, and the Bretton Woods structure of fixed exchange rates, with small permissible variations monitored by the International Monetary Fund was set up and lasted until 1971. In that year, because of the huge outflow of dollars over a twenty-five year period, the United States found it to its best interests to close the gold window—that is, to suspend the commitment to pay out gold for dollars that any nation turned in. Under Bretton Woods the relations of the free world's currencies to one another were fixed in the relation of each to the dollar, which in turn was fixed in value by its relation to the standard "one ounce of gold equals thirty-five dollars." By closing the gold window, the United States shattered that standard, caused the price of an ounce of gold in dollars to soar, destroyed the fixed benchmark according to which all currencies were measured, and ushered in the era of floating exchange rates. In sum, America both made and unmade the Bretton Woods system. In 1945 she persuaded her allies. In 1971 she acted unilaterally and against their wishes.

Under both fixed and floating exchange rates, moreover, the United States has confronted her great power allies with an unpleasant choice. Either they could accept and hold onto the dollars flowing out of the United States and thereby add to their inflation at home by increasing their money supplies; or they could refuse the dollars, watch the value of their currencies in relation to the dollar rise, make their exports more expensive (exports upon which all these nations heavily rely), and threaten a decline in exports with the concomitant risk of a recession. America's economic and military strength has enabled her for over twenty years to confront her great power allies with the choice of inflation or recession for their economies. America did not have to use her military power directly to structure the choice this way nor to make and break the system. Her economic strength, still greater than that of most of her great power allies combined, gave her considerable bargaining power. But without her military preeminence and their military dependence she could never have acted as she did. America used her military power politically to cope with her dollar valuation problem.

In a similar vein, others argue that the United States can no longer use its military power against key Third World nations to achieve its aims because of its dependence on their raw materials or because of its needs to sell them manufactured goods. In order to assess the validity of this argument, four factors must be kept in mind. First, the efficacy of military power should not be confused with the will to use it. In the mid- and late 1970s, as a consequence of the experience with Vietnam, America's foreign policy elite was reluctant to commit American conventional forces to combat. Its calculation has been that the American public would not tolerate such actions, except for the most compelling and extreme of circumstances. The non-use of American military power in Asia, Africa, and Latin America in the late 1970s stems as much from American domestic political restraints as from anything else.

Second, it is important to recall a point made earlier about the inherent limits of military power to achieve economic objectives. A superior military position can give one state a bargaining edge over another in the conduct of their bilateral economic relations, but bargains must still be struck. And that requires compromise by both parties. Only by conquest, occupation, and rule, or by a credible threat to that effect, can one state guarantee that another will conduct its economic relations on terms most favorable to the (would-be) conqueror. Short of that, the economic relations between two states are settled on the basis of each state's perception of its own economic interests, on differences in the strength, size, and diversity of their economies, on differences in the degree to which each state coordinates the activities of its interest groups and hence centrally manages its economy, and on the differential in their military capabilities. Because military power is only one of the ingredients that determine the economic relations between two states, its role is not always, nor usually, overriding. By itself superiority in arms does not guarantee, nor has it ever guaranteed, superiority in economic leverage. In this sense, although there may be clear limits on what the United States through its military power can achieve in its economic relations with the Third World, much of the constraint stems from the limits that inhere in translating military power into economic ends.

Third, America's economic power relative to others has waned in the 1970s. The 1950s were characterized by a United States whose economic and military power far surpassed that of any other nation. With the emergence of the Soviet Union as a global military power in the 1970s, America's freedom to intervene militarily around the world, unimpeded by concerns about the counteractions of another global power, has drastically declined. But America's economic freedom worldwide has also waned. Whether measured by the diminished role of the dollar as the world's reserve currency, by the persistent lack of a favorable trade balance, by a smaller percentage of the world's trade accounted for by American imports and exports, by a decline in the productivity of its labor force, or by a greater dependence on imported raw materials, the United States economy is not as self-sufficient and immune from economic events beyond its borders as it once was. Analysts disagree over the extent to which, and the reasons why, the health of the American economy has become more dependent on the actions of other nations; but they do not disagree on the fact of greater dependence.[2] If the hallmark of the fifties and sixties was America's military and economic preeminence, the hallmark of the seventies has been America's passing the zenith of her power and the consequent waning of this dual preeminence.

A diminishment in the economic power of a state is not easily compensated for by an edge in military capability. When that military edge also wanes, such compensation becomes even more difficult. Although the United States remains the world's strongest economic *and* military power, the gap between her strength in each dimension and that of other nations has narrowed in the seventies from that which was the case in the fifties and sixties. It is therefore wrongheaded to assert that America's diminished ability to get what it wants economically from allies and neutrals is due solely to the devaluation of military power. It is wrongheaded to assert that military power is devalued because it cannot solve economic problems when economic problems have never been readily or totally solved by military measures. It is wrongheaded to blame on military power that which has military and economic causes. The utility of force to a state for compellent purposes does diminish as the relative military power of a state declines. But the utility of force for compellent economic purposes declines even more when a state's economic bargaining power concomitantly wanes.

Fourth, force cannot be efficiently used to achieve goals when ambivalence exists over the goal to be attained. America's increasing dependence on oil imports classically illustrates this problem. Many have taken the decision by the United States not to use military power against OPEC nations in order to get them to lower the price of their oil as a sign of the devaluation of military power in the contemporary world. It would, of course, be absurd to deny the fact that as many of the OPEC nations make strenuous efforts to strengthen themselves militarily, often with American help, the ability of the United States to wield military power against them diminishes. It would be absurd to deny the fact that the potency of the Third World's virulent nationalism has restrained the great powers in their military adventures against those nations. It would be absurd to deny that the 1970s are not different from the 1870s and 1880s, when the European great powers, restrained only by their fears of each other's counteractions, intervened militarily at will in Asia and Africa against poorly armed and politically fragmented "nations." Clearly the political and military conditions for great power military intervention in such areas have drastically changed since then.

It would be equally absurd, however, to ignore the restraint on the use of force imposed by the inherent ambivalence of the United States with regard to the price it should pay for imported oil. In the short term, America's interest is in a stable supply of cheap oil; but if pursued over the long term, such a policy will yield an ever-increasing dependence on foreign oil (as happened by the early 1970s precisely as a consequence of just such a policy), a decline in the replenishment of world oil reserves because of the very cheapness of oil (and especially that of the Middle East), and the lack of a vigorous program to develop alternative energy sources. In the short term, cheap oil reduces America's balance of payments deficit, reduces inflation, and removes a drag on aggregate demand. Over the long term, it promotes greater dependence and rapid depletion of the world's oil reserves. In the short term, expensive oil worsens the nation's balance of payments deficit, increases inflation, and lessens aggregate demand. Over the long term, it promotes conservation, the search for more oil, the development of alternative energy sources, and the likelihood of a decreasing dependence on foreign energy imports.

Faced with such a Hobson's choice, how should America use its military power? It is within her military capability, if she chose to invest the necessary resources, to invade Saudi Arabia, which has a quarter of the world's proven reserves of oil, and secure the oil fields, or better yet, Kuwait, which has smaller though still sizeable reserves, but many fewer people. It would be difficult, but it could be done. *Should* it be done? In the face of the unpleasant choice posed above, and solely on its economic merits, the benefits to the United States of such military intervention are not self-evident. And that is the point. Military power is not useful for solving an economic problem which has no simple or single best solution. Certainly much of America's restraint in her dealings with OPEC, if not her downright ambivalence, stems from an uncertainty over what is in her own best economic interest, or from an unacknowledged but tacit agreement by her foreign policy elite that a rise in the price of imported oil is to America's long-term interest. If it be the latter, then understandably the United States has opted for a stable supply of expensive oil and has used her influence and military power in the Middle East to that end.

American actions aside, the record of the late 1970s simply does not support the assertion that the efficacy of military power is on the wane. Recent Russian successes in Angola, Ethiopia, Southern Yemen, Afghanistan, and Cambodia have all been predicated on the use of Russian military power, sometimes in concert with that of Cuba. Because she continues to pour huge resources into her military machine, Russia evidently does not believe that force has lost its potency. In their relations with one another, conventional military power for the Third World nations remains a vital instrument of foreign policy. Simply recall these events of the last four years: The Tanzanian-Ugandan War, the Northern Yemen-Southern Yemen War, the Ethiopian-Somalian War, the Sino-Vietnam War, the Cambodian-Vietnam War, the Libyan-Egyptian border clashes, the Libyan-backed insurgency in Chad, the Angolan-backed insurgency in southern Zaire, the Moroccan takeover of the Spanish Sahara, and the Algerian-backed Polisaro War against Morocco. Nuclear weapons continue to entice and lure the non-nuclear power. Brazil and Pakistan in particular are in dogged pursuit of them. China urgently seeks to modernize its obsolete military forces. The NATO Alliance has committed itself to a three percent real increase in its military spending. Above and beyond that, sentiment in the United States is building for a tremendous increase in military spending.

The efficacy of force endures. It must. For in anarchy, force and politics are connected. By itself, military power guarantees neither survival nor prosperity. But it is almost always the essential ingredient for both. Because resort to force is the ultimate card of all states, the seriousness of a state's intentions is conveyed fundamentally by its having a credible military posture. Without it, a state's diplomacy generally lacks effectiveness. Force need not be physically used to be politically useful. Threats need not be overtly made to be communicated. The mere presence of a credible military option is often sufficient to make the point. It is the capability to resort to military force if all else fails that serves as the most effective brake against having to do so. Lurking behind the scenes, unstated but explicit, lies the military muscle that gives meaning to the posturings of the diplomats. Diplomacy is the striking of compromises by parties with differing perspectives and clashing interests. The ultimate ability of each to resort to force disciplines the diplomats. Precisely because each knows that all can come to blows if they do not strike compromises do the diplomats engage in the hard work necessary to construct them. There is truth to the old adage: "The best way to keep the peace is first to prepare for war."

NOTES

1. Robert O. Keohane and Joseph S. Nye, *Power and Interdependence: World Politics Transition* (Boston: Little, Brown, 1977), p. 25.
2. For clear statements of two views on the degree of dependence, see Kenneth N. Waltz, *Theory of International Politics* (Reading, MA: Addison-Wesley, 1979), chap. 7, who sees only a slight increase in America's economic dependence on foreign economic activity; and Nye and Keohane, *Power and Interdependence*, chaps. 2, 3, and 8, who see a much greater dependence.

On the "Natural Size" of Great Powers

Paul Kennedy

My invention (if that is the proper word) of the concept of a "natural size" for a country or Power in the international system occurred in the midst of some ruminations of mine upon the controversial issue of the relative decline of the United States in world affairs, and of the analogies which political scientists and historians tend to draw between America's condition today and the position of earlier leading Powers such as Spain or Britain. In making any such analogies, I cautioned, scholars ought not to ignore the "differences in scale" between the United States and those former European Great Powers.

> This can be put another way: the geographical size, population and natural resources of the British Isles would suggest that it ought to possess roughly 3 or 4 percent of the world's wealth and power, *all other things being equal*; but, it is precisely because all other things are *never* equal that a peculiar set of historical and technological circumstances permitted the British Isles to expand to possess, say, 25 percent of the world's wealth and power in its prime; and since those circumstances have disappeared, all that it has been doing is returning down to its more "natural" size. In the same way, it may be argued that the geographical extent, population, and natural resources of the United States suggest that it ought to possess perhaps 16 or 18 percent of the world's wealth and power, but because of historical and technological circumstances favorable to it, that share rose to 40 percent or more by 1945; and what we are witnessing at the moment is the early decades of the ebbing away from that extraordinarily high figure to a more "natural" share. That decline is being masked by the country's enormous military capabilities at

Reprinted from the *Proceedings of the American Philosophical Society* 135 (1991).

present, and also by its success in "internationalizing" American capitalism and culture. Yet even when it declines to occupy its "natural" share of the world's wealth and power, a long time into the future, the United States will still be a very significant Power in a multipolar world, simply because of its size.[1]

Before making additional remarks upon the relative positions of the United States, or Britain, or Japan, a few general observations are in order here.

To begin with, terms such as "natural size" and "shares of world wealth and power" clearly are abstract notions, and somewhat vague ones at that. They invite us to focus upon an important theme, namely, what are the relationships between the physical endowments of a country (its territorial extent, population, resources) and the relative importance it possessed in world history; but because our measurements are bound to be rough and ready, phrases like "16 or 18 percent of the world's wealth and power" suggest a false exactitude. Despite gallant attempts by political scientists to quantify comparative shares of world power, the statistics produced will never be as precise or meaningful a reckoning as, say, shares of world automobile output. And if I use such figures today, they are indeed to be understood as rough and ready.

Second, although we may be employing the term "natural size," in fact what we are interested in is the *opposite*: we are concerned with countries that have assumed an "unnatural" or "abnormal" size in the world affairs relative to their physical endowments. What interests the historian of Great-Power relationships pursuing this line of inquiry is why, for example, it was in the small offshore British Isles in the decades after 1815 that the center of world power lay—and not in the offshore islands of Madagascar, or Taiwan, or Cuba, or Japan; and why, for that matter, it was not in Brazil or Russia or the Congo at that point in history. What special characteristics and advantages did Britain, and before it Venice, Portugal, the Netherlands, *possess*, to allow them to play in their turn a larger role in international affairs than their physical size would at first suggest? Or, to look at a contemporary phenomenon, what special advantages are possessed by Japan, a country with only 0.3 percent of the world's land area, few natural resources, and a mere 2.5 percent of the world's population, that it should contain 80 percent of the world's robots, manufacture three-quarters of the world's memory chips, and so on?

What we are really talking about here, I suspect, is relative efficiency of organization: why and how were the Netherlands better organized than, say, the Ottoman Empire in the eighteenth century?; why and how is South Korea today better organized than Ethiopia? All this begs the obvious question "organized for what?", but I think that the student of international politics can provide the plausible answer: organized for the steady improvement in wealth and standards of living, organized to support and enhance the society's interests in an anarchic and volatile world.

[In examining the "natural size" of Great Powers] we witness a story of replication, of imitation, of attempts to catch up, by countries and societies eager to draw level with—or eclipse—another nation that, at the time, is in the lead. In the seventeenth century, resenting the "unnaturally" large size and influence exerted by the Dutch Republic, the English strove to catch up, by their Navigation Acts, their development of a navy, their rivalry for colonies, their establishment of a stock market, and so on. In the nineteenth century, stimulated by Britain's extraordinary and "unnatural" place in world affairs, Germans strove to follow suit, in adopting the Industrial Revolution, building railways, exporting manufactures, creating shipping lines, establishing colonies, and all the rest. Because the newcomers started later, they could learn from the trail-blazing or lead country's experiences; because they began from a lower base, their rates of growth were relatively faster; and because they had a target, they knew what they were shooting for. By contrast, the then-leading Powers, the Dutch in the seventeenth century, the British in the nineteenth, were much less focused and driven. What they wanted, essentially, was for the *status quo* to remain, so that they could enjoy all the advantages of their Number One position, even if that position was out of proportion to their "natural size." A nation which, like Great Britain, was a small offshore group of islands in the sixteenth century, and then rose to possess an enormous Empire and to be the center of world trade, industry, and finance, did not look with relish at the idea of returning to that earlier status as the twentieth century unfolded.

All of which brings us back, finally, to the condition of the United States in the world, and to the highly charged issue of whether it can retain its position as Number One. So far as I can tell, everyone agrees that its global power and influence after 1945—possessing 50 percent of the world's total Gross National Product, for example, with the only modern industrial base, massive gold and currency reserves, and great military capacities—was artifical and "unnatural," in the sense that so many other nations, in Europe, the USSR, and Japan, were devastated by the war. As they steadily recovered, most of them aided by American support and protection, it was inevitable that the United States' relative share would decrease.

The implication of that line of argument is, however, that the United States is merely returning to its pre–Second World War position, or to its late 1920s position, when it possessed between 33 and 40 percent of world economic power. Yet all the recent evidence—of the current American shares of world manufacturing output, of currency reserves, of high technology, or of R&D levels, trade balances, educational skills—suggests that the United States relative economic position is going to be much lower than the 33 or 40 percent of the interwar years, and much closer to the shares that it possessed in the very early part of this century. And that in turn raises the deeper question: regardless of the short-lived boost which the Second World War gave to the United States' relative world position, did the country not enjoy a set of advantages which had propelled it to become the Number One economic power in any case: a large and protected home market, economies of scale, high levels of industrial investment, modern infrastructure, a good educational system? Because of those advantages, because of the relative efficiency of organization in the United States as compared with other societies, the nation already occupied a position in world economic affairs by 1925 and 1935 that was much larger than its "natural size." What the war did was simply to boost that enhanced position still further, as least for a short while.

The story of America's position in world affairs in the half-century after 1945 may therefore have witnessed two related yet separate processes of relative decline. The first came about because of the erosion of the "effect of the war" factor, that is, as other societies and economies were rebuilt in the late 1940s and 1950s, the American share naturally fell. The second and altogether more insidious factor—and a development which would be denied by many in this country—is that since the 1960s or so the United States has begun to lose those advantages of the relative efficiency of organization that had placed it, economically at least, in the clear Number One position by 1925. Its domestic market was increasingly penetrated by more efficient foreign rivals; its savings ratios, and its levels of investment in commercial research and development, were low; its infrastructure was not being renewed; its youth, not very well educated now compared with those in many advanced societies elsewhere, was drifting away from science, technology, and engineering; consumption had been driven by years of easy credit; rather than by real rises in productivity and income; the trade imbalances had turned the country into the world's greatest debtor, weakened the dollar, and hurt its international credit. Far from the United States being admired and studied for achieving an "unnatural" size in the world, it was Japan that had become the center of attention, at least by the 1980s. How, it was asked, could a country that was only the size of California possess a Gross National Product close to two-thirds that of the entire American economy? What could one learn from Japan's relative efficiency of organization? As I mentioned in my original quotation, these worries are compensated for—at least in some people's minds—by the present military power of the United States and by the globalization of the English language and parts of American culture; but whether they will be enough to arrest any further erosion, back to a more "natural" size of 16 to 18 percent of world power and influence, remains to be seen. The future is open, not closed.

I have offered you some ruminations on the concept of "natural size" in Great Powers (and, for that matter, in small Powers, automobile companies, and soccer associations). It is not, of course, a profound revelation. It is, rather, a figure of speech, or a way of thinking about this complex issue of why certain societies rise and fall, relative to others, in world affairs. That topic *is* certainly of importance, especially to an American public entering the final decade of what some have called the American century. But because it is a complex topic, and a very emotional one, the language and metaphors and analogies that are being deployed may cause as much confusion as they do enlightenment. No one that I know likes the word "decline," even if one modifies it with the adjective *"relative* decline." Whether audiences and readers will prefer the concept of "natural size," and see in that a more detached way of describing the shifting position that countries occupy in world affairs, I cannot say.

NOTE

1. Paul Kennedy, *The Rise and Fall of The Great Powers* (New York: Random House, 1987), pp. 533–534.

Soft Power

Joseph S. Nye, Jr.

The Cold War is over and Americans are trying to understand their place in a world without a defining Soviet threat. Polls report that nearly half the public believes the country is in decline, and that those who believe in decline tend to favor protectionism and to counsel withdrawal from what they consider "overextended international commitments."

In a world of growing interdependence, such advice is counterproductive and could bring on the decline it is supposed to avert; for if the most powerful country fails to lead, the consequences for international stability could be disastrous. Throughout history, anxiety about decline and shifting balances of power has been accompanied by tension and miscalculation. Now that Soviet power is declining and Japanese power rising, misleading theories of American decline and inappropriate analogies between the United States and Great Britain in the late nineteenth century have diverted our attention away from the real issue—how power is changing in world politics.

The United States is certainly less powerful at the end of the twentieth century than it was in 1945. Even conservative estimates show that the U.S. share of global product has declined from more than a third of the total after World War II to a little more than a fifth in the 1980s. That change, however, reflects the artificial effect of World War II: Unlike the other great powers, the United States was *strengthened* by the war. But that artificial preponderance was bound to erode as other countries regained their economic health. The important fact is that the U.S. economy's share of the global product has been relatively constant for the past decade and a half. The Council on Competitiveness finds that the U.S. share of world product has averaged 23 per cent each year since the mid-1970s. The CIA, using numbers that reflect the purchasing power of different currencies, reports that the American share of world product increased slightly from 25 per cent in 1975 to 26 percent in 1988.

These studies suggest that the effect of World War II lasted about a quarter century and that most of the decline worked its way through the system by the mid-1970s. In fact, the big adjustment of American commitments occurred with then President Richard Nixon's withdrawal from Vietnam and the end of the convertibility of the dollar into gold.

The dictionary tells us that power means an ability to do things and control others, to get others to do what they otherwise would not. Because the ability to control others is often associated with the possession of certain resources, politicians and diplomats commonly define power as the possession of population, territory, natural resources, economic size, military forces, and political stability. For example, in the agrarian economies of eighteenth-century Europe, population was a critical power resource since it provided a base for taxes and recruitment of infantry.

Traditionally the test of a great power was its strength in war. Today, however, the definition of power is losing its emphasis on military force and conquest that marked earlier eras. The factors of technology, education, and economic growth are becoming more significant in international power, while geography, population, and raw materials are becoming somewhat less important. . . .

What can we say about changes in the distribution of power resources in the coming decades? Political leaders often use the term "multipolarity" to imply the return to a balance among a number of states with roughly equal power resources analogous to that of the nineteenth century. But this is not likely to be the situation at the turn of the century, for in terms of power resources, all the potential challengers except the United States are deficient in some respect. The Soviet Union lags economically, China remains a less-developed country, Europe lacks political unity, and Japan is deficient both in military power and in global ideological appeal. If economic reforms reverse Soviet decline, if Japan develops a full-fledged nuclear and conventional military capability, or if Europe becomes dramatically more unified, there may be a return to classical multipolarity in the twenty-first century. But barring such changes, the United States is likely to retain a broader range of power resources—military, economic, scientific, cultural, and ideological—than other countries, and the Soviet Union may lose its superpower status.

The Great Power Shift

The coming century may see continued American preeminence, but the sources of power in world politics are likely to undergo major changes that will create new difficulties for all countries in achieving their goals. Proof of power lies not in resources but in the ability to change the behavior of states. Thus, the critical question for the United States is not whether it will start the next century as the superpower with the largest supply of resources, but to what extent it will be able to control the political environment and get other countries to do what it wants. Some trends in world politics suggest that it will be more difficult in the future for any great power to control the political environment. The problem for the United States will be less the rising challenge of another major power than a general diffusion of power. Whereas nineteenth-century Britain faced new challengers, the twenty-first century United States will face new challenges.

As world politics becomes more complex, the power of all major states to gain their objectives will be diminished. To understand what is happening to the United States today, the distinction between power over other countries and power over outcomes must be clear. Although the United States still has leverage over particular countries, it has far less leverage over the system as a whole. It is less well-placed to attain its ends unilaterally, but it is not alone in this situation. All major states will have to confront the changing nature of power in world politics. . . .

Traditionalist accounts of world politics often speak of an international system that results from the balancing strategies of states. Although bipolarity and multipolarity are useful terms, today different spheres of world politics have different distributions of power—that is, different power structures. Military power, particularly nuclear, remains largely bipolar in its distribution. But in trade, where the European Community acts as a unit, power is multipolar. Ocean resources, money, space, shipping, and airlines each have somewhat different distributions of power. The power of states varies as well, as does the significance of nonstate actors in different spheres. For example, the politics of international debt cannot be understood without considering the power of private banks.

If military power could be transferred freely into the realms of economics and the environment, the different structures would not matter; and the overall hierarchy determined by military strength would accurately predict outcomes in world politics. But military power is more costly and less transferable today than in earlier times. Thus, the hierarchies that characterize different issues are more diverse. The games of world politics encompass different players at different tables with different piles of chips. They can transfer winnings among tables, but often only at a considerable discount. The military game and the overall structure of the balance of power dominate when the survival of states is clearly at stake, but in much of modern world politics, physical survival is not the most pressing issue.

. . . At least five trends have contributed to this diffusion of power: economic interdependence, transnational actors, nationalism in weak states, the spread of technology, and changing political issues. . . .

The Changing Face of Power

These trends suggest a second, more attractive way of exercising power than traditional means. A state may achieve the outcomes it prefers in world politics because other states want to follow it or have agreed to a situation that produces such effects. In this sense, it is just as important to set the agenda and structure the situations in world politics as to get others to change in particular cases.

This second aspect of power—which occurs when one country gets other countries to *want* what it wants—might be called co-optive or soft power in contrast with the hard or command power of *ordering* others to do what it wants.

Parents of teenagers have long known that if they have shaped their child's beliefs and preferences, their power will be greater and more enduring than if they rely only on active control. Similarly, political leaders and philosophizers have long understood the power of attractive ideas or the ability to set the political agenda and determine the framework of debate in a way that shapes others' preferences. The ability to affect what other countries want tends to be associated with intangible power resources such as culture, ideology, and institutions.

Soft co-optive power is just as important as hard command power. If a state can make its power seem legitimate in the eyes of others, it will encounter less resistance to its wishes. If its culture and ideology are attractive, others will more willingly follow. If it can establish international norms consistent with its society, it is less likely to have to change. If it can support institutions that make other states wish to channel or limit their activities in ways the dominant state prefers, it may be spared the costly exercise of coercive or hard power.

In general, power is becoming less transferable, less coercive, and less tangible. Modern trends and changes in political issues are having significant effects on the nature of power and the resources that produce it. Co-optive power—getting others to want what you want—and soft power resources—cultural attraction, ideology, and international institutions—are not new. In the early postwar period, the Soviet Union profited greatly from such soft resources as communist ideology, the myth of inevitability, and transnational communist institutions. Various trends today are making co-optive behavior and soft power resources relatively more important.

Given the changes in world politics, the use of power is becoming less coercive, at least among the major states. The current instruments of power range from diplomatic notes through economic threats to military coercion.

In earlier periods, the costs of such coercion were relatively low. Force was acceptable and economies were less interdependent. Early in this century, the United States sent marines and customs agents to collect debts in some Caribbean countries; but under current conditions, the direct use of American troops against small countries like Nicaragua carries greater costs.

Manipulation of interdependence under current conditions is also more costly. Economic interdependence usually carries benefits in both directions; and threats to disrupt a relationship, if carried out, can be very expensive. For example, Japan might want the United States to reduce its budget deficit, but threatening to refuse to buy American Treasury bonds would be likely to disrupt financial markets and to produce enormous costs for Japan as well as for the United States. Because the use of force has become more costly, less threatening forms of power have grown increasingly attractive.

Co-optive power is the ability of a country to structure a situation so that other countries develop preferences or define their interests in ways consistent with its own. This power tends to arise from such resources as cultural and ideological attraction as well as rules and institutions of international regimes. The United States has more co-optive power than other countries. Institutions governing the international economy, such as the International Monetary Fund and the General Agreement on Tariffs and Trade, tend to embody liberal, free-market principles that coincide in large measure with American society and ideology.

Multinational corporations are another source of co-optive power. British author Susan Strange argued in her 1988 book *States and Markets* that U.S. power in the world economy has increased as a result of transnational production:

> Washington may have lost some of its authority over the U.S.-based transnationals, but their managers still carry U.S. passports, can be sub-poenaed in U.S. courts, and in war or national emergency would obey Washington first. Meanwhile, the U.S. government has gained new authority over a great many foreign corporations inside the United States. All of them are acutely aware that the U.S. market is the biggest prize.

This power arises in part from the fact that 34 per cent of the largest multinational corporations are headquartered in the United States (compared to 18 per cent in Japan) and in part from the importance of the American market in any global corporate strategy.

American culture is another relatively inexpensive and useful soft power resource. Obviously, certain aspects of American culture are unattractive to other people, and there is always danger of bias in evaluating cultural sources of power. But American popular culture, embodied in products and communications, has widespread appeal. Young Japanese who have never been to the United States wear sports jackets with the names of American colleges. Nicaraguan television broadcast American shows even while the government fought American-backed guerrillas. Similarly, Soviet teenagers wear blue jeans and seek American recordings, and Chinese students used a symbol modeled on the Statue of Liberty during the 1989 uprisings. Despite the Chinese government's protests against U.S. interference, Chinese citizens were as interested as ever in American democracy and culture.

Of course, there is an element of triviality and fad in popular behavior, but it is also true that a country that stands astride popular channels of communication has more opportunities to get its messages across and to affect the preferences of others. According to past studies by the United Nations Educational, Scientific, and Cultural Organization, the United States has been exporting about seven times as many television shows as the next largest exporter (Britain) and has had the only global network for film distribution. Although American films account for only 6–7 per cent of all films made, they occupy about 50 per cent of world screentime. In 1981, the United States was responsible for 80 per cent of worldwide transmission and processing of data. The American language has become the *lingua franca* of the global economy.

Although Japanese consumer products and cuisine have recently become more fashionable, they seem less associated with an implicit appeal to a broader set of values than American domination of popular communication. The success of Japan's manufacturing sector provides it with an important source of soft power, but Japan is somewhat limited by the inward orientation of its culture. While Japan has been extraordinarily successful in accepting foreign technology, it has been far more reluctant to accept foreigners. Japan's relations with China, for example, have been hampered by cultural insensitivities. Many Japanese are concerned about their lack of "internationalization" and their failure to project a broader message.

While Americans can also be parochial and inward-oriented, the openness of the American culture to various ethnicities and the American values of democracy and human rights exert international influence. West European countries also derive soft power from their democratic institutions, but America's relative openness to immigrants compared to Japan and Europe is an additional source of strength. As European scholar Ralf Dahrendorf has observed, it is "relevant that millions of people all over the world would wish to live in the United States and that indeed people are prepared to risk their lives in order to get there." Maintaining this appeal is important.

In June 1989, after President George Bush criticized the Chinese government for killing student protesters in China, ordinary Chinese seemed more supportive of the United States than ever before. Subsequently, by sending a delegation of too high a level to Beijing to seek reconciliation, Bush squandered some of those soft-power resources. When ideals are an important source of power, the classic distinction between *realpolitik* and liberalism becomes blurred. The realist who focuses only on the balance of hard power will miss the power of transnational ideas. . . .

Americans are rightly concerned about the future shape of a post–Cold War world, but it is a mistake to portray the problem as American decline rather than diffusion of power. Even so, concern about decline might be good for the United States if it cut through complacency and prodded Americans to deal with some of their serious domestic problems. However, pollsters find that excessive anxiety about decline turns American opinion toward nationalistic and protectionist policies that could constrain the U.S. ability to cope with issues created by growing international interdependence. There is no virtue in either overstatement or understatement of American strength. The former leads to failure to adapt, the latter to inappropriate responses such as treating Japan as the new enemy in place of the Soviet Union.

As the world's wealthiest country, the United States should be able to pay for both its international commitments and its domestic investments. America is rich but through its political process acts poor. In real terms, GNP is more than twice what it was in 1960, but Americans today spend much less of their GNP on international leadership. The prevailing view is "we can't afford it," despite the fact that U.S. taxes represent a smaller percentage of gross domestic product than those of other advanced industrial countries. This suggests a problem of domestic political leadership rather than long-term economic decline.

As has happened many times before, the mix of resources that shapes international power is changing. But that does not mean that the world must expect the cycle of hegemonic conflict with its attendant world wars to repeat itself. The United States retains more traditional hard power resources than any other country. It also has the soft ideological and institutional resources to preserve its lead in the new domains of transnational interdependence. In this sense, the situation is quite different from that of Britain at the century's beginning. Loose historical analogies and falsely deterministic political theories are worse than merely academic; they may distract Americans from the true issues confronting them. The problem for U.S. power after the Cold War will be less the new challengers for hegemony than the new challenges of transnational interdependence.

Chapter 5

Foreign Policy and the National Interest

The term *national interest* has a compelling ring. It conveys a sense of urgency, importance, threat, and concreteness. Troops are stationed abroad and wars are fought in its name, covert operations are justified because of it, foreign aid is given to some and denied to others to further its realization, and weapons systems are purchased because the national interest demands it. In fact, it would be a rare foreign-policy initiative that is not justified by reference to a state's national interest. Along with the concept of power, it is one of the central building blocks analysts use to understand and explain the behavior of states in world politics. Unfortunately, just as with the concept of power, the concept of the national interest is not easily defined. At the core of the debate over its definition is the question of whether the national interest should be treated as an objective, measurable asset or a normative political symbol.

National Interest as a Guide to Action

For the national interest to be used as a guide for judging the merits of alternative policy proposals there must be an agreed-on content to its meaning. In studying the concept of the national interest from this perspective, analysts have stressed two points. First, a foreign-policy goal in the national interest should advance truly national goals rather than the interests of specific groups or individuals such as farmers, the government bureaucracy, a political party, the wealthy, or a specific ethnic group. Those critical of a country's foreign policy often argue that special interests rather than national goals are at stake. One particularly influential line of thought, developed to explain U.S. foreign policy but potentially applicable everywhere, argues that the decision-making process has been captured by the military-industrial complex. That is, it is committed to an overly hawkish and conflictual view of international politics, a view that promises to bring individual and collective benefits to its members (the professional military, the arms industry, and politicians) at the expense of the well-being of the rest of society.

Second, it is all but inevitable that the number of possible foreign-policy goals that advance the national interest will exceed the power resources of the state. Some mechanism must be developed for choosing among and making these goals. However, cost alone is held to be an inappropriate standard because although a foreign policy may be very costly, the threat facing the state may be even greater. In such cases the answer is not to avoid undertaking an expensive line of action but to limit the number of objectives a state is pursuing, thereby keeping resources and goals in balance. It is the nature of the threat that must be placed at the center of the ranking system. Foreign policies designed to counter grave and immediate threats to the survival of the state or its political and economic order are more important than those designed to promote its international prestige, dominate a region, or support its allies. In turn, efforts to realize these goals deserve priority over those designed to bring into existence global peace and harmony or a new world order.

Several important but doubtful value assertions need to be brought into the open. First, there is the belief that a correct foreign-policy response exists for every foreign-policy problem, and the challenge is to correctly categorize the problem (and one's power). Then, the solution should be clear and can be arrived at through a deductive decision-making logic in which the costs and benefits of competing courses of action are compared. Second, one state's pursuit of its national interest is likely to place it in conflict with other states. Operating under conditions that border on anarchy, states are placed in a competitive position in the pursuit of power, prestige, and wealth. Self-help and self-interest are the keys to survival under these circumstances. Third, global and national goals constitute two separate and distinct categories of values, which should not be confused. Policymakers who pursue global goals do so at the expense of the national interest, placing them in jeopardy.

Each one of these value assertions can be challenged, and the more one finds them to be troubling or inaccurate the less useful the concept of national interest is likely to be as a guide to policy-making. Correctly categorizing a problem is easier said than done (Was Vietnam in the U.S. national interest? Should the Soviet Union have seen Afghanistan as so important?). Even if there is agreement that solving a problem is in the country's national interest, legitimate disagreements about courses of action are likely to remain (Should Israel trade land for peace? Does Pakistan, a relatively small country between the giant states of India and China, need nuclear weapons?). It is easy to overestimate the amount of conflict in world politics. States do cooperate. Studies have shown that the overwhelming majority of contacts between states are peaceful and, one would assume, in every national interest. Finally, it is not clear to many why global peace, stability, prosperity, and a clean environment are not in every national interest. Their absence would appear to hold the potential for creating severe problems. Some would take the argument even further—that solving these issues are beyond one state's grasp and requires states to cooperate in the name of the global (and national) interest.

National Interest as a Political Symbol

There is a second dimension of the national interest that must be kept in mind at all times. The national interest also serves as a powerful symbol that can be used to sway the course of a policy debate. Viewed in this way, statements calling for policymakers to end apartheid, keep foreign investment out of the United States, balance the budget, or conduct a war on drugs should not be read as objective guides to action. Rather, they are politically oriented calls for protecting values seen as threatened or neglected. Thus, observers have a vantage point from which to chart the policy debate and gauge the influence of competing groups, be they among the public at large or within the policy-making elite. Groups and individuals with differing views of what a country should stand for, what threats face it, or how to go about meeting national security threats will define national interest differently. Thus, it is not uncommon to find the Defense Department opposing high-technology sales to Communist countries for fear of improving their military capability while the Commerce Department has pushed for these very sales, citing competition from foreign firms and balance-of-payments considerations.

As John Lovell notes, when used as a political symbol the concept of national interest can be pitched at different levels of generality. It is important to recognize at which level it is being used because the policy concern varies from level to level. That is, although two people may both be invoking the national interest in presenting their arguments, they may be concerned with two very different policy decisions. At the most concrete level, these arguments deal with strategies, goals, and operational assumptions (The United States should act through the United Nations in opposing Iraq's invasion of Kuwait). At the most abstract level, efforts to manipulate national interest are couched in terms of national identity and purpose (The United States should take the lead in creating a new world order). Between these two extremes we can find competing references focusing on priorities, goals, and broad policy assumptions (Stability in the Persian Gulf is vital to U.S. national security). The American experience suggests that there is a certain logic in how these levels of generality are ordered. Policy debates tend to begin over the particulars of a problem and end at the highest level of generality. Moreover, it is the phrases and catchwords at this level that appear to have the most impact on how the policy is decided.

The National Interest:
From Where Does It Come?

Differences in how to approach the concept of national interest (as a guide to action or a political symbol) are in large part due to a disagreement over where to look for its meaning. Those who see it as a guide to action tend to find its meaning in the power resources of the state and the structure or condition of the international system. From this perspective, as power resources change or the nature of the international system changes, so too should a state's definition of its national interest. For example, as the dominant power after World War II, it was in the U.S. national interest to lead in the global struggle against communism— even to the point of protecting other states when they did little to protect themselves and allowing them to discriminate against American products—because historically the most powerful or hegemonic state benefits most from the way the international system is set up and has the most to lose from its passing. This same line of reasoning leads to the conclusion that if, as some have argued, American power has declined and the cold war has ended, then the United States must redefine its national interest. No longer are global commitments and sacrifice in order. Instead, the United States must behave like a more "normal" state with a more limited definition of its national interest.

Those who view the concept of national interest primarily as a political symbol see its sources in many different areas. Which influence will be the defining one is determined by the dynamics of the political process. Two of the most frequently cited influences are ideology and historical experience. As is shown by the Western debate over Soviet foreign-policy goals, these influences often pull in opposite directions. Soviet national interest as defined by Marxist-Leninist ideology is seen as expansive in nature. Nothing short of the global triumph of communism over capitalism is called for. An emphasis on historical influences leads one to the conclusion that the national interest of the Soviet Union is far more restricted in nature and not much different from that of tsarist Russia: defendable borders, warm-water ports, economic development, and great-power status. Soviet foreign-policy decisions do not necessarily establish which interpretation is correct. Was the Soviet invasion of Afghanistan a self-contained and limited effort to secure a buffer zone around the Soviet border or the first step toward establishing Soviet influence over the entire Persian Gulf, in accordance with an ideologically driven desire for world domination? Is the Soviet interest in arms control a sign that it has limited foreign-policy goals and is willing to work with other states, or is it merely a strategic retreat designed to lull the West into a sense of complacency to ensure the success of some future aggressive act?

Pursuing the National Interest: Foreign Policy

Any discussion of the national interest inevitably leads to an examination of what is meant by foreign policy. For the national interest to be realized, state action of some sort is required, and *foreign policy* is the term given to that course of action. Because a state's foreign policy is supposed to promote the national interest, there is a temptation to see it in terms of a series of rational steps: A problem is identified, solutions are weighed, the solution best suited to solving the problem is selected, and then it is implemented by diplomats and military personnel just as an engineer would work from a blueprint. More often then not, reality is quite different. There is very little that is automatic or straightforward about the formulation or conduct of a state's foreign policy.

One major problem is trying to identify what goals or values a state's foreign policy should promote and protect. Another problem involves a tendency to view all foreign-policy problems as alike, when in fact they can be of quite different origins and thus present policymakers with very different challenges. For example, some foreign-policy problems are inherited from previous presidents and prime ministers, whereas others are being faced for the first time. In the former case, a policymaker's freedom in selecting a foreign policy will probably be restricted by the repercussions of past successes and failures. In the latter case, a policymaker will have far more latitude in selecting an option but perhaps face greater uncertainty over what to do since the problem has not been encountered before.

Analyzing the selected foreign-policy option is made difficult by the fact that a state's foreign policy proceeds at a number of different levels. First, there is a distinction between foreign policy at the level of grand strategy and foreign policy at the level of tactics. For much of the cold war, America's grand strategy was captured in the word *containment*. It provided the overall framework within which the United States sought to protect its national security interests. Covert action, alliances, treaties, embargoes, and arms sales were tactical foreign policies designed to make containment work. One of the major challenges facing policymakers is to ensure that their tactical foreign-policy choices are consistent with their strategic frameworks. If not, they will be left in the unenviable position of winning the war and losing the peace. The lack of fit between tactics and strategy was a major criticism of many U.S. covert actions during the cold war. Concerns for individual career enhancement, bureaucratic imperialism, and "keeping up with the Russians" often seemed to be the primary rationales for many efforts to entrap foreign agents, plant stories in local papers, and secretly bankroll local government officials.

The task of meshing strategies and tactics is likely to become particularly challenging with the passing of the cold war. No longer can the strategic foreign-policy framework be taken as a given, with attention focused almost exclusively on the selection of tactics. Both strategy and tactics will be intensely debated as the outlines of the post–cold war international system take shape. Virtually all observers agree that a very real danger in such times is for tactics to drive strategy. That is, it may prove easier to gain agreement on what should be done in a certain situation (i.e. aiding the Soviet Union, fighting Iraq, and sending peacekeepers to Cambodia) than to gain agreement on why it should be done. To borrow a phrase used in explaining the U.S. involvement in Vietnam, there is the danger of descending down "a slippery slope," ultimately finding themselves in a situation that policymakers never expected to be in and with very little way out.

In looking at how foreign policy is being implemented, we must also differentiate between declaratory and action foreign policy. The distinction is between what is actually done and what is said. For example, the United States has often championed the cause of human rights yet done little in the face of human rights violations; during the cold war the Soviet Union often proclaimed its respect for national sovereignty yet did not hesitate to use local Communist parties to try and overthrow pro-U.S. governments; and Japanese leaders have repeatedly expressed concern over the U.S.-Japanese trade imbalance, yet trade barriers continue.

There are several reasons for this gap in policy. One is that foreign-policy statements are often directed at a different audience than are actions. Whereas actions are directed at other states, statements are frequently made for domestic consumption. A second reason is that it is much easier to stake out verbally a position on an issue or to change that position than it is to implement a diplomatic, military, or economic policy consistent with those statements. For example, incoming administrations routinely changed the name given to U.S. deterrence strategy and the target mix against which U.S. missiles would be directed. Yet a close examination of the actual sites being targeted in the Soviet Union revealed that few actual changes had been made.

Understandable though it may be, the persistence of a gap between declaratory and action foreign policy is not without its dangers. Words do matter. A state that repeatedly says one thing and does another will be looked on with suspicion by other states and will not be regarded as a valuable ally. Words also raise expectations at home. An inability to meet these expectations may cripple a government politically or cause it to undertake an imprudent course of action in the hope of freeing itself from the prison of its own words.

One additional factor promises to complicate both the conduct and analysis of foreign policy in the future. Traditionally foreign policy has been studied apart from domestic policy. Obviously, one reason for doing so is the location of the problems. Foreign-policy problems involve conditions outside of a country, whereas domestic ones occur inside its borders. A more important reason for distinguishing between them has been the belief that the policy-making process operated differently in the two areas. Domestic policy has been seen as driven by the give and take of interest-group lobbying, partisan politics, and the force of public opinion. However, for foreign policy to be effective it has to be immune from these influences. The proper way to make foreign policy has been to concentrate power in a single source—president, prime minister, secretary of state, and so on—and allow experts to work in secret and use their best judgment to address problems that threaten the state's national interest in ways that domestic problems could not.

As world politics enters the twenty-first century, the distinction between foreign and domestic policy is disappearing rapidly. Such pressing policy issues as combating drug use, protecting the environment, improving educational systems, reducing budget deficits, selling military technology, or closing military bases and downsizing military establishments are no longer easily characterized as foreign or domestic problems. Similarly, the process by which foreign policy is made looks increasingly like that which has produced domestic policies. The net effect of these changes is unclear and likely to be debated for some time. On the one hand, there are those who believe that a successful foreign policy requires a strong executive to avoid incoherence and inconsistency. On the other hand, there are those who see the concentration of power in the executive as dangerous and an invitation to abuse. They welcome the increased role of legislatures and interest groups in the conduct of foreign policy and see it as one way of expanding the political agenda so that broader and nontraditional notions of national security might come to guide policy.

The Readings

The decline in power of the Soviet Union and the increased prominence of economic issues have focused attention as never before on Japan. The readings in this section are designed to offer insight into competing views of the Japanese national interest. Shiro Saito's "Japan at the Summit," provides an overview of past Japanese foreign policy themes in relation to the West and to other Asian states. Masaru Tamamoto's "Japan's Search for a World Role," examines the changing relationship between the United States and Japan. He argues that Japan has begun to normalize its foreign policy and that this is a healthy development. Dennis Yasutomo, in "Why Aid? Japan as an 'Aid Great Power,'" offers a more detailed analysis of this important issue.

Bibliography

CLINTON, W. DAVID. "The National Interest: Normative Foundations." *The Review of Politics* 48 (1986).

HOLTSI, OLE, and JAMES ROSENAU. *American Leadership in World Affairs*. Boston: Allen & Unwin, 1984.

JOHNASEN, ROBERT. *The National Interest and the Global Interest*. Princeton, NJ: Princeton University Press, 1980.

KRASNER, STEPHEN. *Defending the National Interest*. Princeton, NJ: Princeton University Press, 1978.

LOVELL, JOHN. "The Idiom of National Security." *Journal of Political and Military Sociology* 11, (1983).

MACRIDIS, ROY (ed.). *Foreign Policy in World Politics*, 7th ed. New York: Prentice Hall, 1989.

MILLS, C. WRIGHT. *The Power Elite*. New York: Oxford University Press, 1956.

MORGENTHAU, HANS. *In Defense of the National Interest*. New York: Knopf, 1951.

SONDERMANN, FRED. "The Theory of the National Interest." *Orbis* 21 (1977).

WOLFERS, ARNOLD. *Discord and Collaboration*. Baltimore: Johns Hopkins University Press, 1962.

Japan at the Summit

Its Role in the Western Alliance and in Asian Pacific Co-operation

Shiro Saito

In December 1987 the new Japanese Prime Minister, Takeshita Noboru, made his first overseas visit, to attend a meeting with the leaders of the Association of South-East Asian Nations (ASEAN) in Manila; the following month he visited the United States to meet President Ronald Reagan. By the time he attended the Toronto summit in June 1988, he had also visited South Korea and Western Europe (twice within a month). These visits represented, both symbolically and practically, the two areas traditionally vital to Japan's national interest and international position: Asia and the West. In the Japanese perception, the two terms imply more than a geographical dimension, for they have existed as the basic framework of the historical pattern of the nation's foreign policy throughout the pre-war and post-war periods.

The history of modern Japan's external relations has proved to be a mixture of aloofness from and intervention in the continent of Asia, and both tendencies have coincided with its alignment with the Western powers. A seclusionist Tokugawa was forced by the Western powers to open the nation to the outside world, not by Asians, and Asian wars led Japan to alliances with the West. The Anglo-Japanese alliance (1902), which first truly placed Japan in the international system against the background of the power balance in the Asian theatre, was replaced by the Four-Power Treaty (1921) and the Nine-Power Treaty (1922) during the great-power rivalry over China. The signing of the Anti-Comintern Pact with Germany (1936) marked the

From *Japan at the Summit* (New York: Routledge, 1990).

beginning of Japan's relations with the Axis powers, and the Tripartite Pact between Germany, Italy, and Japan followed (1940). After the war Japan entered into the alliance with the United States.

Alongside these alliances with the West, Japan's political position in Asia was either interventionist or isolationist. There was no third position based upon a harmonious equal footing. If one compares Japan's Asian involvement before and after World War II, one can see a complete about-face in its conduct, from arrogance to low posture. Partly reinforced by fears of stirring up wartime memories in Asia, and partly as a result of being under the protection of the United States, Japan's self-image as an Asian nation, as well as a member of the Western world, has dictated low-profile policies in every sphere. Nevertheless, given the sharp contrast between political circumspection on the one hand and economic aggressiveness on the other, in both Asia and the West, Japan has been caught in an awkward position. How to overcome this ambiguity will be the most crucial issue for the future of Japan's overall Asia–West relations.

The objectives of this study are, therefore, to discover the relationship and interaction between Japan's policies across Asia and the West in the post-war world, and to look at the possibilities for a coherent strategy for balancing its interests in these broad areas. For Japan will not be able to integrate itself into the international community until it can articulate policy programmes that attempt to unite the various systems of the Asian and Western nations. Perhaps the term 'macro-diplomacy' would serve in this context—a coinage to denote the grasping together of the main forces at work in the various interrelated sectors of the nation's foreign policy. The final target of Japan's macro-diplomacy is twofold: first, to reconcile different overarching geopolitical interests in East Asia and the West; and, second, to assume the political role usually incumbent upon an economic power.

Inevitably, with such a vast theme, the issues have to be dealt with selectively; it is impossible to cover all aspects of Japan–Asia and Japan–West relations. This book therefore focuses on two key areas of the interrelationship: dialogue with Japan's Asian partners through the vehicle of the annual ministerial meetings of ASEAN, and Japan's involvement in Western affairs through its participation in the seven-power economic and political summits. A further word on the framework of the study is needed.

The conventional analysis of Asia divides the continent into regions, such as East Asia, with its sub-regions of North-east and South-east on the periphery of continental China, and South Asia, extending to the Indian subcontinent. A current concept of Asia is an open-ended one, identifying sea-oriented countries under the heading the 'Asian Pacific' or 'Pacific Asian' region. In these terms the Soviet Union cannot be ignored. The problem here is that the conventional definitions obscure the evolving realities in regional affairs on the one hand, and also lead to a certain duplication of old constituencies on the other. Moreover, the perceptual focus of the pivotal region has been shifting over the years and differs from country to country.

Thus, in the post-war period, Japan's primary concern with Asia has been increasingly the rimland of the western Pacific, whereas pre-war Japan often saw Asia as centred on heartland China. One of the main emphases of this study is to explore Japan's relations with the Western Pacific region, including Australia and New Zealand, which may be assumed to be a viable entity linked by seas rather than by land.

As regards 'the West', there is no difficulty about defining it in terms of international politics and the world economy centred on East–West relations. The Western alliance, including Japan, can be clearly identified as a system by its political, economic, and security ties, and it is in this context that Japan is a member of the Western world. Yet, although Japan's relations with the West have been more stable in the post-war period than they were in the pre-war one, there is not total symmetry in the trilateral relationship between North America, Western Europe, and Japan. From the Japanese perspective, the ties with the United States are predominant, especially in terms of the security relationship. Similarly, there is a certain divergence between the policies of the United States and those of the West European countries towards Japan and Asia. The framework of Japan–West relations should, therefore, be set forth in a plural context, and this study endeavours to draw out in particular how the Euro-Japanese relationship fits into the broader Japan–West–East Asia relationship.

The question of Japan's position, respectively, in Asia and the West, as well as its place between the two, is still a constant preoccupation in domestic and foreign-policy circles. Ever since the appearance of an influential essay 'Quit Asia, enter Europe' in the Meiji era, a basic cleavage within national opinion has remained, between the 'Asianists' and those whose priority is the West. To say that Japan's position in Asia and in relation to the Western industrial world resembles that of Britain towards continental Europe and the United States has become axiomatic: both are part of each, but not fully on either side. Japan's place, however, is more detached than Britain's, because Japan's modernization process differed from that of any other country, whereas Britain was part of the mainstream of the world's industrialization from the beginning. 'The very facts of Japanese development have set this nation apart,' an American scholar has observed, with the result that 'it is, but not fully, in Asia. Its problems, as well as its progress, align it naturally with the advanced West, and particularly with the United States, yet the sense of mutual identification on both sides is significantly weaker than one might presume.'

Apart from such considerations, Japan's cultural proclivities for separateness have worked against its becoming a full member of the international community. As a British writer put it: 'The country of the rising sun does not see itself as one nation-state among a lot of others. They are still acting as part of a separate civilization consciously measuring themselves against the Western world.' Another comment made from a different angle: 'The Japanese still view international as well as interpersonal relations in hierarchical terms, and a relationship of equality is difficult for the Japanese.' The former Chancellor of West Germany, Helmut Schmidt, expressed his views in the following strong terms:

> The source of possible future tensions lies in the fact that Japan does not enjoy close relations with her far East and Southeast Asian regions. Relations with China, with all the ASEAN countries and with Korea and Taiwan are normal, but there is no relationship comparable to the conference of the states within the European Community or between the European states on the one hand and the North American states on the other. . . . The Japanese do not seem to be seeking closer friendship with other nations. This insularity may be part of the historic heritage of the long Tokugawa self-isolation; but it has been pursued also in this century.

Some Japanese themselves also admit to 'self-isolation' and argue that 'the dichotomy between the West and Asia continued to be a problem, and Japan remained a loner, not really part of any international system'. But such a dichotomy does not rule out a positive diplomatic stance aimed at achieving a balance between policies designed for the Asian region and those geared to the Western world. Parallel to the cleavage between the Asianists and the Westernizers, there has been a school of thought persistently advocating an independent position which is capable of initiating compatible policies in both directions. Thus, in an article written in 1964, the Japanese foreign Minister, Ohira Masayoshi, declared:

> Japan is a sea-faring nation as a result of her geographical position northeast of the Asiatic continent. So, she is inseparably bound in friendship to our neighbour nations of the continent and to the countries of Southeast Asia. At the same time, we maintain friendly relations with Britain and other European countries as well as with the United States of America. . . . It can be said that for most countries of Asia, the facts of Japan's existence as a free democracy, and her position in the rank of the world's advanced industrial nations, encourage them to give her their trust and reliance and so increase their sense of security. We are convinced that only by a firm adherence to the free world and by a vigorous pursuance of her present policy in Asia can Japan contribute to the stabilization of the Asian region and promote the cause of true world peace.

As is so well expressed in this statement, the very fact of Japan's ambivalent position makes it imperative that it should find a way of using its economic power in the cause of regional prosperity and stability. As will be shown in subsequent chapters, one of the underlying motivations of Japanese foreign policy has been a 'twin-track' diplomacy: one that combines the two principles of the 'ambivalent state', which is both a nation in Asia and a member of the Western world.

At the end of the occupation, Japan turned away from the continent of Asia and away from China, which had been one of its most important pre-war markets, and looked towards the United States and South-east Asia for its trading partners. This was a natural consequence of the changed Asian situation, in which the United States—in the wake of the victory of communism in China and the outbreak of the Korean war—needed Japan's help in stabilizing the Western Pacific region through increasing trade and commerce. In return, Japan was allowed to join, as a donor nation, the Colombo Plan (1950–1), set up by British Commonwealth countries and joined by the United States in South and South-east Asia. There were at this time strong arguments between the Japanese government (Prime Minister Yoshida Shigeru) and Washington about whether the Japanese and South-east Asian economies were complementary in terms of trade and investment, thus making possible long-range economic integration in the region. Launching the bold idea of a kind of 'Marshall Plan for Asia', the Japanese government invited a funding contribution from Washington, and suggested that the Colombo Plan become the organizational focus for a regional development. Although nothing came of this idea at the time, subsequent developments in the mid-1960s led to the positive pursuit of Japan's economic diplomacy.

These early experiences in successful economic diplomacy determined the emphasis in Japanese external relations on South-east Asia—in order to demonstrate Japan's importance as a nation in Asia. Just about all post-war Japanese Prime Ministers (from Yoshida to Takeshita) tried to draw US attention to East and South-east Asia when they visited Washington. They adopted a similar policy for Western Europe, as evidenced by the participation in the Colombo Plan through extending development assistance, and then the admission to the Organization for Economic Co-operation and Development (OECD) on the premiss of joining the Development Aid Committee (DAC). The blurred dichotomy in a 'macro-diplomacy' rendered obsolete the argument of 'Quit Asia, enter Europe' which had carried weight since the Meiji era. Thus, although the policies pursued for greater interdependence between Japan and the Western industrial nations are closely bound up with those of the Asian states, especially the non-communist countries, Japan's position in the structure is asymmetrical: economically, it belongs much more to the US-led Western industrial world than to Asia, to which it is affiliated geographically and culturally; and, in terms of politico-security, it depends most on the US system in the western Pacific. On all counts, it leans lopsidedly towards the other side of the Pacific. . . .

Japan's Search for a World Role

Masaru Tamamoto

The Internationalization of Japanese Foreign Policy

The statecraft of Prime Minister Nakasone tells us something about the limits and possibilities inherent in the nationalist right's vision of Japan. When Nakasone was named prime minister in 1982, speculation arose in both Tokyo and Washington about the extent to which he might try to make Japan more independent of the United States. Nakasone was a self-proclaimed nationalist, the first to become prime minister since Ichiro Hatoyama and Shinsuke Kishi in the 1950s. During his first electoral campaign for parliament, the ex-imperial naval officer flew the national flag on his campaign bicycle in defiance of the U.S.-occupation directive that banned any display of the flag (the directive was part of the effort to eradicate nationalism in Japan). Because of his reputation as a radical nationalist, when Nakasone spoke of pursuing an active foreign policy and of establishing a politically significant place for Japan in the world, many feared the worst.

But Nakasone defied the expectations that many in Tokyo and Washington had of him, for, if anything, his foreign policy brought Japan much closer to the United States. Nakasone defined his foreign policy in terms of a deepened interdependence with the United States. He regarded the U.S.–Japan relationship as a "shared fate" built on cooperation or "equal partnership." On the strategic front, Nakasone brought Japan's defense and foreign aid policies more in line with U.S. strategy than any previous prime minister. Not only did he increase Japan's defense efforts as Washington asked, but he actually began to integrate U.S. and Japanese military strategy and to develop military-related technology with the Pentagon. Under Nakasone, for instance, Japan participated in the SDI (Strategic Defense Initiative) program, and lifted restrictions on the transfer of military goods and technology that had been symptomatic of Japan's avoidance of world political-strategic affairs. Moreover, Nakasone greatly expanded Japan's involvement in U.S.-directed "strategic aid." In the early 1980s, Japan began to allocate considerable economic aid to Turkey, Pakistan and Egypt—countries that were considered geostrategically important to Washington but that promised little in the way of return on investment to Japan. The purpose of such aid was neither to reap future economic benefits nor to cultivate political influence with these countries; it was to support America's global strategy against the Soviet Union.

On the economic front, Nakasone also worked to develop the U.S.–Japan partnership. He established the Maekawa Commission to study domestic reforms for the purpose of alleviating U.S.–Japanese tensions. The policy recommendations of the Maekawa report have led to Japan's present emphasis on domestic-driven growth and to the reforms being made under the Structural Impediments Initiative (SII) talks, including reform of the nation's distribution system and of the government's agricultural support policy. Just as important, Nakasone endorsed the Ministry of Finance's efforts to stabilize the dollar and to increase Japan's contributions to the Baker Plan for Third World debt relief.

Nakasone's statecraft provided an answer to one of the questions that postwar Japanese had about the political intentions of the nationalist right— namely, what is the nationalist right's idea of Japan's place in the world? Behind this question lay the lingering suspicion that the nationalist right harbored ambitions reminiscent of imperial Japan, that it stood for greater political and military independence from the United States. Nakasone's foreign policy showed that the nationalist right does not wish to deviate from the fundamental direction of postwar Japan.

In a sense, Nakasone pursued the only manner of an active foreign policy that Japanese society would permit—a foreign policy that does not challenge American protection of Japan and does not threaten democracy. Although Nakasone and others of the nationalist right do not fully share the concerns many of their compatriots have about the viability of Japanese democracy—for they believe that Japan's democracy is solid—they do nonetheless share the public's conviction that Japan's welfare lies with an enhanced relationship with the United States. It is this shared conviction that allowed the nationalist right to begin to internationalize Japanese foreign policy.

When Nakasone, Ishihara, and others of the nationalist right air their dissatisfaction with the San Francisco framework, therefore, this does not mean that Japan wants to disengage from or challenge the United States.

Rather, it means that they want Japan to shed its political timidity in world affairs—"its pretense of a foreign policy," as Miyazawa says. They believe that Japan, which accounts for upwards of 10 percent of the world's GNP, cannot afford to continue its isolation from world politics, and that the United States and Japan, which together control more than a third of the world's GNP, have shared political responsibilities.

With the internationalization of Japanese foreign policy that was initiated by Nakasone and continued by Noboru Takeshita and Toshiki Kaifu, Japan has in fact begun to shed its willful political innocence. It has started to participate in world political affairs and to direct its wealth for a political purpose. That purpose has not been to expand Japanese power and influence, as many U.S. commentators fear, but to support the United States. Thus the widely held notion that wealth begets political power and that a more active Japanese foreign policy means a more independent foreign policy in the future is too simple, if not mistaken. As Japan's economic wealth has increased it has indeed become more active internationally, but it has become more active in support of U.S. goals.

Much of the worry about a more independent and assertive Japan naturally relates to U.S. dependence on Japanese capital for both domestic and international policy purposes. Japanese financial institutions regularly purchase about one-third of all U.S. Treasury bill issues, and the continued infusion of capital from Japan into the United States is critical to America's ability to run a large budget deficit without triggering a substantial rise in interest rates or inflation. Moreover, Japan's capital contributions to the International Monetary Fund (IMF) and the World Bank and to international development assistance in general are critical to the success of the Brady plan for Third World debt relief and to U.S. policy goals in Latin America and Eastern Europe. If Japan, as a matter of government policy, were to shift its international investment to Asia, or if more Japanese investors were to become attracted to potentially higher yielding German bonds in the future, then the U.S. economy and global strategy would be seriously undermined.

While the Japanese government cannot dictate the investment decisions of private investors, the fear that it would encourage a shift away from supporting the U.S. budget deficit or U.S. international economic goals is misplaced. Among other things, it ignores the extent to which Japan sees its own position and identity tied to that of the United States. The nationalist right recognizes that the world would be a much less hospitable place without U.S. global leadership. Thus, while more Japanese money will undoubtedly go to Germany for purely business reasons, a variety of Japanese institutions—both public and private—will continue to see that the U.S. Treasury bill market is financed and that U.S. development initiatives in the World Bank and IMF are supported. In effect, we are now witnessing an unprecedented arrangement in the history of international relations in which a protectorate is financing the hegemon: Japan, the primary beneficiary of Pax Americana, is underwriting American hegemony and prosperity.

Still, many see a threat to U.S. international leadership in Japan's recent demand for a larger economic role in the world. In the IMF, the World Bank, and other international organizations, Japan has demanded a larger voting share that reflects its growing financial contribution. This demand, however, is entirely in keeping with the notion of U.S.–Japanese partnership that Nakasone enunciated. Japan does not seek to control the largest number of voting shares; it wants the number two position. Nor is Japan seeking to change these U.S.-created institutions; it wants to breathe new life into them. Japan, it is fair to say, has become the champion of the original Principles of the IMF, the World Bank, and the General Agreement on Tariffs and Trade (GATT). It has chosen to respond to U.S. demands for burden-sharing by increasing its support of these U.S.-led institutions. Japan's primary aim, again, has not been to enhance its political and economic power but to strengthen the U.S.–Japanese partnership. Thus when the United States "stole" the Miyazawa Plan for Third World debt relief and renamed it the Brady Plan, Miyazawa was not resentful; the finance ministry was only too happy to offer support for the Brady Plan.

More than anything, the Japanese, especially the "political realists," want clear recognition of their efforts to assume greater global economic responsibilities, especially in the area of international development assistance. This comes at a time when Japan is in the process of shaping a new national consensus commensurate with its position in the world. The consensus that had prevailed in Japan during most of the postwar decades—on the need to catch up with the industrialized West—is no longer meaningful now that Japan's GNP is second only to that of the United States and its per capita income exceeds America's. The new consensus that is emerging sees Japan occupying the number two position in an American world order.

For those who fear the impending rise of Japan, however, Japan's presence in Asia in particular may not seem so reassuring. There it appears that Japan is bent on being number one; its economic clout has attained enormous proportions and continues to grow. Japan has already replaced the United States as the economically dominant power in Southeast Asia, where it leads in trade, investment, and aid. Take the figures for Thailand. In 1988, Japan accounted for 53 percent of all foreign investment in Thailand, the United States for 5.8 percent. Similarly, Japan provided 69.4 percent of Thailand's foreign assistance, the United States 5.3 percent. In the five ASEAN countries, excluding oil- and natural-gas–rich Brunei, Japan accounted for 63.6 percent or $1.68 billion of foreign aid, while the second largest donor, the United States, accounted for 11 percent or $290 million.[1]

Yet it would be a mistake to conclude from this that Japan envisions a Japanese empire in East Asia—a re-creation of the Co-Prosperity Sphere. The Japanese and Southeast Asian economies are closely linked, and there is a clear economic rationale for Japan's deep involvement in the region. The growth of its economic influence in Southeast Asia has been the result of the natural expansion of its industrial program as Japan seeks to tap new markets, invest in promising ventures, and promote a division of labor in the region. However, despite its commanding position in Southeast Asia, Japan has continued to defer to the American order in the region. This can be seen in Japan's divergent approaches to economic relations with the Philippines and Vietnam. While Japan has, at America's request, poured large amounts of money into the Philippines despite its grave doubts about the health of that country's economy, it has not taken full advantage of the trade and investment opportunities it sees in Vietnam out of deference to U.S. policy.

Still, some see signs of an emerging "will to political influence" behind Japan's economic clout. It is true that Japan has begun to take more diplomatic initiatives in the region. In the course of an Asian tour in May, Prime Minister Kaifu expressed a willingness to involve Japan in the political issues of the region. Whereas Kaifu's predecessors had taken great care to avoid entanglement with regional politics for fear of heightening concerns about Japan's involvement in the area—concerns that originate with Japan's conduct during the Pacific War—Kaifu boldly displayed the new face of an internationalizing Japan. In Indonesia, instead of talking vaguely about peace and cooperation and offering increases in aid, as his predecessors had often done, Kaifu expressed his desire to see steps taken toward institutionalizing the transfer of presidential power in that country—a sensitive issue with the Suharto regime. Even in countries where Japan has marginal economic influence, Kaifu spoke with newfound boldness. In India and Pakistan, he made clear Japan's concern about the rumor of war over Kashmir, and he exhorted the two countries to sign the nuclear nonproliferation treaty. Addressing the Indian Parliament, he said that India needs to open its economy to international competition; and in Bhutto's Pakistan, he offered encouraging words for its struggle for democracy.[2] Finally, Japan's hosting of the Cambodian peace talks in June marked its first active participation in diplomatic efforts to resolve that conflict.

While these initiatives represent a significant departure from traditional postwar Japanese diplomacy, Kaifu has simply put into practice what Nakasone meant when he spoke of the "shared fate" between the United States and Japan. Kaifu—who is not a member of the nationalist right and instead belongs to the postwar Japanese tradition of nonideological, pragmatic leadership—is performing his responsibilities in a spirit consistent with Nakasone's internationalization of Japanese foreign policy. Whether the issue is a smooth political succession in Indonesia, nuclear nonproliferation in South Asia, liberalization of the Indian economy, democracy in Pakistan, or settlement of the Cambodian conflict, these concerns reflect political values that the United States and Japan share. And the successful outcome of any of these issues will benefit the two countries. In Kaifu's policy it becomes possible to see the direction Japan is taking as it translates its wealth into political power. Japan's recent Asian initiatives reflect its willingness to remain within the America global framework, based as it is on core political values and goals that Japan shares with the United States.

In its Asian diplomacy Japan can be seen to have adhered to the important lesson it learned from the Pacific War: do not take political initiatives except with the blessing of the hegemonic power, in this case the United States. During the Pacific War, Japan rebelled against the hegemonic order—an order the Japanese referred to then as a "siege by ABCD (American, British, Chinese, and Dutch) powers." After their defeat, the Japanese assigned blame for the ruinous war to the reckless policy of challenging the hegemon. And today, it is clearly understood that Japan's international success derives, in part, from its deference to the hegemonic power—to Britain in the nineteenth century and the United States in the twentieth century. The fall into the valley of darkness during the 1930s and 1940s—the only time when Japan abandoned such deference—is proof to Japan's postwar generation of the validity of this historical interpretation. Whereas many Americans harbor suspicion of Japan because they view that nation in light of its 15-year militarist era, the Japanese see the militarist period as an anomaly in a century otherwise marked by good relations with the Anglo-American hegemon.

For practical reasons, too, Japan does not want to act in Asia without the United States. Japanese leaders fear that America's departure from the region will invite political chaos. After all, it is the American order that has subsumed Asia's suspicions of and antagonisms toward Japan. Asia without the United States would see the elevation of Japan to a position of dominance, and that would bring to the surface latent differences between Japan and the other Asian countries.

Underlying much of the concern about Japan, therefore, is the still largely unspoken fear of Japan's potential military power. In spite of the pacifistic character of Japan in the postwar period, there remains in the United States and throughout Asia a fear of resurgent Japanese militarism. Unless the United States is willing to maintain a substantial military presence in the Pacific indefinitely, Japan, it is increasingly assumed, will do what other rising great powers have done: expand its military power to protect and extend its growing economic reach. Japan has, of course, significantly expanded its military forces over the past decade. Yet, as noted earlier, that expansion has largely been a Japanese response to American demands for greater burden-sharing. It was in response to Washington's demands, for example, that Japan breached its 1-percent-of-GNP ceiling on military spending, that it relaxed its ban on arms exports, and that it extended its naval capabilities to protect the sealanes in and around Japan. For those Americans concerned with the rise of Japan as a great military power, it is ironic that the United States has served as the midwife to the expansion of the Japanese military. Nonetheless, the fact remains that Japan's military policy is subordinate to that of the United States. The most important guideline for Japan's military has been and will be the U.S.–Japan security treaty and America's Asian policy.

It follows, then, that just as the United States possessed the influence to spur Japan's increase in military spending, so too does it possess the ability to discourage its military buildup. What is needed in the Bush–Gorbachev era is American leadership in creating an arms control and disarmament framework for Asia and the Pacific. Thus far the United States has been caught up with the unexpectedly swift turn of events in Europe and has not been able to alter its Asia policy to reflect the changes in Europe and the Soviet Union. But Japan, which manages its military expenditures by five-year plans, is now in the process of drawing up the next plan. The United States can play a pivotal role in determining how much and for what purposes Japan will continue to increase its arms expenditures.

Japan's political leaders now are especially anxious for American strategic leadership. There is belated recognition among them that they will have to respond to Gorbachev's Soviet Union. Until the recent collapse of the East European regimes, the Japanese government had taken a cautious approach toward Gorbachev's future and was thus reluctant to change its Cold War policies. But now, especially given America's supportive response to Gorbachev, Japan's leaders recognize the need for change. Gorbachev is scheduled to visit Tokyo for the first time in 1991. There are indications that he may announce the return to Japan of four disputed northern islands. The islands, which were taken by the Soviets at the end of the Pacific War, are a critical issue in Soviet Japanese relations. Japan claims that until the islands are returned, a peace treaty with the Soviet Union cannot be concluded, and that substantial improvements in economic and other relations cannot be made. Until very recently, Japan had not believed that the Soviet Union would ever relinquish them. The islands issue has provided a convenient excuse to maintain what the Japanese leadership has long thought was the soundest relationship with the Soviet Union—one that was cool, minimal, and distanced. Such a policy served the U.S.–Japanese alliance well. Now that the Soviet Union, contrary to Japan's expectations, seems prepared to adopt a more conciliatory stance, Japan is unprepared for the possibility that the islands might be returned. For this reason, and because relations with the Soviet Union are central to the U.S.–Japan alliance, Japan's leaders await an articulation of American strategic policy in Asia.

The decision the United States makes with respect to its Asian policy will sway the debate in Japan between "political realists" and "military realists"; between the two visions of internationalizing Japan's contributions to the world—one emphasizing foreign aid and one stressing militarization. Because the range of debate between the two camps is narrow (both see strengthened relations with the United States as their goal) the United States is in the position to choose what kind of support it wants from Japan—economic or military, or a mix of the two.

Even the leaders of the nationalist right genuinely feel that a close relation with the United States is more important than the expansion of Japanese military power. During the 1980s, the nationalist right's views on military policy were compatible with American demands for burden-sharing, and American backing of Japan provided the Japanese public, which remains concerned about Japanese rearmament, reason to listen to the nationalist right. Without the support of the United States, the nationalist right's views of the military cannot command a wide audience.

Japan is now beginning to normalize its foreign policy. This is a healthy development. Japan's growing participation in global institutions, its efforts to assume a greater share of its defense, its increasing contributions to economic aid, and its other internationalizing policies are all welcome signs of a more open discourse with the community of nations. Yet for all the concern about the growing influence that accompanies these developments, Japan's will to power is limited. There are no serious views in Japan that challenge the alliance with the United States; Japan wishes to fashion its policies within the broad policy parameters established by American leadership. Crucial to the future of Japanese behavior, therefore, is not any internal design for supremacy but the viability of American global leadership.

But, one may wonder, what are the limits to Japan's deference to the United States? Surely there is a point at which Japan will say no to the United States. It is difficult, however, to determine exactly where that point is, for the Japanese do not seriously imagine such a possibility. Yet one thing is sure: Japan is prepared to meet U.S. demands for greater political, military, and economic contributions toward maintenance of the U.S. global order. Indeed, in some ways, these demands are welcomed in Japan. Demands for burden-sharing offer needed guidelines for a Japanese foreign policy in search of a larger political role in the world. And demands for the removal of structural impediments appeal to Japanese consumers because of the lower prices they will ultimately bring about.

In moving from a completely hesitant to a less hesitant foreign policy stance, Japan has started to voice its opinions on specific U.S. policies but not on America's broader goals. (Recent Japanese criticism of the U.S. budget deficit is one such example.) Japan values its relationship with the United States, although it can do without Washington's emotional outcries. What Japan fears is a protectionist and isolationist United States disengaging from Asia and the world, leaving Japan to fend for itself. Americans who fear the rise of Japan ask at what point Japan will abandon the alliance and emerge as a challenger to the United States. The Japanese respond with a question of their own: what does Japan have to do to maintain the alliance?

NOTES

1. *New York Times*, July 2, 1989.
2. *Far Eastern Economic Review*, May 17, 1990.

Why Aid?

Japan as an "Aid Great Power"

Dennis T. Yasutomo

Japanese aid has come a long way from the periphery to the centre of such an "historic mission." Based on our survey of aid policy's evolution, we can now identify and consolidate five primary reasons for economic aid policy's rise and continued centrality in Japan's foreign policy.

   *(1) **Because it is there.*** Of all diplomatic tools, the Japanese find aid convenient and available. Aid stands out as a relatively benign and flexible policy tool. It is not mired in the political tensions that characterize trade and defense relations with the U.S. and other nations. It has not triggered increasing fears of Japanese domination in the way that increasing Japanese investment in the United States has. As both Inada and Orr note, however, aid friction may become a problem if ODA continues to maintain its central status in Japan's foreign policy.[1] But so far, through the 1980s, aid has received a comparatively warm welcome, with criticism focused on why Japan will not give more (and better), not less, aid.

   Aid resources are also "there." The government finds it relatively easy to get budgetary support for ODA expenditures from the National Diet. And Japan, which became the world's largest creditor nation in the year the debt climbed past $1 trillion and when the U.S. became the largest debtor, now has the resources to partially compensate for aid fatigue and the drop in private flows.

Reprinted by permission. *Pacific Affairs* 62, no. 4 (Winter 1989–90).

(2) Because it works. Aid has been an effective diplomatic tool from Japan's perspective. In the early years, aid served as one means of restoring the severed relations with Asian nations conquered by Japan, restored the flow of raw materials lost after surrender and provided market outlets for the products of the economic miracle. The Tanaka trip enhanced aid's status as a diplomatic tool in Asia, and successive cabinets have incorporated aid as a staple in Japan's Asia policy. Aid currently plays a prominent role in Japanese overtures to ASEAN, China, Burma and Vietnam.

Aid works beyond Asia as well. It served as a major lubricant in restoring the flow of oil to Japan after the first OPEC oil embargo, and it is a useful bargaining tool in relations with Persian Gulf combatants and their allies today. Aid is also contributing toward mitigation of bilateral tensions with the U.S. Washington never accepted Tokyo's suggestion in the early 1980s that aid is a substitute for a military buildup and stronger defense efforts. But with Nakasone's emphasis on defense policy, and with changes in Washington's attitude toward Japan's defense burden-sharing role, Japan now finds Americans more sympathetic to the argument that Japan can contribute more aid because of defense policy limitations. In this sense, it appears that Japan's position has won out.

Aid has thus served as an extremely flexible policy tool, useful in improving relations with Asians, other third world nations, the United States, fellow donor nations and international organizations.

(3) Because it improves Japan's national prestige. The pride that emerged from Japan's attainment of economic great power status extends to its achievement of aid great power status.

The near-obsession with prestige helps explain the consistent Japanese emphasis on the amounts of aid. After all, aid expansion cannot be explained adequately by a Japanese aid philosophy, which has shifted from no philosophy to humanitarianism and interdependence to comprehensive national security to comprehensive economic cooperation. Nor has Japan developed or consistently followed a development philosophy, preferring to piece together themes from American policy (e.g., basic human needs), international organizations (e.g., structural adjustment loans), and international reports (e.g., the Pearson and Brandt Reports). Japan's emphasis on self-help stems from its own development experience, but self-help argues for limited economic assistance, not massive increases.

Japanese aid programs and initiatives have been prepared for maximum public relations effect: Fukuda's $1 billion for his ASEAN trip and his aid doubling pledge for the Bonn summit; Suzuki's aid doubling pledge for the Cancun and Ottawa summits; Nakasone's $20 billion recycling plan and the $500 million Sub-Saharan aid for his Washington visit and the Venice summit; Takeshita's $50 billion for the Toronto summit; Finance Minister Miyazawa Kiichi's debt relief plan for Toronto and the World Bank/IMF meeting; Takeshita's $2 billion ASEAN-Japan Fund for the Japan-ASEAN summit; and Uno's $35 billion recycling pledge for the Paris summit. Japanese aid policy makers acknowledge the need to move away from the fixation on aid amounts, but the diplomatic benefits make it difficult to abandon this kind of aid diplomacy.

(4) Because it's popular. Almost everyone encourages Japan to provide more aid to more recipients. Third world nations appreciate a new source of financing, especially one that pays less attention than multilateral banks and the U.S. to stringent aid conditions. International and multilateral organizations appreciate Japan's readiness to make up for American hesitation on increased multilateral aid since the early 1980s. Fellow donors in DAC appreciate Japan's efforts, in view of their own economic and financial problems and aid fatigue.

Most important, aid has increased steadily in large part because of a national consensus on aid at home. Most Japanese support an increase in, or the same level of, aid expenditures. Labor unions, the media, intellectuals, the business community and all political parties support economic assistance. Domestic controversies center on aid effectiveness and instances of corruption, but the issue is not stoppage but rather reform and improvement of aid-giving procedures.

Reasons for such widespread public support are diverse—humanitarianism, economic well-being, burden sharing, energy resources, and partaking in a nonmilitary international role as part of a historic mission. Aid is flexible enough to garner the support of defense buildup advocates, who can easily accept political and strategic uses of economic aid (though they remain skeptical of its worth compared with an actual arms buildup), and of those inclined toward pacifism. An "aid great power" is not a military great power; nonmilitary statecraft substitutes for military diplomacy. Aid thus inherits the pacifist spirit of the postwar era, which has molded aid into a concrete, activist, global foreign policy tool for a *"heiwa kokka,"* a peace-loving Japan.

Aid has become a potential replacement for the national goals that guided the nation through the economic miracle. Japan has achieved its original postwar goals, and the foreign policy debate in Japan centers on what can serve as the new goals for the next century. Being a great power in terms of giving aid has struck a responsive cord within the nation. Aid fatigue has not afflicted the Japanese yet because aid giving fulfills a basic national need to contribute to the international community.

(5) Because it provides the Japanese with a glimpse of a desired future—a vision of Japan as an activist nonmilitary power contributing in international security and political as well as economic and financial arenas. For the Japanese, aid is an ideal component in their emerging vision of the future. It appeals to the lingering and strong pacifist spirit of the postwar period, provides a nonmilitary means of promoting international stability and economic recovery and conveys an image of involvement and activism that

raises the nation's international stature. It is a policy tool that can respond to both north-south issues, addressing the worsening plight of developing nations, and east-west issues, allowing Japan to play a support role to western nations through nonmilitary means.

This policy tool also responds to the two main themes stressed by the mass media in Japan today: internationalization and new nationalism. Aid's link to internationalization is obvious. It serves as a concrete means of contributing actively and positively to the world community, in service to developing nations and bolsters the efforts of the developed nations and international financial organizations. Aid can also appeal to the newly emerging sense of nationalism as well, for one can detect considerable pride in Japan's ability to catch up to other donor nations. The Japanese enjoy their new status as an "aid great power." Many go on to note the uniqueness of Japan's development experience as a non-western nation that achieved modernization, thus serving as a development model for today's third world. Because of economic success, Japan is the nation best poised to carry on the responsibility and burden of providing substantial amounts of aid to the third world. Thus economic aid has become an "historic mission" that Japan must fulfill in the world for both internationalists and nationalists.

This flexibility in the uses of aid and its appeal at home and abroad explains in large part the rise of aid policy as a convenient, effective and popular policy instrument. It responds to external expectations and fulfills internal aspirations. It has worked relatively well in the past, serves the needs of the present, and the link with Japan's future ensures its continued popularity, expansion and evolution as an integral component of a twenty-first century foreign policy.

This continued prominence and evolution of aid policy also ensures continued complexity in the study of Japanese aid policy, never a simple matter to begin with. The metamorphosis of aid as an increasingly multidimensional and multipurpose policy tool poses new challenges for aid analysts. Aid can no longer be compartmentalized into clear-cut categories, such as economic-commercial, political-diplomatic, strategic or development arenas. It is now all of these and more. The challenge is to delineate and define the "more."

NOTE

1. See Juichi Inada, "Nihon Gaiko ni Okeru Enjo Mondai no Sho-Sokumen," *Kokusai Mondai*, May 1987, pp. 17–18; and Robaato M. Orr, "Nihon no Atarashii Buki: Oda," *Seiron*, January 1988, p. 140. Both Inada and Orr locate the source of aid friction in the commercial arena.

Chapter 6

International System Structure
Power and Values

Over the course of the months leading up to the war with Iraq and the brief period of actual fighting, President George Bush presented the American people with a series of justifications for why the United States needed to take action. None of these evoked as strong a response as that of bringing into existence a "new world order." By their very nature, political slogans are sufficiently vague that anyone can read into them what they will. The concept of a new world order was no different. Was it to be (1) a world without war; (2) a world of increased cooperation among states with divergent political and economic systems; (3) a world populated by capitalist democracies; or (4) simply a world that the United States could walk away from?

In the months that followed the war the most appropriate answer seemed to be "none of the above": (1) There was intense fighting in Yugoslavia and Armenia; (2) the results of the global environmental summit were less than what had been hoped for; (3) a military coup took place in Haiti, human rights violations continued in China, and Kuwaiti leaders complained about unwarranted U.S. pressures to bring about democracy in their country; and (4) even if America wanted to withdraw from the world the influx of Haitian boat people made it clear that the world would find the United States.

Although the absence of confirming data has dampened the initial enthusiasm over the prospect of a new world order it has not led to a rejection of it for at least three reasons. First, the perceived deficiencies of the present international system might not be permanent characteristics but only features of a transitional period from the end of the cold war to the beginning of the new world order. Second, the cold war does appear to be behind us, and the logical question to ask concerns the type of international system that will take its place. Third, from an analytical perspective the type of international system in existence is important because of the hypothesized links between international systems and the behavior of states.

The concept of a system takes as its starting assumption the position that the conduct of foreign policy and the behavior of states are not random but, rather, that patterns exist. The forces that produce these patterns are not found within the states in such areas as interest-group activity, type of government, or economic system. Instead they are found in the way in which the game of world politics is organized and in the linkages that this overall structure creates between the individual parts of the whole. Just as with the human body or the ecological chain of life, changes in the behavior of one part of the system or the injection of a new element into it will change the behavior of other parts of the system and eventually the system itself. Finally, it should be noted that systems can be characterized in many different ways: how well they are able to absorb shocks or harmful actions (stable vs. unstable), how closely linked the actions of one part of the system are to those of another (tight vs. loose), and whether or not they have the ability to accommodate themselves to change and to remain healthy (self-adjusting vs. nonadaptable).

Whereas theorists agree that the constituent parts of the international system (states, international organizations, nonstate actors, etc.) are affected by the makeup of the whole, there is disagreement on what qualities of the international system are most important for shaping state behavior. Here, our focus will be on two attributes: the concentration of power into poles and the dominant value system, which engenders system norms and rules.

System Structure Based on Military Power

At first glance, the number of possible international systems appears to be quite large, limited only by the number of states since each state could serve as a pole—a center of power—in the system. The historical record suggests quite the opposite: Some form of (military) power hierarchy has always existed among states, and certain distributions of power have proven themselves to be so unstable that the resulting systems proved to be short-lived. Consequently, attention has centered on the relative merits of two types of international systems: bipolar and multipolar.

Until recently the debate over which of these two systems was "better" was strictly academic. Although it was recognized that international systems do change, the continued existence of the cold war (a bipolar system) was all but taken as a given. That situation has now changed, making the question of what type of international system the new world order will be a very important one.

A bipolar system is one in which power is concentrated in two poles. These two power centers are pitted against each other in a conflictual relationship that has little room for compromise or peaceful coexistence. Defending its own allies and eliminating the other pole are the primary foreign-policy goals of each power center. Because of the all-encompassing nature of the competition between the two poles, the system tends to be highly inflexible and rigid.

Multipolar systems are characterized by the presence of at least five relatively equal powers, each of which serves as a pole. The primary foreign-policy objective in a multipolar system is not permanent defeat of an enemy, as it is in a bipolar system. Not only are there too many enemies for this to be a realistic objective but also the relationship among power centers is much more flexible, containing elements of cooperation as well as competition. The primary foreign-policy goal is to balance competing power centers. To do so, the most powerful states in the system freely interact with all other powers, creating alliances as needed and breaking them off once the danger of one state or group of states acquiring too much power has passed.

A central point of contention among those who study international systems is whether bipolarity or multipolarity is more likely to produce war. A theoretical case can be made for and against each. Bipolarity could be expected to lead to war because of the high level of tension built into the structure of the system. No conflict is unimportant, and any move by the other power center must be matched. In fact, the image of falling dominoes, often associated with bipolarity, was frequently used by American policymakers to justify U.S. involvement in seemingly out-of-the-way Third World countries facing Communist insurgencies. In defense of bipolarity it could be argued that wars are unlikely because of the high degree of attention focused on the other power center, thereby reducing the incentive to launch a surprise attack, and because of the high degree of control that each power center holds over its allies.

It is this very need to pay attention to several possible enemies that leads some observers to believe that multipolarity is the more war-prone system. Preparations for war are more likely to be unnoticed, and the potential for misinterpreting another state's motives or power potential is similarly increased. Defenders of multipolarity counter by pointing to the conflict-inhibiting properties that are built into the flexibility of a multipolar system. This statement is particularly true for international trade, which binds states together in such a way that they cannot afford to go to war to settle disputes.

Past International Systems

History supports neither position fully. One study found that bipolarity was associated with war in the twentieth century but not in the nineteenth. Another found no relationship at all between the number of poles in the international system and the outbreak of war. Still another found that a unipolar system was the most peaceful. One possible explanation for the inconsistent data lies in the overuse of the terms *multipolarity* and *bipolarity*. For example, it was common to treat the international system as multipolar from the Congress of Vienna in 1814 to the outbreak of World War I in 1914. With the work of Gordon Craig and Alexander George it is possible to identify three different types of multipolar systems between 1815 and 1914. The first is the Congress of Vienna system, which lasted from 1814 to 1854. The principal task of those who gathered in Vienna was not to end a war or punish a defeated state by taking away territory or imposing war damages. Instead they sought to design a system that would prevent future conflicts from erupting into war. At the center of the system they created was the recognition that states must resist any crusade for universal domination; they believed that maintaining a rough equilibrium, or balance of power, among the leading states in the system was the best means for discouraging any state from entering into such a quest.

The second multipolar system was created by German Chancellor Otto von Bismarck in the late 1870s, and it lasted into the first decade of the twentieth century. Bismarck looked favorably on the political status quo in Europe and wished to protect Germany's newfound position of importance. He could not hope to re-create an all-encompassing type of alliance system, like the Congress of Vienna, because the democratic revolutions that swept the continent in 1848 and the surge of nationalism that followed left in their wake an ideological division among the great powers of Europe. Although two opposing alliance systems did not yet exist, there was a great deal of distrust. Bismarck sought to overcome these divisive forces by placing Germany at the center of a complicated system of alliances, many of which were secret. He also entered into a series of political maneuvering designed to prevent any of the other major powers from seeking to increase their power and upset the European status quo.

The third multipolar system existed from 1907 to 1914. At its core were two opposing alliance systems: the Triple Entente of Great Britain, France, and Russia and the Triple Alliance of Germany, Italy, and Austria-Hungary. Without any point connecting them, a role that Bismarck's Germany had sought to play in the second system, this multipolar system soon began to take on the characteristics of a bipolar system, even though it lacked two clearly defined poles. The rigidity of these two alliance systems is cited by many as one of the key factors contributing to the outbreak of World War I following the assassination of Archduke Ferdinand.

What Craig and George's analysis suggests is that the question of which is preferable, a multipolar or a bipolar system, is too simplistic. It is necessary to ask, which multipolar system or which bipolar system? They conclude that although it did not work as envisioned by those who designed it, the Congress of Vienna system is the one that ought to serve as a model for the future.

Knowing what type of international system is most desirable is only a first step toward thinking about world politics in the next century. It is also essential to understand how to bring such a system about and what conditions must be met if it is to work smoothly. Disagreement exists on both points. The primary mechanism for systems change in world politics has been war. One of the most interesting aspects of how the cold war ended was the absence of any defeated and outcast state, such as Nazi Germany or Imperial Japan, from whom war damages are typically sought. Instead, the Soviet Union was seen as a fully legitimate—although seriously weakened—player in the conduct of world affairs.

The transition from cold war to new world order thus promises to be different from the transition that immediately preceded it and led to the creation of the cold war. It is still too early to tell just how different this transition period will be from previous ones. If one accepts Paul Kennedy's argument concerning the rise and fall of great powers, the transition to a new world order can be understood in terms of previous transitions. He argues that great powers inevitably overextend themselves while trying to protect their empires. In the course of doing so they fail to invest enough resources into the economic sector to maintain a flourishing economic base. Over time this policy results in slowed economic performance and decreased military effectiveness. Not burdened by the need to defend a global empire and free to spend on economic growth, a challenging state in the international system will eventually become the dominant state. However, one can argue that the continued presence of large inventories of nuclear weapons in the United States and the former Soviet Union has fundamentally transformed the nature of system change and the role of military power in world politics. Thus, by definition this transformation will be different.

Although they do not address the problem of how to bring about a new version of the Concert of Vienna system, Craig and George do identify the factors that they believe were essential to its proper functioning. First, governments were free from domestic and international pressures that could have forced them to undertake policies that would have led to retaliation by some of the other great powers. Numbered among the "non-constraints" was the absence of pressure from public opinion, from economic interest groups, and from the military. Second, there were no ideological differences among the powers. Finally, with the possible exception of France, all powers subordinated their own goals to the perceived need of maintaining a balance of power. This list is reasonable, but not all commentators would agree with it. For example, Richard Rosecrance, who also believes that a revived Concert of Vienna system would best ensure a peaceful new world order, also suggests three reasons for its success, but they only partly overlap those of Craig and George. First, all of the major powers were actively involved in maintaining the system. Second, there was ideological agreement among the great powers. Third, the great powers renounced territorial expansion and war in favor of advancing liberal democratic values and economic development.

System Structure Based on Economic Power

Whatever a system's formal structure, many regard it as quite possible that economic power rather than military power will serve as the primary measure of a pole's strength. Economic-centered discussions of international systems generally have not been written about in terms of poles or power centers in the same way as have military-centered ones. Interdependence and regime-based theories start from the assumption that power is issue-specific and that relations between states need not be conflictual but instead can be largely cooperative. Dependency theories see economic relations as exploitive but tend to take for granted the existence of a larger military system within which these relations are organized.

One analyst who has written about economic systems in language similar to ours here is Johan Galtung. His work suggests not only that economic- and military-based international systems can be thought of in the same terms but also that they logically follow each other and that they are part of a larger cycle. Galtung argues that the proper way to understand present and past international system structures is in terms of unequal exploitive, or imperialistic, relationships between the center and the periphery states. Center states are those that have the most advanced economic, educational, military, and administrative systems, whereas periphery states have them in only an incomplete or underdeveloped form. Galtung maintains that center states establish vertical relations with portions of the periphery, which they then isolate from other center states and other parts of the periphery. The economic result is that all the periphery's trade is concentrated on one trading partner—the center—and that its economy is organized to meet the needs of the center. The political result is feudalism.

Initially, military power and the physical occupation of the periphery by the center was needed to maintain this international structure. Galtung argues that this is no longer necessary, however, as the mechanisms for domination have evolved over time to become more subtle and less expensive for the center state. Today they are primarily economic, taking the form of multinational corporations, international organizations, private relief agencies, and universities. Galtung predicts that increasingly the mechanism for control will lie in the sphere of (center-controlled) global and instantaneous mass communications. Domination and control will take the form of "cultural imperialism," in which images of the periphery are structured by the center's media. Because of their monopoly the media will determine not only how the periphery is viewed in the center but also how the periphery views its own condition. American TV news coverage of the Persian Gulf war showed the potential inherent in modern mass communication for shaping the global image of an event.

However, a recent study by William Meyer suggests that although some elements of Galtung's vision are in place, the overall effect still falls short of cultural imperialism. He found that a compartmentalized and hierarchical structure exists in international news flows. Eighty-five percent of all the international news coverage in Latin America dealt with events in Latin America or the United States, and 71 percent of those news stories about Latin America came from the United Press International or the Associated Press. Similarly, between 56 and 76 percent of the international news in the major news dailies of Kenya, Zambia, and Zimbabwe dealt with other countries once in the British Empire. Almost one-half of the news stories about former British colonies came from Reuters. Overall, 56 to 76 percent of all international news stories reported by African and Latin American presses originated with one of the major United States, British, or French news agencies. Finally, although regional and local news services do produce more in-depth reporting on development issues than do the major international wire services, and therefore serve as an alternative to these organizations, Third World news agencies are heavily dependent on the major wire services for up-to-the-minute coverage of major global issues.

System Structure Based on Values

The distribution of power is not the only way to think about the structure of an international system. It is also possible to think of it in terms of the underlying values that govern the system's operation. Those who employ this approach start from the position that the conduct of international relations, whether carried out by economic or military means, is always based on some underlying notion of (1) the fundamental nature of relations between political units and (2) what is acceptable behavior. The dominant value system during the cold war was realism. Realism stresses the management and acquisition of power, the inevitability of conflict, and the importance of the state. These themes come together to form the concepts of *realpolitik* and *raison d'etat*. The first term calls for conducting foreign policy on the basis of power politics instead of moral and ethical considerations. The second term states that because the state is the primary actor in world politics, any action that furthers the security of the state is justifiable. In doing so it consigns the rights and concerns of individuals, as well as the idea of global community, to a secondary position.

Viewed from a value perspective, for a new world order to emerge realism must be replaced by another value system. If it is not, replacing bipolarity with multipolarity or some other distribution of power is of little importance. The most frequently discussed alternative to realism is liberalism, which would replace, according to Doyle, the "balancing of enemies with the cultivation of friends." Doyle, a proponent of international liberalism, cautions that a new world order organized along the principles of liberalism does not guarantee peace. He notes that although liberal democracies have not gone to war against one another, there is ample evidence that liberal states are capable of adopting expansionist foreign policies. He also concedes that they have adopted policies of isolationism and appeasement. Still, Doyle maintains that unlike realism, the combination of liberal institutions, liberal ideas and transnational economic ties can provide the basis for a sustained peace. Membership in a liberal community of states brings with it a responsibility to "defend other members of the liberal community, to discriminate in certain instances in their favor, and to override in some (hopefully rare) circumstances the domestic sovereignty of states in order to rescue fellow human beings from intolerable oppression."

Replacing realism with liberalism may very well bring about significant changes in the conduct of world politics. It is not, however, the only possible type of value change that may occur. It is quite possible that world politics in the twenty-first century will be characterized by the coexistence of several different value systems. It is important to recall that realism became a global philosophy of world politics much in the same way that European law became global—with the spread of Western military and economic power. Moreover, thinking about liberalism as the logical successor to realism also reflects a continued tendency to think about world politics from a Western perspective and to pay insufficient attention to non-Western patterns of thought. Of particular importance may be what Michael Haas has described as the "Asian Way" of conducting international relations, which is based on the writings of Confucius, Mohammed, and Buddha. It arose spontaneously across Asia and, in part, represents an "unlearning" of Anglo-European practices.

Six principles lie at the heart of the Asian way. They address both the general nature of international relations and the specific practices that are appropriate for resolving disputes. (1) There must be "Asian solutions for Asian problems." Outsiders do not have enough of an interest in or knowledge of Asian affairs to make a meaningful contribution. (2) Problems must be addressed in a spirit of toleration and partnership. (3) Decisions should be unanimous rather then imposed or forced on reluctant states. (4) Incremental problem solving is stressed over the formulation of grand designs. Unlike Western incrementalism, which focuses on creating problem-solving institutions with carefully defined powers, Asian incrementalism emphasizes informal frameworks and loosely structured organizations. (5) Implementation and matters of principle are kept separate. First an agreement in principle is obtained, and then implementation problems are addressed by lower-level figures. This practice is different from the Western tendency to negotiate agreements only on those matters for which an administrative solution is readily at hand. (6) The Asian Way stresses the collective self rather than individualism. It is not concerned with defeating anyone but with allowing all to work together.

The Readings

The four readings in this section represent a sampling of views concerning the future shape of the international system. In "The Name of the Game," Susan Strange speaks to both the structure of the game of world politics in the next century and the likely values that will govern its conduct. She sees the former as being centered on a contest for control of market shares and the latter as being a civilization of international business. Jessica Mathews, in "Redefining Security," argues that the nature of world politics has been dramatically altered and that population, environmental, and resource questions must now come to dominate world politics. James Goldgeier and Michael McFaul, in "A Tale of Two Worlds," argue that the post–cold war era may look very different from the perspective of Third World states than from that of the rich industrialized states. Democracy and economic prosperity have altered the way in which the latter will conduct international relations. But because these traits are less prevalent in Third World states, power politics can be expected to continue there. Rodolfo Stavehagen, in "Ethnic Conflicts and Their Impact on International Society," explains the persistence of ethnic conflicts and examines their consequences for world politics. He is particularly concerned with the simultaneous internationalizing of ethnic conflicts and the ethnicization of international relations.

Bibliography

CRAIG, GORDON, and ALEXANDER GEORGE. *Force and Statecraft,* 2nd ed. New York: Oxford University Press, 1990.

DOYLE, MICHAEL. "An International Liberal Community." In Graham Allison and Gregory Treverton (eds.), *Rethinking America's Security.* New York: Norton, 1992.

GALTUNG, JOHAN. "A Structural Theory of Imperialism." *Journal of Peace Research* 2 (1971), 81–98.

GILPIN, ROBERT. *War and Change in World Politics.* London: Cambridge University Press, 1981.

HAAS, MICHAEL. "Asian Culture and International Relations." In Jongsuk Chay, *Culture and International Relations.* New York: Praeger, 1990.

KAPLAN, MORTON. *System and Process in International Relations.* New York: Wiley, 1957.

KENNEDY, PAUL. *The Rise and Fall of the Great Powers.* New York: Random House, 1987.

LEVY, JACK. *War in the Modern Great Power System, 1495–1975.* Lexington: University Press of Kentucky, 1983.

MEYER, WILLIAM. "Global News Flows: Dependency and Neoimperialism." *Comparative Political Studies* 22 (1989), 243–64.

NYE, JOSEPH. "What New World Order." *Foreign Affairs* 71 (1992), 83–96.

ROSECRANCE, RICHARD. *Action and Reaction in World Politics.* Boston: Little, Brown, 1963.

ROSECRANCE, RICHARD. "A New Concert of Powers." *Foreign Affairs* 71 (1992), 64–82.

The Name
of the Game

Susan Strange

Imagine a game of poker. It is being played for money. Next night, it is strip poker, played for quite different stakes. The card game apparently has not changed, but the name of the game has.

Something like that happened to international relations in the course of the 1980s. The name of the competitive game between states used to be control of territory. Other states had to be "contained." Buffer zones were needed for protection. Dividing "curtains" hung over big rivers like the Oder and Neisse, or the Yalu in Korea, separating territory on the right bank from territory on the left. Behind each curtain, there were missile bases, guns, and airfields to deter incursions into the territory.

Now the name of the game is world market shares. Export competitiveness is what states need to keep national income rising. And rising national income is what governments need to keep from being thrown out. In order to stay in power, and maintain their authority, governments have to concede to popular demand for participation, or at least for peoples' interests to be taken into account. Social justice involves welfare spending by the state, and that costs money. Rising gross national product, which automatically increases the tax harvest, is the one way government can pay for welfare without raising the level of taxation. Everywhere, from Mexico to the Transkei, from Kiev to Calcutta, people expect governments to see that they

From Nicholas X. Rizopoulos (ed.), *Sea-Changes: American Foreign Policy in a World Transformed* (New York: Council on Foreign Relations, 1990).

get a better standard of living next year than they got last year, and that their voice is more loudly heard in the corridors of power.

In short, more people are demanding more as the price of their acquiescence to hierarchies of power. They want more say and more goods in return for acknowledging the legitimacy of their masters. When rulers first emerged in ancient times, people asked only some security from random violence. To pay the costs of protection, rulers needed land to tax and authority over the farmers creating wealth from the land. So chiefs, lords, kings, and emperors—even popes—coveted land and sought to enlarge their territory. With first the English revolution under Cromwell and then the French Revolution, people began to demand a say in government and the abolition or restriction of absolute rule. Enter the nation-state, self-determination, and the democratic franchise. Territory then became primarily where "our" people lived, not something valuable in itself as a source of either wealth or military manpower. Fighting over it could be justified only in terms of the balance of costs and risks to the people. Thus, by the 1980s, the whole world outside the Middle East saw the futile Iraq-Iran war as a tragic anachronism. Hardly less anachronistic in terms of the mismatch of means and ends, as perceived by the bystanders, was the Falklands war or the U.S. invasion of Panama. Only where the retreat of an empire has left behind a mismatch between people who live on territory and a community that feels emotionally responsible for them—as Turks feel responsible for Turkish Cypriots—are there still places where it looks as though the old game of competition for territory is still played. But it is not really the same game. The reason for the obsolescence of major war, as historian John Mueller has argued, is not just that people fear the catastrophe of nuclear war. It is that the *idea* is dead, or dying.[1]

Elsewhere, the loss of appetite for the control of territory has been a striking feature of recent years. Why did the Soviet Union give up Afghanistan? Why did South Africa give up its claim to Namibia? Why does communal trouble in Kashmir cause so much less apprehension about an Indo-Pakistan war than it would have in the 1940s? Why did the Czechs feel so confident that the Soviet tanks would not be used as they were in 1968? Not so long ago, the postwar retreat from empire by the British, the Dutch, the French, the Belgians, seemed to some Americans the proof of Europe's decadence, or else, perhaps, an enforced concession to pressures from the United States. Now, in hindsight, perhaps the Europeans were just showing a prescient recognition of the changing name of the game, forced on them by a quite exceptional disparity between the benefits of territory and the economic and political costs of holding on to it.

Not since the fifteenth century—or if you count Amsterdam as well as Florence and Venice, not since the seventeenth—has preeminence in the production of wealth been claimed by cities as well as territorial states. Yet the inclusion of Singapore and Hong Kong among the "Asian tigers" underlines the growing irrelevance of territory as the basis of wealth and power.

Forced by their very lack of territory to go full-tilt for export competitive-ness, Singapore and Hong Kong have recognized the new name of the game more quickly than have the United States, the Soviet Union, China, and India, whose big domestic markets lulled them into a false sense of security and economic success.

Conversely, we find players in the new game throwing away cards that they once valued in order to stay at the table. Three examples come to mind. South Africa—persuaded, no doubt, by its powerful banks and trans-national conglomerates—has apparently come to the conclusion that apart-heid is a costly handicap in the game, one that it can no longer afford, even if there are all sorts of difficulties in the shedding of it. Canada, fearful of its vulnerability to U.S. protectionism, has put its national pride and separate identity at severe risk by accepting the U.S.–Canada Free Trade Agreement. The Eastern Europeans have come to the conclusion—as even one day, per-haps, the Soviet Union may—that the economic cost of maintaining the lead-ing role of the party is too great and imposes too big a handicap in the struggle for economic growth, export earnings, and political legitimacy.

The big debates these days in most countries are not about foreign policy. They are about industrial policy. The fact that in the United States no one cares to admit that such a thing as industrial policy exists does not make patriotic Americans' differences about its content any less profound; whether there should be state support for manufacturing industry, what is the proper relation between industry and services, and what rules should apply to for-eign investment by the United States and in the United States are hot issues. The old debates between strategists over weapon systems and the disposition of nuclear capability are fading off the front page—because of detente and arms control agreements, it may be said. But why the optimism about this phase of arms control? Surely, because both superpowers came almost simul-taneously to the same conclusion: military spending was putting such a dead-weight on their economic performance in the competition for market shares that it was preempting those very resources without which social needs and demands could never be met. Both governments instinctively knew and rec-ognized the new game that had to be played. . . .

As more and more enterprises have been drawn into the competitive game of world markets, because they could no longer survive by supplying just the local market, the so-called multinationals have come to occupy a larger and larger part of the current picture of international relations. They are no longer playing walk-on parts, auxiliaries to the real actors. They are at center stage, right up there with the governments.

Indeed, growing numbers of enterprises have begun to resemble states, and sometimes to behave like them, sending diplomatc missions to other firms or to governments; making alliances with other firms or with states; even setting up intelligence departments, which may be described as "research" but may also engage in what governments would recognize as spying. And just as the state was never concerned simply with the pursuit of security, so the transnational corporation is seldom concerned simply with the pursuit of immediate profit. Its products, whether goods or services, are its weapons. Its employees are its armed forces. Its concern is with survival, security against takeover, or dwindling market share. Both firms and states now have the problem of managing multiple agendas; of trading off the pursuit of immediate wealth against the demands of long-term security; and of allocating the proceeds between the bosses, the stockholders, and the workers.

Because this evolution of international business has been going on for so long, it sometimes seems as though nothing new has happened. But the mid-1980s were a milestone as the volume of international production for the first time exceeded the volume of international trade. International trade is when goods or services are bought and sold across frontiers. International production is when goods or services are produced within a country under the global strategy of a foreign-owned and foreign-directed enterprise. When the latter became more important, it marked a significant change in the relation of states to markets and the graduation of transnational enterprises to a significant political role in international affairs—or, as the Council on Foreign Relations prefers to say, foreign relations.

The change is significant because while there is a lot states can do to disrupt, manage, or distort trade, there is much less they can do to disrupt, manage, or distort international production. To put it in a nutshell, states can to some extent control trade because they can bar entry to the territory in which the *national* market functions. They cannot so easily control production that is aimed at a *world* market and that does not necessarily take place within their frontiers. And even when a lot of production for the market is under control—as it was in oil in the 1970s—the market may not be—as the Organization of Petroleum Exporting Countries (OPEC) discovered, to its cost, in the 1980s. When states do try to use their power to influence where and how international production takes place, they find they cannot direct, as with trade. They can only bargain. And the costs to themselves can be very much higher than the rather small costs of indulging in trade protection. For example, when the Brazilian government excluded all the big international computer enterprises from producing in Brazil, it imposed a very high cost on all the local enterprises needing to use the latest and best computers in order to keep up with *their* competitors. When governments have wanted to develop offshore oil fields, they have had to bargain with enterprises possessing the know-how and the risk capital necessary for the operation, and have been obliged to moderate their tax demands and other conditions accordingly. The outcome of bargaining may be to the state's advantage, or to the multinationals'. It is still a bargain. It was much easier—and less costly to the national economy—in war or Cold War to ban some kinds of trade altogether, or in peace arbitrarily to saddle traders with tariffs or quotas.

Henceforward, therefore, diplomacy has to be conceived as an activity with not one, but three dimensions. The first, familiar dimension is the bargaining and exchange of views and information between representatives of governments, the conventional diplomats. The second, newer dimension is the bargaining and exchange of views and information between representatives of enterprises. And the third is the bargaining and exchange of views and information between a government representative on one side of the table and a representative of an enterprise, whether based in the same or in another state, on the other. . . .

To sum up, perhaps the greatest misperception is that the international system of states has not changed—even that it never will. By the end of the 1980s, a metamorphosis of the international political economy had begun: the old, close relationship between state, civil society, and economy is in the process of being replaced by a new relationship between authority and economy, and between authority and society. A global business civilization had emerged, a new international economic order in which authority is far more dispersed, less precisely defined but not totally absent. What, more precisely, does it mean?

The International Business Civilization

In the first place, it is now worldwide, in that the closed societies of China and the Soviet Union began opening up to it in the 1980s. By the end of the decade the alternative path of central planning of the economy was everywhere being abandoned—not only in the Soviet bloc, but in Burma and in several African states. In Europe and Latin America, big state enterprises were being broken up or privatized. Foreign investors were newly welcome. In the summer of 1989, before the autumn revolutions, Soviet managers were sent to the London Business School. All this did not mean, as some wishfully thought, that socialism as an idea was on the rubbish heap. Freedom for the socialist countries was a victory not for undiluted American capitalism, but for the forces of the market, which promised to put more goods in the shops, and popular demands for participation in government—in short, for some form of democratic socialism within the world market economy. It *was* a victory in the sense that the whole idea of creating a separate, centrally planned economic block insulated from world markets was abandoned and implicit assent given to joining up with the business civilization.

However, to say that the business civilization became worldwide is not to say that it is universal, that everyone belongs to it, as people in a territorial empire are its subjects. Civilizations are not like that. Indeed, at this point it may help to distinguish rather more clearly between the concept of civilization and that of empire. They are not the same, though historically they have usually—but not always—closely coincided. A civilization may have a territorial base—China in Confucian civilization, for example. Or it may have just an ideological base in a belief system, presided over by a central authority, in which case it could be called a nonterritorial empire—the Mormon and Catholic churches and the religion of the Aga Khan are examples. The nearest example of the combination of a civilization with a formal, territorial empire of subjects and an informal, nonterritorial empire of *cives* (citizens with civic rights and duties) was Rome. It had a core, south of the Alps, which extended west to Spain and east across the Adriatic, and where the *cives* predominated. In its northern periphery, in Wales or Brittany, or across the sea in North Africa, or among nomads like the Romany (i.e., Gypsy) people, most people were subjects. Among them, old ways, old religions and customs, old social hierarchies, persisted side by side with the new. Willy-nilly, however dissident, it is clear that these peoples were also part of Rome's informal empire, its civilization, for besides the relics of Roman power in the shape of military camps to keep order in the marches of empire, archeologists are still finding the relics of Roman civilization: villas that were outlying farmsteads, with baths and heating systems, coins, and ornaments—all witnesses to common civilized tastes and economic behavior. One could make the same point about ancient Chinese or Islamic civilizations; though sustained by military and political power, they were not coterminous with it in either time or space. And when Britain, with its sterling standard, was the geographic core of the business civilization in the nineteenth century, its tentacles reached out beyond the political empire—for example, into Argentina and the Middle East. And in outlying parts of that civilization, its level of concentration was often low, diluted by dissidents. The robber and folk hero Ned Kelly was not the only "new" Australian in the nineteenth century who rejected the values of British business civilization along with the authority of the government of New South Wales. "Waltzing Matilda" tells of the swagman caught stealing sheep who drowns in the creek, shouting defiance. "You'll never take me alive!" said he.

The international business civilization of today is the same. Its core is in New York—not Washington—and in Chicago and Los Angeles. There are Ned Kellys in each of these places, but these are also the cities where the social and political elites most wholeheartedly accept the values, the mores, the customs, and the taboos of the civilization—as, of course, do their counterparts in London, Tokyo, São Paulo, Sydney, and Taipei. The values are both economic—efficiency, speed, and responsiveness to demand in the production of goods and services—and social—openness to competition and opportunity for social advancement regardless of race, parentage, and soon, perhaps, sex. Particularly on the last issue, practice, as always, falls short of ideology. Women are not yet given equal opportunity; nor are blacks, as a head count of business-class passengers on any airline will show. But the significant point here, as with the other values of the civilization, is that the core is in the lead in bringing about social and economic change. American women have more opportunities than Japanese women; American blacks have more opportunity than Japanese of Korean or Ainu origin. And there is little doubt that where the core has led, the civilization will follow. A harbinger of future sea-change in the late 1980s was the first appearance of a Japanese woman, the Socialist Party's Takako Doi, on the political scene.

A central concern of the civilization is with the securing of property rights, for individuals and for firms. In the realm of ideas, the business civilization has given and, on the whole, despite environmental protests, still gives the benefit of any doubt to science. The scientists exercise authority in a way that in other civilizations the priests have done. The fact that—like priests—they do not always agree does not apparently lessen the legitimacy of their claim to pass judgment.

There is an important point here. The scientists with authority do not have to be American. But in most every field of advanced scientific research, the largest concentrations of authoritative scholars is in the United States—at the Massachusetts Institute of Technology, the Mayo Clinic, Woods Hole; in Silicon Valley and the San Francisco area for advanced electronics; at the Livermore laboratories. Between them, their influence over the preferred directions for scientific inquiry is felt worldwide. Their presence explains why, however poor the showing of American education at the lowest, primary levels, its standards in higher education, especially in the great graduate schools, are superlative. And the research communities based in the territorial United States are often attached to universities, dependent on the U.S. government, on U.S.-based foundations, and on state legislatures and fee income of predominantly American students. This means that the indirect authority exercised in the United States by the government, federal and state, in scientific matters is certainly greater than the governmental authority in any other country.

If the scientists wield one kind of authority in the civilization, the banks and the financial markets wield quite another. In earlier business civilizations, and when they were more fragmented into a series of predominantly national systems, governments reserved to themselves the authority to decide how much credit should be created. Banks were allowed some power to decide on the allocation of the credit they created, but generally not on its amount. Now, with the growth of global capital markets, of Eurobonds and Eurocurrency loans, all governments have given up a large part of their control over the rate at which credit is created. The fact that the U.S. government really has little choice but to bail out the savings and loan institutions for fear of the social consequences of not doing so is just one indication of a significant shift in authority over the world market economy from state to market.

Within the civilization, social groups are increasingly built up within firms, not around places. They are not nearly so closely linked to local communities as they were even 50 years ago. The friendships made by corporate executives and technologists are more and more within the enterprise or, beyond the enterprise, within a particular sector of economic or professional activity. These social networks are increasingly transnational, creating new conflicts of loyalty. The situation for many individuals is becoming much more akin to the civilization of Christendom in the Middle Ages. Then, people had multiple loyalties—to family, to church, to prince, to politico-economic groups like Guelphs and Ghibellines, to guilds, and so forth. Now, once again, individual choices have constantly to be made between conflicting claims. The apparent resurgence of nationalisms long suppressed in some parts of Eastern Europe—Transylvania, for instance—does not change the secular trend in most societies today toward a more fragmented social map.

The notion of citizenship is also undergoing subtle change. At the core of the business civilization in America, there are grades of entitlement to the status of citizen. At the bottom are illegal immigrants who live and work in the country under various degrees of threat to their way of life. At the top are the passport-carrying, job-holding, bona fide U.S. nationals. In between, there are participants in the business civilization who, as residents, enjoy, de facto, many of the rights of nationals. They can come and go freely. They have access to the courts, to schools and universities, and, through health insurance, to doctors and hospitals. Some gain entitlement through wealth, as businessmen; others through knowledge and education, as experts in the arts or entertainment, as well as in science and technology. And outside the United States, there are citizens of the business civilization who may be Swedish, Japanese, Israeli, Brazilian, or of many other nationalities, but who, culturally speaking, are almost identical with the American model. If their command of the grammar of the language is wobbly, or if they speak with a foreign accent, these are weaknesses that have been shared by some top officials and leaders of the U.S. government. As in Rome, in fact, there are grades of citizenship, degrees of entitlement, uniting, not separating, participants in one global civilization. Japanese businessmen dress like Americans. Their wives dress like American wives. Their children jump to the same music, follow the same fads and fashions, eat the same junk food, are even beginning to experiment with the same dangerous drugs. In every country, people are introducing more and more American words into their local languages. They are copying Americans in the taste for travel, for foreign cuisine, for jogging, for a freer and easier style of life. . . .

. . . What we have to think about is how to devise a wholly new system of government for the business civilization of the next century, for the informal empire whose core is still in the United States, however much it may need the consent and cooperation of its junior partner Japan, just as it once needed the consent and cooperation of Britain. That is the task for the 1990s.

NOTE

1. See John Mueller, *Retreat from Doomsday: The Obsolescence of Major War* (New York: Basic Books, 1989).

Redefining Security

Jessica Tuchman Mathews

The 1990s will demand a redefinition of what constitutes national security. In the 1970s the concept was expanded to include international economics as it became clear that the U.S. economy was no longer the independent force it had once been, but was powerfully affected by economic policies in dozens of other countries. Global developments now suggest the need for another analogous, broadening definition of national security to include resource, environmental and demographic issues.

The assumptions and institutions that have governed international relations in the postwar era are a poor fit with these new realities. Environmental strains that transcend national borders are already beginning to break down the sacred boundaries of national sovereignty, previously rendered porous by the information and communication revolutions and the instantaneous global movement of financial capital. The once sharp dividing line between foreign and domestic policy is blurred, forcing governments to grapple in international forums with issues that were contentious enough in the domestic arena.

Despite the headlines of 1988—the polluted coastlines, the climatic extremes, the accelerating deforestation and flooding that plagued the planet—human society has not arrived at the brink of some absolute limit to its growth. The planet may ultimately be able to accommodate the additional five or six billion people projected to be living here by the year 2100. But it

From *Foreign Affairs* 68 (1989). Reprinted by permission of *Foreign Affairs*.

seems unlikely that the world will be able to do so unless the means of production change dramatically. Global economic output has quadrupled since 1950 and it must continue to grow rapidly simply to meet basic human needs, to say nothing of the challenge of lifting billions from poverty. But economic growth as we currently know it requires more energy use, more emissions and wastes, more land converted from its natural state, and more need for the products of natural systems. Whether the planet can accommodate all of these demands remains an open question.

Individuals and governments alike are beginning to feel the cost of substituting for (or doing without) the goods and services once freely provided by healthy ecosystems. Nature's bill is presented in many different forms: the cost of commercial fertilizer needed to replenish once naturally fertile soils; the expense of dredging rivers that flood their banks because of soil erosion hundreds of miles upstream; the loss in crop failures due to the indiscriminate use of pesticides that inadvertently kill insect pollinators; or the price of worsening pollution, once filtered from the air by vegetation. Whatever the immediate cause for concern, the value and absolute necessity for human life of functioning ecosystems is finally becoming apparent.

Moreover, for the first time in its history, mankind is rapidly—if inadvertently—altering the basic physiology of the planet. Global changes currently taking place in the chemical composition of the atmosphere, in the genetic diversity of species inhabiting the planet, and in the cycling of vital chemicals through the oceans, atmosphere, biosphere and geosphere, are unprecedented in both their pace and scale. If left unchecked, the consequences will be profound and, unlike familiar types of local damage, irreversible.

Population growth lies at the core of most environmental trends. It took 130 years for world population to grow from one billion to two billion: it will take just a decade to climb from today's five billion to six billion. More than 90 percent of the added billion will live in the developing world, with the result that by the end of the 1990s the developed countries will be home to only 20 percent of the world's people, compared to almost 40 percent at the end of World War II. Sheer numbers do not translate into political power, especially when most of the added billion will be living in poverty. But the demographic shift will thrust the welfare of developing nations further toward the center of international affairs.

The relationship linking population levels and the resource base is complex. Policies, technologies and institutions determine the impact of population growth. These factors can spell the difference between a highly stressed, degraded environment and one that can provide for many more people. At any given level of investment and knowledge, absolute population numbers can be crucial. For example, traditional systems of shifting agriculture—in which land is left fallow for a few years to recover from human use—can sustain people for centuries, only to crumble in a short time when population densities exceed a certain threshold. More important, though, is the *rate* of growth. A government that is fully capable of providing food, housing, jobs and health care for a population growing at one percent per year (therefore doubling its population in 72 years), might be completely overwhelmed by an annual growth rate of three percent, which would double the population in 24 years. . . .

An important paradox to bear in mind when examining natural resource trends is that so-called nonrenewable resources—such as coal, oil and minerals—are in fact inexhaustible, while so-called renewable resources can be finite. As a nonrenewable resource becomes scarce and more expensive, demand falls, and substitutes and alternative technologies appear. For that reason we will never pump the last barrel of oil or anything close to it. On the other hand, a fishery fished beyond a certain point will not recover, a species driven to extinction will not reappear, and eroded topsoil cannot be replaced (except over geological time). There are, thus, threshold effects for renewable resources that belie the name given them, with unfortunate consequences for policy. . . .

A different kind of environmental concern has arisen from mankind's new ability to alter the environment on a planetary scale. The earth's physiology is shaped by the characteristics of four elements (carbon, nitrogen, phosphorous and sulfur); by its living inhabitants (the biosphere); and by the interactions of the atmosphere and the oceans, which produce our climate.

Mankind is altering both the carbon and nitrogen cycles, having increased the natural carbon dioxide concentration in the atmosphere by 25 percent. This has occurred largely in the last three decades through fossil-fuel use and deforestation. The production of commercial fertilizer has doubled the amount of nitrogen nature makes available to living things. The use of a single, minor class of chemicals, chlorofluorocarbons, has punched a continent-sized "hole" in the ozone layer at the top of the stratosphere over Antarctica, and caused a smaller, but growing loss of ozone all around the planet. Species loss is destroying the work of three billion years of evolution. Together these changes could drastically alter the conditions in which life on earth has evolved.

The greenhouse effect results from the fact that the planet's atmosphere is largely transparent to incoming radiation from the sun but absorbs much of the lower energy radiation reemitted by the earth. This natural phenomenon makes the earth warm enough to support life. But as emissions of greenhouse gases increase, the planet is warmed *un*naturally. Carbon dioxide produced from the combustion of fossil fuels and by deforestation is responsible for about half of the greenhouse effect. A number of other gases, notably methane (natural gas), nitrous oxide, ozone (in the lower atmosphere, as distinguished from the protective ozone layer in the stratosphere) and the man-made chlorofluorocarbons are responsible for the other half. . . .

Absent profound change in man's relationship to his environment, the future does not look bright. Consider the planet without such change in the year 2050. Economic growth is projected to have quintupled by then. Energy use could also quintuple, or if post-1973 trends continue, it may grow more slowly, perhaps only doubling or tripling. The human species already consumes or destroys 40 percent of all the energy produced by terrestrial photosynthesis, that is, 40 percent of the food energy potentially available to living things on land. While that fraction may be sustainable, it is doubtful that it could keep pace with the expected doubling of the world's population. Human use of 80 percent of the planet's potential productivity does not seem compatible with the continued functioning of the biosphere as we know it. The expected rate of species loss would have risen from perhaps a few each day to several hundred a day. The pollution and toxic waste burden would likely prove unmanageable. Tropical forests would have largely disappeared, and arable land, a vital resource in a world of ten billion people, would be rapidly decreasing due to soil degradation. In short, sweeping change in economic production systems is not a choice but a necessity.

Happily, this grim sketch of conditions in 2050 is not a prediction, but a projection, based on current trends. Like all projections, it says more about the present and the recent past than it does about the future. The planet is not destined to a slow and painful decline into environmental chaos. There are technical, scientific and economical solutions that are feasible to many current trends, and enough is known about promising new approaches to be confident that the right kinds of research will produce huge payoffs. Embedded in current practices are vast costs in lost opportunities and waste, which, if corrected, would bring massive benefits. Some such steps will require only a reallocation of money, while others will require sizable capital investments. None of the needed steps, however, requires globally unaffordable sums of money. What they do demand is a sizable shift in priorities.

For example, family-planning services cost about $10 per user, a tiny fraction of the cost of the basic human needs that would otherwise have to be met. Already identified opportunities for raising the efficiency of energy use in the United States cost one-half to one-seventh the cost of new energy supply. Comparable savings are available in most other countries. Agroforestry techniques, in which carefully selected combinations of trees and shrubs are planted together with crops, can not only replace the need for purchased fertilizer but also improve soil quality, make more water available to crops, hold down weeds, and provide fuelwood and higher agricultural yields all at the same time.

But if the technological opportunities are boundless, the social, political and institutional barriers are huge. Subsidies, pricing policies and economic discount rates encourage resource depletion in the name of economic growth, while delivering only the illusion of sustainable growth. Population control remains a controversial subject in much of the world. The traditional prerogatives of nation states are poorly matched with the needs for regional cooperation and global decision-making. And ignorance of the biological underpinning of human society blocks a clear view of where the long-term threats to global security lie.

Overcoming these economic and political barriers wilt require social and institutional inventions comparable in scale and vision to the new arrangements conceived in the decade following World War II. Without the sharp political turning point of a major war, and with threats that are diffuse and long term, the task will be more difficult. But if we are to avoid irreversible damage to the planet and a heavy toll in human suffering, nothing less is likely to suffice. A partial list of the specific changes suggests how demanding a task it will be.

Achieving sustainable economic growth will require the remodeling of agriculture, energy use and industrial production after nature's example—their reinvention, in fact. These economic systems must become circular rather than linear. Industry and manufacturing will need processes that use materials and energy with high efficiency, recycle by-products and produce little waste. Energy demand will have to be met with the highest efficiency consistent with full economic growth. Agriculture will rely heavily upon free ecosystem services instead of nearly exclusive reliance on man-made substitutes. And all systems will have to price goods and services to reflect the environmental costs of their provision. . . .

On the political front, the need for a new diplomacy and for new institutions and regulatory regimes to cope with the world's growing environmental interdependence is even more compelling. Put bluntly, our accepted definition of the limits of national sovereignty as coinciding with national borders is obsolete. The government of Bangladesh, no matter how hard it tries, cannot prevent tragic floods, such as it suffered last year. Preventing them requires active cooperation from Nepal and India. The government of Canada cannot protect its water resources from acid rain without collaboration with the United States. Eighteen diverse nations share the heavily polluted Mediterranean Sea. Even the Caribbean Islands, as physically isolated as they are, find themselves affected by others' resource management policies as locusts, inadvertently bred through generations of exposure to pesticides and now strong enough to fly all the way from Africa, infest their shores.

The majority of environmental problems demand regional solutions which encroach upon what we now think of as the prerogatives of national governments. This is because the phenomena themselves are defined by the limits of watershed, ecosystem, or atmospheric transport, not by national borders. Indeed, the costs and benefits of alternative policies cannot often be accurately judged without considering the region rather than the nation.

The developing countries especially will need to pool their efforts in the search for solutions. Three-quarters of the countries in sub-Saharan Africa, for example, have fewer people than live in New York City. National scientific and research capabilities cannot be built on such a small population base. Regional cooperation is required.

Dealing with global change will be more difficult. No one nation or even group of nations can meet these challenges, and no nation can protect itself from the actions—or inaction—of others. No existing institution matches these criteria. It will be necessary to reduce the dominance of the superpower relationship which so often encourages other countries to adopt a wait-and-see attitude. (you solve your problems first, then talk to us about change).

The United States, in particular, will have to assign a far greater prominence than it has heretofore to the practice of multilateral diplomacy. This would mean changes that range from the organization of the State Department and the language proficiency of the Foreign Service, to the definition of an international role that allows leadership without primacy, both in the slogging work of negotiation and in adherence to final outcomes. Above all, ways must soon be found to step around the deeply entrenched North-South cleavage and to replace it with a planetary sense of shared destiny. Perhaps the successes of the U.N. specialized agencies can be built upon for this purpose. But certainly the task of forging a global energy policy in order to control the greenhouse effect, for example, is a very long way from eradicating smallpox or sharing weather information.

The recent Soviet proposal to turn the U.N. Trusteeship Council, which has outlived the colonies it oversaw, into a trusteeship for managing the global commons (the oceans, the atmosphere, biological diversity and planetary climate) deserves close scrutiny. If a newly defined council could sidestep the U.N.'s political fault lines, and incorporate, rather than supplant, the existing strengths of the United Nations Environment Programme, it might provide a useful forum for reaching global environmental decisions at a far higher political level than anything that exists now.

Today's negotiating models—the Law of the Sea Treaty, the Nuclear Nonproliferation Treaty, even the promising Convention to Protect the Ozone Layer—are inadequate. Typically, such agreements take about 15 years to negotiate and enter into force, and perhaps another ten years before substantial changes in behavior are actually achieved. (The NPT, which required only seven years to complete these steps, is a notable exception.) Far better approaches will be needed.

Among these new approaches, perhaps the most difficult to achieve will be ways to negotiate successfully in the presence of substantial scientific uncertainty. The present model is static: years of negotiation leading to a final product. The new model will have to be fluid, allowing a rolling process of intermediate or self-adjusting agreements that respond quickly to growing scientific understanding. The recent Montreal agreement on the ozone layer supplies a useful precedent by providing that one-third of the parties can reconvene a scientific experts group to consider new evidence as it becomes available. The new model will require new economic methods for assessing risk, especially where the possible outcomes are irreversible. It will depend on a more active political role for biologists and chemists than they have been accustomed to, and far greater technical competence in the natural and planetary sciences among policymakers. Finally, the new model may need to forge a more involved and constructive role for the private sector. Relegating the affected industries to a heel-dragging, adversarial, outsiders role almost guarantees a slow process. The ozone agreement, to cite again this recent example, would not have been reached as quickly, and perhaps not at all, had it not been for the cooperation of the chlorofluorocarbon producers.

International law, broadly speaking, has declined in influence in recent years. With leadership and commitment from the major powers it might
regain its lost status. But that will not be sufficient. To be effective, future
arrangements will require provisions for monitoring, enforcement and compensation, even when damage cannot be assigned a precise monetary value.
These are all areas where international law has traditionally been weak.

This is only a partial agenda for the needed decade of invention.
Meanwhile, much can and must be done with existing means. Four steps are
most important: prompt revision of the Montreal Treaty, to eliminate completely the production of chlorofluorocarbons no later than the year 2000;
full support for and implementation of the global Tropical Forestry Action
Plan developed by the World Bank, the U.N.'s Development Programme, the
Food and Agricultural Organization, and the World Resources Institute; sufficient support for family planning programs to ensure that all who want
contraceptives have affordable access to them at least by the end of the
decade; and, for the United States, a ten-year energy policy with the goal of
increasing the energy productivity of our economy (i.e., reducing the amount
of energy required to produce a dollar of GNP) by about three percent each
year. While choosing four priorities from dozens of needed initiatives is
highly arbitrary, these four stand out as ambitious yet achievable goals on
which a broad consensus could be developed, and whose success would bring
multiple, long-term global benefits touching every major international environmental concern.

Reflecting on the discovery of atomic energy, Albert Einstein noted
"everything changed." And indeed, nuclear fission became the dominant
force—military, geopolitical, and even psychological and social—of the ensuing decades. In the same sense, the driving force of the coming decades may
well be environmental change. Man is still utterly dependent on the natural
world but now has for the first time the ability to alter it, rapidly and on a
global scale. Because of that difference, Einstein's verdict that "we shall require a substantially new manner of thinking if mankind is to survive" still
seems apt.

A Tale of Two Worlds
Core and Periphery in the Post–Cold War Era

James M. Goldgeier
Michael McFaul

As the world moves away from the familiar bipolar cold war era, many international relations theorists have renewed an old debate about which is more stable: a world with two great powers or a world with many great powers.[1] Based on the chief assumptions of structural realism—namely, that the international system is characterized by anarchy and that states are unitary actors seeking to survive in this anarchic system—some security analysts are predicting that a world of several great powers will lead to a return to the shifting alliances and instabilities of the multipolar era that existed prior to World War II.[2] . . .

We challenge both the structural realist predictions and the fundamental assumptions upon which they are based. We argue that balance-of-power politics will not be the defining feature of interactions among great powers in the coming decades, since the nature of states and the nature of the international system differ fundamentally from those described by structural realists. Because the great powers of the future will be *nonunitary actors* focusing primarily on maximizing *wealth* and acting not simply within a system of states but instead within a "great power society,"[3] they will no longer engage in balancing alliances but will settle conflicts and enhance their security through negotiation and compromise rather than through the use or threat of force.

Reprinted from *International Organization* 46:2 (1992), James Goldgeier and Michael McFaul, "A Tale of Two Worlds: Core and Periphery in the Post–Cold War Era," by permission of MIT Press, Cambridge, MA.

In this great power society, the major powers will gravitate toward one set of shared norms—namely, economic liberalism and political democracy. These norms will enhance the incentives to avoid the use of military means to settle disputes between the great powers. In direct contrast to the predictions about the effects of multipolarity offered by many realists, our prediction is that the collapse of communism will continue to move the world closer to an international order governed politically by collective action among the great powers rather than by balance-of-power politics. Conflicts between the great powers will still be common, but they will be played out in boardrooms and courtrooms, not on battlefields or in command and control centers.

The International System Today: A Tale of Two Worlds

The Nature of the State and the System

Assuming that states are unitary actors is counterproductive for developing theories about the behavior of great powers today; the growth of transnational economic interests and the rising constraints of public opinion on foreign policy have diminished the freedom of leaders to conduct foreign policy. A state's ability to conduct a "national" economic policy, for example, is weakened by the international behavior of its firms and by the growing importance of other states' investments in the "national" economy. Expanding trade flows and the accepted "rationality" of an open international market punish state interventions, autarkic systems, or import-substitution strategies.[4] It has become more and more difficult for individual states to regulate the fluidity of capital and the flow of technology transfers, which have both increased.[5] Transnational links and institutions limit the leaders' abilities to conduct mercantilist strategies and weaken the state's control over the domestic economy.[6]

Furthermore, with the collapse of communism—or, more accurately, the collapse of autocratic governments and command economies that followed the Soviet model—leaders are under increasing pressure to adopt international norms about economic liberalism and political democracy. Authoritarian governments face the specter of exclusion from international political regimes such as the European Community if they do not adopt democratic principles. Likewise, state-centered or protectionist economies forfeit access to International Monetary Fund (IMF) credits, World Bank loans, the European Common Market, and U.S. Agency for International Development (AID) assistance if they fail to push the state out of the domestic market and open the economy to the international market.

From within, the state as a unitary actor in foreign policymaking is challenged by both democracy and free markets. Just as American foreign policymakers have had to cope with public constraints on foreign policy since the Vietnam War, Soviet and Russian policymakers in recent years have had to contend with domestic publics that opposed the use of military force at home and abroad. Similarly, state actions that damage individual and corporate gains from an international free market risk domestic resistance and refusal. The "national" interest must now compete with the interests of the "nationals."

Not only are states less unitary, but the effects of international anarchy are less pronounced than in earlier periods.[7] First, the existence of nuclear weapons means that the great powers cannot use war to solve the conflicts that arise between them, and this lessens potential security dilemmas.[8] Disputes between great powers must be settled in more ordered fashions to ensure state survival. Second, the multilateral institutions and international regimes created after World War II to regulate and stimulate a world capitalist economy have served to temper the effects of international economic anarchy by decreasing transaction costs, providing information, and thereby reducing uncertainty.[9] Third, the rise of democratic principles within great powers has contributed to more regular and predictable behavior between the great powers.[10] . . .

While many of the changes affecting the state and the system in the core have similar effects in the periphery, the degree of transformation has been less pronounced for three key reasons. First, as nations in the periphery have not been engaged in massive nuclear arms races, absolute deterrents for military aggression do not exist. On the contrary, military force is still a valued means for influencing outcomes and increasing state power. Second, because sovereignty for many countries in the periphery is newly acquired and often challenged both from within and without, leaders actively (though not necessarily successfully) resist challenges to their control over policy, particularly in the economic sphere.[11] Foreign investment, foreign ownership, and, ultimately, foreign intervention are seen by many in the periphery as tools of the core states to exploit the peripheral states' resources. Different attitudes regarding the relationship of the state to international capitalism have created a multitude of different economic systems in the periphery. With respect to economic principles and practices, while the differences between those of Japan and the United States are large, they pale in comparison with the differences between those of Cuba and Singapore or between those of North Korea and Argentina. Third, predictability based on a set of shared norms does not exist in the periphery, since many regional security systems consist of states with radically different governments, economies, cultures, ethnic groups, and religions. In the Middle East, fundamentalist Muslim states share a regional security system with Israel. In southern Africa, democratic Botswana is surrounded by authoritarian states, both capitalist and socialist. In Southeast Asia, communist-controlled Vietnam and Cambodia share a regional security system with right-wing military regimes. While there are differences between the French and American models of democracy, they are minor in comparison with the differences between political systems in the periphery.

The Goals of States

The core. In the new international system, preserving existence will still be the ultimate objective of the state. For the great powers, however, ensuring survival will be a relatively easy task; core states need not remain "essentially war making machines."[12] A realist would expect that if Germany and Japan grow as great powers and challenge the United States, uncertainties will grow about the threat each poses to the other, and they therefore will be compelled to take internal or external measures to balance one another in the international system. We, however, argue that state survival within the core system of states will be relegated to a perfunctory national objective, and hence the security dilemma will not dominate relations between the great powers.

Beyond mere existence, wealth and power will remain the two overriding goals of all states, but the preference ordering between the two has changed fundamentally in the post–cold war era. Aircraft carriers and nuclear warheads do not generate gold for the national treasury. On the contrary, the experience of the Soviet Union and, to a lesser extent, the United States underscores that military power does not necessarily create economic wealth. Economists in Moscow and abroad concur that Soviet defense spending over the past forty years has stifled efficient resource allocations and stunted nonmilitary growth. The United States has channeled major research and development funds into pursuing military applications of sophisticated technologies, while others—most notably Japan—have nurtured commercial applications of American scientific achievements to generate tremendous economic growth. Two big winners of the cold war were nonparticipants. Japan spent 1 percent of its gross national product on military defense and turned its war-devastated state into the world's second-wealthiest country. Germany followed a similar postwar trajectory.

The end game of the cold war should not lead to the conclusion that military power is not important for the construction and preservation of the core's economic system. American economic hegemony after World War II laid the groundwork for liberal internationalism among capitalist states, while American military prowess contained antisystemic challenges to this order.[13] But in the new order *within* the core states, the norms, rules, and procedures brought into the system by American hegemony have been institutionalized by multilateral regimes, while antisystemic threats are in retreat. The great powers will continue to collide about farm subsidies and import quotas, but no core state or group of leading actors within the core has an interest in undoing the liberal international capitalist system. Even if quibbles between great powers become conflicts, the utility of military power for influencing the outcome of these disputes is rapidly declining.

The periphery. In many parts of the developing world, power and wealth are still linked in ways recognizable to the realists, and the security dilemma is paramount. Military threats from neighbors and internal threats from insurgents continue to threaten the existence of states. Although in historical perspective the conflict in the periphery has been minimal in comparison with that in Europe, interstate conflicts (such as those between Armenia and Azerbaijan, India and Pakistan, Iraq and Kuwait, and Israel and the Arab world) and intrastate wars (such as those in Afghanistan, Angola, Liberia, Peru, and Yugoslavia) will continue to compel leaders in the periphery to seek military power to ensure their rule and preserve the state. Not only can conquering new lands lead to more secure borders, but the addition of population and resources can increase the wealth that supports military power. Iraq's invasion of Kuwait demonstrated that Saddam Hussein discerned a direct relationship between military power and economic gain. Adding the resources of new oil fields would have added to his wealth and thus to his power both in the region and globally.

The convergence of norms among the core states about wealth and power has an effect on the definition of goals in the periphery. Since the world economy is organized and regulated by the core states, peripheral states must accept their rules to participate. Peripheral states that have prospered in the world economy have learned about the capital drains of extensive military budgets and the capital gains of export-led growth. Consequently, a region's military hegemon will not necessarily be the region's economic hegemon. Yet, as long as a regional military hegemon continues to exercise force on occasion, its economically successful neighbors are compelled to expand their military potentials, as Saudi Arabia recently learned. In many regions of the periphery, a relationship, or at least the perception of a relationship, between military power and economic wealth still exists. . . .

The Behavior of States

The core. If the nature of the state and the system as well as the definition of state goals has changed, then the logic of state behavior predicted by realist balance-of-power theory no longer applies. Rather than balancing, core states are seeking to bandwagon, not around a power pole but around a shared set of liberal beliefs, institutions, and practices. Unlike the last multipolar system, the current system offers few incentives for the great powers to engage either in internal or external balancing. . . .

Security is much more easily achieved in an age in which several powers have nuclear weapons than it was in the days when great powers could be conquered. Concerns stemming from international anarchy are therefore less severe now than in the past. A war between great powers simply would be impossible to wage today. Even if Japan and Germany do not build their own nuclear arsenals, they can share the "benefits" of the nuclear world. They cannot contemplate attacks on the five major nuclear powers, but the lack of utility of nuclear weapons (except for deterrence) means that the five nuclear powers will not use nuclear weapons against them either. Mearsheimer argues that "when push comes to shove," traditional security politics rule. But what if push does not come to shove? In that case, a focus on military balancing and alliance formations explains little about the nature of state interaction. . . .

The periphery. The core-periphery divorce accelerated by the end of the U.S.–Soviet rivalry has dramatic military and economic implications. Regarding military matters, the great powers will neither intervene to preserve the security of peripheral states nor constrain the peripheral states from undertaking belligerent actions *unless* core economic interests are threatened. If there is no balancing in the core, there will be no engaging of core states in balancing in the periphery. With the cold war straitjacket removed, wars in the developing world will not be deterred or promoted by the possibility of core state military actions.[14] Rather, core state military engagement in the periphery will be determined primarily by vital interests such as access to oil and strategic mineral supplies and to a lesser extent by special interests of domestic constituents. As in the Iraqi invasion of Kuwait, the absence of true polarity within the core states has removed those international structural constraints which may have inhibited military actions by great powers in the past. But while the great powers will move to protect vital interests, they will not show the same resolve when called upon to protect an African country from invasion or an Asian country from revolution. The relative absence of concern for the civil wars in Liberia, Sudan, and even Ethiopia—the same type of events that only a decade earlier attracted major intervention by great powers—portends a new relationship between the great powers and the regional security systems.

This decoupling of the core state security structure from the peripheral security structures suggests that states in the developing world will have to seek means for enhancing security within their own states or regions. Classic structural realist balance-of-power theory delineates the options available. First, states can devote greater resources both to purchasing weapons and to developing domestic arms production capabilities.[15] The Indian–Pakistani, Israeli–Syrian, and North Korean–South Korean arms races are clear examples of regional balancing by building up domestic arsenals. Not all states, however, have the ability to follow this first course. As a consequence, acquisition of military firepower has not been evenly distributed, and regional hegemons have emerged. To ensure security in these situations, the less militarized states throughout the Third World face the choice of policy options offered by realist theory—that of balancing or bandwagoning. Saddam Hussein's quest for regional hegemony, for example, forced the other Middle Eastern states to act, with Jordon choosing to bandwagon and Egypt, Saudi Arabia, and Syria choosing to balance against the rising threat.

Regarding economic matters, capital and trade flows will circulate within the core, while the periphery will continue to get relatively poorer. Likewise, economic assistance coming from the core will dwindle. The United

States has already reduced its foreign assistance expenditures, while Japan, now the largest aid donor in the world, spends only 0.3 percent of its gross national product on foreign assistance. The assistance that remains available is increasingly devoted to macroeconomic structural adjustment policies and tied to core state export promotion. If peripheral states want to remain linked to the core economies, they will be compelled to accept the terms of North–South trade and investment proposed by the industrialized states and the major international lending institutions.[16]. . .

Conclusion

Pessimists about a future multipolar world rely heavily on the notion that the postwar world has been stable because of bipolarity. . . .

. . . Economic interdependence and political democracy make balance-of-power politics less likely. Nuclear weapons may have induced caution, but they did not stop the United States and Soviet Union from engaging in classic balance-of-power politics. The two superpowers built tremendous arsenals to oppose one another, and they sought allies throughout the globe. They balanced one another—or at least tried to—in places such as Korea, Vietnam, Cuba, Angola, and Afghanistan. Each power feared its ultimate defeat to the other; the United States feared the specter of world communism, while the Soviet Union feared capitalist encirclement.

As the great powers come to share norms about economics and politics, the rationale for building arms and seeking allies among these major states is weakened, and the cost of pursuing these activities is increased. While power may be redistributed among more than just two countries, threats will not be. Unitary actors seeking to survive in an anarchic environment engage in arms races and alliance formation. Nonunitary actors seeking to maximize wealth in a great power society do not.

Technological, political, and economic factors have not changed traditional state relationships in the periphery. The desire of many of the poorer states to move closer to the core in order to reap the economic benefits may induce cooperation rather than conflict. But the traditional linkages between wealth and military power in the periphery, the concern with achieving state sovereignty against internal and external military threats, and the continued disputes over territorial boundaries will all be forces for old-style power politics among the smaller regional powers. In the periphery, as in the core, the likelihood of war will be lower in those regions which enjoy both greater economic interdependence and more political democracy.

NOTES

1. We define a "great power" as a country possessing the will and the capability to alter events throughout the international system. For more on the debate about whether a bipolar or multipolar world is more stable, see Kenneth N. Walta, *Theory of International Politics* (Reading, MA: Addison-Wesley, 1979); Richard Rosecrance,

"Bipolarity, Multipolarity and the Future," *Journal of Conflict Resolution* 10 (September 1966): 314–327; Karl Deutsch and J. David Singer, "Multipolar Power Systems and International Stability," *World Politics* 16 (April 1964): 390–406; and John Lewis Gaddis, "The Long Peace: Elements of Stability in the Postwar International System," *International Security* 10 (Spring 1986): 99–142.

2. See, for example, Thomas J. Christensen and Jack Snyder, "Chain Gangs and Passed Bucks: Predicting Alliance Patterns in Multipolarity," *International Organization* 44 (Spring 1990): 137–168; and John J. Mearsheimer, "Back to the Future: Instability in Europe After the Cold War," *International Security* 15 (Summer 1990): 5–56. In other articles, Snyder focuses more heavily on domestic institutions and the internal and external factors that influence them. See, for example, Jack Snyder, "Averting Anarchy in the New Europe," *International Security* 14 (Spring 1990): 5–41.

3. The term "great power society" is derived from the conception of "international society" in Hedley Bull's *The Anarchical Society: A Study of Order in World Politics* (London: Macmillan, 1977), pp. 12–14. In an international society, state interaction is influenced by a set of shared norms about permissible and impermissible behavior. These norms provide a basis for order that is absent in an anarchical environment. Our modification simply stresses that the conditions of an international society outlined by Bull are present within the core states but are not extended throughout the world. . . .

4. See Robert O. Keohane, *After Hegemony: Cooperation and Discord in the World Political Economy* (Princeton, NJ: Princeton University Press, 1984), p. 253.

5. See Raymond Vernon, "Japan, the United States, and the Global Economy," *Washington Quarterly* 13 (Summer 1990): 57–68; and Donald Puchala, "The Pangs of Atlantic Interdependence," in *The United States and the European Community: Convergence or Conflict?* ed. H. M. Belien (The Hague: Nijgh & Van Ditmar Universitair, 1989): pp.131–146. For an alternative argument examining how states can regulate foreign investment and do have the power to conduct a national economic strategy, see Simon Reich, "Roads to Follow: Regulating Direct Foreign Investment," *International Organization* 43 (Autumn 1989): 543–584.

6. For recent brief reports, see "The Myth of Economic Sovereignty," *The Economist*, June 23, 1990, p. 67; and "Business Without Borders," *U.S. News and World Report*, July 16, 1990, pp. 29–31. For a scholarly analysis, see Helen Milner, "Trading Places: Industries for Free Trade," *World Politics* 40 (April 1988): 350–376.

7. On the problems of defining anarchy and its effects, see Robert Axelrod and Robert O. Keohane, "Achieving Cooperation Under Anarchy: Strategies and Institutions," in *Cooperation Under Anarchy*, ed. Kenneth Oye, (Princeton, NJ: Princeton University Press, 1986), pp. 226–254.

8. For an analysis of how nuclear weapons affect the structure of the international system, see Steve Weber, "Realism, Detente, and Nuclear Weapons," *International Organization* 44 (Winter 1990): 55–82.

9. See Stephen Krasner, ed., *International Regimes* (Ithaca, NY: Cornell University Press, 1983); Keohane, *After Hegemony;* and Keohane and Nye's discussion of "processes" in Robert O. Keohane and Joseph S. Nye, Jr., "Power and Interdependence Revisited," *International Organization* 41 (Autumn 1987): 725–753.

10. Bull, *The Anarchical Society*, pp. 243–248; Stanley Kober, "Idealpolitik," *Foreign Policy* 79 (Summer 1990): 13–18; and Immanuel Kant, *Perpetual Peace* (1796) (Los Angeles: U.S. Library Association, 1932); Michael Doyle, "Liberalism and World Politics," *American Political Science Review* 80 (December 1986): 1151–1169; Michael Doyle, "Kant, Liberal Legacies, and Foreign Affairs" (2 parts), *Philosophy and Public Affairs* 12 (1983): 204–235 and 323–353.

11. On sovereignty in the Third World, see Robert H. Jackson and Carl G. Rosberg, "Why Africa's Weak States Persist: The Empirical and the Juridical in Statehood," *World Politics* 35 (October 1982): 1–24; Stephen Krasner, *Structural Conflict: The Third World Against Global Liberalism* (Berkeley: University of California Press, 1985); and Jeffrey Herbst, "War and the State in Africa," *International Security* 14 (Spring 1990): 117–139.

12. This definition is in Robert Gilpin's, *War and Change in World Politics* (Cambridge: Cambridge University Press, 1981), p. 131. Similarly, Carr asserted that "every act

of the state, in its power aspects, is directed to war." See E. H. Carr, *The Twenty Years Crisis, 1919–1939* (London: Macmillan, 1940), p. 139.

13. Regarding economic hegemony, see Keohane, *After Hegemony*, pp. 135–181; Robert Gilpin, *The Political Economy of International Relations* (Princeton, NJ: Princeton University Press, 1987); and Stephen Krasner, "State Power and the Structure of International Trade," *World Politics* 28 (April 1976): 317–347. Regarding military prowess, see John Lewis Gaddis, *Strategies of Containment: A Critical Appraisal of Postwar American National Security Policy* (Oxford: Oxford University Press, 1982).

14. Jose Thiago Cintra, *Regional Conflicts: Trends in a Period of Transition* (London: Institute for International Strategic Studies, Spring 1989), pp. 94–108.

15. For a discussion of these capabilities, see Andrew L. Ross, "World Order and Third World Arms Production," in *The Implications of Third World Military Industrialization: Sowing the Serpents' Teeth*, ed. James Everett Katz (Lexington, MA: Lexington Books, 1986), pp. 277–292.

16. See Krasner, *Structural Conflict;* and Keohane, *After Hegemony*, p. 253.

Ethnic Conflicts
and Their Impact
on International Society

Rodolfo Stavenhagen

The Persistence of Ethnic Conflicts

A survey on states in armed conflicted in 1988 reports that of a total of 111 such conflicts in the world, 63 were internal and 36 were described by the authors as "wars of state formation", that is, conflicts involving one government and an opposition group demanding autonomy or secession for a particular ethnic or region.[1] In fact, in recent years, the number of classic inter-state wars has been decreasing and the number of intra-state conflicts, particularly in Third World countries, increasing. Another report tells us that "state-sponsored massacres of members of ethnic and political groups are responsible for greater loss of life than all other forms of deadly conflict combined. . . . On average, between 1.6 and 3.9 million unarmed civilians have died at the hand of the state in each decade since the end of World War II. . . ."[2]

Despite such evidence, relatively little attention has been paid over the years to ethnic conflicts by specialists of peace and conflict research and of international relations.[3] More attention has been given to inter-state confrontations of the traditional type. . . .

Reprinted from *International Social Science Journal* no. 127 (1991), pp. 117–32.

Types of Ethnic Groups in Conflict

In order to place ethnic conflicts into proper perspective, it may be useful briefly to refer to different kinds of situation in which ethnic groups interact within a wider framework. But even before this, it will be necessary to provide a minimum working definition of ethnic groups, because the term is used rather loosely in the literature and there is no general consensus regarding this concept.[4] For brevity's sake, an ethnic group or ethnic is a collectivity which identifies itself and is identified by others according to ethnic criteria, that is, in terms of certain common elements such as language, religion, tribe, nationality or race, or a combination thereof, and which shares a common feeling of identity with other members of the group. True, such a definition raises more questions than it answers, but it may serve a useful purpose in introducing the rest of this article.

Ethnic groups so defined may also be considered as peoples, nations, nationalities, minorities, tribes or communities, according to different contexts and circumstances. Frequently, ethnic groups are identified in terms of their relationships with similar groups and with the state. In fact, many ethnic conflicts in the world result from problems arising out of changes in the position of an ethnic group within the wider society. Let us identify a number of different kinds of situations which are common around the world:

(a) Ethnic groups within a state which identifies itself as being multi-ethnic or multi-national. Such groups may base their identity on language (as in Belgium and Switzerland), religion (as do Sikhs, Muslims and Hindus in India; Christians and Muslims in Lebanon), nationality (as in the Soviet Union) or race (South Africa). In such cases, ethnic groups which are different from the dominant or majority nationality may or may not enjoy special legal status, and they are usually in a minority and non-dominant position.

(b) Ethnic groups within a state which does not formally recognize its own multi-ethnic composition, such as France, Japan, Indonesia, Turkey, Portugal and numerous African countries. Here minorities may be regionally based such as Bretons and Corsicans in France, or Scots and Welsh in Britain; or they may be racial (as Blacks in the United States), religious (as the Copts in Egypt or the Baha'i in Iran), linguistic (as the Berbers in Algeria), or tribal (as in Afghanistan); or a combination of several of these elements.

(c) National minorities which identify with their ethnic kin in a neighbouring state in which they may have majority status (such as the Hungarians in Rumania, the Turks in Bulgaria, the Albanians in Yugoslavia, the Chicanos in the United States).

(d) Multiple ethnic groups within a state in which none enjoys a particularly dominant position, specifically in recently independent, formerly colonial countries, in which the state itself is a relatively weak, artificial construct; this situation tends to prevail in Africa south of the Sahara.

(e) Ethnic minorities which straddle international boundaries and with minority status in each one of the countries, as in the frontier areas in

Southeast Asia, the Basques in Spain and France, and the Kurds in the Middle East.

(f) Ethnic immigrants and refugees resulting from extensive migrations, particularly from the Third World countries into other Third World countries or into industrialized nations. Whereas in earlier centuries European settlers colonized numerous areas around the world, and their descendants constitute ethnic groups in many countries (sometimes as minorities, or else as majorities), in recent decades migratory flows have turned around the Third World immigrants are now settling their former metropolises, constituting ethnic enclaves in numerous countries and giving rise to serious social and cultural problems.

(g) Indigenous and tribal peoples constitute a special case of ethnic groups, generally being regarded as minorities, because of the historical circumstances of their conquest and incorporation into new state structures as well as their attachment to their land and territory and their secular resistance to genocide, ethnocide and assimilation. Indigenous peoples are found mainly in the Americas, Australia and New Zealand, but numerous south and southeast Asian tribal peoples are nowadays also considered as indigenous, as well as the Inuit and Sami in the far north.[5]

This schematic classification does not exhaust all possibilities of situations in which ethnic groups interact, and there may be overlapping between the categories. It is, however, a useful device to identify situations in which ethnic conflicts tend to occur.

The Internationalization of Ethnic Conflicts

At first glance, most contemporary ethnic conflicts appear to be mainly internal matters of nation-states. Ethnic groups confront each other within the framework of an existing society; or else an ethnic struggles over rights and power with a central government; state policies may be questioned and perhaps altered; the legal position or status of an ethnic minority may be modified. To the extent that the modern international system is based on the principle of state sovereignty, such internal matters are conveniently kept outside the concerns of the international community. This may be the ideal situation to which contemporary spokesmen adhere, but in fact ethnic conflicts and the situation of ethnic minorities have long had international implications, and they still do so today. . . .

Ethnic Kin Abroad

There may be a number of reasons why an ethnic conflict spills over national boundaries and involves outside actors. A common occurrence is that an ethnic group in conflict has ethnic affenes or kin in other countries. Thus, the Sri Lankan Tamils, the Kurds, the Basques, the Sikhs, the Miskitos, the

Ulster Catholics, the Turks in Cyprus and Bulgaria, the Albanians in Yugoslavia, the Hungarians in Rumania, among others, have ethnic kin groups in other, generally but not always, neighbouring countries where they seek and often obtain political and material support. The Tamil insurgency finds support in Tamilnadu across the Palk strait; militant Basques in southern Euzkadi find refuge in the Pays Basque in France and so do members of the IRA in the Republic of Ireland. Sikh communities in Britain and Canada support the struggle of the Sikhs in the Punjab. Kurdish nationalist militants in Iran, Iraq, Turkey and Syria have found support in neighbouring countries according to the unstable and moving circumstances of Middle Eastern politics. Miskito refugees from Nicaragua were harboured by the Miskito communities in neighbouring Honduras before returning home as circumstances changed. Thus ethnic kin abroad may be a potent factor in the evolution of an apparently purely domestic ethnic conflict.

A *caveat* is in order here. The idea of an ethnic conflict being a purely internal or domestic matter of states is simply one more statist myth. In fact, if an ethnic group is involved in a conflict, it is quite logical that in terms not of a fictitious *raison d'état*, but also of a, perhaps equally fictitious, *raison d'ethnie*, ethnic kin, no matter where, should provide support to their ethnic affenes regardless of international borders or the question of state sovereignty. This is obviously a controversial issue, because what may seem logical to the members of an ethnie is deemed highly dangerous and subversive by states. A case in point: when the conflict between the Miskitos and the revolutionary Nicaraguan government was at its height, a number of international indigenous organizations suggested that the indigenous had the responsibility to come to the aid of their embattled brethren. Of course, the Nicaraguan government, which at that time was itself the victim of external intervention, considered this posture to be a clear invitation for further interference into its sovereign affairs. Most governments react in similar fashion and often attempt to downplay the local causes of an ethnic conflict by attributing it simply to foreign interference in its internal affairs.

Outside Ideological Support

There may be other reasons for external participation in an ethnic conflict. The most common element has to do with the ideological sympathies that one of the parties in the conflict may command amongst outside actors, and these in turn may see in an ethnic conflict an opportunity to extend their influence and strengthen their ideology. Much has been written about the involvement of Ghadafi's Libya in a number of such conflicts: its support for extremist nationalist movements such as ETA and the IRA, and the role it has played in supporting the Moro rebellion in the Philippines and then arranging for negotiations between the Moro leadership and the Phillipine government. Leftist movements in the 1970s and 1980s supported "national liberation movements" in various parts of the world. Conservative groups, in

turn, provided moral and sometimes material support to embattled governments of similar ideological persuasion trying to cope with ethnic uprisings.

Concerned Neighbours

Some foreign interventions have nothing to do with ethnicity or ideology, but
simply with geopolitics. Neighbouring countries can easily be drawn into an
ethnic conflict for their own political reasons of state. Thus, for example,
both Iran and Iraq have given support to the Kurds fighting against the state
in the neighbouring country, and yet have been accused of repressing the
Kurds in their own territories. India has accused Pakistan of abetting the
extremist Sikh nationalist movement in the Punjab as well as the Kashmir
Muslim uprising for geopolitical reasons of its own. And the government of
India, in turn, has been accused of doing similar mischief in both Sri Lanka
and Tibet.

Involved Superpowers

Finally, superpower involvement has increased, as ethnic conflicts multiplied
around the world. The Soviet Union, for its own political interests, has intervened in the ethnic conflict in Ethiopia, first supporting one side, and then
the other, with little regard for either ideology or ethnicity. The United States
has systematically supported the Christians in Lebanon, the Miskitos against
the Sandinista government of Nicaragua, the Sri Lankan government against
the Tamil insurrection, the Philippine government against the Moros and the
tribal uprisings, the Ovambos against the Angolan government, and the
Hmong against the Vietnamese government, among others. In early 1990,
the Soviet Union's three Baltic republics declared their independence unilaterally and received sympathetic understanding in the West, from the very
sources which would not countenance the independence of the Basques, the
Northern Irish, the Quebecois or Puerto Rico.

The Burden of History

A number of ethnic/nationalist movements today are carry-overs from earlier
periods of state-formation and empire-building and as such carry with them
the international implications of these processes. Currently, the Baltic republics in the Soviet Union express anew a long suppressed nationalist tendency
and question the secret agreements between Stalin and Hitler which allowed
the Soviet Union to annex the three independent Baltic states in 1940. The
Puerto Rico independence movement still rejects the island's incorporation
into the United States as a result of the 1898 Spanish-American war. Several
ethnic groups in India, who would have opted for independence if they had
had an opportunity to do so, reject the way the formation of the Indian state

impinged upon their own sovereignty (Sikkim, tribal peoples of Bihar and Assam). A similar case can be made for the Karen and Shan in Burma, as well as East Timor and West Papua, which are now a part of Indonesia. The conflicts in Western Sahara and Cyprus have a similar origin. Some of these cases have been dealt with by the United Nations in its specialized organs, particularly when the issue of "self-determination of peoples" is involved. But in general, the United Nations tends to favour the respect of state sovereignty over its sympathy for the self-determination of non-state peoples, except in some cases of flagrant decolonization, such as Namibia.

The Changing Ethno-Demographic Balance

When ethnic conflicts arise as a result of migrations and the changing demographic equilibrium of certain countries, then the "home country" of the migrants may express some concern at the international or bilateral level for the well-being of its offspring. Thus, India expresses interest in the fate of Indians in East Africa or the Pacific (Uganda, Fiji). China casts a paternal eye over millions of overseas Chinese in Southeast Asia and elsewhere. Turkey and Algeria, among others, sign agreements with Western European governments concerning the situation of their migrant workers in the latter countries.

Direct Intervention

The Indo–Sri Lankan Accord of 1987 is one recent example of direct formal intervention by a regional power in a domestic ethnic conflict. Several precedents made this intervention almost inevitable, as mentioned before. Furthermore, as an increasingly assertive regional power, India was worried about the geopolitical implications of instability on its southern flank. India had offered its good offices to mediate, with little success, between the Tamil insurgents and the Sri Lankan government. By the terms of the Indo–Sri Lankan Accord of 1987, Indian troops were to disarm the Tamil guerrillas, and the Sri Lankan government would recognize certain of the legitimate demands of the Tamil movement. In fact, however, Indian troops helped to repress several of the Tamil factions, at great cost of human lives, and were seen in Sri Lanka, by both Tamils and Sinhalese, as a new occupation force. In 1990, the Indians withdrew. In the Sri Lankan example, outside intervention followed an almost predictable pattern. At first India discreetly sympathized with one of the parties in conflict (the Tamils), then it tried its hand at mediation; subsequently it intervened militarily as 'pacifier', with a restricted mandate; thereafter it was accused of trying to impose its own *Diktat* on the parties in conflict, and finally it was rejected by all parties concerned.

The Ethnicization of International Relations

In Sri Lanka, as in the case of Euzkadi, Ulster, Cyprus and many others, it might be said that an internal ethnic conflict 'spilled over' into the international arena and became internationalized. However, it often happens that international relations between states become 'ethnicized' when potential or actual ethnic conflict occurs. Some countries' foreign policies are clearly inspired by ethnic sympathies or considerations. It is unnecessary to recall the aggressive use Nazi Germany made of ethnic Germans abroad in preparation of the Second World War. Colonial powers, up to very recently, used to couch their colonial designs in terms of racial supremacist theories. Whenever there are 'white' victims in some political disturbance in a Third World country, Western governments and public opinion are particularly concerned, and little attention is paid to the more numerous local victims. US foreign policy, in particular, is especially sensitive to the desires of American interest groups who lobby Congress and the White House. Thus, though the American government's interests lie with the white supremacist South African regime, it cannot ignore the pressures of the Afro-American community against apartheid, expressed, among others, through public demands for economic sanctions against South Africa. One of the reasons for America's continued support for Israel is the strength of the Jewish-American lobby on Capitol Hill. Arab-Americans are just beginning to understand the importance of such activity in order to express their own support for the arab cause. US support for Poland over the years was as much a function of anti-Soviet ideology as of the pressures of the Polish community in the United States.[6]

Public Opinion, NGOs and Ethnic Conflicts

The internationalization of ethnic conflict has other aspects besides the direct or indirect intervention of neighbouring states or superpowers. World public opinion, particularly in the West, can be swayed by the use of the mass media. Let us simply recall the media-wide coverage which the Palestinian *Intifadah* and the Black resistance in South Africa received for a time, till Israel and the South African governments, respectively, imposed severe restrictions on such coverage. Almost overnight, world public concern dropped. The Palestinians and the Shiites in Lebanon, among others, have learned how to make use of the power of the international media in order to make an impact on, or garner the sympathy of (the two being of course not always identical), world public opinion.

To the extent that so many ethnic conflicts today occur in the Third World, numerous nongovernmental organizations and voluntary agencies who work in Third World countries sometimes play a role in international involvement. They may become external advocates of the cause of some ethnic group in conflict. The Kurds, the Miskitos, the Tamils, the East-Timorese, the South African Blacks and others can count on the support and sympathy of numerous such organizations which operate out of Western Europe and North America, and which not only provide external publicity to the ethnic group's cause, but also channel resources and all sorts of aid to such groups. Donor agencies from the industrialized world play an increasingly important role in the development projects of many underdeveloped countries. While some of the aid goes directly to local projects and helps people at the grassroots level, very often it is channelled through local government agencies. Ethnic groups in conflict with a state frequently complain that such aid does not reach them, or is withheld from them and actually reinforces the power of the state. Under such circumstances, donor agencies may threaten to withdraw or withhold their contributions to a certain country, thus attempting to influence the behaviour of a government in relation to such a conflict. Examples are the pressures put on the Sri Lankan government by numerous donor agencies to change its policies *vis-à-vis* the Tamils. Similar pressures were exerted upon the Sudanese government in relation with the conflict in southern Sudan or Ethiopia as regards the conflict in Tigre and Eritrea. Governments, of course, react negatively to such policies, considering them to be undue interference in their internal affairs.

The United Nations

Another significant and potentially more effective form of international concern is being expressed through the United Nations system. While the UN is scrupulously respectful of the sovereignty of states, in principle it can become involved in ethnic conflicts (as in other kinds of internal conflict) under three distinct mandates: (a) when a conflict represents a clear danger to the maintenance of peace, (b) when it is a problem of decolonization, and (c) when it involves serious human rights violations. The UN has undertaken peace-keeping missions in some ethnic conflicts (Lebanon, Cyprus), but only when the conflict had already become internationalized and an external country had intervened. In terms of the United Nations' role in the process of decolonization, the General Assembly has adopted numerous resolutions regarding the right of self-determination of peoples, but these have not always been heeded by the states which exercise power over the territory and people concerned. Cases in point are Western Sahara and East Timor. . . .

Consequences of Internationalization

The internationalization of ethnic conflicts may have different kinds of consequences for the conflict itself. One scholar distinguishes five patterns:

(a) the exacerbation of the conflict through foreign intervention;
(b) the prolongation of the conflict as the result of the intervention of outside interests;
(c) the moderation of conflict because of international concern and pressures;

(d) conciliation of the parties to a conflict due to the mediation or intervention of an outside party;

(e) supercession of the conflict, in other words, the ethnic conflict may be superseded by the non-ethnic and particular interests of outside parties and turn into another kind of conflict altogether.[7]

Conclusions

The study of the internationalization of ethnic conflicts and the ethnicization of international relations is just beginning. Social science and international theory have as yet made few contributions to this emerging field. The world importance of ethnic conflicts can no longer be denied or neglected. As the major ideological conflicts of the twentieth century fade into the background, conflicts of identity and values, that is, protracted ethnic conflicts, will surely become more salient and more virulent. New forms of conflict management and resolution must be found. Ethnically defined non-state peoples are becoming new international actors as the traditional functions of the state become transformed. Third parties (whether states or nongovernmental organizations become involved in the ethnic conflicts. The international community, and particularly the regional and universal multilateral organizations, must rise to meet the challenge posed by ethnic groups in conflict.

NOTES

1. Peter Wallensteen, ed., *States in Armed Conflict 1988* (Upsala: Upsala University, Department of Peace and Conflict Research, July 1989), Report No. 30.

2. Barbara Harff and Ted Robert Gurr, "Genocides and Politicides Since 1945: Evidence and Anticipation", *Internet on the Holocaust and Genocide*, Jerusalem: Institute of the International Conference on the Holocaust and Genocide, Special Issue 13 (December 1987).

3. Kumar Rupesinghe, "Theories of Conflict Resolution and Their Applicability to Protracted Ethnic Conflicts", in *Ethnic Conflicts and Human Rights*, ed. Kumar Rupesinghe (Oslo: The United Nations University and Norwegian University Press, 1988); also Michael Banks, "The International Relations Discipline: Asset or Liability for Conflict Resolution?" in *International Conflict Resolution, Theory and Practice*, ed. Edward E. Azar and John W. Burton (Sussex: Wheatsheaf Books, 1986).

4. A useful tool in ethnicity research is Fred W. Riggs, ed., *Ethnicity, Intercocta Glossary, Concepts and Terms used in Ethnicity Research*, International Conceptual Encyclopedia for the Social Sciences, Volume 1 (Honolulu: International Social Science Council, 1985).

5. On indigenous peoples, see Independent Commission on International Humanitarian Issues, *Indigenous Peoples, A Global Quest for Justice* (London: Zed Books, 1987).

6. Kenneth Longmyer, "Black American Demands," and Daud J. Sadd and G. N. Lendermann, "Arab American Grievances," *Foreign Policy*, no. 60 (Fall 1985), special section on "New Ethnic Voices."

7. Ralph R. Premdas, "The Internationalization of Ethnic Conflict: Theoretical Explorations." Paper presented to the ICES International Workshop on Internatalization of Ethnic Conflict, 2–4 August, 1989, Colombo, Sri Lanka.

Chapter 7

International Law and Organization

The formulation of international law and the establishment of international organizations are two of the most prominent ways in which policymakers have sought to ameliorate the conflictual and competitive tendencies of world politics. International law consists of a series of rights and duties which taken together constitute a code of conduct for states. Whereas international law starts from the premise of sovereign states acting independently in the pursuit of their foreign-policy goals, international organizations assume the need for joint action. But rather then rely on informal consultation or ad hoc decision-making procedures to produce the needed action, states have made an effort to institutionalize cooperative behavior through international organizations.

At their core, international law and international organizations represent reformist approaches to the problems of managing international relations. Their purpose is not to replace the existing international system with a more visionary one but to make it work better. Modest though this objective may at first seem, it is not one that has been easily achieved. As a result, international law and international organizations frequently find themselves under attack by both conservative and radical critics. Conservatives point to their failures as sufficient proof of why states should not put much confidence in their ability to further national interests. Radicals cite these same failures as evidence of the need to move beyond reformist approaches and to embrace more far-reaching ones that hold the promise of restructuring world politics.

Although international law and international organizations try to serve as a counterweight to the anarchic properties of world politics in different ways, their efforts are rooted in a similar logic. First, both seek to encourage cooperation by clarifying rules, norms, and principles so that policymakers can more readily see what type of behavior is expected of states. Second, both seek to encourage desired forms of behavior by attaching costs to actions that violate international standards. Third, both serve to increase the sense of community that exists among states by providing forums for the exchange of ideas and the identification of common interests. When successful, the net result of these efforts is an increase in the confidence of policymakers that other states will act in a predictable and cooperative way. This belief, in turn, encourages policymakers to reciprocate with equally predictable and cooperative behavior of their own.

Any projection of the role of international law and international organization into the twenty-first century must take into account the four sets of issues that follow. There is no correct choice for any of these alternatives; each approach has its strengths and weaknesses. But choices have to be made either by default or by design, and the choices made will set the parameters within which international law and international organization will operate in the twenty-first century.

Setting International Norms

The first issue involves a determination of the proper role of international law and international organizations in setting global norms. One possibility is that they should be in the forefront of efforts to create a global consensus on furthering such values as human rights, environmental protection, disarmament, or economic well-being. Alternatively, they might best be seen as mechanisms for codifying an international consensus on an issue only after it has been reached.

Uncertainty over which role international organizations are best suited to play can be seen in the differing approaches to integration theory. The three most prominent strategies for bringing about regional integration are federalism, functionalism, and neofunctionalism. From a federalist perspective, the proper way to achieve attitudinal change among policy-making elites and the population at large is first to create political institutions whose legal and bureaucratic reach extends across national boundaries. Functionalists believe that the only way to achieve integration is through a process of technical self-determination. Unlike the federalists, seen as simply attempting to replace current states with larger ones, the functionalists' goal is to make the state irrelevant. The key is to allow transnational boundary-crossing efforts to evolve spontaneously in those areas where cooperation is necessary for policy success. A value consensus on such matters as human rights and protecting the environment will evolve naturally. Neofunctionalism occupies a middle ground between these two positions. Although it is skeptical of federalism's ultimate aims, it is also uncomfortable with the functionalist belief that integration will evolve on its own. Neofunctionalists assert the need for an engineering approach whereby policy areas with high integrative potential are structured in such a way as to stimulate and sustain the integration process.

Controversy over the intellectual roots of international law virtually guarantees disagreement over whether it should follow or lead in forging a global value consensus. The two most frequently held starting points are natural law and positivist traditions. The former holds that a universal and unchanging set of laws governs human relationships and provides a standard for judging the behavior of states. The positivist position maintains that international law does not stem from a set of underlying moral principles but consists only of those points that states have agreed to abide by. In concrete terms, whereas natural-law scholars are willing to embrace international customs and traditions as a source of international law, positivists hold that only treaties and agreements freely entered into can provide a basis for it.

These uncertain intellectual roots plus the complexity of world politics produce gaps in the coverage of international law. One of the most important involves the place of the individual. Historically, international law sought to govern the relations between states. With the growth of international organizations in the post–World War II period, international law was broadened to bring them under its reach. Although this extension was relatively noncontroversial (in large part because states are members of and control international organizations), the further extension of international law to cover individuals has generated far more debate.

One type of "individual" that has sought standing in international law is multinational corporations. Because their existence was not formally recognized by international law, their only method of protesting unfair treatment by a government was through their home country. Corporations found that depending on governments to protect them from the actions of other governments was both time-consuming and often unsatisfying. Thus they have sought the right to represent themselves at arbitration hearings and other international legal forums.

The increased attention on human rights also raises the question of individual standing in international law. Bringing an end to torture and other gross abuses of human rights is only one part of the problem. Additional problems are found in such areas as large-scale refugee flows, protection of indigenous people, and population control efforts. As with corporations, the issue here is not just content coverage but standing. Can an individual bring suit against a state in an international court of law? In the European Court of Human Rights, for example, technically speaking the litigants are a state and the European Commission of Human Rights.

Regionalism Versus Globalism

The second issue involves a choice between regionalism and globalism, that is, determining the proper scope of international law and international organizations. Should they aspire to be global in their coverage, or is the world community better served by stressing regional laws and organizations?

Although its name suggests otherwise, modern international law is not international in the sense of representing a blending of moral and ethical traditions from around the world. Its base is European law, and it became international with the global spread of European military and economic power. The

European character endured even when European military and economic power receded for two reasons. First, it was replaced by American and Soviet power. Although both of these states have traditionally seen themselves as culturally distinct from Europe, they have also been heavily influenced by its intellectual traditions. Second, the cold war competition between the United States and the Soviet Union inhibited the expression of local or regional interpretations on the proper nature of international law. As the ability of the two states to project their power globally declined and the cold war ended, the grip of European values on international law has weakened. The situation would now seem ripe for the development of a truly "international" law.

But how is this to be done? Not only are Western values often different from those held elsewhere in the world, but feminist analysts point out that even the European heritage of international law represents a very limited and biased reading of the Western experience. That is, it rests on the gender-based distinction between public life and private life, a distinction that condemns women to subordinate status. In human rights, feminist critics point out that international law makes at least two unwarranted assumptions. First, it assumes that women's rights can be protected simply by extending legal coverage. As Hilary Charlesworth, Christine Chinkin, and Shelley Wright point out, protecting women's rights also often requires the extension of social, economic, and cultural rights. Second, international law assumes that human rights legislation affects men and women equally, which is not necessarily the case. Protecting communal or group rights may have the effect of harming women or denying them individual rights if the group they are part of—the group or community whose rights are being protected—discriminates against women.

The dilemma of choosing between regionalism and globalism also confronts architects of international organizations. On one level the coexistence of regional and international organizations does not present as many problems as it does for international law. Membership in international organizations is voluntary, and it can therefore be assumed that states joining an international organization are willing to abide by its laws. Moreover, since like-minded states tend to join together more often than do ideologically incompatible ones, most international organizations should be relatively free of value conflict.

The crux of the problem lies in two areas. First, just as with states under international law, ultimately regional international organizations will come into conflict with one another or their jurisdictions will cross with those of a global organization. For example, the post–World War II international trading system was based on the principle of free trade and operated under the loose guidance of the General Agreement on Tariffs and Trade (GATT). To hasten European economic recovery and to lessen the appeal of communism, GATT permitted European states to practice protectionism and encouraged the formation of the Common Market. Now, however, the very strength of European Community (EC) economic institutions is one of the major threats to free trade and a prime building block of exclusive regional trading zones. Rather then being complementary institutions, the EC and GATT appear to be locked in a zero-sum game, whereby the stronger one becomes stronger and the other becomes progressively weaker. Similarly, the prolonged indecision or unwillingness of NATO, the United

Nations, or the EC to take military action to end the Yugoslavian civil war points to the potential problems inherent in regional and global organizations with overlapping jurisdictions.

The second problem is uncertainty over the proper end point for integration efforts, regardless of which of the three integration theories is being championed. For the federalist, when does one stop trying to create a larger state? Does one end with a United States of Europe, or is the only true ending place a single world government? Defining a United States of Europe as the end point of European integration only raises another set of questions. What are the boundaries of Europe? Most are probably willing to acknowledge that the states that were once part of Communist East Europe should be included, but what about Kazakstan, Armenia, Georgia, or other parts of the former Soviet Union?

Because neofunctionalist and functionalist strategies for integration seek to make the state irrelevant, they do not have to answer these questions. The problems they face are somewhat different. The key to success lies in generating a momentum for integration that reaches out to incorporate more and more sectors. Neofunctionalists and functionalists constantly must address questions of which sectors to integrate next and how to keep the momentum going. The perceived need to expand inevitably brings them into conflict with other organizations, as is evident in the EC's interest in acquiring a military arm (bringing it into potential conflict with NATO), setting environmental standards (where it has moved ahead of agreed-on minimum standards in the Montreal Protocol), and setting monetary policy (where its policies have run counter to those of the International Monetary Fund).

Informal Versus Formal

A third choice in designing international law and organizations concerns highly formalized structures versus informal arrangements periodic meetings, and understandings. The debate over how best to proceed in organizing environmental conferences illustrates the two basic options available. The first option replicates the strategy used in the Law of the Sea Conference. At its core lies the negotiation of a comprehensive agreement covering all aspects of the problem, which then must be accepted as a package deal. The second option is based on efforts to regulate the use of chlorofluorocarbons (CFCs). It involves a set-by-step approach whereby a general framework is agreed on and then a series of separate protocols are negotiated for various problems. Another key part of this strategy is that significant modifications of the agreement can take place over time without reratification.

Dissatisfaction with both the pace of the Law of the Sea negotiations (more then twelve years) and the results (the United States refused to sign the treaty) led policymakers to embrace the framework/protocol model. The successful conclusion of a conference on protecting the ozone layer in Montreal in 1987 plus the strengthening of that agreement in the 1990 London Revisions to the Montreal Protocol have sparked further interest in this approach.

However, James Sebenius warns that too much might have been read into the success of the CFC negotiations. Before the start of the comprehensive

Law of the Sea conference there had been two smaller conferences, both of which failed to produce agreements on protecting the ocean's resources or defining international boundaries. Each conference was organized around the idea of producing agreements in specific and limited areas. Thus, it was the failure of the framework/protocol approach that led to the organization of a comprehensive conference.

Sebenius goes on to note that international negotiations over unsettled environmental issues, such as those relating to climatic change (the greenhouse effect) will be even more complex then those conducted at either the CFC or Law of the Sea talks. It may well be necessary to make trade-offs between issues if an agreement is to be reached, and the existence of a single, comprehensive package makes it easier for policymakers to negotiate and sell the trade-offs to their domestic constituencies than does a series of single-issue agreements. Single-issue agreements tend to produce a scoreboard mentality, in which each country counts an agreement as a win or a loss.

Finally, we should remember that the adoption of a framework/protocol strategy does not guarantee the speedy drafting of international laws to protect the environment or the quick establishment of international organizations to deal with environmental problems. It took over five years to negotiate the Montreal Protocols on CFCs—actually, ten years if one dates the beginning of the process to the United Nation's 1977 Action Plan to Protect the Ozone Layer.

Concern over the length of time that it takes to negotiate international agreements and set up international organizations has led some to call for abandoning this strategy completely. In its place they want a greater reliance on informal agreements and unilateral national action. The possibility of pursuing such an alternative strategy was brought into focus by the rate at which unilateral U.S. and Soviet military reductions outpaced efforts to write minimum figures into treaties. Advocates of this approach argue that the resulting "agreements" will be far more responsive to changes in international conditions, policy priorities, and technology.

A strategy of solving global problems by unilateral national action and informal agreements has its drawbacks. James Goodby notes that one of the advantages of formal agreements is their ability to serve as a buffer or restraining force at those times when national policymakers are inclined to take action that would violate the terms of an agreement. He also notes that signing a treaty is not the end of the arms-control process. As with any international agreement, differences of interpretation will arise, as will issues that were not addressed in the agreement. Formally negotiated agreements can provide mechanisms for dealing with such disputes and keep them from becoming major points of controversy.

Solution or Problem

Supporters of international law and organization take it as all but a given that "more" is better, that the more international laws and the more international organizations there are the better off the global community will be. But is this necessarily true? Might international law and international organizations be part of the problem of managing world politics rather then a solution to it?

Giulio Gallarotti recognizes that poorly constructed international organizations can have harmful effects, but he also suggests that excessive amounts of "good" international organizations can have a destabilizing effect on international relations, for example, when international organizations try to manage tightly coupled systems. This problem is essentially an engineering or technical one and comes about because policymakers act without a full understanding of the problem they are dealing with. He cites as a good example, efforts by the Group of 7 (United States, France, Italy, Germany, Japan, Great Britain, and Canada) to manage international exchange rates by adopting a plan in 1987 to strengthen the position of the U.S. dollar. However, because international money markets interpreted the move as a sign of the dollar's continued weakness rather than a sign of growing strength, it had the opposite effect and the value of the dollar fell.

Three other negative consequences from the activities of good international organizations are political in nature. First, these organizations can become what Gallarotti describes as a "source of moral hazard." That is, by mitigating the negative effects of irresponsible state behavior, international organizations reduce the incentives for states to change their counterproductive acts. For example, a resource-sharing arrangement through the International Energy Agency allows states to continue to waste energy resources because they know they can get help, and the escape clauses of GATT provide added protection to distressed industries.

Second, the presence of good international organizations can have a destabilizing effect by discouraging states from investigating longer-term solutions to problems. Food aid as it was conducted in the 1970s is now thought to have encouraged Third World states to neglect domestic agricultural production, which would have brought them closer to self-sufficiency. Speaking more generally, former U.N. Secretary General Perez de Cuellar noted that there was a tendency for states to feel that the passage of a resolution relieves them of the need to take further action on a problem.

A third problem arises when otherwise good international organizations become the object of international competition between states or a tool of a member state. Gallarotti notes that the former frequently occurred to the United Nations during the height of the cold war and that the United States has often used the Organization of American States to justify its actions.

The same set of concerns might be applied to international law. Consider the problem of developing laws to govern the environment. Are the full ramifications of controlling CFCs and other harmful pollutants fully understood? Might it be that by trying to establish laws in such a highly complex area, the problem could be made worse or new ones could be created? Will the adoption of international laws protecting the environment bring to an end state efforts to seek alternatives to current policies, and will it actually encourage states to continue polluting the environment because laws have been passed to "solve" the problem. Finally, the 1992 World Environmental Summit Conference in Rio de Janeiro provides ample evidence of how the writing of international law may become a battleground between states and actually retard the prospects for saving the environment.

The Readings

The four readings in this section cover international law and a wide range of international organizations including multinational companies. In "The European Community in the New Europe," Stephen George examines the debate over the future of the European Community (EC), giving special attention to the impact of events in Eastern Europe in the late 1980s and the EC's actions in the war against Iraq. Tad Daley, in "Can the U.N. Stretch to Fit Its Future?" provides us with a look at the U.N.'s ability to keep the peace in the next century. "Toward a Feminist Analysis of International Law," by Hilary Charlesworth, Christine Chinkin, and Shelley Wright, argues that presently international law provides inadequate protection for women. Kenny Bruno, in "The Corporate Capture of the Earth Summit," argues that corporate influence undermined the efforts of environmentalists to pass a meaningful treaty at the 1992 Earth Summit.

Bibliography

AKEHURST, MICHAEL. *A Modern Introduction to International Law*, 6th ed. Boston: Unwin, Hyman, 1987.

BENEDICT, RICHARD. *Ozone Diplomacy*. Cambridge, MA: Harvard University Press, 1991.

CHARLESWORTH, HILARY. Christine Chinkin, and Shelley Wright, "Feminist Approaches to International Law," *American Journal of International Law* 85 (1991), 613–45.

GALLAROTTI, GIULIO. "The Limits of International Organization: Systematic Failure in the Management of International Relations." *International Organization* 45 (1991), 183–220.

GOODBY, JAMES. "Can Arms Control Survive Peace," *Washington Quarterly* 13 (1990), 93–104.

KARNS, MARGARET, and KAREN MINGST. (eds.). *The United States and Multilateral Institutions: Patterns of Changing Instrumentality and Influence*. Boston: Unwin, Hyman, 1990.

LINDBERG, LEON, and PHILIPPE SCHMITTER (eds.). *Regional Integration*. Cambridge, MA: Harvard University Press, 1971.

OXMAN, BERNARD, DAVID CARON, and C. BUDERI. *Law of the Sea: U.S. Policy Dilemma*. San Francisco: ICS Press, 1983.

REISMAN, W. MICHAEL, and ANDREW WILLARD. *International Incidents: International Law That Counts in World Politics*. Princeton, NJ: Princeton University Press, 1988.

ROCHESTER, J. MARTIN. "The Rise and Fall of International Organization as a Field of Study." *International Organization* 40 (1986), 753–75.

SEBENIUS, JAMES. "Designing Negotiations Toward a New Regime." *International Security* 15 (1991), 110–48.

YOUNG, ORAN. "Regime Dynamics: The Rise and Fall of International Regimes." *International Organization* 36 (1982), 277–98.

The European Community in the New Europe

Stephen George

Precisely what the position of the European Community (EC) will be in the new Europe that is now emerging is difficult to say, but it is bound to play an important role. That role will be determined partly by the overall shape of the new European architecture and partly by the future character of the EC itself. At the time of writing both these issues were under intensive discussion—the general shape of Europe in a variety of forums, the future character of the EC in an intergovernmental conference (IGC) on political union.

In this article an attempt is made to review the way in which the events in Eastern Europe at the end of the 1980s interacted with a debate that had already begun on the future nature of the EC and its relationship both to the member states and to other organisations such as the Western European Union (WEU), which were being spoken about as elements in the new European architecture.

Views on the Organisation of Europe

There have always been different views about how Europe ought to be organised. Perhaps the two most influential and contrasting positions are those of the federalists and of the intergovernmentalists. Federalists have long

From *Political Quarterly*, 1992 (Supplement), pp. 52–63. Reprinted by permission of *Political Quarterly*.

argued that some form of federal European state is necessary to deal with the problems of interdependence and to make Europe an effective actor in world affairs. The European Community has been seen by federalists as the basis of this future European super-state. Intergovernmentalists, on the other hand, have argued that the problems can be dealt with by co-operation between sovereign independent states, without the apparatus of a federal structure. They have tended to stress the dangers both for the national cultures of the states of Europe and for individual freedom of a super-state emerging.

In the past France has provided representatives of both voices in this debate. Jean Monnet, who devised the plans for both the European Coal and Steel Community and the European Atomic Energy Community, and who also promoted the idea of the European Economic Community, could be taken as representative of the federalist line of thinking, although it is probable that he would not have accepted the title of federalist himself. Charles de Gaulle was the clearest French representative of the intergovernmental approach to the problems of Europe, and the scourge of the federalist tendency within the EC in the 1960s.

More recently the French President François Mitterrand has adopted the rhetoric of federalism in his approach to the EC. Ironically, given de Gaulle s opposition to British membership of the EC, it is the British government that has generally carried the torch of intergovernmentalism since Britain became a member in 1973; and when she was prime minister Margaret Thatcher came to be seen as a second de Gaulle on European matters, especially following her strong restatement of the intergovernmental position in her speech at the College of Europe in Bruges in September 1988.

That speech marked an important stage in an argument about the future of the EC which was already raging fiercely when the collapse of communism in Eastern Europe caused it to be extended into a debate about the position of the EC in the wider Europe.

The Debate About the Future of the EC

In 1985 the European Community embarked on a project to free the internal market of non-tariff barriers to trade by the end of 1992. This led to a rapid revival of economic activity, as companies engaged in investment and mergers in anticipation of the new competitive climate to come. It also led to a dispute between the member states about the extent of the programme upon which they had embarked. The British government in particular seemed to want the '1992 project' to comprise no more than the freeing of the market. But for other actors the project had further aspects.

For the European Commission there seemed to be at least four other aspects to the programme. One was inauguration of a European programme of research in advanced technologies; a second was monetary union; a third was the so-called 'social dimension' to 1992; and a fourth was institutional reform to strengthen central decision-making in the EC. All but the first of these were challenged by Thatcher in her Bruges speech; but, in the weeks that followed, the leaders of the other member states almost all criticised the Bruges speech and defended the extended concept of 1992 as envisaged by the Commission.

Thatcher's critique of the extended concept of 1992 was based on the traditional tenets of intergovernmentalism: that 'willing and active cooperation between independent sovereign states is the best way to build a successful European Community'. Other elements came into the critique; that minimal government is the best form of government; that social regulations simply 'raise the cost of *employment* and make Europe's labour market less flexible'; that Europe should not be protectionist. These were the fundamentals of Thatcherism as an economic and social programme, and the Bruges speech was an application of them to the European level. But the essential ground on which Thatcher took her stand was that of intergovernmentalism, and the other member states found themselves arguing the case for some degree of federalism in contrast.

There was thus disharmony in the EC about its future direction in the late 1980s. There was also a problem about the relationship of the post-1992 EC with its neighbours. In 1987 Turkey revived its application for membership; and in the course of 1989 and 1990 some members of the European Free Trade Association (EFTA) declared their intention to apply for full membership in order to be inside the single market. The Commission of the EC declared in its response to the Turkish application that there could be no question of a further enlargement until after 1992, and restated this position in response to an Austrian approach in July 1989. So the issue was held over, but remained a cause for concern.

Onto this scene swept the collapse of communism in East and Central Europe. The rapidity with which events unfolded in the course of 1989 caught everybody by surprise. The declaration by the new regimes in Czechoslovakia, Hungary, and Poland that they would be seeking eventual membership of the EC both brought the membership issue into sharper focus and fed into the disputes between the member states about the extent of the 1992 programme.

Nobody denied that the hope of membership had to be held out to these states in order to assist them in their transition to capitalism, and to help to stabilise democracy there. Thatcher was quick to claim that developments strengthened her arguments against the surrender of further sovereignty to the central institutions. She argued that these states had only just reclaimed their sovereignty from the Soviet Union, and would not be willing to see it handed over to supranational institutions in Brussels and Strasbourg. She also argued that the rate of progress towards monetary union and social harmonisation ought to be slowed because they would take the EC further away from any position that the Central European states could hope to attain in any reasonable period of time and so make it more difficult for them to join.

Against that, Jacques Delors, the President of the Commission, argued in a speech at the College of Europe in October 1989 that the developments in Eastern Europe actually made it necessary for the EC to move more rapidly towards political union, otherwise it would be pulled apart. A similar analysis was put to the European Parliament by François Mitterrand in speeches in October and November 1989.

What particularly worried Delors and Mitterrand in the latter months of 1989 was the progress towards the reunification of Germany following the collapse of the German Democratic Republic. The way in which the Federal German government dealt with this matter was surprisingly direct and effective, but it involved no consultation with either the Commission or Germany's supposedly closest ally, France. Up to that point the French and Germans had worked in tandem to push forward the closer integration of the EC, and had developed mechanisms for close bi-lateral collaboration on foreign policy and defence. The sight of the Federal German government going off on its own caused great concern in both Brussels and Paris.

In its defence the German government argued that it did not have the time to consult, so rapid was the pace of events, and in November 1989 Chancellor Kohl joined President Mitterrand in calling for the EC to strengthen its bonds so that it could act as a model of democracy and freedom for the East European states. Mitterrand summarised the new Franco–German line when he told the European Parliament that, 'The Community's role is to realise that it is the only attractive force on this continent. It must be a guiding light and a beacon across the horizon'.

In April 1990 the German Chancellor joined with the French President in sending a letter to the Irish Taoiseach, Charles Haughey, whose government held the Presidency of the EC Council of Ministers during the first half of that year. The letter called for the acceleration of political unity within the EC in response to the developments in Eastern Europe, and for an IGC on political union. Predictably the British government rejected the logic of the argument that the Franco–German letter put forward. In a speech in Paris the British Foreign Secretary, Douglas Hurd, said of the initiative on political union, 'I do not find persuasive the argument that we must accelerate the pace of political integration in the Community precisely because of these dramatic events. The Community is not a vehicle that necessarily requires radical redesign when the landscape through which it is travelling changes'. Nevertheless, he also added that if the other member states wished to convene an IGC, the British government would participate.

Intergovernmental Conferences

It is a requirement of the founding treaties of the EC that any amendments to those treaties be preceded by an IGC, which then proposes amendments to a meeting of the heads of government. Any amendments agreed by the heads of government then have to be ratified by national parliaments.

One IGC had been held in 1985–86, resulting in the Single European Act of 1987. One of the innovations in the Single European Act was that the European Monetary System (EMS) for the first time became part of a consti-tutional document, and it was therefore necessary to convene an IGC in order to implement the proposed move towards monetary union. This con-ference was agreed at the Strasbourg meeting of the European Council in December 1989, on a majority vote of eleven to one with Britain voting against. The IGC on political union which was proposed by the French and German governments was agreed on the basis of the same majority at the Dublin meeting of the European Council in June 1990. The two IGCs were to run in parallel, starting in December 1990. Agreement to this second IGC was conditioned by a number of factors. Perhaps first in importance was concern about the new Germany. Not only would the emerging state be an economic giant, there was also concern about the possibility of a revival of German nationalism following re-unification. Political union could tie down the new Germany, something that the Federal German government welcomed as much as did France and Germany's other neighbours.

A second consideration was the realisation that the demands for en-largement of the EC could not forever be resisted. There was a real prospect of a future EC of over 20 member states, and such a large organisation would not be able to operate effectively unless there was more recourse to majority voting in the Council of Ministers and some greater delegation of authority to the Commission. There was also a strong feeling among some member states, especially perhaps in Germany and Italy, that the EC risked looking hypocritical if it continued to preach the virtues of democratic gov-ernment and to refuse membership to states that did not sustain democratic systems, while at the same time having a serious democratic deficit in its own decision-making procedures. There was a case to be made out therefore for increasing the powers of the European Parliament.

Another very important area for the IGC was that of security and defence. Proposals for an extension of Community competence to these areas had been around for some years, but had always been resisted by the Irish government because of what it saw as the conflict with its state's neutrality. There was also a neutrality problem for some of the prospective member states that were currently in EFTA.

The British government, too, had difficulties about seeing the EC acquire a defence dimension, both because of its attachment to the ideal of national sovereignty, for which an independent national defensive capability is crucial, and because of the importance that it attached to the Atlantic Alliance and to keeping the United States involved in the defence of western Europe. One of Thatcher's 'guiding principles' in the Bruges speech had been that, 'Europe must continue to maintain a sure defence through NATO'.

What brought security and defence to the top of the agenda was the risk of instability in the very backyard of the EC. The collapse of communism in Eastern Europe allowed the re-emergence of nationalist sentiments, and the revival of national rivalries that had been buried for decades under the blanket of communist rule. Also, the process of transition to capitalism was likely to be difficult even for the northern states of Eastern Europe, and even more so for the southern states such as Albania, Bulgaria and Romania. If regional conflicts did break out, it was unlikely that the EC would be able to sit back and not get involved. However, it was also unlikely that any one state would be happy to see another become involved in a policing operation within Europe in the way that French policing operations in francophone Africa had been tolerated in the past. Added to these considerations, and very influential, was the attitude of the Bush administration in the United States.

The Attitude of the United States

US attitudes to the EC have always moved along a spectrum between the ideas of partnership and rivalry. The partnership pole represents the idea of burden-sharing; the United States has frequently looked for the West Europeans to help in the tasks of stabilising the capitalist system both economically and militarily. On the other hand, there has been frequent retreat from this position when the EC has begun to act independently. The ideal of successive US administrations seems to have been for an EC that would help the United States without challenging its authority.

After the arrival in office of the Bush administration the tenor of US policy towards the EC swung decidedly to the burden-sharing pole. A widely reported speech by Secretary of State James Baker in Berlin in December 1989 stressed the need for the Europeans to get their act together and make the EC into a useful partner in stabilising the new Europe that was emerging. This line ran directly counter to Thatcher's argument that there was no need for greater political unity or for monetary union. Her vision of an EC of independent nation states did not coincide with the desire of the US administration to have a clearly identifiable partner with which it could do business, and one with the capability to act decisively in a crisis. . . .

The basis for this US attitude was largely economic although it also recognised the realities of domestic politics in the United States. The hard economic fact that the Bush administration had to deal with was the twin deficits on the budget and the balance of payments, a legacy of the profligate Reagan years. This relative penury was instrumental in the decision to allow the West Europeans to take the lead in the reconstruction of the economies of Central and East Europe. The European Bank for Reconstruction and Development, which began work informally in September 1990 and was officially inaugurated in March 1991, drew half of its capital from Western Europe and only one quarter from the United States, a balance reflected in the nomination of a Frenchman, Jacques Attali, as its head. . . .

The Gulf Crisis

Just as with the collapse of communism in Eastern Europe, the fragmented and slow reaction of the Community states to the crisis in the Gulf was claimed by both sides in the argument over the future of the EC as support for their case.

On 30 August 1990 Thatcher told a conference of the European Democratic Union in Helsinki that all the rhetoric about a common security policy contrasted with the hesitant reaction of some countries when practical measures were required, and repeated a favourite theme, that some other members of the EC were strong on words and weak on action. The clear implication was that the EC was not ready for closer political unity.

In September 1990 the Italian Foreign Minister and then current President of the Council of Ministers, Gianni de Michelis, told journalists that the Community's reaction to the crisis showed the need for the EC to take on a military capability, and that Italy would bring forward a proposal that the Western European Union (WEU) be incorporated into European Political Co-operation (EPC), the intergovernmental mechanism through which the member states of the EC try to co-ordinate their positions on questions of foreign policy. The aim of this incorporation of WEU would be to give the EC an effective defence and security dimension.

WEU is an organisation that was set up in the 1950s in the aftermath of the collapse of a proposal for a European Defence Community. Its importance has been overshadowed by NATO, but it was revived in the 1980s as a means of allowing those Community states that so wished to discuss defence-related issues without bringing defence into the forum of EPC where it would embarrass Ireland, and possibly also Denmark and Greece. These three Community members are not members of WEU.

When the Italian proposal was initially discussed by Foreign Ministers in early October 1990 there was no strong support from other states for the absorption of WEU into the EC, but there was support from both France and Germany for some aspects of the co-ordination of both foreign policy and security policy being decided by majority vote within the EPC framework, a position that the British government was unable to support. Douglas Hurd did, however, admit that the weak response to the Gulf crisis indicated that something must be done.

Eventually, after the change of British prime minister, the outcome of this line of thinking appeared in the form of the British paper to the IGC on political union. Hurd outlined these proposals in the 1991 Winston Churchill Memorial Lecture. He made it clear that the British government could neither accept the Italian proposal for WEU to be incorporated into EPC, nor the Franco-German proposal for majority voting to be extended to EPC. At the same time he dismissed the argument of more anti-European voices in the Conservative Party that the failure of the EC to respond effectively to the Gulf crisis meant that a common foreign policy was not feasible. On the contrary, he argued that greater unity was necessary to contribute to 'a more peaceful and orderly world'. To facilitate greater unity, the British paper to the IGC would endorse another idea that also had the support of the French, German, and Italian governments: that WEU should become part of some form of European union which would group the EC, EPC, and WEU as three related but distinct entities co-ordinated through the European Council.

Defence would thus be incorporated into an overall framework that would allow it to be handled on an intergovernmental basis alongside the supranational EC and the intergovernmental EPC. Such a multi-faceted entity would allow Britain to be a fully involved member of the new European union, whilst allowing states such as Ireland, which had doubts about the incorporation of the defence element, to play a full role in two of the three forums and absent themselves, or have only observer status, in the third. These ideas were eventually formulated by the Luxembourg presidency of the EC in April 1991 into a 95-page paper which was referred to as the 'non-paper'; this became the text around which the discussions in the IGC centred.

The Nature and Role of the EC in the New Europe

Already, before the two IGCs began work in December 1990, the debate on the future of the EC in the new Europe had come to centre around the two issues of the degree of supranationalism or of intergovernmentalism that should prevail in its internal arrangements, and the extent to which the EC would take on new functions, particularly with respect to external relations. There was no disagreement that certain economic, diplomatic, and possibly even security functions would have to be performed in the new Europe, and that they would not be performed willingly nor easily by the United States. The disagreement was over whether they should be performed by the EC acting as a sort of European super-state.

The strong intergovernmental line taken by Mrs. Thatcher while she was the British prime minster made the debate appear polarised, Britain against the rest. In fact there were serious doubts in many quarters in the EC about the apparent ambition of Jacques Delors to increase the power and authority of the Commission; but it was difficult for the leaders of states where European integration remained a popular concept to appear to side with Thatcher, who had been consistently presented as an enemy of closer unity.

On the other hand, there was also considerable concern in Europe about the position of the newly united Germany, and a strong feeling even amongst those who had previously been allies of the British that it was necessary to constrain this new Germany by strengthening the European framework within which it had to operate, even if that meant some further surrender of their own national sovereignty. This applied particularly to Denmark, which changed its stance from support for the Thatcher line of a Europe of sovereign states to a more pragmatic and flexible position. Despite the apparent anti-German sentiments of some members of the Thatcher government, perhaps including the prime minister herself, the same conclusion was not drawn in London.

The removal of Thatcher from the leadership in November 1990 made it much easier to reach a consensus on both monetary union and political union. John Major's more pragmatic approach brought Britain into line with the position of those other EC states that were both suspicious of the ambitions of Delors and fearful of the potential for domination by the new Germany. Major's conciliatory and low-key style made it easier for other governments to express reservations about too large an increase in the power of the central institutions of the EC without appearing to side with an 'anti-Community' position. It may also have forced them to some extent to do so because the British government could no longer be relied upon to block unwelcome measures of centralisation.

On monetary union, the IGC began to move away from the precise timetable that had apparently been agreed at the Rome meeting of the European Council in October 1990, when Mrs Thatcher had isolated herself and pushed potential allies into the arms of the advocates of the Delors plan. There was increasing acceptance that economic convergence must precede any attempt to move to a monetary union, and discussion around how to achieve economic convergence without an unacceptable degree of direct intervention in the internal economic policy-making of member states made the evolutionary character of the British plan for a 'hard Ecu' as a parallel to national currencies seem increasingly attractive, especially in the context of a British government which was prepared to stress that this *was* an alternative route to monetary union and not a route devised to avoid that destination, as Thatcher had tended to imply.

On political union, the Luxembourg presidency's 'non-paper', while still containing elements over which there was less than total agreement, summarised the way in which thinking had been moving. It rested on the concept of a European Union, with the European Council at its summit, and incorporating within it the EC as one element, but also separate elements of a more intergovernmental nature to deal with external relations, including external security, and with internal aspects of security such as co-operation to control crime and terrorism.

The competences of the EC would be extended to give it a firmer role in social affairs, transport policy, technological research, and energy, and new competences in the areas of health, education, tourism, and cultural policy; but the risk of a creeping further extension of its role was to be removed by an explicit commitment to the principle of 'subsidiarity' (that the member states should continue to perform all functions that they had not agreed to cede to the EC because they could be better performed at that level). There was also a proposal to extend the powers of the European

Parliament, which angered Jacques Delors because it implied a downgrading of the role of the Commission in the legislative process of the EC. The external policy and internal security aspects would not come under the EC institutional rules, and would continue to be governed by the principle of consensus. Defence would be handled through WEU, with the possibility that it might be incorporated as an extra element in the Union following the expiry of its existing treaty in 1996.

While a lot of issues remained to be decided, the shape could be seen here of an agreement that would take account of the concern not to create too powerful and centralised an EC, while at the same time tying Germany into a firmly restricting set of obligations, and making provision for the performance of the functions that would have to be performed by some European actor both in the new Europe and in the emerging new world order. Rather than a new superstate, what seemed to be emerging was an economic and social grouping that could continue to act as a magnet to the states of Central and Eastern Europe, combined with a new Congress of Europe.

Can the U.N. Stretch to Fit Its Future?

Tad Daley

Shortly before the first-ever United Nations Security Council summit convened in New York on January 31, a reporter asked British Prime Minister John Major whether he would recommend changing the composition of the council. The best response Major could muster was: "Why break up a winning team?" Following the summit, a reporter asked Russian President Boris Yeltsin whether he would propose permanent Security Council membership for Germany and Japan. "I think you're confusing me with someone else," he said.

Questions about the composition of the Security Council are often side-stepped these days. There is no good answer to them. The idea that the five great powers of the world of 1945 should forever retain the leading role in the maintenance of international peace and security simply doesn't play well anymore with the rest of the planet.

In a declaration issued at the summit, the Security Council invited Boutros Ghali, the new secretary-general, to recommend by July 1 steps the United Nations might take to strengthen its capacity for "preventive diplomacy, peacemaking, and peacekeeping."

Ghali may well produce some bold initiatives—all of which, as the declaration stipulated, will fall "within the framework and provisions of the Charter." But pressures to open the U.N. Charter have been building for many years, and they are likely to increase. The weakness of the arguments for indefinitely retaining the San Francisco Charter will likely soon produce other initiatives that go far beyond those that Ghali is likely to suggest in July.

A Peace Army

Because the U.N. Secretariat must now improvise each new operation from scratch, support is growing for ideas such as a standing system of logistical and financial support for peacekeeping efforts, a military staff college for training peacekeeping officers, and even a standing rapid deployment force for peacekeeping actions. French President François Mitterrand proposed such a force in his summit speech, pledging French willingness to commit 1,000 troops within 48 hours in a crisis.

Mitterrand did not specify whether the troops for this U.N. force would remain with their respective national military establishments until mobilized by the United Nations, or instead form a standing U.N. army. He was also unclear whether the authority to dispatch such a force would lay with the Security Council or the secretary-general. Mitterrand did suggest, however, that the rapid deployment force could operate under the command of the U.N. Military Staff Committee, which consists of the chiefs of staff of the "Perm Five" states. The Military Staff Committee has never commanded a force in the U.N.'s 47-year history, and the Charter provides no guidelines for how the Perm Five might reach consensus decisions. Boris Yeltsin of Russia generally endorsed Mitterrand's proposal in his own summit speech, although he added that the "expeditious activation" of such a force should occur "upon the decision of the Security Council."

An effective U.N. rapid deployment force would possess several key elements: The United Nations must be able to discern that an outbreak of violence is imminent, either through its own intelligence sources or "borrowed" intelligence information from member nations. There must be authority to dispatch such a force, as Austrian Chancellor Franz Vranitzky's summit statement suggested, *before* a conflict ignites, and without necessarily obtaining the consent of all the parties to the potential conflict. Most important, the secretary-general must have the blanket authority to dispatch the force on his own initiative, without Security Council authorization. Such authority is essential to avoid "telegraphing the punch," even if that might sometimes act as a deterrent. Other mechanisms exist for such public deterrent efforts. While a July 1990 Security Council debate might have deterred Saddam Hussein's invasion of Kuwait, it might also have moved him to invade earlier.

Deployment of a U.N. force could be followed by compulsory U.N. mediation or by a hearing before the World Court. If a U.N. rapid deployment force had existed in the summer of 1990, and if the World Court had been prepared to hear the kinds of disputes (slant drilling, maritime access, and the like) that Iraq had with Kuwait, and if the world community had previously displayed a consistent commitment to the enforcement of international law, Iraq might never have invaded at all.

The summit declaration also noted with approval that the General Assembly had recently created a global arms registry for tracking transfers of conventional weapons. The British and the Japanese have gone further by pushing for a registry that would track both transactions and national inventories in conventional, nuclear, biological, and chemical weapons. Such an all-embracing register could deter both recipient and supplier, as in the famous phrase underlying American securities-disclosure laws: "Sunlight is the best of disinfectants." With the Perm Five countries accounting for nearly 90 percent of arms sales around the world, exposing the full range of arms trafficking ought to be a natural role for tomorrow's United Nations.

Beyond Peacekeeping

The U.N. role is likely to continue to expand beyond international security concerns into areas such as temporary governmental administration (now under way in Cambodia), election monitoring, humanitarian assistance, and disaster relief. The British have been pressing for the establishment of a new high-level U.N. position—a permanent undersecretary-general for disaster relief. The aid provided to victims of the May 1991 Bangladesh cyclone by American marines, who happened to be on their way home from the Persian Gulf, only underscored the inadequacy of the present system.

The maintenance of a healthy and sustainable biosphere may be the most important policy imperative facing the human community. Global environmental changes have made absolute national sovereignty over territories of importance to all of humankind—such as the Amazon rainforests—increasingly anachronistic. The U.N. Conference on Environment and Development, which convenes in June in Brazil, may go a long way toward creating an unprecedented body of global environmental law, as well as the enforcement mechanisms that global environmental protection will probably require.

Other problems, including drug trafficking, terrorism, AIDS, and sundry financial flim-flams—such as those perpetrated by the Bank of Credit and Commerce International—increasingly transcend national boundaries, and demand U.N. attention. But some attention must also be focused on the nearly universal Third World fears that the U.N.'s renaissance will be dominated by a First World perspective. The concerns of developing countries—such as debt, low prices for raw materials, and economic development—cannot be brushed aside. At the summit, several leaders of developing nations spoke passionately of the vast waste of human capital engendered by perpetual poverty.

In the broadest sense, the coming decades will demand larger roles for international institutions in the *management* of environmental degradation, population growth, energy exhaustion, and the global movements of capital, goods, services, information, and people. Will the scale of management of human affairs keep up with the continuously increasing degree of global interdependence? The international community must address that question today, not tomorrow.

Fading Sovereignty

Article 2, Paragraph 7 of the U.N. Charter prohibits U.N. intervention "in matters essentially within the domestic jurisdiction of any state." Nevertheless, we may be seeing the creeping emergence of a doctrine of humanitarian intervention in the internal affairs of sovereign states. An important theme in the speeches of the fifteen leaders gathered for the summit was the need to protect human rights everywhere. While most of the leaders spoke favorably of human rights as a common global value, some suggested even more directly that this value could be superior to national sovereignty.

Russia's Yeltsin, for instance, said that human rights "are not an internal matter of states, but rather obligations under the U.N. Charter," and maintained that the Security Council had a "collective responsibility for the protection of human rights and freedoms." And Secretary-General Ghali, echoing his predecessor, Javier Perez de Cuellar, said that "the misuse of state sovereignty may jeopardize a peaceful global life. Civil wars are no longer civil, and the carnage they inflict will not let the world remain indifferent."

Although Germany was not represented at the summit, Foreign Minister Hans-Dietrich Genscher had gone even further last fall in a speech to the General Assembly: "Today sovereignty must meet its limits in the responsibility of states for mankind as a whole. . . . When human rights are trampled underfoot, the family of nations is not confined to the role of spectator. . . . It must intervene."

The most notable event to date on the sovereignty front has been the haven for Kurds carved out of northern Iraq. Although the sponsors of U.N. Resolution 688 in April 1991 argued that the situation with Kurdish refugees threatened international stability, in reality external military intervention was used inside Iraq to prevent the Iraqi government from committing acts of aggression against its own people on its own territory.

Saddam Hussein's behavior also revived the idea of establishing an international criminal court that could not only try violators of international conventions regarding such matters as terrorism and drug trafficking, but also heads of state who violate international law through acts of international or internal aggression. Security Council Resolution 731, issued in January, also stepped into this territory. The resolution demands that Libya surrender the two intelligence agents accused of the bombing of Pan Am Flight 103.

Not only does the resolution call upon Libya to subordinate its own procedures regarding extradition, but it implies, perhaps for the first time, that
the writ of the Security Council extends not just to states, but to individuals
anywhere in the world.

But the use of economic sanctions as a mechanism to pressure states
to mend their ways may soon come up for reexamination. Economic sanctions are generally thought to be a lesser form of coercion than direct military action. Yet, as British journalist Edward Pearce has pointed out, although
the international community condemns biological warfare, the economic sanctions preventing the repair of damaged Iraqi power plants and sewage treatment facilities have resulted in epidemic levels of cholera in Iraq. "That is
different from deliberately seeding and spreading the cholera virus," says
Pearce, "in the same way that manslaughter is different from murder."

The economic embargoes against Iraq—and now Haiti—are aimed
directly at the removal of their governing regimes. But it is unclear how these
sanctions can accomplish their desired ends. If Iraqi opposition forces could
not overthrow Saddam Hussein at his weakest moment in the spring of 1991,
sanctions that harm rulers less than the ruled seem hardly likely to increase
the opposition's prospects.

In Haiti, where the economic embargo is hitting the general population far harder than the rich and well-connected, the policy, rather than
giving Haitians the incentive and the wherewithal to overthrow the military
regime, has instead resulted in a massive refugee crisis off the coast of the
United States. Something has gone awry in the international system when we
impose harsh and effective economic sanctions on a country, and then repatriate the consequent refugees because their motives are economic rather
than political.

If it has become legitimate for the international community to endeavor to remove a governing regime, direct international removal efforts
may be undertaken in the not-too-distant future. It may soon become widely
accepted that world standards and laws apply to every individual on the
planet, and that the international community will intervene to enforce those
standards and laws. Whether this process continues in an evolutionary or
revolutionary fashion, we may be witnessing the beginnings of a sea change
in human history.

Taxation Without Representation

As the U.N.'s role in world affairs continues to expand, so too will pressure
increase to bring the composition of the Security Council in line with the
contemporary realities of international power. The framers of the Charter
envisioned a dynamic institution that would evolve over time. Article 109
provides for the convening of a "General Charter Review Conference" upon
the approval of the two-thirds of the member states, including any nine

members of the Security Council. And Article 108 allows Charter amendment upon the approval of two-thirds of the member states, including all five permanent members of the Security Council.

Japan and Germany, the second and third largest financial contributors to U.N. activities, are the two states most commonly cited as deserving permanent membership on the Security Council. Indeed, Japan contributes more to the United Nations than Britain and France combined, and thus already has considerable clout. The new secretary-general's first high-level appointment was Japan's Yasushi Akashi, who was named special representative to oversee the multibillion dollar U.N. peacekeeping operation in Cambodia. Tokyo's U.N. ambassador, Yoshio Hatano, reportedly reminded Ghali beforehand that Japan had pledged to pick up fully half the tab for the massive operation.

But Japan is not satisfied with only this intangible influence in U.N. decision making. Although the possibility of a Security Council membership for Japan has been long discussed, Japanese Prime Minister Kiichi Miyazawa was particularly direct at the summit, saying that membership on the council must be "more reflective of the realities of the new era." In case anyone failed to get the message, his press secretary, Masamichi Hanabusa, later said Tokyo expected a Security Council seat by 1995, the U.N.'s fiftieth anniversary. Otherwise, he added, Japan would increasingly resent "taxation without representation."

Germany's approach is more low-key. In the short term, Germany seems to hope that Britain and France will informally "Europeanize" their seats as the European Community draws closer together. (Bonn, however, was reportedly miffed that it had not been consulted by London or Paris in preparation for the summit.) In the long term, German Chancellor Helmut Kohl said shortly before the summit that he was "strictly opposed" to Germany itself putting the Security Council issue on the table, but that he could imagine the European Community acquiring a permanent seat at some point.

Merging British, French, and German interests into a single European Community seat would require amending both Article 23 (which names the permanent members of the Security Council) and Article 4 (which limits U.N. membership to "states"). Once that Pandora's box is opened, all sorts of issues emerge. What about developing nations of increasing weight—such as India, Brazil, Nigeria, Egypt, and Indonesia? Indian Prime Minister P.V. Narasimha Rao made a strong case at the summit for expanding the Security Council's representation if it hopes to maintain political and moral effectiveness. And shortly after the summit, Nigerian President Ibrahim Babangida said that "to retain the structure of the Security Council in its present form is to run the risk of perpetuating what is at best a feudal anachronism."

What exactly are the criteria for selection as permanent members of the Security Council? Political power? Economic power? Military power? (The Perm Five happen to be the five major nuclear-weapon states.) Regional representation? Perhaps most important, if the Security Council expands its permanent membership, how can it retain the ability to act decisively?

Decisiveness or Democracy?

Italian Foreign Minister Gianni de Michelis called for major Charter revisions in a speech to the General Assembly in September 1991. He proposed expanding the number of both permanent and rotating members of the Security Council, but not necessarily extending the right of veto to the new permanent members. He also suggested "a system of weighted voting in both the General Assembly and the Security Council."

Over the years, many weighted voting schemes have been discussed. Some would give added weight to the population of a member state, or to its financial contribution. Some would award a degree of representation to stateless ethnic groups—Kurds and Sikhs, for example. Others envision a bicameral system much like the U.S. Congress, with citizens all over the world electing local representatives to a "U.N. House" and national representatives to a "U.N. Senate."

Many U.N. watchers argue that any conceivable recomposition of the Security Council would tremendously complicate the process of reaching consensus, and might paralyze the United Nations again, just when it is beginning to fulfill its post–Cold War potential. Although the veto has become a rarity in recent years, it is not difficult to imagine circumstances in which it could again be regularly employed. In November 1990, the "Soyuz" group of deputies in the Supreme Soviet stated plainly that they would have vetoed Resolution 678 on the use of force against Iraq. Conservative Soviet commentator B. Zanegin said after the war that "the U.N. Security Council can serve as an instrument for legalizing unilateral decisions by the U.S. and imposing them on the world community." The new world order, he added, basically amounts to a "U.S. dictatorship or hegemony" that is exercised through the Security Council.

But if a more conservative leadership should again come to power in Moscow, it is not clear that they would fail to cooperate in the Security Council. A conservative Russia would still be a nation in decline. Even a single Security Council veto might lead Western states to reconsider the large-scale aid programs now under way. And a return to a "Mr. Nyet" approach could simply cause the United States and the West to again pursue their interests outside the U.N. framework, leaving Russia with virtually no voice in global political affairs.

Nevertheless, objective perceptions of national interest are seldom the sole determinants of a state's foreign policies. A central objective of a right-wing Russian leadership, however harmful to Russian interests, might be simply to reverse the national humiliation stemming from the recent Russian subservience to the United States in the international arena. Future Russian Security Council vetoes, exercised as a means of demonstrating national pride and independence, are far from inconceivable.

In addition, Chinese Prime Minister Li Peng struck a discordant note at the summit when he insisted that China would consistently oppose all external interventions in the internal affairs of sovereign states "using human rights as an excuse." The stridency of Li's speech suggests that we could see the emergence of the Chinese veto as well. Many Third World nations are deeply disturbed by the sovereignty issue. China may see an opportunity to stand at the head of the developing world as the great defender of sovereignty, opposing and vetoing all proposed U.N. interventions in "domestic affairs."

The various democratic decision-making structures around the world today are rarely paralyzed into complete inaction. Though often contentious in their procedures, they usually manage to produce some kind of public policy, however imperfect. Is there something fundamentally different about a global decision-making structure? If "decisive action" were the sole U.S. value, the president would be allowed to act, in all cases, without congressional authorization. "Democratization, at the national level," said Ghali in his summit statement, "dictates a corresponding process at the global level."

If Not Now, When?

The post–Cold War world will require global institutions with the power and authority to address the increasingly global issues of the new millennium. That is why, shortly after the Gulf War ended, the Stockholm Initiative on Global Security and Governance received the endorsement of international luminaries including Benazir Bhutto, Willy Brandt, Jimmy Carter, Vaclev Havel, Robert McNamara, Julius Nyerere, and Eduard Shevardnadze. The initiative proposes measures such as "the elaboration of a global law enforcement mechanism," "the levying of fees on the emission of pollutants affecting the global environment," "a review of both the composition of the Security Council and the use of the veto," and the convening of "a World Summit on Global Governance, similar to the meetings in San Francisco and Bretton Woods in the 1940s."

Any new world order centered around the San Francisco Charter stands hostage to the prevailing political winds in Moscow and Beijing. Any opening of the Charter must endeavor to at least limit the Security Council veto so that some types of collective U.N. action can be undertaken even in the face of disagreement among the great powers. The protracted conflict between the United States and the Soviet Union was, after all, why the United Nations was essentially irrelevant for its first four decades.

The international community can pretend that the potential for paralysis-by-veto no longer exists, and it can keep bringing more and more issues to the Security Council in the hope that all will go well. Or it can begin seriously laying the groundwork, perhaps to coincide with the U.N.'s fiftieth anniversary in 1995, for an Article 109 Charter Review Conference.

"I am not an advocate for frequent changes in laws and constitutions," said Thomas Jefferson, in words inscribed on the Jefferson Memorial. "[But] as circumstances change, institutions must also advance to keep pace with the times. We might as well require a man still to wear the coat which fitted him when a boy, as require civilized society to remain ever under the regimen of their barbarous ancestors."

The San Francisco coat of the 1940s no longer fits the world of the 1990s. There are few worse things we could do to the legacy of Roosevelt, Churchill, and the U.N.'s other founders than to cast in stone the global structures they created for the world of their day. Politics, as every undergraduate knows, is the art of the possible. A great deal more is possible today, as we emerge from the Cold War era, than was possible when we entered it a half century ago.

Toward a Feminist Analysis of International Law

Hilary Charlesworth
Christine Chinkin
Shelly Wright

How can feminist accounts of law be applied in international law? Feminist legal theory can promote a variety of activities. The term signifies an interest (gender as an issue of primary importance); a focus of attention (women as individuals and as members of groups); a political agenda (real social, political, economic and cultural equality regardless of gender); a critical stance (an analysis of "masculinism" and male hierarchical power or "patriarchy"); a means of reinterpreting and reformulating substantive law so that it more adequately reflects the experiences of all people; and an alternative method of practicing, talking about and learning the law.[1] Feminist method must be concerned with examining the fundamentals of the legal persuasion: the language it uses; the organization of legal materials in predetermined, watertight categories; the acceptance of abstract concepts as somehow valid or "pure"; the reliance in practice on confrontational, adversarial techniques; and the commitment to male, hierarchical structures in all legal and political organizations.

Christine Littleton has said, "Feminist method starts with the very radical act of taking women seriously, believing that what we say about ourselves and our experience is important and valid, even when (or perhaps especially when) it has little or no relationship to what has been or is being said *about* us."[2] No single approach can deal with the complexity of international legal organizations, processes and rules, or with the diversity of women's experiences within and outside those structures. In this section we look at two interconnected themes developed in feminist accounts of the law that suggest new ways of analyzing international law.

Critique of Rights

The feminist critique of rights questions whether the acquisition of legal rights advances women's equality. Feminist scholars have argued that, although the search for formal legal equality through the formulation of rights may have been politically appropriate in the early stages of the feminist movement, continuing to focus on the acquisition of rights may not be beneficial to women. Quite apart from problems such as the form in which rights are drafted, their interpretation by tribunals, and women's access to their enforcement, the rhetoric of rights, according to some feminist legal scholars, is exhausted.

Rights discourse is taxed with reducing intricate power relations in a simplistic way. The formal acquisition of a right, such as the right to equal treatment, is often assumed to have solved an imbalance of power. In practice, however, the promise of rights is thwarted by the inequalities of power: the economic and social dependence of women on men may discourage the invocation of legal rights that are premised on an adversarial relationship between the rights holder and the infringer. More complex still are rights designed to apply to women only such as the rights to reproductive freedom and to choose abortion.

In addition, although they respond to general societal imbalances, formulations of rights are generally cast in individual terms. The invocation of rights to sexual equality may therefore solve an occasional case of inequality for individual women but will leave the position of women generally unchanged. Moreover, international law accords priority to civil and political rights, rights that may have very little to offer women generally. The major forms of oppression of women operate within the economic, social and cultural realms. Economic, social and cultural rights are traditionally regarded as a lesser form of international right and as much more difficult to implement.[3]

A second major criticism of the assumption that the granting of rights inevitably spells progress for women is that it ignores competing rights: the right of women and children not to be subjected to violence in the home may be balanced against the property rights of men in the home or their right to family life. Furthermore, certain rights may be appropriated by more powerful groups: Carol Smart relates that provisions in the European Convention on Human Rights on family life were used by fathers to assert their authority over ex nuptial children.[4] One solution may be to design rights to apply only to particular groups. However, apart from the serious political difficulties this tactic would raise, the formulation of rights that apply only to women, as we have seen in the international sphere, may result in marginalizing these rights.

A third feminist concern about the "rights" approach to achieve equality is that some rights can operate to the detriment of women. The right to freedom of religion, for example, can have differing impacts on women and men. Freedom to exercise all aspects of religious belief does not always benefit women because many accepted religious practices entail reduced social positions and status for women.[5] Yet attempts to set priorities and to discuss the issue have been met with hostility and blocking techniques. Thus, at its 1987 meeting the CEDAW Committee adopted a decision requesting that the United Nations and the specialized agencies

> promote or undertake studies on the status of women under Islamic laws and customs and in particular on the status and equality of women in the family on issues such as marriage, divorce, custody and property rights and their participation in public life of the society, taking into consideration the principle of El Ijtihad in Islam.[6]

The representatives of Islamic nations criticized this decision in ECOSOC and in the Third Committee of the General Assembly as a threat to their freedom of religion.[7] The CEDAW Committee's recommendation was ultimately rejected. The General Assembly passed a resolution in which it decided that "no action shall be taken on decision 4 adopted by the Committee and request[ed that] the Committee . . . review that decision, taking into account the views expressed by delegations at the first regular session of the Economic and Social Council of 1987 and in the Third Committee of the General Assembly." CEDAW later justified its action by stating that the study was necessary for it to carry out its duties under the Women's Convention and that no disrespect was intended to Islam.

Another example of internationally recognized rights that might affect women and men differently are those relating to the protection of the family. The major human rights instruments all have provisions applicable to the family. Thus, the Universal Declaration proclaims that the family is the "natural and fundamental group unit of society and is entitled to protection by society and the State." These provisions ignore that to many women the family is a unit for abuse and violence; hence, protection of the family also preserves the power structure within the family, which can lead to subjugation and dominance by men over women and children.

The development of rights may be particularly problematic for women in the Third World, where women's rights to equality with men and traditional values may clash. An example of the ambivalence of Third World states toward women's concerns is the Banjul Charter, the human rights instrument of the Organization of African Unity.[8]

The Charter, unlike "western" instruments preoccupied with the rights of individuals, emphasizes the need to recognize communities and peoples as entities entitled to rights, and it provides that people within the group owe duties and obligations to the group. "Peoples'" rights in the Banjul Charter include the right to self-determination, the right to exploit natural resources and wealth, the right to development, the right to international peace and security, and the right to a generally satisfactory environment.

The creation of communal or "peoples'" rights, however, does not take into account the often severe limitations on the rights of women within these groups, communities or "peoples." The Preamble to the Charter makes specific reference to the elimination of "all forms of discrimination, particularly those based on race, ethnic group, colour, sex, language, religion or political opinion." Article 2 enshrines the enjoyment of all rights contained within the Charter without discrimination of any kind. But after Article 2, the Charter refers exclusively to "his" rights, the "rights of man." Articles 3–17 set out basic political, civil, economic and social rights similar to those contained in other instruments, in particular the International Covenants, the Universal Declaration of Human Rights (which is cited in the preamble) and European instruments. Article 15 is significant in that it guarantees that the right to work includes the right to "receive equal pay for equal work." This right might be useful to women who are employed in jobs that men also do. The difficulty is that most African women, like women elsewhere, generally do not perform the same jobs as men.

Articles 17 and 18 and the list of duties contained in Articles 27–29 present obstacles to African women's enjoyment of rights set out elsewhere in the Charter. Article 17(3) states that "[t]he promotion and protection of morals and traditional values recognized by the community shall be the duty of the State." Article 18 entrusts the family with custody of those morals and values, describing it as "the natural unit and basis of society." The same article requires that discrimination against women be eliminated, but the conjunction of the notion of equality with the protection of the family and "traditional" values poses serious problems. It has been noted in relation to Zimbabwe and Mozambique that

> [t]he official political rhetoric relating to women in these southern African societies may be rooted in a model derived from Engels, via the Soviet Union, but the actual situation they face today bears little resemblance to that of the USSR. In Zimbabwe particularly, policy-makers are caught between several ideological and material contradictions, which are especially pertinent to women-oriented policies. The dominant ideology has been shaped by two belief-systems, opposed in their conceptions of women. Marxism vies with a model deriving from pre-colonial society, in which women's capacity to reproduce the lineage, socially, economically and biologically, was crucial and in which lineage males controlled women's labour power.[9]

This contradiction between the emancipation of women and adherence to traditional values lies at the heart of and complicates discussion about human rights in relation to many Third World women. The rhetoric of human rights, on both the national and the international levels, regards women as equal citizens, as "individuals" subject to the same level of treatment and the same protection as men. But the discourse of "traditional values" may prevent women from enjoying any human rights, however they may be described.[10]

Despite all these problems, the assertion of rights can exude great symbolic force for oppressed groups within a society and it constitutes an organizing principle in the struggle against inequality. Patricia Williams has pointed out that for blacks in the United States, "the prospect of attaining full rights under the law has always been a fiercely motivational, almost religious, source of hope." She writes:

> "Rights" feels so new in the mouths of most black people. It is still so deliciously empowering to say. It is a sign for and a gift of selfhood that is very hard to contemplate restructuring . . . at this point in history. It is the magic wand of visibility and invisibility, of inclusion and exclusion, of power and no power. . . .[11]

The discourse of rights may have greater significance at the international level than in many national systems. It provides an accepted means to challenge the traditional legal order and to develop alternative principles. While the acquisition of rights must not be identified with automatic and immediate advances for women, and the limitations of the rights model must be recognized, the notion of women's rights remains a source of potential power for women in international law. The challenge is to rethink that notion so that rights correspond to women's experiences and needs.

The Public/Private Distinction

. . . Here we show how the dichotomy between public and private worlds has undermined the operation of international law, giving two examples.

The Right to Development

The right to development was formulated in legal terms only recently and its status in international law is still controversial.[12] Its proponents present it as a collective or solidarity right that responds to the phenomenon of global interdependence, while its critics argue that it is an aspiration rather than a right.[13] The 1986 United Nations Declaration on the Right to Development describes the content of the right as the entitlement "to participate in, contribute to, and enjoy economic, social, cultural and political development, in which all human rights and fundamental freedoms can be fully realized." Primary responsibility for the creation of conditions favorable to the right is placed on states:

> States have the right and the duty to formulate appropriate national development policies that aim at the constant improvement of the well-being of the entire population and of all individuals, on the basis of their active, free and

meaningful participation in development and in the fair distribution of the benefits resulting therefrom.[14]

The right is apparently designed to apply to all individuals within a state and is assumed to benefit women and men equally: the preamble to the declaration twice refers to the Charter exhortation to promote and encourage respect for human rights for all without distinction of any kind such as of race or sex. Moreover, Article 8 of the declaration obliges states to ensure equality of opportunity for all regarding access to basic resources and fair distribution of income. It provides that "effective measures should be undertaken to ensure that women have an active role in the development process."

Other provisions of the declaration, however, indicate that discrimination against women is not seen as a major obstacle to development or to the fair distribution of its benefits. For example, one aspect of the right to development is the obligation of states to take "resolute steps" to eliminate "massive and flagrant violations of the human rights of peoples and human beings." The examples given of such violations include apartheid and racial discrimination but not sex discrimination.

Three theories about the causes of underdevelopment dominate its analysis: shortages of capital, technology, skilled labor and entrepreneurship; exploitation of the wealth of developing nations by richer nations; and economic dependence of developing nations on developed nations.[15] The subordination of women to men does not enter this traditional calculus. Moreover, "development" as economic growth above all takes no notice of the lack of benefits or disadvantageous effects this growth may have on half of the society it purports to benefit.

One aspect of the international right to development is the provision of development assistance and aid. The UN General Assembly has called for international and national efforts to be aimed at eliminating "economic deprivation, hunger and disease in all parts of the world without discrimination" and for international cooperation to be aimed, inter alia, at maintaining "stable and sustained economic growth," increasing concessional assistance to developing countries, building world food security and resolving the debt burden.

Women and children are more often the victims of poverty and malnutrition than men. Women should therefore have much to gain from an international right to development. Yet the position of many women in developing countries has deteriorated over the last two decades: their access to economic resources has been reduced, their health and educational status has declined, and their work burdens have increased. The generality and apparent universal applicability of the right to development, as formulated in the UN declaration, is undermined by the fundamentally androcentric nature of the international economic system and its reinforcement of the public/private distinction. Of course, the problematic nature of current development practice for Third World women cannot be attributed simply to the international legal formulation of the right to development. But the rhetoric of international law both reflects and reinforces a system that contributes to the subordination of women.

Over the last twenty years, considerable research has been done on women and Third World development.[16] This research has documented the crucial role of women in the economies of developing nations, particularly in agriculture. It has also pointed to the lack of impact, or the adverse impact, of "development" on many Third World women's lives. The international legal order, like most development policies, has not taken this research into account in formulating any aspect of the right to development.

The distinction between the public and private spheres operates to make the work and needs of women invisible. Economic visibility depends on working in the public sphere and unpaid work in the home or community is categorized as "unproductive, unoccupied, and economically inactive." Marilyn Waring has recently argued that this division, which is institutionalized in developed nations, has been exported to the developing world, in part through the United Nations System of National Accounts (UNSNA).

The UNSNA, developed largely by Sir Richard Stone in the 1950s, enables experts to monitor the financial position of states and trends in their national development and to compare one nation's economy with that of another. It will thus influence the categorization of nations as developed or developing and the style and magnitude of the required international aid. The UNSNA measures the value of all goods and services that actually enter the market and of other nonmarket production such as government services provided free of charge. Some activities, however, are designated as outside the "production boundary" and are not measured. Economic reality is constructed by the UNSNA's "production boundaries" in such a way that reproduction, child care, domestic work and subsistence production are excluded from the measurement of economic productivity and growth. This view of women's work as nonwork was nicely summed up in 1985 in a report by the Secretary-General to the General Assembly, "Overall socio-economic perspective of the world economy to the year 2000." It said: "Women's productive and reproductive roles tend to be compatible in rural areas of low-income countries, since family agriculture and cottage industries keep women close to the home, permit flexibility in working conditions and *require low investment of the mother's time.*"

The assignment of the work of women and men to different spheres, and the consequent categorization of women as "nonproducers," are detrimental to women in developing countries in many ways and make their rights to development considerably less attainable than men's. For example, the operation of the public/private distinction in international economic measurement excludes women from many aid programs because they are not considered to be workers or are regarded as less productive than men. If aid is provided to women, it is often to marginalize them: foreign aid may be available to women only in their role as mothers, although at least since 1967 it has been recognized that women are responsible for as much as 80 percent of the food production in developing countries. The failure to acknowledge women's significant role in agriculture and the lack of concern about the impact of development on women mean that the potential of any right to development is jeopardized from the start.

Although the increased industrialization of the Third World has brought greater employment opportunities for women, this seeming improvement has not increased their economic independence or social standing and has had little impact on women's equality. Women are found in the lowest-paid and lowest-status jobs, without career paths; their working conditions are often discriminatory and insecure. Moreover, there is little difference in the position of women who live in developing nations with a socialist political order.[17] The dominant model of development assumes that any paid employment is better than none and fails to take into account the potential for increasing the inequality of women and lowering their economic position.

As we have seen, the international statement of the right to development draws no distinction between the economic position of men and of women. In using the neutral language of development and economics, it does not challenge the pervasive and detrimental assumption that women's work is of a different—and lesser—order than men's. It therefore cannot enhance the development of the group within developing nations that is most in need. More recent UN deliberations on development have paid greater attention to the situation of women. Their concerns, however, are presented as quite distinct, solvable by the application of special protective measures rather than as crucial to development.

The Right to Self-Determination

The public/private dichotomy operates to reduce the effectiveness of the right to self-determination at international law. The notion of self-determination as meaning the right of "all peoples" to "freely determine their political status and freely pursue their economic, social and cultural development" is flatly contradicted by the continued domination and marginalization of one sector of the population of a nation-state by another. The treatment of women within groups claiming a right to self-determination should be relevant to those claims. But the international community's response to the claims to self-determination of the Afghan and Sahrawi people, for example, indicates little concern for the position of women within those groups.

The violation of the territorial integrity and political independence of Afghanistan by the Soviet Union when it invaded that country in 1979, and other strategic, economic, and geopolitical concerns, persuaded the United States of the legality and morality of its support for the Afghan insurgents. In deciding to support the rebels, the United States did not regard the policies of the *mujahidin* with respect to women as relevant. The mujahidin are committed to an oppressive, rural, unambiguously patriarchal form of society quite different from that espoused by the socialist Soviet-backed regime. Indeed, Cynthia Enloe notes that "[o]ne of the policies the Soviet-backed government in Kabul pursued that so alienated male clan leaders was expanding economic and educational opportunities for Afghanistan's women." A consequence of the continued support for the insurgents was the creation of a vast refugee flow into Pakistan. Of these refugees, 30 percent were women and 40 percent were children under thirteen. The mullahs imposed a strict fundamentalist regime in the refugee camps, which confined women to the premises, isolated them, and even deprived them of their traditional rural tasks. There is no indication that any different policy would be followed if the mujahidin were successful and able to form a government in Afghanistan. Indeed, this marginalization and isolation of Afghan women is being projected into the future, as the educational services provided by the UN High Commissioner for Refugees are overwhelmingly for boys. The vital impact of education on women and its effect in undermining male domination have been well documented.

Morocco's claims to Western Sahara and the Polisario resistance to those claims have led to the establishment of Sahrawi refugee camps in Algeria that are mainly occupied by women and children. In these camps, however, women have been able to assert themselves: they have built hospitals and schools, achieved high rates of literacy, and supported "the right of the woman and the mother," as well as the "fight for independence." The international community, through the International Court of Justice and the General Assembly, has reiterated the right of the people of Western Sahara to self-determination. Despite this legal support, the Sahrawis' only backing comes from Algeria, while Morocco is backed, inter alia, by France and the United States. The determination of these women to keep alive a "democracy, based on proportional representation, with centralised and equal distribution, full employment, [and] social and political parity between the sexes" in the adverse conditions of refugee camps has received little international support.

The international community recognizes only the right of "peoples" to self-determination, which in practice is most frequently linked to the notion of the independent state. Women have never been viewed as a "people" for the purposes of the right to self-determination. In most instances, the pursuit of self-determination as a political response to colonial rule has not resulted in terminating the oppression and domination of one section of society by another.

States often show complete indifference to the position of women when determining their response to claims of self-determination; the international invisibility of women persists. Thus, after the Soviet Union vetoed a Security Council resolution on the invasion of Afghanistan, the General Assembly reaffirmed "the inalienable right of all peoples . . . to choose their own form of government free from outside interference" and stated that the Afghan people should be able to "choose their economic, political and social systems free from outside intervention, subversion, coercion or constraint of any kind whatsoever." The General Assembly's concern was with "outside" intervention alone. Women arguably suffer more from "internal" intervention: women are not free to choose their role in society without the constraints of masculine domination inside the state and are constantly subject to male coercion. The high-sounding ideals of noninterference do not apply to them, for their self-determination is subsumed by that of the group. The denial to women of the freedom to determine their own economic, social and cultural development should be taken into consideration by states in assessing the legitimacy of requests for assistance in achieving self-determination and of claims regarding the use of force.[18]

NOTES

1. Wishnik, "To Question Everything: The Inquiries of Feminist Jurisprudence," *Berkeley Women's Law Journal*, 1 (1985): 64.
2. Littleton, "Feminist Jurisprudence: The Difference Method Makes," *Stanford Law Review* 41 (1989): 751, 764.
3. See, for example, Cranston, "Are There Any Human Rights?" *Daedalus* 113 (1983).
4. Smart, *Feminism and the Power of Law* (New York: Routledge, 1989), p. 145.
5. See, for example, Arzt, "The Application of International Human Rights Law in Islamic States," *Human Rights Quarterly* 12 (1990):202, 203.
6. U.N. Document E/1987/SR.11, in Byrnes, *Report on the Seventh Session of the Committee on the Elimination of Discrimination Against Women and the Fourth Meeting of States Parties to the Convention on the Elimination of All Forms of Discrimination Against Women* (Hubert Humphrey School of Public Affairs, University of Minnesota, Minneapolis, MN: International Women's Rights Action Watch, 1988), p. 13.
7. Ibid.
8. African Charter on Human and Peoples' Rights, adopted June 27, 1981, Organization of African Unity Document CAB/LEG/67/3/Rev.5 reprinted in *International Legal Materials* 21 (1982).
9. Jacobs and Tracy, "Women in Zimbabwe: Stated Policies and State Action," *Women, State, Ideology: Studies from Africa and Asia* in Afshar (ed.), (New York: Macmillan, 1988).
10. Amos and Parmar, "Challenging Imperial Feminism," *Feminist Review* 17 (1984).
11. Williams, "Alchemical Notes: Reconstructing Ideals from Deconstructed Rights," *Harvard Civil Rights–Civil Liberties Law Review* 22 (1987).
12. Alston, "Making Space for New Human Rights: The Case of the Right to Development," *Harvard Human Rights Yearbook* 3 (1988); and Rich, "The Right to Development: A Right of Peoples," in Crawford (ed.), *The Rights of Peoples* (New York: Oxford University Press, 1988).
13. See, for example, Brownlie, "The Right of Peoples in Modern International Law," in *The Rights of Peoples*.
14. General Assembly Resolution 41/128, Article 2 (3), December 4, 1986.
15. Thomas and Skeat, "Gender in Third World Development Studies: An Overview of an Underview," *Australian Geographical Studies* 28 (1990).
16. The first major study was Boserup, Women's Role in Economic Development (London: Allen & Unwin, 1970). For a valuable review of the literature see Thomas and Skeat, "Gender in Third World Development Studies."
17. Molyneux, "Women's Emancipation Under Socialism: A Model for the Third World," *World Development* 9 (1982).
18. Chinkin, "A Gendered Perspective to the International Use of Force," *Australian Yearbook of International Law* 12 (1992).

The Corporate Capture of the Earth Summit

Kenny Bruno

Rio De Janeiro—In his last press conference as Secretary-General of the United Nations Conference on Environment and Development, Maurice Strong admitted that he was "really disappointed" in the failures of the Earth Summit. But he left unanswered—and unasked—the question of why the conference had failed. As people around the world attempt to understand why their governments did not implement measures to address the environmental and development crises, they should look closely at the influence of the world's most powerful economic actors, multinational corporations (also known as transnational corporations or TNCs).

Earth Summit negotiatiors set their goal as nothing less than moving the course of human activities onto a sustainable path. Given this lofty objective, it would have been logical to confront multinational corporations, since they are the entities primarily responsible for ozone depletion, global warming, toxic contamination, pesticide proliferation, international trade in hazards and other practices which threaten human health and the environment.

Instead, throughout the UNCED process, corporations enjoyed special access to the Secretariat, and the final UNCED documents treat them deferentially.

Corporate influence on the Earth Summit undermined Agenda 21, rendered the Climate Convention toothless and weakened the Biodiversity Convention, which was nonetheless rejected by the United States. In addition,

Reprinted with permission of *Multinational Monitor*. Individual subscription $25/year. P.O. Box 19405, Washington, DC 20036.

through an enormous public relations drive, corporate leaders themselves attempted to take over the UNCED stage to claim that they have voluntarily turned the corner onto a new path of sustainability.

The business vision on this "new" path still centers around economic growth, with free trade and open markets as prerequisites. Meanwhile, business leaders envision linking environmental protection to profitability, through a system in which all of nature is priced and patented. This is "sustainable development" according to the global corporations. And in Rio, UNCED—made up of representatives of virtually every government in the world—came close to adopting this vision of free market environmentalism as its own.

Maurice Strong: Businessman as Environmentalist

The choice of Maurice Strong—a multimillionaire Canadian businessman with interests in oil, real estate, mining and ecotourism—as UNCED Secretary-General was an early sign that the business perspective would have extraordinary clout at UNCED. In his opening speech to an UNCED preparatory conference in New York, Strong laid his philosophy on the table and called on UNCED to be compatible with the General Agreement on Tariffs and Trade (GATT), an international trade agreement which emphasizes open markets and is strongly supported by internationally oriented companies. This emphasis on free trade is embodied in Principle 12 of the Rio Declaration and allows GATT to cast its shadow over UNCED. As Kristen Dawkins of the Minneapolis-based Institute for Agriculture and Trade Policy says, "UNCED has bought the TNCs' plan for free trade to reign supreme over environmental protection in the New World Order. Principle 12 has the power to render environmental agreements moot."

Strong never denied close links with business during the UNCED process. At one meeting in Rio, he responded to criticism of this special relationship by saying, "How can we achieve [sustainable development] without the participation of business?"

The Business Council for Sustainable Development

Early in the UNCED process, Strong appointed Swiss industrialist Stephan Schmidheiny as his chief advisor for business and industry. Schmidheiny in turn gathered 48 top executives from companies like DuPont, Shell, Dow, Ciba-Geigy and Mitsubishi to form the Business Council for Sustainable Development (BCSD). The centerpiece of the BCSD's energetic effort was the book *Changing Course*, which lays out the multinational corporate vision of free-market environmentalism.

Throughout the UNCED process, the BCSD had special access to Strong, access which was unavailable to nongovernmental organizations, trade unions and groups representing women, youth, farmers and indigenous peoples. Strong even reported that he and DuPont Chief Executive Officer Edgar Woolard had edited a chapter of *Changing Course* together.

Strong's role as an apologist for industry intensified in the week before the official opening of UNCED. On the Friday before UNCED officially began, Strong could be found at a BCSD press conference, watching a high-tech Kodak-produced slide show of Brazilian flora, and fawning over Schmidheiny and the BCSD. "No contribution [to UNCED] has been more important than yours," he told Schmidheiny in front of scores of reporters.

ICC Guts Agenda 21

Two days earlier, with the presence of the King and Queen of Sweden drawing a flock of photographers, Strong delivered a similar paean to the plenary session of a 3-day meeting of the International Chamber of Commerce (ICC). The "deep appreciation" of the secretary-general was even more striking in this context, since the ICC has been a leading lobby against proposals to regulate the environmental practices of businesses.

During the fourth UNCED preparatory committee meeting in New York, Sweden and Norway introduced detailed Agenda 21 proposals. Based on recommendations of the United Nations Centre on Transnational Corporations, the proposals included some of the very same measures supported by the BCSD and ICC in written politics. However, after lobbying by ICC members back in Stockholm and in New York, these proposals were dropped. The final draft of Agenda 21 contains no proposals for controlling multinational corporations. Instead, it discusses the important role business and industry have to play in environmental protection and emphasizes voluntary measures that corporations are already taking.

This type of tactic was typical of the strategies used by the BCSD and ICC throughout the UNCED. While the slick and highly visible BCSD publicized its commitment to full environmental cost accounting, the ICC lobbied to remove such accounting measures from Agenda 21. While the BCSD touted the "changing course" of industry, the ICC systematically made sure that no changes harmful to its interests were made. About half of the BCSD companies are on the board of the ICC.

The Climate Convention

Three hundred scientists from 40 countries make up the International Panel on Climate Change (IPCC). Their report "Climate Change: The IPCC Scientific Assessment," states explicitly that the only hope for avoiding unprecedented and ecologically disastrous global warming is to make deep cuts in carbon dioxide emissions. The Climate Convention, which does not obligate any country to emissions reductions, therefore ranks as one of UNCED's most devastating failures.

In part, the weakness of the Convention represents the payoff of the work of the Global Climate Coalition, an industry lobby which was active throughout the two-year negotiating process. At the last session of the pre-conference negotiations, the Coalition passed out fliers which claimed, contrary to all the evidence amassed by the IPCC, that no environmental benefit will be achieved by stabilizing carbon dioxide emissions.

Shell and Du Pont, both members of the Coalition, are also members of the BCSD, and claim to embrace the "precautionary approach" to global warming. But a look underneath the fancy green language of "eco-efficiency," "no-regrets," and "precautionary principles," reveals that the oil industry still plans to burn "all the oil" it can find. After the BCSD press conference in Rio, Italian oil giant ENI President Gabriele Cagliari was asked if the world can burn all the oil on the planet and call it sustainable. Cagliari, who is also a BCSD member, squirmed slightly and answered, "Yes."

The Biodiversity Convention

On June 7, with the Rio conference less than half over, Schmidheiny, Cagliari and the other BCSD executives who had come to Rio left town, saying their work was done. Indeed it was. Two days earlier, the *New York Times* printed a leaked memo revealing that the White House had rejected the recommendation of William Reilly, chief administrator of the Environmental Protection Agency and the leader of U.S. delegation in Rio, to allow Brazil to try to renegotiate the biodiversity treaty, preferring to reject the treaty outright. Pointing out that he is "the president of the United States, not president of the world," President Bush explained that "in biodiversity it is important to protect our rights, our business rights."

The BCSD may have left town, but Bush was watching out for business interests. It was the corporations involved in biotechnology, including BCSD member companies like DuPont and Ciba-Geigy, whose concerns about profits from intellectual property rights had prompted Bush to sabotage the Biodiversity Convention.

Business Sponsorship of UNCED

Business influence was pervasive at UNCED in subtler ways as well. A handful of big companies, including Ashai Glass, Atlantic Richfield, ICI, Swatch and 3M, were major funders of Ecofund, a Washington, D.C.–based non-profit group set up to help finance the conference.

Business sponsorship extended to the Global Forum, the huge alternative summit for nongovernmental organizations. A report released by a group of student activists during UNCED detailed the environmentally destructive practices of Global Forum sponsors Petrobras, the Brazilian oil company, and Companhia Vale Do Rio Doce, a major Brazilian mining company.

Whether companies knew it or not, big business even had a man working for its interests in one of the more remote corners of the Rio meetings, the non-governmental organizations' negotiations of a treaty on TNCs. But the negotiations coordinator for the TNC treaty turned out to be Patrick McNamara, a representative of a group called "Business Transformations." This group is dedicated to working "with business" to help industries incorporate values such as "love, compassion [and] environmental protection," into their operations. After a struggle with others interested more in how to control TNCs than in how to raise the consciousness of business executives, McNamara agreed to relinquish his role as coordinator, but continued to attend meetings of the group.

TNCs, Development and Rocinha

UNCED's official pro-multinational corporation rationale is that these companies are the engines of economic growth which will provide resources for environmental protection and jobs for eliminating poverty. Rio was an interesting site for UNCED, because the poverty which "development" is meant to eradicate is on grotesque display. On their way to and from the conference each day, thousands of delegates and journalists passed through a tunnel underneath Rocinha, Latin America's largest *favela*, or shantytown, which is built on one of Rio's dramatic limestone hills.

On the first Saturday during the conference, NGO representatives and reporters gathered in Rocinha, high above the Hotel Intercontinental, were a week earlier, ICC executives had expressed pious concern for the world's poor. In a neighborhood Samba school, the NGO members listened to community leaders describe what UNCED had meant to them—tanks, soldiers, one disappearance and two killings since the Brazilian government increased security for the conference.

Compared to other similar places, Rocinha is a success story. After a tough struggle over the last few years, the shantytown's residents have seen some improvements in living conditions: it is no longer run by drug dealers, some of the neighborhoods are prospering and a leading candidate for mayor is from the *favela*. Nevertheless, the entire economy of Rocinha, including its schools, hospitals and sewage systems, is outside the official economy, and the signs of poverty are everywhere. It is a giant reminder of how growth and development, anachronistically peddled by multinational corporations and the World Bank at Rio, have failed to trickle even a minimal portion of wealth down to millions of people in Brazil and around the world.

Next on the TNC Agenda: GATT vs. UNCED

But UN and government officials seem to have ignored the failure of the market era and economic growth to provide environmental protection and eradicate poverty. By the time UNCED was over, multinational corporate executives could happily note that they had prevented international governmental meddling in corporate affairs and ushered in the era of free market environmentalism. Big business will now be relatively free to pursue its full agenda in the current GATT negotiations.

Judging from Rio, there will be opposition. Before the conference, non-governmental organizations aggressively challenged the role of multinational corporations in UNCED, starting with the release of a pamphlet called the "Greenpeace Book on Greenwash," an exposé of the BCSD and the environmental records of nine prominent companies. Two days later, when the BCSD began its meeting in Copacabana, the Greenpeace ship Rainbow Warrior blockaded the port of BCSD member Aracruz Celulosa and a coalition of indigenous people and Aracruz workers protested company policies. Almost every day saw a new counterattack against multinationals, and skeptics of corporate environmentalism from North and South sprouted up everywhere in the Global Forum.

The world's governments let corporate greenwash taint UNCED, but the thousands of NGOs gathered in Rio were resentful of the special influence corporations grabbed for themselves at the conference. The move into the era of free trade and free market environmentalism will only intensify the battle between environmentalists and multinational corporations. As Indian ecologist and feminist Vandana Shiva told a group discussing multinationals' role at UNCED, "Governments have abdicated their responsibilities; now it's between TNCs and citizens to fight it out directly."

Chapter *8*

Military Security

Today more so than in the past, it is recognized that threats to a state's security can spring from a variety of sources and take any number of forms. They may be economic (a trade embargo or a suddenly weakened currency), political (a break in diplomatic relations or the expulsion of refugees), environmental (global warming or damage from an oil spill), or cultural (the loss of national identity through the dominating influence of foreign news media or the advertising efforts of multinational corporations). Still, the most intensely studied threats to a state's security are those associated with military actions undertaken by a hostile state.

The central role played by military issues in strategic thought stems from what realist writers on world politics perceive to be the near anarchic nature of the international system. States are seen as operating in an environment in which considerations of international law, morality, and public opinion have only a limited ability to restrain the often hostile actions of other states. In the final analysis states can rely only on their own resources to protect their security, and the primary mechanism for holding other states in check is military power.

Two military security problems that have dominated the policy agenda in the post–World War II era and will continue to be of major importance in the twenty-first century are nuclear deterrence and international crisis management. After examining these areas we will consider four possible ways of short-circuiting the security dilemma: the replacement of nuclear deterrence by the principle of reassurance, the establishment of a collective security system, arms control, and disarmament.

Nuclear Deterrence

For American and Soviet military planners, the primary security problems of the cold war centered on the use of nuclear weapons. Until the arrival of the nuclear era it was commonly assumed that military power, whether a battleship, bomber, or infantry platoon, could be used in three different ways with equal effectiveness. First, military power could be used in combat to defend one's territory or seize the territory of others. Second, it could be used to compel another state to undertake a course of action that it would not otherwise choose. Third, it could be used to deter another state from carrying out policies it wished to pursue. The immense destructive power of nuclear weapons led most strategists to conclude that they could not be used in all these ways, and a consensus soon emerged that the only mission for which nuclear weapons were well suited was deterrence.

Although the specifics of the various deterrence strategies adopted by the United States and the Soviet Union often changed, the underlying logic of nuclear deterrence did not. Strategists started from the assumption of rationality. Policymakers were seen as making a series of cost-benefit calculations over what goals they wished to achieve and the price they were willing to pay to realize them. For deterrence to work, the cost of pursuing a certain goal had to become unacceptable. The strategy of the United States was to threaten to retaliate against the aggressor with an overwhelming amount of nuclear weapons, which would leave its society, economy, and leadership structure in ruins. The Soviet Union sought to deter the United States both by threatening a second-strike retaliation and by claiming the ability to fight and win a nuclear war.

Successful deterrence requires more than military capacity, however. The threat must also be credible. In part, credibility is a function of what is being protected. A willingness to fight a nuclear war to protect one's homeland from attack is credible. Fighting a nuclear war to protect an ally is not as credible, and the less important the ally the less credible the pledge becomes. Because neither superpower was content merely to protect its homeland from attack by the other, policymakers were forced to find ways of bolstering their credibility. Among the favored strategies were signing treaties; publicly pledging support for an ally; setting up trip-wires or imaginary lines, which once crossed automatically set in motion a military response; and boxing oneself into a corner so that it was politically impossible to back down and not carry out one's policy.

The final element in the construction of a successful deterrence policy is that it must be communicated to the adversary in a clear and timely fashion. Whereas surprise is often a highly valued commodity in military strategy, it has little place in deterrence. Deterrence succeeds because the enemy believes that the cost of aggression will be too high. Similarly, trip-wires are effective only if everyone recognizes them as such and they are not mistaken for a half-hearted commitment. In the final analysis, because deterrence forces are designed not to be used, deterrence has failed once fighting begins even if the enemy is then easily defeated. Communicating a deterrence policy to an adversary is complicated by several factors. Cultural barriers and differing value systems can often distort messages, causing them to be misinterpreted or even unrecognized. Governments are not unitary actors. They are made up of large bureaucratic organizations that often have quite different views of the world and may be in competition with one another for influence over policy and budgetary resources. Thus, communicating the existence of a trip-wire or new military capability to the ministry of defense may produce quite a different response than if it were to go through the foreign office or an intelligence agency.

Critics of deterrence argue that when discussed separately the various elements of a successful deterrence strategy pose few analytical difficulties. Problems arise, however, when they are combined into a single package. For example, it is assumed that governments are rational, but as already noted, governments are made up of competing bureaucracies. The assumption of rationality is further undermined by the need of a state to limit drastically its flexibility in order to make its threat credible. Finally, the assumption of rationality is called into question by studies of crisis decision making, which suggest that members of small decision-making groups are particularly vulnerable to internal group pressures that may lead to flawed decisions.

Conceptual problems have plagued deterrence theory from the outset and led many to question its value in providing military security. The end of the cold war and demise of the Soviet Union present yet another set of challenges to deterrence theorists. From its very inception deterrence theory took for granted the existence of a bipolar nuclear world in which there was only one nuclear adversary of consequence. This is no longer the case. Although the United States remains the preeminent nuclear power, it now faces the prospect of having to deter several nuclear states with varying goals and value systems. None of these states will have the ability, either acting alone or in unison, to threaten the physical security of the United States, but they may have the ability to alter regional power balances and significantly raise the costs of U.S. intervention around the world. Under these circumstances the military and political value of its nuclear weapons will be severely diminished unless new deterrence strategies are developed.

International Crises

The onset of an international crisis signals a sudden and critical departure from the normal conduct of international relations. Along with the element of surprise and a sense of urgency, crises carry a large measure of uncertainty over how they will end. All too often they have ended in war. During the cold war the link between war and crisis appeared to weaken, making the problem of international crisis management seem less urgent. At first this weakening was due to the overwhelming fear that were a superpower crisis to get out of control it might result in a nuclear World War III. Later, it seemed to be the product of an increased capacity of American and Soviet policymakers to manage international crises and establish informal ground rules governing crisis behavior.

One of the fears most frequently expressed is that with the end of the cold war, international crises will become even more numerous and dangerous. Several factors are at work here. The first involves a reevaluation of the role played by nuclear weapons in preventing a clash between the United States and

Soviet Union. John Mueller argues that contrary to popular belief, the large number of nuclear weapons in U.S. and Soviet inventories did not place restraints on their behavior. In fact, he argues, nuclear weapons were largely irrelevant to peace during the cold war.

Second, studies of crisis decision making suggest that the self-confidence policymakers have acquired may be misplaced and overstated. Rather then being good at crisis management, policymakers were often lucky. For example, Scott Sagan in his study of nuclear alerts and crisis management concludes that frequently "civilian authorities did not understand the military operations they were contemplating." He also offers evidence that the Joint Chiefs of Staff had placed the military on a higher alert than the Secretary of Defense had intended; that military commanders had taken it upon themselves to place their forces on a high state of alert without formal presidential authorization; and that because they had inadequate military forces, commanders had been unable to implement an alert order in the instructed manner.

Richard Betts's examination of the way in which American presidents employed nuclear threats during crises also contains unsettling implications for future crisis management. He found that presidents and their advisors often appeared to make nuclear threats without carefully thinking through the consequences of their actions. He also found that U.S. and Soviet leaders differed in how they reacted to crises. The decisions of American leaders were governed more by how politically important the issue was than by relative military capabilities. Soviet leaders, however, appeared to "let military prudence override political interests." This difference is significant for two reasons. First, it always produced a situation in which the Soviet Union backed down. Second, there is no guarantee that in future crises Russian, Iraqi, or other leaders may not operate on the same principle as U.S leaders. Should this happen war would seem to be the almost unavoidable outcome.

A final reason for concern over the onset of international crises in the future is a potential failure by policymakers to recognize that not all crises are identical. Strategies that might succeed in one crisis may intensify another and make its peaceful resolution more problematic. Richard Lebow distinguishes among three types of international crises. In a justification-of-hostilities crisis the instigating state has already made a decision to go to war and is manufacturing a crisis solely for this purpose. The most common form is the brinkmanship crisis, which occurs when one state deliberately creates a crisis to gain a military or political advantage over another state by forcing it to back down from the brink of war. Unlike the justification-of-hostilities crisis, in a brinkmanship crisis the initiating state is not committed to fighting a war. Quite the opposite, it hopes to realize its goals strictly through the threat of force. The most unmanageable type of crisis is the spinoff. As its name implies this type is often an offshoot of a larger crisis or problem that is being contested at the time. It literally sneaks up on states because their attention is focused elsewhere, and it is this lack of preparation and foresight that makes a spinoff crisis so dangerous. Steps that might have been taken to defuse the crisis in its early stages are not employed, and actions taken elsewhere may unintentionally compound the problem.

Alternative Security Policies

Although the exercise of military power is necessary for the survival of the state, many also recognize that its use may very well be self-defeating. That is, rather than increase the security of a state the use of military power may actually serve to lessen it. The reason for this effect is thought to lie in the *security dilemma*. That is, the pursuit of power by state A in the name of national security will lessen the security of others around it. The proper response by policymakers in these states is to acquire more military power. The net result of this decision will be to lessen the value of the security just purchased by state A, perhaps even placing state A in a more insecure position than before. Confronted with this situation, state A must once again seek to acquire more military power, thereby setting in motion further military buildups by other states.

Janice Gross Stein proposes that policymakers give serious consideration to replacing, or at least supplementing, deterrence with reassurance strategies as one way of lessening the grip of the security dilemma. She argues that such a change is necessary because deterrence is not a universally appropriate strategy but may at times be provocative, ineffective, or irrelevant. It is provocative when instead of convincing an adversary not to act, it frightens the state into taking the unwanted action. It is ineffective when the deterrence threat is not recognized by the adversary and irrelevant when the adversary has already made an irrevocable decision to proceed. Verbal assurances and nonprovocative actions can compensate for these potential deficiencies.

Stein characterizes reassurance strategies as prenegotiation strategies. Their purpose is to alter the conditions under which states consider the use of force and to "persuade the adversary that negotiation is a serious alternative." She identifies four such strategies: the exercise of restraint, the creation of norms of competition, the making of irrevocable commitments, and regime building. Like deterrence strategies, reassurance strategies presume the existence of hostile or adversarial relationships between states. Unlike deterrence strategies, however, reassurance strategies do not assume that states are opportunistic in nature and always ready to turn an adversary's weakness to their own advantage. Rather, they assume that states are primarily concerned with meeting their own needs and compensating for their own weaknesses.

Charles and Clifford Kupchan suggest a second alternative to deterrence as a means of realizing military security. They assert that the military and political landscape of Europe has been transformed to the point that it is now possible to establish an effective collective security system. All of the necessary preconditions for such a system are now either in place or emerging: (1) No single state can be so powerful that it can resist an opposing coalition of forces, (2) the major powers must have compatible views on what constitutes an acceptable and stable international order, and (3) elites must share an awareness of international community and a desire to preserve it.

Kupchan and Kupchan recognize that collective security systems in their ideal form are inherently fragile. First, it is extremely difficult to assemble and maintain a system in which all states participate. Second, policymakers are not inclined to make automatic and binding commitments to oppose aggression. To compensate for these two points of weakness, Kupchan and Kupchan propose establishing a European collective security system that draws heavily on the notion of an informal concert of the major European powers. Operating through a consensual decision-making process, these states would decide which acts of aggression merit a response and which do not. The concert would also be able to act in other ways to deal with conflict, such as taking preemptory action, imposing sanctions, mobilizing forces, and holding emergency meetings.

Kupchan and Kupchan conclude that the general framework for such a collective security system already exists in the Conference on Security and Cooperation in Europe (CSCE), and they propose creating a two-tiered structure within it. In addition to the current body to which all members belong, there would be a security group, made up of the major European powers, that would have jurisdiction over such topics as national boundaries, arms control, and peacekeeping. The core of this body would consist of the United States, Great Britain, France, Germany, and Russia. Other states might be added on a rotating basis, much as in the U.N. Security Council. Initially the CSCE Security Group would coexist with NATO, but over time NATO would transfer more responsibility to it and would ultimately dissolve.

The third and fourth alternative policies are arms control and disarmament. Disarmament seeks to eliminate weapons. Whether the goal is complete and total disarmament, the reduction or elimination of selective weapons systems, or the elimination of weapons from specific regions, disarmament plans are rooted in the assumption that weapons themselves are a primary cause of international conflict. Arms-control efforts start from a very different premise. Although recognizing that weapons can aggravate military security problems, advocates of arms control assume that the root causes of these problems are political. Accordingly they seek to place restraints on the use of weapons rather than limits on their numbers.

Over the past several years the distinctions between arms control and disarmament have become blurred. Not only do international agreements combine elements of each, but also the policy-making community has begun to use *arms control* as a generic term for all efforts at curbing military competition between states. However, it is important to be sensitive to the differences between the two approaches for several reasons. First, arms control and disarmament were long considered to be incompatible with each other. They were seen as representing an either/or situation, and trying to pursue both policies at once would only undermine a state's security. Beginning in the late 1960s, however, policymakers attempted to combine both under the heading of arms limitation. The limited support and widespread criticism that arms-limitation efforts received (i.e., SALT I and SALT II) in the United States raise the possibility that the original practitioners of arms control and disarmament may have been correct.

Second, because arms control and disarmament proceed from different assumptions, they are not interchangeable. Not only will one approach be more suitable for dealing with certain types of problems, but also the prerequisites for their successful use will be different. For example, disarmament efforts often degenerate into international propaganda campaigns designed to make one state appear to be aggressive and the other a champion of peace. Regional disarmament proposals have met with the greatest success prior to the introduction of weapons systems in a given region. Once a military capability and interest in using it exist, disarmament plans begin to encounter difficulties.

It is hardly surprising that the focal point of arms-control and disarmament efforts during the cold war was on reducing and restraining the nuclear capabilities of the United States and the Soviet Union. The end of the cold war has not meant an end to the dangers inherent in U.S. and Russian nuclear weapons. Large numbers of strategic nuclear weapons continue to exist (disarmament), and nuclear testing continues (arms control). What the end of the cold war has done is to expand the number of security issues for which arms control and disarmament measures might be crafted.

Along with this continued concern for U.S. and Russian nuclear forces, five other security issues are likely to compete for space on the arms-control and disarmament agenda in the next century: conventional weapons, arms transfers, chemical and biological weapons, naval forces, and nuclear proliferation. None of these security issues is truly a new problem. Negotiations on conventional weapons in Europe have been underway since 1973, for example. Some, like naval forces, have only been dealt with infrequently and half-heartedly. Others, such as biological and chemical weapons, appear periodically and are addressed with great fervor for a short time only to disappear from view as the crisis passes.

Nuclear proliferation and arms transfers promise to be two of the most pressing and complex issues both because of the numbers of states whose agreement will be necessary to make any agreement work and because of the technical complexity involved. Consider just two issues. First, at what point can a state be said to have "gone nuclear"? Must it possess a deliverable nuclear capability (and if so, how far must it be capable of delivering such a weapon or by what means?), must it have successfully tested a nuclear device, or must it just possess the knowledge to build a bomb? An answer to this question must be given before the task of controlling nuclear proliferation can be addressed. Second, what is the best point to deal with the problem of arms transfers? Can, or must, one limit the activity of individual firms who sell technology openly on the international market, or is it enough simply to control sales by the military establishments of one state to that of another? If one is going to limit or restrain the sale of technology, how does one deal with the many dual-use technologies that presently exist? Moreover, who should be responsible for verifying that the agreed-on limits and restraints are in place? Can national verification programs be entrusted with this responsibility, or must an international or regional organization assume this task?

The Readings

The first reading, by George Quester, examines "The Future of Deterrence" in the post–cold war world. In "Four Decades of Nuclear Nonproliferation," Lewis Dunn evaluates the record of international attempts at furthering nuclear nonproliferation in terms of wins, losses, and draws. In "Windows of Opportunity," Richard Ned Lebow examines whether states really start military conflicts because they think they can win, as is usually believed to be the case. In "The United States and the Politics of Conflict in Developing Countries," Todd Greentree calls for a selective engagement and puts forward criteria to follow now that the policy of containment can no longer guide U.S. foreign policy.

Bibliography

BETTS, RICHARD. *Nuclear Blackmail and Nuclear Balance.* Washington, DC: Brookings Institutions, 1987.

BUZAN, BARRY. *An Introduction to Strategic Studies,* New York: St. Martins Press, 1987.

GEORGE, ALEXANDER, PHILIP FARLEY, and ALEXANDER DALLIN. (eds.), *U.S.-Soviet Security Cooperation.* New York: Oxford University Press, 1988.

JERVIS, ROBERT. *The Illogic of American Nuclear Strategy.* Ithaca, NY: Cornell University Press, 1984.

KUPCHAN, CHARLES, and CLIFFORD KUPCHAN. "Concerts, Collective Security, and the Future of Europe." *International Security* 16 (1991), 114–61.

LEBOW, RICHARD. *Between Peace and War: The Nature of International Crisis.* Baltimore: Johns Hopkins University Press, 1981.

LYNN-JONES, SEAN. et al. (eds.). *Nuclear Diplomacy and Crisis Management: An International Security Reader.* Cambridge, MA: MIT Press, 1990.

MILLER, STEVEN. (ed.). *Strategy and Nuclear Deterrence: An International Security Reader.* (Princeton, NJ: Princeton University Press, 1984.

MUELLER, JOHN. "The Essential Irrelevance of Nuclear Weapons." *International Security* 13 (1988), 55–79.

SAGAN, SCOTT. "Nuclear Alerts and Crisis Management." *International Security* 9 (1985), 99–139.

STEIN, JANICE. "Reassurance in International Conflict Management." *Political Science Quarterly* 106 (1991), 431–51.

TETLOCK, PHILIP., et al. (eds.). *Behavior, Society, and Nuclear War,* Vols. 1 and 2. New York: Oxford University Press, 1989,1991.

WESTON, BURNS. (ed.). *Toward Nuclear Disarmament and Global Security: A Search for Alternatives.* Boulder, CO: Westview, 1984.

The Future of Nuclear Deterrence

George H. Quester

Nuclear deterrence has been burdened with problems for decades. However, the revolutions in Eastern Europe and the even more revolutionary developments in what used to be known as the Soviet Union may be transforming these problems and posing fundamental questions about the future of nuclear deterrence itself.

Prior to the dissolution of the Warsaw Pact, analysts had four main concerns about nuclear deterrence: the problem of maintaining adequate retaliatory forces; the problem of maintaining command and control to prevent unauthorized nuclear attacks; the problem of reconciling nuclear deterrence to Western moral traditions; and the problem of extending nuclear deterrence to prevent conventional attacks. Dramatic changes may take place in each of these areas due to the recent transformation of the strategic landscape.

Retaliatory Capabilities

Deterrence theory has always maintained that both sides must be able to launch a formidable countervalue attack even after absorbing a counter-force attack designed to prevent such retaliation. If either side was able to neutralize the other's forces, nuclear deterrence would fail.

From *Survival* 34 (Spring 1992). Reprinted by permission of International Institute for Strategic Studies.

Recent developments might affect this nuclear deterrence problem in three different ways. First, substantial reductions in the nuclear arsenals of the United States and the former Soviet Union, enshrined in the Strategic Arms Reduction Talks (START) Treaty and envisioned in radical proposals for even deeper cuts in strategic forces, raise questions about the viability of strategic retaliatory forces and, therefore, strategic stability. Some now maintain that each side should reduce its arsenal from 10,000–12,000 weapons to 3,000; others maintain the number should be even less than 1,000. With smaller arsenals on each side, the retaliatory force left after a counter-force attack would also be smaller. At what point would this become too small to deter? Although many are opposed to the maintenance of excess capabilities in the arsenals of the two sides, one could hardly endorse further major reductions if this would increase the chances of an all-out nuclear war taking place.

One of the most important aspects of the strategic balance is crisis stability, which revolves around calculations and perceptions about the value of launching a first strike should nuclear war appear imminent. Neither side should ever be thrust into a 'use them or lose them' position with regard to its nuclear retaliatory forces. Therefore, it is fundamental to inquire whether crisis stability will be enhanced or degraded as the arsenals on each side are reduced. The United States will almost certainly then not elect to go below 3,000 warheads.

Second, British, French and Chinese nuclear forces continue to complicate strategic calculations in several interesting ways. Balance-of-power theory maintains that the existence of third, fourth and fifth powers helps to dissuade the first from attacking the second, and vice versa, because the other powers could intervene and exploit whatever attrition occurred as a result of the initial conflict. Alternatively, an aggressive power could attack all of the other major powers in the system, but this would dilute the attack and make defeat more likely. The existence of medium-sized powers thereby helps to reinforce the stability of the central balance between the superpowers. British, French and Chinese forces have effectively helped to maintain this balance for decades. . . .

An interesting analogy to what might emerge from this process can be found in the discussions that took place in the 1930s about an 'Air Locarno' as the solution to the balance of power in the air.[1] Air planners between the wars had come to be concerned about a 'knockout blow', by which one air force might catch another on the ground and impose a total defeat in a first strike, even if the two air forces were equally matched. If there were as many as four such air forces, however, the arithmetic made it much less likely that any single force could launch a sneak attack and disarm the other three. The existence of medium-sized arsenals therefore helped to stabilize the relationship between the two leading powers. In short, British, French and Chinese nuclear forces could play an even more important role in the future than they have in the past.

Third, Western decision-makers and analysts have long wondered how much retaliatory punishment was needed to deter the other side from attacking. Another important by-product of recent events in the former Soviet Union is that Western decision-makers and analysts can at last expect to have some of their questions answered. Refreshingly candid strategic analysis has emerged from Soviet defence intellectuals in the past five years, and this has gone a long way towards dispelling the idea that the Soviet leadership 'did not understand deterrence' or that the strategic reasoning developed and articulated in the English-speaking world was somehow 'ethno-centric' and peculiar to Western culture.

The West has, thus, throughout the nuclear age, been bothered by elementary doubts about whether deterrence was viable and whether it was needed. Were Soviet leaders deterred by the prospect of massive destruction? Would Soviet leaders have contemplated aggression if their civil defence preparations could have kept casualties down to the levels suffered in World War II? Were Soviet leaders interested only in 'winning', meaning counter-value threats did not act as a reliable deterrent? To look at this problem from another angle, is it possible that the Soviet Union would not have attacked the United States or Western Europe, even if American and other Western nuclear forces had not been developed? Is it possible that there was no need for nuclear deterrence?

The *glasnost* and chaos sweeping the former Soviet Union may soon shed more light on such questions, freeing the West at last from the conjectures of the past. The level of forces needed for deterrence can be set more precisely once it can be determined how close the Soviet Union came to exploiting capabilities 'gaps' or 'windows of opportunity' in the past.

Nuclear Command and Control

Although there is some good news as far as the stability of the strategic balance is concerned, the situation appears much grimmer when one turns to the problem of command and control. Recent developments in the former Soviet Union have aggravated some basic problems.

Nuclear deterrence has always depended on the ability of the major powers to maintain responsible command and control of their forces, so that nuclear attacks could not be launched without proper authorization. Western leaders and analysts, therefore, have long wanted the Soviet Union to take two steps the United States and its allies had already taken: conduct psychological tests of the officers who handle nuclear weapons and install physical security devices such as Permissive Action Links (PALs) on nuclear weapon systems. The available evidence suggests that in the 1980s the Soviet Union astutely shared Western concerns about the importance of maintaining adequate command and control of nuclear forces and that it had its nuclear weapons under very close control.

With the break-down of central authority in the Soviet Union, it is possible that the newly independent republics will insist on dividing up the Soviet nuclear arsenal. Much depends on what the leaders of the new republics want. They may simply want a *safety-catch* veto over the firing of the Commonwealth's nuclear weapons; this would safeguard the status of the republics that handed over nuclear weapons to Russia and keep the balance of military power in the Commonwealth from tipping precipitously in Moscow's direction. If this is all the non-Russian republics want, the West has little to worry about. But if the non-Russian republics want the ability to fire weapons on their own, the situation is much more menacing. The global community would then be facing a very serious nuclear proliferation problem.

Unfortunately, there are other command-and-control problems to consider, including the possibility of more coup attempts in Moscow, of coups and insubordination elsewhere in the Commonwealth and of civil wars among the republics or factions within the armed forces. A related problem is that one or more Central European states might seek to acquire nuclear weapons should Russia or the Ukraine attempt to reimpose hegemony on the region or if the Ukraine retains complete control over nuclear forces stationed on its territory.

. . . The main threat the West faces is not an all out, co-ordinated attack by the new Commonwealth, but rather a smaller, unco-ordinated and perhaps unauthorized attack from some unknown quarter. The case for ballistic missiles or a Global Protection Against Limited Strikes (GPALS) system, has always been stronger in the context of threats such as these, as opposed to the robust Soviet threat the West faced for so long.

Advocates of total nuclear disarmament or deep cuts in the superpower arsenals are also at least partially vindicated, given these emerging and potential command-and-control problems. If there had not been *so many* warheads added to the superpower arsenals on each side in previous decades, the command-and-control problem would be more manageable today. If each side had not felt the need for mobile missiles (in response to concerns about maintaining adequate retaliatory capabilities), worries about the whereabouts of these weapons would not be an issue today. Much of President George Bush's September 1991 disarmament initiative—eliminating mobile basing of missiles, taking bombers off runway alert and putting the bombs in secure shelters, taking naval nuclear weapons off ships and placing them in secure facilities on shore, eliminating ground-based tactical nuclear weapons altogether—astutely reflects such concerns.

The Immorality of Nuclear Deterrence

A problem that has continued to trouble many is the immorality of nuclear deterrence. Contrary to Western philosophical tradition, nuclear deterrence calls for the punishment of the innocent to deter the potentially guilty. The mechanism of nuclear deterrence is analogous to attempts to deter people from murder by threatening, if they themselves cannot be punished, to punish their spouse and children instead. In other areas of public policy, punishment of civilian hostages has long been condemned as barbaric. If such punishment is tolerated in an attempt to prevent nuclear war, this amounts to a grand exception to the rule.

Throughout the years, one has frequently heard the disingenuous argument that 'military targets' have been found in every major city of the Soviet Union. While the US Strategic Air Command would have been bombing 'military targets' in its response to whatever had caused an all out war, at least as far as official rhetoric was concerned, it has long been understood that there would have been a great deal of collateral 'bonus' damage to the civilian population and industry of the Soviet Union if such an attack took place. Even if this collateral damage was officially 'inadvertent', to avoid too blatant a contradiction of the laws of war and of traditional morality, the threat of such damage had to be accepted as a preventative measure in the first place. It was assumed that Soviet leaders did not want to see 50 million or more Soviet citizens killed (whether or not these citizens were dedicated communists) and would thus think twice before sending tanks into Germany.

These moral conundrums posed at least three problems during the Cold War era. First, when Americans or others were forced to contemplate how nuclear deterrence actually worked, as in the 1983 Letter of the Roman Catholic Bishops, they tended to be repulsed.[2] Some analysts conjectured that nuclear deterrence could not last out the century, on the grounds that a moral moment of truth would lead all decent human beings to reject it.[3]

Second, when military planners on either side took these moral issues seriously, they were led in the direction of developing counter-force options. Their goal became devising ways of putting the other side's military forces, including its strategic nuclear forces, at risk. This, of course, threatened to undermine the most basic prerequisites of deterrence.

Third, in the West, there is a moral compunction to avoid threatening the innocent, but there are fewer qualms about punishing the guilty. Did nuclear deterrence lead the West to label its adversaries as guilty parties, as aggressors? Did it induce animosity where none previously existed? When German and Japanese cities were fire-bombed during World War II and then Hiroshima and Nagasaki were attacked with atomic weapons, the Allies told themselves that most of the Germans were Nazis and that the Japanese were barbaric imperialists. (The Allied air forces also pretended to themselves that targets of a military nature were being attacked.) The countervalue components of nuclear deterrence are easiest to swallow when one believes oneself to be at war with the other side's entire population because they are all 'working in military factories' or because they all are enthusiastic about their nation's aggressive, militaristic policies.

Duplicating this line of thinking has been difficult in the nuclear age and will become even more difficult now that the Cold War is over. The West opposed the Soviet Union for decades because it was opposed to communist dictatorships, not because it found the Soviet peoples hateful. . . .

Extended Nuclear Deterrence

The fourth and final problem has been most troubling during the course of the Cold War. This is the problem of extending the US nuclear umbrella to protect regimes that were vulnerable to Soviet conventional attack. This problem was easily manageable during the short period when the United States had a nuclear monopoly; however, once the Soviet Union developed atomic bombs, some were concerned that the threat of nuclear attack would have to be held in reserve, to deter its equivalent, thereby leaving many countries vulnerable to Soviet conventional attacks. . . .

From a hardline Soviet perspective, the spread of democratic forces eliminated much of what was worth fighting for in the first place. At the same time, the disarray within the former Soviet Union vitiates the need and the opportunity to extend nuclear deterrence.

One can thus outline at least three possible scenarios for the future of extended nuclear deterrence. First, if conventional forces are ultimately balanced, the realization of what former Secretary of Defense McNamara has advocated for years may occur—the elimination of flexible response and extended nuclear deterrence. As long as nuclear weapons exist, one can not totally dismiss what many have called 'existential deterrence', the inherent possibility that, if any nation possessing nuclear weapons experiences a disastrous conventional military defeat, it might still bring these weapons into use. Yet, nuclear deterrence would not be extended more than this should things move in that direction.

Second, if Russia comes to dominate the Commonwealth and if it feels threatened by the conventional forces on the Commonwealth's borders, the possibility remains, as noted, that Russia might adopt a flexible response policy and pose the threat of first use.

Third, if Russia or the Commonwealth were to regain much more than this minimum level of cohesion, if it were to come back in the next decade 'leaner and meaner', still exploiting its geographically central position, the West might feel by the end of the century that it faced another Cold War. The conventional Western frontier would no longer be the Elbe, of course, but the Bug, with NATO thus having more room for manoeuvre and more conventional forces; however, there might be a temptation to rely on extended nuclear deterrence for the protection of Poland, Czechoslovakia and other European powers, rather than waste resources on more costly conventional defences.

The first of these worlds would be one of 'conventional deterrence', in which the disincentive to attack rests more on a lessened probability of military success in either direction than on a threat of horrendous destruction. Pessimists are fond of noting that historically there have been many conventional 'deterrence failures', but no nuclear failures. Opponents of extended nuclear deterrence can always respond by noting the enormity of the calamity if nuclear deterrence fails and by expressing the hope that improvements in East–West political relations will remove most incentives for war.

'Peace Dividends' and Nuclear Proliferation

A great number of people around the world will react to these questions with astonishment and indignation, on the grounds that the dramatic changes in the Soviet Union and in East–West relations surely render such strategic questions obsolete. . . .

Rather than further developing the argument that the end of the Cold War may not always reduce the risks of armed conflict, it is useful to try to relate this to nuclear deterrence. One comes then to the issue of nuclear proliferation, which has all along been capable of upsetting any and all of the current presumptions about deterrence. What can now be expected about the rate of proliferation? And, if such weapons spread to a large number of countries, what will this mean for the future of nuclear deterrence?

Nuclear proliferation almost always undermines the reliability of command and control. The more separate triggers there are, the more there is a risk of someone pulling a trigger 'for no good reason'. Deterrence thus fails by definition.

Concerns about the survivability of retaliatory forces are more unevenly affected. The proliferation of independent nuclear forces may make it more unlikely than ever that a successful general nuclear strike could be undertaken. In this case, no single country might be able to establish a global nuclear monopoly by landing a 'splendid first strike'. However, fledgling nuclear forces will often look like attractive targets, thus creating a dangerous period of passage until they can be wedded to secure and reliable second-strike delivery systems.

Moral issues are compounded by the spread of nuclear weapons, at least insofar as a need to project evil onto the people being targeted may poison political relationships among many countries. Too often, for example, the 'traditional rivalry' between Brazil and Argentina is glibly spoken of, as if these two states had been at war with each other repeatedly throughout the years. Yet, the introduction of nuclear arsenals on each side might make this rivalry much more real, for the first time resembling the confrontations that have often characterized Europe.

For these three reasons, the proliferation of nuclear weapons should thus be rejected. In a fourth area—the feasibility of extended nuclear deterrence—the possible attractions of nuclear proliferation emerge. Any 'pariah state' threatened by the conventional forces of its neighbours and shunned by the international community may be tempted to acquire nuclear weapons as a way of deterring attack because no existing nuclear-weapons state will make the necessary commitments to intervention and escalation. Israel, Taiwan and South Africa come to mind in this regard. . . .

The lessons of the Iraqi invasion of Kuwait are thus quite mixed insofar as nuclear proliferation is concerned. By making Iraqi interest in acquiring nuclear weapons one of the reasons for resisting Saddam Hussein and by getting international backing on this issue, the United States amplified a growing worldwide consensus against nuclear proliferation. By directing so much attention at obtaining reassurances that Iraq had not yet acquired nuclear weapons, however, the same operations may have driven home the point that future aggressors should make proliferation their first venture.

NOTES

1. See Royal Institute of International Affairs, *Documents on International Affairs*, vol. 1 (London: Oxford University Press, 1936), pp. 27, 36.
2. *The Challenge of Peace: God's Promise and Our Response* (Washington, DC: National Conference of Catholic Bishops, 1983).
3. See, for example, Fred Iklé, "Can Nuclear Deterrence Last Out the Century?" *Foreign Affairs* 51, no. 2 (January 1973): 267–285.

Four Decades of Nuclear Nonproliferation

Some Lessons from Wins, Losses, and Draws

Lewis A. Dunn

For more than four decades, the United States has opposed the spread of nuclear weapons to other countries. This basic policy has rested on the belief that nuclear proliferation would result in new threats to U.S. security, heighten global and regional instabilities, and quite possibly lead to the use of nuclear weapons. That assumption continues to guide U.S. policy today.

Over the years, U.S. nuclear nonproliferation efforts have relied on three broad sets of specific actions that constitute the basic building blocks of U.S. policy in this area. Initiatives have been launched and measures have been taken in order to reduce the political incentives that could lead countries to acquire nuclear weapons; technical obstacles have been created in order to make acquisition more difficult; and international nonproliferation institutions have been established.

It is especially timely to reconsider the record of nuclear nonproliferation efforts over the course of the past decade. With open or unacknowledged nuclear proliferation throughout the world, such an analysis could provide useful insights for renewed attempts to head off a world of many nuclear weapon states. Equally, with policy attention focusing on the problems of chemical weapons and missile proliferation, examination of the nuclear nonproliferation experience could provide lessons for those two areas.

This article offers some reflections on nuclear nonproliferation wins, losses, and draws. It focuses on both the policies pursued and the results

Reprinted by permission of *The Washington Quarterly* 13 (Summer 1990) and the Aspen Strategy Group.

achieved. In some cases, whether to categorize given policies and their results as wins, losses, or draws is open to differing interpretations; readers undoubtedly will strike their own balance. By way of conclusion, some lessons for chemical weapons and missile nonproliferation are drawn from the nuclear nonproliferation record.

Nuclear Nonproliferation Wins

There are five acknowledged nuclear weapon states: the United States (1945), the Soviet Union (1949), the United Kingdom (1952), France (1960), and China (1964). In addition, India detonated a nuclear explosive device in 1974, but claimed it was only for peaceful purposes; and Israel is believed publicly to have manufactured nuclear weapons.[1] Top officials in both South Africa and Pakistan have stated publicly that their countries have "the capability" to make nuclear weapons should they desire to do so.[2]

Today, proliferation is quite different from what many officials and observers in the late 1950s and early 1960s thought would be the case. Back then, it was feared widely that 15–20 states, if not more, would possess nuclear weapons by the mid-1970s. Behind the difference between past predictions and the current situation are a series of nuclear nonproliferation wins.

Decisions by West European Countries Not to Acquire the Bomb

In thinking about steps to slow overt or unacknowledged nuclear proliferation, we rightly focus on today's so-called problem countries, such as Pakistan, India, North and South Korea, Taiwan, Israel, Iran, Iraq, Libya, Syria, and South Africa. Two decades ago, however, the list of problem countries was quite different. Rather than Third World countries, that list included the West European countries of France, West Germany, Italy, Switzerland, and Sweden. Japan also should be put in the category of early potential problem countries, even though there was considerably less serious discussion of nuclear weapons acquisition there. With the exception of France, all of these countries eventually chose not to acquire nuclear weapons.

The decision by West European countries and Japan to renounce nuclear weapons is a clear, and often forgotten, nuclear nonproliferation success. Renunciation, however, was not a foregone conclusion: at differing times in the 1950s or 1960s, acquisition of nuclear weapons was an open question in virtually all of the above mentioned countries. Several countries, including Sweden and Switzerland, had nuclear weapon programs. For West Germany and Japan, their subsequent adherence to and ratification of the 1968 Nuclear Non-Proliferation Treaty (NPT), rather than reserving the nuclear option, was not an open and shut issue. . . .

Third World Incentives
and the Nuclear Nonproliferation Norm

The establishment and strengthening of the nuclear nonproliferation norm is another closely related success. The norm has helped contain the spread of nuclear weapons to the Third World, while reinforcing the decisions of most Western countries to renounce nuclear weapons. . . .

This norm probably has been most important in containing proliferation incentives in those Third World countries that are not today's problem countries, but that could have been driven to seek nuclear weapons by fear of their neighbors' long-term intentions, by prestige, or by the simple belief that sooner or later all important countries would have nuclear weapons. This group includes, for example, Indonesia, the Philippines, Singapore, Venezuela, Mexico, Chile, Egypt, Algeria, Nigeria, and Yugoslavia. At the same time, the norm of nuclear nonproliferation, as discussed more fully below, also appears to have constrained the efforts of Third World problem countries such as Pakistan to acquire a nuclear weapon capability. Concern about hostile foreign reaction undoubtedly partly explains, for instance, the decision not to move to open pursuit of a nuclear weapons capability in several problem countries, such as India and Pakistan. Finally, this norm has helped to prevent the reconsideration of earlier decisions by most Western countries to opt for nonnuclear status.

The Nuclear Supply Regime

Beginning in the mid-1950s, U.S. policymakers also took the lead in establishing a set of international institutions, procedures, and agreements to regulate peaceful nuclear cooperation and the supply of nuclear materials, facilities, and technology to other countries, which became a nuclear supply and export control regime. This regime now consists of U.S. conditions for agreements on bilateral cooperation; International Atomic Energy Agency (IAEA) safeguards that monitor the peaceful uses of nuclear energy; the so-called Zangger trigger lists that specify the items that NPT nuclear suppliers can export under safeguards, which have become the basis for rejecting export requests from problem countries; and the London Nuclear Suppliers' Guidelines that extend controls to technology and include commitments to restraint in the transfer of sensitive reprocessing and enrichment equipment or technology. At present, efforts are underway to extend the nuclear export control and supply regime to meet the challenges posed by the so-called dual-use exports, items with both nuclear and nonnuclear uses, and by new enrichment technologies. . . .

Winning Widespread Adherence to the NPT

Widespread adherence to the NPT also stands out as a nonproliferation success by helping to establish a norm of nuclear nonproliferation. In adhering to the NPT, moreover, nearly 140 countries have renounced the right to manufacture or acquire nuclear weapons. Although in a few cases this undertaking might be open to question, for virtually all others, adherence both significantly binds a country's future policy and provides reassurance to its neighbors. In addition, the legal obligations assumed by state-parties under Article III of the NPT have been a major foundation for nuclear supplier restraint and export controls. Similarly, for many countries, the acceptance of IAEA safeguards on all of their peaceful nuclear activities rests on their NPT obligation, also under Article III. . . .

Regularizing U.S.–Soviet Nonproliferation Discussions

Another example of successful institution-building is the pattern of regular bilateral discussions between the United States and the Soviet Union on nuclear nonproliferation that has been established. Begun sporadically in the late 1970s, these exchanges have taken place approximately every six months since 1983. The discussions have ranged across the nuclear nonproliferation agenda, and also have proved relatively insulated from the ups and downs of the broader political relationship. For example, even as the Soviet delegation was walking out of the Geneva nuclear negotiations in 1983, the Soviet Union was proposing a new round of nonproliferation talks. . . .

Nuclear Nonproliferation Losses

The record also contains a number of nuclear nonproliferation losses, suggesting the limits of what U.S. nuclear nonproliferation policy can accomplish and of U.S. readiness to pay a political or domestic price for that goal.

Additional Nuclear Weapon States: Could More Have Been Done?

The failure to prevent additional countries from acquiring nuclear weapons or a nuclear weapons capability is the most obvious nuclear nonproliferation loss. In addition to the five acknowledged nuclear weapon states, four other countries widely are assumed either to possess nuclear weapons capability or to be able to acquire it within the short-term. At the same time, the pattern of this additional proliferation activity has changed. Since China detonated a nuclear weapon in 1964, no other country openly has opted for nuclear weapons status. Instead, a new group of neither acknowledged nuclear weapon states nor questioned nonnuclear weapon states is emerging. . . .

The NPT Holdouts

That a group of countries have refused to sign the NPT, despite U.S. efforts to convince them to do so, is another nuclear nonproliferation loss. Four of these NPT holdouts are high on all lists of problem countries: Pakistan,

India, Israel, and South Africa. The other countries that appear to be further away from possession of a nuclear weapons capability include Argentina, Brazil, and Chile in Latin America, and Algeria in Africa, France and China, also holdouts, are nuclear weapon states. . . .

The reasons for nonadherence vary. For virtually all holdout countries, refusal to adhere is, in part, a means to keep open the option to make nuclear weapons. Rejection of adherence also is buttressed in some cases, such as India, Argentina, and Brazil, by arguments about the NPT's discriminatory character. These arguments emphasize that nuclear weapons states are not required to renounce their nuclear arsenals, nor do they have to accept IAEA safeguards on their peaceful nuclear activities. For China, nonadherence is a residue of earlier attitudes that stressed the benefits for communism of the proliferation of nuclear weapons. French nonadherence is tied up as much with Gallic pride and the logic of independence as with French criticism of the NPT's discriminatory elements. Some French NPT critics also claim to be concerned that adherence to the NPT would make it more difficult to continue the testing of nuclear weapons.

Widespread Civilian Use of Plutonium

The growing prospect of the widespread commercial use of plutonium is a somewhat different nuclear nonproliferation loss. Although estimates vary, several tens of thousands of kilograms of separated plutonium could be circulating in international commerce by the year 2000. Most of this plutonium will be used as nuclear fuel in light-water reactors in Japan, France, West Germany, Switzerland, and some other West European countries. With time, South Korean again could seek access to plutonium for use in its substantial civilian nuclear power program. . . .

The increased commercial use of plutonium and its frequent international shipment will place new strains on the ability of countries to ensure its adequate physical security. The risk of plutonium theft, whether by terrorists, extortionists, radical governments, or thieves could well be high. Problems with tracking and accounting for large shipments and stocks of plutonium—especially because some amount in use always will be unaccounted for—will open up the possibility of insider collusion in any such thefts.

Failures of Nuclear Supplier Cooperation

Overall, most nuclear suppliers often have taken quite seriously their responsibilities for nuclear export controls. Nonetheless, periodic failures of nuclear supplier cooperation constitute another nuclear nonproliferation loss, one with implications for other areas of nonproliferation export controls. Two types of supply failure have occurred: specific export control breakdowns and broader inability among the major nuclear suppliers to agree to hold regular multilateral discussions of nonproliferation.

At one time or another, the export control system of virtually all nuclear suppliers has failed to block exports of concern to a problem country, despite good faith efforts by the supplier. Also, there have been instances in which the nuclear export control bureaucracy of a given country has not paid sufficient attention to potentially troublesome exports or to entreaties to stop particular exports of nonproliferation concern. . . .

Nuclear Nonproliferation Draws

Still other developments of the past decades fall into the category of nuclear nonproliferation draws. For this category, the jury is still out. There have been both positive and negative consequences, or there has been a mixture of both success and failure.

Containing the Openness and Scope of Nuclear Weapons Programs

Although U.S. policies have not been successful in preventing completely the proliferation of nuclear weapons or nuclear weapons programs, they have contributed to constraining the openness and scope of nuclear weapons activities in current problem countries. This comprises a nuclear nonproliferation draw. These countries still may proceed to open nuclear weapons programs and eventual deployments; but their current unacknowledged moves toward or apparent acquisition of a nuclear weapons capability are less damaging than open proliferation.

There are several reasons to believe that this outcome is less dangerous. On balance, the unacknowledged possession of nuclear weapons likely will have a less corrosive impact on the perception that widespread proliferation still is avoidable. Such possession probably will have less impact on the incentives of countries other than regional rivals to acquire nuclear weapons. In turn, constraining the size of a country's nuclear weapons program—in terms of the amount of nuclear weapons materials and weapons—can help reduce the threat of nuclear theft or nuclear gifts. Scarce nuclear assets are easier to keep track of and too dear to give away for political, ideological, and economic reasons. Moreover, to the extent that future new nuclear weapon states move beyond small unacknowledged capabilities, crisis instability, and the risk of accidental, unintended, or intentional use of nuclear weapons likely would increase. . . .

Some Nuclear Weapons Program Shutdowns?

It is well known that in the mid-1970s both South Korea and Taiwan had active nuclear weapons programs, but under political pressure from the United States, both countries shut down such activities. Nonetheless, this termination must be considered only a nuclear nonproliferation draw, because under certain circumstances both programs could spring back to life. . . .

The Treaty of Tlatelolco: An Almost Nuclear-Free Zone

Although the Treaty of Tlatelolco provides the legal framework to make Latin America a nuclear weapons-free zone, it only can be considered a nuclear nonproliferation draw. Chile and Cuba have not signed, Argentina has not ratified, and despite having signed and ratified, Brazil has yet to wave it into force. As such, the Treaty of Tlatelolco remains as much a nuclear nonproliferation promise as reality.

The United States and Latin American countries repeatedly have urged Argentina, Brazil, and Chile to take the needed steps to bring Tlatelolco fully into force. In response, the latter countries have made various arguments, from calling into question whether the United States was abiding by its obligations under the Treaty to calling for special provisions to safeguard their peaceful nuclear activities. Still, the underlying explanation of their reluctance to bring the Treaty fully into force has been a desire to preserve a nuclear weapons option.

Nonetheless, the Treaty does serve to constrain their activities, to a degree. Brazil, for example, has stressed that in accordance with international law it will take no action inconsistent with Tlatelolco. By its very existence, the Treaty also adds to the norm of nuclear nonproliferation. Moreover, both Argentina and Brazil at some point could decide to adhere. For instance, if fears of a nuclear arms race fueled by mutual suspicions were to grow in Buenos Aires and Brasilia, full adherence to Tlatelolco would offer a ready-made vehicle to provide needed reassurance. Here, too, the jury is still out and some measure of success has occurred.

Nonuse of Nuclear Weapons

Although not the direct result of U.S. nuclear nonproliferation policy, the nonuse of nuclear weapons over the past four decades also has had important nuclear nonproliferation benefits, and, therefore, deserves brief mention.

In particular, nonuse has contributed significantly to the emergence and widespread acceptance of the belief that nuclear weapons were not simply advanced conventional weapons. This oft-remarked nuclear taboo, in turn, has affected the calculations of some of the first generation problem countries regarding the benefits and need for nuclear weapons. Nonuse also supported the growth in the 1960s and 1970s of the norm of nuclear nonproliferation.

More widespread nuclear weapons proliferation, however, could lead to a future use of nuclear weapons. Depending on the specifics, such use could either greatly strengthen the nuclear taboo and associated nonproliferation norm, or undermine it. For that reason and because it had little to do with nonproliferation per se, nonuse is considered a draw. . . .

Conclusion

Looking back at the record of four decades of nuclear nonproliferation wins, losses, and draws makes clear both the potential influence and the continuing limits of U.S. efforts to prevent the further spread of nuclear weapons around the globe. Both what the United States realistically can hope to do and what it cannot do need to be taken into account in revamping U.S. nuclear nonproliferation policies in the decades ahead. Equally, the lessons of the record of the past decades need to be reflected in the new measures now rising to prominence in order to prevent the spread of chemical weapons and missiles. To do so could increase measurably the prospects for their success.

NOTES

1. For a detailed discussion of recent revelations about Israeli capabilities, see Frank Barnaby, *The Invisible Bomb* (London: I.H. Tauris & Co., 1989).
2. See *Time*, March 30, 1987, p. 42; *New York Times*, August 14, 1986; for an overview of the current nonproliferation situation, see Leonard S. Spector, *The Undeclared Bomb* (Cambridge, MA: Ballinger, 1988).

Windows of Opportunity

Do States Jump Through Them?

Richard Ned Lebow

A "window of opportunity," a period during which a state possesses a significant military advantage over an adversary, has been a central concern of American strategic analysis. . . . Several times in the past, American intelligence and defense experts have worried that such windows were about to open because of some reputed Soviet military capability; the "bomber gap," "missile gap," and the "ABM gap" were all predictions of this kind that failed to materialize. . . .

History indicates that wars rarely start because one side believes it has a military advantage. Rather, they occur when leaders become convinced that force is necessary to achieve important goals. War as Clausewitz observed—and the Soviets proclaim—is an extension of politics by other means. Its scope, strategy, and timing are determined, if often imperfectly, by the political objective for which the war is fought. Relative military advantage is merely one component of any decision regarding war. It is by no means even the most important one as examples can be drawn from every era of states' knowingly starting wars without a military advantage.[1]

Window of vulnerability arguments also tend to ignore the host of nonmilitary factors which can influence leaders in the direction of peace. This article explores the importance of two such constraints: the absolute cost of war in human and economic terms and the personal reluctance of leaders to assume responsibility for it. . . .

Reprinted from *International Security* 9:1 (1984), Richard Lebow, "Windows of Opportunity: Do States Jump Through Them?" by permission of MIT Press, Cambridge, MA.

Three Windows of Opportunity

One way of analyzing the importance of nonmilitary considerations in decisions about peace and war would be to examine several instances in which peace was preserved even though a calculus of cost and gain of strategic interests ought to have pointed towards war. The most dramatic situations of this kind would be those in which policymakers decided against war with an apparently irreconcilable adversary despite their expectation that the military balance, seen at the time as highly favorable to themselves, would worsen dramatically in the near future. In keeping the peace they refused to exploit the advantages of a window of opportunity. Three twentieth-century examples come to mind: Germany in several crises prior to 1914, the United States in the 1950s, and the Soviet Union in the late 1960s.

Between 1891, the year of the Franco–Russian alliance, and the outbreak of war in 1914, Germany had a pronounced but gradually declining military edge over its two continental adversaries. The General Staff's solution to the problem posed by the prospect of a two-front war was the ill-fated Schlieffen Plan which aimed to defeat Germany's adversaries sequentially. The Plan was made possible by the slow rate of Russian mobilization which was expected to give Germany just enough time to overwhelm France by means of a lightning offensive before having to confront massive Russian armies on the eastern borders.[2]

From 1905 on, the German General Staff were increasingly concerned about the pace of Russian railway construction and military reforms. They feared that these activities would speed up Russian mobilization and make Russia's army more effective, thereby rendering the Schlieffen Plan unworkable. The generals repeatedly urged the Kaiser and the Chancellor to wage a preventive war against Russia and France while victory was still possible. In 1905, in 1909, and again in 1912, Germany's leaders rejected the pleas of the generals despite their recognition of the worsening military situation. In 1914, when Germany did go to war, it was the result of a crisis initiated by Austria; at the outset neither the Kaiser nor the Chancellor expected that German support for Austria would lead to anything more than a localized Balkan conflict. What is surprising given the assumptions of deterrence theory and the window of vulnerability thesis is not that Germany stumbled into a European war in 1914 but that it consciously rejected such a war on three previous and more favorable occasions.

American restraint towards the Soviet Union during the years when Washington had a near monopoly in deliverable nuclear weapons constitutes a more recent example of a state's failure to exploit an apparent window of opportunity. Despite widespread recognition that the Soviets would sooner or later develop the means to make the continental United States vulnerable to attack, American leaders rejected the possibility of preventive war. They did this even though many officials feared that the Soviets would be tempted to start a nuclear war as soon as they acquired the strategic wherewithal to do so. Throughout this period, from roughly 1950 to 1965, American policymakers also refrained from attempting to exploit their nuclear superiority to roll back Soviet influences in central Europe, a policy rejected in practice because of the attendant risk of war. The Cold War rhetoric of Dulles and Kennedy aside, caution was the order of the day. Only in Cuba in 1962 did an American president deliberately pursue a policy that was seen at the time to court some risk of nuclear war. But this was done in circumstances in which, from Washington's perspective, the Americans were on the defensive and responding to a Soviet initiative which they believed to threaten the political and strategic status quo.

The Soviet Union evidenced similar self-restraint *vis à vis* its Chinese adversary in the late 1960s and the early 1970s. The Soviet image of China at that time as an implacable and irrational foe apparently led to serious consideration in Moscow in 1969–1970 of a preventive strike against Chinese nuclear facilities in order to deny Peking a nuclear capability. Soviet leaders decided against such a strike even though it meant accepting their own certain vulnerability in the not so distant future.[3]. . .

Despite the imperfect correspondence between these cases and what might be considered an "ideal type" window of opportunity situation, there is still enough of a fit to talk about the cases as constituting windows. In all three instances, the extreme hostility and aggressive character of the adversary was taken as a given. In all three, the state in question possessed a significant if not always overwhelming military advantage. And each of the adversaries was expected to improve his military capability in the near future to the point where that advantage was no longer decisive or even disappeared altogether. Without undue exaggeration, proponents of preventive war could and did argue that their adversary was on the verge of acquiring the means of threatening the very survival of their state. Preventive war promised to ward off this military threat. It also held out the prospect of victory at less cost than a future war whose outcome would be uncertain. A decision based solely upon calculations of strategic cost and gain might well have dictated a decision in favor of war. This failed to happen, we must conclude, because of the salience of other, nonmilitary considerations in the minds of the policymakers in all three cases.

Absolute versus Relative Costs

The most obvious nonmilitary considerations are those of a political nature. Leaders who believe that their national interests require military action can still be constrained by public opinion or other domestic political forces. Prior to 1914, Austrian leaders were prevented by Hungarian opposition from starting a war with Serbia; only Germany's "blank check" and subsequent pleas for decisive action enabled them to overcome this obstacle in July 1914. Pacific or divided public opinion forestalled American intervention in the two world wars until either enough American ships had been sunk or the country itself had been attacked. French and British leaders were similarly constrained from acting against Hitler in the mid-1930s at a time when Germany might easily have been crushed. Ronald Reagan confronted public opposition to his administration's efforts to expand America's military role in Central America.

A second consideration militating against war can be its expected costs. In some circumstances they may be high enough to dissuade policymakers from using force regardless of the magnitude of the expected gains. Window of vulnerability arguments and deterrence theory in general conceive of political and military costs in relative terms. They describe the calculus of decision as a comparison of cost and gain, with the rational policymaker moved to adopt the initiative in question to the extent that the gains outweigh the costs. The nature and magnitude of costs are not considered in and of themselves; they take on meaning only in comparison to the expected gains. Such a theoretical formulation ignores the reality that *absolute* costs, when sufficiently great, are a very important consideration for policymakers. . . .

Moral and Psychological Costs

Third party estimates of the cost and gain of any foreign policy initiative are always based on tangible strategic and political considerations. The better analyses of this kind also include some consideration of the expected bureaucratic and domestic political effects of the policy in question. Even these assessments invariably ignore the moral and psychological dimension of decisions. However, these "hidden" costs and gains can be extremely important, even decisive, in affecting decisional outcomes. . . .

Important decisions generate internal conflict because policymakers are likely to experience opposing tendencies to accept and reject a given course of action. Decisional conflict and the stress it generates become acute when a policymaker realizes that there is a risk of serious loss associated with any course of action open to him. The stress can become crippling if this loss is perceived to entail the sacrifice of values that are extremely important to the policymaker. In these circumstances, he will be burdened with anticipatory feelings of shame, guilt, and related feelings of self-deprecation, which lower his self-esteem. A policymaker tends to cope with such situations by procrastinating, shifting responsibility for decision, and by "bolstering."[4] These affective responses detract from the quality of decision-making but are functional in the sense that they facilitate coping with stress. They may even be necessary for the policymaker to move confidently towards a decision.

It is difficult to conceive of a decision more fraught with stress than one to start a nuclear war. Mere contemplation of the act and its expected consequences—let alone its unexpected consequences—could be expected to arouse considerable anxiety on the part of almost any policymaker seriously considering it as an option. For this reason alone it is ludicrous to suppose that an American president or Soviet Premier could wake up one morning, decide that the correlation of forces was favorable, and so calmly give the order to push the button. Policymakers and people with any kind of ordinary feelings and emotions would find it difficult to assume responsibility for the death of untold millions of people and, should the war get out of hand, perhaps the destruction of society itself. Leaders who seriously contemplated the use of such destructive weapons would have a real need to do something in advance to reduce their anxiety and anticipatory guilt feelings before they could actually authorize a nuclear strike. . . .

Implications

If comparisons of military capability are theoretically misleading, they are also politically dangerous. They encourage exaggerated perceptions of threat to the extent that they rely on worst case analysis, an evil seemingly endemic to force comparisons and strategic exchange models devised by professional military and civilian analysts. As a general rule, these analysts are most sensitive to the capabilities of their adversary and the deficiencies of their own forces. They must also base their models on uncertain and incomplete data about the performance characteristics and operational reliability of weapons on both sides, but especially those of the adversary. The less that is known about the qualities of the other side's weapons, the greater the tendency to assign high values to them in order to be on the "safe side." In dynamic analyses, this bias can be further compounded by the choice of a war scenario that is particularly favorable to the enemy. In a strategic exchange this is likely to be a "bolt-from-the-blue" strike at a time when one's own forces are "ungenerated," that is in a day-to-day state of readiness. Rigging the situation in this way results in an extremely threatening picture of the strategic balance.

When worst case analysis is used by both sides, it means that they will interpret a situation of strategic parity as one of imbalance favoring their adversary. This will encourage both states to augment or modernize their arsenals in order to redress the balance. This in turn will aggravate the tensions between them as each side will interpret any arms buildup as proof of the other's hostile intentions given its belief that its adversary already possesses an advantage. The current Soviet and American inability to agree about either the conventional or nuclear balance in Europe offers a telling example of just how this dynamic operates.[5] It illustrates how asymmetrical perceptions of military balance are an important structural cause of arms races.

When perceptions of imbalance are wedded to fears of windows of vulnerability, threat perception becomes more exaggerated still. For now, the adversary is seen not only to have the wherewithal to carry out an effective attack but also the incentive to do so. Such an analysis, we have argued, is intellectually naive. It is also a poor predictor of state behavior. Germany went to war in 1914 even though its perceived window of opportunity was more pronounced in 1905, 1909, and 1912. To the extent that German leaders were influenced at all by relative military capabilities, it was by the fact that Germany's advantage was seen to be rapidly *diminishing* in 1914; they went to war to forestall a window of vulnerability. And even that, we have tried to show, was an insufficient condition for war. Germany's leaders also required a decisional context that permitted them to deny all responsibility of war to themselves. The United States failed to exploit its window in the 1950s and early 1960s. So did the Soviet Union *vis à vis* China a decade later.

If states often fail to exploit windows of opportunity, they also start wars at inauspicious moments judged in terms of relative military capabilities. World War II is a case in point. Hitler, a leader certainly unconstrained by the usual political and moral considerations, failed to time his war to correspond with the period of Germany's maximum expected military advantage. German military planners predicted that this would not be until about 1943. Hitler chose war in 1939 and there is evidence that he would have actually preferred it in 1938 when Germany was even less prepared. Hitler had a personal timetable. His obsession with his health, fear of a premature death, and belief that only he could lead Germany to victory drove him to provoke war while he was fifty and still healthy. The Argentine invasion of the Falklands provides a more recent example. Had the Argentines postponed their attack one more year the British would have decommissioned so many of the ships vital to their invasion force, among them the aircraft carrier *Hermes*, that an effort to retake the Falklands would probably no longer have been considered a viable policy option. The Argentine *junta* did not wait because their action was taken in response to internal political need, not external military opportunity.[6]

As war is an extension of politics by other means, its objectives and timing are generally determined by *political* considerations. Attempts to predict war on the basis of the military balance are therefore likely to be misleading. In the first instance, they will encourage predictions of wars that never come to pass. They will also make analysts insensitive to the prospects of war in situations where the military balance is not favorable to the would-be aggressor. The Israeli intelligence failure in October 1973 has been attributed to this latter phenomenon.[7]

There is another danger to window of opportunity analysis. When leaders believe in windows they risk making themselves vulnerable to them. If an adversary can gain a military advantage, or merely convince the other side that it possesses one, it can exploit its putative advantage for political ends. Hitler did this in the 1930s. He succeeded in portraying German military might, especially airpower, as much greater than it was at the time. Fear of German power overlaid on French and British expectations that Hitler would not hesitate to resort to war to achieve his goals was one of the principal causes of appeasement.

To the degree that American leaders are convinced that the Soviet Union would start a war simply because the "correlation of forces" was favorable to it, they open themselves up to political blackmail should Soviet leaders ever succeed in convincing the United States that they possess a significant strategic advantage. Given the baneful effects of worst case analysis, Moscow would not really need much of an advantage to attempt to convince Washington of its superior prowess. Fortunately, the Soviet Union has for the time being chosen to downplay rather than exaggerate its strategic capability. This does not detract from the political truth that the kinds of window of vulnerability scenarios that have been widely publicized in recent years do a serious disservice to the real interests of the United States to the extent that they are taken seriously by policymakers.

NOTES

1. This argument is developed more fully by Richard Ned Lebow, "Misperceptions in American Strategic Assessment," *Political Science Quarterly* 97 (Summer 1982): 187–206.
2. On the Schlieffen Plan see Gerhard Ritter, *The Schlieffen Plan*, trans. Andrew and Eva Wilson (New York: Praeger, 1958); Lancelot L. Farrar, Jr., *The Short War: German Policy, Strategy, and Domestic Affairs: August-December, 1914* (Santa Barbara, CA: ABC-CLIO, 1973), pp. 10–33.
3. Marvin Kalb and Bernard Kalb, *Kissinger* (Boston: Little Brown, 1974), pp. 258–261; John Newhouse, *Cold Dawn, The Story of SALT* (New York: Holt, Rinehart & Winston, 1973), pp. 164, 188–189; and Henry Kissinger, *White House Years* (Boston: Little, Brown, 1979), p. 183.
4. Irving L. Janis and Leon Mann, *Decision-Making: A Psychological Analysis of Conflict, Choice, and Commitment* (New York: Free Press, 1977), pp. 74–95.
5. For documentation of this phenomenon see the twin articles by Raymod L. Garthoff, "The Soviet SS-20 Decision," *Survival* 25 (May–June 1983): 110–119; and "The NATO Decision on Theater Nuclear Forces," *Political Science Quarterly* 98 (Summer 1983): 197–213.
6. Richard Ned Lebow, "Miscalculation in the South Atlantic: The Origins of the Falkland War," *Journal of Strategic Studies* 6 (March 1983): 5–35.
7. The Agranat Report, *A Partial Report by the Commission in Inquiry to the Government of Israel* (Jerusalem: Government Printing Office, April 2, 1974).

The United States
and the Politics of Conflict
in Developing Countries

Todd R. Greentree

Criteria to Follow the Demise of Containment

The fundamental reduction in U.S.–Soviet confrontation essentially removes global containment as the unifying rationale for U.S. involvement in Third World conflicts. It is also now possible to argue that the U.S. has been freed to attend to the problems of the developing world, but the delinking of the relatively small conflicts in the Third World from significance as arenas for bipolar geostrategic competition in reality lessens rather than increases the rationale for U.S. involvement in every corner of the globe.

While the absence of a cumulative threat to the U.S. from Third World conflicts reduces the motivations for U.S. involvement, it does not eliminate them. Rather, this transformation, and the resulting change in the U.S. role in the world, requires careful reassessment of U.S. policy and strategy. Two general questions need to be addressed: First, which of a multiplicity of conflicts throughout the Third World truly affect U.S. interests to a degree warranting involvement? And second, how should the U.S. be involved?

As a starting point, it is apparent that some of the conflicts in which the U.S. is engaged are residual in terms of containment—El Salvador and Afghanistan, for example. The country-specific and regional implications of each conflict must be analyzed in terms of corresponding U.S. internal and

Reprinted from *The United States and the Politics of Conflict in Developing Countries*, Center for Low-Intensity Conflict, Langley Air Force Base, Va., 1990.

external objectives. For example, the primary motivation for contemporary U.S. involvement with the Philippine counterinsurgency, which has flared on and off since the U.S. first intervened in 1898, will become contingent on the redefinition of the U.S. role in Southeast Asia, and specifically the future of the U.S. military bases there. But the degree of U.S. determination to maintain the bases will in turn affect and be affected by the dynamics of Philippine politics and the course of U.S.–Philippine relations. If the Philippine bases are no longer essential to the U.S. regional security role, what is the degree of political and financial commitment the U.S. wishes to sustain there?

Similar issues arise regarding Latin America, and particularly Central America. Is the region a vital sphere of interest, and is the objective of excluding foreign powers, first defined under the Monroe Doctrine in 1829, still a valid rationale for military involvement there?

In addition to specific regional threats, what other types of conflicts in the Third World may require U.S. engagement? For example, the world's population has been projected to nearly triple from 5.3 billion to 14 billion over the next century without additional control measures.[1] The bulk of this increase will occur primarily in the Third World. If resource and population pressures add to internal conflict, particularly in countries of strategic significance for the United States, such as Mexico, when and how should the U.S. be engaged?

Military Action and the Brushfire Corollary

In addition to determination of threats, the manner of U.S. engagement must also come under scrutiny. On the military side, it appears to have become fairly well embedded within the government that U.S. combat troops will not be committed to long-term internal conflicts in the Third World. Rather, the approach is to provide indirect assistance, either to a government or insurgent movement. At the other side of the spectrum, a precedent if not a consensus has been established for direct military action with circumscribed and clearly defined objectives more akin to special operations in specific contingencies, such as counterterrorism, or the invasion of small countries in Latin America.

Major ambiguities remain, however, in the spectrum of military action. For example, U.S. military involvement in counter-narcotics operations is subject to several ambiguities, including its impact on the political power of host country armed forces, and the differing orientation of these governments, which tend to favor economic rather than military solutions.

The essential judgment regarding military action is the truism in Low Intensity Conflict that, if military action is required, the problem has already advanced to a critical degree. The application of the other tools of U.S. policy that are intended to resolve the underlying causes of conflict—support for long-term democratic and economic development—may come too late and run afoul of the contradictions and limits to reform.

These are twin weaknesses of U.S. action in Third World conflict: to engage seriously only when conflict has emerged, and to assume the ability to resolve crises through the direct application of resources. This might be termed the "brushfire corollary," a chronic problem deriving from the global spread of U.S. commitments where the demand for resources and policy attention in countries generally on the geopolitical periphery far exceeds the capabilities of the U.S. government.

Such brushfire situations contain a fundamental paradox. If a country is peripheral, why apply scarce resources and attention when crisis is at a low level? Other constraints to policy include legal requirements and ethical ideals, the total nature of the conflicts as opposed to limited external objectives, and the limits to reform within Third World countries. For example, in El Salvador it has proven possible to prevent the FMLN guerrillas from coming to power, but the cost has already been over 5 billion dollars and ten years in a very small country of five million people.

Correspondingly, given a high degree of commitment, it is extremely difficult to construct a disengagement strategy without it being perceived as a defeat. This is especially true when government or insurgent armed forces have obtained significant force buildups dependent on U.S. support.

Some Guidelines

The main conclusion of this analysis might imply a pessimistic assumption of U.S. engagement in conflict in the Third World. It is true that when judged in terms of the broadly stated objectives of building the basis for internal democratic and economic development, the record is not particularly good. When judged in terms of the external objective of preventing forces hostile to the United States from increasing their power, the record is better.

At present, the diminishing of containment as a national security justification for involvement in Third World conflict exposes the definition of U.S. interests to a new range of ambiguities regarding the where and how of U.S. policy. This would be relatively simple, for example, for direct threats to major sea lines of communication or terrorist acts against U.S. citizens. It is less clear, for example, where internal revolts seem to threaten U.S. interests or challenge U.S. prestige.

A set of general policy guidelines do emerge from the historical and theoretical elements of this analysis:

1. Determine how a specific conflict is linked to specific U.S. interests, with emphasis on the involvement of foreign powers or other geopolitical dimensions.
2. Distinguish between internal and external objectives.
3. Understand the nature of the conflict; analyze the specific internal dimensions of a conflict in terms of economic, political, social, and military factors.
4. Limit escalation and mobilization.

5. Assess the degree of engagement, ranging from minor assistance to full invasion, likely to be required to achieve specific defined objectives.
6. Avoid committing U.S. troops to protracted conflicts and attempting to apply conventional U.S. military doctrine.
7. Determine obstacles to achieving objectives in terms of resources and the limits to reform.
8. Emphasize support for a functioning and legitimate political entity.

Selective Engagement

The essential conclusion suggested here is that no single unifying principle replaces global containment as a rationale for U.S. involvement in Third World conflict. The general objective of excluding foreign powers as a function of the balance of power must now be further refined in terms of specific interests in specific countries and regions.

Such a policy might be termed "selective engagement". Selective engagement signifies recognition of the multiple ambiguities, contradictions, and limits to U.S. involvement in Third World conflicts. As a conceptual guide to strategy, it confirms the U.S. commitment to deterring aggression and to democratic reform, but it applies resources to pursue those objectives with circumspection. Selective engagement recommends against proclaiming too ambitious a "mission" in protracted conflicts, but at the same time encourages rapid action free from idle threats in specific short-term contingencies. It also recognizes the ambiguities of this type of conflict and the political uncertainty of the outcome, and particularly the need for perseverance. Finally, selective engagement in the context of declining East-West conflict suggests the possibility of increased opportunities for UN peacekeeping or other forms of international cooperation to deal with Third World conflict.[2]

The restructuring of U.S. forces to provide for small specialized forces trained and equipped to cope with low-intensity conflicts in the Third World is an important asset, but does not in itself justify involvement. Engagement must focus on political objectives, with careful attention to the contradictions and limitations imposed by both the situation and the U.S. system.

Although not applicable to all situations, Sir Robert Thompson's prescription for counterinsurgency is an excellent example of the clarity of purpose the U.S. should strive for:

> Government must have clear political aim—To establish and maintain a free, independent, and united country which is politically and economically stable and viable; The government must function in accordance with the law; the government must have an overall plan; the government must give priority to defeating the political subversion, not the guerrillas; in the guerrilla phase of an insurgency a government must secure its base areas first.[3]

As a mature nation, the U.S. should come to grips with these problems, and should do so effectively and consistently, within a context of democratic political debate about interests and goals.

NOTES

1. Susan Oakie, "World Population Tallied," *Washington Post*, February 26, 1990, p. 8.
2. Commission on Integrated Long-Term Strategy, "Discriminate Deterrence," January 1988.
3. Sir Robert Thompson, *Revolutionary War in World Strategy, 1945–69* (London: Taplinger, 1970), p. 126.

Chapter 9

The International Economy

Today, domestic economies isolated from the world economic system cannot hope to provide adequately for their societies; thus participation in the world economy is a necessity rather than a choice. As the world economy becomes increasingly interdependent, states' options to act autonomously are limited.

We will address three important issues related to interdependency. The first is the flow of public funds in the form of foreign aid, particularly the perception that more than thirty years of aid has neither alleviated poverty nor accomplished industrialization in the poorest countries. The second is control of multinational corporations, a major source of private finance. The third is the European Community. The movement toward European economic unity has made enormous headway since the establishment of the EEC (European Economic Community) in 1957. A united Europe challenges U.S. and Japanese economic dominance in the international economy and raises questions about the extent to which national economies can go beyond interdependence to integration.

Foreign Aid

Economic development requires a surplus of capital. In those states that industrialized early, this surplus came largely from increasingly productive agriculture both at home and in colonial possessions. Today, capital-poor countries must turn to those with a surplus for loans and aid to finance industrialization. The source of this capital can be public or private. In this section we will look at public assistance.

The Bretton Woods agreement set up the World Bank to assist in rebuilding the countries devastated by World War II. In the postwar period the rebuilding of Europe was the first priority of the bank. Although less developed countries wanted World Bank funds for development, the wealthier states argued that expanded trade opportunities, external capital from private sources, and domestic capital would be adequate. The World Bank as originally instituted was to loan money at market rates and was not really intended as a device to secure the industrialization of the less developed world. It was not until 1956 that the International Finance Corporation was established as a subsidiary to the World Bank, to promote private investment in less developed countries. In 1960 the International Development Agency was established to make loans at below-market rates.

Three criteria distinguish foreign aid from other financial flows. First, the assistance must be public or at least noncommercial in intent. Second, the assistance must be rendered on concessional terms; that is, loans must be made at below-market interest rates and for extended repayment periods. Third, the assistance should be designed to aid in development or redistribute income, and not for military uses.

In the 1950s, with the cold war at the forefront of foreign relations, foreign aid became an important policy tool of the United States. It was believed that economically developed states would be more stable and less prone to Communist influence. External capital would provide the means for this economic growth. During this period most aid (about 91 percent) was bilateral and in the form of outright grants. The major donor was the United States.

During the 1960s and 1970s, multilateral institutions (particularly the World Bank) became somewhat more important for the dispersal of aid, and new donors—Europe in the 1960s and the OPEC nations in the 1970s—entered the arena. Loans, as opposed to outright grants, became more common. By the 1980s, 28 percent of foreign aid was channeled through multilateral institutions. Although the United States continued to be the world's largest donor in terms of absolute amount, several other countries gave higher percentages of their GNPs.

There is considerable continuity in the factors characterizing foreign aid. First, most aid remains bilateral. Second, there is a general agreement among donors (both individual countries and multilateral institutions) that aid should not compete with private capital. Thus, most aid is for the development of infrastructure to support industry rather than for industrial projects themselves. Third, aid is usually granted on conditional terms, which may be very specific requirements that purchases are donor country products or may be more vague and related to overall economic policy. Finally, most aid is loaned, not granted outright. Presently about 70 percent of foreign aid is in the form of loans granted at concessional terms.

The philosophy behind foreign aid is that financial transfers can be used to supplement deficient capital and push the less developed country into self-sustaining growth. Although most economists continue to support aid, some have questioned whether it does in fact promote growth or instead substitutes for domestic savings (thus retarding self-sustaining development) while exacerbating balance-of-payments deficits (through requirements that aid be spent on donor country exports and through loans). Recently, development analysts have suggested again that trade rather than aid is the best route to industrialization.

An underlying goal of aid by the capitalist countries of the North was to ensure that as development occurred in the South, it would take a capitalist form. In this respect, aid has been remarkably successful. The capitalist world economy has become increasingly interdependent, and few states are significantly outside it. By other measures, the success of development aid programs is mixed at best. Only nineteen of ninety-five less developed countries have maintained consistent economic growth in the period from 1950 to 1987, more than 1 billion people in the developing world live in poverty, and a number of developing economies are facing crushing external debt. Many countries of the South now find themselves in a condition of "aid dependency"; they need aid at current levels merely to maintain their present poor standard of living. The Organization for Economic Cooperation and Development (OECD), a consortium of wealthy states, reports that the most troubling shortcoming of aid is that it has contributed only slightly to reducing poverty, especially in the rural areas of very poor countries.

There are a number of reasons for this failure, some of which are related to the characteristics of the aid regime. Most aid is bilateral, and for most donors its major purposes have had nothing to do with development or reducing poverty. In 1986 only 8 percent of U.S. aid could be classified as development assistance to low-income countries. Donors have a variety of motives for granting aid, but political and economic reasons predominate over humanitarian ones. There is a tendency for donors to fund infrastructure that helps their own multinational firms, and they will not usually provide funds for recurrent costs. The predominant needs of the poor include education and health programs; and for both, recurrent costs are a major portion of the expenses.

Other problems rest with the recipient countries' policies or the design of the programs. Programs targeted at the basic needs of the poor, no matter how successful in the short run, may be undermined by macroeconomic policies such as those governing agricultural pricing or land tenure. Programs run by foreign experts outside the country's existing institutions are less likely to be continued once initial funding is stopped than those involving domestic bureaucracies.

Most observers agree that aid programs need to be overhauled. Studies of completed projects have found that to be successful aid projects need to take into account nationwide economic policies, include the participation of the target population, be flexible, require recipients to expend some of their own labor and resources, and be as simple in design as possible. The World Bank recommends that the economy-wide policies of countries should be examined for their effects on the poor. In those countries where there is a commitment to alleviating poverty, the Bank recommends a number of different ways to deliver aid programs. In countries without such poverty-reducing economic policies, the Bank suggests that a limited quantity of humanitarian aid should be carefully directed at highly targeted groups. Although the Bank agrees that trade is the best way to finance industrialization and that there should be increasing reliance on trade, it argues that many of the world's poorest countries are not yet ready to be weaned from direct transfers in the form of aid.

Controlling Multinational Corporations

Public funds are only one source of international financial transfers. Private funds are transferred through commercial loans and through direct investment in an economy by multinational corporations. These transfers constitute a major source of capital for development and economic growth.

Direct investment in a domestic economy by a foreign firm is considered one of the most significant threats to economic sovereignty in an increasingly interdependent world. A number of factors make the control of multinational corporations (MNCs) an important consideration. Size alone makes MNCs important—in 1985, the sales of each of the top ten MNCs were more than the gross domestic products of each of 104 countries. The MNCs give a global dimension to production, marketing, and investment—increasing the interdependence of economies and making independent action on the part of states harder—and their characteristics facilitate their own independence from state control. They tend to be centralized and mobile, and their production and marketing activities are well integrated. Decisions about where to invest and what goals to pursue are made at corporate headquarters, although in many instances firms have considerable flexibility in where to locate.

Given the size of these firms and their importance to state economies, their desires must be taken into account by policymakers when domestic economic policy is formulated. Firms may make campaign contributions, lobby policyholders directly, bribe officials, or even support the overthrow of those in office. The MNCs are difficult to police because they operate in a number of different jurisdictions. Through astute management and manipulation of trade with subsidiaries, large MNCs may avoid taxation without breaking laws. Attempts by state governments in the United States to solve this problem by figuring taxes according to worldwide profits, adjusted for amount of activity in a particular locality, have met with failure. Firms refuse to invest in localities that follow this policy.

Less developed countries charge that their sovereignty is threatened by not only the MNCs but also their home governments. They point to instances when the home countries of MNCs have intervened in their affairs to protect these firms. Some see a threat to their culture and way of life in that foreign investment Westernizes their population through production and marketing. There is evidence that a new managerial class has emerged in less developed countries that has adopted many of the liberal beliefs held by Western economic elites and exercises considerable political influence. The less developed states have found MNCs particularly difficult to control, given the states' limited institutional and tangible resources, but recently the countries of the South have shown increasing sophistication at monitoring these firms more effectively.

The major concern for the more developed states (also a concern for the less developed economies) is their ability to recognize economic goals. Decisions critical to a state's welfare may be made at a foreign firm's headquarters. Of particular concern are those industries, such as communications or finance, that are vital to a state's economy. There have been instances when the home government of a firm has persuaded it to act in ways beneficial to the home state's economy but damaging to its hosts'. Even firms headquartered in a state can pose problems. Corporate goals and national goals are not necessarily synonymous, so there is no guarantee that a German firm, say, will pursue policies helpful to Germany. This statement holds more for firms operating internationally than for those more closely tied to a domestic economy.

The predominant method of controlling MNCs is through restrictions on initial investment. Key sectors of the economy may be closed entirely to direct foreign investment. Countries may also have agencies for reviewing the impact of investment on the economy before it is approved. Once an investment is made, existing laws governing commerce and existing agencies monitor MNCs in the same way they monitor domestic firms.

In spite of concerns about control, most countries try to attract investment. Where capital is scarce, foreign investment can overcome the gap between what exists and what is needed for economic growth. Foreign investment can remedy problems arising from low savings or balance-of-payments deficits and an inadequate tax base by infusing capital. Also, multinational investment may provide missing technology and managerial skill. The competition for investment makes the control of MNCs even more problematic, since states that restrict initial investment or enact policies designed to control investment once in place often find that foreign investors simply go elsewhere.

The European Community

When it was founded in 1957, the European Economic Community had as its short-term objective the removal of obstacles to trade within its boundaries. This goal required that there be no customs duties or quotas on goods moving within the EEC and uniform customs duties on goods entering any member country from outside the EEC. In addition, citizens and businesses of member states were able to operate freely across borders. Taxation and benefits had to apply equally to all citizens of member states working anywhere within the EEC, and governments could not make policies to help their own citizens or businesses in competition with those of other member states. Finally, there could be no restrictions on the free transfer of capital from one member state to another.

Over the next few decades, the EEC grew in membership and progressively adopted directives aimed at facilitating the free movement of peoples and goods across borders—although there were significant problems along the way. France originally opposed the admission of Great Britain, which was not admitted until 1973, and there have been disagreements over special treatment for Commonwealth members, budgetary matters, and agricultural policy. Economic problems during recessions have led periodically to movements for protection within the EEC.

In the 1980s the movement toward a single European market gained momentum, culminating with the agreement to adopt the Single European Act (SEA) in 1987. The European economies had been slow to recover from the effects of rising oil prices, and voters had expressed increasing dissatisfaction with economic performance. The appeal of a unified market better able to compete with the Americans and Japanese was strong.

The SEA set 1992 as the date for the creation of a true common market, as the original agreement signed in 1957 did not stipulate an integrated, single market. Although a uniform external tariff was established and tariffs were removed within the European Community (EC), customs procedures differ from state to state. Member countries must not treat the citizens (or businesses) of member states within their borders differently than they treat their own citizens, but there is no requirement that these regulations be the same in all member states. Different standards for production, procurement, and licensing and different fiscal systems remain in existence. The SEA set the goal of eliminating all barriers to the movement of capital, goods, persons, and services within the EC. Once in effect, economic policy applying to marketing goods and services acceptable anywhere in the EC must be acceptable everywhere in the EC. Standardizing rates for the value-added tax will also be accomplished, with the eventual movement toward common income taxes and corporate taxes. The actual negotiations to remove the fiscal, technical, and physical barriers still separating the members of the EC have been long and difficult and still continue.

These and other provisions are intended to boost trade within the EC. As firms relocate to areas with lower labor and transportation costs, consumers within the EC should enjoy lower prices and EC goods should become more competitive internationally.

There will be adjustment costs as well as benefits. Unemployment may rise in some areas as firms move toward cheaper labor. Small and mid-sized firms may not prosper as well as larger ones that can realize economies of scale. The United States and others external to the EC fear that these costs will be passed on to them through new external barriers.

During the 1990s the membership of the EC is expected to grow—from twelve to perhaps as many as twenty-five members. In October 1991 the EC and EFTA (European Free Trade Association) agreed to a European Economic Area (EEA), which will create a market of 380 million people and account for 40 percent of world trade. The trade agreement did not satisfy EFTA members that want full membership in the EC. All of the members of EFTA (Finland, Austria, Sweden, Malta, Cyprus, Norway, and Switzerland) are expected to be admitted without much difficulty, but the poorer nations of Eastern Europe also want to join. Their membership would double the regional aid budget and require revisions in industrial, farm, and budgetary policy.

One immediate concern caused by the expected increase in membership is that decisions will be harder to reach. Thus, it is argued, the organization needs to be reformed now while the membership is still smaller. France in particular has called for faster progress on questions of monetary and political union. There are suggestions to replace the current commission and rotating presidency with a single body and to institute new voting rules in the Council of Ministers. Present voting rules leave large countries underrepresented relative to their populations. The inclusion of new states, many of which are small, would exacerbate this problem. There is considerable opposition in member countries (especially Germany, which has a federal system) to a strong central EC government.

Monetary and political union remains problematic. In December 1991 the EC agreed to move toward a common currency and foreign policy. A common currency alone will have far-reaching consequences for individual economies, given the importance of monetary policy. The agreement would provide for a single currency and a central bank. Individual states would lose the power to set interest rates independently or to value their own currencies. Margaret Thatcher, while prime minister of Britain, was probably the most vocal opponent, citing a loss of sovereignty. Although her successor, John Major, is considered to be more favorably inclined toward integration, Britain remains a major dissenter on the issue of greater unity. States in Europe began voting in the spring of 1992 on whether to amend their constitutions to accommodate the Maastricht Treaty. The French National Assembly voted yes. A referendum in Ireland approved the treaty, but in Denmark citizens voted no. The present governing structure of the EC puts considerable power in the Brussels bureaucracy. The elected parliament is weak. Some observers believe that the governing institutions of the EC will have to be restructured before the Maastricht Treaty will be approved. One argument holds that if a less powerful state holds the presidency in a crisis the EC will not be effective in making foreign-policy decisions. Some have called for a prime minister of Europe. Germany and France want more movement toward federalism, whereas Britain is reluctant to approve changes that give the EC more political power.

The Readings

The first reading, "Can the Interdependent World Political Economy Survive?" by Robert Gilpin, presents a theoretical overview of the world economy from three different perspectives. The next two readings deal with aid and development. "Seven Basic Questions About the Future," published by the United States Agency for International Development, addresses questions now being considered by those responsible for developing and managing U.S. foreign aid policy. The article by Robin Broad, John Cavanagh, and Walden Bello, "Development: The Market Is Not Enough," challenges some of the assumptions commonly made by policymakers and argues that the growth of the free market is not sufficient to ensure development; democracy and respect for human rights will also be important factors in sustainable growth. The final reading examines issues associated with the international monetary system. In "Reinvigorating the Global Economy," Sherle Schwenninger presents an overview of the subject and suggests how problems might best be addressed.

Bibliography

BLAKE, DAVID, and ROBERT WALTERS. *The Politics of Global Economic Relations*. Englewood Cliffs, NJ: Prentice-Hall, 1987.

EVANS, PETER. *Dependent Development: The Alliance of Multinational, State, and Local Capital in Brazil*. Princeton, NJ: Princeton University Press, 1979.

HUNTINGTON, SAMUEL P. "The U.S.—Decline or Renewal?" *Foreign Affairs* 67, No. 2 (Winter 1988).

KRASNER, STEPHEN. *Defending the National Interest: Raw Materials Investments and U.S. Foreign Policy*. Princeton, NJ: Princeton University Press, 1978.

LENIN, V. I. *Imperialism: The Highest Stage of Capitalism*. New York: International Publishers, 1939.

NYE, JOSEPH. "Understanding U.S. Strength." *Foreign Policy*, 72 (Fall 1988), 105–29.

SPERO, JOAN. *The Politics of International Economic Relations*. New York: St. Martin's Press, 1991.

STRANGE, SUSAN. "Protectionism and World Politics." *International Organization* 39, No. 2 (Spring 1985), 233–60.

WALLERSTEIN, IMMANUEL. *The Politics of the World Economy*. Cambridge, Eng.: Cambridge University Press, 1964.

Can the Interdependent World Political Economy Survive?

Three Perspectives on the Future

Robert Gilpin

In this brief article . . . my purpose is to present and evaluate three models of the future drawn from current writings on international relations. These models are really representative of the three prevailing schools of thought on political economy: liberalism, Marxism, and economic nationalism. Each model is an amalgam of the ideas of several writers who, in my judgment (or by their own statements), fall into one or another of these perspectives on the relationship of economic and political affairs.

Each model constitutes an ideal type. Perhaps no one individual would subscribe to each argument made by any one position. Yet the tendencies and assumptions associated with each perception of the future are real enough; they have a profound influence on popular, academic, and official thinking on trade, monetary, and investment problems. One, in fact, cannot really escape being influenced by one position or another.

The Sovereignty-at-Bay Model

I label the first model *sovereignty at bay*, after the title of Raymond Vernon's influential book on the multinational corporation.[1] According to this view, increasing economic interdependence and technological advances in communication and transportation are making the nation state an anachronism. These

Reprinted from *International Organization* 29 (Winter 1975), Robert Gilpin, "Can the Interdependent World Economy Survive? Three Perspectives on The Future," by permission of MIT Press, Cambridge, MA.

economic and technological developments are said to have undermined the traditional economic rationale of the nation state. In the interest of world efficiency and domestic economic welfare, the nation state's control over economic affairs will continually give way to the multinational corporation, to the Eurodollar market, and to other international institutions better suited to the economic needs of mankind.

Perhaps the most forceful statement of the sovereignty-at-bay thesis is that of Harry Johnson—the paragon of economic liberalism. Analyzing the international economic problems of the 1970s, Johnson makes the following prediction:

> In an important sense, the fundamental problem of the future is the conflict between the political forces of nationalism and the economic forces pressing for world integration. This conflict currently appears as one between the national government and the international corporation, in which the balance of power at least superficially appears to lie on the side of the national government. But in the longer run economic forces are likely to predominate over political. . . . Ultimately, a world federal government will appear as the only rational method for coping with the world's economic problems.[2]

Though not all adherents of the sovereignty-at-bay thesis would go as far as Johnson, and an interdependent world economy is quite conceivable without unbridled scope for the activities of multinational corporations, most do regard the multinational corporation as the embodiment par excellence of the liberal ideal of an interdependent world economy. It has taken the integration of national economies beyond trade and money to the internationalization of production. For the first time in history, production, marketing, and investment are being organized on a global scale rather than in terms of isolated national economies. The multinational corporations are increasingly indifferent to national boundaries in making decisions with respect to markets, production, and sources of supply.

The sovereignty-at-bay thesis argues that national economies have become enmeshed in a web of economic interdependence from which they cannot easily escape, and from which they derive great economic benefits. Through trade, monetary relations, and foreign investment, the destinies and well-being of societies have become too inexorably interwoven for these bonds to be severed. The costs of the ensuing inefficiencies in order to assert national autonomy or some other nationalistic goal would be too high. The citizenry, so this thesis contends, would not tolerate the sacrifices of domestic economic well-being that would be entailed if individual nation states sought to hamper unduly the successful operation of the international economy.

Underlying this development, the liberal position argues, is a revolution in economic needs and expectations. Domestic economic goals have been elevated to a predominant position in the hierarchy of national goals. Full employment, regional development, and other economic welfare goals have become the primary concerns of political leadership. More importantly, these goals can only be achieved, this position argues, through participation in the world economy. No government, for example, would dare shut out the multinational corporations and thereby forego employment, regional development, or other benefits these corporations bring into countries. In short, the rise of the welfare state and the increasing sensitivity of national governments to the rising economic expectations of their societies have made them dependent upon the benefits provided by a liberal world-economic system.

In essence, this argument runs, one must distinguish between the creation of the interdependent world economy and the consequences of its subsequent dynamics.[3] Though the postwar world economy was primarily a creation of the United States, the system has since become essentially irreversible. The intermeshing of interests across national boundaries and the recognized benefits of interdependence now cement the system together for the future. Therefore, even though the power of the United States and security concerns may be in relative decline, this does not portend a major transformation of the international economy and political system.

The multinational corporation, for example, is now believed to be sufficiently strong to stand and survive on its own. The flexibility, mobility, and vast resources of the corporations give them an advantage in confrontations with nation states. A corporation always has the option of moving its production facilities elsewhere. If it does, the nation state is the loser in terms of employment, corporate resources, and access to world markets. Thus the multinationals are escaping the control of nation states, including that of their home (source) governments. They are emerging as sufficient powers in their own right to survive the changing context of international political relations.

On the other hand, it is argued that the nation state has been placed in a dilemma it cannot hope to resolve.[4] It is losing control over economic affairs to transnational actors like the multinational corporation. It cannot retain its traditional independence and sovereignty and simultaneously meet the expanding economic needs and desires of its populace. The efforts of nation states to enhance their security and power *relative* to others are held to be incompatible with an interdependent world economy that generates *absolute* gains for everyone. In response to the growing economic demands of its citizens, the nation state must adjust to the forces of economic rationality and efficiency. . . .

The sovereignty-at-bay view also envisages a major transformation of the relationships among developed and underdeveloped countries. The multinational corporations of the developed, industrial economies must not only produce in each other's markets, but the locus of manufacturing industry will increasingly shift to underdeveloped countries.[5] As the economies of developed countries become more service oriented, as their terms of trade for raw materials continue to deteriorate, and as their labor costs continue to rise, manufacturing will migrate to lesser-developed countries. United States firms already engage in extensive offshore production in Asia and Latin America. Western Europe has reached the limits of importing Mediterranean labor, which is the functional equivalent of foreign direct investment. Japan's favorable wage structure and undervalued currency have eroded. With the end of the era of cheap energy and of favorable terms of trade for raw materials, the logic of industrial location favors the underdeveloped periphery. Increasingly, the multinational corporations of all industrial powers will follow the logic of this manufacturing revolution. Manufacturing, particularly of components and semiprocessed goods, will migrate to lesser-developed countries.

This vision of the future has been portrayed most dramatically by Norman Macrae, in an issue of *The Economist,* who foresees a world of spreading affluence energized perhaps by "small transnational companies run in West Africa by London telecommuters who live in Honolulu?"[6] New computer-based training methods and information systems will facilitate the rapid diffusion of skills, technologies and industries to lesser-developed countries. The whole system will be connected by modern telecommunications and computers; the rich will concentrate on the knowledge-creating and knowledge-processing industries. More and more of the old manufacturing industries will move to the underdeveloped world. The entire West and Japan will be a service-oriented island in a labor-intensive global archipelago. Thus, whereas the telephone and jet aircraft facilitated the internationalization of production in the Northern Hemisphere, the contemporary revolution in communications and transportation will encompass the whole globe.

"The logical and eventual development of this possibility," according to management consultant John Diebold, "would be the end of nationality and national governments as we know them."[7] This sovereignty-at-bay world, then, is one of voluntary and cooperative relations among interdependent economies, the goal of which is to accelerate the economic growth and welfare of everyone. In this model, development of the poor is achieved through the transfer of capital, technology, and managerial know-how from the continually advancing developed lands to the lesser-developed nations; it is a world in which the tide of economic growth lifts all boats. In this liberal vision of the future, the multinational corporation, freed from the nation state, is the critical transmission belt of capital, ideas, and growth.

The Dependencia Model

In contrast to the sovereignty-at-bay vision of the future is what may be characterized as the *dependencia* model.[8] Although the analysis underlying the two approaches has much in common, the dependencia model challenges the partners-in-development motif of the sovereignty-at-bay model. Its Marxist conception is one of a hierarchical and exploitative world order. The sovereignty-at-bay model envisages a relatively benevolent system in which growth and wealth spread from the developed core to the lesser-developed periphery. In the dependencia model, on the other hand, the flow of wealth and benefits is seen as moving—via the same mechanisms—from the global, underdeveloped periphery to the centers of industrial financial power and decision. It is an exploitative system that produces affluent development for some and dependent underdevelopment for the majority of mankind. In effect, what is termed transnationalism by the sovereignty-at-bay advocates is considered imperialisin by the Marxist proponents of the dependencia model. . . .

In this hierarchical and exploitative world system, power and decision would be lodged in the urban financial and industrial cores of New York, London, Tokyo, etc. Here would be located the computers and data banks of the closely integrated global systems of production and distribution; the main computer in the core would control subsidiary computers in the periphery. The higher functions of management, research and development, entrepreneurship, and finance would be located in these Northern metropolitan centers. "Lower" functions and labor-intensive manufacturing would be continuously diffused to the lesser developed countries where are found cheap pliable labor, abundant raw materials, and an indifference to industrial pollution. This global division of labor between higher and lower economic functions would perpetuate the chasm between the affluent northern one-fifth of the globe and the destitute southern four-fifths of the globe.

The argument of the dependencia thesis is that the economic dependence of the underdeveloped periphery upon the developed core is responsible for the impoverishment of the former. Development and underdevelopment are simultaneous processes; the developed countries have progressed and have grown rich through exploiting the poor and making them poorer. Lacking true autonomy and being economically dependent upon the developed countries, the underdeveloped countries have suffered because the developed have a veto over their development:

> By dependence we mean a situation in which the economy of certain countries is conditioned by the development and expansion of another economy to which the former is subjected. The relation of interdependence between two or more economies, and between these and world trade, assumes the form of dependence when some countries (the dominant ones) can expand and be self-sustaining, while other countries (the dependent ones) can do this only as a reflection of that expansion, which can have either a positive or negative effect on their immediate development.[9]

Though this particular quotation refers to trade relations, much of the dependence literature is addressed to the issue of foreign direct investment. In content, most of this literature is of a piece with traditional Marxist and radical theories of imperialism. Whether because of the falling rate of profit in capitalist economies or the attraction of superprofits abroad, multinational corporations are believed to exploit the underdeveloped countries. Thus, Paul Baran and Paul Sweezy see the multinational necessarily impelled to invest in lesser-developed countries.[10] Constantine Vaitsos has sought to document the superprofits available to American corporations in

Latin America.[11] The message conveyed by this literature is that the imperialism of free investment has replaced the imperialism of free trade in the contemporary world.

The Mercantilist Model

A key element missing in both the sovereignty-at-bay and the dependencia models is the nation state. Both envisage a world organized and managed by powerful North American, European, and Japanese corporations. In the beneficial corporate order of the first model and the imperialist corporate order of the second, there is little room for nation states, save as servants of corporate power and ambition. In opposition to both these models, therefore, the third model of the future—the mercantilist model—views the nation state and the interplay of national interests (as distinct from corporate interests) as the primary determinants of the future role of the world economy.[12]

According to this mercantilist view, the interdependent world economy, which has provided such a favorable environment for the multinational corporation, is coming to an end. In the wake of the relative decline of American power and of growing conflicts among the capitalist economies, a new international political order less favorable to the multinational corporation is coming into existence. Whether it is former President Nixon's five-power world (US, USSR, and China, the EEC, and Japan), a triangular world (US, USSR, and China), or some form of American-Soviet condominium, the emergent world order will be characterized by intense international economic competition for markets, investment outlets, and sources of raw materials.

By *mercantilism* I mean the attempt of governments to manipulate economic arrangements in order to maximize their own interests, whether or not this is at the expense of others. These interests may be related to domestic concerns (full employment, price stability, etc.) or to foreign policy (security, independence, etc.).

This use of the term *mercantilism* is far broader than its eighteenth-century association with a trade and balance-of-payments surplus. The essence of mercantilism, as the concept is used in this article, is the priority of *national* economic and political objectives over considerations of *global* economic efficiency. The mercantilist impulse can take many forms in the contemporary world: the desire for a balance-of-payments surplus; the export of unemployment, inflation, or both; the imposition of import and/or export controls; the expansion of world market shares; and the stimulation of advanced technology. In short, each nation will pursue economic policies that reflect domestic economic needs and external political ambitions without much concern for the effects of these policies on other countries or on the international economic system as a whole.

The mercantilist position in effect reverses the argument of the liberals with respect to the nature and success of the interdependent world economy. In contrast to the liberal view that trade liberalization has fostered economic growth, the mercantilist thesis is that several decades of uninter-rupted economic growth permitted interdependence. Growth, based in part on relatively cheap energy and other resources as well as on the diffusion of American technology abroad, facilitated the reintroduction of Japan into the world economy and the development of a closely linked Atlantic economy. Now both cheap energy and a technological gap, which were sources of rapid economic growth and global interdependence, have ceased to exist. . . .

Malevolent mercantilism believes regionalization will intensify interna-tional economic conflict. Each bloc centered on the large industrial powers— the United States, Western Europe, Japan, and the Soviet Union—will clash over markets, currency, and investment outlets. This would be a return to the lawlessness and beggar-thy-neighbor policies of the 1930s.

Benign mercantilism, on the other hand, believes regional blocs would stabilize world economic relations. It believes that throughout modern history universalism and regionalism have been at odds. The rationale of regional blocs is that one can have simultaneously the benefits of greater scale and interdependence and minimal accompanying costs of economic and political interdependence. Though the material gains from a global division of labor and free trade could be greater, regionalism is held to provide security and protection against external economic and political forces over which the nation state, acting alone, has little influence or control. In short, the organization of the world economy into regional blocs could provide the basis for a secure and peaceful economic order.

A Critique of the Three Models

Sovereignty at Bay

Fundamentally, the sovereignty-at-bay thesis reduces to a question of interests and power: Who has the power to make the world economy serve its inter-ests? This point may be best illustrated by considering the relationship of the multinational corporation and the nation state. In the writings I identified with the sovereignty-at-bay thesis, this contest is held to be most critical.

On one side of this contest is the host nation state. Its primary source of power is its control over access to its territory, that is, access to its internal market, investment opportunities, and sources of raw material. On the other side is the corporation with its capital, technology, and access to world mar-kets. Each has something the other wants. Each seeks to maximize its benefits and minimize its costs. The bargain they strike is dependent upon how much one wants what the other has to offer and how skillfully one or the other can exploit its respective advantages. In most cases, the issue is how the benefits and costs of foreign investments are to be divided between the foreign corpo-ration and the host economy.

The sovereignty-at-bay thesis assumes that the bargaining advantages are and always will be on the side of the corporation. In contrast to the corporation's vast resources and flexibility, the nation state has little with which to bargain. Most nation states lack the economies of scale, indigenous technological capabilities, or native entrepreneurship to free themselves from dependence upon American (or other) multinational corporations. According to this argument, the extent to which nation states reassert their sovereignty is dependent upon the economic price they are willing to pay, and it assumes that when confronted with this cost, they will retreat from nationalistic policies.

In an age of rising economic expectations, the sovereignty-at-bay thesis rests on an important truth: A government is reluctant to assert its sovereignty and drive out the multinational corporations if this means a dramatic lowering of the standard of living, increasing unemployment, and the like. But in an age when the petroleum-producing states, through cooperation, have successfully turned the tables on the multinational corporations, it becomes obvious that the sovereignty-at-bay thesis also neglects the fact that the success of the multinational corporation has been dependent upon a favorable political order. As this order changes, so will the fortunes of the multinationals.

A reversal of fortunes has already been seen in the case of the oil multinationals. The significance of the offensive by the oil-producing states against the large international oil companies is not merely that the price of oil to the United States and to the rest of the world has risen but also that the United States may lose one of its most lucrative sources of investment income. The oil crisis and Arab oil boycott which followed the 1973 Arab-Israeli war was a profound learning experience for Europe, Japan, and even the United States. The oil boycott and the behavior of the oil multinationals set into motion a series of events that [helped to] transform national attitudes and policies toward the oil multinationals. The sudden appreciation of how vulnerable governments were to the policies of the oil multinationals and how far their "sovereignty" had been compromised awakened them to the inherent dangers of overdependence on the corporations and their policies. . . .

The case of oil and the oil multinationals is perhaps unique. Yet it does suggest that nation states have not lost their power or their will to act when they believe the multinational corporations are threatening their perceived national interests and sovereignty. The experience of the oil boycott and the role of the multinationals in carrying it out reveal the extent to which the operators and the success of these corporations have been dependent upon American power. With the relative decline of American power and the rise of governments hostile to American interests and policies, this case history at least raises the question of how the weakening of the Pax Americana will affect the status of other American multinational corporations throughout the world.

Dependencia

The weakness of the dependencia, or ultraimperialism, model is that it makes at least three unwarranted assumptions. In the first place, it assumes much greater common interest among the noncommunist industrial powers—the United States, Western Europe, and Japan—than is actually the case. Secondly, it treats the peripheral states of Asia, Africa, Latin America, Canada, and the Middle East solely as objects of international economic and political relations. Neither assumption is true. As the first assumption is considered in more detail in the next section, let us consider the second for a moment.

After nearly two centuries, the passivity of the periphery is now past. The Soviet challenge to the West [during the Cold War] and the divisions among the capitalist powers themselves [gave] the emerging elites in the periphery room for maneuver. These nationalist elites are no longer ignorant and pliable colonials. Within the periphery, there [were] coalescing centers of power that will weigh increasingly in the future world balance of power: China, Indonesia, India, Iran, Nigeria, Brazil, and some form of Arab oil power. Moreover, if properly organized and led, such centers of power in control over a vital resource, as the experience of the Organization of Petroleum Exporting Countries (OPEC) demonstrates, may reverse the tables and make the core dependent upon the periphery. For the moment at least, a perceptible shift appears to be taking place in the global balance of economic power from the owners of capital to the owners of natural resources.[13]

The third unwarranted assumption is that a quasi-Marxist theory of capitalist imperialism is applicable to the relationship of developed and lesser-developed economies today. Again, I illustrate my argument by considering the role of the multinational corporation in the lesser-developed countries, since its allegedly exploitative function is stressed by almost all dependencia theorists.

The dependencia theory undoubtedly has a good case with respect to foreign direct investment in petroleum and other extractive industries. The oil, copper, and other multinationals have provided the noncommunist industrial world with a plentiful and relatively cheap supply of minerals and energy. The dramatic reversal of this situation by the oil-producing countries in 1973–74 and the steady rise of prices of other commodities support the contention that the producing countries were not getting the highest possible price and possibly not a just price for their nonrenewable resources. But what constitutes the just price for a natural endowment that was worthless until the multinationals found it is not an easy issue to resolve.

With respect to foreign direct investment in manufacturing, the case is far more ambiguous. Even if technological rents are collected, does the foreign corporation bring more into the economy in terms of technology, capital, and access to world markets than it takes out in the form of earnings? The research of Canadian, Australian, and other economists, for example, suggests that it does. They find no differences in the corporate behavior of domestic and foreign firms; on the contrary, foreign firms are given higher marks in terms of export performance, industrial research and development, and other economic indicators. Nonetheless, it would be naive to suggest that no exploitation or severe distortions of host economies have taken place.

On the other hand, it may not be unwarranted to suggest that a strong presumption exists for arguing that in terms of economic growth and industrial development, foreign direct investment in *manufacturing* is to the advantage of the host economy. A major cause of foreign direct investment is the sector specific nature of knowledge and capital in the home economy.[14] In order to prevent a fall in their rate of profits through overinvesting at home or diversifying into unknown areas, American corporations frequently go abroad to guard against a lower rate of profit at home rather than because the superprofits abroad are attractive. Insofar as this is true, and there is sufficient evidence to warrant its plausibility, foreign direct investment benefits both the corporation and the host economy at a cost to other factors of production in the home economy. Thus, though the Marxists may be right in saying that there is an imperative for capitalism to go abroad, the effect is not to exploit but to benefit the recipient economy—a conclusion, by the way, that Marx himself would have accepted.[15]. . .

The dependencia argument that foreign direct investment by multinational corporations preempts the emergence of an indigenous entrepreneurial middle class and creates a situation of technological dependence provides a clue to what is the central concern of dependence theory. Though most frequently couched solely in economic terms, the concepts of underdevelopment and dependence are more political than economic in nature. They involve an assessment of the political costs of foreign investment. They refer both to the internal political development of the recipient country and its external relations. As one of the better dependence theorists has put it, the problem "is not so much growth, i.e., expansion of a given socio-economic system, as it is 'development,' i.e., rapid and fundamental politico-socioeconomic transformation."[16] In other words, foreign direct investment fosters an international division of labor that perpetuates underdevelopment and politico-economic dependencia.

This distinction between *growth* and *development* is crucial.[17] Economic growth is defined by most development economists simply as an increase in output or income per capita; it is essentially a positive and quantitative concept. The concepts of development and underdevelopment as used by dependence theorists are primarily normative and qualitative; they refer to structural changes internal to the lesser-developed economy and in external relations with the developed world. Dependencia theory really calls for a change in the current international division of labor between the core and the periphery of the international economy, in which the periphery is a supplier of raw materials and whose industries are branch plants of the core's multinational corporations.

Whatever its economic merits, the dependencia model will continue to generate opposition against the structure of the contemporary world economy and the multinational corporation throughout the underdeveloped periphery of the world economy. As these peripheral societies grow in power, one can anticipate that they will undertake initiatives that attempt to lessen their dependence upon developed countries.

Mercantilism

It seems to me that mercantilists either ignore or ascribe too little significance to certain primary facts. Although the relative power of the United States has declined, the United States remains the dominant world economy. The scale, diversity, and dynamics of the American economy will continue to place the United States at the center of the international economic system. The universal desire for access to the huge American market, the inherent technological dynamism of the American economy, and America's additional strength in both agriculture and resources—which Europe and Japan do not have— provide a cement sufficient to hold the world economy together and to keep the United States at its center.[18]

Furthermore, the United States can compensate for its loss of strength in one issue area by its continued strength in another. For example, the American economic position has indeed declined relative to Europe and Japan. Yet the continued dependence of Europe and Japan on the United States for their security provides the United States with a strong lever over the economic policies of each.

Thus, the fundamental weakness of the mercantilist model is the absence of a convincing alternative to an American-centered world economy. Western Europe, the primary economic challenger to the United States, remains internally divided; it is as yet unable to develop common policies in such areas as industry and energy or with respect to economic and monetary union. It is merely a customs union with a common agricultural policy. Moreover, like Japan, it continues to be totally dependent upon the United States for its security. As long as both Europe and Japan lack an alternative to their military and economic dependence on the United States, the mercantilist world of regional blocks lacks credibility. . . .

Yet sufficient tensions and conflict of interests remain within this world economy to prevent one from dismissing so quickly the mercantilist thesis. Undoubtedly, the interstate conflict that will be the most vexing is the growing demand and competition for raw materials, particularly petroleum. . . . In the longer term, these changes have put the industrial powers in competition for . . . limited resources. They are also competing for export markets in order to finance these vital imports and for the capital the oil-producing states now have to invest. Thus, whereas in the past America's virtual control over the noncommunist world's supply of petroleum was a source of unity, today the United States is struggling with other industrial powers to insure its own position in a highly competitive environment.

The other reason for believing that there may be some validity in the mercantilist vision of the future is the weakening of political bonds between the United States, Western Europe, and Japan. During the height of the cold war, the foreign economic policies of these three countries were complementary. Potential conflicts over economic matters were subordinated to the necessity for political unity against the Soviet Union and China. The United States encouraged export-led growth and accepted anti-American trade discrimination in order to enable Japan and Europe to rebuild their shattered economies. Reciprocally, Japan and Europe supported the international position of the dollar. Through foreign direct investment, American corporations were able to maintain their relative share of world markets. Neither the Europeans nor the Japanese challenged America's dominant position with respect to the industrial world's access to vital raw materials, particularly Middle Eastern petroleum.

Until the early 1970s, the political benefits of this arrangement were regarded as outweighing the economic costs to each partner. With the movement toward détente and with the revival of the European and Japanese economies, however, the political benefits have receded in importance and the concern over costs has increased. As a consequence, the United States and its industrial partners now desire reforms of the world's trading and monetary systems that would enable each to pursue its own particular set of interests and to limit that of the others. For example, the United States has proposed reforms of the trade and monetary systems that would limit the ability of the Europeans and the Japanese to run up huge trade surpluses. Europe and Japan, for their part, desire to preserve this scope and to limit the privileges of the United States as world banker. . . .

Conclusion

In conclusion, what does this redistribution of world power imply for the future of the interdependent world economy? Today, the liberal world economy is challenged by powerful groups (especially organized labor) within the dominant economy; the dominant economy itself is in relative decline. With the decline of the dominant economic power, the world economy may be following the pattern of the latter part of the nineteenth century and of the 1930s and may be fragmenting into regional trading and monetary blocs. This would be prevented, of course, if the United States, as it is presently trying to do, were to reassert its waning hegemony over Western Europe, Japan, and the rest of the noncommunist world economy.

In the wake of the decline of American power and the erosion of the political base upon which the world economy has rested, the question arises whether the wisest policy for the United States is to attempt to reassert its dominance. May not this effort in the areas of trade, money, investment, and energy exacerbate the conflicts between the United States, Western Europe, and Japan? If so, a future that could be characterized increasingly by benign mercantilism could well be transformed into its more malevolent relative. If this were to happen, the United States and its allies would be the losers.

This admonition suggests that the United States should accept a greater regionalization of the world economy than it has been wont to accept in the past. It implies greater representation and voice for other nations and regional blocs in international economic organizations. While such a policy of retrenchment would no doubt harm the interests of American corporations and other sectors of the American economy, the attempt to hold on to rather than adjust to the shifting balance of world power could be even more costly for the United States in the long run.

In a world economy composed of regional blocs and centers of power, economic bargaining and competition would predominate. Through the exercise of economic power and various trade-offs, each center of the world economy would seek to shift the costs and benefits of economic interdependence to its own advantage. Trade, monetary, and investment relations would be the consequence of negotiations as nation states and regional blocs sought to increase the benefits of interdependence and to decrease the costs. This in fact has been the direction of the evolution of the international economy, from a liberal to a negotiated system, since the rise of large and rival economic entities in the latter part of the nineteenth century.

Therefore, debate and policy planning today should not focus on economic independence or dependence but on the nature and consequences of economic interdependence. Economic interdependence may take many forms; it may affect the welfare of nations in very different ways. Some will emphasize security; others, efficiency, low rates of inflation, or full employment. The question of how these benefits and costs will be distributed is at the heart of the increasingly mercantilistic policies of nation states in the contemporary world.

NOTES

1. Raymond Vernon, *Sovereignty at Bay* (New York: Basic Books, 1971).
2. Harry G. Johnson, *International Economic Questions Facing Britain, the United States, and Canada in the 70's*, British-North American Research Association, June 1970, p. 24.
3. Samuel Huntington, "Transnational Organizations in World Politics," *World Politics* 25 (April 1973): 361.
4. Edward L. Morse, "Crisis Diplomacy, Interdependence, and the Politics of International Economic Relations," *World Politics* 24, supplement (Spring 1972): 123–150.
5. John Diebold, "Multinational Corporations—Why Be Scared of Them?" *Foreign Policy*, no. 12 (Fall 1973): 79–95.
6. "The Future of International Business," *The Economist*, January 22, 1972.
7. Diebold, "Multinational Corporations," p. 87.
8. The literature on dependencia, or underdevelopment, has now become legend. One of the better statements of this thesis is Osvaldo Sunkel, "Big Business and 'Dependencia': A Latin American View," *Foreign Affairs* 50 (April 1972): 517–531. For an excellent and critical view of the dependencia thesis, see Benjamin J. Cohen, *The Question of Imperialism—The Political Economy of Dominance and Dependence* (New York: Basic Books, 1973), chap. 6.
9. Quoted in Cohen, *The Question of Imperialism*, pp. 190–191.
10. *Monopoly Capital—An Essay on the American Economic and Social Order* (New York: Monthly Review Press, 1966).

11. Constantine Vaitsos, "Transfer of Resources and Preservation of Monopoly Rents," Economic Development Report No. 168, Development Advisory Service, Harvard University, 1970. (Mimeographed.)

12. See, for example, David Calleo and Benjamin Rowland, *America and the World Political Economy* (Bloomington: Indiana University Press, 1973). Mercantilism is also the real theme of Ernest Mandel's *Europe vs. America—Contradictions of Imperialism* (New York: Monthly Review Press, 1970).

13. See C. Fred Bergsten, "The Threat From the Third World," *Foreign Policy*, no. 11 (Summer 1973): 102–124.

14. This point is developed in US Congress, Senate Committee on Labor and Public Welfare, *The Multinational Corporation and the National Interest* (report prepared for the Committee), 93rd Cong., 1st sess., 1973, Committee print.

15. Karl Marx, "The Future Results of British Rule in India," in *Karl Marx on Colonialism and Modernization*, ed. Shlomo Avineri (Garden City, NY: Doubleday, 1968), pp. 125–131.

16. This distinction is developed by Keith Griffin, *Underdevelopment in Spanish America* (Cambridge, MA: M.I.T. Press, 1969), p. 117.

17. For a more detailed analysis of the distinction, see J. D. Gould, *Economic Growth in History* (London: Methuen and Co., 1972), chap. 1.

18. A forceful statement of this position is Raymond Vernon, "Rogue Elephant in the Forest: An Appraisal of Transatlantic Relations," *Foreign Affairs* 51 (April 1973): 573–587.

Seven Basic Questions About the Future

United States Agency for International Development

Much has changed since President Kennedy's clear-cut 1963 definition of U.S. foreign aid as a phased, finite means of helping countries to achieve self-reliance. . . . Layer upon layer of new objectives—often unrelated or conflicting—have been piled onto American foreign assistance by succeeding Congresses and Administrations.

Even if such a wide range of competing objectives could be pursued indefinitely—and growing fiscal constraints combined with domestic and defense priorities make this increasingly unlikely—does the scatter-gun assistance policy that results truly serve America's national interests and the interests of mankind? And what new demands are likely to be made on our already strained official development resources?

In the end, making America's contribution to global development work—and making it better serve our own vital interests—means answering seven bottom-line questions:

1. How Do We Define Success?

Who is responsible and how can we measure success? With so many different objectives, every program is a success by someone's standards, a failure by another's. Good short-term economic growth can be successfully implemented

From *Development and the National Interest* (Washington, DC: U.S. Agency for International Development).

by pumping aid into a small country's malfunctioning economy. But is it a real long-term solution?

Low or negative growth may, in turn, have nothing to do with the basic soundness of either a country's long-term policies or the aid it is receiving.

How can global assistance objectives be reconciled with the need to focus on country-specific requirements and the comparative advantage of different development institutions? Clearly, no single government agency can be made responsible for working on every development priority in every country. The fact that a particular issue is important does not necessarily indicate which particular agency—domestic or foreign, private or governmental—is best suited to work on it. What are the limits on government initiative, particularly in the face of increasingly important and self-sustaining informal sectors?

Similarly, how can humanitarian progress that, in the past, has helped reduce infant mortality and boost life expectancy be sustained when further gains require new sorts of domestic institutions? How will poor countries or individuals afford the rising costs of sustained progress in health or education?

And while official U.S. aid shrinks as a force for global development, can the broader American contribution, in the form of intellectual creativity, leadership, technical expertise, private voluntary assistance, private investment, and enlightened trade and financial policies be a driving engine for development?

Increasingly, how much the U.S. Government spends is not a reasonable measure of how much America achieves, in the absence of reliable, objective-oriented information. Without such information, how can Administrations test their policies? How can Congress—much less the general public—decide what works and what does not? And how can we avoid the perverse incentive to focus on instant success stories that may generate the next round of appropriations but divert development strategy from long-range progress?

2. What Are Our Strategic Interests?

Are American strategic interests changing? The Central American Initiative launched by the National Bipartisan Commission on Central America is the latest major foreign aid effort tied to a direct communist threat. While firmly grounded on strategic national interests, will it succeed in fostering development in Central America that will make political stability possible? In the past, such American efforts have both succeeded and failed. In any event, will an increasingly skeptical Congress be willing to provide both the long-term funding *and* the executive flexibility to make success possible?

Similarly, in the aftermath of the Soviet withdrawal from Afghanistan, can we expect another massive outflow of American assistance dollars? Will these, and other strategic considerations such as the continuous rise in base rights allocations, remain the only growing part of the assistance budget, at the expense of development elsewhere? Alternatively, could a possible decline in East-West tensions mean less strategic aid requirements from both U.S. and U.S.S.R. client states and allies?

3. What Are Our Humanitarian Interests?

Humanitarianism remains a major motivation for American foreign aid. Americans always have been, and always will be, eager to help victims of natural disasters around the world. We need only recall, most recently, the massive official and private sector relief assistance Americans rushed to the victims of the Armenian earthquake.

But what about endemic poverty and economic dislocations sometimes imposed upon developing countries by their own governments? Even if it were affordable, should the U.S. become the automatic source of last resort whenever a developing country faces the economic and human consequences of its own mistaken policies?

Costs are rising along with demands, even as aid resources contract. How much can be done, how much should be done, and where? And from a humanitarian point of view, is it time to realize that the current international safety net only works when host governments allow it to?

4. What Are Our Economic Interests?

Has U.S. foreign assistance served our own economic interests? Certainly the reconstruction of Western Europe and Japan contributed to American prosperity, although this was an unexpected benefit from what were then seen as national security oriented programs. Since then, the economic returns have been more mixed, and development assistance has, in general, not been linked directly to U.S. economic interests.

- In the years ahead, will economic considerations play a larger role in U.S. foreign policy? Should the pressures of a more competitive international economy force an overhaul of development assistance?
- At what point should assistance oriented efforts give way to programs more directly focused on cooperation and mutual gain? What parts of the U.S. Government should be involved in managing these evolving economic relationships?
- Should the U.S. phase out its assistance programs in those countries which are becoming important trading partners? In the past, economic growth has increased mutually beneficial trade and investment and justified reducing or closing assistance programs.

■ How can we compete with export promoting programs that other countries call development assistance? Is the answer to re-direct existing aid flows to promote commercial advantage or to take a stronger negotiating stance, backed by a big war chest, with our competitors?

5. How Can We Reconcile Sovereignty and Assistance?

One of the most humbling lessons for enthusiastic boosters of development in the 1980s has been how comparatively small their impact is likely to be. In the last analysis, does not progress in any LDC [less developed country] depend on its own decisions and policies? Foreign resources, including aid, can preserve incomes and provide short-term relief in the face of natural disasters. The result, however, is maintaining the status quo, not development—*unless* the host country firmly commits itself to growth and opportunity-oriented domestic policies.

While it makes sense to mold foreign assistance programs to encourage such policies, each sovereign state must ultimately chart its own developmental course. No one else has a right—much less an obligation—to do so. The degree to which U.S. development assistance can influence such policy choices is thus severely limited. American aid has helped the people of countries like Korea to score impressive development gains, but it was the people and policies of the host countries that ultimately made their national development efforts work. Ultimately, the credit or blame for development success or failure—and the responsibility to choose its own path to development—can only reside with each sovereign state.

Indeed, to the extent that the U.S. does influence development, it is our broader economic and trade policies, the dynamic growth of the American economy, and the foreign investment decisions of our vast private sector that have the greatest impact on developing nations.

6. How Relevant Is Foreign Assistance to Development?

Perhaps the single greatest challenge to many major developing nations today is foreign debt, a problem current foreign assistance programs do little or nothing to address. Strategic aid, sometimes in the form of direct payment transfers, has little bearing on development pure and simple. Some critics even argue that the allocation of strategically-linked assistance would be more appropriately handled directly by the State Department, and that is not, strictly speaking, development aid. And . . . the trade component of economic development is largely the domain of other federal agencies and departments. How much of a relevant role does this leave for U.S. development assistance as currently structured?

7. Finally, and Most Importantly, How Can We Better Match U.S. Assistance to the National Interest?

Above all, successful development means successful growth; anything less is nothing more than a thinly disguised dole fostering dependence instead of development. To be distributed, wealth must first be produced. For poverty to be reduced, wealth must be increased. And the production of wealth—of economic growth and individual opportunity—is a vital factor in the development of strong, stable democratic social values. Wise men have understood this greater dimension of wealth since ancient times, as witnessed by the Athenian historian Thucydides' proud assertion, "Wealth to us is not merely material for vain glory but an opportunity for achievement; and poverty we think it is no disgrace to acknowledge but a real degradation to make no effort to overcome."

Forty years ago, America made an investment in the future that broke all of the conventional rules of the day. In the wake of the Second World War, we reached out and provided economic assistance to the war-torn nations of Europe and Asia, to those who had been our adversaries as well as to our allies.

Through programs of economic assistance, the Marshall Plan and Point Four, and through the international organizations that we and our allies created, we expressed our conviction that America's security and its future prosperity depend on the fortunes of many nations—on global peace and prosperity.

We believed then, and we believe now, that the economic development of other nations is in our national interest. However, we also recognize that much of what has haphazardly evolved as development assistance over the past four decades has not worked, has sometimes not even been aimed at the correct objectives, and, above all, has been overtaken by events.

Well-intended calls for a "New Marshall Plan" for the Philippines, Central America, or any other strategic region in a real or perceived state of crisis overlook historical reality. The Marshall Plan—and similar post–war recovery assistance to Japan—was a straightforward, finite program of reconstruction. Sophisticated, industrialized societies with skilled work forces, managerial cadres, and long-established competitive economies were helped to rebuild, and to resume their place in the ranks of developed nations.

This was a magnificent undertaking, and it succeeded admirably. But it has little to do with today's development challenges, the most important of which deal with countries that have little in common—culturally, economically, politically, or geographically—with Japan and the Marshall Plan's West European beneficiaries of nearly half a century ago. The Marshall Plan nursed a series of modern but war-devastated national economies back to health. Once the patients were up and around again, they were out of the hospital and on their own.

Today's development is a matter of construction, not reconstruction. Many of the countries with the greatest needs—including many of the countries of greatest strategic importance to the U.S.—are fragile societies in their economic and political infancy as independent states. Others, while older, have been plagued by chronic social and economic instability since birth.

Development for these countries means far more than putting a good system back into operation by repairing it; it means evolving not only an entirely new atmosphere of individual rights and incentives but, in many cases, a whole new way of thinking. . . .

This kind of development is long-term work, and most of the work, while it can be marginally assisted by friendly outside agencies, must be done by the governments and people of the countries themselves.

No Marshall Plan existed in the 17th, 18th, and 19th centuries when Britain and Western Europe developed into global trading powers and modern industrial states, during Japan's initial drive to modernization in the second half of the 19th century, or during the first century and a half of America's own history when a small coastal cluster of mainly agricultural colonies evolved into a mighty transcontinental industrial power. In all three cases, development was the work of many generations, was largely accomplished internally, and has continued because of deeply imbedded domestic institutions that promote economic growth, competition, and trade by rewarding individual enterprise.

Conversely, we have seen New Economic Order after New Economic Order emphasizing state control and the abolition of property rights collapse under the weight of their own folly, and more and more wounded societies in the communist world as well as the developing world turn belatedly to growth and market oriented policies.

America's interest in promoting this global awakening to the realities development is threefold:

- From a purely humanitarian standpoint, we know that economic growth is the only way out of long-term poverty and suffering for any society in any part of the world—the only way it can provide its people with the permanent means of bettering their lives.
- From an economic standpoint, we know that America, and the world, will benefit from the greater prosperity, trade, and stability that such development can bring.
- From the bottom-line view of our own strategic national interest, we know that in the long run, peace and prosperity can only exist in a world consisting of secure nations bound together by positive economic relationships and a shared interest in continued growth and cooperation.

The seven basic questions this report poses go to the very heart of development aid. They are fundamental. Current structures and concepts are based on a past which no longer exists. The challenges of today's problems, and tomorrow's, cannot be met with yesterday's solutions, suitable as they may have been to yesterday's problems.

America's role in global development remains pivotal, but actual government programs play a supporting part at best to the contributions of the

U.S. private sector, overseas investment, the contributions of the American education system as university to the world, the massive humanitarian and developmental efforts of American private voluntary organizations, and, most of all, the growth-oriented example and wealth-generating dynamism of the American economy itself.

Radically reshaping future official assistance programs to face new realities and complement these greater unofficial American contributions to global development must be both an immediate concern and a major long-term national priority. Nothing less will serve the national interests of the United States.

Development

The Market Is Not Enough

Robin Broad
John Cavanagh
Walden Bello

As the 1990s begin, the development debate has all but disappeared in the West. Monumental changes in Eastern Europe and Latin America are widely interpreted as proof of the superiority of development models that are led by the private sector and oriented toward exports. Free-market capitalism is said to have prevailed because only it promises growth and democracy for the battered economies of Africa, Asia, and Latin America. World Bank President Barber Conable summed up this prevailing view in remarks made in February 1990: "If I were to characterize the past decade, the most remarkable thing was the generation of a global consensus that market forces and economic efficiency were the best way to achieve the kind of growth which is the best antidote to poverty."

Ample evidence exists, however, to suggest caution in the face of triumphalism. Warning signs are surfacing in South Korea and Taiwan, the miracle models of capitalist development. After decades of systematic exploitation, the South Korean labor force erupted in thousands of strikes during the late 1980s, undermining the very basis of that country's export success. Meanwhile, decades of uncontrolled industrial development have left large parts of Taiwan's landscape with poisoned soil and toxic water.

Additional evidence reveals extensive suffering throughout Africa, parts of Asia, and Latin America, where privatized adjustment has been

Reprinted with permission from *Foreign Policy* 81 (Winter 1990–91). Copyright 1990 by the Carnegie Endowment for International Peace.

practiced for more than a decade in a world economy of slower growth. As the United Nations Children's Fund noted in its 1990 annual report, "Over the course of the 1980s, average incomes have fallen by 10 per cent in most of Latin America and by over 20 per cent in sub-Saharan Africa. . . . In many urban areas, real minimum wages have declined by as much as 50 per cent." The World Bank estimates that as many as 950 million of the world's 5.2 billion people are "chronically malnourished"—more than twice as many hungry people as a decade ago.

In Latin America, people are talking about a lost decade, even a lost generation. In Rio de Janeiro, the lack of meaningful futures has given birth to a new sport: train surfing. Brazilian street children stand atop trains beside a 3,300 volt cable that sends trains hurtling at speeds of 120 kilometers per hour. During an 18-month period in 1987–88, train surfing in Rio produced some 200 deaths and 500 gruesome injuries. "It's a form of suicide," said the father of a *surfista* who was killed. "Brazilian youth is suffering so much, they see no reason to live."

This generalized failure of development in the 1980s is producing a very different kind of consensus among people the development establishment rarely contacts and whose voices are seldom heard. A new wave of democratic movements across Africa, Asia, and Latin America is demanding another kind of development. Through citizens' organizations millions of environmentalists, farmers, women, and workers are saying they want to define and control their own futures. They are beginning to lay the groundwork for a new type of development in the 1990s—one that emphasizes ecological sustainability, equity, and participation, in addition to raising material living standards.

The false impression that the free-market model has triumphed in development is rooted in three misconceptions about the past decade:

- that the newly industrializing countries (NICs) of East Asia were exceptions to the "lost decade" and continue to represent models of successful development;
- that socialist command economies in Eastern Europe or the developing world failed principally because they did not use market mechanisms;
- that the export-oriented structural adjustment reforms that were put in place in much of the developing world have laid the groundwork for sustained growth in the 1990s. . . .

Most developing countries . . . fall neither into the category of the NICs nor into the socialist world. For the development establishment, the lesson drawn from the experience of the NICs and the socialist countries is that developing countries' only hope rests with exporting their way to NIC status through the purgatory of structural adjustment. Dozens of countries across Africa, Asia, and Latin America have been force-fed this harsh prescription.

Supervised by the World Bank and the International Monetary Fund (IMF), these adjustment packages mandate severely cutting government spending to balance budgets, eliminating trade barriers and social subsidies, encouraging exports, tightening money policies, devaluing currencies, and dismantling nationalist barriers to foreign investment.

Part of the West's sense of triumph flows from a feeling that a world-wide consensus has developed about the necessity of these reforms. But many Western development authorities ignore that this "consensus" has been pushed on developing-country governments with a heavy hand. After borrowing sprees in the 1970s most developing countries ran into debt-servicing difficulties in the 1980s. Creditor banks, using the World Bank and IMF as enforcers, conditioned debt rescheduling on acceptance of export-oriented structural adjustment packages. In fact, many least-developed countries (LDCs) faced serious external constraints on export opportunities—from growing protectionism in developed-country markets to increased substitution for raw-material exports.[1]

The Failures of Structural Adjustment

The strategy urged on the LDCs suffers from other shortcomings as well. Structural adjustment in practice has damaged environments, worsened structural inequities, failed even in the very narrow goal of pulling economies forward, and bypassed popular participation. Now many of the democratic movements expanding across the globe are rejecting the profoundly undemocratic approach of structural adjustment.

Ecological sustainability has been undermined in country after country. In their frenzy to export, countries often resort to the easiest short-term approach: unsustainable exploitation of natural resources. The stories of ecological disasters lurking behind export successes have become common: Timber exporting has denuded mountains, causing soil erosion and drying critical watersheds. Cash crop exports have depended on polluting pesticides and fertilizers. Large fishing boats have destroyed the coral reefs in which fish breed and live. Tailings from mines have polluted rivers and bays.

One example is the production of prawns in the Philippines. Prawns were one of the fastest growing Philippine exports during the 1980s and are heavily promoted throughout Asia by some U.N. and other development agencies. By 1988, Philippine prawn exports had reached $250 million, ranking them fifth among the country's exports. The government's Department of Trade and Industry is seeking to boost that figure to $1 billion by 1993.

Prawn farming requires a careful mixture of fresh and salt water in coastal ponds. Vast quantities of fresh water are pumped into the ponds and mixed with salt water drawn from the sea. But some rice farmers in the Philippines' biggest prawn area fear that as salt water seeps into their nearby lands, their crop yields will fall as they have in Taiwan. Other farmers complain that not enough fresh water remains for their crops. In one town in the heart of prawn country, the water supply has already dropped 30 per cent: Potable water is being rationed. Like many cash crops, prawns do little to increase equity. Invariably, they make the rich richer and the poor poorer, weakening the prospect for mass participation in development. In one typical Philippine province, the substantial initial investment of approximately $50,000 per hectare limited potential prawn-pond owners to the wealthiest 30 or 40 families, including the province's vice governor, the ex-governor, and several mayors. Moreover, as the wealthy renovated old milkfish ponds into high-tech prawn ponds, the supply of milkfish, a staple of the poor, fell and its price rose.

Structural adjustment hurts the poor in other ways, too. As government spending is reduced, social programs are decimated. One May 1989 World Bank working paper concluded that a byproduct of the "sharply deteriorating social indicators" that accompany contractionary adjustment packages is that "people below the poverty line will probably suffer irreparable damage in health, nutrition, and education." Another World Bank working paper, published in September 1989, on Costa Rica, El Salvador, and Haiti suggested that the concentration of land in the hands of a few, along with population growth, was a major cause of environmental degradation. Skewed land distribution, it argued, pushed marginalized peasants onto fragile ecosystems. However, as the report noted, the adjustment programs in these countries failed to address distributional issues, focusing instead on correcting "distorted prices." In this regard, Taiwan and South Korea offer historical precedents: Their economic success rested on an initial redistribution of the land. Although some recent agricultural policies have been biased against the peasantry, extensive land reforms in the 1950s helped create the internal market that sustained the early stages of industrialization.

The failures of structural adjustment in the areas of environment and equity might appear less serious if the adjustment packages were scoring economic successes. They are not. The first World Bank structural adjustment loans were given to Kenya, the Philippines, and Turkey a decade ago; none can be rated a success story today. A new U.N. Economic Commission for Africa study has highlighted the World Bank's own findings that after structural adjustment programs, 15 African countries were worse off in a number of economic categories.[2]

None of these examples is meant to deny that developing countries need substantial reforms, that some governments consistently overspend, or that markets have an important role to play. Rather, the lesson of the 1980s teaches that there are no shortcuts to development. Development strategies will not succeed and endure unless they incorporate ecological sustainability, equity, and participation, as well as effectiveness in raising material living standards.

Countries focusing on any of these principles to the exclusion of others will probably fall short in the long run, if they have not already. The World Bank and the IMF, either by ignoring these first three principles in their structural adjustment reforms or, at best, by treating them as afterthoughts, have adjusted economies to the short-term benefit of narrow elite interests. Their fixation on high gross national product growth rates ensures that the costs in terms of people and resources will mount and overwhelm an economy at a later date, much as they have in South Korea and Taiwan.

People Power

While governmental approaches to development are failing across Africa, Asia, and Latin America, development initiatives are flourishing among citizens' organizations. Indeed, a natural relationship exists between the two levels. The failure of governments in development has given birth to many citizens' initiatives.

Popular organizations are taking on ecological destruction, inequitable control over resources and land, and governments' inability to advance the quality of life. And often the people are struggling in the face of government and military repression. Many citizens' groups are pushing for a central role in development—a concept they do not measure solely in terms of economic growth. At the core of almost all these movements lies an emphasis on participation of members in initiating and implementing plans, and in exercising control over their own lives. Hence, democracy becomes the central theme. . . .

Ultimately, the greatest successes in sustainable development will come when citizen groups seat their representatives in government. Governments that are more representative can help transform sustainable development initiatives into reality. Such governments can help build up an economic infrastructure and an internal market, create a network of social services, and set rules for a country's integration into the world economy. These three tenets do not represent another universal model to replace those of free marketeers, Marxist-Leninists, or the World Bank; the past four decades are littered with the failures of universal models. However, the outlines of a more positive government role in development can be sketched using the principles of ecological sustainability, equity, participation, and effectiveness.

South Korea and Taiwan offer positive lessons for the ideal governmental role in the economy. The main lesson is not that the government should be taken out of the economy. Instead, the NICs' experiences suggest that success depends on governments standing above vested interests to help create the social and political infrastructure for economic growth. Indeed, though it may sound paradoxical, one needs an effective government to create the market.

The problem in many developing countries is not too much government, but a government that is too tangled in the web of narrow interest groups. The Philippine government, for example, serves as the private preserve of special economic interests. In South Korea, on the other hand, the weakness of the landed and business elite allowed the government to set the direction for development in the 1960s and 1970s. Without an assertive government that often acted against the wishes of international agencies and big business, South Korea would never have gained the foundation of heavy and high-technology industries that enabled it to become a world-class exporter of high value-added commodities.

Placing governments above the control of economic interest groups presents no easy task in countries where a small number of powerful families control much of the land and resources. To increase the chances of success, strong citizens' groups must put their representatives in government, continue to closely monitor government actions, and press for redistributive reforms that weaken the power of special interests.

While independent governments can help push economies through the early stages of development, progress to more mature economies seems to require more market mechanisms to achieve effective production and distribution. For market mechanisms to work, however, there must first be a market. And for the majority of the developing world, creating a market with consumers possessing effective demand requires eliminating the severe inequalities that depress the purchasing power of workers and peasants. The "how to" list necessitates such steps as land reform, progressive taxation, and advancement of workers' rights.

Pragmatism is also essential for the integration of developing countries into the world economy. The choice facing these countries should not be viewed as an ideological one between import substitution and export-oriented growth, neither of which alone has generated sustainable development. Basing development on exports that prove to be ecologically damaging not only ignores sustainability, it fails to ask the more fundamental question of whom development should benefit. But building an export base on top of a strong internal market does make sense. In this scheme, foreign exchange receipts would shift from primary commodities to processed commodities, manufactures, and environmentally sensitive tourism. China, India, South Korea, and Taiwan all based their early industrial development on slowly raising the real incomes of their domestic populations. Each opened up to varying degrees to the world market and to foreign capital only after substantial domestic markets had been developed and nurtured. . . .

Democratic participation in the formulation and implementation of development plans forms the central factor in determining their medium- and long-term viability. This, however, is a controversial premise. Indeed, such a pronounced emphasis on democracy flies in the face of political scientist Samuel Huntington's claim in the 1960s that order must precede democracy in the early stages of development. Many still believe authoritarian governments in Eastern Europe, South Korea, and Taiwan served as the catalysts for industrialization that in turn created the conditions for advancing democracy.

Experiences of the last two decades suggest otherwise. Africa, home to dozens of one-party authoritarian states, remains a development disaster. Argentina, Brazil, the Philippines, and other Asian and Latin American countries ruled by authoritarian governments have suffered similar fates. As political scientist Atul Kohli has documented, the economies of the relatively democratic regimes in Costa Rica, India, Malaysia, Sri Lanka, and Venezuela have "grown at moderate but steady rates" since the 1960s and income inequalities have "either remained stable or even narrowed."

Moreover, in South Korea and Taiwan, authoritarian characteristics of the government were not responsible for industrialization and growth. Far-reaching land reforms and each state's ability to rise above factions in civil society deserve credit for sparking growth. The only "positive" growth impact of repression by these governments was to hold down wage levels, thereby making exports more competitive. Yet heavy dependence on exports no longer serves as an option in today's increasingly protectionist global markets. The percentage of imports into the major developed countries that were affected by nontariff barriers to trade rose more than 20 per cent during the 1980s, a trend that is likely to continue. In this hostile global economic climate, respect for workers' rights can lead to the creation of local markets by increasing domestic buying power. Democratic development therefore implies shifting emphasis from foreign to domestic (or, for small countries, to regional) markets. This shift meets more needs of local people and takes into account the difficult world market of the 1980s and 1990s.

The portrait painted at the outset—of a global development crisis masked by triumphant Western development orthodoxy—was a decidedly gloomy one. Why then should citizens' movements pushing for more equitable, sustainable, and participatory development stand a chance in the 1990s? Much of the answer lies in the extraordinary possibilities of the current historical moment.

Development After the Cold War

For four decades, the Cold War has steered almost all development discussions toward ideological arguments over capitalism versus communism, market versus planning. It has also diverted public attention away from nonideological global concerns (such as environment, health, and economic decay) and toward the Soviet Union as the source of problems. Hence, the dramatic winding down of the Cold War opens great opportunities for development.

At the very minimum, real debate should now become possible, getting beyond sharply drawn ideological categories in order to discuss development in more pragmatic terms. What are the proper roles of government and market? If one values both effectiveness and equity, what kind of checks should be placed on the market? What do the experiences of Japan, South Korea, and Taiwan offer to this discussion?

The 1990s provide other opportunities to cut across Cold War polarities. Paranoid Cold War governments often saw communists lurking behind popular organizations fighting for a better society. But citizens' movements played a central role in the recent transformation of Eastern Europe. A greater openness should emerge from this phenomenon. Not only should governments and development experts treat such nongovernmental organizations with the respect they deserve, but they should realize that these groups have vital roles to play beyond the reach of governments and individuals.

Beyond the Cold War, global economic shifts also offer new possibilities for the sustainable development agenda. While much attention has been focused on the relative decline of the United States, this shift offers potentially positive openings. A decade of unprecedented U.S. military spending, for example, has bequeathed fiscal deficits that preclude significant increases in foreign aid. This situation adds impetus to proposals that the United States give less but better aid. That can be accomplished by slashing military aid that in areas like Latin America has often been used to suppress citizens' movements, and by redirecting development assistance away from unaccountable governments and toward citizens' organizations.

Likewise, persistent trade deficits are pushing the U.S. government to restrict imports that enter the domestic market with the assistance of unfair trade practices. The United States could assist developing-country movements for equity and workers' rights by implementing existing legislation that classifies systematic repression of worker rights as an unfair trading practice. Finally, the failure of the Baker and Brady plans to halt the pile up of debt should reopen the door for substantial debt plans that shift payments toward sustainable development initiatives.

Japan's displacement of the United States as the world's most dynamic large economy and biggest aid-giver provides perhaps more intriguing questions about development efforts in the next decade. Japan stands at a juncture fraught with both danger and opportunity. It can take the easy road and mimic what the United States did: ally with local elites and subordinate development policy to security policy. Or Japan can practice enlightened leadership by divorcing the two policies and opening up the possibility for a qualitative change in North-South ties. Will Japan seize the opportunities? During the Marshall plan years, the United States bestowed substantial decision-making power on the recipient governments. Can Japan, using that experience as a starting point, broaden the decision-making group to include nongovernmental organizations? In fact, voices within Japan are calling for the Japanese government to redirect its aid flows to include citizens' organizations. As a January 1990 editorial in the *Asahi Evening News* commented:

> It is a task for Japan in the 1990's to provide aid for welfare and growth purposes according to the needs of the receiving countries as well as increase the total amount. It is also necessary to invite the participation of the people in the receiving countries so that its benefits will not be taken up exclusively by a particular group of leaders and bureaucrats.

The question also remains whether Japan will follow the U.S. example of using the World Bank and IMF as extensions of its aid, commercial, and trade policies, further eroding the credibility of these institutions in the Third World. Perhaps Japan's ascension will encourage these institutions to delve more objectively into the development lessons of Japan, South Korea, and Taiwan, thus adding realism to their prescriptions.

Finally, both Japan and the United States will have to face the need to respect the emerging citizens' movements as the groups reach out internationally to work with one another. The realization that governments suffer from severe limits in the development field should not be seen as negative. Rather, this understanding opens a variety of possibilities for new forms of government-citizen initiatives. In February 1990, for instance, African nongovernmental organizations, governments, and the U.N. Economic Commission for Africa jointly planned and participated in a conference that adopted a strong declaration affirming popular participation in development. NGOs may also enjoy an enhanced role at the 1992 U.N. Conference on Environment and Development in Brazil as the realization spreads that governments alone can do little to stop forest destruction and other activities that contribute to the emission of greenhouse gases.

In the face of such opportunities, the seeming death of the development debate in the industrial world represents an enormous travesty. Rekindling that debate, however, requires listening to new approaches from the rest of the world. Excessive confidence in free-market approaches melts when one examines the mounting crises in the supposed success stories of South Korea and Taiwan. Exciting alternatives to the dominant development paradigms are emerging in the hundreds of thousands of citizens' groups that flourish amid adversity and repression in Africa, Asia, and Latin America. These voices must be heard in the development establishments of Washington, Tokyo, and Bonn.

NOTES

1. See Robin Broad and John Cavanagh, "No More NICs," *Foreign Policy* 72 (Fall 1988): 81–104.
2. For another view regarding Africa, see Stephen Brent, "Aiding Africa," *Foreign Policy* 80 (Fall 1990): 121–140.

Reinvigorating the Global Economy

Sherle R. Schwenninger

The current global macroeconomic outlook poses an unprecedented challenge for the system of G–3 management that we rely on to manage the world economy. Each of the three major economic powers is undergoing structural changes that limit its ability to pursue expansionary policies. Yet a particularly untimely world recession threatens because of inadequate global demand and potential liquidity squeezes. The Bush administration has not had a strategy for dealing with this situation except to call repeatedly for Germany and Japan to cut their interest rates. Washington's proposals have not gotten far with Tokyo and Frankfurt because they believe that looser monetary policies would only make their own national economic situations more unmanageable. Moreover, they are not in the mood to be pushed around by Washington, for both of them see Washington's economic mismanagement in the 1980s as in part responsible for the current crisis.

Japan, for instance, has resisted Washington's call for concerted interest rate reductions, because it remembers all too well what happened when the last big exercise of this kind was undertaken in the 1980s. Today, it is struggling with problems that it believes are not entirely of its own making, since asset inflation was a product of previous Japanese efforts to bolster, at Washington's request, domestic demand and help stabilize the dollar. Normally responsive to American pressures during an election year, Tokyo has grown weary of Washington's incessant demands and its lack of appreciation for past services rendered. Japan was reportedly ready to embark on a new global partnership with the United States at the time of President Bush's visit to Tokyo this past January, but the president ignored Japan's proposals and instead made auto import quotas the focus of his visit, much to the embarrassment of Prime Minister Kiichi Miyazawa. Now worried by Washington's growing "isolationism" and its emphasis on a North American free-trade agreement, Tokyo has begun to tend more actively to business in its own region—even to the point of trying to ensure that Asia's dwindling capital surpluses are retained within the region to offset potential shortages.

Germany, too, has given the administration's proposals the cold shoulder. The view in Bonn is that Washington should clean up its own economic house before it tells others what to do. Hard-pressed by the costs of unification, Bonn is hardly receptive to yet more American demands, especially those that are contrary to its own perceived national interests. Moreover, German officials believe they already have done their fair share. After all, Germany contributed $12 billion to Desert Storm and has shouldered most of the financial burdens of assistance to Eastern Europe and the former Soviet Union while Washington has barely lifted a finger. Indeed, Bonn has begun to turn the burden-sharing argument around on Washington, demanding with ever more urgency that the United States do more to aid the transformation process in the former Soviet empire.

The administration has no choice but to accept and work within (or around) Germany's and Japan's structural constraints. Whining to Bonn and Tokyo about interest rates, as it has begun to do, or trying to use its waning leverage in military security matters, as it tried to do following the Gulf War, will not get Washington very far and may only make things worse. But accepting Bonn's and Tokyo's limits does not justify administration inaction, especially given the stakes involved. For there are a number of ways to reconcile German and Japanese interests with our own and still address the underlying problems in the world's macroeconomic situation. But to do so, the administration will need to show more sympathy than it has thus far shown not only for supporting growth and development outside the industrial world, but also for using the facilities of the international financial institutions in creative ways that expand global demand and ease world liquidity shortages.

In light of the constraints on expansionary policies, particularly monetary stimulus, in each of the three major economies, what is called for is a world public sector–supported economic recovery.[1] In other words, the United States, with the support of Europe and Japan, should intervene to expand demand at the global level rather than at the national level by using the IMF, the World Bank, and the regional development banks such as the European Bank for Reconstruction and Development (EBRD). Such global measures would not, of course, substitute entirely for national policies—or for the deeper structural changes necessary for more balanced economic growth. But Germany, Japan, and the United States would all have more room to pursue expansionary policies if these were supplemented by world public sector initiatives aimed at relieving liquidity shortages and supporting growth and development in Eastern Europe and the developing countries.

Slow growth and austerity in the developing world and the former Soviet empire constitute one of the principal problems in the world macroeconomic outlook as well as one of the principal shortcomings in the Plaza Accord strategy. Restarting growth there would add buoyancy to a sluggish world economy and create additional demand for U.S. and Western exports. Yet current assistance levels to these regions are inadequate either to aid the transition to democracy or to provide a real boost to the world economy. A number of world public sector efforts to increase global demand by stimulating growth in the developing world can be devised with little cost to the Western taxpayer and with little long-term inflationary risk. The administration should start by focusing on those efforts that could be readily implemented within the next six to nine months, a critical period for both the world economy and the post–Cold War transition in Eastern Europe and the developing world.

To begin with, the United States should work within the IMF to support a onetime issue of special drawings rights (SDR) by the IMF, as requested by Japan and the developing countries. Such an issue would help alleviate world credit strain caused by the temporary collapse of Japan and Germany as capital-exporting nations and would help ease the anticipated imbalance between world investment needs and savings. If the industrialized nations gave up their SDRs to the developing countries and the former republics of the Soviet Union, these countries would be able to borrow more money from the IMF. This would provide a critical supplement to current inadequately funded assistance programs.

Japan has repeatedly proposed a onetime SDR issue, most recently at the 1991 annual IMF–World Bank meeting. The IMF is reportedly studying the idea, at Japan's request, for presentation at the next IMF–World Bank meeting this fall. The Bush administration, however, has opposed the idea on the official grounds that it would be inflationary. But it would be no more inflationary than the Fed printing money. Indeed, an SDR issue could be a less inflationary way to meet the U.S. goal of lower world interest rates than would a further easing of monetary policy in individual national economies. By spurring productive activity that could generate an increase in savings over the medium term, such an additional injection of liquidity into the world economy would ease the world's capital shortage without sparking inflation in the near term. For example, development economist Lance Taylor of MIT has estimated that in the current situation every dollar of assistance to the developing countries increases output two or three times, because the ability to use existing economic capacity has in many countries been sharply reduced by the scarcity of imports.[2] In other words, the new capital flows associated with an SDR issue would unclog existing bottlenecks in many developing countries (although probably not in the former Soviet Union), allowing capital in place to operate more efficiently.

The real reason for the administration's objection, it seems, is that the Treasury Department and the large U.S. commercial banks profit handsomely from the current scarcity of SDRs. This is because the current dollar-based international payments system forces the central banks of developing countries to borrow (or exchange) large sums from U.S. financial institutions in order to maintain a supply of Treasury bonds and other U.S.-denominated currency to meet loan payments as well as to finance trade.[3] But it would be tragic if the Bush administration let such narrow special interests stand in the way of a measure that would restart growth in areas of geoeconomic interest to the United States.

To make a sizable SDR issue more attractive to the United States, a portion of the credit provided by the issue could be set aside for purchases of capital goods from the industrialized donor countries. The attraction of this scheme is that it would create external demand for the capital-goods industries of the West, which would allow the United States and other producers to expand exports while building the productive capacity of the emerging market-based economies. In other words, it would provide the same combination of self-interest and altruism as the Marshall Plan did.

An SDR issue would be the most direct and effective way to address today's global macroeconomic problems: it would ease the liquidity squeeze, increase global aggregate demand, expand America's export markets, alleviate austerity in struggling democracies, and cost the Western taxpayer little. For these reasons, it should form the heart of any world public sector–supported economic recovery. But an SDR issue alone is not likely to be of sufficient magnitude to address the current recessionary pressures in the world economy. It will therefore need to be supplemented by several other world public sector measures designed to expand global demand and ease liquidity problems.

One such measure would be for the World Bank to expand and front-load its lending over the next year. Recent capital increases have left the World Bank significant "headroom" to expand lending at this time. The Bank's statutory lending limit is $152.3 billion, nearly $62 billion more than its outstanding loans of $90.6 billion. The Bank could readily accelerate and expand loans for public infrastructure development and social services in Eastern Europe as well as in Latin America and Africa. For there are a number of urgent needs in these regions in the areas of road construction, rail modernization, environmental and nuclear power cleanup, and telecommunications. Many of the projects now on the drawing boards could be accelerated and expanded without sacrificing environmental or loan quality. So could programs to meet education, health, and nutritional needs, as well as other social Keynesian measures. At the same time, in order that this expansion of lending does not disrupt the Bank's regular lending programs, the United States, as the Bank's largest shareholder, could ask for an immediate increase in the Bank's statutory lending limit with an understanding that capital increases could be paid over a three-year period. Such an increase would in effect increase the Bank's gearing ratio without compromising the

Bank's credit rating. It would thus give Bank lending an additional stimulative effect.

A second measure deserving U.S. support would be an initiative to expand current debt relief efforts to include multilateral debt forgiveness. As it is, the Brady Plan and other debt relief programs apply only to commercial debt or official government debt, not to loans from the IMF and other multilateral agencies. . . . This has created a rather perverse situation in which most African and Caribbean and some Latin American countries are sending more money back to the IMF and World Bank than they are receiving in new IMF and World Bank loans and credits. As an interim measure to help correct this situation, the United States could support the suspension of interest payments on developing country loans from the World Bank and the IMF while a plan is worked out for debt forgiveness for the most hard-pressed debtor countries. A suspension of interest payments would work as an injection of capital, allowing developing countries to increase investment and consumption.

A third set of measures would involve addressing the special conditions in Eastern Europe and the former Soviet Union, where growth has declined because of the collapse of intraregional trade and the rush toward open economies. To help ease these problems, the United States should bring together the officials of the IMF and the EBRD to establish a hard-currency (payments) clearing union for Eastern Europe and the republics of the former Soviet Union. The establishment of such a payments union, backed by $10–15 billion in hard currencies, would help to reverse the spiral downward of East–East trade that resulted from the disintegration of the ruble-based COMECON trading bloc in 1989. The collapse of East–East trade has greatly aggravated the already immense difficulties of the transition to a market economy in all Central and East European countries. In fact, restarting Eastern trade is essential to any program for economic recovery and development. An East European clearinghouse could be modeled on the successful experience of the European Payments Union, which aided West European recovery following World War II.

At the same time, the United States should use its weight within the IMF and the World Bank to encourage a slower transition to an open market economy in Eastern Europe and the former Soviet Union. When state-dominated economies are plunged into a Western market and opened up to Western competition, the value of many factories and other business enterprises vanishes, wiping out capital. But with a more gradual transition, including a period of protection for domestic industries, some of the enterprises in the nonmilitary sector that are now running losses could continue to function by transforming themselves into efficient operations. Both of these measures—an IMF-supported dollar-based East European Payments Union and a policy favoring a slower transition to an open market economy—would be in U.S. geoeconomic interests, since they would help ease pressure on world capital markets and increase global demand.

Finally, in order to counteract the inflationary expectations these world public sector initiatives would create, the United States should also pursue a number of proposals to redress the longer-term imbalance between world savings and world capital needs. In this regard, the administration should more actively support the IMF's effort to shift wasteful public spending—in particular, military spending—to more productive uses. The best way to do so would be for Washington to move more quickly to cut its own military budget in line with new security realities. Beyond this, it is time for the United States to take the lead in establishing a modern system of global taxation to support world public sector needs. Given the backlog of unmet needs ranging from the global environment to U.N. peacekeeping, we can no longer afford to rely on "involuntary" national contributions, which depend on the courage of national politicians. Calls for the wealthy countries to increase international development and environmental assistance have largely gone unheeded over the years, except by the most internationalist-minded middle-power nations, such as Canada and Sweden. If international agencies are to have the resources they need to address critical transnational problems, then we will need to move to a system of value-added taxes that would be collected automatically when goods and services cross national borders. Under such a system, those who benefit most from world trade—for example, rich consumers and transnational corporations—would pay the greater share. A one percent levy on all traded goods and services would yield approximately $50 billion for world public sector uses. This sum could be increased by placing a higher levy on certain kinds of trade—such as arms transfers—that the world community wishes to discourage.

Together, these and other world public sector measures would help the United States and the other G–7 nations cope with an unfavorable world macroeconomic environment that now threatens world recession and increased global conflict. The underlying rationale of such a world public sector program is that in today's climate, a globally applied macroeconomic stimulus would be less inflationary and thus less disruptive to sustained economic growth in the long run than more stimulative domestic policies. It would also be more effective in helping correct current account imbalances. Such a program would not only create new markets for U.S. goods, thereby helping to sustain an export-led recovery, but relieve pressure on the U.S. market for other countries' goods.

As importantly, such a program would yield an important security dividend. Directing more public capital into the depressed areas of the world economy that are undergoing painful structural adjustment transitions would help ease the potential for political turmoil in those regions without undermining the discipline required for adjustment efforts to succeed. By restoring economic growth in those areas, it could also help improve profits and thus ease capital shortages in the medium term. Finally, a world public sector program would point the way to the longer term institutional reform that is now needed to maintain a growing and healthy world economy. . . .

NOTES

1. This section of the article is based on a paper prepared for the Cuomo Commission on Trade and Competitiveness.
2. Cited by Peter Passell, "Capital Squeeze: Guess Who Pays," *New York Times*, May 2, 1990.
3. Keith Bradsher, "Discord Is Said to Stall Plan to Raise I.M.F. Loan Aid to Ex-Soviets," *New York Times*, April 20, 1992.

Chapter *10*

Environmental Issues

Historically, international issues tended to be regional in impact and could be analyzed from a power perspective. In fact, for many analysts the term *international relations* by definition implied a struggle for power. The last few decades have seen the emergence of a set of issues, global in scope, that require the development of new perspectives. These complex problems, generally referred to as global issues, illustrate interdependence among the world's states and defy solutions based on power politics. Some of the more pressing issues concern the global environment, including pollution, global warming, ozone depletion, food production, management of the commons, and resource depletion and species loss.

The deterioration of the global environment ensues partially from pollution. International concerns focus on pollutants that travel across borders either through the contamination of rivers and oceans or through the air. Interest in water contamination has centered on oil transport, as oil spills and chronic oil pollution in the oceans have received considerable international attention. In the atmosphere, acid rain, global warming, and depletion of the ozone have been the subject of a number of international conferences and conventions. Acid rain results when sulphur dioxide and nitrogen oxide are released by industry, and it is responsible for widespread damage to forests and lakes in the Northern Hemisphere. Global warming, or the greenhouse effect, refers to the buildup of carbon dioxide (CO_2) in the atmosphere. CO_2 is released by burning fossil fuels and through deforestation. There is considerable disagreement about the extent of the buildup and its consequences. Many environmental scientists argue that the gas will produce a greenhouse effect, trapping sunlight on the earth's surface and increasing global temperatures. This global warming will result in changed weather patterns and a rise in the level of the oceans as the polar icecaps melt. Others argue that an increasing cloud cover may actually lower global temperatures.

An equally important problem is ozone depletion. High in the atmosphere, a layer of ozone protects life on Earth from deadly exposure to solar radiation. The release of chlorine atoms into the atmosphere breaks up the ozone molecule. The use of chlorofluorocarbons (CFCs) and the release of methane through rice cultivation on wetlands and the raising of livestock are major sources of chlorine atoms. It is generally accepted that a small decrease in the ozone layer will have serious consequences for health worldwide. Already, significant holes in the ozone have been observed over the polar regions, and recently a significant reduction in the winter ozone layer over the United States has been documented.

Another set of environmental issues concerns resource depletion. Population pressures threaten the world's food supply, and international cooperation is essential in distributing food to areas where there are serious shortages. Nonrenewable resources such as petroleum, metals, and other minerals are being used in ever-increasing amounts. Although the extent of undiscovered reserves is unknown, mineral deposits are nevertheless finite and extraction is expected to become more rather than less expensive. Access to resources concentrated in particular countries and regions raises concerns about national security, in addition to environmental issues, and thus complicates international cooperation. Additionally decisions must be made about the exploitation of the commons, that is, areas that are not included within national borders. How are the minerals and other resources that may exist in deep seabeds, in Antarctica, and in outer space to be distributed among the world's countries?

Environmental Issues

James Harf and Thomas Trout have identified five characteristics that define global issues: (1) transcendence of national boundaries, (2) incapacity for autonomous action, (3) a present imperative, (4) requirement for policy action, and (5) persistence. All of these apply particularly well to environmental issues. First, environmental problems transcend national and regional boundaries. Pollution affects an area far beyond its original source. Population pressures in the tropics can lead to deforestation, which affects the climate worldwide. The introduction into the atmosphere of CFCs in the United States can affect the ozone layer over Antarctica. Few issues illustrate the increasing interdependence of states more clearly than those involving the environment.

Second, cooperation is required if we are to find a solution to today's problems. No state acting alone can solve them. We cannot erect a barrier to prevent airborne pollutants from entering our atmosphere. Similarly no action on the part of any country will stop ocean pollution, as long as others continue to empty pollutants into their rivers and streams. Even where specific policies are pursued within states, the effects can be mitigated by activity elsewhere. The U.S. ban on the production and use of CFCs will not prevent ozone depletion if other states continue to manufacture and use these chemicals. Not only do environmental issues require cooperation among states, but they also call for coordination among other international actors, including nongovernmental organizations.

Third, environmental issues are a present imperative; that is, they impel us to seek a resolution. Although governments disagree on such factors as which issues should be addressed first, what solutions should be devised, and who should bear the costs, they are nevertheless in agreement that some concerted action must be taken. The present imperative does not prevent the governments of less developed countries from arguing that the industrialized states have contributed disproportionately to environmental problems in the course of their development. Thus they argue that the brunt of the costs for preserving the environment should be borne by these wealthier states and that their own opportunities for development must not be compromised.

Fourth, these issues require policy action for their solution, and to be successful compliance must be widespread. Although such policies may rely on voluntary compliance rather than coercion and on individual or organizational rather than government action, it is expected that the most successful policies will involve formal international agreements and some measure of coercion in the form of sanctions.

Finally global issues and particularly environmental issues are characterized by persistence. Dennis Pirages refers to the necessity for an "anticipatory perspective," that is, planning for future contingencies. If each country continues to pursue its own short-term interests, environmental problems will be exacerbated and, in the view of many, will become intractable. Similarly, crisis management will not solve such problems as resource depletion and pollution but in the long run will result in a decline in the quality of life. Thus it becomes essential to plan for future generations even if it means denying present interests. The necessity for planning is complicated by the pace of change. Not only do environmental conditions themselves change fairly rapidly when viewed in a historical perspective, but so does environmental science. Methods of forecasting, data collection, and analysis are developing rapidly. Disagreements over projections are common and make long-range planning difficult. For these reasons, many argue that scientists will play increasingly prominent roles in provoking international action and in negotiating agreements. For example, the thinning of the ozone layer would never have come to the attention of policymakers without scientific knowledge and the concerted actions of scientists to provoke action. Increasing collaboration between scientists and government officials is likely in addressing environmental issues in the twenty-first century.

Environmental issues can be approached in a number of ways. One is through the establishment of international regimes. A second option is to expand the focus from environmental issues in isolation to one that includes other concerns, such as sustainable development. A third possibility is that environmental issues will increasingly be approached from the perspective of power politics. Conflict over scarce resources is almost certain to be an important item on the international agenda in the future. These approaches are only a few of many possibilities; and because they are not mutually exclusive, in the next century we can expect to see them in various combinations.

International Regimes

Ultimately environmental challenges are beyond manipulation by individual nation-states and are a fertile area for the development of international regimes, which are structured but often informal patterns of cooperation among states on a particular issue. Norms, rules, principles, institutions, and procedures pertaining to a common issue make up international regimes; they do not have to be formal agreements or treaties. Regimes facilitate shared interests, impose constraints on state behavior, and help states develop habits of cooperation.

Examples of formal international regimes that have developed around environmental issues include the following:

> Convention on International Trade in Endangered Species of Wild Fauna and Flora, 1973
>
> Convention for the Protection of the Ozone Layer, 1985, and the 1987 protocol
>
> Antarctic Treaty, 1959; Convention on the Conservation of Antarctic Marine Living Resources, 1980; and Antarctic Minerals Convention, 1988
>
> Convention for the Protection of the Mediterranean Sea Against Pollution, 1976, and related protocols
>
> Convention on Early Notification of a Nuclear Accident, 1986; and Convention on Assistance in the Case of a Nuclear Accident or Radiological Emergency, 1986

One advantage of regimes is the facilitation of planning based on expectations concerning state behavior. Without the ability to plan for the environment, states will be forced into crisis management, or "fire fighting." Regimes also help in dealing with the complex interlocking relationships among population, international economy, technological development, and environmental quality.

Thus far, those regimes that exist tend to focus on relatively narrow issues. The U.N. Conference on Environment and Development (popularly known as the Rio Summit), held in Rio de Janeiro in June 1992, illustrates some of the difficulties surrounding the development of broader regimes. One hundred and seventy-eight nations came together to reach agreements on the Earth Summit treaty, three proposals for environmental protection, and Agenda 21. The Earth Summit Treaty, which comprises 27 principles for the management of planetary resources, was approved by the delegates. Additional agreements were reached on Agenda 21, which contains 800 measures for action from which each country can choose. Both of these texts are so broad that agreements could be reached without sacrificing state sovereignty. Disagreements centered around the more specific proposals to protect forests and biodiversity. A third agreement on the world's climate contains no timetable and was thus agreed to only in principle. The United States declined to sign the biodiversity agreement, arguing that it threatened biotech industries. The agreement on forest management was opposed by Brazil, Indonesia, and Malaysia, which do not wish to give up the right to exploit their forests.

Sustainable Development

Sustainable development is defined as economic and technological development that meets present human needs without compromising the ability of future generations to meet future human needs. It does not require a particular economic strategy or political ideology, and can be tailored to meet different cultural expectations. Nevertheless, it requires renewable resources to be used with attention to their place in the ecosystem as well as the ability to replenish them, nonrenewable resources to be conserved so that supplies are not exhausted before alternatives are developed, and free goods like air and water to be preserved in a healthy state.

Presently China, India, Bangladesh, and Indonesia contain nearly half the world's population. If these countries were to achieve the same standard of living (and level of consumption) now found in developed countries, the strain on the world's environment would be enormous. For less developed countries to increase their energy consumption to levels now found in the industrialized states, we would need five times the energy now produced. The Earth cannot support all its people in the standard of living presently enjoyed by those in developed countries without serious changes in lifestyle.

The idea of sustainable development, however, does not rest simply on conservation. It rejects the notion that to save the environment we need to preserve the status quo or prevent additional growth. It recognizes the rights of people in the less developed countries to economic development and an improved standard of living. It ties together political, economic, and social issues by emphasizing the right of citizens to participate in political decisions, an economic system that will generate sustained surpluses and technology, an international system that fosters sustainable patterns of trade and finance, a system of production that respects the environment, and a regime that is flexible and self-correcting. Sustainable development will not be achieved by law alone but through a network of community support and changes in the attitudes and procedures of public and private sector institutions.

Achieving sustainable growth will not be easy but will require fundamental changes in social, political, and economic institutions. Wealth will have to be distributed more equitably among and within nations. The amount of energy and natural resources expended in products will have to be reduced. Environmental calculations will have to be fully integrated into policy at all levels of government rather than considered as a separate issue. New technologies using resources more efficiently and forecasting environmental consequences will have to be developed, and population growth must be slowed.

Presently there is relatively little progress in these areas, and in some cases there is deterioration. Population pressures are usually studied as a significant problem only in the less developed countries, but in fact people in the countries of the North consume much greater portions of the world's resources than their numbers would suggest. Some of these countries have programs that encourage population growth. Meanwhile, population growth rates remain high in the South, threatening fragile environments.

Many governments in both the North and the South pursue policies that are not eco-friendly. Agricultural subsidies encourage overproduction and the degradation of the land as well as the overuse of energy. Other policies encourage deforestation or discourage the development of alternative energy sources.

Power Politics

The global environment has not been absent from traditional international relations concerns. A state's access to resources is considered in estimations of power and in questions of national security. Competition over resources is recognized as an important source of international conflict, especially when environmental concerns are tied to security issues. Population pressures, resource depletion, and the resulting persistent poverty lead to domestic instability, spilling over into regional conflict. Drought and famine lead to refugee flows across international borders.

Resource scarcity is expected to become an increasingly important issue in the next century. The 1992 gulf war is an example of the lengths to which countries will go to protect supplies of an important resource like oil. Other resources may be equally conflictual. In deserts, water is a scarce and valuable commodity. Jordan, Israel, Egypt, Morocco, Algeria, and Saudi Arabia are all countries that face declining water supplies. Rivers and aquifers cross international borders, and disputes are likely among countries sharing this valuable resource. One state's actions in damming and irrigation can have profound effects on its neighbors. Tension has already developed over Turkish plans to dam the Euphrates, diverting much of its flow away from Syria and Iraq. Turkey has accused Syria of a plot to blow up the Ataturk Dam. In 1989, Syrian MIGs shot down a Turkish survey plane within Turkey's borders. Earlier, in 1975, Syria and Iraq nearly went to war over Syria's reduction of the Euphrates at the Ath-Thawrah Dam. Although the United Nations has made an effort to anticipate water crises, it lacks the power to enforce settlements among countries.

Resource conflicts will continue to inspire power politics in the future. Resource management is viewed as essential to regional and international security and is likely to be linked to other political disputes. For example, in the Middle East, the Palestinian question is also linked to the availability of water, particularly on the West Bank. Conflict in one area is likely to spill over into another, and resolutions of political problems without consideration of resources are unlikely.

In addition to these kinds of concerns, however, is a recognition that environmental issues also challenge the system in ways requiring coordinated action not related solely to interstate rivalry and conflict. The degradation of the environment cannot be blamed on any one country and cannot be solved by applying military force. Ultimately, it threatens all human life regardless of nationality.

The Readings

The readings in this chapter illustrate the range of environmental issues confronting the international community as well as the complexities involved in addressing them. Lester Brown, "Assessing the Planet's Condition," provides an overview of the environmental problems facing the planet. Olav Stokke, "The Northern

Environment: Is Cooperation Coming?," writes about a little discussed problem and frames his discussion around the concept of regimes. Both of these articles are written from the perspective of the developed nations of the Northern Hemisphere. "Environment, Oceans, and Energy," by the Commission on the South, a group of leaders from twenty-seven developing countries, takes a look at some of the same issues from a southern perspective and illustrates attempts at cooperation now under way in the commons area.

Bibliography

BENEDICK, RICHARD. *Ozone Diplomacy*. Cambridge, MA: Harvard University Press, 1991.

BROWN, LESTER. *The State of the World 1990*. New York: Norton, 1990.

HARDIN, GARRETT. "The Tragedy of the Commons." *Science* 162 (1968).

HARF, JAMES E., and THOMAS B. TROUT. *The Politics of Global Resources: Energy, Environment, Population, and Food* Durham, NC: Duke University Press, 1986.

HUGHES, BARRY. *World Futures*. Baltimore: Johns Hopkins University Press, 1985.

MATHEWS, JESSICA. "Redefining Security." *Foreign Affairs,* Spring 1989.

MEAD, MARGARET. "The Underdeveloped and the Overdeveloped." *Foreign Affairs*, Fall 1962.

MEADOWS, DONELLA, DENNIS MEADOWS, JORGEN TANDERS, and WILLIAM BEHRENS. *The Limits to Growth*. New York: Signet, 1972.

PIRAGES, DENNIS. *Global Technopolitics: The International Politics of Technology and Resources*. Pacific Grove, CA: Brooks/Cole, 1989.

STARR, JOYCE. "Water Wars." *Foreign Policy* 82 (Spring, 1991).

WIRTH, DAVID. "Climate Chaos." *Foreign Policy* 74 (Spring 1989).

YOUNG, ORAN. "The Politics of International Regime Formation." *International Organization* 43 (Summer 1989).

Assessing the Planet's Condition

Lester R. Brown

Despite the worldwide growth in the environmental movement since the watershed of Earth Day 1970, the degradation of the Earth has accelerated. No comparable two-decade period in human history has witnessed such a wholesale destruction of the natural systems and resources on which civilization depends.

Since 1970, the Earth's human inhabitants have increased by 1.6 billion. While gaining new residents, the planet has lost trees and topsoil. Over the last 20 years, it has lost well over 500 million acres of tree cover, an area roughly the size of the United States east of the Mississippi, and an estimated 480 billion tons of topsoil, more than the amount on all U.S. cropland.

Atmospheric carbon-dioxide levels have risen 9 percent in the last two decades, and levels of other greenhouse gases, including methane, nitrous oxides, and CFCs, have risen even more. With six of this century's warmest years occurring during the 1980s, the greenhouse effect appears to be more than a scientific hypothesis.

Scientists studying the stratospheric ozone layer tell us the Earth has lost 2 percent or more of this protective shield over the last 20 years. We're warned that a small hole now appears above the North Pole, joining the huge hole that opens up over Antarctica during the Southern Hemisphere spring.

Twenty years ago, it was understood that the acid rain caused by

EPA Journal 16 (July/August 1990).

fossil fuel burning in automobiles and power plants was capable of leaving lakes acidic and lifeless, but it was not until the early 1980s that scientists pegged acid rain with destroying forests. Now the connection is painfully obvious. More than half of West Germany's forests are showing signs of damage from a combination of air pollution and acid rain. In East Germany, 22 percent of all trees are reportedly dead.

Air pollution, too, is far worse today than it was 20 years ago. Despite improvements in selected cities in the industrial North, the overwhelming trend has been toward deteriorating air quality. In literally hundreds of cities, air pollution has reached health-threatening levels, with concentrations of pollutants well above the tolerance limits established by the World Health Organization.

The biological impoverishment of the Earth is continuing and quickening. Australia has lost 18 of its 200 mammal species since European settlement. Another 40 species are threatened. According to the Polish Academy of Sciences, the pollution of that country's air, water, and soil with toxic materials and the associated die-off of forests and other natural vegetation are expected to eliminate 20 percent of the country's flora and 15 percent of its fauna before the end of the century. Disturbing as these losses are, they are dwarfed by those from the burning of Brazil's rain forest. Worldwide, countless thousands of plant and animal species have disappeared since 1970.

The accumulation of toxic chemicals in soil and water has continued unabated over the last 20 years. In the United States, there are 1,163 toxic waste sites in urgent need of cleanup. Other parts of the world, such as Eastern Europe, areas of China, and Brazil's heavily industrialized south, face even more serious hazardous-waste issues.

The most profound and immediate consequence of global environmental degradation, one already affecting the welfare of hundreds of millions, is the emerging scarcity of food in developing countries. All the principal changes in the Earth's physical condition—eroding soils, shrinking forests, deteriorating rangelands, expanding deserts, acid rain, ozone depletion, the buildup of greenhouse gases, air pollution, and the loss of biological diversity—are having a negative effect on food production. Spreading hunger in both Africa and Latin America during the 1980s, a worldwide fall of 6 percent in per-capita grain production from the historic high in 1984, and the one-third rise in world wheat and rice prices over the last two years may be early signs of the trouble that lies ahead.

The Challenge Before Us

An environmentally sustainable global economy is one where trees cut and those planted are in balance, where soil erosion does not exceed new soil formation, where carbon emissions do not exceed carbon fixation, where human births and deaths are in balance, where the ozone layer is stable, and where the extinction of plant and animal species does not exceed the rate at which new species evolve.

We can achieve these goals by stabilizing population size, increasing energy efficiency, shifting to renewable energy sources, reusing and recycling materials, phasing out CFCs, and halting agricultural practices that erode soils and reduce the land's inherent productivity. Although these steps can be simply stated, achieving them will require an unprecedented political mobilization. They call not for fine-tuning, but for a fundamental restructuring of the global economic system.

Stabilizing Population Size

In a world where the growth in human numbers appears to be out of control, 14 countries, all in Europe, have stabilized their population size. In these countries, which contain just over 5 percent of the world's people, births and deaths are essentially in balance. Other countries, including Japan, France, and Finland, appear headed for zero population growth in the not-too-distant future. In contrast, the populations of India, Ethiopia, Nigeria, and Mexico are projected to double or triple before stabilizing late in the next century.

The record addition of 88 million people to world population in 1989 represents the difference between 143 million births and 55 million deaths. Assuming no change in death rates, stabilizing world population thus means reducing the number of births by a staggering 61 percent.

Avoiding a wholesale deterioration in living conditions in much of the world may depend on cutting world population growth sharply, perhaps in half by the year 2000. Difficult though this may appear, it is not impossible. Two countries have cut their population growth rates in half within less than a decade. Japan did so beween 1948 and 1955. China matched this performance between 1970 and 1976, during the years immediately before the one-child family was adopted as a social goal. Thailand came close to cutting its population growth in half between 1975 and 1983.

The difficulty of slowing world population growth cannot be overestimated. The only thing more difficult than quickly stabilizing population size will be living with the consequences of failing to do so.

Raising Energy Efficiency

Just as achieving a satisfactory balance between food and people depends on reducing family size, so stabilizing climate depends on reducing energy use. One of the legacies of abundant fossil fuels in the industrial countries and plentiful wood fuel supplies in developing countries is an extraordinarily inefficient set of energy technologies.

Two basic uses of energy, transportation and cooking, illustrate the potential for raising the energy efficiency of the world economy. The average automobile in the U.S. fleet gets 17 miles per gallon, three times as much fuel per mile traveled as the most efficient cars now on the market. Similar energy inefficiencies exist in Third World villages, where stoves commonly used for cooking use four times as much wood as the most efficient new designs.

Redesigning the system can sometimes offer greater savings than substituting more efficient technologies. A combination of public transport and bicycle-friendly transportation systems can dramatically reduce dependence on automobiles. In countries such as Bolivia, Guatemala, and Sierra Leone, exciting gains have been made by replacing wood stoves with solar-box cookers. Using sunlight to cook food directly is far more efficient than first converting it into wood and then cutting and transporting the wood.

Harnessing the Sun's Energy

Energy reaching the Earth from the Sun takes many different forms. Hydropower taps the energy in the hydrological cycle, which is driven by heat from the Sun evaporating water. Wind power taps the energy in the movement of air driven by the differential heating rates of the Earth's surface. Buildings designed by solar architects exploit the Sun's energy for heating during the winter. Photovoltaic cells convert sunlight into electricity. Solar thermal plants concentrate sunlight on vessels containing water or other liquids to power steam turbines and generate electricity. Through photosynthesis, plants store energy from the Sun in various forms, such as the wood of trees or the sugar in cane, that can be used to produce fuel alcohol.

Photovoltaic cells, by themselves, show the potential for a solar-based world economy. They were first used commercially on Earth-orbiting satellites. Indeed, a phone or facsimile from the United States to Europe is relayed by satellites running on electricity generated from photovoltaic cells.

As the cost of manufacturing photovoltaic cells dropped, they became competitive as the power source for pocket calculators. Third World governments are finding it cost-effective to use photovoltaics to provide power for villages not linked to electricity grids. Some 5,000 villages in India now get their electricity from free-standing photovoltaic installations. Indonesia is beginning to install photovoltaic arrays in 2,000 villages. With costs continuing to fall, this source of electricity is poised for a period of rapid growth during the 1990s.

Perhaps the most promising solar technology is the solar thermal power plant, which concentrates sunlight to produce the steam that spins electrical generators. Power plants using this technology and incorporating recent design advances convert a phenomenal 22 percent of sunlight into electricity. An 80-megawatt plant built by the Luz Corporation in the Mojave Desert is generating electricity at a cost of 8 cents per kilowatt hour, compared with roughly 12 cents for nuclear power and 6 cents for coal-fired power plants. Luz believes it can eventually supply 35 percent of U.S. electricity needs with this technology. Because of its high efficiency and low cost, electricity from solar thermal plants could eventually be used to break down water through electrolysis to produce hydrogen for use as an automotive fuel.

Solar thermal technology could convert semi-arid regions into major power-producing zones. One can easily picture a day when solar thermal plants along the North African coast will produce cheap electricity that is transmitted by cable under the Mediterranean Sea to Europe. Or, that region might supply the cheap electricity needed to produce hydrogen from water. The gas would be fed into the existing system of pipelines that now moves natural gas from Algeria to Italy.

If the international community could be persuaded to levy a carbon tax, one that reflected such indirect costs of fossil-fuel burning as air pollution, acid rain, and global warming, the spread of these technologies would be greatly enhanced. In much of the world, energy from solar thermal plants would be cheaper than energy from fossil fuels. Such a tax would move the world quickly toward an energy economy that could last forever.

Reusing and Recycling Materials

The enormous one-way flow of materials through throwaway economies accounts for a large share of the world's fossil-fuel use, air pollution, water pollution, and acid rain. The alternative to a disposable society is one that reuses and recycles. The first priority is to avoid the unnecessary use of materials in the first place. At the industrial level, this may mean the elimination of unnecessary layers of packaging; at the personal level, it may mean replacing throwaway paper or plastic grocery bags with canvas bags that can be used again and again. It means using hand towels instead of paper towels, handkerchiefs instead of tissues.

The next step in the hierarchy involves reuse. Environmentally, the ideal system would be one where beverage containers made of a durable material, such as glass, would be used interchangeably for all beverages. Standardized containers of one cup, one quart, and half gallon, for example, could be used for fruit juice, milk, carbonated beverages, and beer. Reusing such a bottle would involve simply cleaning it and replacing the old label with a new one. A computerized inventory of all containers in a system would permit their efficient movement from supermarket or other collection points to wherever they were needed. Canada has taken a step in this direction with standardized beer containers used by all breweries.

After the reuse option, the recycling of glass containers, aluminum cans, used automobiles, waste paper, and other materials comes next. The Netherlands and Japan, for example, already recycle half or more of all their waste paper. This contrasts with less than a third in the United States and United Kingdom. The story is the same for glass. The Netherlands recycles

53 percent, compared with only 12 percent in the United Kingdom and 10 percent in the United States.

In some instances, a new technology, such as the electric arc steel furnace, which depends exclusively on scrap metal, is boosting the recycling prospect. In the United States, the amount of steel produced by electric arc furnaces has increased from 8 percent in 1960 to an estimated 36 percent in 1990. All this comes from recycled scrap. With comprehensive recycling, mature industrial societies with stable populations can operate largely with material already in the economic system, using virgin ores only for supplemental purposes. It may be only a matter of time until national governments are mandating source separation and recycling as some local governments are already doing.

Reforesting the Earth

Each year during our lifetimes, the Earth's tree cover is smaller than the year before. Reversing this trend depends on dealing with the causes. In the Brazilian Amazon, rain forest is burned to make room for cattle or crops; in India, deforestation proceeds in ever-widening circles around cities as residents forage for firewood; in Southeast Asia, foreign timber firms are overcutting the forests; and in Europe, air pollution and acid rain are killing trees.

Brazil is taking its first steps to slow the loss of its forests by removing tax subsidies for forest clearing and by enforcing the requirement of a permit before burning. In India, more efficient fuelwood stoves and solar cookers can help stem deforestation. In Southeast Asia, stabilizing forest cover depends on a change in logging practices, one that moves away from forest mining toward sustained yields and ecological protection. In Europe, maintaining forests lies more in reducing air pollution and acid rain.

The other basic remedy is planting trees. Unfortunately, the history of recent decades is strewn with Third World reforestation failures. Only South Korea has succeeded in dramatically increasing its tree cover. A well-organized program launched in the early 1970s to reforest its once denuded hills and mountainsides enabled this thriving country to cover an area with trees that is roughly two-thirds that planted in rice.

China launched an ambitious tree-planting effort in the 1970s, one intended to increase the country's tree cover from 13 percent of its land area to 20 percent by the year 2000. A combination of low survival rates and the enormous surge in demand for housing during the decade-long boom following economic reform in the late 1970s prevented any increase in tree cover. In fact, demand for forest products continues to outstrip the sustainable yield of China's forests.

India, which together with fellow population giant China holds half of the developing world's people, launched a plan to plant five million hectares of trees per year beginning in 1984. Actual plantings, though, have not averaged more than 1.5 million hectares. On balance, India, like China, is still losing tree cover.

Some industrial countries are launching massive tree-planting programs, largely for environmental reasons. Australia announced a national environmental plan for the 1990s, which included the planting of a billion trees, roughly 70 trees for each Australian. If successful, this effort would restore two-thirds of the tree cover lost since European settlement.

In early 1990, the United States announced a plan to plant a billion trees a year during the decade. If successful, this effort would cover some 16 million acres with trees, an area more than one-fifth that planted in corn. This would dwarf any past tree-planting efforts, including the 2.2 million acres planted with trees under the Department of Agriculture's Conservation Reserve Program from 1986 through 1989.

Reversing the Earth's deforestation will not be easy, but of all the principal actions needed to create an environmentally sustainable global economy, it may be the easiest.

Soil Stabilization

As the 1990s begin, the world's farmers are losing an estimated 24 billion tons of topsoil from their cropland each year, an amount roughly equivalent to the topsoil covering Australia's wheatland. A world that each year loses this much topsoil and adds some 90 million people is in obvious trouble.

Restoring the Earth's tree cover will do double duty to preserve soils by reducing rainfall run-off and lessening wind erosion. As with reforestation, however, soil stabilization success stories are few. Among the major food-producing countries, only the United States, which was losing 1.6 billion tons of topsoil annually in excess of new soil formation, has a successful erosion-reduction program.

This program takes effect in two five-year phases. From 1986 through 1990, the goal was to convert the most highly erodible cropland into either grassland or woodland before it became wasteland. The 34 million acres converted through 1989, roughly one-tenth of all U.S. cropland, has reduced soil erosion by some 600 million tons, or roughly one-third of the total erosion.

The second phase, from 1990 through 1995, requires that for the remaining highly erodible land, farmers implement a plan approved by the Soil Conservation Service if they wish to maintain their eligibility for federal farm programs. This program is expected to eliminate another 300 to 500 million tons of annual soil loss, reducing U.S. soil losses by 0.9–1.1 billion tons, or nearly 70 percent. This success on U.S. cropland, which accounts for one-sixth of the world grain harvest, is a landmark achievement, a breakthrough for the entire world.

Unfortunately, none of the other three major food-producing countries, the Soviet Union, China, and India, which are losing as much or more soil than the United States, has an effective program to check their losses. For countries that cannot easily retire their most erodible cropland, terracing and contouring to check water erosion, planting hedges and tree belts to check wind erosion, and other stringent conservation measures are needed. Reducing soil erosion in the remainder of the world will not be easy, but with the U.S. model to draw upon, it will be easier.

The Decade of Reckoning

The gap between what needs to be done to reverse the environmental degradation of the planet and what is actually being done is growing wider year by year. There is little precedent for the scale of activity needed during this decade. Modest increases in energy-efficiency investments or family-planning budgets will not suffice. A wholesale reordering of priorities like that occurring after World War II is in order.

Time is of the essence. Species lost cannot be recreated. Soil washed away may take centuries, if not millennia, to replace, even under careful management. Once the Earth gets warmer, there will be no practical way of cooling it.

The issue is not whether we will survive as a species but under what conditions we will be living in the future. By the end of this decade, we either will have rallied and turned back the threatening trends, or environmental deterioration and economic decline will be feeding on each other.

The Northern Environment
Is Cooperation Coming?

Olav Schram Stokke

The industrialization of the North implies common opportunities as well as shared problems among the Arctic states. Today the idea of cooperation is much in vogue in political rhetoric, as shown by Gorbachev's Murmansk speech and the recent Finnish initiative to set up an Arctic conference on environmental issues of the North. The purpose of this article is to describe, explain, and project the pace and form of Arctic cooperation. The focus is on science, resource extraction, and environmental management, and toward the end I will comment on the interplay of the Nordic and Artic levels.

In general, the Arctic environment is vulnerable to industrialization for a cluster of reasons. A harsh climate means greater strain on the equipment employed. Accidents are more likely, and efforts to rectify damage will be hampered by long distances and poor infrastructure. Low temperatures inhibit the natural assimilation and breakdown of pollutants, and a disruption of one link in the simple ecosystems may have serious implications for the rest. Improved catching and localization technology have boosted efficiency in the extraction of living resources to the point of eradication, and some of the most important Arctic fish stocks are threatened by overexploitation. The degree of marine pollution in the Arctic is still very low and for the most part originates outside the region itself. The current spread of offshore petroleum activities may threaten this situation. Moreover, while most of it originates further south, the winter and spring concentration of air pollutants

From *The Annals of the American Academy of Political and Social Science* 512 (1990). Copyright © 1990. Reprinted by permission of Sage Publications, Inc.

such as sulphur dioxide in the Arctic is as high as in the northeastern United States. Some alarming reports indicate a thinning of the ozone layer above the Arctic. The so-called greenhouse effect will entail regional temperature rises above the global average, effecting a melting of the ice cap, with serious if yet unclear consequences for global climatic conditions.

The Whats and Whys of Arctic Cooperation

By "cooperation" I mean coordination of policy in order to realize mutual gains or avoid mutual losses. Cooperation may be ad hoc or tacit, but more often it requires a mechanism I term regimes and define as "practices consisting of recognized roles linked together by clusters of rules or conventions governing relations among the occupants of these roles," in "well-defined activities, resources, or geographical areas."[1] Regimes may facilitate cooperation by changing the structure of actor incentives in a number of ways. Clearly, there may be instrumental reasons for complying with a regime, such as fear of being punished by other states or in domestic elections. Usually, however, the compliance decision will be the result of standard operating procedures rather than a calculus of costs and benefits. In this article I shall focus on the information of cooperative regimes in the Arctic. While the concept is often given broader meaning, I will concentrate on regimes that are formalized by international agreements.

A regime involves a set of rights and rules and usually a more or less formalized procedure for handling social or collective choice. Two dimensions of this concept are especially salient for our discussion. One is the breadth of the regime, or the number of members. Judging from the many bilateral agreements concluded in the Arctic in the past decade, narrow regimes seem easier to establish than broad ones. In many situations, however, the actors will have no incentive to join a regime unless it involves a critical minimum of others. A second dimension is the depth of the regime, or the extent to which it limits the autonomy of states in a given issue area. At a moderate level, a regime may imply no more than an obligation to exchange information. It is less shallow if it involves mechanisms for joint planning or regulation, as do the fisheries and environmental commissions in the Barents Sea. At an exalted level, regimes may provide instruments for joint enforcement of regulations, but usually this is left to the participant states. Clearly, shallow regimes are generally easier to negotiate than deep ones because they infringe less on the sovereign rights of states. Yet they may for the same reason be less effective in realizing cooperative gains.

Explaining the Formation of Regimes

. . . The process of regime formation will vary fundamentally with the clarity of the national interests involved. Clarity is the degree of domestic consensus about what the national interest is on a particular issue. If the interests are very clear, the process will be structured and predictable, and the potential for cooperation can be analyzed by a straightforward assessment of cost efficiency, externalities, and competition. If, on the other hand, the state decision makers perceive themselves as weakly or ambiguously affected by the possible regime, the negotiations are likely to be more anarchical and more prone to the situational factors highlighted by Young.[2] States are the main actors in the model and they are clearly satisficers. Yet, by contending or confirming the established definition of national interest, nongovernmental organizations can significantly influence political processes. The main thesis of this article is that many of the traditional Arctic policy issues are being invaded by various domestic or even transnational interest groups that stress the benefits and not the dangers of cooperation. The public is more aware of environmental issues and less afraid of military ones than in the early 1980s. This increases the leeway of state policymakers engaged in international negotiations, and we can expect Young's situational factors to grow in importance . . .

Regime Opportunities in the Arctic

With the exception of the Svalbard Treaty and the 1973 Polar Bear Convention, there are no circumpolar environmental or resource regimes in the Arctic today. Generally, bilateral agreements are the most common, and the regimes are fairly shallow.

Scientific Cooperation

Ever since the Phipps expedition in 1775 or the better-known first Polar Year in 1882–83, there have been many efforts to organize multilateral cooperation in Arctic science. Many analysts have commented on their lack of success.[3] Today, however, there are two processes under way that challenge pessimism. A network of recent and fairly comprehensive bilateral agreements is emerging in the science area, often crossing the East-West divide.[4] I will look more closely at a second process, the movement toward setting up an International Arctic Science Committee.

How clear-cut are the national interests involved? The policy arena varies from country to country, but in general there seem to be two types of concerns that compete for the definition of national interests. One is a knowledge-motivated interest in pooling resources, in order to avoid duplication and secure access to data from the full circumpolar area. Not surprisingly, the major domestic proponents are members of the scientific community, in all the Arctic states. At this level, the problem is the benign one of realizing cost efficiency. However, when moving from basic to applied science, concerns of another kind appear. Certain fields of Arctic research have military or direct industrial applications and are thus highly competitive:

oceanography, physics of the upper atmosphere, and Arctic engineering. Still, as the proprosed agreement will clearly enable the avoidance of sensitive areas in the cooperative programs, the intensity of these other concerns must be deemed low. It is not surprising that in both the United States and the Soviet Union, the Ministry of Foreign Affairs has played a secondary role in the process.[5]

The lack of clear national interests of a competitive kind leads us to expect a fairly anarchical process, with ample room for action for entrepreneurial groups eager to reap cooperative gains. This would go a long way toward explaining developments in the early phase of the preparations for the International Arctic Science Committee. An informal international network of scientists developed an organizational model that was apparently much influenced by two salient solutions, namely, the Antarctic Treaty System and later the Scientific Committee on Antarctic Research, confined to the nongovernmental level. The more concrete the plans, however, the more they touched upon symbolic, competitive issues, such as the breadth of the regime. This issue was brought to a head when West Germany, France, and Great Britain declared to the United States their interest in joining the decision-making machinery of the new organization. The process was rendered less anarchical by the introduction of dormant competitive concerns such as U.S. loyalty to allies and a long-standing Soviet position that Arctic affairs should be dealt with by Arctic states alone. But, as the negotiations are now at an advanced stage, it seems unlikely that this element will kill the regime. A probable outcome is a privileged position for the so-called Arctic Eight in the central decision-making bodies but a larger role for the more broadly based scientific working groups.

Groundfish: Exploitation and Management

With the introduction of 200-mile economic zones, the cross-boundary interdependence in the fishery area was sharply reduced, and the existent regimes are predominantly bilateral. The 1982 Law of the Sea Convention sets up a global regime to be specified differently in each region depending on the biological distribution of the fish stocks. I shall focus on two regions, the Bering Sea and the Barents Sea.

In the Bering Sea, off Alaska, industry-level cooperation in the exploitation of groundfish has been very intense since the United States set up its 200-mile zone. The main actors were foreign fishing companies and U.S. trawler owners, who lobbied for continued foreign quotas in the zone in return for at-sea processing and marketing services. The Alaskan infrastructure was unable to assimilate all the fish taken in the Bering Sea and Gulf of Alaska. Thus, at an early stage, U.S. interests were reasonably clear and compatible with cooperation, and a number of international fisheries agreements were concluded with long-distance fishing nations. The main actors were Japanese, Soviet, and U.S. industry organizations, with the Soviets as front-runners. As they had previously set up similar arrangements with Norwegian firms in the Barents Sea, this option stood out as a possibly salient solution to the problem posed by the U.S. phasing-out policy. Complementary capabilities and probable synergy effects made the issue very benign, but there was also an element of competition for the raw material between the foreign factory vessels and domestic processors. U.S. legislation settled this issue to the benefit of the processors. Only moderate at first, this competition was intensified as a U.S. fleet of factory trawlers emerged in the late 1980s. As the domestic factory-trawler owners were able to redefine the perceived U.S. interests at the cost of the small joint-venture trawler owners, industry-level cooperation in the U.S. Arctic zone was terminated in 1988. It is unlikely to reappear. Cooperation might occur in Soviet waters, but only for a limited period. The complementarity on which it will be based is as vulnerable in the Soviet setting as in American.

Instead, groundfish cooperation is likely to move from exploitation to the management area, where it has been negligible in the past. With the U.S. stakes in the Arctic groundfish industry so much higher than before and the health of the pollack stocks in partial jeopardy, the need for coordinated action by the two coastal states increases. An immediate task is to improve knowledge about the marine ecosystems. U.S.-Soviet coordination in this area will probably increase, both bilaterally and within a broader Pacific framework. There are three multilateral processes under way: the growing activity of the International North Pacific Fisheries Commission groundfish group, the series of international scientific symposia on Bering Sea groundfish, and the efforts to establish the Pacific Council for the Exploration of the Seas. Moreover, if they can take the lead in setting up an international groundfish commission for this area, the United States and the Soviet Union will enhance their ability to regulate troublesome third-country fishing in the Donut Hole, a high-sea area located between their zones. Realizing these gains from bilateral cooperation involves no significant problems of externality or competition. Cross-boundary stock interdependences are probably moderate, and the two coastal states serve different markets.

In the Barents Sea the policy arena has been very different, for three reasons. Because of the link in international law between exercised authority and claims to sovereignty, the issue of cooperative management by Norway and the Soviet Union is deeply embedded in the territorial disputes in these waters. Second, Norway's domestic fisheries sector is regulated by a detailed network of explicit rights and obligations. Any cooperative effort that is perceived to infringe upon the interests of certain subsectors is likely to be effectively resisted. Third, overcapacity has marked the fishing fleets of both coastal states for the last 15 years. Accordingly, there is scant room for anarchical processes in the formation of regimes; and cooperation has proceeded in a cautious manner. The 1978 Grey Zone agreement allows regulation of fishing operations in the disputed section of the Barents Sea by separate systems of enforcement. The Grey Zone is not identical with the disputed area, thus reducing the basis for creeping jurisdiction and, with it, a basic competitive element in the problem of shared management. The second competitive element, distribution of shared stocks, has been removed in a manner that reminds us of Young's concept of a salient and apparently equitable solution. Norway and the Soviet Union have settled on fixed keys based on rough, one-shot assessments of biological abundance.[6] Thus cooperative bilateral management has proceeded far in the Barents Sea. The current resource crisis has also enhanced the potential for cooperation on the exploitation of groundfish. The Soviets need hard currency and lack the ability to process high-quality products for Western markets. In the past years agreements have been set up to allow direct deliveries from Soviet vessels to Norwegian processors short on raw material. This is still a small-scale phenomenon, highly vulnerable to changes in the domestic supply situation; but it might spill over to other sectors such as the ship-building and equipment industries.

Bilateral but fairly deep fisheries regimes are already in operation in the Arctic. There is no reason to expect broader membership in these regimes, but conditions are favorable for increased coordination of management in the Bering Sea and, to a lesser extent, exploitation in the Barents Sea.

Arctic Oil and Gas

Today there is very little cooperation in the area of mineral exploitation in the Arctic. Apart from a dormant Norwegian-Icelandic accord, no specific regimes exist to regulate such cooperation. When discussing future prospects, we must distinguish between disputed and undisputed waters. The disputed boundaries in the Barents, Bering, Chukchi, and Beaufort seas involve problems of the most malign type, as cooperative arrangements might subvert national claims to shelf resources. The issues under explicit negotiation have not proceeded beyond the specification of property rights. These issues involve hard-core national interests. Accordingly, entrepreneurial actors who may benefit from cooperation will have a hard time persuading governments to give concessions in order to achieve cooperation. Nor is there great urgency to enter the disputed areas, as vast areas of undisputed waters are still unexplored. This may explain why the Soviet proposal for a joint development zone in the Barents Sea, deemed reasonable by outside analysts[7] and clearly modeled on the rather successful Grey Zone agreement, was rebuffed by Norwegian authorities demanding a clear boundary line. In undisputed waters the cooperative problem seems more benign, especially between Western oil companies and the Soviet Union. The Soviets have already invited a number of West European companies to participate in the exploitation of their Arctic shelf resources. They have relaxed domestic restrictions on the size and transfer of foreign ownership shares in joint ventures. The employment of more cost-efficient Western technology may enable the Soviets to identify and extract resources earlier and probably at a lower cost than without cooperation.

Two competitive elements may obstruct the realization of this integrative potential, however. An argument against licensing technology is the fear of nourishing the growth of a strong competitor. On the other hand, the Finnish experiences of joint ship construction with Soviet partners suggest that the deterioration of a technological advantage is a slow process, especially in an area so close to the technology frontier. Likewise, the very strict regulations on technology transfers from Western countries to Eastern-bloc states, coordinated through an increasingly formal organization called COCOM, is gradually being phased out. Another competitive element is the issue of marketing. Because of the depressed state of world oil markets, some cooperative efforts have stumbled over disagreement on market channels. Nevertheless, industrial cooperation within undisputed areas of the Soviet Union would not require much political innovation as the restrictions on technology transfers dwindle and the competitive elements become surmountable. The main obstacle to cooperation is beyond the control of Northern government and oil companies; it is, namely, the state of the international oil markets, which may not encourage large-scale investments in the Arctic frontier areas. Still, as shown by the recent lease sales in the Chukchi Sea, the oil industry is still willing to put money into high-risk, long-term exploration.

The Arctic Environment: Marine Pollution

In recent years a number of bilateral and fairly shallow environmental agreements have emerged in the Arctic. Due to increased petroleum activity and the related density of shipping operations, a need for deeper international cooperation in the area of marine pollution is probably growing. Today there are no agreed-upon emission standards corresponding to those found in the North Sea or the Baltic.

When assessing the problem structure of marine pollution, we must bear in mind that it is a strongly contested issue in all Arctic states. The traditional predominance of industrial concerns is in a decline. Nongovernmental organizations are very active in this area, operating within as well as outside the regular political channels. Decision makers have scant knowledge about the costs of various measures, including that of nonaction. Thus, in general, this is a changing policy arena where the domestic actors are many and national interests unclear. A rather anarchical policy process is likely to evolve, sensitive to situational factors such as sudden crises, salient solutions, and entrepreneurial activity.

This statement needs to be qualified. A shallow regime concerned mainly with the exchange of information and some coordination of scientific operations would clearly be cost-efficient. The present network of bilateral environmental and scientific agreements in the Arctic states may be able to tap parts of this potential. Still, broadening the membership would be more efficient and would not introduce significant externalities or competition. Such a broadening of existent regimes may actually be propelled by entrepreneurial spillover from the cooperative institutions in the scientific area. The problem of negotiating an explicitly regulative regime is more malign. The costs of conforming to given rules will depend on unevenly distributed factors, like the volume and composition of industrial production and the command of reasonably clean technologies. Therefore the specific rules are bound to be strongly contested by the participants to a regime even though the notion that regulations will be collectively helpful may not. There is a model for a solution to this type of problem, exemplified by the United Nations Environmental Programme's Regional Seas Programme. A broad umbrella agreement is negotiated and later specified through protocols when perceived national interests permit. In the highly topical area of Arctic shipping, the 1973/1978 MARPOL convention could be useful, as all the Arctic states are members. As pointed out by Roginko, it might be possible to achieve a "special area" status for the Arctic Oceans, which would imply especially strict regulations. Due to the density of boundary disputes in Arctic waters, cooperative systems of compliance control and enforcement will be very difficult to achieve.

Thus, as long as the regime proposals are fairly shallow or general at first, they are not likely to infringe upon clearly defined interests in any of the Arctic states. On the contrary, there is considerable domestic goodwill to be won by showing political strength in this area. This implies that external shocks like the recent tanker accident off Alaska and entrepreneurial activity such as the Finnish initiative to organize a broad ministerial convergence on the environment may push marine pollution to the top of the Arctic policy agenda.

A Special Role for the Nordic Countries?

In this setting, the Nordic countries may prove important to the realization of Arctic cooperation in two ways. First, it may seem farfetched to search for salient Nordic solutions to be emulated by the broader set of Arctic states. Despite strong cultural homogeneity and deep economic interdependence, Nordic cooperation has not been a linear success story. Many ambitious attempts to set up regional regimes in the strategic and economic areas have failed, largely because of centrifugal forces toward broader solutions in the North Atlantic Treaty Organization, the European Free Trade Association, and the European Community. Whenever this has happened, the Nordic countries have settled for less controversial mechanisms for coordination. While there are a number of institutions, the dense network of informal intra-Nordic contacts at almost every level of political activity is equally important. Thus both the incrementalist response to setbacks and the low-key nature of Nordic coordination may provide lessons for the Arctic process.

Second, as demonstrated also by the Finnish Initiative, the Nordic states are particularly well suited to act as entrepreneurs for cooperative processes in the Arctic, for three reasons. It is a matter of routine to coordinate their own positions on issues related to Arctic cooperation, and together they make up five of the eight Arctic states. Also, geography implies that they are ill served by tensions in the region, and this provides a strong incentive to promote cooperative solutions to collective problems. Finally, their very smallness and varying strategic orientations have often led the Nordic states to see themselves as East-West bridge builders.

Concluding Remarks

Current Arctic regimes are narrow and shallow. In the areas of science, petroleum development, fisheries management, and marine protection, however, the predominance of military considerations is increasingly being challenged in key Arctic states. Scientists, industrial firms, and environmental organizations portray the problems in terms of cost efficiency rather than competition. The assessment of national interests is less straightforward than before; the positions of various Arctic players are being loosened up. Accordingly, the process of Arctic regime formation will be more influenced by accidental situational factors. Today these are very favorable for cooperation, due to the sense of urgency present in certain areas, the entrepreneurial activity of some actors, and the presence in each issue area of cooperative salient solutions.

NOTES

1. Oran R. Young, *International Cooperation: Building Regimes for Natural Resources and the Environment* (Ithaca. NY: Cornell University Press, 1989), pp. 12–13.
2. Oran R. Young, "The Politics of Regime Formation: Managing Natural Resources and the Environment," *International Organization* 43, no. 3 (Summer 1989).
3. Willy Ostreng, "Polar Science and Politics: Close Twins or Opposite Poles in International Cooperation," in *International Resource Management*, ed. S. Andersen and W. Ostreng (London: Belhaven Press, 1989).
4. Olav Schram Stokke, "The Arctic: Towards a Cooperate Region?" *International Challenges* 8, no. 4 (1988): 18–26.
5. Oran R. Young, *The Arctic in World Affairs* (Seattle: Washington Sea Grant Program, 1989), p. 29.
6. Brit Floistad and Olav Schram Stokke, "Common Concerns—National Interests: Norway, the Soviet Union and the Barents Sea Fisheries," *International Challenges* 9, no. 2 (1989).
7. Robert L. Friedheim, "The Regime of the Arctic—Distributional or Integrative Bargaining?" *Ocean Development and International Law* 19 (1988): 504.

Environment, Oceans, and Energy

Commission on the South

The protection of the environment is a matter of global concern calling for global measures. However, the manner in which the North is attempting to define the issues introduces an element of potential North-South conflict. This must be avoided, since the only possible way forward is through global co-operative efforts.

With regard to the depletion of the ozone layer due to the emission of chlorofluorocarbons (CFCs) and the destruction of rain forests, the North is in effect demanding that the South should give priority to environmental protection over development objectives. It is also attempting to put in place mechanisms for Northern monitoring and control over development policies in the South that could have environmental implications.

This is unacceptable on several counts. Singling out developing countries as a main source of the threat to the global environment obscures the fact that the ecological stress on the global commons has in large part been caused by the North. The North, with only 20 percent of the earth's population, accounts for 85 percent of the global consumption of non-renewable energy. Its burning of fossil fuel—coal, oil—is by far the most important source of gases harming the atmosphere, particularly carbon dioxide, which causes the greenhouse effect . . . and sulphur dioxide, which produces acid rain. Similarly, the threat to the earth's ozone layer from the emission of chlorofluorocarbons is largely the outcome of the consumption patterns of the North and is attributable to the wide use of such products as refrigerators and aerosols. And the threat to marine life in the world's oceans is again largely due to the industrial effluents and toxic wastes originating in the countries of the North, and to over-fishing by their fishing enterprises.

The North has already used much of the planet's ecological capital. It will have to take important measures to adjust its patterns of production and consumption in order to mitigate the clear threat to the earth's environment. It will also have to reduce its consumption of certain key natural resources, such as non-renewable fossil fuels, to accomodate the industrialization and economic development of the South.

. . . The South cannot accept that its development should be arrested in order to conserve the environment. The real choice is not between development and the environment, but between environment-sensitive and environment-insensitive forms of development. The former calls for large-scale investments which the South can hardly make unaided.

We believe that it is in the North's own interest to assist the South in safeguarding the environment. Technical and financial assistance from the North will be essential to enable the South to use its natural resources in an efficient manner compatible with the protection of the environment. Similar assistance will be required to reduce the pollution of the global commons that industrialization and urbanization in the South will inevitably entail.

Should the North be prepared to finance a substantial part of the cost of switching to environment-sensitive patterns of growth and consumption in the South, a negotiated agreement could provide for reciprocal obligations on the part of the governments of the South. A concerted attack on global poverty has to be an integral part of the efforts to protect the environment. Measures taken in this connection must of course respect the sovereignty of national governments and their right to determine their national conditionality—to be added to that imposed on the South by the international financing institutions—is utterly unacceptable.

The South's commitment to a global approach is signified by the proposal made by India at the Non-Aligned Summit in Belgrade in September 1989 for the establishment of a Planet Protection Fund under the auspices of the United Nations. The proposal envisages annual contributions to the Fund at the rate of 0.1 percent of GDP by all countries, except the least developed. The Fund would be used for developing or purchasing conservation-compatible technologies in critical areas, which could then be brought into the public domain for the benefit of both developing and developed countries. Additional resources for the Fund could be mobilized, for instance through a levy on the consumption of pollutants in the North. This type of tax is well known at the national level, taxes on petrol for automobile engines being a prime example. Its extension to the international field would be testimony to the North's commitment to a global effort to protect the environment.

Important steps toward introducing a global approach to some of these issues are the adoption in 1988 of United Nations General Assembly resolution 43/53 on the Protection of the Global Climate, the conclusion of the 1985 Vienna Convention for the Protection of the Ozone Layer and the 1987 Montreal Protocol, and the creation of the Intergovernmental Panel on Climatic Change by the United Nations Environment Programme and the World Meteorological Organization.

A global approach also informs the Declaration of the Hague, signed in 1989 by twenty-four Heads of State and Government or their representatives, which deals with the subjects of climate change, the warming of the atmosphere, and the deterioration of the ozone layer. The Declaration states the principle that developing countries have a right to fair and equitable compensation for the burden they may bear in carrying out decisions taken to protect the atmosphere, in recognition both of their development needs and of their lesser responsibility for the deterioration of the atmosphere. Much will depend on the operational guide-lines and the mechanism devised to implement this principle.

The Oceans and the United Nations Convention on the Law of the Sea

A particularly important topic of international environmental policy is the treatment of oceans. The enormous wealth of the world's oceans and their potential for hastening economic development led developing countries in the late 1960s to propose that this wealth should be declared part of the common heritage of humankind.

The United Nations Convention on the Law of the Sea of 1982 offers a comprehensive institutional and legal framework for the embodiment of this principle. It provides an internationally agreed regime for the management of the oceans, based on the principle of equity in the use of their resources. It gives to coastal states permanent sovereignty over natural resources within an Exclusive Economic Zone of 200 nautical miles. It establishes an International Seabed Authority to regulate the exploitation of the international waters, sea-bed, and subsoil, notably sea-bed mining. The Authority has the power to levy an international tax or royalty on the exploitation of these resources, and developing countries participate as equals in its decision making.

The Convention establishes a structured relationship between ocean-mining companies and the International Authority, which in effect goes beyond issuing a code of conduct for multinational corporations. It provides for regional co-operation, especially in the management of living resources and in the protection of the marine environment, as well as for the establishment of regional centres to advance marine sciences and to facilitate the transfer of technology. The first such centre has been set up in the Mediterranean, and similar centres are to be set up in the Caribbean and Indian Ocean regions.

The Convention reserves the use of the high seas, the international sea-bed area, and marine scientific research for peaceful purposes, and provides a system for the settlement of disputes. While the relevant articles need further interpretation and progressive development, they provide a basis for the denuclearization and demilitarization of ocean regions such as the Indian Ocean, the Mediterranean, the sea of Japan, and the Southern Ocean.

The Convention is a legal instrument which integrates development, the environment, and the issues of disarmament and peace in the overall goal of sustainable development. It is necessary that all states should ratify the Convention on the Law of the Sea and bring it into force as soon as possible. A forum should be created within the United Nations system for the discussion of ocean affairs in an integrated manner, in line with the recognition in the preamble to the Convention that the problems of the oceans are closely interrelated and should be considered together. Other conventions and treaties dealing with marine affairs should be harmonized, wherever required, with the Convention on the Law of the Sea. These should include in particular the treaty banning nuclear weapons and other weapons of mass destruction from the sea-bed.

The problems which may arise in the management of the international sea-bed may differ from those arising in the management and possible exploitation of other global commons such as Antarctica and outer space. However, any international regime in these areas must also be based on their acceptance as part of the common heritage of mankind. Regulation on the basis of agreements involving only a small group of technologically developed states should be clearly rejected. It is necessary that the 1959 Antarctica Treaty, which expires in 1991, should be succeeded by a new treaty inspired by a vision of the continent as part of the global commons—and of the common heritage of all countries.

An International Regime for Energy

Fluctuations in the international supply and price of energy, notably oil, have a profound influence on the world economy. The sharp increase in prices in 1973–74 made oil a key factor in most countries' balance of payments, inflation, and growth. The economic slow-down in the developed countries in the mid-1970s was related to the 'oil shock', as was the recession which began in the 1980s. Higher oil prices, while dramatically boosting the foreign exchange surpluses of the oil-exporting countries of the South, also placed a heavy burden on the South's oil importers. The reversal of the price trend in the 1980s, notably from 1986 onwards, also had significant effects on both oil producers and consumers. Volatility in prices has continued to be a feature of the world oil market.

So far, a global energy/oil crisis has been averted because of improvements in the energy efficiency of the economies of the North, and because of the modest rate of growth of the large countries of the South. A higher growth rate in these countries would stimulate a rising demand for oil and eventually put further pressure on energy supplies. The likely entry of the countries of Eastern Europe into the world market for petroleum, in consequence of a reduction of supplies from the USSR, adds to the uncertainty of the world oil market.

An agreed international regime for energy is therefore necessary, so that the development of the South is not impeded by the failure to provide for an orderly expansion and fair allocation of exhaustible energy resources. The South would need to be actively assisted to develop substitutes for fossil fuels and also to adopt techniques for conserving energy to the maximum extent possible.

The global economy needs a regime for energy that would be both stable, in that it would minimize disruptive fluctuations in supply and prices, and fair to both producers and consumers, assuring reasonable and remunerative prices as well as predictable access to supplies. The two objectives are interrelated, since fair prices will encourage an orderly expansion of production and so minimize the occurrence of both gluts and shortages. The scramble for supplies which marks periods of scarcity would be eliminated, and all countries would be assured of supplies to meet their needs.

Chapter *11*

Humanitarian and Moral Issues

Under the broad heading of human and moral issues, we can include such topics as human rights, that is, issues involving a state's treatment of its inhabitants; response to human tragedy, catastrophes from famine and other natural disasters, and war; and chronic poverty and underdevelopment, mortality and other health concerns, food production and distribution, education, and standard of living. Increasingly important are population-related problems, such as AIDS, the rise in ethnic tensions in Eastern Europe and elsewhere, and the degradation of the environment.

Traditionally, international relations has been characterized by binary thinking—a state can base its policies on *either* humanitarian concerns *or* national security. Conflicts between the two are seen as inevitable, and when they occur, it is realistic to believe that national interest must predominate. The international system is viewed as a Hobbesian world—a state of anarchy in which everyone is driven by self-interest. The principal actors in the international system are states, and states are the basic unit of analysis. The key concepts are conflict, power, and hierarchy. This paradigm, by defining what elements are relevant, ensures that security issues will be paramount. Even for the United States, where moral values have always been important to its citizens and appeals to morality are central to the American tradition, actual foreign policy has been driven by self-interest.

In spite of this preoccupation with power, conflict, and security, humanitarian and moral issues have not been ignored. In the realist system there have always been constraints on behavior, limits beyond which one must not go even in the interest of national security. Similarly, there is a role for ideals. Although they may not drive policy, they inform policy and they are used to justify one's own actions and condemn the actions of others.

Many analysts argue that our old ways of doing business in the international system cannot address the urgency of human and moral issues in the future. We will look at some ways in which these issues have been addressed in the past and discuss prospects for the future.

Human Rights

Respect for human rights was placed on the international agenda with the passage of the Universal Declaration of Human Rights by the U.N. General Assembly in 1948. This document urges governments to work toward the fulfillment of political, economic, and social rights, including the right to freedom of conscience and expression; participation in government; freedom from arbitrary imprisonment and torture; work in just conditions; the formation of trade unions; and a decent standard of living sufficient to provide for food, clothing, shelter, and medical care. Clearly the existence of the declaration has not ended human rights abuses. Although most states profess to recognize basic human rights, they do not agree on exactly what these rights are. States have been reluctant to provide mechanisms for the enforcement of rights that would challenge state sovereignty. For example the International Covenant on Civil and Political Rights, although submitted to the U.S. Senate in 1974, was not approved until spring 1992. Human rights violations, while deplored, are usually seen as being within the province of domestic rather than international politics; most countries, the United States included, have generally allowed other international interests to take precedence over the rights of citizens in other countries.

World response to apartheid illustrates how progress in the recognition of human interests occurs only slowly when direct threats to national security are not perceived by major players. Human rights violations in South Africa first gained U.N. attention in 1946. After the National Party achieved a majority in South Africa in 1948, it swiftly enacted legislation that systematically solidified apartheid, a legal, social, political, and economic system of separate and unequal citizenship for whites and nonwhites. Other African states hoped to use the United Nations as a forum for combating apartheid. However, although the vast majority of members agreed that the system was deplorable, it was perceived primarily as a human rather than a security issue and little progress was made toward its demise.

In the early 1950s the General Assembly appointed a commission to study the situation, and it issued a report characterizing apartheid as being dangerous to peaceful international relations. The U.N. Charter states that its first purpose is

> To maintain international peace and security, and to that end: to take effective collective measures for the prevention and removal of threats to the peace and

for the suppression of acts of aggression or other breaches of the peace, and to bring about by peaceful means, and in conformity with the principles of justice and international law, adjustment or settlement of international disputes or situations which might lead to a breach of the peace.

By defining the situation as a threat to world peace, the commission hoped to induce action. Various resolutions were passed by the General Assembly in the following years, requesting that South Africa review its policies. After police fired on demonstrators at Sharpeville, killing a number of unarmed demonstrators, including young children, the Security Council passed a resolution stating that the situation was dangerous to world peace and instructed Secretary-General Hammarskjold to visit South Africa and to work with that government to uphold the U.N. charter. His appeals to the South African government had no more effect on policy than had repeated U.N. resolutions.

In 1962, the General Assembly asked members to sever diplomatic relations, close their ports to South African shipping and aircraft, boycott all South African products, and suspend all exports and travel. The African states wanted a blockade, but the United States and Britain were opposed. They did not agree that apartheid was a threat to international peace within the meaning of Article 39 of the Charter, nor was the situation high on their lists of security concerns. They refused to support collective action. Trade with South Africa was economically important to Britain, and both Britain and the United States expressed fear that a blockade would lead to war and to worsening conditions within South Africa.

The African states, having failed to achieve an economic blockade, attacked on another front, the International Court of Justice. South Africa governed Namibia (formerly South West Africa) through a U.N. mandate. The League of Nations had established a British mandate over this former German colony after the defeat of Germany in World War I. This mandate was executed by South Africa, which tried (unsuccessfully) to annex the area. After World War II, the United Nations allowed South African administration to continue but refused to allow annexation by South Africa and required regular reports on conditions in the territory. South Africa had submitted no reports since 1948. In 1960 the Organization of African Unity (OAU)—through Ethiopia and Libya, former members of the League of Nations—initiated a case before the court claiming that the mandate agreement had been violated. Not only had South Africa failed to report on conditions, but also it had illegally extended the policy of apartheid beyond its own borders and into Namibia. Although the court had initially agreed to hear the case, in July 1966 it ruled that the plaintiffs had no standing in the matter. In October the General Assembly resolved (114 votes to 2 with 2 abstentions) to terminate the mandate, and in 1970 the Security Council declared South Africa's occupation of Namibia illegal. Even so it was not until the late 1970s that South Africa began to make plans to withdraw. This decision was made not because of U.N. pressure but for security reasons. Angola's independence from Portugal had given anti–South African guerrillas fighting in Namibia a nearby base of operations. South Africa feared an increasingly intense battle to retain control of

Namibia and preferred instead to attempt to set up a government there that would be less hostile to its interests. Nevertheless, Namibia did not become fully independent until 1990.

In the 1970s economic sanctions against South Africa were not particularly effective, and in the late 1970s there was even a period of economic growth. But in the 1980s, changes began to occur. As repression increased, international opinion became more and more united against the South African government. Western firms, including a number of American companies, scaled down their investments. Violence within the country increased, and a growing number of white South Africans began to pressure the government for change. Officially the United States and Britian, under Reagan and Thatcher, respectively, continued to argue against economic sanctions, but congressional action and public opinion in the United States suggested that widespread sanctions were inevitable. Although the net effect of economic sanctions on South Africa appears to have been meager, the psychological impact contributed to a breakdown in white support for apartheid. With the election of F. W. de Klerk, the South African government began its dismantlement. More than forty years had passed since apartheid first gained international attention.

Population Issues and Emergency Relief Aid

Generally, altruism is regarded as the least important reason for granting foreign aid; most analysts argue that the primary motivations are political and economic. States give aid to extend influence, to shore up friendly regimes, to undermine hostile regimes, to create markets, and to grant capital for the purchase of the grantor's goods. These types of aid are bilateral and continue to constitute the greatest proportion of aid given. In contrast, emergency assistance in response to human tragedy is thought to be altruistic, and an important role in its administration is played by nongovernment organizations (NGOs) and intergovernment organizations (IGOs). The best known are the agencies of the United Nations, such as UNICEF and the World Health Organization, and private organizations like CARE, the International Red Cross, and OXFAM. These organizations depend in part on donations from individuals and corporations, but the larger share of the assistance they provide is supplied by donor countries. Governments channel large amounts of emergency assistance through these organizations because they have relief structures in place throughout the world.

Many observers argue that these organizations are the best way to provide emergency assistance because they are not motivated by political concerns. However, the line between apolitical humanitarian aid and assistance tied to political issues is not always clear. States respond more quickly to disasters in those countries with whom they have historical ties. Thus former colonies often receive more emergency relief from their former occupiers than from elsewhere. Aid is also more prompt when there is a domestic constituency in the donor country that can be mobilized to support it. This constituency may be made up of ethnic or religious groups, sympathetic political groups, or even economic interests that would benefit from the shipment of aid. When the General Accounting Office recommended a greater role for IGOs in dispensing humanitarian aid, Henry Kissinger disagreed: ". . . Disaster relief is becoming increasingly a major instrument of our foreign policy. The assistance we can provide to various nations may have a long-term impact on US relations with those nations and their friends." In theory, natural disasters do not call forth political considerations to the same extent as those caused by human intervention, such as war. However, in practice it is sometimes difficult to separate the two. The Ethiopian famine in the 1980s was only partly caused by drought. The civil war there was certainly a factor—some observers claim that it was the cause—and assistance was affected by concerns about which side in the conflict was being helped.

Aid channeled through IGOs and NGOs is also subject to political uses. These organizations can be affected by political pressure, especially from states like the United States that are major contributors. The U.S. withdrawal of support in the 1980s for family-planning agencies that include abortion as an option is an example. Donor governments may turn to multilateral assistance to get around political opposition at home or to try to legitimize an issue in the eyes of the world.

Development Assistance

Emergency relief efforts were never intended to resolve long-term population problems, for which the international response has been development assistance. Historically, high growth rates were seen in positive terms because large populations were a source of military and economic strength. In the last few decades, however, most of the population growth has taken place in the less developed countries. When it outstrips economic growth rates, it increases poverty and strains the ability of the state to provide basic human services.

In August 1974, the first World Population Conference was sponsored by the United Nations. Representatives from 136 nations met and approved a World Population Plan of Action, which stated that all couples and individuals have a basic right to decide freely and responsibly the number and spacing of their children and should have access to the information and means to do so. In August 1984, the International Conference on Population was held in Mexico City, where 149 nations reaffirmed the plan of action adopted ten years earlier. The international response has been directed toward raising the standard of living and encouraging family planning. The U.S. withdrawal of support from the U.N. Population Fund and International Planned Parenthood and the opposition of the Catholic church to contraception have hindered the success of population control programs.

Development assistance has been largely bilateral and has followed the basic philosophy that economic growth is by definition good. Much past assistance was designed to raise national incomes, and relatively little attention was given until recently to income distribution. Overall economic growth was expected gradually to raise the standard of living of the poor as well as that of the elite.

In the 1970s directly raising the standard of living of the poor became a priority. This "basic human needs" approach to development questioned the validity of the trickle-down theory, pointing to higher levels of absolute poverty those states experiencing overall growth. More recently, specialists have argued that attention to the needs of the poor must be accompanied by considerations of macroeconomic policies. The World Bank recommends that ongoing development assistance be tied to domestic policies that exhibit a commitment to fighting poverty through structural reforms. These strategies certainly contain a moral dimension: improving the quality of individuals' lives, even in those cases in which political and economic interests are predominant. What has not been considered is the long-term effect of continued economic growth on the environment and the ways in which this omission threatens humanity and thus human values.

Human Needs and the Future of the International System

Population issues are becoming increasingly important in world affairs; the perception that they are largely within the province of humanitarian concerns and thus are safely left to NGOs and IGOs is changing. Enduring poverty is not the only issue here. Increasingly attention is being focused on the effects of population growth on the environment. Between 1970 and 1990, approximately 1.6 billion people were added to the world's population, and as a consequence the world's resources are being depleted, forests are shrinking, and deserts are growing. In an attempt to produce adequate food we are "borrowing from the future," to use Lester Brown's phrase. He notes that the growth in world food production that occurred during the late 1970s and early 1980s came from increasingly fragile land and overpumped aquifers. As a consequence the level of growth in production has declined and has not kept up with population growth. For the world as a whole, the annual growth in grain production from 1984 to 1990 was 1 percent, while population growth was nearly 2 percent.

Three different perspectives for addressing these issues are found in realism, feminism, and ecology. Both feminist and ecological theory argue for a fundamental shift in the way diplomacy is conducted. The realist approach merely defines these problems in terms of power politics.

Certainly there are problems arising from population growth that threaten international security. Environmental degradation increases poverty and thus contributes to instability, to natural disasters, and to refugee flows and economic migrants. Differential growth rates among ethnic groups can exacerbate existing tensions and threaten existing institutions. Any of these threats to security may be met in part with traditional forms of diplomacy. The primary actors will be state-level policymakers acting from perceived national interests.

Feminists, however, find this business-as-usual approach inadequate. They call for a shift in focus beyond crisis management to prevent problems from worsening. Traditionally, world affairs have revolved around the interaction of elites—politicians and technocrats—but actions designed to address population growth and the environmental concerns associated with it depend on individual action. Feminists believe that basic values must be changed and individual behavior altered. Economic growth cannot be seen in uncritically positive terms because growth without changes in patterns of consumption and waste management cannot be sustained indefinitely.

A number of analysts have argued that the field of international relations requires new theoretical paradigms if it is to address current problems. Feminists charge that past theories were constructed by men working with male models of reality. Its approaches omit the experience of women, resulting in a dichotomy between public and private spheres of activity. This distinction between public and private action must be broken down and more attention given to areas formerly ignored such as human issues. The male perspective has also resulted in a focus on conflict and competition, rather than on cooperation and accommodation, and on hierarchical relationships rather than networks. The conception of what constitutes a social being is an important part of this worldview.

In the international realm there is no agreement on acceptable behavior and no common power to ensure conformity to such behavior. The dominant paradigm sees the individual as competitive, self-interested, and destructive. Belief in this image prescribes a set of rational behaviors for states operating in such a system. Feminism suggests that this view is gender-biased; that is, women are absent entirely from this formulation and from the theories that follow from it. The distinctions drawn concerning public and private life reinforce this bias. A state's security concerns, as a consequence, often do not take into account the interests of its citizens. Theory that emphasizes security issues will not address human and moral issues until they reach the point of crisis and then will be poorly equipped to offer long-term solutions. Refugee politics is an excellent example of this phenomenon. Ignoring the underlying causes of refugee flows means that responses to them will be highly politicized at worst and short-term crisis management at best.

Ecologists challenge development theories that focus on growth as progress. They see reality in terms of cycles rather than a linear progression. They envision a future world arena in which ideologies will play a limited role. When states are actors, their relationships with nature will take precedence over relations with one another. Common goals and cooperation will be the hallmark of this system. The behavior of individual citizens, who must be encouraged to act responsibly, and the quality of the lives of individuals will be the major concerns. Diplomacy will involve complex negotiations concerning waste disposal, species protection, sharing of resources, and development of environmentally friendly technology. Power will be derived from environmental and economic leadership rather than from military might. Given the need for international agreement and cooperation, the United Nation's importance to international affairs will increase.

Even realists ponder whether the values that have played a part in international politics can continue to do so in a system with rapid population shifts. Much attention has been focused on population growth per se and not on its characteristics. Most of the future growth will occur in the less developed world. Eventually this burgeoning population will result in a shift in influence, both politically and economically, from the states of the industrial North to those of the South. These states may not be guided by the same value systems that have shaped international politics in the past.

The Readings

Louis Henkin, in "The Universality of the Concept of Human Rights," discusses whether the issue of human rights as currently defined reflects a Western bias. He argues that the concept is universal and widely accepted by non-Western as well as Western cultures. Rensselaer Lee's "The Political Economy of the Andean Cocaine Industry," considers the implications of the drug trade. This problem illustrates the way in which human issues are not easily settled by power politics. Refugee problems are commonly thought about in humanitarian and legal terms. In "Predicting State Response to Refugees," Glenn Hastedt and Kay Knickrehm show the political side of this problem by focusing on the response of receiving states to large movements of refugees across their borders.

Bibliography

BROWN, LESTER. *State of the World 1991.* New York: W. W. Norton, 1991

EBERSTADT, NICHOLAS. "Population Changes and National Security." *Foreign Affairs,* Summer 1991, pp. 115–31.

GALLAGHER, DENNIS. "The Evolution of the International Refugee System." *International Migration Review* 23, no. 3 (1989), 579–97.

GRANT, REBECCA and KATHLEEN NEWLAND (eds.). *Gender and International Relations.* Bloomington, IN: Indiana University Press, 1991.

KENT, RANDOLPH. *Anatomy of Disaster Relief: The International Network in Action.* New York: Pinter Publishers, 1987.

NICHOLS, BRUCE, and GIL LOESCHER. *The Moral Nation: Humanitarianism and U.S. Foreign Policy Today.* Notre Dame, IN: University of Notre Dame Press, 1989.

REPETTO, ROBERT. "Population, Resources, Environment: An Uncertain Future" *Population Bulletin.*

RUNYON, ANNE SISSON, and V. SPIKE PETERSON. "The Radical Future of Realism: Feminist Subversions of IR Theory." *Alternatives* 16 (1991), 67–106.

SYLVESTER, CHRISTINE. "The Emperor's Theories and Transformations: Looking at the Field Through Feminist Lenses." In Dennis Pirages (ed.), *Transformations in the Global Political Economy.* New York: Macmillan, 1990.

The Universality of the Concept of Human Rights

Louis Henkin

Discussion of the universality of the concept of human rights begs for definition and interpretation of terms. I offer a word about the concept of human rights, another about universality.

Human Rights

Human rights are not the equivalent of justice, or "the good society," or, as some think, democracy, although the human rights idea is related to all of these. Briefly, the human rights idea declares that every individual has legitimate claims upon his or her own society for certain freedoms and benefits. Few, if any, human rights are absolute; they are prima facie rights and may sometimes bow to compelling public interest. Ronald Dworkin suggested that human rights ordinarily "trump" other public interests.

These claims upon society are not for some general and inchoate category of what is good; they have been authoritatively defined. They are specified in the Universal Declaration of Human Rights and in various other international instruments. The rights specified are commonly divided into two categories. Civil and political rights include rights to life and physical integrity; freedom from torture, slavery, and arbitrary detention; and rights

From *The Annals of the American Academy of Political and Social Science* 506 (1989). Copyright © 1989. Reprinted by permission of Sage Publications, Inc.

to fair criminal process; as well as rights of personhood and privacy; freedom of conscience, religion, and expression; and the right to vote and participate in government. The other category comprises economic and social rights. These are essentially those associated with the welfare state: the right to work, to eat, to obtain health care, housing, education, and an adequate standard of living generally. A people's rights to self-determination and sovereignty over natural resources have been appended to the human rights catalog in two international covenants. Controversial candidates for inclusion as human rights are rights to peace, economic development, and a healthy environment.

The idea of human rights is a political idea with moral foundations. It is an expression of the political relationship that should prevail between individual and society. It implies that there are limitations on government, including limits on what can be done to the individual even for the welfare of the majority, the public interest, the common good. There are even limitations on law; one may think of human rights as a kind of higher law. The human rights idea implies individual entitlement and corresponding obligations on society. Our rights are not granted by society; we enjoy them not by the grace of society and not only because it may be good societal policy to respect them. Rather, we are entitled to them.

Implicit in the idea of human rights is a commitment to individual worth. The individual counts, and counts independently of the community. The idea suggests equality of human beings, not hierarchy among them. It implies that values of liberty and autonomy are sometimes more important than values of order. Justice Cardozo wrote of "ordered liberty."

Where the idea of human rights comes from is not agreed upon. In the contemporary world, human rights claims are justified rhetorically as required by human dignity, and by goals of freedom, justice, and peace.

Universality

The term "human rights" suggests the rights of all human beings anywhere and anytime. The principal contemporary articulation of human rights, the Universal Declaration of Human Rights, claims and prescribes universality.

The universality of human rights has been challenged from several perspectives. The idea has had an uphill struggle from political and philosophical acceptance. The strongest challenge has been to claims of cultural universality.

The political and philosophical idea of human rights has not always been universal, and it has not been universal for very long. It finds its authentic origins in the seventeenth century in the natural rights of John Locke. In America, we tend to proclaim Thomas Jefferson's restatement of Locke in the Declaration of Independence. But the idea was rejected by traditionalists such as Edmund Burke. It was rejected by progressives, even such eminent progressives as Jeremy Bentham. Bentham said: "Natural rights is simple nonsense: natural and imprescriptible rights, rhetorical nonsense—nonsense upon stilts." An American thinker once wrote that natural rights have been as much "the shield of conservatism as the sword of radicalism."[1]

In the nineteenth and early twentieth centuries, the idea of natural rights was challenged by positivists. It has been denied by utilitarianism, which implies that one can sacrifice individuals to achieve the greatest good of the greatest number or the maximum of total happiness. The idea of human rights has been attacked by socialists. Communitarians generally see human rights as egocentric, egotistic, and divisive. The human rights idea has also been challenged as undemocratic when claims to individual rights conflict with the will of the majority.

This political idea, so self-evident to Americans, took root in very few places. It found fertile soil in the United States in 1776 when Jefferson proclaimed it and the states included it in their constitutions; in 1789 Congress adopted what became the Bill of Rights. It is sobering to note, however, that while we amended the Constitution to include the Bill of Rights and continued to recite the Declaration of Independence, we maintained slavery for another eighty years, maintained racial discrimination for a hundred years more, and limited suffrage until recently. Minorities and women continue to claim invidious discrimination.

Our partner in the idea of rights in the eighteenth century, France, proclaimed its great Declaration of the Rights of Man and of the Citizen in 1789, then shelved it for about 150 years. Great Britain, our mother-in-law, continues to reject the idea of rights in constitutional principle, in favor of parliamentary supremacy. One hardly need mention countries in the twentieth century that rejected the idea of human rights in principle as well as in fact, in the name of fascism, national socialism, and Stalin's socialism.

Religions, too, have challenged the idea of rights. At various times, almost every religion—including Protestantism, whose stress on the individual contributed to the idea—has not received the idea of human rights warmly. Religions have not tended to favor ideas that could be seen as essentially anthropocentric. Autonomy and liberty have not been religious values and have been seen as anarchic.

Finally, some cultural anthropoligists have charged that natural rights is a Western idea and that imposing it on others is cultural imperialism. In any event, they insisted, there is little hope for human rights if the world's cultures are not receptive to the idea.

Emerging Universality

The human rights idea was not universal not too long ago. I believe it has now achieved universality in significant respects.

Political universality today can hardly be denied. World War II and the full realization of the enormities of Adolf Hitler ushered in what I have called "the age of rights." Human rights has been accepted as the idea of our times; no other political idea—not socialism; not capitalism; not even democracy, however defined, usually undefined—has received such universal acclaim. All states have accepted the idea of human rights in some form. Universal condemnation of apartheid, for example, also implies universal acceptance of the idea of rights.

The second half of this century has given the idea legal universality as well. The concept of human rights has been enshrined in the U.N. Charter, to which virtually all states are parties. The Universal Declaration of Human Rights has been accepted by virtually all states. The international covenants and conventions on human rights have been widely adhered to, and there is a customary law of human rights binding on all states.

The concept of human rights has been incorporated in virtually all state constitutions. Where it has not been fully incorporated, there is continuous demand for its inclusion and for constitutional guarantees of rights. Even the Soviet Union, even China have included human rights in their recent constitutions.

Needless to say, universal political and even legal acceptance does not guarantee universal respect for human rights. Many will see such acceptance as rhetoric or even hypocrisy. I have been sometimes tempted to offer two cheers for hypocrisy in human rights. Two cheers—though not three—recognize that "hypocrisy is the homage that vice pays to virtue"; it is important that the concept of human rights is the virtue to which vice has to pay homage in our time. Acceptance, even hypocritical acceptance, is a commitment in principle to which one can be held accountable. Hypocrisy requires concealment that can be uncovered. This homage is reflected even in the phenomenon of emergency rule that prevails in many countries today. When a country declares emergency rule, it declares its situation to be abnormal. In principle, emergency rule is only temporary. Regardless of how long it lasts, it continues to be abnormal.

There can be little doubt about the fact of the constitutionalization and the internationalization of human rights in our time, and of the popularity of the idea—in all senses of "popularity." With those political developments, even philosophical and religious opposition to the idea has been muted if not erased.

We may be approaching universality even among philosophers. Natural rights have had a rebirth. Philosophers who continue to eschew natural rights may nonetheless recognize a sense of common moral intuition that provides a basis for human rights. In any event, the human rights movement does not invoke natural rights with its historical baggage, and the battles with positivism are now moot since human rights are now established in positive national and international law. Philosophers, such as Professor Cranston in Great Britain, who continue to object to economic and social rights as rights do not challenge the concept of human rights and indeed reaffirm it, and other philosophers have shouted him down on economic and social rights, too.

The others I have mentioned—the utilitarians, the communitarians, the socialists—may continue to be opposed to the idea in abstract theory, but none of them is now prepared to submerge the individual completely. Utilitarians will not sanction slavery, or torture, even "for the greatest good." Communitarians increasingly recognize that a legitimate community can be maintained only with respect for individual human rights. Socialism recognizes that socialism is acceptable and viable only if it has a human face.

All the major religions have begun to emphasize their individualist, universalist, this-worldly—rather than other-worldly—elements. They have played down doctrines that are in tension with human rights, such as intolerance of other religions and subordination of women. Some fundamentalist actions taken in the name of Islam, however, continue to resist this trend. The rights of individuals now commonly are seen by all religions as a floor, a minimum requirement for the good society, especially in modern urban industrialized society. All societies and all religions today have accepted the notion of rights to have basic human needs satisfied. Modernization has brought the human rights idea even to the illiterate villager. In all parts of the world, it is increasingly recognized, the village will need law, institutions, education, organization, and human rights if it is to be part of modern society.

Cultural Receptivity

The core of the continuing challenge to the universality of human rights today is cultural. Essentially, the claim is that the concept of human rights is a Western idea, imposed on the rest of the world, and that many cultures are resistant and unreceptive to the idea.

That the idea has been imposed by the West is debatable. The idea of human rights has been accepted by leaders in every country, embraced not only by the early Western-educated elites but also by contemporary leaders. The Third World has had its Nyereres committed to human rights, not only its Idi Amins. Much of the resistance to human rights is resistance not to the idea of human rights but to some of its politics in the United Nations, to external scrutiny rejected as interference, to the imposition of sanctions for human rights violations—for example, by the United States—but not to the idea of human rights.

In any event, many contemporary ideas in the political world are Western—the concept of the state, socialism, the idea of the United Nations. Development is a Western concept, universally acclaimed. No one claims that these ideas are anything other than Western, yet no one claims that they are therefore culturally foreign and unacceptable.

Human rights may be a Western idea, but the West has not been more receptive to it than have other regions and cultures. The ideas hardly flourished in the West before World War II, and it was in the West that Hitler perpetrated his monstrous deeds.

The political idea of human rights is rooted in interpersonal morality. The issue, I believe, is not the universality of the political idea but of the underlying morality. The question is whether the moral values of human rights are universal, whether the specifics in the catalog of rights in the Universal Declaration of Human Rights respond to that common morality. The important issue, moreover, is not even whether human rights reflects a common morality, but whether the morality it reflects, now universally politically prescribed, is culturally acceptable or will be rejected as foreign matter.

I am persuaded that there is, universally, a common contemporary moral intuition that responds to, and will not reject, most of the provisions in the Universal Declaration, those that constitute the core of human rights. I think there is universal cultural receptivity to the right to life and physical integrity; to freedom from torture, slavery, and arbitrary detention; to due process of law and the right not to suffer cruel punishment; to a right to property. These rights correspond to those alluded to in the phrase "consistent patterns of gross violations of internationally recognized human rights," a term of art in both U.N. doctrine and U.S. legislation. There is no reason to assume cultural resistance to universal political participation. There is surely no cultural resistance to societal responsibility for meeting basic needs for food, housing, health care, education, and the care of children and the aged.

On the other hand, some rights in the Universal Declaration are not universally favored and may meet cultural resistance. I cannot conclude that freedom of expression is universally accepted or even acceptable; I am not confident even about freedom of conscience and religion. Equality is not yet universally welcomed, and discrimination on grounds of race, ethnicity, or gender will be difficult to eradicate. The world has moved, but it has not yet moved far enough.

The world has been moved to accept new ideas, and in my view it is more receptive to the idea of human rights than to many others. The idea of human rights has been on the world scene for only some forty years. It has faced an uphill struggle in many countries, Western as well as Eastern, in the First and Second as in the Third World. Its political and legal acceptance has been universal, and philosophical and ideological resistance to it has subsided. The conception of human rights, and most of the rights in the authoritative catalog of human rights, I conclude, conform to a common moral intuition that is virtually universal today, and those rights are in fact congenial—or acceptable—to the principal cultures. Serious violations of these rights in many countries reflect, I think, not cultural resistance but political-social-economic underdevelopment and instability, and a still underdeveloped culture of constitutionalism, including an inability to keep the army in its barracks.

Some rights, on the other hand—freedom of expression, religious and ethnic equality, and the equality of women—appear not yet to be acceptable in fact in a number of societies. In that sense, those rights are not yet universal. I do not think that it is impossible to make them universal, but it will take dedicated effort by those who care.

NOTE

1. Jerome Frank, "Interpretations of Modern Legal Philosophers," in *Interpretations of Modern Legal Philosophies: Essays in Honor of Roscoe Pound*, ed. Paul L. Sayre (New York: Oxford University Pres, 1947), p. 223.

The Political Economy of the Andean Cocaine Industry

Rensselaer W. Lee III

. . . U.S. and Latin American efforts to curb the supply of cocaine have failed abjectly. Some 300 to 400 tons of cocaine may flow into U.S. markets yearly; as University of Michigan researcher Lloyd Johnston notes, "the supply of cocaine has never been greater in the streets, the price has never been lower, and [the] drug has never been purer."[1] South American coca cultivation increased 44 percent from 1985 to 1989 according to the State Department's Bureau of International Narcotics Matters.[2] The U.S. government plans to spend $2.2 billion on narcotics-related programs in the Andean countries over the next five years, but even this sum is a pittance when compared to the South American cocaine industry's earnings of $9 to $10 billion a year. Anyhow, more resources may not be the answer. Structural barriers block effective drug enforcement in poor countries, and such barriers could well be insurmountable.

First, Andean governments worry about the impact of successful drug-control programs. The consequences would be exacerbated rural poverty and new legions of the unemployed, both of which would strengthen anti-democratic or communist movements. Imagine 200,000 coca-growing peasants marching on Bolivia's capital, La Paz. In Peru and Colombia, the war against drugs has proved difficult to reconcile with the struggle against communist insurgency. The threat of eradication alienates coca growers from the government and enhances the appeal of insurgent groups. In the Upper

From *Orbis: A Journal of World Affairs*, Spring 1991, published by the Foreign Policy Research Institute.

Huallaga Valley, for example, the U.S.-backed eradication effort has doubtless driven many peasants into the ranks of Sendero Luminoso. In Colombia, the government's persecution of the Medellin drug lords has tied down roughly one-third of Colombia's 110,000-man army, mostly in occupying estates belonging to traffickers. Such a huge diversion of manpower has enabled guerrilla organizations to regroup, expand their strength, and launch new offensives against military and civilian targets.

Second, many Latin Americans see the economic benefits of drug trafficking. Colombia's controller general, Rodolfo Gonzales, has publicly hailed the contribution of drug dollars to national economic growth. Leading bankers in Peru talk about the importance of cocaine earnings in stabilizing the country's currency. Bolivia's president Victor Paz Estenssoro remarked in 1986 that "cocaine has gained in importance in our economy in direct response to the shrinking of the formal economy."[3]

Third, Latin Americans tend to see U.S.-imposed drug enforcement measures as infringements on their national sovereignty. According to recent polls, two-thirds of Colombians oppose the extradition of drug traffickers to the United States.[4] This feeling may be heightened because some of the leading candidates for extradition, such as Colombia's Pablo Escobar and Bolivia's Roberto Suarez, provide support for charitable activities and so are popular in their countries. Arresting and extraditing such traffickers would be difficult politically. Officials undoubtedly recall the violent anti-American outbursts in Honduras following the April 1988 extradition of Juan Matta Ballestreros, a narcophilanthropist who cultivated a Robin Hood image.

Fourth, governments often exercise little or no control over territories where drug production flourishes, for these are remote from metropolitan centers, relatively inaccessible mountainous or jungle terrains which are patrolled by guerrillas or other hostile groups. In this way, drug traffic encourages territorial disintegration. The Peruvian government, for example, is losing control over the Upper Huallaga Valley, the region which ships its most important export, coca paste, to Colombia and in return receives money, weapons, and some economic leadership. Colombian aircraft maintain this connection by flying in and out of Peruvian airspace with virtual impunity. Colombian middlemen increasingly buy paste directly from peasants in the Valley rather than through Peruvian dealers. The Upper Huallaga is becoming less a part of Peru and more a part of Colombia.

Finally, corruption severely undermines criminal justice systems in cocaine-producing countries. Law enforcement in Latin American countries often represents simply a way to share in the proceeds of the drug trade: the police take bribes not to make arrests and seizures. When the police do make successful busts, the drugs are often resold on the illicit market.

These barriers mean that anti-drug activities in Latin American countries are largely cosmetic. Governments draw up elaborate plans to eradicate coca—the police make a few highly publicized arrests and cocaine seizures, fly around the countryside in helicopters, terrorize villages, and knock out an occasional cocaine laboratory—but with little effect. The core structure of the cocaine industry remains, and the industry's agricultural base continues to expand. Farmers in the Upper Huallaga Valley plant four to five acres for every hectare of coca eradicated, according to a professor at the Agrarian University of Tingo María, the capital of an important cocaine-growing province in the Valley.

At the same time, governments resist the only effective method for controlling coca cultivation, herbicides. Herbicides toxic enough to kill the hardy cocaine bush may also be dangerous to agricultural crops, wildlife, fish, and even humans. The herbicide tebuthiuron ("Spike"), manufactured by Eli Lilly, is "one of a class of toxins that has caused liver damage and testicle tumors in rats." Lilly has refused to sell the herbicide to the State Department, apparently fearing a rash of liability lawsuits stemming from improper use.[5]

Governments fear ecological damage from the use of toxic chemicals, but they are even more concerned about the social effects: the prospects of massive rural unemployment and (in Colombia and Peru) the aggravation of a festering insurgency problem.

As a result, Bolivia has ruled out chemical eradication entirely. In Colombia, an experimental spraying program has been halted because the government is reportedly afraid of "criticism by environmentalists, the political opposition and peasants involved in drug cultivation." In Peru test spraying has been underway since October 1987; however, the Peruvian government's willingness to move toward full-scale chemical eradication seems contingent on assurances "that the herbicide is not harmful to other plants, animals and human beings." Given the recent publicity surrounding "Spike" and other toxic chemicals, the Peruvian government may opt to remain at the testing stage indefinitely.[6]

The U.S. Policy Dilemma

A 1988 Department of State report noted that Latin American governments do not yet recognize that coca growing and cocaine trafficking "pose serious threats to their own survival."[7] Be that as it may, many Andean leaders are concerned that the suggested cures would be worse than the disease.

To a degree, that concern must also be the concern of Washington, which wants to encourage stable, economically viable governments in the region; to promote democracy; and to suppress leftist insurgent movements. America's war against its drug addiction is not necessarily compatible with these other priorities, at least in the short run. In fact, the argument can be made that the United States and its Latin American allies have a common interest in minimizing the intensity of the drug war. Yet this may be hard for Washington to do—there are real public pressures to do just the opposite. A *New York Times*/CBS News poll shows that Americans perceive drug trafficking as a more important international problem than arms control, terrorism, Palestinian unrest in Israel, or the situation in Central America. Another poll reports that Americans perceive stopping the drug dealings of anti-communist leaders in Central America as more important (by a vote of three to one) than fighting communism in the region. A third poll notes a public preference for U.S. government policies that reduce the supply of illicit drugs entering the United States over policies that focus on persuading Americans to stop using drugs. A *Wall Street Journal*/NBC News poll in September 1989 showed that Americans by a 58 percent to 34 percent margin favored sending troops to fight drug trafficking in Colombia if the government there requested them.[8]

Nevertheless, the State Department report is certainly correct if it means that the status quo is not in the long-term interests of the Latin American countries. At issue is not so much democracy as the deterioration and de-modernization of political and economic institutions. As U.S. Ambassador to Colombia Charles Gillespie recently remarked, "The traffickers have already penetrated the fabric of Colombian life. . . .[T]his penetration will lead not to the downfall of Colombia and its institutions but rather to a serious and lasting corruption."[9] Other political problems include the governments' weakening hold on their territories, their deteriorating reputation, and discrimination against their citizens and products.

Unfortunately, there may be no useful way to upgrade the war against cocaine that is not counterproductive. Virtually every prescription under discussion carries major disadvantages.

Enhancement of Drug-Fighting Capabilities in Producer Countries

Under this proposal, Andean governments would be provided with firepower, transport, communications, and intelligence support to establish their authority in drug-trafficking zones and destroy the cocaine industry's infrastructure. But the prevailing pattern of corruption in Andean countries makes many U.S. observers skeptical of the utility of such buildups. RAND economist Peter Reuter has suggested that better-equipped governments might mean no more than greater payoffs from the drug traffickers.[10]

Direct U.S. Military Intervention

The classic example of the approach was Operation Blast Furnace, the U.S. army-supported operation against cocaine laboratories in Bolivia in the summer of 1986. Blast Furnace was apparently a technical success since it virtually shut down the Bolivian cocaine trade for three months, but such operations can undermine the political legitimacy of host governments. All segments of Bolivia's political establishment condemned the government for inviting in American forces, and a leader with less stature than Victor Pas

Estenssoro probably could not have survived the political fallout. South American countries today do not want foreign military forces stationed in their territories. Sending in military units or even large numbers of armed Drug Enforcement Agency agents risk landing the United States in a Vietnam-type morass: an unpopular confrontation with a powerful and elusive enemy on the enemy's own turf.

Income Replacement

"If we are to make a difference in cocaine control," declares a Department of State report, "a massive infusion of economic assistance will be required."[11] Such assistance compensates countries for the economic and social costs of shutting down cocaine production. Possible measures include hard currency loans to compensate for the reduced flow of dollars and lowering import barriers for legitimate products, such as textiles and sugar.

But what about the hundreds of thousands of small farmers who cultivate coca? A coca farmer in the Bolivian Chapare can net up to $2,600 per hectare per year, over four times what he can earn from cultivating oranges and avocados, the next most profitable traditional crops. Thus crop substitution offers few attractions. The U.S. government is now indirectly paying $2,000 for each hectare of coca eradicated in Bolivia, but the Bolivian government estimates that the social costs of eradication—the cost of redirecting farmers into the licit agricultural economy—would be at least $7,000 per hectare. For Bolivia, where coca grows on 50,000 to 70,000 hectares, the cost of total eradication would be a mind-boggling $350 to $490 million. Even if the money were available, it might be misspent; there are persistent rumors that some coca farmers in the Upper Huallaga Valley and the Chapare have used the cash payments for eradication to underwrite the costs of planting new coca fields in other locations.

Sanctions

Perennially popular with Congress, this course of action includes withholding aid, prohibiting trade, cutting off international lending, and restricting the flow of travelers. Yet the record shows few cases where sanctions have achieved the desired objective. To cut off aid to the Andean countries would probably provoke intense anti-Yankee feelings, poison the diplomatic atmosphere, and reduce the resources available for anti-drug campaigns.

In addition, sanctions are a blunt instrument for specific problems. Thus, when Jorge Ochoa was released from a Colombian jail on December 30, 1987 (the second such release in sixteen months), the U.S. government singled out Colombian passengers and products for special customs checks at U.S. ports of entry. Yet the Colombian government had no jurisdiction over the criminal court judge who ordered Ochoa's release, and it had taken extraordinary measures to ensure that Ochoa could not escape from jail.

Hence, the U.S. sanctions were misplaced—they will not bring Ochoa back to jail, nor will they make Colombia's criminal justice system less porous. Worse, they doubtless added to the unpopularity of the war against drugs. As Carlos Mauro Hoyas, Colombia's recently murdered attorney general, remarked, "Reprisals against innocent tourists create anger and resentment as well as a sort of solidarity with the drug bosses, not as traffickers but as fellow Colombians."[12]

Negotiating Cutbacks in Drug Production

This approach requires a dialogue with the Escobars, the Ochoas, the Rodriguez Gachas, and the other chief executives of the cocaine industry. The idea of a dialogue has enormous public support in Colombia. Supporters include a number of distinguished figures: a former head of Colombia's State Council (the country's top administrative court), a former acting attorney general, two Catholic bishops (of Popayan and Pereira), the mayor of Medellin, the president of the Chamber of Representatives, and several congressmen and academics. An ABC/*Washington Post* poll released in February 1990 indicated that nearly six out of ten Colombians favor giving amnesty to drug traffickers if they abandon the drug traffic, free their hostages, and end the violence.[13] The traffickers themselves made a formal offer to the government in 1984—to withdraw from the cocaine industry, to dismantle their laboratories and airstrips, and to repatriate their capital. In return, they wanted guarantees against extradition, which would have amounted to a safe haven in Colombia. The Medellin mafia advanced similar peace initiatives in September 1988 and January 1990. The Colombian government has said officially that it will not negotiate with traffickers.

Certainly, selective amnesty arrangements for criminals can and have been tried as tools of law enforcement. (The United States has its own witness protection program, for example.) Cocaine chiefs could reveal much about the structure and operations of the international cocaine industry—its supply channels, distribution networks, personnel policies, financing, and the names of corrupt U.S. officials who abet the trade. They could also provide information about guerrilla operations, for the two often use the same territory, the same clandestine methods, the same smuggling channels, even the same overseas banks.

Yet it is hard to see how the proposal would work in practice. For example, monitoring an amnesty arrangement—the repatriation of capital and the shutting down of a multi-billion-dollar industry—would present fundamental problems. How many Colombian and American law enforcement officials would it take to oversee such a program, and who would monitor the monitors? Too, the traffickers might be unable to deliver on their promises. Is the cocaine industry so tightly structured that a few kingpins can command a larger number of lieutenants to order an even larger number of managers, suppliers, and transporters to withdraw from a business that earns so much? Possibly, but an amnesty might constitute little more than a retirement program for the chief executives of the cocaine industry. They would have to make a practical demonstration of their market power—say, by shutting down 80 percent of Colombian cocaine production for a six-month period. A negotiated settlement is at best a futuristic option. The idea has some theoretical merit, but it would be extremely difficult to implement.

These difficulties suggest that curbing the supply of cocaine from producer countries may not be effective, no matter how much money the United States government devotes to overseas programs.

Are there better ways to spend the U.S. drug-enforcement dollar? The options seem to be increased interdiction, stepped-up enforcement against drug dealers and pushers, and such demand-reduction steps as stiffer penalties for users, "Just Say No" programs, and drug testing. Many U.S. experts expect these measures also may not work very well. Moreover, as the national controversy over drug testing indicates, there are political and legal limits to controlling drug consumption, just as there are limits to controlling production in the Andean countries. Short of legalizing cocaine use (which carries the danger of stimulating even more addiction) or changing the habits and preferences of U.S. consumers, there seems to be no way out of the cocaine morass.

The solution, if there is one, lies not in the Andean jungles but in the United States. The six million people who now consume cocaine must be persuaded to change their habits and preferences. Perhaps they will grow tired of cocaine and switch to designer drugs; or perhaps they will find more productive and healthy forms of recreation.

NOTES

1. Quoted in *The New York Times*, April 12, 1988.
2. State Department, *International Narcotics Control Strategy Report* (Washington, D.C., Bureau of International Narcotics Matters, 1987), p. 24, hereafter INCSR; *New York Times*, March 2, 1990.
3. "Reactivación Economica por Dinero Caliente," *El Espectador*, October 3, 1987; "Directive del BCR del Peru Habla Sobre Narcodolares," *El Comercio*, October 8, 1987; *Washington Post*, July 17, 1986.
4. *Washington Post*, February 2, 1988, and ABC/*Washington Post*, Columbia Poll, February 8, 1990.
5. *The Washington Times*, June 8, 1988.
6. INCRS, March 1, 1988, pp. 8, 75, and 91, *New York Times*, June 28, 1988.
7. INCRS, 1988, p. 8.
8. Michael McQueen and David Shribman, "Battle Against Drugs Is Chief Issue Facing Nations," *The Wall Street Journal*, September 22, 1989, pp. A1, A14.
9. Quoted in *The Los Angeles Times*, February 21, 1988.
10. Congressional Research Service, *Combatting International Drug Cartels: Issues for U.S. Policy*, Report for the Caucus on International Narcotics Control, U.S. Senate (Washington, D.C.: Government Printing Office, 1987), p. 13.
11. INCSR, 1988, p. 8.
12. *New York Times*, January 13, 1988.
13. ABC/*Washington Post*, Colombia Poll, February 8, 1990.

Predicting State Response to Refugees

The Decision Logic of Receiving States

Glenn Hastedt
Kay Knickrehm

From the perspective of policymakers, the challenges to a state presented by a sudden and large-scale refugee flow are immediate, direct, and far-reaching. Contrary to the conventional wisdom of only a decade ago, refugee and migratory movements are not on the decline. The number of people involved in these flows has been relatively constant throughout the twentieth century, and the conditions most commonly associated with generating refugee flows and labor migrations show few signs of abating.

These movements directly challenge one of the most fundamental principles of sovereignty: that states decide whom to admit to their territory and under what conditions. Confronted with large numbers of individuals seeking entry into the state, policymakers have few viable options at their disposal. Admitting all who have arrived may invite economic chaos and social unrest. Refusing to permit entry to everyone may escalate regional tensions and bring pressure from other states to modify this policy. Selectively admitting certain refugees is a nonoption given the numbers involved, the short time frame for action, and the failure of this strategy when applied to labor migrations.[1]

The challenges have far-reaching consequences because of the need to balance the human rights concerns of the refugees with calculations of national security, economic well-being, and cultural integrity.[2] The cultural and economic identity of the refugee is of key importance in these calculations. No host state will readily allow its social order to be disrupted by the sudden influx of minority groups, nor does it wish to have domestic problems exacerbated by the influx of workers who cannot be readily absorbed into the economy.

Meeting these challenges will require not only great amounts of will and money but also a greater understanding of the underlying dynamics of refugee flows. A first step in developing such an understanding is to construct frameworks capable of performing two tasks: comparing refugee flows to one another and comparing refugee flows to other types of international flows (i.e., technology, capital, and information). In this essay, we employ such a framework to show that at least insofar as the response patterns of the receiving states are concerned, regularities can be identified that transcend the great diversity of detail and the complexity found in individual case studies. This framework is rooted in the literature of international relations theory and in the assumption that there are different issues in the field of world politics.

Figure 1 illustrates the decision-making paths and their consequences. The underlying logic of a state's response to a large-scale refugee flow depends on whether the problem is seen as involving or not involving national security concerns. Once the receiving state defines the flow as a national security issue, most other concerns become secondary. Another major factor concerns relations between the sending and receiving states. When relations are hostile, the refugees will be accepted regardless of the complexity of their individual motivations. They are seen as contributing to the receiving state's power equation, even if only symbolically. When the sending and receiving states have friendly or neutral relations, refugees are unlikely to be welcomed, particularly when there are significant regime similarities. The composition and causes of the flow become important, as well as the interests of international organizations, and the autonomy of state-level decision makers is reduced. In either instance, national security concerns remain paramount and make it extremely unlikley that a refugee regime can operate.

A Framework for Studying Refugee Flows

Ultimately it is the receiving state's response to the flow of refugees that establishes the conceptual boundaries for how the problem will be approached. Therefore, for constructing an issue area framework, the key definitions of the problem are those adopted by the receiving state. This initial definition establishes the parameters within which other variables operate.

The receiving state may define the refugee flow as a national security problem under a number of different conditions; however, the most likely situation (and the most tension-filled one) occurs when relations between the sending and receiving states are severely strained (Category I). In this case, the problem is likely to be approached from the traditional realist perspective on world politics, and the primary concern of policymakers will be with the impact of this flow on the state's power position. If the refugees are seen as

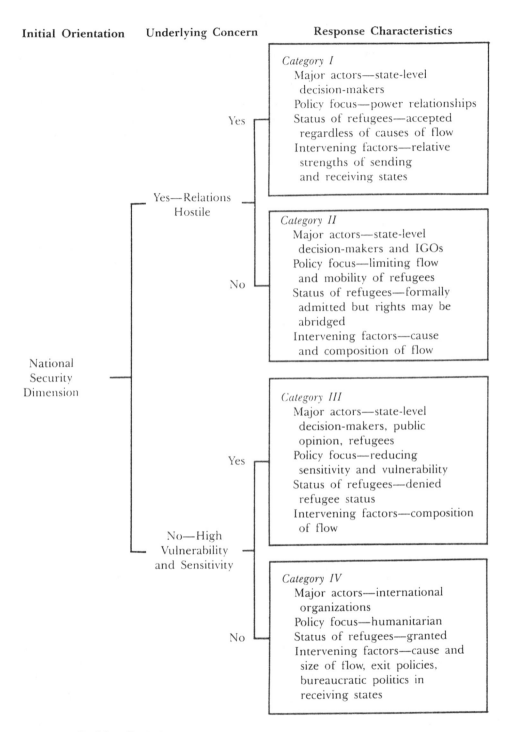

FIGURE 1. Decision Context.

contributing to the state's power base they will be accepted with little acrimony, regardless of such factors as the cause and composition of the flow, domestic variables like economic conditions and bureaucratic procedures, and so on. Refugees may increase a state's power in two ways. First, they may add to the state's military capabilities by increasing or augmenting the size of its military establishment. Second, their presence may make a powerful symbolic statement about the receiving state's foreign-policy goals and vision of its place in the international system. The sense of national purpose or resolve surrounding such a vision is an important ingredient in a state's power potential.

The bilateral bargaining process will be competitive and zero-sum in nature, and the relative power of the two states becomes an important consideration. If the power capabilities of the two states are grossly unequal, the dominant state will attempt to impose a solution if the opportunity presents itself. In this circumstance nonstate actors may assume relatively little importance. The United Nations High Commissioner for Refugees (UNHCR) will not be welcomed, and mediating efforts by regional organizations may be ignored. The more evenly matched the capabilities of the sending and receiving state, the greater the likelihood of stalemate. Power equality also increases the likelihood that third-party mediation, such as by the UNHCR, will take place.

In either instance policymakers will rely heavily on threats of punishment and offers of rewards. Little attention will be given to appeals to a common interest or shared visions of the world. Overall, the emphasis on power and the sense of threat make the probability of conflict in the short term greater here than in any of the other categories. Given the belief that the problem is important to national security, policymakers in the receiving state will be reluctant to surrender decision-making power, thus reducing the influence of nonstate actors and diminishing the impact of other variables such as the ethnic composition of the refugees, the domestic economy, and the interests of international organizations.

The sending and receiving states need not be hostile to each other for a national security orientation to take place, but the consequences will be different from those in Category I. When the sending and receiving states are friendly or at least neutral, the refugees themselves may be perceived as a threat to national security. This circumstance is particularly likely when the receiving state is suffering from or is threatened by significant internal unrest. Refugees from a friendly neighbor will often constitute a potentially subversive force in the receiving society when regime similarities exist between the sending and receiving states. When relationships between states are largely neutral, the refugees pose a danger to that neutrality if the sending state mounts attacks into refugee camps across the border. Under these conditions, the policymakers will attempt to restrict the entry of refugees. However, a number of factors limit the options of policymakers in this situation. An important consideration is the immediate cause of the refugee flow. According to international convention, a refugee is one who has fled a state for fear of political persecution. There are no special provisions or rights for labor migrants; those fleeing drought, famine, or natural disasters; or those fleeing a general condition of societal unrest. Difficulties arise from the fact that all refugee flows comprise individuals with a wide variety of motives. The overwhelming majority of refugees are politically passive. They are more likely to be caught up in events than they are to be autonomous actors making their way from one state to another.[3] Where borders are reasonably secure, the receiving state may confront the problem by refusing to grant refugee status and by turning back potential refugees. Where the refugees are the victims of war and borders are vulnerable, it becomes more difficult for the receiving state to classify the refugees as ordinary migrants. Here the influence of nonstate actors becomes more important. Because the refugees are unwelcome, international organizations, including the UNHCR, are likely to express an interest in their protection. In addition, the situation is likely to be complicated by the interests of other states in the region or by the superpowers, who may view the refugees as potential warriors for their own foreign policy objectives.

Although the potential for cooperation between states is higher here than in Category I and regional tensions may be reduced, the refugees are less likely to be treated well. There will be states who are reluctant to classify as refugees those fleeing a similar and/or friendly regime. Those denied protection face extradition to their homeland or must try to survive as illegal aliens. Once granted refugee status, the refugees may find the receiving state unable or unwilling to protect them. Guerillas who hide behind noncombatant refugees further imperil their situation, even where they have been granted refugee status, by exposing them to raids across borders and harassment by security forces in the receiving state.

When the receiving state does not perceive a national security dimension, the accompanying tensions will be approached from the perspective of interdependence (Category III) or a tragedy of the commons (Category IV). When the issue is bilateral, the interdependence perspective dominates. This perspective involves a recognition that military force will be of limited utility in gaining policy objectives. Furthermore, policymakers are seen as having limited control over events, and the events themselves are seen as being highly interconnected with other events. Two alternative strategies are open to the receiving state. It may attempt to link the refugee issue to other issues, thereby making trade-offs and compromises easier, or it may attempt to subdivide the issue into smaller problems in order to accomplish the same ends.

At least in the short run, the potential for cooperation is greater in Category III than in the other categories. In the absence of a we-they dichotomy, attention is more readily focused on the problem at hand and away from the identity of the sending state or the political orientation of the refugees. This view facilitates the task of reaching an agreement because it directs attention to the concrete aspects of the problem and away from the symbolic and transcendent dimensions.[4] However, the cooperation may be only short-lived if the negotiated solution is acceptable to the states involved but not necessarily to the refugees. If the conditions motivating the flow are left unaddressed, the flow may resume and be even more difficult to deal with, given the once-failed effort to cooperate on a solution.

When the problem is not defined in national security terms, the setting appears ideal for the operation of the type of humanitarian-oriented refugee regime commonly envisioned by observers. A key factor in the decision-making context is the degree of sensitivity and vulnerability to the refugee flow by the receiving state. Sensitivity refers to how quickly changes in one country bring about changes in another and how great the effects are. Vulnerability refers to the costs imposed on a state by external events. The two dimensions interact to place restraints on how long policymakers in the receiving state can pursue a negotiated solution and what types of concessions they are willing to make. The greater the sensitivity, the less time available to search for mutually acceptable alternatives. The greater the vulnerability, the greater the demands placed on the sending state for concessions.

The sending state has considerable leverage in the bargaining process. The limited utility of military force and the limited control that the receiving state has over events make its cooperation vital to a low-cost resolution of the problem. By pleading an inability to control the refugee flow or by demonstrating a willingness to manipulate it, the sending state is in a position to extract concessions from the receiving state. There are, however, inherent limits to such a strategy. Pressured by sensitivity and vulnerability considerations, the receiving state may redefine the problem so that it includes a national security dimension and seek to impose its will on the sending state. Such an eventuality is greatest when the underlying relations between the sending and receiving states are unfriendly. Under these conditions confrontation and posturing will dominate the negotiating process and prevent a settlement from being reached. The more amicable these relations are, the greater the reliance on economic, diplomatic, and humanitarian instruments in reaching an agreement. It must be stressed, however, that although an agreement will be easier to reach, it may not address the underlying problems that produced the refugee flow. Morrison notes that in most cases the linkage between U.S. economic instruments and migratory "push" factors are indirect; complex; and in the long run, weak.[5] Sensitivity and vulnerability considerations thus present a constant challenge to the effective operation of a refugee regime because it is how policymakers evaluate their presence or absence and not the origins of the refugee flow that determines a state's response in the absence of national security threat.

The bilateral dimension, when coupled with the absence of a national security orientation, makes Category III likely to yield a situation in which the receiving state has little control over events. Although high vulnerability and sensitivity may create pressures for a quick solution, circumstances prevent such a solution from being implemented.

When the receiving state does not define the flow in terms of national security considerations, and sensitivity and vulnerablity are low, a tragedy-of-the-commons approach to solving refugee-related tensions is produced. This approach is most likely to occur when the response to the flow is multilateral. In this case, the solution to the problem is pursued through a global or regional approach, in which all share responsibility for the resolution and in which all will be affected by the outcome. To the recognition of interdependence between states, found in Category III, is added the assumption that definitions of the national interest must be both forward looking and coupled with definitions of regional or global interest. Interdependence leaves open to policymakers the option of pursuing a zero-sum strategy in furthering state objectives. A tragedy-of-the-commons perspective does not. It necessitates a concern for common goals and a non–zero-sum view of the world.

A considerable amount of effort will be required in bargaining over definitions, rights, and responsibilities. At the same time, the absence of a threat suggests that the potential for cooperation is great. That this may be the case is supported by functionalist and neofunctionalist studies of integration, which show that the greatest strides toward upgrading definitions of the common interest are made in policy areas where concrete bargaining is possible and national security concerns are of secondary importance. However, the absence of a sense of threat may cause states to put forward only a token or minimal effort at meeting their commitments.

Past experience suggests that such efforts will barely be enough to meet the problem, will have little spillover effect, and may just postpone the ultimate resolution of the issue. Neither the League of Nations nor the United Nations has been particularly successful in attacking the root causes of large-scale refugee flows. They have pursued strategies of response rather than of anticipation and prevention. Each crisis is approached individually with an emphasis on the immediate needs of the refugees involved rather than on long-term solutions to the general causes of the problem.

The likely failure of the spaceship-earth solution raises the question of what to try next. While staying within the parameters of a tragedy-of-the commons view, the receiving state still has two options. The first is a lifeboat ethics solution in which the state attempts to shut off its borders and deny entry to all refugees. A second option is a policy of refugee triage, in which the receiving state accepts some refugees but determines who they are and on what grounds they will be admitted. It is important to stress that in advancing a response of either lifeboat ethics or refugee triage, policymakers still accept a tragedy-of-the-commons definition of the problem. These policies are being adopted because of the failure of the international community to respond in the necessary manner. The extent to which such policies succeed in reducing tensions or in meeting the needs of the refugees depends on factors largely beyond the control of the receiving state. If the flow is reduced or cut off, the policies may succeed as a sense of normality returns to the nature of interstate relations. If not, the receiving state may change its definition of the problem to include a national security dimension and/or to view it as a basically bilateral problem. In either case it would no longer view the refugee crisis as a tragedy-of-the-commons problem.

NOTES

1. G. Tapinos, "European Migration Patterns," in *United States Immigration and Refugee Policy*, ed. M. Kirtz (Lexington, MA: Lexington Books, 1983).
2. M. Teitelbaum, "Right vs. Right," *Foreign Affairs* 59 (1980): 21–59.
3. E. Kunz, "The Refugee, in Flight," *International Migration Review* 7 (1973): 125–46.
4. R. Mansbach and J. Vasquez, *In Search of Theory* (New York: Columbia University Press, 1981).
5. T. Morrison, "The Relationship of U.S. Aid, Trade and Investment to Migration Pressures in Sending Countries," *International Migration Review* 16 (1982): 4–26.

Chapter *12*

Forecasting the Future

No state wishes to go blindly into the future. Policymakers are well aware of the dangers inherent in confusing friend and foe, of becoming too closely tied to one state or alienated from another, and in choosing between a policy of self-sufficiency and one of dependence on foreign resources. Yet, regardless of their political ideology or level of economic development, foreign policy planning has never been a strong suit of states.

The early post–World War II experience of the United States is not atypical. Determined to be better prepared for the postwar era than they were for the start of World War II, policymakers established a long-term planning unit within the State Department and staffed it with highly skilled professionals. This strategy quickly proved its worth. The planning unit was responsible for such policies as the Marshall Plan for European economic recovery and NSC-68, which served as the blueprint for military rearmament after the start of the Korean War. It was not long, however, before long-range forecasting started to atrophy. Under the pressure of coping with major international problems on what seemed to be an almost daily basis, high-level policymakers began to place greater value on forecasting efforts that addressed their concrete, immediate policy problems and not those in the more distant future. They also came to feel that they could not afford to have some of their best analysts working on long-range problems when they were needed simply to get through current difficulties.

No matter how understandable it may be, however, a focus on the immediate future does not free policymakers from the need to think about the more distant future. And more is required than just collecting data, predicting events, and plotting trends. Policymakers have to understand why events are expected to unfold in a certain pattern and what will be its foreign policy consequences. Otherwise, efforts at forecasting the future amount to little more then fortune-telling. In looking to the future, analysts of world politics have been particularly concerned with three questions: (1) Why is it so hard to look into the future? (2) How does one go about constructing alternative world futures? (3) How can one do a better job of forecasting the future of world politics.

Surprise in World Politics

To be surprised is to be taken unawares. Surprise in world politics is rarely, if ever, total. The "bolt from the blue" military campaign is more the stuff of fiction than of reality. The calm of peace is not abruptly shattered by the onset of international violence. There is always some warning, so that military surprise becomes a matter of degree: when, where, why, or how the attack occurs. The United States knew that Japan was planning to launch an attack. The failure was to anticipate correctly where the attack would occur. American officials had concluded that the Philippines and not Pearl Harbor was the logical place for Japan to attack. In 1973 the Israelis possessed Egypt's war plans, yet they were caught unprepared when the Yom Kippur war broke out. Their plans called for an attack only after Egyptian forces would be able to control the air space over the battlefield. Correctly concluding that Egypt did not have such a capability, Israel discounted warnings that war was imminent. What Israeli leaders did not understand was that Egyptian President Anwar Sadat was so frustrated by the Middle East status quo that he was willing to fight a war that he might lose. The same holds true for diplomatic surprise. Nixon's 1971 televised announcement that he would be going to China startled the world. But had they been looking, analysts could have seen evidence of movement in this direction as early as Nixon's first inaugural address. In fact, Michael Handel asserts that there were at least 100 different warning signs or indicators pointing to this change in U.S. foreign policy.

A more detailed review of startling events—Hitler's attack on the Soviet Union in 1941, the 1967 Arab-Israeli war, the Ribbentrop-Molotov pact, Sadat's expulsion of Soviet military advisors from Egypt, the Soviet Union's invasions of Czechoslovakia and Afghanistan, the 1968 Tet offensive in Vietnam, the terrorists' attack on U.S. Marines in Beirut, the Chinese intervention into the Korean War, the Falkland/Malvinas Islands war between Argentina and Great Britain, the taking of U.S. hostages in Iran, and Iraq's attack on Kuwait—would reveal three other important points about surprise in world politics.

First, surprise itself is of very little importance. Given the complexity and number of events, it is not unexpected that policymakers are often caught off guard. Surprise only becomes significant for the conduct of world affairs when it negates the assumptions or premises on which important policies are based. For example, surprise acts to multiply military power. Estimates suggest that the combat capabilities of states that initiate a surprise attack are almost doubled and that the act of surprise can change the casualty rate in favor of the attacker from 1:1 to 5:1. A similar effect holds for diplomatic surprise. Nixon's trip to China fundamentally reoriented American foreign policy and changed the game of world politics from one of a bipolar struggle between the United States and the Soviet Union into a tripolar contest. Sadat's peace initiative to Israel did the same for the Middle East, as it could no longer be assumed that the Arab world would be united in its opposition to the existence of a Jewish state.

Second, surprise occurs despite warnings. Although it is common to blame intelligence failures, the problem often lies not with the collection of data or the construction of forecasts but with the inability or unwillingness of policymakers to respond to the information they are given. Barton Whaley notes in his account of Hitler's attack on the Soviet Union that Stalin "received more and better information on the approaching danger . . . than did any other leadership of an attacked country in the history of modern warfare." Others in Moscow shared his disbelief. As the invasion began, Soviet forces on the border alerted Moscow: "We are being fired upon. What shall we do?" Moscow responded, "You must be insane." Roberta Wohlstetter records that the U.S. response to news of Pearl Harbor was not much different. Secretary of the Navy Knox, on hearing of the attack, responded, "This can't be true . . . [it] must mean the Philippines."

The reason for this unwillingness to believe intelligence reports lies with the nature of the policy-making process and the ways in which intelligence organizations operate within it. It must be recognized that policymakers do not sit back and passively take in information. They interact with it, picking and choosing which pieces are relevant to their needs and which are not, and the most important perceptual filter is their immediate concerns and policy preoccupations. Concerned with stabilizing a government or bolstering a regime, policymakers become insensitive to warnings that the leaders they are dealing with are not as trustworthy as they would like them to be or that the resulting weapons flow is creating a very real security problem for neighboring states. This logic is being used to explain the Bush administration's failure to anticipate the actions of Iraq's Sadam Hussein. Contingency plans and a firm personal commitment to a given course of action can have the same blinding effect. Committed to stopping the spread of communism, U.S. policymakers needed little information to "see" communism in Third World revolutionary movements. Similarly, the complete confidence that American officials had in the ability of the Shah of Iran to survive skewed U.S. intelligence efforts. Analysts complained that "you couldn't give away intelligence on the Shah."

At times tunnel vision grows out of biases deeper than the attachment to a line of policy or preoccupation with a problem. It may also stem from a false set of starting assumptions that are widely held throughout the policy-making process and guide the formulation of policy. Examples are Israel's 1973 failure to anticipate Egypt's attack, the British belief that Argentina would not go to war over the Falkland/Malvinas Islands until negotiations failed, and the U.S. belief that North Korea would attack South Korea only as part of a more general conflict. One of the more telling consequences of this occurrence is to distort further intelligence-gathering and reporting efforts. In 1973 Israeli intelligence suppressed warnings of the upcoming attack because it was known that high-ranking officials rejected this interpretation of the data. The Soviet intelligence system hedged its reports on Hitler's preparations for an attack because it was known that Stalin believed these warnings to be provocations designed to lure Russia into war with Germany.

Finally, there is the problem of alert fatigue. Intelligence makes its impact through its ability to jolt policymakers out of their normal routine and to force them to realize that events are moving in an unexpected and dangerous direction. The problem is that it is quite possible to be overwarned. Individuals and organizations can not stay at high levels of alert indefinitely. The more often one is warned, the more accustomed one becomes to the situation. Repeated too often, the warning becomes routine, thereby negating the ability of intelligence to alert policymakers and bring about a creative response. Crying wolf is especially difficult to overcome in dealing with terrorism. One officer told the House committee investigating the terrorist attack on the Marines in Beirut, which killed 241 U.S. soldiers, "Since we have been here, we have, I think, counted a hundred car bomb threats." Another noted that once a threat was received regarding a blue Mercedes and added, "There are quite a few blue Mercedes in Lebanon."

Surprise is inevitable because of the difficulties involved in predicting future events and trends. In part this is a product of the inherent ambiguity of evidence. It is only with 20-20 hindsight that the difference between a signal and "noise," the natural background clutter of useless information, is clear. Major events do not come in neat packages. The closer one looks at the details of a terrorist attack, border skirmish, or diplomatic breakthrough, the more loose ends one encounters. On the eve of Pearl Harbor there was a great deal of evidence to support all of the wrong interpretations of the last-minute signals that were being received.

Added to the problem of noise are the actions of other states. Paradoxical as it may at first sound, success in warning can be indistinguishable from failure because the attacker always has the option of changing its plans. Warnings of an attack may therefore be correct even if no attack is forthcoming. Had Israel mobilized in October 1973 as it did in May, Sadat might not have attacked. Japanese plans called for aborting the attack on Pearl Harbor if its attack fleet was discovered. Indecision on the part of policymakers can similarly complicate an issue because of the contradictory signals that they send. On more than one occasion, contradictory diplomatic signals were sent by China to the Nixon administration because of conflicts within the Chinese Communist party.

Surprise presents policymakers with two problems as they look into the twenty-first century. First, with declining resources at their disposal, coping with the negative effects of surprise will be an even bigger problem than it was in the past, especially in the military area. No longer will policymakers be able to protect their states by having large standing armies capable of meeting every contingency. Flexibility rather than redundancy will be the key to successful planning. In turn, designing an effective flexible force is complicated by the general uncertainty that surrounds world politics at the present time. Second, because the nature of world politics is changing, policymakers need to be sensitive to new types of surprises. Until now the focus of research has been on diplomatic and military surprise. But in the twenty-first century it may be that environmental, economic, and technological surprises will hold the greatest potential for undermining critical policy assumptions.

Constructing Alternative World Futures

One of the major complaints of the study and practice of world politics is that it is too negative. The tendency is to take the status quo as a given and reject the possibility of major changes. Bureaucratic inertia, vested personal interests, domestic political pressures, and international system constraints are seen as conspiring to prevent much more than incremental change. All too often the favored solution to a stubborn international problem appears to be the resurrection of previous, and often failed, proposals. Generals fight the last war, and diplomats negotiate the last peace. Many analysts see a need to move beyond what presently exists—and perhaps even beyond what is possible—to what is desirable. For them the problem of looking into the future is not so much dealing with surprise as it is building a better international system, and doing so requires thinking about two questions: (1) What values do we want to see furthered? (2) How do we get there?

One set of answers is given by the World Order Models Project (WOMP), established in the early 1960s to find creative ways of educating people on the task of eliminating war as a social institution. The founders of WOMP felt that three factors were responsible for the lack of creative thinking about world politics. One was the belief that social science research should be value-free, a position WOMP believes is ethically misleading and politically and historically irrelevant. Strict empiricism is seen as leading only to descriptive accounts of the present global condition and relatively simple extrapolations of current trends into the future. The other two factors were an attachment to the nation-state as the unit of analysis and culture-bound thinking about world problems.

As it evolved over time, WOMP has come to identify four major global problems: war, poverty, social injustice, and environmental decay. In its view any desirable future world order must address these problems and promise hope of their elimination. Current thinking, with its acceptance of the state system and willingness to seek "peace" within it, is seen by WOMP as an inadequate response. As Richard Falk notes, moderation of interstate conflict tends to produce a toleration of poverty, repression, environmental decay, and inequality in world politics. Moreover, traditional state-oriented diplomatic solutions tend to displace and undermine visions of planetary unity and the interests of the global community.

It is not enough to identify values that need to be stressed or problems that need to be solved. It is also necessary to find methods of realizing those goals. In Falk's words it is important to identify "relevant utopias." Two types of global transformation to new world orders are possible, according to WOMP. The first involves the continued gradual evolution of the current world order, which WOMP contends is inadequate to meet the mounting challenges in the four strategic values. It argues for the adoption of a conscious reform strategy to move the world in the desired direction. At the heart of this strategy are what Falk refers to as "nonviolent options which not only encourage the presentation of demands for change but which also favor the implementation of a mandate for change." Included among these options are value change through education; the growth of pro–world order organizational activism; and institutional innovation at the community, regional, and global level that will encourage the growth of a new global consciousness.

This approach to a new world order is not the only possible way to proceed. In fact, WOMP fully expected to be the forerunner of other attempts to model new world orders, and many efforts have followed. Barry Hughes suggests that it is possible to categorize the writings of futurists by how they treat world development issues: population, economics, technology, raw materials, energy, and the environment. Hughes suggests that the two most important underlying dimensions of these writings are their approaches to political ecology and to political economy. The former is concerned with the relationship between people and their biological and physical surroundings. Hughes sees two different value approaches here: modernist and neotraditionalist. Modernists are convinced of humankind's ability to master the environment through the application of technology and rational thought. Neotraditionalists are skeptical of efforts to "solve" environmental problems and see the environment as fragile and easily destroyed.

Political economy involves the relationship between economic and political activity. Hughes sees three different value systems operating here. The first is classical liberalism, which holds that government intervention into the economy ought to be minimal and stresses the free market as the route to development. The second is internationalism, which sees the free market as an imperfect institution for dealing with development and urges government intervention to accelerate growth and break the poverty cycle. The third is the radical perspective, which sees free markets as a tool of domination and calls for Third World countries to break away from the capitalist system or change it through revolution.

As the radical perspective makes clear, nonviolence is not the only possible way to obtain a desired world future at either the international or the community level. Ethnic and religious groups have frequently turned to terrorism and other forms of violence in an effort either to bring down a government or to secure what they perceive to be denied human rights. Historically, violence played a central role in securing and protecting the rights of workers. Hitler sought to establish his vision of a future world order through both domestic and international violence of the most extreme kind. Most recently, the United States and its allies chose war over nonviolent means to defeat Iraq in the name of protecting and nurturing a new world order.

Forecasting the Future

For most of us there is an almost inescapable inclination to look back to the past for guidance when thinking about the future, and policymakers and analysts are no different. There is certainly nothing wrong in doing so. History has much to teach us about both the present and the future. However, studies have shown that policymakers tend to misuse history seriously in thinking about the future.

Four mistakes are particularly common. First, policymakers tend to focus almost exclusively on what occurred rather than why it occurred. What future policymakers will remember about the early 1990s is that Iraq invaded Kuwait, Yugoslavia succumbed to a bitter civil war, and a global environmental conference was held. But why these events took place will not be remembered with equal clarity.

Second, to the extent that policymakers do try to understand why events occurred, they tend to assume that important events have important causes. They feel that something as important as the collapse of the Soviet Union must have been brought about by equally important causes, and often they seek those causes in their own strategies and tactics. Little importance is given to the role of such largely invisible factors as standard operating procedures, bureaucratic ineptitude, careful staff work, or chance.

Third, the tendency is to project history into the future in a linear fashion, with no appreciation for the changed context of events. Because no Communist government had ever been overthrown, it was assumed by many conservatives that Communist governments could not and would not be overthrown in the future. Therefore, the only viable strategy for U.S. policymakers was to stop them from coming into power in the first place. Those who opposed the Vietnam war projected a similar historical straight line into the future, with the cry of no more Vietnams. At the tactical level this type of thinking results in an overattachment to successful policies and a total abandonment of failed ones. Because a policy has worked in the past, the assumption is that it will work in the future. In fact, the success of that policy may have been heavily dependent on circumstances that no longer exist, and a strategy that failed earlier may now be the correct one.

Fourth, the history we learn best appears to be the history we experience firsthand. The problem is that too much attention is paid to these events while the lessons of others are ignored. The lessons the United States has learned from Vietnam are the lessons of its experience there and not those of the French, who preceded it in defeat. The same holds true for the Soviet Union. By all accounts it failed to learn the proper lessons from Vietnam and walked blindly into its own Vietnam in Afghanistan.

Richard Neustadt and Ernest May are sensitive to the ways in which policymakers misuse history. They are also convinced that this need not be the case. Two of their proposals are worth noting because they are relatively simple and straightforward. First, one way of making better use of historical analogies in trying to solve current problems is to identify systematically the likenesses and differences in the two situations. For example, one of the most frequently employed analogies in US foreign policy is "Munich." The implied lessons speak to the dangers inherent in trying to appease a dictator (Hitler) bent on future conquests. The question Neustadt and May want policymakers to ask is "just how much is the situation today (in Korea, Vietnam, Iraq, etc.) like that in Munich in 1939 and how is it different?" Second, the evidence in front of policymakers should be divided into three categories: known, unknown, and presumed. Thus policymakers will be forced to reexamine the available information and it become more fully aware of where they are reaching for analogies and where they are operating on the basis of solidly held data.

Finally, we end with the question of what makes a good forecast. The immediate answer that comes to mind is accuracy. A good forecast is one that correctly predicts the future. Yet, is accuracy alone enough of a standard or even the proper standard for all cases? Accuracy in forecasting tends to improve the closer the future and the more routine the event. It is not hard to predict incremental change. The challenge is to be right about sudden and major departures from the norm and to be right for the correct reasons.

It can be said that accuracy is a poor measure of the worth of a forecast for the types of surprises that will be most disruptive to world affairs and to efforts to construct alternative world futures. The most valuable forecasts will describe the future environment in terms useful to policymakers and clarify their thinking about the future. Accuracy is certainly an important component of any attempt to clarify the future, but it is not the only one. A forecast that is wrong but that causes policymakers to reevaluate critically their core assumptions can be deemed successful. So, too, is one that provokes policymakers to think about problems or options in new terms.

The Readings

Each of these readings presents a different vantage point on the challenge of looking into the future. "Desert Storm and the Lessons of Learning," by Joseph Collins, a professional military officer, presents a practitioner's perspective on how to look for lessons from the Iraq War. "Will More Countries Become Democratic?," by Samuel Huntington, is concerned with domestic affairs and was written in the mid 1980s before the end of the cold war. The merits of Huntington's arguments can now be judged with reference to events in Russia, Eastern Europe, and the Third World. In contrast, "U.S. Security in a Separatist Season," by Stephen Cohen was written after the end of the cold war and is concerned with foreign policy. He examines the factors that are eating away at the legitimacy of the modern state and speculates on their larger implications for U.S. security. "The Global 2000 Report to the President," was written by a U.S. government commission. In his environmental message to Congress on May 23, 1977, President Jimmy Carter directed the Council on Economic Quality and the Department of State to work together with other federal agencies to draft a report on the "probable changes in the world's population, natural resources, and environment through the end of the century" in order to provide a "foundation. . .[for] longer-term planning."

Bibliography

ASCHER, WILLIAM. *Forecasting: An Appraisal for Policy-Makers and Planners*. Baltimore: Johns Hopkins University Press, 1978.

BERES, LOUIS, and HARRY TARG. *Reordering the Planet: Constructing Alternative World Futures*. Boston: Allyn Bacon, 1974.

BETTS, RICHARD. *Surprise Attack: Lessons for Defense Planning*. Washington, DC: Brookings Institution, 1982.

CHOURCRI, NAZLI, and THOMAS ROBINSON. *Fore-*

casting in International Relations. San Francisco: Freeman, 1978.

FALK, RICHARD. *A Study of Future Worlds*. New York: Free Press, 1975.

HANDEL, MICHAEL. *The Diplomacy of Surprise: Hitler, Nixon, Sadat*. Cambridge, MA: Center for International Affairs, Harvard University, 1981.

HUGHES, BARRY. *World Futures: A Critical Analysis of Alternatives*. Baltimore: Johns Hopkins University Press, 1985.

JERVIS, ROBERT. *Perception and Misperception in International Politics*. Princeton, NJ: Princeton University Press, 1976.

KOTHARI, RAJNI. *Footsteps into the Future: Diagnosis of the Present World and a Design for an Alternative*. New York: Free Press, 1974.

MAY, ERNEST. *"Lessons" of the Past: The Use and Misuse of History in American Foreign Policy*. New York: Oxford University Press, 1973.

NEUSTADT, RICHARD, and ERNEST MAY. *Thinking in Time: The Uses of History for Decision Makers*. New York: Free Press, 1986.

WHALEY, BARTON. *Codeword BARBAROSA*. Cambridge, MA: MIT Press, 1973.

WOHLSTETTER, ROBERTA. *Pearl Harbor: Warning and Decision*. Stanford, CA: Stanford University Press, 1962.

ZIMMERMANN, WALTER, and ROBERT AXELROD. "The 'Lessons' of Vietnam and Soviet Foreign Policy." *World Politics* 34 (1981), 1–24.

Desert Storm
and the Lessons of Learning

Joseph J. Collins

Desert Storm promises to rank with "1914," "Munich," and "Vietnam" as a powerful source of lessons for policymakers. Our involvement began with a clear-cut case of Iraqi aggression, followed by a million-soldier conflict. It ended in a decisive military victory for the US-led Coalition. The war was media-intensive, and, along with the events that followed, it had wide-ranging political consequences, some of which are still taking shape. Burned into our collective consciousness, Desert Storm will, for better or worse, be a benchmark for future US defense policy and military art.

It is axiomatic that those who fail to heed the lessons of history are doomed to repeat its follies. However, the sages rarely remind us how difficult this learning process is. A full disclosure would show that decision makers, uniformed and civilian, often fail to learn effectively from experience. Their mistakes range from costly to catastrophic.

Complex operations like Desert Shield and Desert Storm will require careful evaluation, not only in light of what happened there, but also in light of what we know about learning from war. Five observations, informed by interpretive history and the emerging literature about Desert Storm, will move us toward that end.

■ *First, accurate and timely lessons count, but even concerted effort is no guarantee of success in learning them.*

Reprinted from *Parameters* (July/August 1992). © *1992 Joseph J. Collins.*

In postwar eras, learning failures have been frequent and costly. Three types of learning failures are common: linear projection, in which the future is seen as a direct extrapolation from events of the past; hasty, ill-considered adaptations; and fixation on past individual or national successes.

The much-belittled generals who have prepared to fight the last war are familiar figures. In varying degrees, they all projected the future as a linear development from a key event in the past. Before World War I, European military leaders misjudged the balance between offensive and defensive combat, believing that short, decisive wars—like the Franco-Prussian War—would be the norm. Frontal assaults, profligate slaughter, and four years of destructive trench warfare were the result of these and other misjudgments. Had European leaders correctly estimated the battlefield effects of their weaponry, they might have used better military judgment in the war. Perhaps if they had understood the paralyzing advantages of the defense and the high casualties inherent in offensives, they might have avoided war altogether.

Astoundingly, despite considerable effort on its part, France made a reciprocal error in the interwar years. Based on its experience in World War I, it overemphasized the power of the defense. Although France took account of mechanization, its "new weapons essentially remained tied to old ideas." With a force equivalent to Germany's in size and in number of weapon systems, France and its allies were defeated in six weeks by an army with more refined concepts and a better sense of the possible.[1]

In a similar vein, there have been instances in which overzealous leaders have hastily seized on incorrect lessons of the recent past and later paid a stiff price for their mistake. For example, in 1939, Stalin—having purged many of his armor experts—concluded, based on the experience of the Spanish Civil War and the control problems his tank formations experienced in Poland, that large tank formations were unwieldy and ineffective. He ordered the immediate reorganization of his embryonic tank corps into smaller units for infantry support. After Germany's successful blitzkrieg in France, Stalin changed his mind, but it was too late. In June 1941, the Soviet army was caught between organizational designs. The rest, as they say, is history.

Professor Robert Jervis reminds us that past success can also be the cause of future failure. As though blinded after a brilliant flash of light, leaders tend to see current situations as resembling those of past policy successes. Dazzled by their own statesmanship or the nation's good fortune, they overestimate the degree to which national policy was central to success and apply a previously successful policy to changed circumstances.

Jervis notes, for example, that in 1941 Japan believed it could fight a limited war with the United States because it had done so 36 years previously with Czarist Russia. A successful covert operation in Guatemala in 1954 inspired 1961's Bay of Pigs fiasco. Norway thought it could stay out of World War II because it had successfully remained neutral in World War I.[2] Other analysts have noted the discomfiting role that Soviet success in Czechoslovakia in 1968 played in their invasion of Afghanistan in 1980.[3]

In the case of Desert Storm, Saddam's strategy was to absorb the effects of our air attack and inflict great casualties on the Coalition on the ground, where he believed he held a comparative advantage. An attempt to widen the war by missile strikes on Israel would further threaten the Coalition and add to the carnage. He apparently believed that the Western public would quickly demand an end to a highly destructive war, leaving Saddam with at least part of Kuwait and, more important, the scepter of Arab leadership.

Drawing on the legacy of his recent victory over Iran to accomplish these ends, Saddam Hussein deployed his forces in Kuwait in an inflexible manner, with immobile front-line infantry units dug in as if they were waiting for an Iranian frontal assault. They were backed by only slightly more flexible counterattack forces. Iraq's poor intelligence and inflexibility transformed tactics that had worked well against Iran on Iraqi territory into a catastrophic failure when they were used to counter a more mobile Coalition in Kuwait.

The causes of all of these failures to learn effectively are as varied as the cases: stupidity, poor information, misperception, the stress of time, organizational predilections, politics, and inflexible or inaccurate military doctrine. Historian Jay Luvaas made a comment seven years ago which serves as an apt warning to those who would know and apply the lessons of Desert Storm:

> We should understand the reasons why military men in the past have failed sometimes to heed the correct lessons. Often, it has been the result of an inability to understand local conditions or to accept another army or society on its own terms. Sometimes, the guidance to observers has been so specific that the major lessons of war went unheeded simply because observers had not been instructed to look in different directions. . . . Sometimes, doctrine has narrowed the vision or directed the search, as in the case of the French army after World War I. Often, there has been a failure to appreciate that once removed from its unique context, a specific lesson loses much of its usefulness.[4]

■ *Second, the lessons one learns are influenced—for better or worse—by interests, ideology, and perception.*

What's good for the goose may seem foul to the gander. Consider the lessons of Vietnam and their effect on Soviet policy toward Afghanistan. Two experienced US analysts concluded that while the lessons the United States drew from Vietnam would have counseled restraint by the USSR in Afghanistan, "the lessons the Soviets drew . . . did not warn them of the dangers of such an intervention by Soviet forces. On the contrary, the frequent assertion that aid from the Soviet Union and other socialist countries had been important in Vietnam may have increased their propensity to intervene in Afghanistan."[5]

Different countries may draw different lessons from Desert Storm. Some may believe that if they step out of line, the world policeman will arrest them. Others may step up their efforts to develop military power for their own purpose or to compete with the United States. In that light, the effect of Desert Storm on China and the states of the former Soviet Union should be carefully weighed.

The Russian military will have a strong incentive to learn from Desert Storm. The war was the general staff's worst nightmare: the revolution in military affairs (which they had talked about for over a decade) arrived while they were preoccupied with domestic matters and years behind in some conventional technologies. Russian experts might perceive that the Gorbachev-era doctrine of "reasonable sufficiency," which relies on a stiff defense followed by a counterattack, is outmoded after Desert Storm. Accordingly, a reinvigorated general staff might, some years hence, return to more offensive operational concepts, a traditional bias. While the military's defense of the quality of the weapons provided by the USSR to Iraq often appeared hollow and self-serving, real concerns could, in the long term, push more resources into the research and development accounts to improve air defense and continue development of their "reconnaissance-strike complexes" (space-based reconnaissance, surveillance, and target-acquisition systems linked in real time to long-range strike means). In all, based on "their" lessons from Desert Storm, we may expect a long-term effort from aspiring world powers to redress US advantages in military power. One of these powers will surely be the entity that we now hesitatingly call Russia.[6]

Other states may also attempt to change the security calculus in a given region by improving their forces and weapon inventories. It is a safe bet that trends in the proliferation of nuclear, chemical, and biological weapons will continue or accelerate. The Department of Defense estimates that by the year 2000, 15 developing nations will have a ballistic missile capability; eight of these nations may also be nuclear-capable. Thirty nations may have chemical weapons; ten may have biological weapons. More than a dozen developing nations already possess large and capable armored forces. Other potential opponents, noting US superiority in conventional warfare, may hone their skills in insurgency or other forms of low-intensity conflict. In brief, there will be as many sets of Desert Storm lessons as there are learners. We need to be aware of both "our" lessons and "their" lessons.

■ *Third, technology-inspired lessons from a single war are likely to have a very short life, and a single war will seldom prove the long-term utility of any branch of service or component of the force.*

Tracing the development and use of weapon systems and forces across a few wars permits useful observations. In Israel's Six Day War of 1967, the tank-fighter combination was king. However, in the Yom Kippur War in 1973, air defense and antitank guided missiles provided a serious challenge to their opposing systems. In 1973, to meet the new threat, the Israeli Defense Forces needed more infantrymen, mortars, and armored personnel carriers, all of which had been downplayed after 1967. In 1982 in

Lebanon, the fighter aircraft, aided by drones and electronic warfare equipment, soundly defeated air defense systems. In Desert Storm, the stealth fighter, precision-guided munitions, and the attack helicopter became key variables in both the air war and the armor battle. They also soundly defeated Iraqi air defenses.

In the tanker war in the Persian Gulf, surface naval vessels carried the day, but in Desert Storm, except for their yeoman work on the blockade and their use as cruise missile platforms, they were less important. In the past, the Navy's carrier-based fighters have often been the only air support for US forces in Third World contingencies. In Desert Storm, they were an adjunct to the more numerous and better-equipped Air Force fighters. Neither of these combat air elements played a decisive role in Urgent Fury (Grenada) or Just Cause (Panama), but land-based air was the principal weapon for almost 90 percent of Desert Storm. Eight Army and two Marine divisions—overall, a relatively large and heavy land force—carried the 100-hour land battle. Unlike in Grenada, the Marines did not make an amphibious landing, although the existence of that capability created an effective deception, keeping at least six Iraqi divisions oriented on the coastal defense mission.

These cases exemplify no easily discernible pattern or trend. Even holding the human factor constant, one war's experience with forces and weapon systems is an imprecise guide to the course of the next conflict. The utility of a particular service or branch has varied with the character of a particular war. Moreover, weapon-system lessons from today's war may be barely applicable to tomorrow's. Next month you may have to make significant changes; by next year the changes may be extreme, even if you happen to be in the same theater.

Thus, while Desert Storm demonstrated the value of the stealth fighter and the need for real-time reconnaissance and strike assets for use against relocatable targets like the SCUD missile, it did not, by itself, make a convincing case for the stealth bomber or any particular stealth fighter. The Patriot missile's success against the SCUD did not justify any particular SDI system, although it did point out the need for theater protection against an ever-growing arsenal of ballistic missiles. In a similar vein, Desert Storm alone cannot justify a greater (or lesser) role for any of the services or any of their primary conventional capabilities.

Overall, success in past battles is only one input in the development of weapon systems and the design of forces. Technological possibilities, threat capabilities, and doctrine will also play key roles. If anything, the wars discussed above suggest that no one can safely predict which of the services will be the centerpiece of the next conflict, pointing toward the necessity of a balanced force and robust unified commands, fully capable of tailoring and employing the forces needed.

Finally, analysts should be aware that the efficacy of various weapon systems or major force components may change drastically, even within the same war. While this was not a factor in Desert Storm, it is an important issue for both lesson-learners and lesson-appliers. One clear example of this phenomenon was General MacArthur's use of strategic air power. In World War II, MacArthur, poor in ground forces, used long-range bombers to great effect against the Japanese. In 1950, he used them with marked success against relatively heavy North Korean formations and later predicted great success if Chinese formations were to intervene. However, he failed to understand that strategic air power would not be equally effective against the lighter, more flexible, night-moving Chinese People's Liberation Army. The Eighth Army and X Corps paid for his miscalculation.[7]

■ *Fourth, learning about war is complicated by the human factor, which includes the state of unit and individual training, as well as other intangibles such as individual morale, esprit de corps, and discipline.*

The experience of modern wars suggests that human factors are more powerful than technology. (In that light, we can only applaud DOD's fierce defense over the last decade of expenditures for the recruitment and retention of quality personnel, the sine qua non of military power.) Moreover, it is particularly hard to separate technological considerations from their human aspects. On this issue, the findings of the Center for Strategic and International Studies in its report, *The Gulf War: Military Lessons Learned,* appear sound: "High technology weapons and military systems are useless in the abstract. . . . US investment strategy must reflect that international coalitions, training, strategy, and other factors are just as important to winning wars as expensive weapons."[8]

These seemingly obvious facts may well be disputed in years to come. The advocates of high-technology weapon systems have already begun to overstate the benefits of such weapons. For example, former Under Secretary of Defense William Perry, writing in *Foreign Affairs,* claimed:

> In Operation Desert Storm the United States employed for the first time a new class of military systems that gave American forces a revolutionary advance in military capability. Key to this capability is a new generation of military support systems—intelligence sensors, defense suppression systems, and precision guidance subsystems—that serve as "force multipliers" by increasing the effectiveness of US weapon systems. An army with such technology has an overwhelming advantage over an army without it, much as an army equipped with tanks would overwhelm an army with horse cavalry.[9]

Dr. Perry also asserts that we can now pursue a purely conventional deterrent against conventional aggression in Europe and Korea and that our advantage in military technology is mainly responsible for our "thousand-to-one" performance advantage in fighting Iraqi forces.

While Dr. Perry richly deserves an opportunity to salute the systems that he played such a key role in developing, past wars as well as Desert Storm suggest that his conclusions are, at best, incomplete. First, while an army with tanks might well "overwhelm an army with horse cavalry," poorly equipped conventional forces (e.g. Israel in 1948, Chad versus Libya in 1987) have defeated those with vast technological or force advantages. Also, the possession of radically advanced systems is by itself no guarantee of victory. The V2 and the world's first jet fighter couldn't save Hitler. Soviet tanks and attack helicopters failed to provided the edge in Afghanistan. In low-intensity conflict, use of intangible strengths to thwart technological prowess has made peoples' war an effective alternative to matching the great powers in the area of high-tech weapons. Recall that the American technological edge over the Viet Cong and North Vietnam was far more pronounced than that enjoyed over the Iraqis; yet the United States lost the Vietnam War.

Were Dr. Perry's observations completely accurate, quality conventional forces might exert a stronger deterrent power than they do. Up to now, the most remarkable aspect of purely conventional deterrence has been the frequency with which it has failed, including, most recently, in Kuwait. We can hope that Desert Storm has changed that, but we can't bet the national interest on it, especially since potential aggressors may perceive today's high-technology weapons as less overwhelmingly punishing than their area-weapon predecessors. Compare the widespread destruction from strategic bombing in Europe in World War II with the relatively small damage produced by precision-guided munitions in Baghdad. Future opponents may well accept the risk of surgical strikes if they believe carpet bombing to be improbable.

Dr. Perry's dramatic conclusions are based on a unique and somewhat unusual case. Although he does mention some environmental factors, his analysis of intelligence adjuncts, defense-suppression systems, and precision-guided munitions falls short of an integrated view of this particular conflict. He does not consider the linkage of soldiers and machines to doctrinal concepts, nor does he estimate the effects of other factors, such as the quality of Coalition strategy. In short, we cannot evaluate high technology as an isolated variable. Analysts need more cases—especially ones involving more even matches—before we can draw measured conclusions about the awesome capabilities of today's weapons, as well any newly found deterrent capability they might possess.

Analyzing the human factor is also essential for understanding how thoroughly our attack debilitated the enemy forces. For example, it is difficult to overestimate the psychological disorientation and lack of agility in Iraqi command echelons. It would, in more than a few instances, be hard to overestimate the extent and effect of Iraqi incompetence. In part from the Coalition's excellent deception plan and in part from Iraqi inadequacies, the fog of war covered and mystified Iraqi command elements. A force that fought well when it faced a less capable foe on a more predictable battlefield virtually came apart when confronted by a first-class opponent. One example speaks volumes: the senior Iraqi officers who surrendered to General Schwarzkopf had no idea how many Iraqi prisoners the Coalition held, nor could they believe an accurate trace of US forward positions which were behind what they thought were Iraqi "lines."[10]

With examples like this in plentiful supply, we must exercise great caution in making definitive judgments about the effects of our high-technology weapons.

■ *Fifth, every outcome of war is environmentally conditioned.*

War outcomes are affected by environmental factors. Here we use "environment" not just in the sense of geographical and climatic factors, but rather to signify the broad battlefield milieu, the innumerable surrounding conditions under which the tasks of war are accomplished. For example, among the most telling conditions for the great victory in the Desert Storm air war were these: lopsided US technological and skill advantages; open desert terrain; blind and unsynchronized Iraqi air defenses; an inadequate number of air defense weapons and launchers; and an enemy air force that did not fight. Given similar conditions, we can confidently predict success in any future air war! Of course, if you vary these conditions, you vary the degree of difficulty our pilots will face and the degree of success they will achieve.

In its first report on the war, *Conduct of the Persian Gulf Conflict: An Interim Report to the Congress*, the Department of Defense emphasizes environmental conditions for understanding war outcomes. As Secretary Cheney notes in the introduction:

> This war, like every other, was unique. We benefited greatly from certain of its features—such as the long interval to deploy and prepare our forces—that we cannot count on in the future. We benefited from our enemy's near-total international isolation. . . . We received ample support from the nations that hosted our forces and relied on a well-developed coastal infrastructure. . . . And we fought in a unique desert environment. . . . Enemy forces were fielded largely in terrain ideally suited to armor and air power and largely free of noncombatant civilians.[11]

Rarely have we had such a cooperative enemy, one who failed to attempt to stop our methodical buildup, even when a few brigade-sized armored raids could have had significant effects on our initial force deployment. His failure to use chemical weapons made our task easier. Finally, in the early stages of the conflict, Saddam's air force, inexperienced though it was, could have mounted token resistance, but he sent them to a sanctuary on the territory of his former arch-enemy. Such behaviors, to say the least, add to the uniqueness of this conflict and point to the need for experts on political culture and aberrant psychology to play a role in determining what lessons can be drawn from it.

Although large and impressive, Desert Storm was not an all-encompassing case, nor is it one that should, in isolation, be used to radically alter US force structure or budget priorities. Clearly, US forces—even when oriented on regional contingencies—must be prepared for operations across a wide spectrum of potential conflicts. Indeed, some analysts think that low-intensity conflict is a much more likely model for future US engagement than is mid-intensity warfare. A few even believe that our success in Desert Storm will encourage opponents to opt for other methods, such as terrorism and insurgency. Regarding the higher-intensity end of the spectrum, Secretary Cheney reminded us that the tasks of future war might well be more challenging than those of Desert Storm:

> We should also remember that much of our military capability was not tested in Operations Desert Shield and Desert Storm. There was no submarine threat. Ships did not face significant anti-surface action. We had little fear that our forces. . . would be attacked on their way to the region. There was no effective attack by aircraft. . . . Chemical warfare and biological warfare. . . were never employed. American amphibious capabilities. . . were not tested on a large scale under fire. Our Army did not have to fight for long. Saddam Hussein's missiles were inaccurate. As such, much of what was tested needs to be viewed in the context of the unique environment and conflict we are addressing.[12]

Conclusions

At this point in its evaluation, the Department of Defense has articulated the most obvious lessons of Desert Storm, those that it assumes will be most useful for determining the outline of future defense policy. The DOD report concludes that "five general lessons stand out":

- Decisive presidential leadership set clear goals, gave others confidence in America's sense of purpose, and rallied the domestic and international support necessary to reach those goals;
- A revolutionary new generation of high-technology weapons, combined with innovative and effective doctrine, gave our forces the edge;
- The high quality of our military, from its skilled commanders to the highly ready, well-trained, brave, and disciplined men and women of the US armed forces, made an extraordinary victory possible;
- In a highly uncertain world, sound planning, forces in forward areas, and strategic air and sea lift are critical for developing the confidence, capabilities, international cooperation, and reach needed in times of trouble;
- It takes a long time to build the high-quality forces and systems that gave us success.[13]

These lessons, even allowing for their self-congratulatory tone, are a useful start point for the detailed, multilevel analysis that must be conducted over the next few years by the services, the Joint Staff, and the theater commands. With a new strategy oriented on regional conflict, the US defense establishment must examine in detail a number of issues: campaign planning, anti-missile tactics, defense against chemical attack, and fratricide. The use of reserve forces to support rapid deployments in response to regional conflicts, the issue of women in combat, and our national and theater capability for the production of military intelligence also require careful attention. Similarly,

Desert Storm has particularly valuable implications for coalition formation, the use of economic blockades, combined war funding, the role of the United Nations in regional conflicts, war termination, and post-conflict humanitarian operations. The war may offer no surefire lessons on coordinating policies for arms control and arms sales, but speculation will abound on these issues, and they too must be analyzed.

Desert Storm was a vivid reminder that we must also pay more attention to strategic lift. For example, James Blackwell of the Center for Strategic and International Studies here details our national sealift problem during the prelude to the war:

> The Navy had only eight fast sealift ships that were capable of rapidly loading tanks and armored personnel carriers. . . . These were designated to go to Savannah, Georgia, to load out the 24th Infantry Division and could steam to the Persian Gulf in about ten days. But some of the ships were slow to get to port, and once loaded, two of them broke down en route. . . . One of the fast sealift ships, in fact, took so long to repair that it arrived after the slow boats.

The Ready Reserve Fleet of smaller, slower ships fared even worse:

> Only 21 percent of the 98 ships in the reserve fleet were ready on time, and 60 percent showed up as much as ten days late during the first month of the deployment. Only 73 ships were able to be readied for service during Desert Shield, forcing the Transportation Command to rely on chartering commercial ships to make up the shortfall in shipping requirements.[14]

In the future, we will have a smaller force, based in the continental United States. We may not have the luxury of a six-month buildup to respond effectively to a regional contingency. We will need reliable air and sea lift, better (though not necessarily in larger quantities) than what we had available for Desert Storm, a model in scale and complexity for the regional conflicts that we'll have to be ready for. Decisions on lift should not be service decisions alone because the problem is interagency in nature and strategic in its effects. Future decisions about strategic air and sea lift require the closest scrutiny by the National Command Authorities.

To develop and disseminate lessons learned, analysis must center not only on input from Desert Storm itself, but also upon the methodology of historical assimilation, that is, upon a sound system for mastering the intricacies of learning from history as well as integrating the resulting lessons into future policy and training efforts. This is far easier said than done. Soldiers in the field will look for simple, easy-to-apply lessons, scholars will favor nuance, and politicians may opt for bumper stickers. Clearly, we could get lost in a thicket of lessons drawn for various purposes and audiences.

Some key consumers, like the Army's National Training Center, should become laboratories to ensure that tactical lessons are tested and remembered. John Gooch and Eliot Cohen suggest the need for "an institutional locus for applied historical study" to facilitate learning. They further suggest: "Military organizations should inculcate in their members a relentless empiricism, a disdain for a priori theorizing if they are to succeed. The 'learners' in military organizations must cultivate the temperament of the historian, the detective, or the journalist rather than the theoretical bent of the social scientist or philosopher."[15]

Given the particular difficulty of learning from success, our Desert Storm learners might do well to study specifically how other complex organizations have done it effectively. While learning must also encompass political and strategic lessons, one interesting case of tactical and operational application was documented in Williamson Murray's study of the German military's efforts to learn from their success in Poland in 1939 the wherewithal to prepare for their invasion of France in 1940. This learning exercise was comprehensive, painfully frank, and usefully integrated into German training programs for newly organized units. Murray noted that "the higher the headquarters, the more demanding and dissatisfied were commanders with operational performance." Command emphasis was to expose, not to paper-over, mistakes. Learning, not blame, was the focus.[16]

In short, institutional integrity enabled the German army to improve on success and not be blinded by it. Their newly mobilized units entered battle with France and Britain having been trained by combat veterans and schooled in the lessons of Poland. Of course, the professionalism of the German army did not, by itself, lead to strategic or political wisdom. Germany's battlefield successes no doubt encouraged Hitler's strategic blunders. That too bears some reflection.

Finally, those who attempt to learn from Desert Storm must be aware that history does not teach, it enlightens, not with the searchlight of maxims, but with the reflected glow of analogies. The art of learning from experience begins with understanding linkages and the conditions under which events took place. At the highest level, the application of this knowledge—be it by soldiers or civilians—must be done in a comparative framework, guided by a rigorous skepticism, and ever mindful of the dominant role played by a human opponent who may choose to play by different rules than our own. As Jay Luvaas has noted, "insight gained" might be a more appropriate term than "lessons learned."

The future of the US armed forces is in the hands of those who must reconcile a rapidly changing strategy, a shifting strategic environment, and a shrinking resource base with the lessons of Desert Storm and other recent military operations. At stake is the fate not only of the best armed forces we have ever had, but, more important, of the nation and its preparedness to meet unforeseen contingencies that may or may not resemble Desert Storm. To meet the storms of the future in all their infinite variety, our leaders will require the wisdom of Solomon, as well as a sound understanding of where that wisdom came from and what its limitations are.

NOTES

1. The quotation is from Robert Doughty, *The Seeds of Disaster: The Development of French Army Doctrine, 1919–1939* (Hamden, Conn.: Archon Books, 1985), p. 11. For historical material concerning the world wars, see Jack Snyder, *The Ideology of the Offensive: Military Decision Making and the Disasters of 1914* (Ithaca, N.Y.: Cornell Univ. Press, 1984), especially pp. 9–40 and 99–205; and Barry R. Posen, *The Sources of Military Doctrine: France, Britain, and Germany Between the World Wars* (Ithaca, N.Y.: Cornell Univ. Press, 1984) especially pp. 7–80 and 220–224. On the subject of how decision makers learn, see Ernest R. May, *"Lessons" of the Past: the Use and Misuse of History in American Foreign Policy* (New York: Oxford Univ. Press, 1973), especially pp. ix–xiv. For a practical guide for using history in decision making, see Richard E. Neustadt and Ernest R. May, *Thinking in Time: The Use of History for Decision Makers* (New York: Free Press, 1986), pp. 252–270.

2. Robert Jervis, *Perception and Misperception in International Politics* (Princeton, NJ: Princeton Univ. Press, 1976), pp. 217–282.

3. Joseph Collins, *The Soviet Invasion of Afghanistan: A Study in the Use of Force in Soviet Foreign Policy* (Lexington, Mass.: Lexington Books, 1986), pp. 77, 81.

4. Jay Luvaas, "Lessons and Lessons Learned: A Historical Perspective," in Robert E. Harkavy and Stephanie G. Neuman, eds., *The Lessons of Recent Wars in the Third World: Approaches and Case Studies, Volume I* (Lexington, Mass.: Lexington Books, 1985), p. 68.

5. William Zimmerman and Robert Axelrod, "The Lessons of Vietnam and Soviet Foreign Policy," *World Politics*, 34 (October 1981): 19–20.

6. For an early look at the Russian/Commonwealth reaction, see Stephen J. Blank, *The Soviet Military Views Desert Storm* (Carlisle Barracks, Pa.: Strategic Studies Institute, 1991), especially pp. 20–26. The author's use of the terms "Russia" and "Russian" in the text does not mean to suggest that he rules out a commonwealth-level reaction. Rather, it was felt that "Russian" more clearly described the most probable focus of activity, as well as the nationality of the relevant strategic culture.

7. Eliot A. Cohen and John Gooch, *Military Misfortunes: The Anatomy of Failure in War* (New York: Free Press, 1990), pp. 177–180, 192–193.

8. James Blackwell, Michael J. Mazarr, and Don Snider, Project Directors, *The Gulf War, Military Lessons Learned: Interim Report of the CSIS Study Group on Lessons Learned from the Gulf War* (Washington, D.C.: Center for Strategic and International Studies, 1991), pp. v–vi.

9. William Perry, "Desert Storm and Deterrence," *Foreign Affairs*, 70 (Fall 1991): 66–82.

10. Department of Defense, *Conduct of the Persian Gulf Conflict: An Interim Report to the Congress*, July 1991, pp. 4–10.

11. Ibid., pp. I-3 to I-4. As this manuscript was being written in February 1992, the Department of Defense had just completed a new three-volume report over 1,000 pages in length.

12. Dan Bolger, "The Ghosts of Omdurman," *Parameters*, 21 (Autumn 1991): 38–39.

13. Department of Defense, *Conduct of the Persian Gulf Conflict*, pp. I-4 to I-5.

14. James Blackwell, *Thunder in the Desert* (New York: Bantam Books, 1991), p. 98.

15. Cohen and Gooch, pp. 236–237.

16. Williamson Murray, "The German Response to Victory in Poland: A Case Study in Professionalism," *Armed Forces and Society*, 7 (Winter 1981): 285–298. The quotation is from p. 286.

Will More Countries Become Democratic?

Samuel P. Huntington

What are the prospects for the emergence of more democratic regimes in the world? . . . This issue is important for at least four reasons. First, the future of democracy is closely associated with the future of freedom in the world. Democracies can and have abused individual rights and liberties, and a well-regulated authoritarian state may provide a high degree of security and order for its citizens. Overall, however, the correlation between the existence of democracy and the existence of individual liberty is extremely high. Indeed, some measure of the latter is an essential component of the former. Conversely, the long-term effect of the operation of democratic politics is probably to broaden and deepen individual liberty. Liberty is, in a sense, the peculiar virtue of democracy; hence, if one is concerned with liberty as an ultimate social value, one should also be concerned with the fate of democracy.

Second, the future of democracy elsewhere in the world is of importance to the United States. The United States is the world's premier democratic country, and the greater the extent to which democracy prevails elsewhere in the world, the more congenial the world environment will be to American interests generally and the future of democracy in the United States in particular. Michael Doyle has argued quite persuasively that no two liberal societies have ever fought each other.[1] His concept of liberalism differs from the concept of democracy employed in this paper, but the point may well be true of democratic regimes as well as liberal ones. Other things being

From *Political Science Quarterly* 99 (1984).

equal, non-democratic regimes are likely to pose more serious challenges to American interests than democratic regimes.

Third, "a house divided against itself," Abraham Lincoln said, "cannot stand. . . . This government cannot endure permanently half-slave and half-free." At present the world is not a single house, but it is becoming more and more closely integrated. Interdependence is the trend of the times. How long can an increasingly interdependent world survive part-democratic and part-authoritarian and totalitarian? At what point does interdependence become incompatible with coexistence? For the Soviet bloc and the Western World, that point may still be some distance in the future, but tensions arising out of the growing interaction between totally different political systems are almost inevitably bound to increase. At some point, coexistence may require a slowing down or halting of the trends toward interdependence.

Fourth, the extension or decline of democracy has implications for other social values, such as economic growth, socioeconomic equity, political stability, social justice, and national independence. In societies at one level of development, progress toward one or more of these goals may be compatible with a high level of democracy. At another level of socioeconomic development, conflicts may exist. The question of the appropriateness of democracy for poor countries is, in this context, a central issue. But even highly developed societies may achieve their democracy at some sacrifice of other important values, such as national security. . . .

Preconditions of Democratization

In 1970, Dankwart Rustow published a penetrating article on "transitions to democracy," in which he criticized studies that focused on "preconditions" for democratization because they often tended to jump from the correlation between democracy and other factors to the conclusion that those other factors were responsible for democracy. They also tended, he argued, to look for the causes of democracy primarily in economic, social, cultural, and psychological, but not political, factors.[2] Rustow's criticisms were well taken and helped to provide a more balanced view of the complexities of democratization. It would, however, be a mistake to swing entirely to the other extreme and ignore the environmental factors that may affect democratic development. In fact, plausible arguments can be and have been made for a wide variety of factors or preconditions that appear to be associated with the emergence of democratic regimes. To a large extent these factors can be grouped into four broad categories—economic, social, external, and cultural.

Economic Wealth and Equality

. . . The correlation between wealth and democracy is . . . fairly strong. How can it be explained? There are three possibilities. First, both democracy and wealth could be caused by a third factor. Protestantism has, for instance, been assigned by some a major role in the origins of capitalism, economic development, and democracy. Second, democracy could give rise to economic wealth. In fact, however, high levels of economic wealth require high rates of economic growth and high rates of economic growth do not correlate with the prevalence of democratic political systems. Hence, it seems unlikely that wealth depends on democracy, and, if a connection exists, democracy must depend on wealth.

The probability of any causal connection running from wealth to democracy is enhanced by the arguments as to why this would be a plausible relationship. A wealthy economy, it is said, makes possible higher levels of literacy, education, and mass media exposure, all of which are conducive to democracy. A wealthy economy also moderates the tensions of political conflict; alternative opportunities are likely to exist for unsuccessful political leaders and greater economic resources generally facilitate accommodation and compromise. In addition, a highly developed, industrialized economy and the complex society it implies cannot be governed efficiently by authoritarian means. Decision-making is necessarily dispersed, and hence power is shared and rule must be based on consent. Finally, in a more highly developed economy, income and possibly wealth also tend to be more equally distributed than in a poorer economy. Since democracy means, in some measure, majority rule, democracy is only possible if the majority is a relatively satisfied middle class, and not an impoverished majority confronting an inordinately wealthy oligarchy. A substantial middle class, in turn, may be the product of the relatively equal distribution of land in agrarian societies that may otherwise be relatively poor, such as the early nineteenth century United States or twentieth century Costa Rica. It may also be the result of a relatively high level of development, which produces greater income equality in industrial as compared to industrializing societies. . . .

Social Structure

A second set of often-discussed preconditions for democracy involves the extent to which there is a widely differentiated and articulated social structure with relatively autonomous social classes, regional groups, occupational groups, and ethnic and religious groups. Such groups, it is argued, provide the basis for the limitation of state power, hence for the control of the state by society, and hence for democratic political institutions as the most effective means of exercising that control. Societies that lack autonomous intermediate groups are, on the other hand, much more likely to be dominated by a centralized power apparatus—an absolute monarchy, an oriental despotism, or an authoritarian or totalitarian dictatorship.[3] This argument can be made on behalf of groups and pluralism in general or on behalf of particular groups or types of pluralistic structure which are singled out as playing a decisive role in making democracy possible. . . .

The theory that emphasizes traditional pluralism is, in a sense, the opposite of the one that emphasizes wealth as a precondition of democracy. The latter makes democracy dependent on how far the processes of economic development and modernization have gone. The traditional pluralism theory, in contrast, puts the emphasis on where the process started, on the nature of traditional society. Was it, in Gaetano Mosca's terms, primarily a "feudal" or a "bureaucratic" society? If pushed to the extreme, of course, this theory implies societal predestination: it is all determined in advance that some societies will become democratic and others will not. . . .

External Environment

External influences may be of decisive importance in influencing whether a society moves in a democratic or non-democratic direction. To the extent that such influences are more important than indigenous factors, democratization is the result of diffusion rather than development. Conceivably, democracy in the world could stem from a single source. Clearly it does not. Yet it would be wrong to ignore the extent to which much of the democracy in the world does have a common origin. In 1984, Freedom House classified fifty-two countries (many of them extremely small) as "free." In thirty-three of those fifty-two countries, the presence of democratic institutions could be ascribed in large part to British and American influence, either through settlement, colonial rule, defeat in war, or fairly direct imposition (such as in the Dominican Republic). Most of the other nineteen "free" countries where democracy had other sources were either in Western Europe or in South America. The extension of democracy into the non-Western world, insofar as that has occurred, has thus been largely the product of Anglo-American efforts. . . .

In large measure, the rise and decline of democracy on a global scale is a function of the rise and decline of the most powerful democratic states. The spread of democracy in the nineteenth century went hand in hand with the Pax Britannica. The extension of democracy after World War II reflected the global power of the United States. The decline of democracy in East Asia and Latin America in the 1970s was in part a reflection of the waning of American influence.[4] That influence is felt both directly, as a result of the efforts of the American government to affect political processes in other societies, and also indirectly by providing a powerful and successful model to be followed.

Regional external influences can also have a significant effect on political development within a society. The governments and political parties of the European Community (EC) helped to encourage the emergence of democratic institutions in Spain and Portugal, and the desire of those two countries plus Greece to join the community provided an additional incentive for them to become democratic. Even beyond the confines of the EC, Western Europe has generally become defined as a community of democratic nations, and any significant departure by one nation from the democratic norm would clearly create a major crisis in intra-European relations. In some measure, a similar development may be taking place among the countries of the Andean Pact. The departure from the Pact of Chile and the addition of Venezuela in the mid-1970s, plus the transitions to democracy in Ecuador and Peru, then laid the basis for identifying pact membership with the adherence to democratic government.

In some regions, but most notably in Latin America, regional trends may exist. By and large, Latin American governments moved in a democratic direction in the late 1950s and early 1960s, then in an authoritarian direction in the late 1960s and early 1970s, and then once again in a democratic direction in the late 1970s and early 1980s. The reasons for these regional shifts are not entirely clear. They could be a result of four factors: simultaneous parallel socioeconomic development in Latin American societies; the triggering of a trend by the impact of one "pace-setting" Latin American society on its neighbors; the impact on Latin America of a common external influence (such as the United States); or some combination of these factors.

Cultural Context

The political culture of a society has been defined by Sidney Verba as "the system of empirical beliefs, expressive symbols, and values which defines the situation in which political action takes place."[5] Political culture is, presumably, rooted in the broader culture of a society involving those beliefs and values, often religiously based, concerning the nature of humanity and society, the relations among human beings, and the relation of individuals to a transcendent being. Significant differences in their receptivity to democracy appear to exist among societies with different cultural traditions.

Historically, as many scholars have pointed out, a high correlation existed between Protestantism and democracy. In the contemporary world, virtually all countries with a European population and a Protestant majority (except East Germany) have democratic governments.[6] The case of Catholicism, particularly in Latin countries, on the other hand, is more ambivalent. Historically, it was often argued that a natural opposition existed between Catholicism and democracy. By and large, democratic institutions developed later and less surely in European Catholic countries than in Protestant ones. By and large, however, these countries also developed later economically than the Protestant countries, and hence it is difficult to distinguish between the impact of economics and that of religion. Conceivably, the influence of the latter on politics could have been mediated through its impact on economic development and the rise of an entrepreneurial class. With economic development, however, the role of the church changed, and in most Catholic countries now the church is identified with support for democracy.

Islam, on the other hand, has not been hospitable to democracy. Of thirty-six countries with Moslem majorities, Freedom House in 1984 rated twenty-one as "not free," fifteen as "partially free," none as "free." The one

Islamic country that sustained even intermittent democracy after World War II was Turkey, which had, under Mustapha Kemal, explicitly rejected its Islamic tradition and defined itself as a secular republic. The one Arab country that sustained democracy, albeit of the consociational variety, for any time was Lebanon, 40 to 50 percent of whose population was Christian and whose democratic institutions collapsed when the Moslem majority asserted itself in the 1970s. Somewhat similarly, both Confucianism and Buddhism have been conducive to authoritarian rule, even in those cases where, as in Korea, Taiwan, and Singapore, economic preconditions for democracy have come into being. In India and Japan, on the other hand, the traditional Hindu and Shinto cultures at the very least did not prevent the development of democratic institutions and may well have encouraged it.

. . . It seems reasonable to expect that the prevalence of some values and beliefs will be more conducive to the emergence of democracy than others. A political culture that values highly hierarchical relationships and extreme deference to authority presumably is less fertile ground for democracy than one that does not. Similarly, a culture in which there is a high degree of mutual trust among members of the society is likely to be more favorable to democracy than one in which interpersonal relationships are more generally characterized by suspicion, hostility, and distrust. A willingness to tolerate diversity and conflict among groups and to recognize the legitimacy of compromise also should be helpful to democratic development. Societies in which great stress is put on the need to acquire power and little on the need to accommodate others are more likely to have authoritarian or totalitarian regimes. Social scientists have attempted to compare societies along these various dimensions, but the evidence remains fragmented and difficult to systematize.[7] In addition, of course, even if some beliefs and values are found to correlate with the presence of democratic institutions, the question still remains concerning the relationship among these in a developmental sense. To what extent does the development of a pro-democratic political culture have to precede the development of democratic institutions? Or do the two tend to develop more simultaneously with the successful operation of democratic institutions, possibly created for other reasons, generating adherence to democratic values and beliefs?

Processes of Democratization

The classic model of democratization that has infused much discussion of the subject is that of Britain, with its stately progression from civic rights to political rights to social rights, gradual development of parliamentary supremacy and cabinet government, and incremental expansion of the suffrage over the course of a century. It is basically a linear model. Dankwart A. Rustow's model, based on Swedish experience—national unity, prolonged and inconclusive political struggle, a conscious decision to adopt democratic rules, habituation to the working of those rules—also involves a relatively simple linear progression. These "ingredients," he has argued, "must be assembled one at a time." These linear models primarily reflect European experience during the century ending in 1920 and the experience of some Latin American countries (such as Argentina until 1930 and Chile until 1973).

Two other models have generally been more relevant than the linear model to the experience of Third World countries. One is the cyclical model of alternating despotism and democracy. In this case, key elites normally accept, at least superficially, the legitimacy of democratic forms. Elections are held from time to time, but rarely is there any sustained succession of governments coming to power through the electoral process. Governments are as often the product of military interventions as they are of elections. Such interventions tend to occur either when a radical party wins or appears about to win an election, when the government in power threatens or appears to threaten the prerogatives of the armed forces, or when the government appears incapable of effectively guiding the economy and maintaining public order. Once a military junta takes over, it will normally promise to return power to civilian rule. In due course, it does so, if only to minimize divisiveness within the armed forces and to escape from its own inability to govern effectively. In a praetorian situation like this, neither authoritarian nor democratic institutions are effectively institutionalized. Once countries enter into this cyclical pattern, it appears to be extremely difficult for them to escape from it. In many respects, countries that have had relatively stable authoritarian rule (such as Spain and Portugal) are more likely to evolve into relatively stable democracies than countries that have regularly oscillated between despotism and democracy (such as Peru, Ecuador, Bolivia, Argentina, Ghana, Nigeria). In the latter, neither democratic nor authoritarian norms have deep roots among the relevant political elites, while in the former a broad consensus accepting of authoritarian norms is displaced by a broad consensus on or acceptance of democratic ones. In the one case, the alternation of democracy and despotism *is* the political system; in the other, the shift from a stable despotism to a stable democracy *is a change* in political systems.

A third model is neither linear nor cyclical but rather dialectical. In this case, the development of a middle class leads to increased pressures on the existing authoritarian regimes for expanded participation and contestation. At some point, there is then a sharp break, perhaps in the form of what I have elsewhere called the "urban breakthrough," the overthrow of the existing authoritarian regime, and the installation of a democratic one.[8] This regime, however, finds it difficult or impossible to govern effectively. A sharp reaction occurs with the overthrow of the democratic system and installation of a (usually right-wing) authoritarian regime. In due course, however, this regime collapses and a transition is made to a more stable, more balanced, and longer-lasting democratic system. This model is roughly applicable to the history of a number of countries, including Germany, Italy, Austria, Greece, and Spain. . . .

Possibility of Regime Changes

In terms of these generalizations, prospects for democratic development in the 1980s are probably greatest in the bureaucratic-authoritarian states of South America. Cultural traditions, levels of economic development, previous democratic experience, social pluralism (albeit with weak bourgeoisies outside Brazil), and elite desires to emulate European and North American models all favor movement toward democracy in these countries. On the other hand, the polarization and violence that has occurred (particularly in Argentina and Chile) could make such movement difficult. The prospects for a relatively stable democratic system should be greatest in Brazil. Beginning in the early 1970s, the leadership of the Brazilian regime began a process of *distensão*, gradually relaxing the authoritarian controls that had been imposed in the 1960s. By the early 1980s, Brazil had acquired many of the characteristics of a democratic system. The principal deficiency was the absence of popular elections for the chief executive, but those were generally viewed as certain to come sometime in the 1980s. The gradualness of the Brazilian process, the relative low level of violence that accompanied it, and the general recognition among elite groups of the importance of not disrupting it in any way, all seemed to enhance the prospects for democracy.

In Argentina, the economic and military failures of the authoritarian regime led to a much more dramatic and rapid transit to democracy in 1983. The probabilities of this replacement being sustained would seem to depend on three factors: the ability of the Alfonsín government to deal with the economic problems it confronted; the extent to which Peronista, as well as Radical, elites were willing to abide by democratic rules; and the extent to which military leadership was effectively excluded from power or came to identify its interests with the maintenance of a democratic regime. The two other southern cone countries with bureaucratic-authoritarian regimes, Chile and Uruguay, are the two South American countries that did have the strongest democratic traditions. As of 1984, however, in neither country had authoritarian rule lost its legitimacy and effectiveness to the point where it could no longer be maintained and a replacement process could occur (as in Argentina). Nor had the leaders of either regime embarked on a meaningful transformation process to democratize their system (as in Brazil). The Brazilian and Argentine changes, however, cannot fail to have impact on political development in the smaller countries.

The probability of movement in a democratic direction in the East Asian newly industrializing countries is considerably less than it is among the Latin American B-A states. The economic basis for democracy is clearly coming into existence, and if their economic development continues at anything like the rates it did in the 1960s and 1970s, these states will soon constitute an authoritarian anomaly among the wealthier countries of the world. The East Asian countries generally have also had and maintained a relatively equal distribution of income. In addition, the United States, Britain, and Japan are the principal external influences on these societies. All these factors favor democratic development. On the other side, cultural traditions, social structure, and a general weakness of democratic norms among key elites all impede movement in a democratic direction. In some measure, the East Asian states dramatically pose the issue of whether economics or culture has the greater influence on political development. One can also speculate on whether the spread of Christianity in Korea may create a cultural context more favorable to democracy.

Among other less economically developed East Asian societies, the prospects for democracy are undoubtedly highest but still not very high in the Philippines. The Marcos government is not likely to attempt to transform itself, and hence efforts to create a democratic system must await its demise. At that time, American influence, previous experience with democracy, social pluralism (including the influence of the Catholic Church), and the general agreement among opposition political leaders on the desirability of a return to democracy, should all provide support for movement in that direction. On the other hand, military leaders may not support democratic norms, and the existence of a radical insurgency committed to violence, plus a general proclivity to the use of violence in the society, might make such a transition difficult. Conceivably, Philippine development could follow the lines of the dialectical model referred to earlier, in which (as in Venezuela) an initial experience with democracy is broken by a personalistic authoritarian interlude that then collapses and a new, more stable democratic regime is brought into existence by agreement among political leaders. The Philippine Betancourt, however, may well have been gunned down at the Manila airport.

Among Islamic countries, particularly those in the Middle East, the prospects for democratic development seem low. The Islamic revival, and particularly the rise of Shi'ite fundamentalism, would seem to reduce even further the likelihood of democratic development, particularly since democracy is often identified with the very Western influences the revival strongly opposes. In addition, many of the Islamic states are very poor. Those that are rich, on the other hand, are so because of oil, which is controlled by the state and hence enhances the power of the state in general and of the bureaucracy in particular. Saudi Arabia and some of the smaller Arab oil-rich Gulf countries have from time to time made some modest gestures toward the introduction of democratic institutions, but these have not gone far and have often been reversed.

Most African countries are, by reason of their poverty or the violence of their politics, unlikely to move into a democratic direction. Those African and Latin American countries that have adhered to the cyclical pattern of alternating democratic and authoritarian systems in the past are not likely to change this basic pattern, as the example of Nigeria underlines, unless more fundamental changes occur in their economic and social infrastructure. In South Africa, on the other hand, the relatively high level of economic development by African standards, the intense contestation that occurs within the minority permitted to participate in politics, the modest expansion of that minority to include the Coloureds and Asians, and the influence of Western democratic norms, all provide a basis for moving in a more democratic direction. However, that basis is countered on the other side by the inequalities, fears, and hatreds that separate blacks and whites.

In some small countries, democratic institutions may emerge as a result of massive foreign effort. This did happen in the Dominican Republic; in 1984 it was, presumably, happening in Grenada; it could, conceivably, happen at extremely high cost in El Salvador.

The likelihood of democratic development in Eastern Europe is virtually nil. The Soviet presence is a decisive overriding obstacle, no matter how favorable other conditions may be in countries like Czechoslovakia, Hungary, and Poland. Democratization could occur in these societies only if either the Soviet Union were drastically weakened through war, domestic upheaval, or economic collapse (none of which seems likely), or if the Soviet Union came to view Eastern European democratization as not threatening to its interests (which seems equally unlikely).

The issue of Soviet intervention apart, a more general issue concerns the domestic pattern of evolution within Communist states. For almost four decades after World War II, no democratic country, with the dubious possible exception of Czechoslovakia in 1948, became Communist and no Communist country became democratic through internal causes. Authoritarian regimes, on the other hand, were frequently replaced by either democratic or Communist regimes, and democratic regimes were replaced by authoritarian ones. In their early phase, Communist states usually approximated the totalitarian model, with ideology and the party playing central roles and massive efforts being made to indoctrinate and mobilize the population and to extend party control throughout all institutions in the society. Over time, however, Communist regimes also tend to change and often to become less totalitarian and more authoritarian. The importance of ideology and mobilization declines, bureaucratic stagnation replaces ideological fervor, and the party becomes less a dedicated elite and more a mechanism for patronage. In some cases, military influence increases significantly. The question thus arises: Will Communist authoritarian regimes, absent Soviet control, be more susceptible to movement toward democracy than Communist totalitarian regimes?

The answer to that question may well depend on the extent to which Communist authoritarian regimes permit the development of a market-oriented economy. The basic thrust of communism suggests that such a development is unlikely. Communism is not, as Karl Marx argued, a product of capitalist democracy; nor is it simply a "disease of the transition" to capitalist democracy, to use Rostow's phrase.[9] It is instead an alternative to capitalist democracy and one whose guiding principle is the subjection of economic development to political control. Even if it becomes more authoritarian and less totalitarian, the Communist political system is likely to ensure that economic development neither achieves a level nor assumes a form that will be conducive to democracy.

The United States and Global Democracy

The ability of the United States to affect the development of democracy elsewhere is limited. There is little that the United States or any other foreign country can do to alter the basic cultural tradition and social structure of another society or to promote compromise among groups of that society that have been killing each other. Within the restricted limits of the possible, however, the United States could contribute to democratic development in other countries in four ways.

First, it can assist the economic development of poor countries and promote a more equitable distribution of income and wealth in those countries. Second, it can encourage developing countries to foster market economies and the development of vigorous bourgeois classes. Third, it can refurbish its own economic, military, and political power so as to be able to exercise greater influence than it has in world affairs. Finally, it can develop a concerted program designed to encourage and to help the elites of countries entering the "transition zone" to move their countries in a more democratic direction.

Efforts such as these could have a modest influence on the development of democracy in other countries. Overall, however, this survey of the preconditions for and processes of democratization leads to the conclusion that, with a few exceptions, the prospects would improve significantly only if there were major discontinuities in current trends—such as if, for instance, the economic development of the Third World were to proceed at a much faster rate and to have a far more positive impact on democratic development than it has had so far, or if the United States reestablished a hegemonic position in the world comparable to that which it had in the 1940s and 1950s. In the absence of developments such as these, a significant increase in the number of democratic regimes in the world is unlikely. The substantial power of anti-democratic governments (particularly the Soviet Union), the unreceptivity to democracy of several major cultural traditions, the difficulties of eliminating poverty in large parts of the world, and the prevalence of high levels of polarization and violence in many societies all suggest that, with a few exceptions, the limits of democratic development in the world may well have been reached.

NOTES

1. Michael W. Doyle, "Kant, Liberal Legacies, and Foreign Affairs, Part I," *Philosophy and Public Affairs* 12 (1983): 213ff.
2. Dankwart A. Rustow, "Transitions to Democracy: Toward a Dynamic Model," *Comparative Politics* 2 (1970): 337ff.
3. For a balanced analysis of these see Robert A. Dahl, *Dilemmas of Pluralist Democracy: Autonomy vs. Control* (New Haven, CT: Yale University Press, 1982).
4. Samuel P. Huntington, *American Politics: The Promise of Disharmony* (Cambridge, MA: Harvard University Press, 1981), pp. 246–259.
5. Sidney Verba, "Comparative Political Culture," in *Political Culture and Political Development*, ed. Lucien Pye and Sidney Verba (Princeton, NJ: Princeton University Press, 1965), p. 513.

6. For a statistical correlation between Protestantism and democracy see Kenneth A. Bollen, "Political Democracy and the Timing of Development," *American Sociological Review* 44 (1979): 572–587.

7. See Pye and Verba, *Political Culture and Political Development*; Robert Dahl, *Polyarchy* (New Haven, CT: Yale University Press, 1971), pp. 124–187; Gabriel Almond and Sidney Verba, *The Civic Culture* (Princeton, NJ: Princeton University Press, 1963); David McClelland, *The Achieving Society* (Princeton, NJ): Van Nostrand, 1961).

8. Samuel P. Huntington, *Political Order in Changing Societies* (New Haven, CT: Yale University Press, 1968), pp. 72–78.

9. Walt W. Rostow, *The Stages of Economic Growth* (Cambridge: Cambridge University Press, 1960), p. 162.

The Global 2000 Report to the President

A Report Prepared by the Council on Environmental Quality and the Department of State

The President's directive establishing the Global 2000 Study called for a "study of the probable changes in the world's population, natural resources, and environment through the end of the century" and indicated that the Study as a whole was to "serve as the foundation of our longer-term planning." The findings of the Study identify problems to which world attention must be directed. But because all study reports eventually become dated and less useful, the Study's findings alone cannot provide the foundation called for in the directive. The necessary foundation for longer-term planning lies not in study findings *per se*, but in the Government's continuing institutional capabilities—skilled personnel, data, and analytical models—for developing studies and analyses. Therefore, to meet the objectives stated in the President's directive, the Global 2000 Study was designed not only to assess probable changes in the world's population, natural resources, and environment, but also, through the study process itself, to identify and strengthen the Government's capability for longer-term planning and analysis.[1]

Building the Study

The process chosen for the Global 2000 Study was to develop trend projections using, to the fullest extent possible, the long-term global data and models routinely employed by the Federal agencies. The process also in-

From The Global 2000 Report to the President (Washington, D.C.: The Government Printing Office, 1980).

cluded a detailed analysis of the Government's global modeling capabilities as well as a comparison of the Government's findings with those of other global analyses.

An executive group, established and co-chaired by the Council on Environmental Quality and the State Department, together with a team of designated agency coordinators, assisted in locating the agencies' experts, data, and analytical models. A number of Americans from outside Government and several people from other countries advised on the study structure. The agencies' expert met occasionally with some of these advisors to work out methods for coordinating data, models, and assumptions.

Overall, the Federal agencies have an impressive capability for long-term analyses of world trends in population, resources, and environment. Several agencies have extensive, richly detailed data bases and highly elaborate sectoral models. Collectively, the agencies' sectoral models and data constitute the Nation's present foundation for long-term planning and analysis.

Currently, the principal limitation in the Government's long-term global analytical capability is that the models for various sectors were not designed to be used together in a consistent and interactive manner. The agencies' models were created at different times, using different methods, to meet different objectives. Little thought has been given to how the various sectoral models—and the institutions of which they are a part—can be related to each other to project a comprehensive, consistent image of the world. As a result, there has been little direct interaction among the agencies' sectoral models.

With the Government's current models, the individual sectors addressed in the Global 2000 Study could be interrelated only by developing projections sequentially, that is, by using the results of some of the projections as inputs to others. Since population and gross national product (GNP) projections were required to estimate demand in the resource sector models, the population and GNP projections were developed first, in 1977. The resource projections followed in late 1977 and early 1978. All of the projections were linked to the environment projections, which were made during 1978 and 1979.

The Global 2000 Study developed its projections in a way that furthered interactions, improved internal consistency, and generally strengthened the Government's global models. However, the effort to harmonize and integrate the Study's projections was only partially successful. Many internal contradictions and inconsistencies could not be resolved. Inconsistencies arose immediately from the fact that sequential projections are not as interactive as events in the real world, or as projections that could be achieved in an improved model. While the sequential process allowed some interaction among the model's sectors, it omitted the continuous influence that all the elements—population, resources, economic activity, environment—have upon each other. For example, the Global 2000 Study food projections assume that the catch from traditional fisheries will increase as fast as world population, while the fisheries projections indicate that this harvest will not increase over present levels on a sustainable basis. If it has been possible to link the fisheries and food projections, the expected fisheries contribution to the human food supply could have been realistically reflected in the food projections. This and other inconsistencies are discussed in detail in the Technical Report.[2]

Difficulties also arise from multiple allocation of resources. Most of the quantitative projections simply assume that resource needs in the sector they cover—needs for capital, energy, land, water, minerals—will be met. Since the needs for each sector are not clearly identified, they cannot be summed up and compared with estimates of what might be available. It is very likely that the same resources have been allocated to more than one sector.

Equally significant, some of the Study's resource projections implicitly assume that the goods and services provided in the past by the earth's land, air, and water will continue to be available in larger and larger amounts, with no maintenance problems and no increase in costs. The Global 2000 Study projections for the environment cast serious doubt on these assumptions.

Collectively, the inconsistencies and missing linkages that are unavoidable with the Government's current global models affect the Global 2000 projections in many ways. Analysis of the assumptions underlying the projections and comparisons with other global projections suggest that most of the Study's quantitative results understate the severity of potential problems the world will face as it prepares to enter the twenty-first century.

The question naturally arises as to whether circumstances have changed significantly since the earliest projections were made in 1977. The answer is no. What changes have occurred generally support the projections and highlight the problems identified. The brief summaries of the projections (beginning on the next page) each conclude with comments on how the projections might be altered if redeveloped today.

The Global 2000 Study has three major underlying assumptions. First, the projections assume a general continuation around the world of present public policy relating to population stabilization, natural resource conservation, and environmental protection. The projections thus point to the expected future if policies continue without significant changes.

The second major assumption relates to the effects of technological developments and of the market mechanism. The Study assumes that rapid rates of technological development and adoption will continue, and that the rate of development will be spurred on by efforts to deal with problems identified by this Study. Participating agencies were asked to use the technological assumptions they normally use in preparing long-term global projections. In general, the agencies assume a continuation of rapid rates of technological development and no serious social resistance to the adoption of new technologies. Agricultural technology, for example, is assumed to continue increasing crop yields as rapidly as during the past few decades, including the period of the Green Revolution. . . . The projections assume no revolutionary advances—such as immediate wide-scale availability of nuclear fusion for energy production—and no disastrous setbacks—such as serious new health risks from widely used contraceptives or an outbreak of plant disease severely affecting an important strain of grain. The projections all assume that price, operating through the market mechanism, will reduce demand whenever supply constraints are encountered.

Third, the Study assumes that there will be no major disruptions of international trade as a result of war, disturbance of the international monetary system, or political disruption. The findings of the Study do, however, point to increasing potential for international conflict and increasing stress on international financial arrangements. Should wars or a significant disturbance of the international monetary system occur, the projected trends would be altered in unpredictable ways.

Because of the limitations outlined above, the Global 2000 Study is not the definitive study of future population, resource, and environment conditions. Nor is it intended to be a prediction. The Study does provide the most internally consistent and interrelated set of global projections available so far from the U.S. Government. Furthermore, its major findings are supported by a variety of nongovernmental global studies based on more highly interactive models that project similar trends through the year 2000 or beyond.

Major Findings and Conclusions

If present trends continue, the world in 2000 will be more crowded, more polluted, less stable ecologically, and more vulnerable to disruption than the world we live in now. Serious stresses involving population, resources, and environment are clearly visible ahead. Despite greater material output, the world's people will be poorer in many ways than they are today.

For hundreds of millions of the desperately poor, the outlook for food and other necessities of life will be no better. For many it will be worse. Barring revolutionary advances in technology, life for most people on earth will be more precarious in 2000 than it is now—unless the nations of the world act decisively to alter current trends.

This, in essence, is the picture emerging from the U.S. Government's projections of probable changes in world population, resources, and environment by the end of the century, as presented in the Global 2000 Study. They do not predict what will occur. Rather, they depict conditions that are likely to develop if there are no changes in public policies, institutions, or rates of technological advance, and if there are no wars or other major disruptions. A keener awareness of the nature of the current trends, however, may induce changes that will alter these trends and the projected outcome.

Principal Findings

Rapid growth in world population will hardly have altered by 2000. The world's population will grow from 4 billion in 1975 to 6.35 billion in 2000, an increase of more than 50 percent. The rate of growth will slow only marginally, from 1.8 percent a year to 1.7 percent. In terms of sheer numbers, population will be growing faster in 2000 than it is today, with 100 million people added each year compared with 75 million in 1975. Ninety percent of this growth will occur in the poorest countries.

While the economies of the less developed countries (LDCs) are expected to grow at faster rates than those of the industrialized nations, the gross national product per capita in most LDCs remains low. The average gross national product per capita is projected to rise substantially in some LDCs (especially in Latin America), but in the great populous nations of South Asia it remains below $200 a year (in 1975 dollars). The large existing gap between the rich and poor nations widens.

World food production is projected to increase 90 percent over the 30 years from 1970 to 2000. This translates into a global per capita increase of less than 15 percent over the same period. The bulk of that increase goes to countries that already have relatively high per capita food consumption. Meanwhile per capita consumption in South Asia, the Middle East, and the LDCs of Africa will scarcely improve or will actually decline below present inadequate levels. At the same time, real prices for food are expected to double.

Arable land will increase only 4 percent by 2000, so that most of the increased output of food will have to come from higher yields. Most of the elements that now contribute to higher yields—fertilizer, pesticides, power for irrigation, and fuel for machinery—depend heavily on oil and gas.

During the 1990s world oil production will approach geological estimates of maximum production capacity, even with rapidly increasing petroleum prices. The Study projects that the richer industrialized nations will be able to command enough oil and other commercial energy supplies to meet rising demands through 1990. With the expected price increases, many less developed countries will have increasing difficulties meeting energy needs. For the one-quarter of humankind that depends primarily on wood for fuel, the outlook is bleak. Needs for fuelwood will exceed available supplies by about 25 percent before the turn of the century.

While the world's finite fuel resources—coal, oil, gas, oil shale, tar sands, and uranium—are theoretically sufficient for centuries, they are not evenly distributed; they pose difficult economic and environmental problems; and they vary greatly in their amenability to exploitation and use.

Nonfuel mineral resources generally appear sufficient to meet projected demands through 2000, but further discoveries and investments will be needed to maintain reserves. In addition, production costs will increase with energy prices and may make some nonfuel mineral resources uneconomic.

The quarter of the world's population that inhabits industrial countries will continue to absorb three-fourths of the world's mineral production.

Regional water shortages will become more severe. In the 1970–2000 period population growth alone will cause requirements for water to double in nearly half the world. Still greater increases would be needed to improve standards of living. In many LDCs, water supplies will become increasingly erratic by 2000 as a result of extensive deforestation. Development of new water supplies will become more costly virtually everywhere.

Significant losses of world forests will continue over the next 20 years as demand for forest products and fuelwood increases. Growing stocks of commercial-size timber are projected to decline 50 percent per capita. The world's forests are now disappearing at the rate of 18–20 million hectares a year (an area half the size of California), with most of the loss occurring in the humid tropical forests of Africa, Asia, and South America. The projections indicate that by 2000 some 40 percent of the remaining forest cover in LDCs will be gone.

Serious deterioration of agricultural soils will occur worldwide, due to erosion, loss of organic matter, desertification, salinization, alkalinization, and waterlogging. Already, an area of cropland and grassland approximately the size of Maine is becoming barren wasteland each year, and the spread of desert-like conditions is likely to accelerate.

Atmospheric concentrations of carbon dioxide and ozone-depleting chemicals are expected to increase at rates that could alter the world's climate and upper atmosphere significantly by 2050. Acid rain from increased combustion of fossil fuels (especially coal) threatens damage to lakes, soils, and crops. Radioactive and other hazardous materials present health and safety problems in increasing numbers of countries.

Extinctions of plant and animal species will increase dramatically. Hundreds of thousands of species—perhaps as many as 20 percent of all species on earth—will be irretrievably lost as their habitats vanish, especially in tropical forests.

The future depicted by the U.S. Government projections, briefly outlined above, may actually understate the impending problems. The methods available for carrying out the Study led to certain gaps and inconsistencies that tend to impart an optimistic bias. For example, most of the individual projections for the various sectors studied—food, minerals, energy, and so on—assume that sufficient capital, energy, water, and land will be available in each of these sectors to meet their needs, regardless of the competing needs of the other sectors. More consistent, better-integrated projections would produce a still more emphatic picture of intensifying stresses, as the world enters the twenty-first century.

Conclusions

At present and projected growth rates, the world's population would reach 10 billion by 2030 and would approach 30 billion by the end of the twenty-first century. These levels correspond closely to estimates by the U.S. National

Academy of Sciences of the maximum carrying capacity of the entire earth. Already the populations in sub-Saharan Africa and in the Himalayan hills of Asia have exceeded the carrying capacity of the immediate area, triggering an erosion of the land's capacity to support life. The resulting poverty and ill health have further complicated efforts to reduce fertility. Unless this circle of interlinked problems is broken soon, population growth in such areas will unfortunately be slowed for reasons other than declining birth rates. Hunger and disease will claim more babies and young children, and more of those surviving will be mentally and physically handicapped by childhood malnutrition.

Indeed, the problems of preserving the carrying capacity of the earth and sustaining the possibility of a decent life for the human beings that inhabit it are enormous and close upon us. Yet there is reason for hope. It must be emphasized that the Global 2000 Study's projections are based on the assumption that national policies regarding population stabilization, resource conservation, and environmental protection will remain essentially unchanged through the end of the century. But in fact, policies are beginning to change. In some areas, forests are being replanted after cutting. Some nations are taking steps to reduce soil losses and desertification. Interest in energy conservation is growing, and large sums are being invested in exploring alternatives to petroleum dependence. The need for family planning is slowly becoming better understood. Water supplies are being improved and waste treatment systems built. High-yield seeds are widely available and seed banks are being expanded. Some wildlands with their genetic resources are being protected. Natural predators and selective pesticides are being substituted for persistent and destructive pesticides.

Encouraging as these developments are, they are far from adequate to meet the global challenges projected in this Study. Vigorous, determined new initiatives are needed if worsening poverty and human suffering, environmental degradation, and international tension and conflicts are to be prevented. There are no quick fixes. The only solutions to the problems of population, resources, and environment are complex and long-term. These problems are inextricably linked to some of the most perplexing and persistent problems in the world—poverty, injustice, and social conflict. New and imaginative ideas—and a willingness to act on them—are essential.

The needed changes go far beyond the capability and responsibility of this or any other single nation. An era of unprecedented cooperation and commitment is essential. Yet there are opportunities—and a strong rationale—for the United States to provide leadership among nations. A high priority for this Nation must be a thorough assessment of its foreign and domestic policies relating to population, resources, and environment. The United States, possessing the world's largest economy, can expect its policies to have a significant influence on global trends. An equally important priority for the United States is to cooperate generously and justly with other nations—particularly in the areas of trade, investment, and assistance—in seeking solutions to the many problems that extend beyond our national boundaries. There are many unfulfilled opportunities to cooperate with other nations in efforts to relieve poverty and hunger, stabilize population, and enhance economic and environmental productivity. Further cooperation among nations is also needed to strengthen international mechanisms for protecting and utilizing the "global commons"—the oceans and atmosphere.

To meet the challenges described in this Study, the United States must improve its ability to identify emerging problems and assess alternative responses. In using and evaluating the Government's present capability for long-term global analysis, the Study found serious inconsistencies in the methods and assumptions employed by the various agencies in making their projections. The Study itself made a start toward resolving these inadequacies. It represents the Government's first attempt to produce an interrelated set of population, resource, and environmental projections, and it has brought forth the most consistent set of global projections yet achieved by U.S. agencies. Nevertheless, the projections still contain serious gaps and contradictions that must be corrected if the Government's analytic capability is to be improved. It must be acknowledged that at present the Federal agencies are not always capable of providing projections of the quality needed for long-term policy decisions.

While limited resources may be a contributing factor in some instances, the primary problem is lack of coordination. The U.S. Government needs a mechanism for continuous review of the assumptions and methods the Federal agencies use in their projection models and for assurance that the agencies' models are sound, consistent, and well documented. The improved analyses that could result would provide not only a clearer sense of emerging problems and opportunities, but also a better means for evaluating alternative responses, and a better basis for decisions of worldwide significance that the President, the Congress, and the Federal Government as a whole must make.

With its limitations and rough approximations, the Global 2000 Study may be seen as no more than a reconnaissance of the future; nonetheless its conclusions are reinforced by similar findings of other recent global studies that were examined in the course of the Global 2000 Study. . . . All these studies are in general agreement on the nature of the problems and on the threats they pose to the future welfare of humankind. The available evidence leaves no doubt that the world—including this Nation—faces enormous, urgent, and complex problems in the decades immediately ahead. Prompt and vigorous changes in public policy around the world are needed to avoid or minimize these problems before they become unmanageable. Long lead times are required for effective action. If decisions are delayed until the problems become worse, options for effective actions will be severely reduced.

NOTES

1. A more detailed discussion of the Global 2000 Study process is provided in *The Global 2000 Report to the President*, vol. 2, *Technical Report*, "Preface and Acknowledgements," and chap. 1, "Introduction to the Projections."
2. *Technical Report*, "Closing the Loops," chaps. 13 and 14.

U.S. Security
in a Separatist Season

Stephen P. Cohen

August 14 [1992] is the first anniversary of the KGB-led coup that tried to preempt the new Union treaty in the Soviet Union. The failure of the coup led to the discrediting of the KGB, the downfall of the Communist Party, and the dissolution of the Soviet Union. The entity that was both feared and misunderstood for so many years came to a symbolic end when Mikhail Gorbachev, already stripped of his party chairmanship, resigned as president of the (former) Soviet Union on December 24, 1991.

Because the world still saw things in terms of an ideological struggle between West and East, many of us in the West were justifiably excited by the collapse of communism. However, insufficient attention has been paid to the broader implications of the breakup of the Soviet *state*. This was the second instance since the end of World War II of a modern multi-ethnic state collapsing—the destruction of Pakistan in 1971 (midwifed by the armed intervention of neighboring India) was the first. (Ironically, Pakistan itself was evidence of the difficulty of state-making—it was conceived in violence when the British left India in 1947.)

With separatist movements cropping up throughout the Middle East, Southern and Central Asia, and parts of Europe, it is important to understand that the Soviet Union disintegrated not only because of the political and economic collapse of communism, and the enfeeblement of its security forces, but because the Soviet state was under extraordinary pressure from within and without. It may turn out that the crisis of the multi-ethnic state, not the disappearance of communism, will be the most profound political event of our generation.

This breaking-up process has far-reaching implications for U.S. foreign policy. In recent decades, Americans seem to have a special problem in determining if, where, and how Washington should intervene in a world made up of states of unequal power, stability, and importance.

Americans under 60 have lived their entire adult lives during one of two titanic struggles. The first was against the Nazi and Japanese empires in World War II, the second against Leninist structures and Stalinist expansionism in the Cold War. Yet traditional American isolationism survives, most recently speaking with the voice of television commentator and presidential candidate Patrick Buchanan. For some conservatives, the United States, as God's chosen country, can only be contaminated by contact with a corrupt world and scheming foreigners.

But nowadays, the conservative right has a new ally: the burnt-out left, still obsessed with the non-interventionist "lessons" of the Vietnam war. They think that America is corrupt—that it has failed to live up to its own ideals. To them, Washington cannot act abroad without creating victims.

Together, the two isolationisms threaten the rational conduct of foreign affairs. Without a significant, dramatic international threat, internationalisms of all varieties face tough going in the next decade. This could be dangerous to world peace. The fate of the political entities that develop and control nuclear weapons, that oppress or liberate their own people, should be of central concern to policymakers. But it is hard to think about (and even harder to make policy about) such entities at a time when the state is disintegrating in so many parts of the world, and isolationist rhetoric shadows political discourse.

What is eating away at the legitimacy and power of the state—the entity that was the building block of international politics for the past two hundred years? Five factors have undercut the moral, economic, military, and political foundation of the modern, Western-style state.

■ **The state has lost its monopoly over information.** Galloping technologies have weakened the ability of the state to control the information flowing to its citizens. The two revolutionaries of our era are not Marx and Lenin, but Bell Labs and the Boeing Corporation—inventors, respectively, of the transistor and the wide-bodied jet. The transistor and its solid-state progeny have put modern communications receivers in the hands of individuals, families, and small groups. State broadcasting systems everywhere are forced to compete with the BBC, CNN, and the private Singapore-based Star radio and television services.

Meanwhile, jumbo jets make it possible for people and goods to move cheaply and rapidly across frontiers. In some cases this has meant new horizons and new ideas; in others, it has enabled older ties and linkages to extend across the world. Terrorists of all nationalities, for example, not only blow up jumbo jets but they ride in them, commuting between target state and safe haven.

The electronic and air travel revolutions have enabled ideas and people to move over and through iron and bamboo curtains. Although modern police states have used advanced electronics to spy upon and control their own populations, the race has been won by the "offense." At least temporarily, the bureaucracies of bugging and terror have been outmaneuvered by VCRs, cassette tape-recorders (crucial in overthrowing the Shah of Iran), small transistor radios, short-wave and satellite broadcasting systems, and discounted air tickets.

■ **The state cannot protect its citizens in wartime.** When Ronald Reagan said in 1985 that a nuclear war could not be fought, and, if fought, could not be won, he kicked away one of the most important props of the state since the mid-eighteenth century: the argument that it protected its citizens from the depredations of foreigners.

Ironically, the spread of nuclear weapons after 1945 at first seemed to strengthen the hand of the state. At no time in history did any state command such enormous military power as did the United States and the Soviet Union during the period of American and Soviet nuclear hegemony from 1950–1990. Even today, hawks in India, Pakistan, Iraq, North Korea, and other near-nuclear states seek nuclear weapons for statist, not strategic, reasons. Yet, the breakdown of the Soviet Union suggests a very different lesson: mere possession of nuclear weapons is not enough to prevent the breakup of a state, let alone to insure the physical protection of its citizens from external attack—except by mutual suicide.

Indeed, as a state appears to become strong through the possession of nuclear weapons, its citizens become vulnerable, undefendable targets of the nuclear weapons of other powers. Short of developing a perfect strategic defense system, no state can ever again promise its citizens physical security. Reagan's staunch support of the Strategic Defense Initiative was no whim. He understood that nuclear weapons had transformed the role of the state, and only through a miracle of technology might the modern state regain one of its key functions.

■ **The state no longer insures economic prosperity.** States once claimed, sometimes erroneously, that only they could insure economic growth and justice within a given territory. The nineteenth-century model of the self-contained state embodied an evolution from basic agriculture, through a trading economy, to industrial self-reliance—dramatically symbolized, in the last century, by steel mills and rail networks, and today, by aircraft industries and nuclear power plants.

But the nineteenth-century model has been supplanted by a new model. Sub-national regions and territories try to link up with larger economic entities: a multi-national corporation, or a Japanese auto firm, or an American clothing retailer. Mayors and governors from Kansas to Guangzhou compete with each other for the favor of Mitsubishi or Motorola. They demand that their national governments either subsidize the process or get out of the way.

And, if the weather and geography are suitable, some regional leaders calculate that they can become stand-alone "tourist destinations." All they need is a beach or mountain scenery, and the jumbo jets bearing German and Japanese tourists will come, just as soon as the concrete hardens at the spanking new international airport.

Kashmiris, for example, looking at Nepal and Sri Lanka, have calculated that a regular air link with Europe and Northeast Asia could quadruple their income from tourists—and payments would be in hard currencies, not in Indian rupees. Only the Indian state—controlled by a New Delhi elite—seems to stand in their way.

■ **The state has lost its monopoly on justice.** Aristotle taught us that the object of politics is justice. Until very recently it was understood that the state—a Western invention—provided the context in which individuals and groups achieved justice. Further, it was also assumed that a large and powerful state could best guarantee justice within its borders, and secure justice vis-à-vis potentially hostile neighbors.

That is no longer true. International organizations, human rights groups, and self-appointed spokesmen for democracy all challenge the state's claim to be the moral arbiter of its citizens' lives. When backed by the power of international lending institutions, or by the Japanese Export-Import Bank, or by the U.S. Congress, these arguments carry unprecedented weight, and they have the unintended consequence of giving aid and comfort to some who would destroy certain states.

Earlier this year, all of the South Asian states jointly challenged the linkage of human rights and international loans. India and its neighbors are democracies with fairly good human rights records, but they resent—as violations of sovereignty—the application of human rights criteria by foreign institutions. They also fear that separatist groups will see this as an international endorsement of their aims and methods.

And, from a new quarter, Islamic movements not only challenge the dominance of secularized Western notions of justice and freedom, they undercut the grounds on which many rulers govern in secular Muslim-majority states or in states (such as India and the Philippines) that have large Muslim populations.

■ **The state is being attacked from within.** Multi-ethnic states are everywhere trembling in the aftermath of the breakup of the Soviet Union and the civil war in Yugoslavia. A once-heretical question is again being raised: Why should there be one China? Or one India? Or only two South Asian Islamic republics—Pakistan and Bangladesh? Or one Iraq, or one Sri Lanka? Why not three, or four, or five, or twenty?

Three generations ago, the great nationalist leaders forged anti-colonial movements by arguing that India, or the Dutch East Indies, or the

Gold Coast, could achieve "unity in diversity," that they could manage their complex societies better than foreign imperialists.

Today, separatist ethnic, regional, linguistic, and religious groups have turned the argument inside out. Contemporary Nehrus, Nkrumahs, Jinnahs, and Titos argue that there can be greater economic progress, military security, and political justice in *diversity*—that the big-state apparatus is irrelevant in an era of global economic linkages and unusable military power. And, the new sub-national leaders see foreign lending agencies and human rights groups (which in America includes the far right as well as elements of the left) as allies, not enemies, as they press the case that the parts of the state are greater than the whole.

Larger Implications

What does the crumbling of the state hold for the future? Four points seem to be crucial for the international community to keep in mind.

- The classical state is not dead, even in those cases where new states rise from the corpse of the old. The state remains the model for those who would destroy it. We are not likely to see the new states of the world pass up the opportunity to acquire all of the trappings of sovereignty: their own airlines, armies, navies, and even nuclear weapons programs.

But the new rulers will be sabotaged by the same forces that brought down their predecessors: an emerging global economy, new international standards of state behavior and human rights, and populations that cannot be easily controlled. Thus, there may be more states (the breakup of the Soviet Union and Yugoslavia has alone created 20 new ones), but their governments will be weaker. The entire foreign office of Kazakhstan consists of eight people, yet it is a republic that nominally controls hundreds of nuclear weapons.

- The proliferation of states, either through the voluntary reorganization of existing entities (the Soviet pattern) or through civil war and chaos (first Pakistan, and more recently Yugoslavia, Ethiopia, and possibly Iraq) will interact with a second proliferation process—the rapid spread of weapons of mass destruction. Nuclear weapons and missiles are, respectively, 50- and 60-year-old technologies. These technologies have been mastered by thousands of scientists and technicians around the world.

The more unstable and nervous of the new state entities will reach for such weapons technologies and hope that they will insure the survival of the regime and of the state. But the lesson of the Soviet and Iraqi cases should not be forgotten: The disposition of these technologies is not solely dictated by old notions of national "sovereignty"; these weapons are of widespread concern beyond the state borders, and their spread may justify international or unilateral intervention.

Establishing nuclear non-proliferation as a firm international norm is important now, and it should be a factor that determines the conditions under which the United States supports—or refrains from supporting—states under attack.

■ It is unlikely that the state will be replaced by either global or regional political institutions as the unit of international politics. For better *and* for worse, we will have a world of states, not a world of effective international or regional organizations. The United Nations and one or two regional organizations may play a useful role in cushioning the impact of state breakup, or in some cases preventing it, but they will not attract the loyalty of great numbers of people, nor can they meet basic economic, moral, and political needs of sizable numbers of people.

While it is important to support nascent regional organizations, such as the South Asian Association for Regional Cooperation (SAARC) and the Association of Southeast Asian Nations (ASEAN), these groupings are no substitute for great-power engagement in regional security matters. The involvement may be intrusive and even violent in cases where some states are trying to destroy others (the Middle East, certainly), or advisory in regions where there is a prevalence of vulnerable multi-ethnic states (South Asia). And great-power involvement may be vital in areas that lack any regional organization—especially Northeast Asia, the most dangerous area of all, where a divided state, Korea, interacts with a volatile combination of nuclear-weapons powers, advanced economies, and historical antagonisms.

■ It is time to abandon the deceptive vocabulary used to classify large numbers of states. In the 1950s, the euphemisms "developing" and "emerging" replaced "backward" and "undeveloped," which in their day were polite substitutes for "wogs" or "natives." But in the 1970s, another term arrived, further corrupting the discourse on state-building. "Third World" began as a euphemism for the "non-aligned," but then it acquired a vague social, political, and moral content.

To the right, Third World states were somehow poor, somehow threatening, and generally a danger to the rest of us when they fell upon one another, or acquired weapons of mass destruction. On the left, there was an effort to create the illusion of a class of states with shared moral qualities, a group that represented more than the sum of its parts. However, while the First and Second Worlds have conceptually vanished, the Third World remains, still shaped by Cold War constructs.

Thus, virtually every public figure today proclaims the existence of a "Third World" located somewhere along the Mexico-Bombay-Manila axis. Weirdly, China is not a "Third World" country, but India—with two hundred [million] of its eight hundred million possessing a European living standard—is.

Western leaders, steeped in Cold War visions of strong enemies, long ignored the transformation of weak states into stronger states. Our understanding of the deeper destructive processes at work in many states around the world (and not all of them are poor, southern, or non-aligned) may have been compromised by such terms as "Third World," "South," and other euphemisms.

State Building

In the United States, academic and government strategists who speak enthusiastically of a new world order need to look more carefully at the friable and imperfect material they are working with.

In a speech last November, John Reichart, a member of the State Department's Policy Planning Staff, characterized the "new world order" as an era of hope based on "cooperative diplomacy," adherence to human rights, and the spread of market economies. The deplorable "old world order" was epitomized by containment, "a negative strategy." Containment was "what we were against"; the new world order is "what we are for."

But policymakers need to devote as much attention to an understanding of the units out of which we are constructing a new world order as they do to the nature of that order. The fall of communism was an astonishing event, but so, in its own way, has been the breakup of the Soviet state. Other than China, there are no more communisms of consequence left to fall.

Nevertheless, the state in many parts of the world is under attack and most will not go as quietly. Their leaders have not lived under the shadow of nuclear terror for two generations, as did the leaders of the United States and the Soviet Union. Further, in most cases these leaders see the West as a threat, not as a potential friend. For the leaders of such states, and for those who would challenge them, weapons of mass destruction are likely to be seen as part of the solution, not as part of the problem.

The cliché of the day in the Pentagon and among its friends on the right is that our unstable new world is "more dangerous than ever." Meanwhile, on the left, there has been a convenient rediscovery of "human rights" violations and a growing indignation over state violence, coupled with virtual silence about the separatists, narco-terrorists, and murderers who are trying to tear apart a number of states. But between those who assume that there is nothing wrong with the state, and those who argue that there is nothing right with most states—between threat-of-the-day thinking on one hand and indignant liberal isolationism on the other—there is a prudent center.

Chester Bowles, a New Dealer who became an undersecretary of state in the Kennedy administration, understood that state building was an important national security interest of the United States. But Bowles failed as a strategist because he was not single-minded enough for the pugnacious Cold Warriors who surrounded him. They saw Bowles's interest in state building in Africa, Latin America, and Asia in a purely Cold War framework, not as an important aim in itself.

But Bowles was right. Today, many years after Bowles left the scene, multi-ethnic states are fragmenting, and the United States must make the best of it. Rather than observe from afar, we must have a foreign policy that takes this into account, especially when many of these states (or their successors) will have access to instruments of mass destruction. These states, in particular, need our understanding, assistance, and perhaps direct intervention to achieve the kind of stability that benefits them individually, and the world collectively.